THOSE WONDERFUL WIND MACHINES
MW00358457
The best of ALL sailing worlds.
Sailing Illustrated
Volume II
by Patrick M. Royce
1
2
3
4
5
8
9
14
15
16
17
18
19
20
21
22
23
24
25
26
27
28
29
30
31
32
33
34
35
36
37
38
39
40
41
How many wind machines can you recognize?
ROYCE'S SAILING ILLUSTRATED

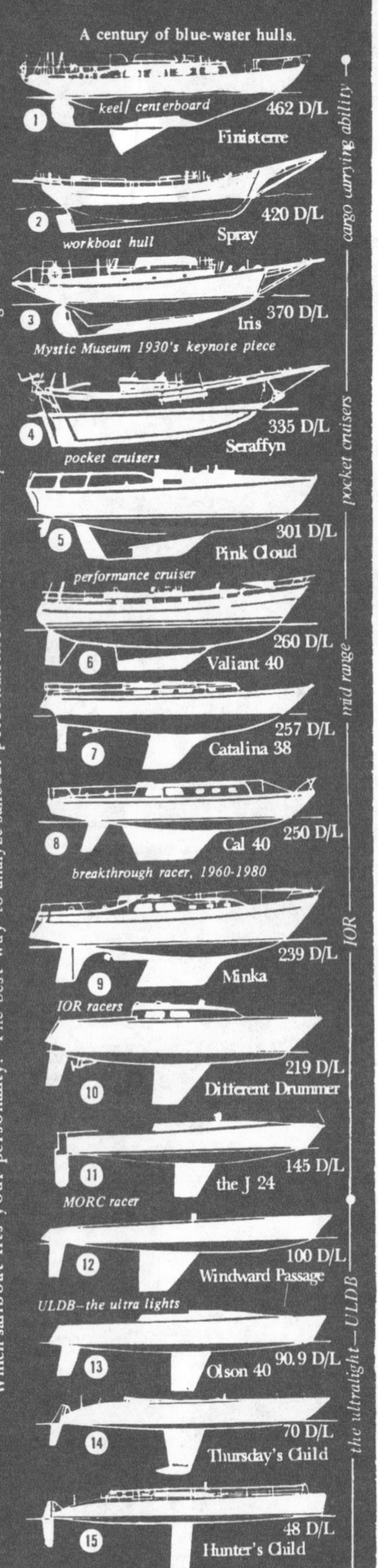

A century of blue-water hulls.
1 keel/ centerboard 462 D/L Finisterre
2 workboat hull 420 D/L Spray
3 370 D/L Iris
Mystic Museum 1930's keynote piece
4 335 D/L Seraffyn
pocket cruisers
5 301 D/L Pink Cloud
performance cruiser
6 260 D/L Valiant 40
7 257 D/L Catalina 38
8 250 D/L Cal 40
breakthrough racer, 1960-1980
9 239 D/L Minka
IOR racers
10 219 D/L Different Drummer
11 145 D/L the J 24
MORC racer
12 100 D/L Windward Passage
ULDB–the ultra lights
13 90.9 D/L Olson 40
14 70 D/L Thursday's Child
15 48 D/L Hunter's Child
cargo carrying ability
pocket cruisers
mid range
IOR
the ultralight—ULDB
Which sailboat fits your personality? The best way to analyze sailboat personalities is with their Displacement to Length ratios.

Royce Publications

The best of all sailing worlds, and the best of all powerboating worlds.

Box 1967, Newport Beach
CA 92663, USA
(714) 642-4430
FAX (714) 646-SAIL

D/L definition- see pages 18-21
Volume I *Sailing Illustrated.*

Sailing Illustrated- Volume II
1985, 1996 by Patrick M. Royce
former name ***Homestudy Guide***

Researched, illustrated, written by, and all type set by its author Patrick M. Royce

***Sailing Illustrated* I and II,** are dedicated to Hilda Royce, my first mate and bride of over 50 years marriage, and holding.

This book began as an elusive goal, a six year project continually defying completion, requiring her love, patience, and backing, plus two years for this revision. We hate to think the price of this book if its retail price resulted from charging for our hours invested.

Ben Burns, M.D. Ben became fully involved with this book. For over three years he spent most weekends and several nights a week as idea sparring partner and proof reader.

Ben was the rare friend few meet in a lifetime, with a passion for sailing. He helped with the final check before the printer. Ben was buried at sea shortly before he was to receive the first copy of our book.

It is time to look back as age 75 rapidly approaches. How wonderful the memories are with over 40 years serving the sailing public, with customers sometimes as many as three generations in the same family.

While in Tahiti visiting sailboats at the crossroaads of the Pacific... none were from the U.S. All had old copies of our sailing book. One book on the same sailboat from New Zealand, had crossed the Pacific to the U.S. three round trips under three owners after launching in Baltimore. How many storms had it seen?

We also give thanks to Ken Hoffmann and ***DELTA Litho*** for their continual help to print our books to excellent standards thru the years. ***Thanks Team!***

Distributed by **Gordon Soules Book Publishers Ltd.** • 1354-B Marine Drive, West Vancouver BC Canada V7T 1B5
• 620-1916 Pike Place, Seattle WA 98101 US
E-mail: books@gordonsoules.com
Web site: http://www.gordonsoules.com
(604) 922 6588 Fax: (604) 688 5442

ISBN 0-911284-07-9

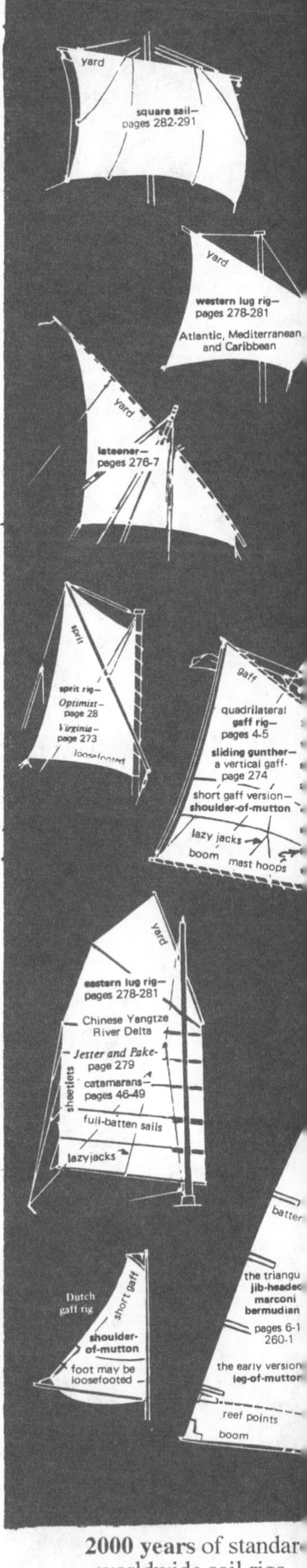

yard
square sail– pages 282-291
yard
western lug rig– pages 278-281
Atlantic, Mediterranean and Caribbean
yard
lateener– pages 276-7
sprit
sprit rig– Optimist– page 28
Virginia– page 273
gaff
quadrilateral gaff rig– pages 4-5
sliding gunther– a vertical gaff- page 274
short gaff version– shoulder-of-mutton
lazy jacks
boom
mast hoops
yard
eastern lug rig– pages 278-281
Chinese Yangtze River Delta
Jester and Pake- page 279
catamarans– pages 46-49
sheetlets
full-batten sails
lazyjacks
Dutch gaff rig
short gaff
shoulder-of-mutton
foot may be loosefooted
reef points
boom

2000 years of standar
worldwide sail rigs.

How many one-design dinghies can you recognize?
Sunfish
Olympic Star
Snipe
Lightning
Optimist
Lido 14
Laser
Force 5
Olympic Finn
Thistle
Olympic Sailboard
Olympic Tornado Cat
Hobie 16
Naples Sabot
Olympic Flying Dutchman
Malibu Outrigger
Penguin
Coronado 15
Kite

Find your subjects with our chapter flipping indexes, also back cover.

Our publications are listed page 50.

The WONDERFUL WIND MACHINE evolution.

A

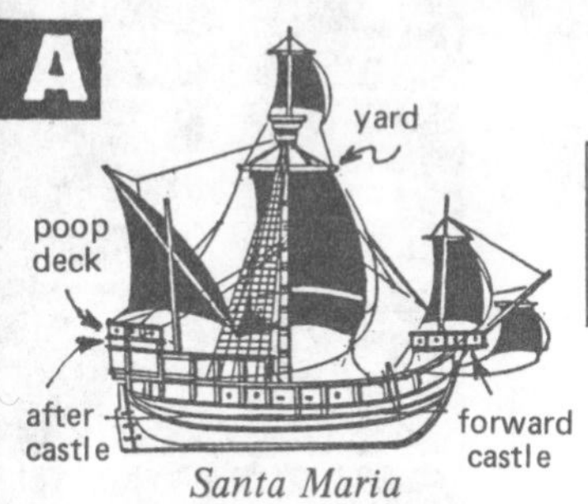

yard
poop deck
after castle
forward castle

Santa Maria

Introduction—*we show a variety of sailing vessels and rigs which had to survive,perform,and withstand the test of time in endless ocean and wind conditions. These vessels were products of different environments and time periods,using materials and technology available at the time.*

> Man roamed the oceans downwind under square sails for many centuries. When headed by the wind his alternatives were to anchor...or break out the oars. You may have felt better ideas were needed if the pirates were moving up on your stern...or you were the pirate with the good guys pulling ahead.

The yard was tilted,then moved to a fore and aft position to become the ***lug sail*** (1) for windward work. Luggers to 80' long were popular with pirates laying in wait for Spanish merchant vessels filled with looted treasures on their return to Europe. The luggers,hidden ashore,were ready to charge out to capture these sluggish vessels becalmed in the lee of tropical Caribbean islands.

the Chinese lug rig

Chinese sailors used the lug rig made of native materials adding full length battens (2). Though Chinese traders for many centuries roamed as far west as Africa their efficient sails were ignored by builders in other countries.

the modern lug rig

The modern lug rig **Pake** (3) using the latest in materials and technology.

history of the lateener

The ***lateen rig*** (4) dating back to early Phoenician traders is an outgrowth of the lug rig adapted by Arab sailors. The Arab lateeners followed the monsoon wind patterns for centuries sailing yearly to Africa and India,then when the monsoons reversed direction,they sailed their lateeners back to their Red Sea home ports.

the beach boat

The **Malibu** ***outrigger*** (5) using a modified lateen rig was our first practical beach boat later obsoleted by the Hobie cats. The popular **Sunfish** (6) uses a lateen rig.

the sprit rig— rowboat to barge

The ***sprit rig*** (7) uses a diagonal gaff across a mainsail which was first used in rowboats as the wind came up is represented today by the **Optimist pram** (7). The sprit rig has been used for over three centuries on London's **Thames Barges** (8) often 80' long and 20' wide with 16' long lee boards. These sailing barges were often operated by a man,boy,and dog,still carrying working sails in a force 6 wind.

all-weather cutter

Outside English harbors were ***all-weather sailing vessels*** represented by the **West County Pilot Cutter** (9) on harbor pilot duty. It carries a loose-footed mainsail with a short gaff,plus a topmast and topsail for light weather,down to a spitfire jib (small, stout inner jib) during a bad storm for harbor pilot duty. The **Revenue Cutter**,text page 289,was somewhat similar,also carrying sails for all-weather sailing use.

gaff-rigged catboat

The **Cape Cod** ***catboat*** (10) averaging 25' long with an 11' beam was designed for the New England area with shallow harbors. After the gaff-rigged main was secured out of the way it became an excellent fishing workboat with a large cockpit to handle nets and lines plus a large fish hold below in the cabin. It didn't have speed back to the market yet what was the hurry with other fishermen sailing similar slow rigs.

Sailing Illustrated Volume II

The **sliding gunther** (11) belongs to the gaff-rig family,with the gaff raised parallel to the mast with all spars short enough to be stored into the dinghy when not in use.

the GAFF rig

> We have followed the square sail thru the lugger and lateener,and from the sprit rig to the ***gaff-rigged mainsail*** (10),the British call the ***quadrilateral mainsail rig***.

the MARCONI rig

> The ***Bermudian sloop rig*** (12) appeared with a triangular mainsail in the Caribbean around 1830...called the ***marconi rig*** by Americans always ready to adapt slang terms due to resemblence to early Marconi wireless tower supports.

fractional sloop rig

The best way to define sloop rigs is to begin with identical hulls carrying identical sail areas with different rigs. The 3/4,7/8,15/16 ***fractional sloop rigs*** (13) use the tallest mast with a small jib,as the jibstay doesn't go to the top of the mast. The tall mast is especially important for dinghies sailing on inland lakes to catch upper breezes when shorter mast rigs are becalmed,plus flexible masts for better sail control.

masthead sloop rig

headsail sloop rig

The jibstay goes to the top of the mast of a ***masthead sloop rig*** (14) permitting the use of much larger jibs. IOR Rules favor the ***headsail sloop rig*** (15) with a shorter main, the larger jib providing its major drive force upwind,the spinnaker,downwind.

The ***cutter*** (16) normally carries two jibs with the mast stepped farther aft than on a sloop. The first Valiant 40 cutter shown,successfully finished the first 1982 BOC singlehanded race clockwise around the world,sailed by Dan Byrne. The start and finish was Newport,RI,with three stops in Cape Town,Sydney,and Rio.

Hobie 16,P cat,P 2/18

Both **Hobie 16** (17) and the original **Pacific Cat** (18) carry ***full-batten mainsails***, with medium aspect ratio sail rigs,while the later **P 2/18** (19) has a high aspect ratio sail rig.

stayless catboat rigs

Stayless catboat rigs (20), (21) ,use full-batten mainsail rigs. They are designed for one person operation with sails raised,and lowered between lazy jacks,see **pages 119, 124.**

This is a new version of an old idea,that evolved rapidly in its first decade to provide a new approach to future sailors on large sailboats with small crews.

sailors
helping
sailors
WIND MACHINES thru the centuries
the lugger
2
text-281
junk
rig
rig
text-279
3
modern
rig
4
text-277
rig
the lateener
5
text-44
6
text-26
rig
Fill in missing words—
the sprit rig
text-16, 273
7
t-23
rig
8
Thames Barge
rig
Revenue
Cutter—
text-291
9
text-265
English Pilot
gaff or quadrilateral rig
text-5
10
Cape Cod
text 273
11
gunter
marconi or bermudian rig
text-263
12
arly
rig
13
text-263
airfoils
above
waterfoils
below
sloop
14
text 263
sloop
15
sloop
sloop rigs vs
cutter rig
16
text-265
rig
5
the full-batten mainsail
t-48
7
cat
18
text-46
cat
19
text-49
cat
20
text-4
catboat rig
21
catboat rig

TWO MASTED VESSELS MAY HANDLE EASIER

Motorsailer...a better term is needed.

The term **motorsailer** is fifty years old,defining a sailboat with an auxiliary engine which was a rarity in the early days.Since it is a rarity today to find cabin sailboats without an inboard engine or an outboard motor...the term motorsailer has outlived its descriptive usefulness.Our interest today becomes the performance percentage under sail and under power.

We define a sailboat with the **Minka** 23 a token example,having a full sail rig plus a 30 hp engine able to push it at hull speed even in storm conditions,pg. 72, a 100% sail 100% power rig.When applied to the underrigged **Newporter ketch** 24 it has an 85%/100% rig while the 50%/100% rig 25 uses power most of the time changing to sail at upper force 5.**Windward Passage** 31 has a small engine barely able to move her around the docks,which is fully retracted and its opening sealed,with a 100%/5% rating.A 30%/30% rating would indicate the worst of both sail and power, for dockside sailing.

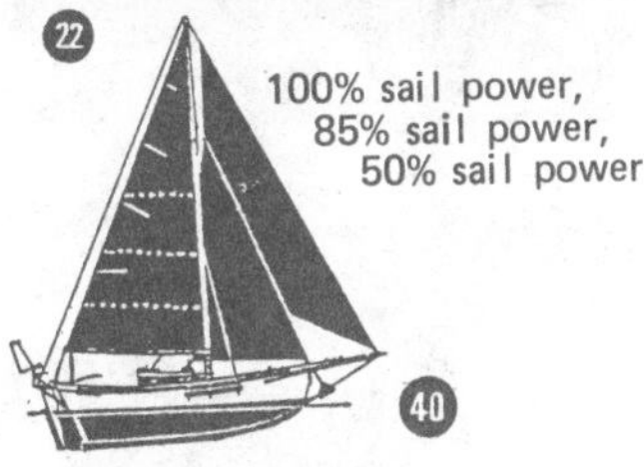
22
100% sail power,
85% sail power,
50% sail power
40

The divided rig for sailboats longer than 35'-see page G 7.

The term ***yacht*** has been overused and clouded in powerboat advertising...originally referred to ***vessels used for pleasure or state occasions*** including the President's yacht, and your dinghy,while a ***rowboat*** by legal definition,still remains a rowboat.A sailing vessel carrying square sails on three or more masts is a ***full-rigged ship*** 22 while other sailing vessels are called by their rig,one-design class,racing rating,or individual names.

Slocum's ***Spray*** 28 , Pardey's ***Seraffyn*** 40, Hiscock's ***Wanderer II,*** and other pure sailboat have sailed around the world using wind power alone,without any auxiliary engine power aboard.On the other extreme is a powerboat 26 using ***steadying sails*** to reduce rolling motion in a seaway,while workboat 27 uses an ***aft sail*** to hold the bow to windward, eliminates the need for anchoring while handling lobster pots,etc.

the YAWL rig

The rudder post is carried between masts of a yawl making it easy to recognize in the distance with its small mizzen or jigger.Our examples **Spray** 28 ,**Iris** 29 ,and **Finisterre** 30 are of similar length,made to different technologies available at the time.

the KETCH rig

The rudder post is carried aft of both masts on a ketch. **Windward Passage** 31 was ketch rigged from 1968 to 1983 when it was redesigned to become a sloop rig.

double ender downwind rolling potentials?

The most famous early ketch design is the **Tahiti ketch** 32 .With all of its rave notices however,an owner with many miles on his Tahiti summarized,"The true double-ender would be ideal *if* you could sail it around the world on a beam reach".The marconi-rigged **Newporter ketch** 24 began production with gaff rig on both masts.

the fascinating **Cascade**

The cat/ketch **Cascade** 33 was designed to challenge the IOR racing sailboat formula with fascinating results best shown with its high aspect ratio sail rig and waterfoils, next to the low aspect ratio Tahiti ketch sail rig.**Cascade** started a new trend for cruising sailboats with one of the early cat/ketches 34 shown.

the log canoe that forgot to stop growing

The Chesapeake Bay area produced unusual sailboat designs,yet few can compare with the ***log canoe*** **Flying Cloud** 35 ,carrying fore and afters,squaresail, topsail, and kite.Early gentlemen colonists bartered log canoes from indians.Since work such as paddling was beneath their dignity,sails were added to the dug-out canoes.Other colonists began competing with longer hulls and soaring sail rigs.A crew member climbs out on the ***boomkin*** as the wind increases to prevent the bow from digging in,while others climb out on ***planks on the high side*** to prevent a capsize.

the SCHOONER rig

Schooners carry two or more masts of equal height,or the after mast is taller. This rig seems peculiar to the U.S. as foreign sailors joining us for an afternoon sail are continually asking questions about,and taking photos of our various local schooners.

traditional schooner rig

topsail schooner rig

The **traditional schooner rig** 36 carries a gaff-headed foresail,plus one or two jibs. It can become a **topsail schooner** 37 when square sails are added to the forward mast of the traditional schooner rig.

staysail schooner

the hermaphrodite brig

The **staysail schooner rig** 38 carries a staysail between the masts,plus one or more jibs, becoming a **hermaphrodite brig** 39 when square sails are added to the forward mast.

the fisherman

Atlantic fishermen returning from the Grand Banks often dried nets in the upper areas of their schooner rigging,finding seaweed in the nets seemed to improve their speed.When gambling and racing become more remunerative than their fish cargo, the nets were replaced with a new sail called the ***fisherman*** on the return voyage.

the trained sailor has MANY advantages

If you enjoy sailing on a variety of craft,take time to understand the big ones as their owners are always looking for new,trained,congenial crew members.

Study the standing and running rigging patterns of two-masted sailboats.While their patterns may seem more complex at first, theyoften provide more flexibility under autopilot,permitting single-handed operation for raising the sails and steering the sailboat.Don't permit the size to bluff you as ***a big sailboat is often a big dinghy*** which is often easier to operate than a smaller sloop...docking is another issue.

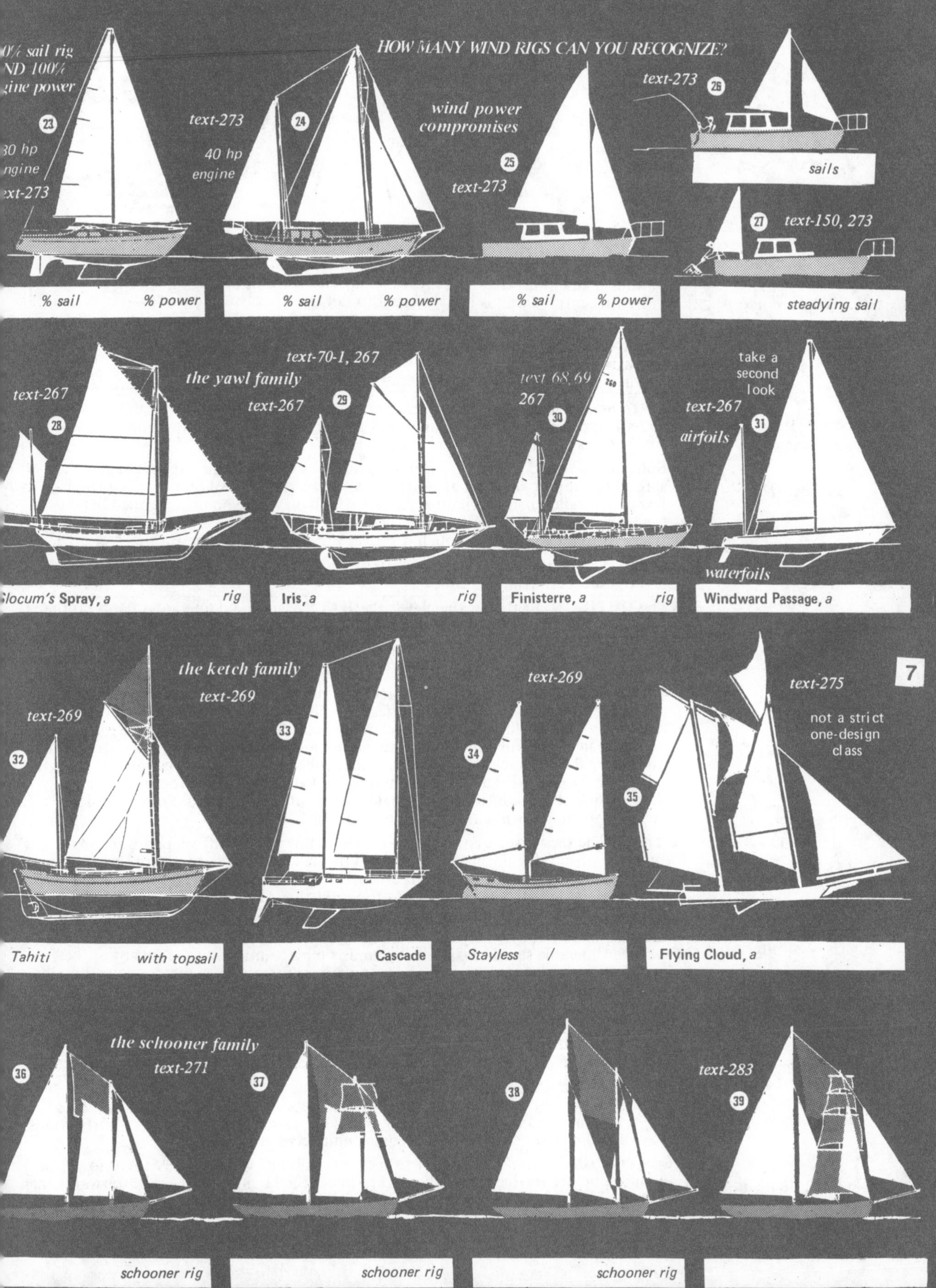
HOW MANY WIND RIGS CAN YOU RECOGNIZE?
0% sail rig
ND 100%
gine power
23
30 hp
ngine
xt-273
% sail
% power
text-273
24
40 hp
engine
% sail
% power
wind power
compromises
25
text-273
% sail
% power
text-273
26
sails
27
text-150, 273
steadying sail
text-267
28
locum's Spray, a
rig
the yawl family
text-70-1, 267
text-267
29
Iris, a
rig
text 68, 69
267
30
Finisterre, a
rig
take a
second
look
text-267
airfoils
31
waterfoils
Windward Passage, a
the ketch family
text-269
text-269
32
Tahiti
with topsail
33
/
Cascade
text-269
34
Stayless
/
text-275
not a strict
one-design
class
35
Flying Cloud, a
the schooner family
text-271
36
schooner rig
37
schooner rig
38
schooner rig
text-283
39

MAINSAIL and JIB–BASIC TERMS,RAISING SAILS

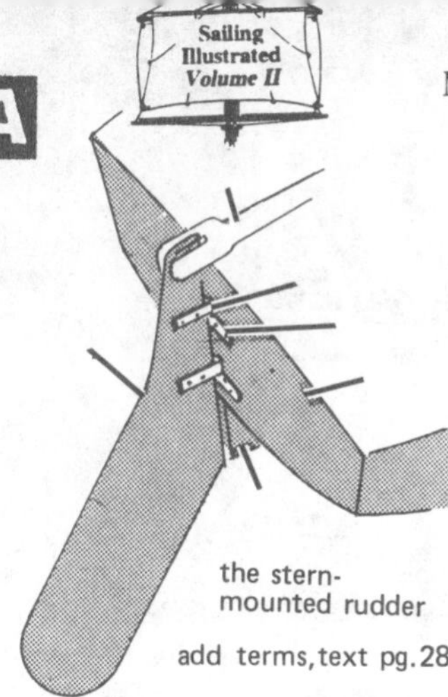
Sailing
Illustrated
Volume II

the stern-mounted rudder

add terms,text pg.28

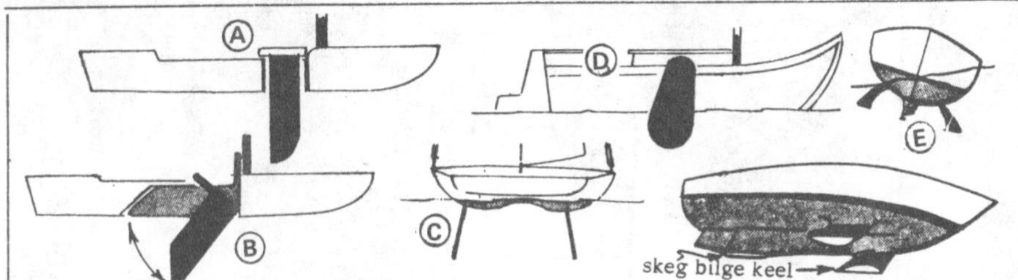
A
D
E
B
C
skeg bilge keel

The **daggerboard** Ⓐ is a high aspect waterfoil to compensate for the sideway force mostly on dinghies when sailing upwind.It is raised progressively from a reach to a broad reach where it may be fully raised. The **centerboard** Ⓑ waterfoil provides a similar function while it pivots on a pin.The **scow** Ⓒ requires twin daggerboards or twin centerboards as it is designed to sail at an excessive heel angle.

Dutch sailing vessels developed the **leeboard** Ⓓ to resist the sideway force for upwind sailing.Since Holland has considerable tidal ranges,their hulls are designed to be aground at low tide,with the leeboard fully raised for protection.The English **twin bilge keel hull** Ⓔ is designed to go aground at low tide and stay upright.

STANDING rigging

- **Fixed or standing rigging** supports the mast fore and aft with jibstay and backstay... and athwartship by shrouds.Standing rigging tension is with a screw adjustment using turnbuckles or shroud adjusters...also with hydraulic adjusters.

spreaders???

- **Spreaders** ⓯ are small athwartship bars or tubes to spread the support angle of a shroud to support the mast athwartship so it can stay "in column".We've seen a few cabin trailersailers without spreaders which may have an uncontrolled bend tendency in a strong wind that may lead to a dismasting,see text page 113,which is also difficult to adjust...though it proves very efficient for the Hobie 14 and 16.

RUNNING rigging

- **Running rigging is adjustable**...consisting of halyards to raise and secure the sails, and the sheets to trim the sails.

BASIC SAIL TERMS

The OUTHAUL hauls out the clew...the HALYARD (Haul up yards) hauls up the head of a sail...the **DOWNHAUL hauls down the tack** of the mainsail.

- Turn to page 7 of your text to add basic sail terms to the small mainsail at right... then add the additional terms to the larger traditional Lightning rig.

the MAINSAIL
tack
clew
head
slides or slugs
downhaul

- **The mainsail.**Secure the **tack** to the tack fitting on the forward end of the boom... then take the mainsail **clew** which goes aft while feeding the slides on the foot into the boom track,finally securing the clew to its outhaul fitting.Secure the main halyard to the **head** of the sail which you start raising,progressively feeding the slides onto the external mast track,text page 88,or into the internal track if the luff has slugs, text page 97,so the head of the mainsail is hauled almost to the top of the mast. Add sufficient tension to the **downhaul**,then cleat the downhaul.Proper tension for outhaul and downhaul is shown on text page 93.

the JIB
tack
luff snaps

- **The jib.**The **tack** is secured to the stemhead fitting,the jib **luff snaps** are snapped onto the jibstay,the jib sheets are secured to the **clew** then fed aft thru their fairleads which changes the sheet angle to the winch.When ready,the jib is rapidly raised with its halyard till the luff is taut but not too tight,then the halyard tail is cleated.

cleating the halyard tails

- **Halyard tails.**The **mainsail halyard** is cleated on,and cleated to the **starboard side** of the mast...while the **jib halyard** is carried on,and cleated to the **port side** of the mast with considerable standardization.It sounds simple...until you are forward of the mast looking aft when raising halyards,sometimes forgetting to reverse your thinking. Add stick-on labels to jib and mainsail halyard winches to avoid this confusion.

folding,stowing sails

Sail handling,cabin sailboats 22' to 30' long. Text pages 96-97 cover the folding sequence of a mainsail,stuffing it into a sailbag,and securing it to a boom for storage.

mainsail tension adjusts

Text pages 92-93 illustrate halyard,outhaul,and downhaul mainsail tension methods. What clues tell you when the tension is too tight...and when it is too slack.

add a topping lift

While the topping lift is seldom found on sailboats under 26' long,active sailboats 23' and longer should require topping lifts while raising sails in strong or puffy winds, page 92,when the boom lift can become an unnecessary hazard.

efficient jib handling

For sailboats 22' to 30',we prefer to secure the jib luff to the jibstay,then stow it in a sailbag before leaving the dock...also to lower the jib into the sailbag afterwards,then unsnapping the hanks for storage.The jib sheet should have a Swedish snap hook for efficiency,and easy handling.

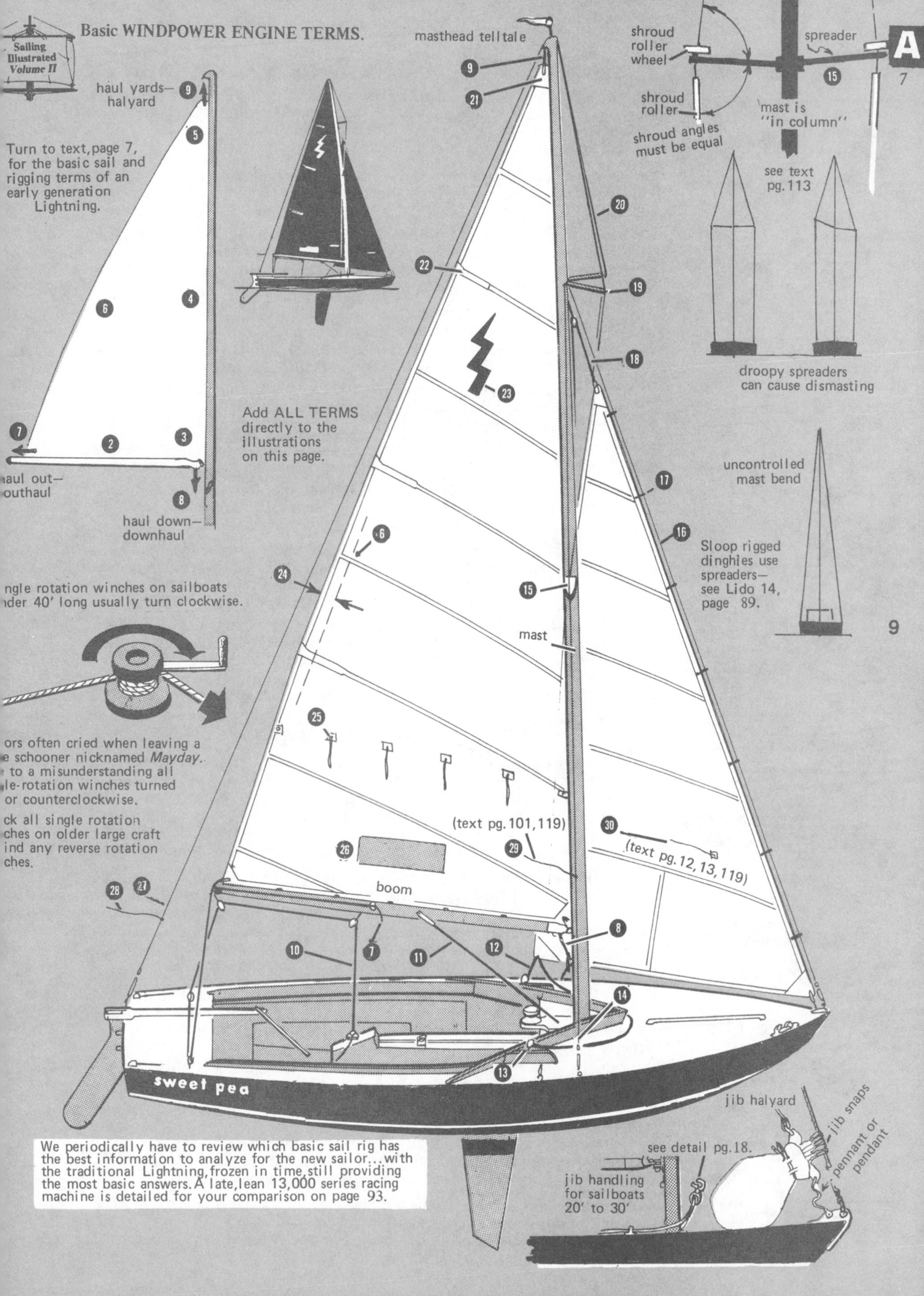

Sailing Illustrated Volume II
Basic WINDPOWER ENGINE TERMS.
A
7
9
masthead telltale
haul yards—
halyard
Turn to text, page 7, for the basic sail and rigging terms of an early generation Lightning.
aul out—
outhaul
haul down—
downhaul
Add ALL TERMS directly to the illustrations on this page.
ngle rotation winches on sailboats
nder 40′ long usually turn clockwise.
ors often cried when leaving a
e schooner nicknamed Mayday.
to a misunderstanding all
le-rotation winches turned
or counterclockwise.
ck all single rotation
ches on older large craft
ind any reverse rotation
ches.
shroud roller wheel
shroud roller
shroud angles must be equal
spreader
mast is "in column"
see text pg. 113
droopy spreaders can cause dismasting
uncontrolled mast bend
Sloop rigged dinghies use spreaders— see Lido 14, page 89.
mast
boom
(text pg. 101, 119)
(text pg. 12, 13, 119)
sweet pea
jib halyard
jib snaps
pennant or pendant
see detail pg. 18.
jib handling for sailboats 20′ to 30′
We periodically have to review which basic sail rig has the best information to analyze for the new sailor...with the traditional Lightning, frozen in time, still providing the most basic answers. A late, lean 13,000 series racing machine is detailed for your comparison on page 93.

A

Sailboat AIRFOILS above the water...and WATERFOILS below, are equally critical.

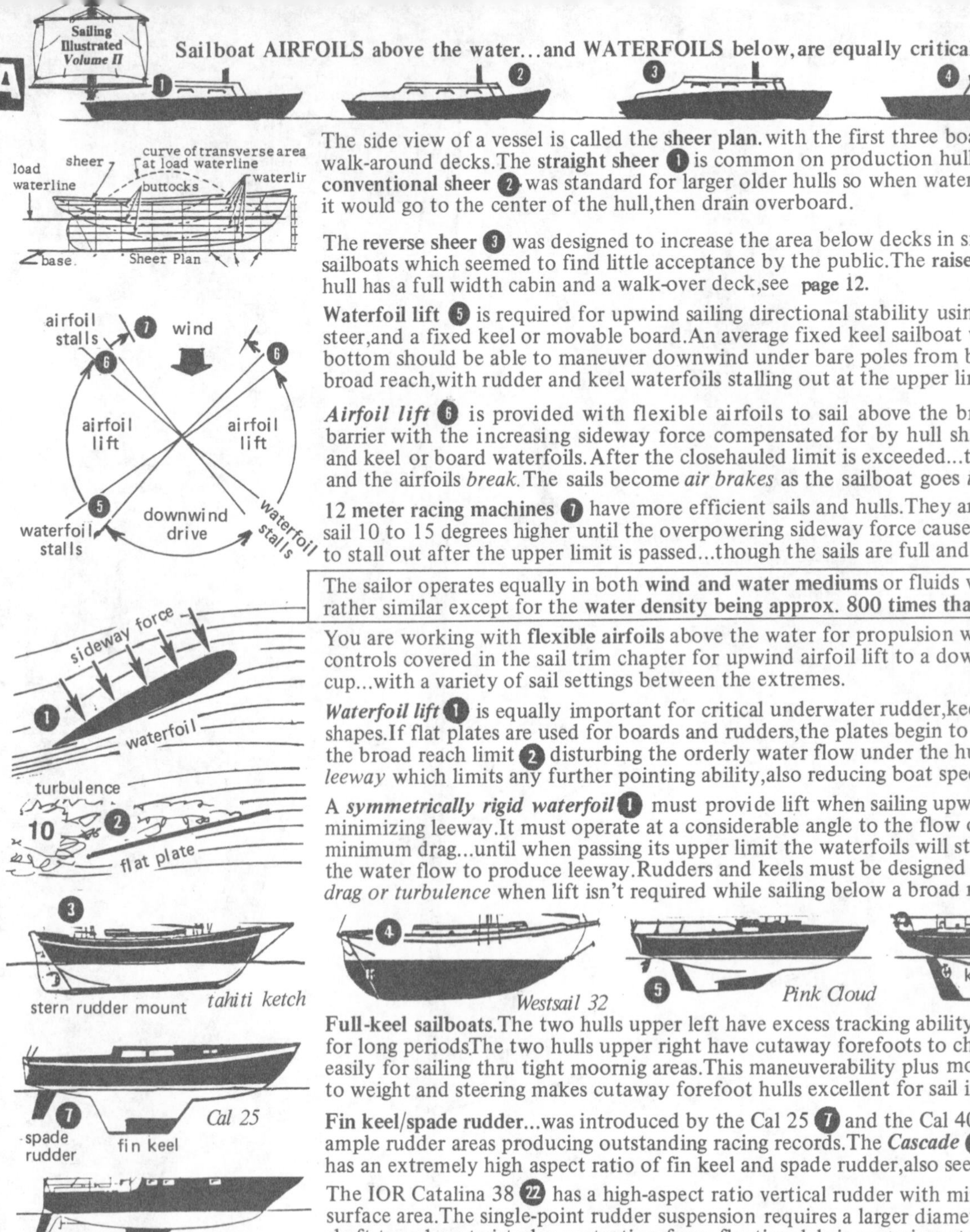
1
2
3
4
load waterline
sheer
curve of transverse area at load waterline
waterline
buttocks
base
Sheer Plan
airfoil stalls
7
wind
6
6
airfoil lift
airfoil lift
5
waterfoil stalls
downwind drive
waterfoil stalls
sideway force
1
waterfoil
turbulence
10
2
flat plate

The side view of a vessel is called the **sheer plan.** with the first three boats having walk-around decks. The **straight sheer** (1) is common on production hulls, while the **conventional sheer** (2) was standard for larger older hulls so when water came aboard it would go to the center of the hull, then drain overboard.

The **reverse sheer** (3) was designed to increase the area below decks in smaller cabin sailboats which seemed to find little acceptance by the public. The **raised deck** (4) hull has a full width cabin and a walk-over deck, see **page 12.**

Waterfoil lift (5) is required for upwind sailing directional stability using a rudder to steer, and a fixed keel or movable board. An average fixed keel sailboat with a clean bottom should be able to maneuver downwind under bare poles from broad reach to broad reach, with rudder and keel waterfoils stalling out at the upper limit.

Airfoil lift (6) is provided with flexible airfoils to sail above the broad reach barrier with the increasing sideway force compensated for by hull shape, rudder, and keel or board waterfoils. After the closehauled limit is exceeded...the sails *lift* and the airfoils *break.* The sails become *air brakes* as the sailboat goes *into irons.*

12 meter racing machines (7) have more efficient sails and hulls. They are able to sail 10 to 15 degrees higher until the overpowering sideway force causes the hull to stall out after the upper limit is passed...though the sails are full and pulling.

The sailor operates equally in both **wind and water mediums** or fluids which are rather similar except for the **water density being approx. 800 times that of air.**

You are working with **flexible airfoils** above the water for propulsion with many controls covered in the sail trim chapter for upwind airfoil lift to a downwind air cup...with a variety of sail settings between the extremes.

Waterfoil lift (1) is equally important for critical underwater rudder, keel and board shapes. If flat plates are used for boards and rudders, the plates begin to stall out at the broad reach limit (2) disturbing the orderly water flow under the hull. This causes *leeway* which limits any further pointing ability, also reducing boat speed.

A ***symmetrically rigid waterfoil*** (1) must provide lift when sailing upwind while minimizing leeway. It must operate at a considerable angle to the flow of water with minimum drag...until when passing its upper limit the waterfoils will stall, disturbing the water flow to produce leeway. Rudders and keels must be designed for *minimum drag or turbulence* when lift isn't required while sailing below a broad reach.

3
stern rudder mount *tahiti ketch*

4 *Westsail 32* 5 *Pink Cloud* keel rudder mount *Sea Sprite*

Full-keel sailboats. The two hulls upper left have excess tracking ability to hold course for long periods. The two hulls upper right have cutaway forefoots to change tack easily for sailing thru tight moornig areas. This maneuverability plus more sensitivity to weight and steering makes cutaway forefoot hulls excellent for sail instruction.

7 spade rudder fin keel *Cal 25*

Fin keel/spade rudder...was introduced by the Cal 25 (7) and the Cal 40 (21) both with ample rudder areas producing outstanding racing records. The ***Cascade*** (8) for comparison has an extremely high aspect ratio of fin keel and spade rudder, also see **page 42.**

8 *Cascade* considerable rudder/skeg rake

The IOR Catalina 38 (22) has a high-aspect ratio vertical rudder with minimum wetted surface area. The single-point rudder suspension requires a larger diameter rudder shaft to reduce twist, plus protection from floating debris, porpoises, etc.

Rudder skegs. Performance cruisers (19), (20) have rudders suspended on strong, full-length skegs to protect their rudders in a grounding, and from floating debris plus porpoises. ***Cascade*** also carries its high-aspect ratio rudder on a full length skeg.

9 10 full fin keel winglet keel

Winglet keel. Our Australian friends introduced this concept in 1984 on its 12 meter ***Australia II***, **page 99** ...which may become standard 12 meter equipment. The winglet keel was next introduced on the Contessa 36 having a 1.4 meter dockside draft instead of the regular 1.9 meter regular fin keel draft. Both keels may have similar draft when sailing upwind due to angle of winglet, see illustration at left.

11 *patented Scheel Keel*

The winglet keel is questionable for cruising sailboats going thru tight moorings and anchorages, becoming an excellent chain and rope catcher, plus kelp. It may also be a hazard for our underwater friends the porpoises and pilot whales.

the Star bulb keel 12

Shallow, low-ballast keel...is the winglet keel advantage. It is also the theory for the 1911 Star bulb-keel design, and the ***Scheel Keel*** at left. Draft is reduced and resistance to heel increased, producing a stiffer boat for upwind sailing performance.

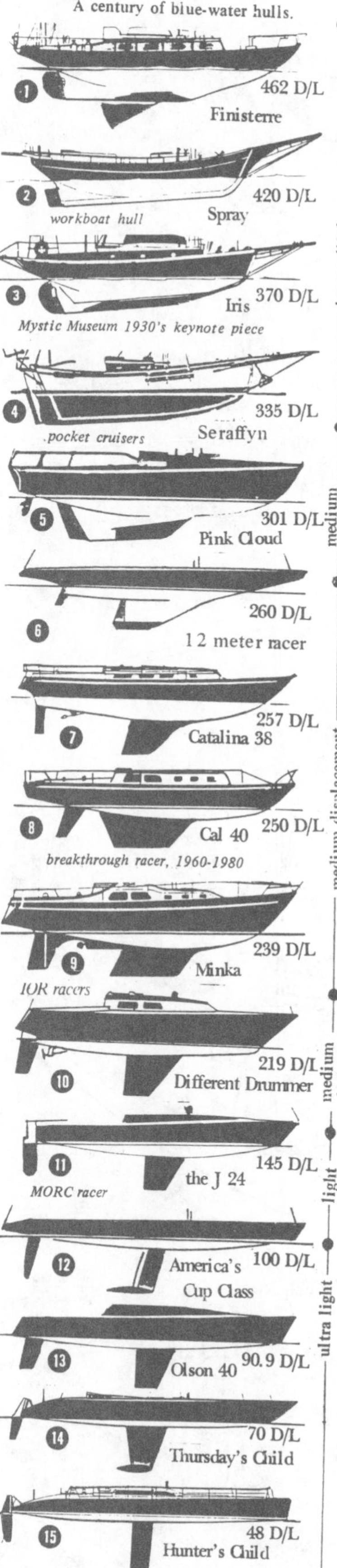

Which sailboat fits your personality? The best way to analyze sailboat personalities is with their Displacement to Length ratios.
A century of blue-water hulls.
1
462 D/L
Finisterre
2
420 D/L
workboat hull
Spray
3
370 D/L
Iris
Mystic Museum 1930's keynote piece
4
335 D/L
pocket cruisers
Seraffyn
5
301 D/L
Pink Cloud
6
260 D/L
12 meter racer
7
257 D/L
Catalina 38
8
250 D/L
Cal 40
breakthrough racer, 1960-1980
9
239 D/L
Minka
IOR racers
10
219 D/L
Different Drummer
11
145 D/L
the J 24
MORC racer
12
100 D/L
America's Cup Class
13
90.9 D/L
Olson 40
14
70 D/L
Thursday's Child
15
48 D/L
Hunter's Child
heavy displacement
medium heavy
medium displacement
medium light
light
ultra light

1960 hull extremes.
13
easy turning
14
excellent tracking
A

1960 hull extremes

1960 hull extremes are the **Columbia 5.5** ⓭ with high aspect ratio airfoils above,and waterfoils below,with minimum wetted surface and long overhangs.The short keel is excellent for short tacks,though tiring to hold a long course.The heavier 5.5 fiberglass hull wasn't competitive with lighter stiffer 5.5 wooden hulls.

The heavy displacement 48' **Taku** ⓮ shows the opposite extreme. The full-length keel follows square rigger concepts that a hull should hold course with minimum rudder attention for long periods,due to its excessive tracking ability,see page **36, comiing about.**

We provide a visual pattern of a hundred years of blue-water hulls from the traditional workboat design on one extreme,to a racing maxi on the other.If ocean sailing interests you... which design fits your personality, kind of sailing,and bank account (oilwells,timber,diamond mines?).

- *The deep-sea hull design* requires a fascinating mix of science,art,and native savvy.A good,efficient hull requires a balanced blend of numerous complex factors producing sailboats with widely varying personalities. If all factors of one hull can be applied to a new design with one change, the performance factors resulting may be considerably different.
- *Tracking ability* resulting from the delicate balance of hull and sail rig, is the primary factor to consider.The ocean sailboat should be able to sail itself for long periods with correct sail trim and weight trim...while the rudder is only used for minor steering corrections and changing tack. ***Avoid*** sailboats with ***undersize rudders.*** Their limited steering ability is an unnecessary hazard,especially when sailing downwind with chute up.
- *Traditional cruising hulls* are designed for maximum cargo carrying capacity,and to protect you in bad weather when you can no longer operate the boat.Their long keels provide excellent tracking ability... also protecting the rudder when going aground.
- *The one-piece cruising hull and rudder waterfoil* limits upwind pointing ability,similar to the limited pointing ability of a catboat.The large underwater surfaces develop considerable parasitic drag as hull speed is approached,page 77. If a true cruising hull design is chosen,the primary factor is for everyone to arrive fresh and relaxed,while due to limited speed and pointing ability,the desire to break port to port elapsed time records...becomes a minor factor.
- *ULDB racing performance* is the primary consideration on long lean strong hulls with minimum wetted surface,not for cargo-carrying ability.
- *ULDB tracking ability is provided by leverage* or distance between fin keel and high aspect ratio rudder,page 42. Water flowing between keel and rudder waterfoils provide upwind lift for racing pointing and footing ability similar to the slot between main and jib,page 33. Minimum parasitic drag surface area is required for good downwind tracking ability at surfing speeds to 20 knots.
- *Workboat hull loading,* the primary requirement of ***Spray,*** is better defined with Scandinavian fishing trawlers,ocean workboats built to standards little changed in over 70 years.They were designed to carry ***heavy weight loads*** for long periods at sea while towing a net,providing an easy ride below and topside in stormy weather.

  When some of these trawlers were built in Norway for use as yachts for local owners,page 135, they were nicknamed *martini mixers* as they rolled miserably,sometimes in a one-reef ocean.Sailors enjoyed their secret while listening to endless trawler-owner complaints who only carried enough provisions and weight aboard for short cruises.
- *ULDB hull loading.* Our ocean greyhounds are similar to weight sensitive light airplanes-if either are to perform to their maximum designed racing potentials.Contact designer or builder for racing maximum weight specifications and loading distribution...also for coastal cruising limits,see page 71 for weight of water and fuel.For a rebuttal to ULDB cruising potentials--port to port time will be reduced considerably requiring less water,food,and cargo as compared to a similar length heavy cruiser traveling the same distance.

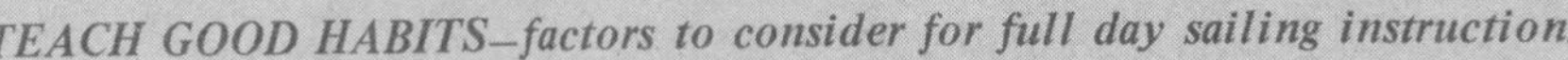

TEACH GOOD HABITS—factors to consider for full day sailing instruction.

The Lido 14 is excellent for sailing in protected waters.

Training sailboats require more planning to teach good habits.

Necessary basic rigging controls for upwind and downwind sailing.

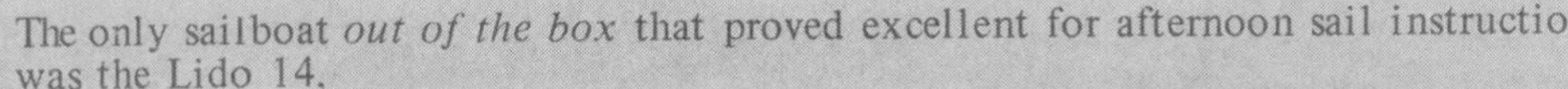

The only sailboat *out of the box* that proved excellent for afternoon sail instruction was the Lido 14.

It didn't provide the answer for new sailors wanting ocean sailing exposure.

We taught on a wide variety of keel boats from small to large with one thing in common...they all had *loose ends.* These ranged from a hinderance to annoyance to hazards for sail instruction such as blocked visibility due to a high cabin and deck sweeping jib...a better answer was required.

Our search led to the 24' sailboat below providing three major answers...good visibility, minimum size, and a large, comfortable cockpit for full day sail instructions. We installed the running rigging and controls to provide the necessary, no-frill basic sail adjustments which were customer tested with endless students. Little did we realize that 20 years later, the same little sailboat would become the benchmark for our book to give you a good starting point for ocean sailing.

The single purpose of a training sailboat, is to prepare students with a sufficient foundation so they can climb aboard their new sailboat which may be considerably different, study the rigging and hardware, raise sails, then enjoy a pleasant, spirited, and uneventful sail.

Factors to consider—heavy displacement with weight sensitivity, and good maneuverability. Helmsman should have good visibility on the boat 23' to 25' long. It can be overpowered intentionally, if required, eliminating the spade rudder. It should be limited to basic controls with slow acting winches, fast acting jib and mainsail cam cleats.

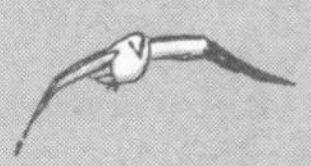

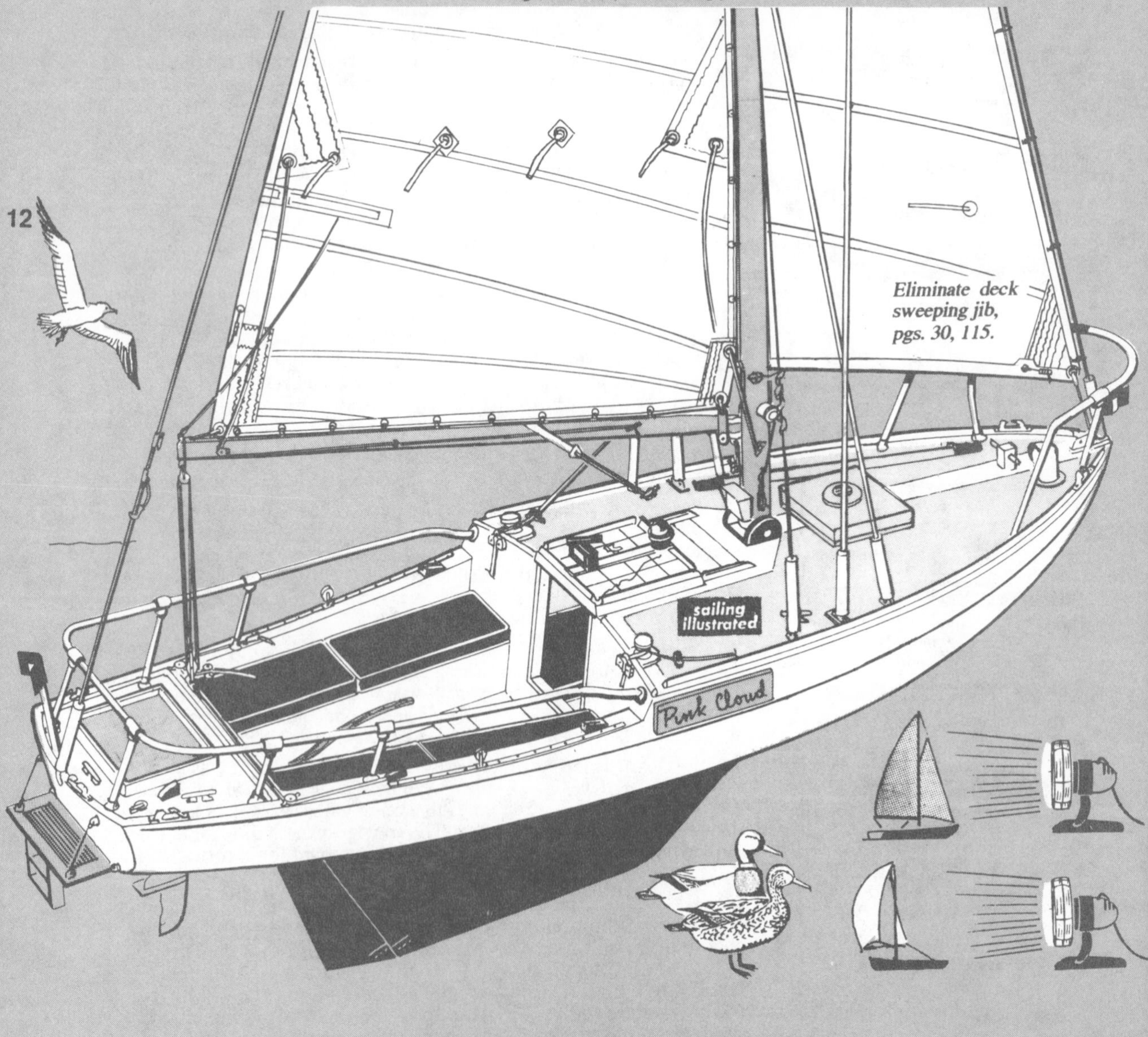

Eliminate deck sweeping jib, pgs. 30, 115.

sailing illustrated

Pink Cloud

Sailing
Illustrated
Volume II

JOIN US FOR A SAIL–

This guide sequence was developed from the patterns tested for our full day sailing lessons on the water...hopefully covering 20 nautical miles by the end of the day. We invite you along for one of these session to develop a better understanding to help you use this information to the best advantage for your type of sailing and sailing area.

The first hour is spent adding the names and discussing the reasons for the wide variety of sail rigs shown on pages 5 and 7. The terms were then added to basic Lightning rigging, sail, hull, and rudder details, Page 9.

After a five minute break students begin exploring the standing and running rigging details of the *Pink Cloud* for familiarity, which were added to an illustration similar to the one at left.

After these basic terminology pages are completed, the boat leaves the dock downwind under bare poles. This provides an hour exposure to the tiller movement, eventually going up to a broad reach stall on one tack, to a broad reach stall on the other tack,

The sails are then raised upwind or downwind following the patterns covered on page 43. The boat was under full sail for the rest of the day with at least four hours on the ocean so students become familiar with the language, rudder action, sail trim, weight trim, and the various courses, plus considerable exposure to the wind force scale, page 73.

Around 1600 the sailboat enters the harbor to begin sailing closehauled thru the moorings which provides a sudden shock... until realizing it is the same patterns as on the ocean. Students rapidly learn the reason for continually *backing the jib*, page 36, to provide considerable maneuverability in tight quarters, to spin a boat in its own length if required.

Critical sailboat balance moves from theory to reality about this time continually insisting on finger-tip steering since it is the only way a sailboat can talk back to you, page 75, to tell you it is in tune...or out of tune. *The moment a skipper has a tight grip on the tiller, ALL communications immediately cease between skipper and sailboat.*

The next exposure is to make a few stops next to a mooring on various courses, page 47, using our *air brakes* as preparation to sailing into our slip at the dock. After that students help me stow the sails followed with refreshments plus a last exchange of ideas, and the session is over. Then when I'm alone begins a revue of ideas developing during the day that can be used to improve our publications and future sailing lessons.

To summarize– around 20% of the day was spent to develop then test their foundation in language and the mechanics of wind power...with the sailboat underway for several hours providing 80% of the exposure. The numerous apprehensions of my sailing companions slowly give way to an understanding of the unique new motions and sensations of sail. They soon adapt to and enjoy the sensation of heeling on a sailboat underway which the confused subconscious mind fights...then accepts.

Children are action oriented.

Most adults are talk oriented...while kids 9 to 15 are action oriented, continually analyzing the motion of a sailboat. This becomes a pleasant surprise to parents who didn t realize their lack of talking was due to concentrating on coordination.

Junior yacht club sailing programs set the age minimum at nine, as word complexity is too difficult for eight year olds, and some nine year olds. We faced an interesting problem in teaching brothers age 7 and 8.

We made a simple sailboat model with a 15'' stick for a mast. Strong threads were used for halyards and sheets, with sails made from model airplane silk. The boys played with this model in front of an electric fan for endless hours, sometimes as early as 5 a.m.

Three weeks later the little tykers rented a 12' catboat for a two hour sail, then docked it without my help, as I was just a passenger. I had a surprise in meeting their first instructor I didn't know about. He stormed down the dock in a huff angrily demanding, ''What have you done... those boys were impossible to teach!'' The answer became obvious as I had observed him talking continuously in previous sailing lessons.

After adding sail, standing rigging, running rigging, and hardware terms to the Pink Cloud at left, repeat the sequence with the high technology FD on the following page. This exposure will provide a good foundation to begin a study of marine hardware which will grow in complexity in this book, especially Dinghy chapter H, and the boats you may sail on. Spend considerable time analyzing pages 128-138, at your leisure. Later you will understand methods to protect expensive seagoing metals.

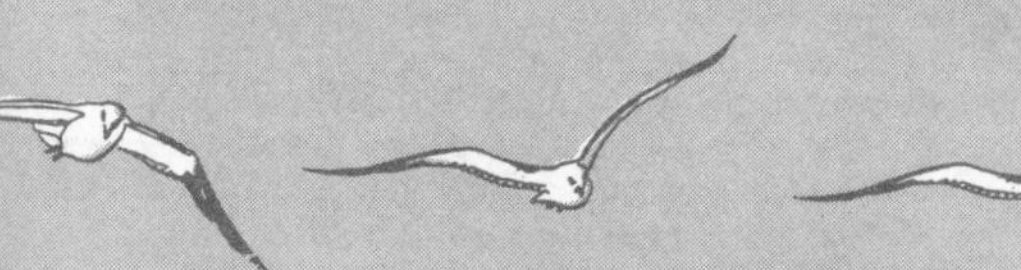

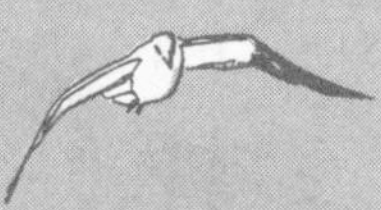

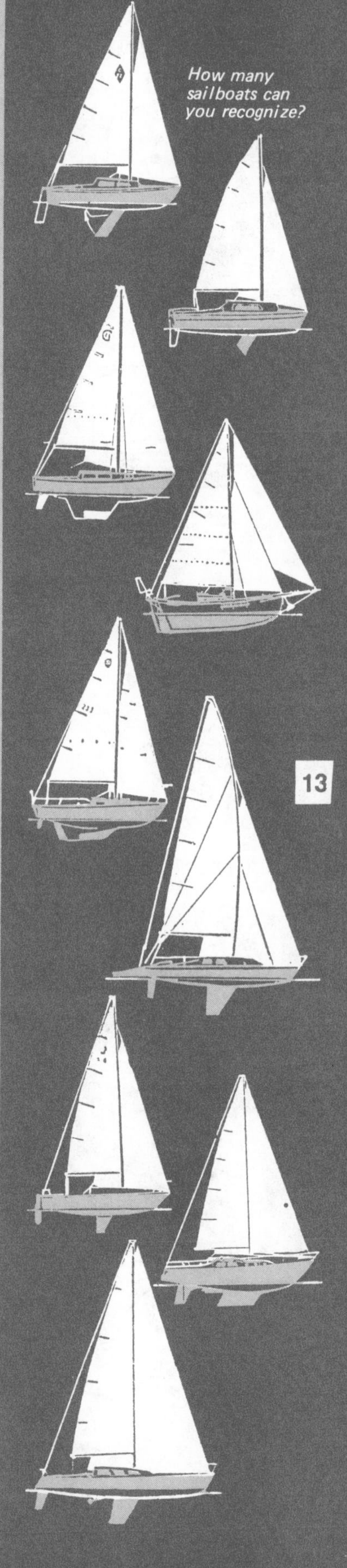
How many sailboats can you recognize?

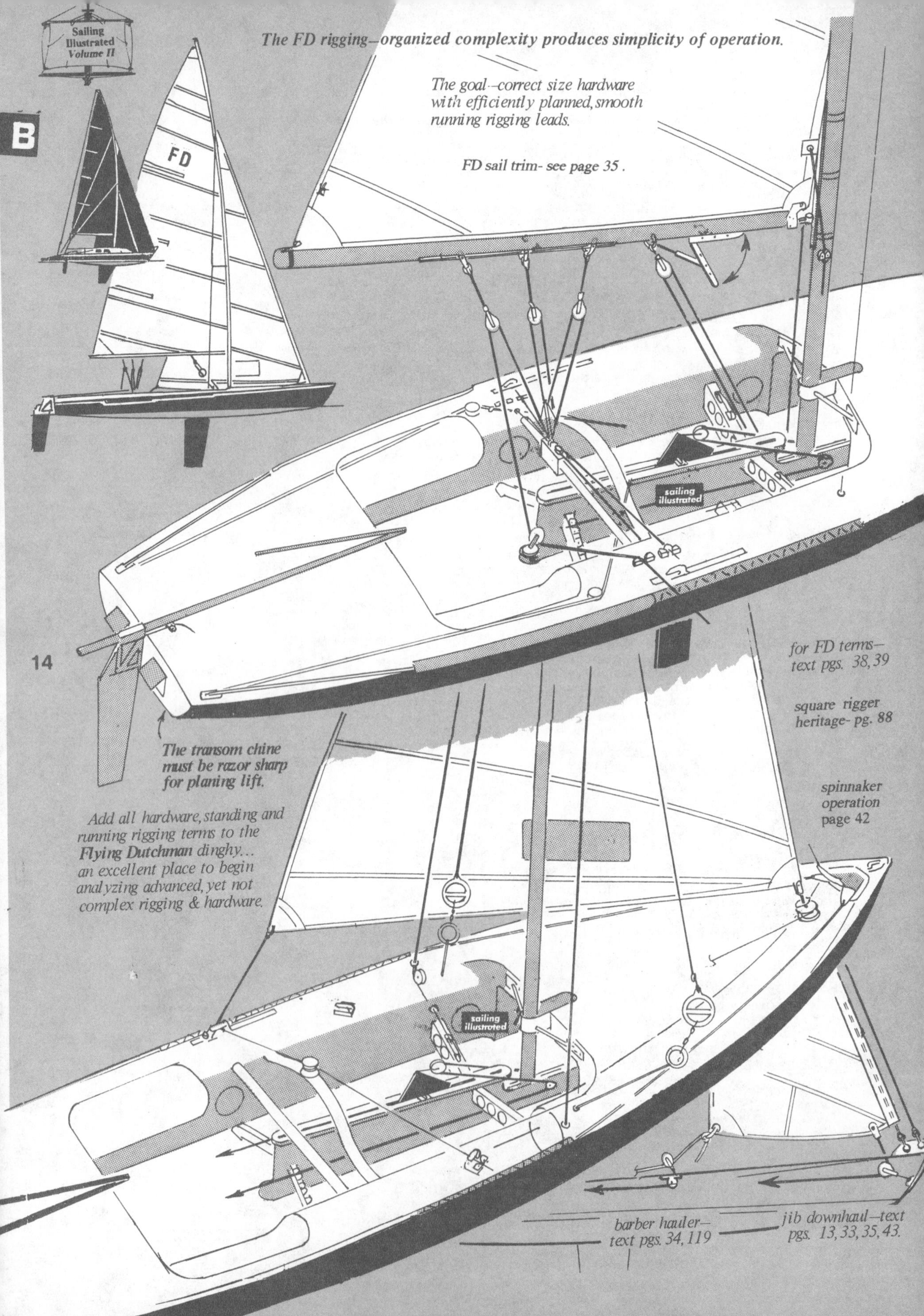
Sailing Illustrated Volume II
B
The FD rigging—organized complexity produces simplicity of operation.
The goal—correct size hardware with efficiently planned, smooth running rigging leads.
FD sail trim- see page 35 .
FD
sailing illustrated
14
for FD terms— text pgs. 38, 39
square rigger heritage- pg. 88
The transom chine must be razor sharp for planing lift.
spinnaker operation page 42
Add all hardware, standing and running rigging terms to the Flying Dutchman dinghy... an excellent place to begin analyzing advanced, yet not complex rigging & hardware.
sailing illustrated
barber hauler— text pgs. 34, 119
jib downhaul—text pgs. 13, 33, 35, 43.

THE COMPLEX MARINE HARDWARE LANGUAGE.

Sailing
Illustrated
Volume II

It wasn t one of my better days...

A customer entered a busy marine hardware store to buy a special snap shackle for his new sailboat.Both customer and clerk were going thru a Charlie Chaplin pantomine with hands plus words,as the customer tried to show the function of the snap shackle so the clerk could find the right part...that produced smiles from nearby customers.

The customer wearing a big smile walked out of the store with his precious snap shackle in his hand.I was the next customer...also having to go thru a similar pantomine with the same clerk to define the function of the part I wanted to buy.

The clerk,a long time acquaintance,tried to hold a straight face...changing to a smug grin as he listened to a sailing author he expected would have the part name without a second thought.

Such is the practical reasoning for studying this **marine hardware chapter...to help you become THE local expert** the next time you buy that special marine hardware part.

This analysis will also help you develop a practical awareness to the continual flow of excellent new marine hardware entering the sailing market.

For a quick review–***standing rigging*** consists of shrouds and stays which are fixed,or permanently rigged to support the mast...while ***running rigging*** covers all adjustable systems that raise and control the sails including halyards, sheets,preventers,and vangs...also running backstays page 122.

Take ample time to list as many callouts as possible on the ***Pink Cloud****, pg. 12, While of pre 1970 vintage,it is just as practical today to provide a basic foundation with simple,functional standing and running rigging for your analysis.*

Before you update the rigging of a sailboat,or rig a new craft,take time to plan all rigging systems so they are ***simple,functional,and efficient.*** If you are rerigging a class sailboat for racing,study any new hardware that will make rigging adjustments faster and easier...within the class rules.

The next step is to study hardware and rigging requirements of the high technology Flying Dutchman to provide a foundation in modern dinghy, IOR, and ULDB rigging methods and theories.The FD is a research class in which you build or buy the hull,mast,and sails.Specific hardware and rigging methods are not specified leaving their choice to the requirements of skipper and crew..

Study the details of the marine hardware chapter,then analyze the varied dinghy chapter running rigging systems to perform similar functions on various hulls.

If you are interested in the latest hardware and rigging for racing sailboats under 30',order the latest ***Marine Racing Hardware Catalog*** and ***Expanded Rigging Systems*** from Seaway Marine,the address is on page 16. Its Founder and President,Harrison Hine,is an active racing competitor.He personally installed 17 rigging systems using 138 blocks on his Star,page 81, text pg.43. His rigging systems and hardware have been standard factory installed equipment for many class sailboats beginning with Hobie 14,16,and 18.

When contacting local Star owners wanting to detail one of their class boats that might be a potential Olympic competitor,many of the Stars suddenly moved as far away as Santa Barbara and Sacramento so I couldn't learn,then report their secrets.When Harrison found about it thru the grapevine he grinned, giving me a call,"You can detail my Star if desired with its rigging about in the middle of the class"...thanks,Harrison.

We have to continually update many of our one-design illustrations to keep pace with the rapidly changing hardware and rigging ideas entering the market. On one extreme is tremendous hydraulic forces and hardware to bend IOR masts,pg.104,and on the other is the stayless rig philosophy.

The 55' tri *Crusader* left New York Harbor 10/23/83 to sail to San Francisco attempting to beat existing square rigger records.After rounding the Horn,then sailing 300 miles northwest,the top of the mast was carried away in 45 knot winds.On 12/15/83 the port hull of the tri filled with water when it slammed into the 200' rescue vessel.The three crew members were saved in a hazardous rescue though the tri was lost.

Tri replacement cost was $250,000. Reputed cause of dismasting...a $15 shackle failed near the top of the mast,designed to withstand pressures to 6000 pounds. Sailors are continually searching for stronger,lighter hardware to reduce the weight and windage, especially in the upper part of the mast,but where is the limit.

A famous poem inspired by Napoleon defines the problem...*For want of a nail a shoe was lost,and for want of a shoe a horse was lost...*the story of the Battle of Waterloo. If that first minor failure can just be eliminated.......

The best reason we can provide for a thorough understanding of marine hardware is the loss of a $250,000 vessel..by failure of a $15 shackle.

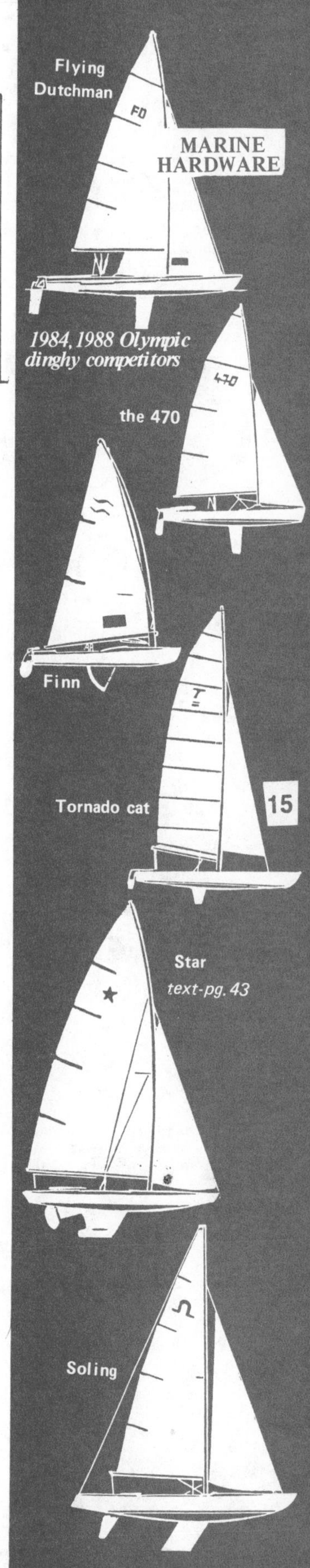
Flying
Dutchman
FD
MARINE
HARDWARE
1984,1988 Olympic
dinghy competitors
470
the 470
Finn
Tornado cat
15
Star
text-pg. 43
Soling

The racing sailor needs *total confidence* in his equipment *to be competitive.*

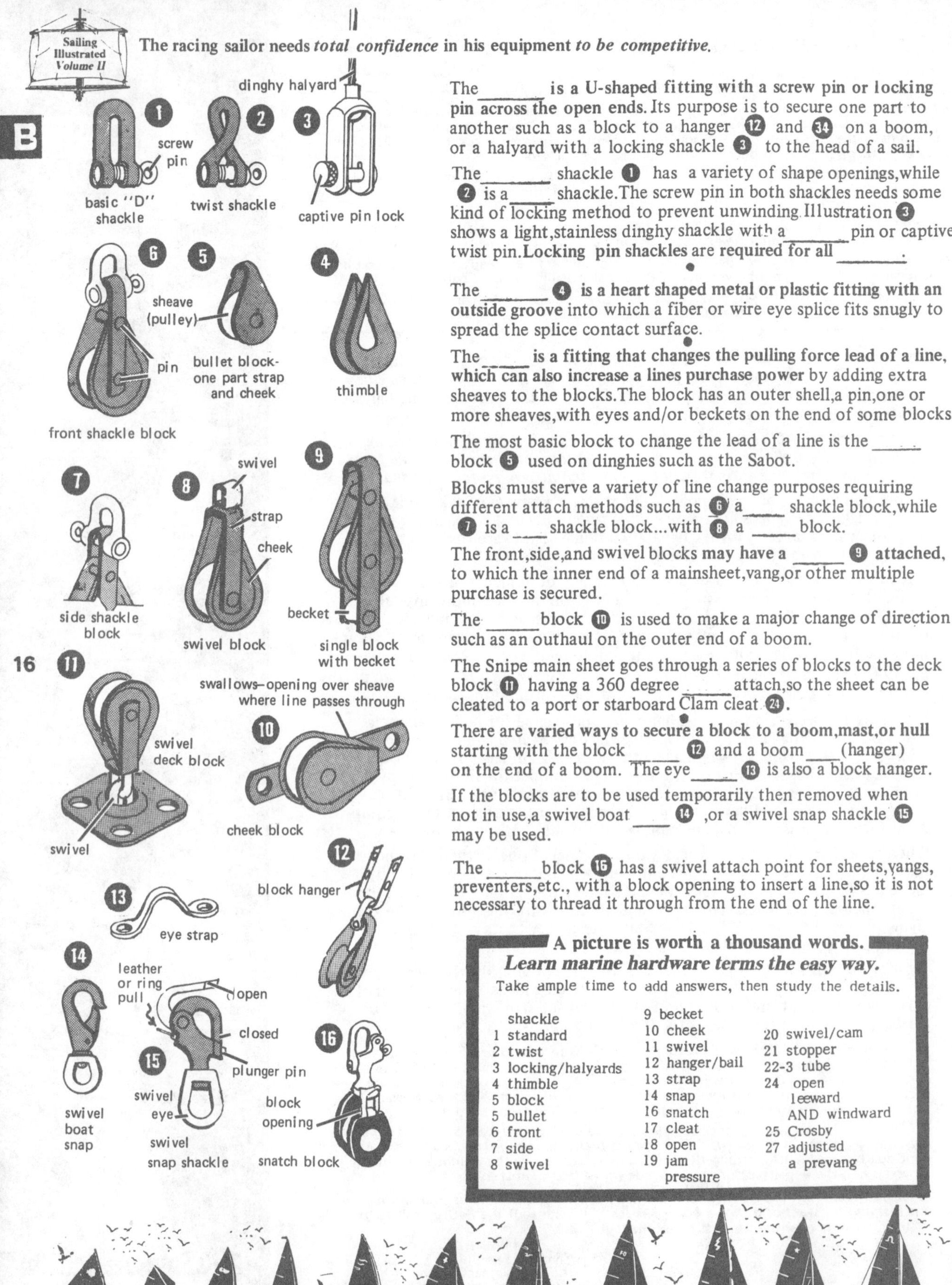

dinghy halyard
1
2
3
screw pin
basic "D" shackle
twist shackle
captive pin lock
6
5
4
sheave (pulley)
pin
bullet block- one part strap and cheek
thimble
front shackle block
swivel
9
7
8
strap
cheek
becket
side shackle block
swivel block
single block with becket
11
swallows–opening over sheave where line passes through
10
swivel deck block
swivel
cheek block
12
block hanger
13
eye strap
14
leather or ring pull
open
closed
16
15
plunger pin
swivel eye
block opening
swivel boat snap
swivel snap shackle
snatch block

The______ is a U-shaped fitting with a screw pin or locking pin across the open ends. Its purpose is to secure one part to another such as a block to a hanger ⓬ and ㉞ on a boom, or a halyard with a locking shackle ❸ to the head of a sail.

The______ shackle ❶ has a variety of shape openings, while ❷ is a_____ shackle. The screw pin in both shackles needs some kind of locking method to prevent unwinding. Illustration ❸ shows a light, stainless dinghy shackle with a______ pin or captive twist pin. **Locking pin shackles** are required for all ______.

The______ ❹ is a heart shaped metal or plastic fitting with an outside groove into which a fiber or wire eye splice fits snugly to spread the splice contact surface.

The_____ is a fitting that changes the pulling force lead of a line, which can also increase a lines purchase power by adding extra sheaves to the blocks. The block has an outer shell, a pin, one or more sheaves, with eyes and/or beckets on the end of some blocks.

The most basic block to change the lead of a line is the_____ block ❺ used on dinghies such as the Sabot.

Blocks must serve a variety of line change purposes requiring different attach methods such as ❻ a____ shackle block, while ❼ is a____ shackle block...with ❽ a _____ block.

The front, side, and swivel blocks **may have a _____ ❾ attached,** to which the inner end of a mainsheet, vang, or other multiple purchase is secured.

The ______block ❿ is used to make a major change of direction such as an outhaul on the outer end of a boom.

The Snipe main sheet goes through a series of blocks to the deck block ⓫ having a 360 degree _____ attach, so the sheet can be cleated to a port or starboard Clam cleat ㉔.

There are **varied ways to secure a block to a boom, mast, or hull** starting with the block _____ ⓬ and a boom____(hanger) on the end of a boom. The eye_____ ⓭ is also a block hanger.

If the blocks are to be used temporarily then removed when not in use, a swivel boat____ ⓮, or a swivel snap shackle ⓯ may be used.

The______block ⓰ has a swivel attach point for sheets, vangs, preventers, etc., with a block opening to insert a line, so it is not necessary to thread it through from the end of the line.

A picture is worth a thousand words.
Learn marine hardware terms the easy way.
Take ample time to add answers, then study the details.

shackle
1 standard
2 twist
3 locking/halyards
4 thimble
5 block
5 bullet
6 front
7 side
8 swivel
9 becket
10 cheek
11 swivel
12 hanger/bail
13 strap
14 snap
16 snatch
17 cleat
18 open
19 jam pressure
20 swivel/cam
21 stopper
22-3 tube
24 open leeward AND windward
25 Crosby
27 adjusted a prevang

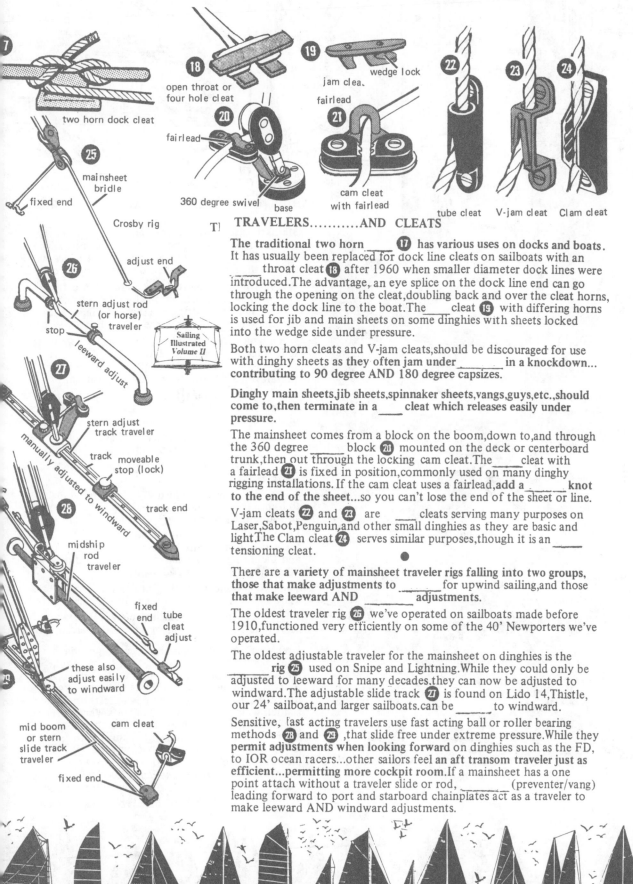

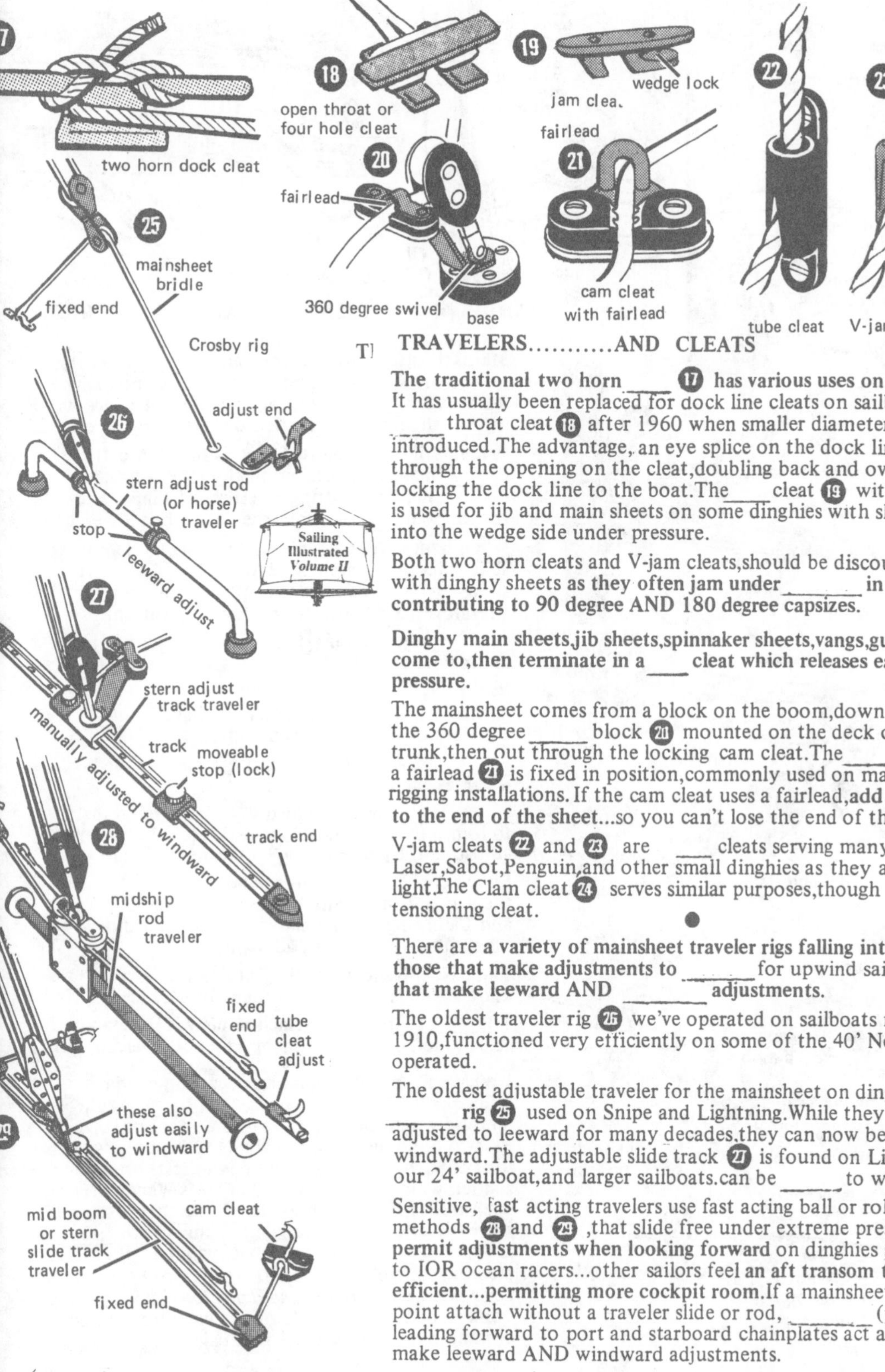
two horn dock cleat
open throat or
four hole cleat
jam clea.
wedge lock
fairlead
fairlead
360 degree swivel
base
cam cleat
with fairlead
tube cleat
V-jam cleat
Clam cleat
mainsheet
bridle
fixed end
Crosby rig
adjust end
stern adjust rod
(or horse)
traveler
stop
leeward adjust
stern adjust
track traveler
manually adjusted to windward
track
moveable
stop (lock)
track end
midship
rod
traveler
fixed
end
tube
cleat
adjust
these also
adjust easily
to windward
mid boom
or stern
slide track
traveler
cam cleat
fixed end
Sailing
Illustrated
Volume II

TRAVELERS...........AND CLEATS

The traditional two horn____ (17) has various uses on docks and boats. It has usually been replaced for dock line cleats on sailboats with an _____ throat cleat (18) after 1960 when smaller diameter dock lines were introduced.The advantage, an eye splice on the dock line end can go through the opening on the cleat,doubling back and over the cleat horns, locking the dock line to the boat.The____ cleat (19) with differing horns is used for jib and main sheets on some dinghies with sheets locked into the wedge side under pressure.

Both two horn cleats and V-jam cleats,should be discouraged for use with dinghy sheets **as they often jam under_______ in a knockdown... contributing to 90 degree AND 180 degree capsizes.**

Dinghy main sheets,jib sheets,spinnaker sheets,vangs,guys,etc.,should come to,then terminate in a____ cleat which releases easily under pressure.

The mainsheet comes from a block on the boom,down to,and through the 360 degree_____ block (20) mounted on the deck or centerboard trunk,then out through the locking cam cleat.The_____cleat with a fairlead (21) is fixed in position,commonly used on many dinghy rigging installations. If the cam cleat uses a fairlead,**add a_____ knot to the end of the sheet**...so you can't lose the end of the sheet or line.

V-jam cleats (22) and (23) are ____ cleats serving many purposes on Laser,Sabot,Penguin,and other small dinghies as they are basic and light.The Clam cleat (24) serves similar purposes,though it is an ____ tensioning cleat.

•

There are a variety of mainsheet traveler rigs falling into two groups, those that make adjustments to _______ for upwind sailing,and those **that make leeward AND ________ adjustments.**

The oldest traveler rig (26) we've operated on sailboats made before 1910,functioned very efficiently on some of the 40' Newporters we've operated.

The oldest adjustable traveler for the mainsheet on dinghies is the _______ rig (25) used on Snipe and Lightning.While they could only be adjusted to leeward for many decades,they can now be adjusted to windward.The adjustable slide track (27) is found on Lido 14,Thistle, our 24' sailboat,and larger sailboats.can be _____ to windward.

Sensitive, fast acting travelers use fast acting ball or roller bearing methods (28) and (29) ,that slide free under extreme pressure.While they **permit adjustments when looking forward** on dinghies such as the FD, to IOR ocean racers...other sailors feel **an aft transom traveler just as efficient...permitting more cockpit room.**If a mainsheet has a one point attach without a traveler slide or rod, ________ (preventer/vang) leading forward to port and starboard chainplates act as a traveler to make leeward AND windward adjustments.

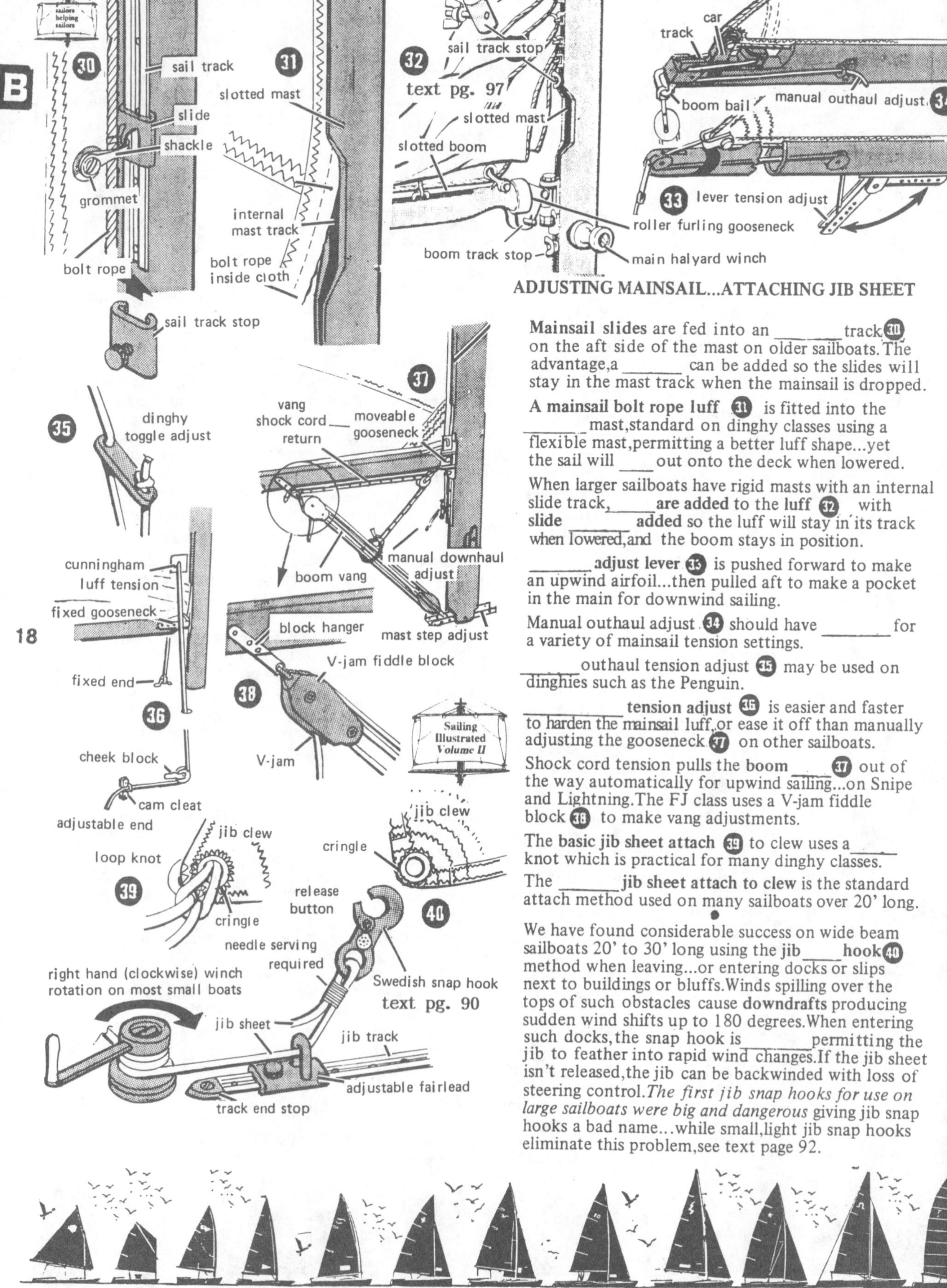
sailors helping sailors
B
30
sail track
slide
shackle
grommet
bolt rope
sail track stop
31
slotted mast
internal mast track
bolt rope inside cloth
32
sail track stop
text pg. 97
slotted mast
slotted boom
boom track stop
roller furling gooseneck
main halyard winch
track
car
boom bail
manual outhaul adjust
34
33
lever tension adjust
35
dinghy toggle adjust
37
vang shock cord return
moveable gooseneck
boom vang
manual downhaul adjust
mast step adjust
cunningham luff tension
fixed gooseneck
fixed end
36
cheek block
cam cleat
adjustable end
block hanger
V-jam fiddle block
38
V-jam
Sailing Illustrated Volume II
39
jib clew
loop knot
cringle
jib clew
cringle
40
release button
needle serving required
Swedish snap hook
text pg. 90
right hand (clockwise) winch rotation on most small boats
jib sheet
jib track
adjustable fairlead
track end stop

18

ADJUSTING MAINSAIL...ATTACHING JIB SHEET

Mainsail slides are fed into an _______ track (30) on the aft side of the mast on older sailboats. The advantage, a _______ can be added so the slides will stay in the mast track when the mainsail is dropped.

A mainsail bolt rope luff (31) is fitted into the _______ mast, standard on dinghy classes using a flexible mast, permitting a better luff shape...yet the sail will ____ out onto the deck when lowered.

When larger sailboats have rigid masts with an internal slide track, _____ **are added** to the **luff** (32) with **slide** _______ **added** so the luff will stay in its track when lowered, and the boom stays in position.

_______ **adjust lever** (33) is pushed forward to make an upwind airfoil...then pulled aft to make a pocket in the main for downwind sailing.

Manual outhaul adjust (34) should have _______ for a variety of mainsail tension settings.

_______ outhaul tension adjust (35) may be used on dinghies such as the Penguin.

_________ **tension adjust** (36) is easier and faster to harden the mainsail luff, or ease it off than manually adjusting the gooseneck (37) on other sailboats.

Shock cord tension pulls the **boom** ____ (37) out of the way automatically for upwind sailing...on Snipe and Lightning. The FJ class uses a V-jam fiddle block (38) to make vang adjustments.

The **basic jib sheet attach** (39) to clew uses a _____ knot which is practical for many dinghy classes.

The _______ **jib sheet attach to clew** is the standard attach method used on many sailboats over 20' long.

We have found considerable success on wide beam sailboats 20' to 30' long using the **jib** ____ **hook** (40) method when leaving...or entering docks or slips next to buildings or bluffs. Winds spilling over the tops of such obstacles cause **downdrafts** producing sudden wind shifts up to 180 degrees. When entering such docks, the snap hook is _______ permitting the jib to feather into rapid wind changes. If the jib sheet isn't released, the jib can be backwinded with loss of steering control. *The first jib snap hooks for use on large sailboats were big and dangerous* giving jib snap hooks a bad name...while small, light jib snap hooks eliminate this problem, see text page 92.

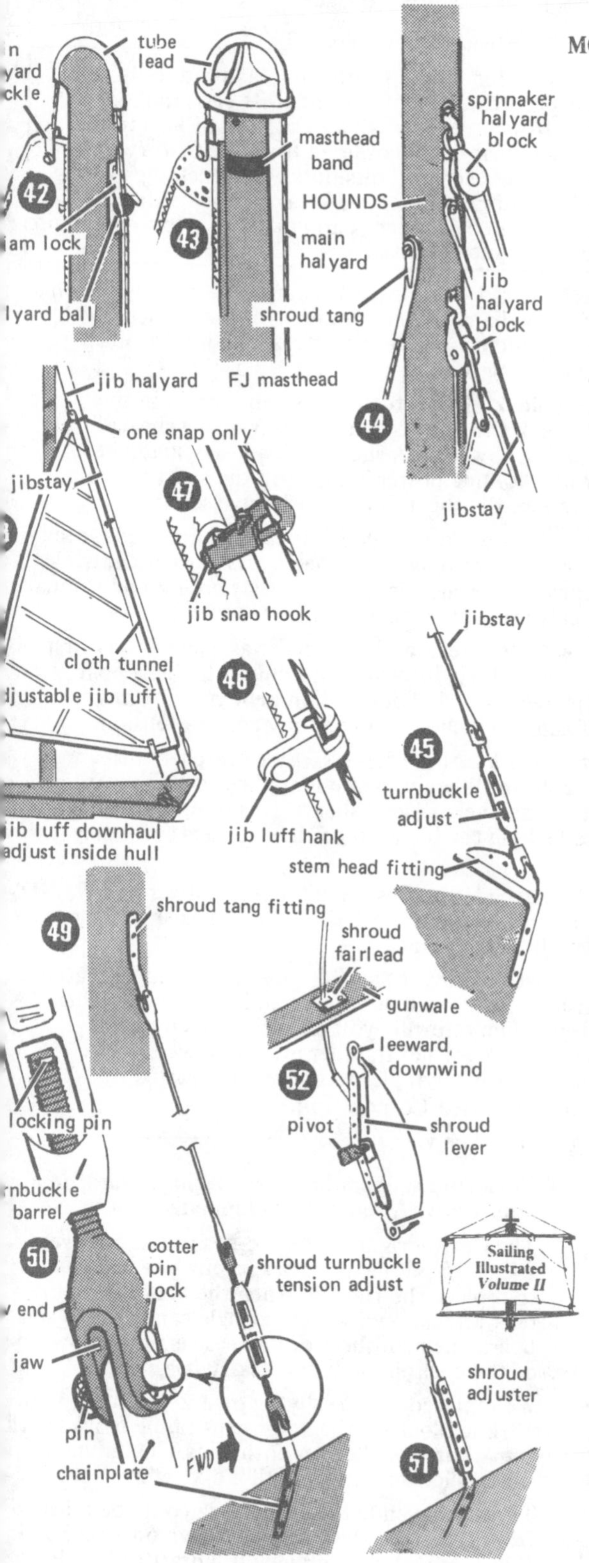

MORE HARDWARE DETAILS

Basic ____ and ______ rudder attachment

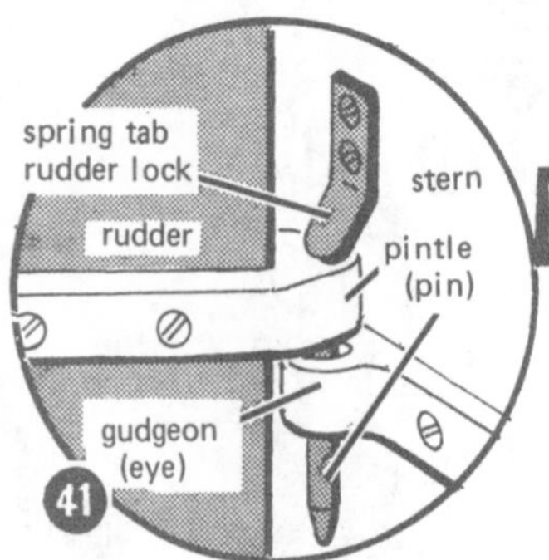

spring tab rudder lock
stern
rudder
pintle (pin)
gudgeon (eye)
41

One of the first items to consider when buying a dinghy is to add a spring tab or other kind of a rudder____ as shown at right.

Without a locking method it is easy to lift the rudder out of the gudgeons when underway.

The **external _______ halyard** may lead through a tube on top of the mast (42) and (43) on Snipe and FJ classes, to make a 180 degree lead turn. This tube reduces masthead windage and weight.

The **mainsail halyard** ____ is used on Snipe and Star classes, fits into a V-jam lock with mainsail luff tension applied with the cunningham downhaul.(36) .

The **HOUNDS** (a British term) **is the______ area of a** fractional rig **dinghy mast** (44) where the shrouds, jibstay, jib halyard, and spinnaker block are installed.

The **jibstay** is bolted to a_____fitting on a fractional rig mast, goes to a ________ fitting on the bow (45) with a turnbuckle used to adjust jibstay tension.

Snipe, Lightning, Star, and other classes often use a **jib tack** _________(48) so jib luff adjustments can be made from the cockpit. The jib wire luff rides inside the sail cloth tunnel. This adjustment was very popular in the 1960's before Dacron cloth had been fully stabilized.

The **upper shroud attach** to the mast, and the lower shroud attach parts are called _____(49) 19

Shroud tension is adjusted with__________ (50) attached to chainplates bolted to the hull. After shroud and stay adjustments have been completed, ______ pins should be added to eliminate turnbuckles from unwinding, or–

A new 30' sailboat launched in the Chicago area was dismasted two days later. The rigger forgot to add locking pins to the turnbuckles that unwound.. which can also occur to new metals during the first month or so on the ocean before sufficient corrosion begins to retard turnbuckle unwinding potentials.

Positive **locking shroud**________ (51) are used on some dinghies where weight and windage factors are involved, secured to the chainplates...or below deck adjuster shown at left.

International 14, Thistle, and FD classes have taken shroud adjusting to the ultimate, using a **shroud lever** (52) **to cast off the**_______**shroud for downwind sailing.**

tube lead
yard ...ckle
42
...am lock
...lyard ball
masthead band
HOUNDS
43
main halyard
shroud tang
FJ masthead
spinnaker halyard block
jib halyard block
44
jibstay
jib halyard
one snap only
jibstay
47
jib snap hook
cloth tunnel
...djustable jib luff
46
...ib luff downhaul adjust inside hull
jib luff hank
jibstay
45
turnbuckle adjust
stem head fitting
49
shroud tang fitting
shroud fairlead
gunwale
leeward, downwind
52
pivot
shroud lever
locking pin
...rnbuckle barrel
50
cotter pin lock
...end
jaw
pin
chainplate
FWD
shroud turnbuckle tension adjust
Sailing Illustrated Volume II
shroud adjuster
51

Marine hardware answers pages 18, 19.

30 external/stop	36 vang	44 upper
31 slotted/fall	37 vang	45 tang/stem
32 slides/stop	39 loop/Swedish	49 tangs
33 outhaul	40 snap/released	50 turnbuckle/locking
34 markings	pintle/gudgeon/lock	51 adjuster
35 toggle	42 main	52 leeward
	42/36 lock	

Many races are won by INCHES, OUNCES, and/or SECONDS proving the importance of hardware details.

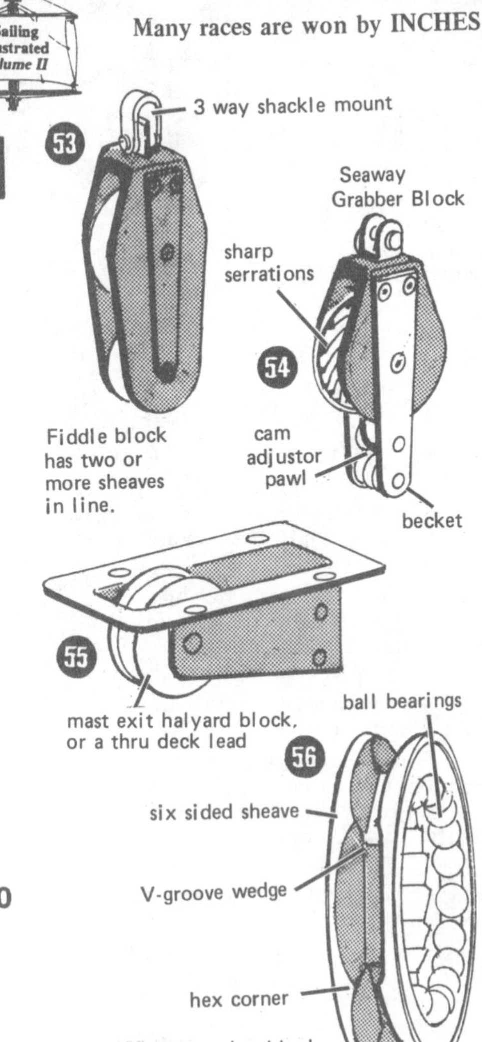

53
3 way shackle mount
Fiddle block has two or more sheaves in line.
54
Seaway Grabber Block
sharp serrations
cam adjustor pawl
becket
55
mast exit halyard block, or a thru deck lead
56
ball bearings
six sided sheave
V-groove wedge
hex corner
the hexaratchet block

Sailboat Parts Catalogs

Catalina Yachts of Woodland Hills, California, has produced fully illustrated, excellent parts catalogs of several of its class sailboats. Each part is covered from stem to stern and bottom of keel to masthead, with part numbers that can be ordered from the factory. Parts commonly available such as screws, bolts, nuts, washers, clamps, wiring, etc., are listed so they can be bought in a local marine hardware store. The availability of such excellent parts catalogs help to maintain interest and longevity of such classes..

The **fiddle block** (53) is used in multi-part mainsheet and vang systems. The sheaves of differing diameters are in line with each other which reduces the twisting tendency and resulting chafe of lines against each other while increasing purchase power.

The **Seaway grabber block** (54) has teeth serrations angled in the direction of pull to suck the line down into the V-shape sheave. It has exceptional holding power for a sheet with a heavy load, yet with a light grip. When holding power is eased on the sheet, the cam adjustor pawl helps ease the sheet out of the sheave serrations.

A **thru deck block** (55) is used on dinghies for control line leads going thru decks and bulkheads from halyards, sheets, lifts, guys, etc.,...while an **exit block** performs the same function on masts, booms, and spinnaker poles for internal halyards, outhauls, and other leads.

My first exposure with the hexaratchet block was when it was first introduced in 1968 with little information, while detailing a boat builders Soling. The owners verbal description kept growing more hilarious and confusing...which was beyond my comprehension.

The ***Harken hexaratchet block*** (56) has a six-sided ratchet with a V-groove inside the sheave. When pressure is applied to the line, it pulls the line deeper into the six-sided sheave. This wedges the line into the **V**-grooves, locking the line into the hex corners as loading is increased.

When pressure is eased the **V**-grooves force the line outward, **UPWARD and off the hex corners**...to the smooth side of the sheave which runs smoothly and freely in a light wind.

The **Force 5** board boat detailed page **84**, uses a Harken hexaratchet block for its mainsheet turn block, has a 17:1 holding power under load, with a 180 degree line return. If you can examine Olympic sailboat contenders...check for hexaratchet **muscle power blocks.** All 1984 Finns racing in the Olympics were built and rigged by the Harken brothers Vanguard Corporation.

20

Can rigging and hardware be improved on your sailboat?

single mainsheet release

port and starboard cam cleat releases

The Crosby rig—a man overboard hazard.

● **Will better hardware and rigging methods permit easier, faster, more efficient operation of your boat?**

Many sailboats, dinghies to larger older racing and cruising boats could use a few to several rigging and hardware improvements to trim the sails easier and faster, with better efficiency. The purpose of this chapter is to help you evaluate such ideas since there are so many variables in today's sailboats.

● **Does your sailboat have any rigging hazards in a knockdown...that can be eliminated?**

The Crosby rig mainsheet (25) is found on several 24' to 25' sailiboat classes having **one jam cleat** to replace the traveler. When the boat has a port tack knockdown with the single cam cleat to starboard, the mainsheet cam release is on the low side of the cockpit...an unnecessary hazard.

We replaced the Crosby rig on a 24' sailboat with a triple block on the boom, plus fiddle blocks with cam cleats installed on both ends. The 76' mainsheet is longer with a smaller diameter.

The double-ended mainsheet rig could be released from the high side in a knockdown on either tack. It also provided many new full draft to flat draft adjustments with minimum strength required.

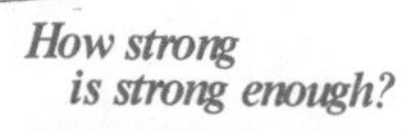

FLOTSAM & JETSAM–3 strand nylon,polyethylene floater...and a grommet punch

B

How strong is strong enough?

AVOID wood screws!

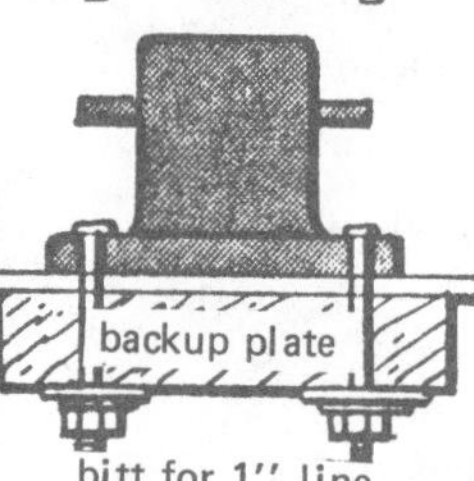
backup plate

"Every piece of dinghy hardware ,and its installation,should be strong enough to lift both the boat and its crew without failing"...was the philosophy of Earl Elms,6'4" tall and very muscular reigning Snipe World Champ for a decade.

A dusty May,1964 clipping from **Proceedings of the Merchant Marine Council** which is just as applicable today states....

"A recent casualty occurred during an attempt to refloat a grounded cruiser with the aid of a nylon towing line.When a strain was placed on the line,the towing cleat on the cruiser suddenly pulled free and became a lethal projectile under the impetus of the violently recoiling line.

"The cleat struck a man,entering the left side of his back.Death was instantaneous.. **Its elasticity...makes it extremely dangerous.**It will recoil like a rubber band when suddenly released from strain".

We'd also like to add that a person should not stand in line with any rope under tension,especially 3 strand nylon,due to its recoil hazard ***IF a cleat or block fails.***

A wood screw doesn't have sufficient bite to hold a cleat in fiberglass when under tension.If a machine screw,washer,and nut,are used to bolt a cleat to a fiberglass deck...the fiberglass under pressure may open sufficiently for the washer and nut to pop out with the cleat no longer under tension,flying through the air...while the hole no longer under pressure shrinks back to its normal size.

Cleats on fiberglass decks need ¼,½,to ¾" ***backup plates*** made of exterior plywood to provide resistance to the strain of a cleat under pressure over a sufficient area so that the bolts or machine screws holding the cleat will not pull loose.Others prefer a thinner metal backup plate to serve the same purpose.

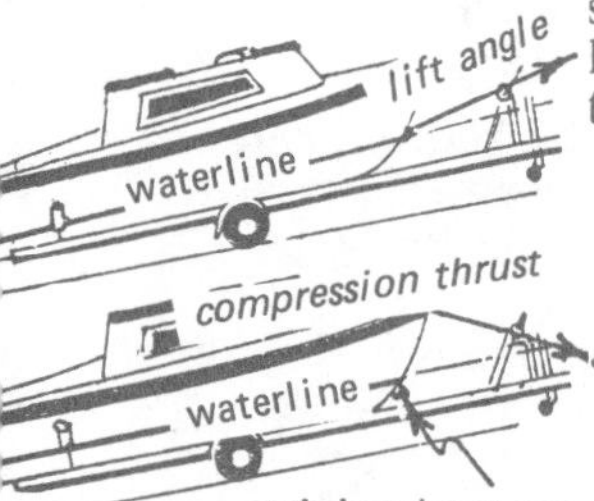
backup plate
bitt for 1" line

Many bow and stern cleats are questionable for cabin sailboat use in ocean conditions, since in case a tow is required,the bow cleat should be able to handle a one inch tow line.The bitt shown at left is much lighter,which takes a lot less space,is large enough to handle a one inch tow line.,with a backup block and double washer support.

lift angle

waterline

The portable sailboat bow eye location is critical.A slight *lifting angle is needed* to help lift the boat onto the trailer with minimum effort.A downward pull of even a couple of degrees develops a compression thrust of the hull against the trailer frame,considerably increasing tension on the line to the winch.*The bow eye MUST be made of stainless...*if the eye is chrome plated, what metal does the chrome cover?

compression thrust

waterline

stainless bow eye

We were involved in a difficult rescue having to move in close to the disabled power-boat to pick up their tow line,followed by a long tow.Research to pass a tow line from one boat to another while staying far enough apart...proved a more common problem than we had realized,see text page 203.

Our testing with a ***braided heaving line*** soon found it almost foolproof for most sailors,while 3 strand,had problems.A professional seaman coiling a 3 strand heaving line line in the morning,may recoil it again in the afternoon if it hadn't been used,to avoid kinks.If a left hander coiled his 3 strand heaving line,then gave it to a right hander (and vice versa)snafu's seemed inevitable.

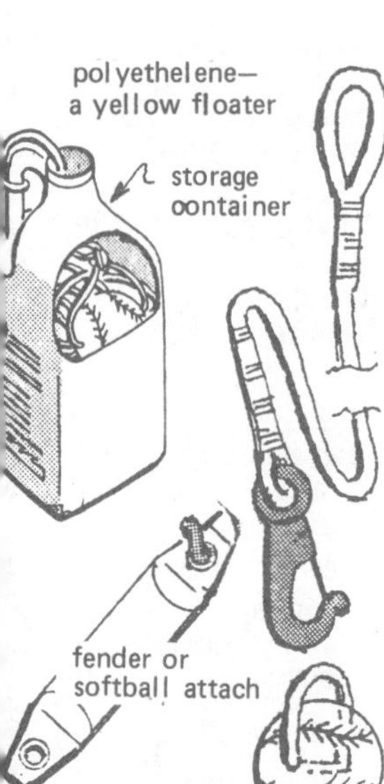
polyethelene–
a yellow floater
storage
container
fender or
softball attach

A commercial airline pilot,preparing his schooner for a South Sea cruise,stopped by our boat to ask the kind of heaving line we preferred.I picked up the plastic container shown at left.After walking to the end of the dock I heaved the softball a full 50' handing the container to him,then returning to work on my sailboat.

He was quiet when returning the heaving line,finally saying,"I completed a 747 survival school ditching program.None of our pilots had any luck with the 3 strand heaving line that was supplied as it continually fouled up...while your heaving line worked every time".

Add a **grommet punch** to your sail kit,though local ones seemed overly expensive. *Exceptions*–N.A.Taylor,Inc.,makes an excellent simple grommet punch we used to make name board covers,and a cockpit cover.Cruising boats should carry a kit aboard with varied punches,snaps,rivets,and a vise plier attachment for cloth and leather– Time Saver Tool Corp.,6806 Indianapolis Blvd.,Hammond IN 46324.

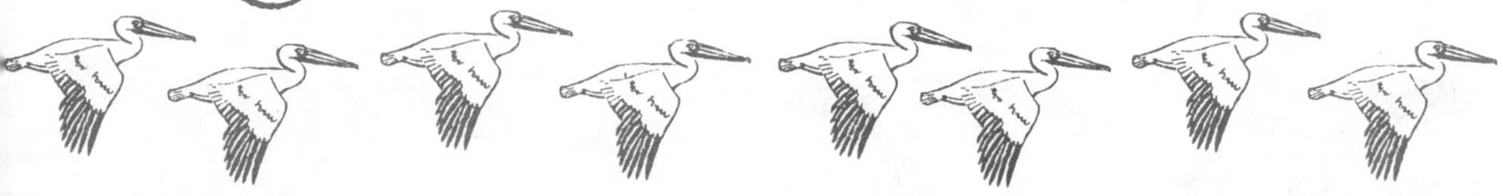

Sailing
Illustrated
Volume II
B

TEST and EXPAND your marine hardware knowledge

Refinements are continuous. Parts and rigging methods shown provide a foundation for the new sailor,plus crew and skippers with some experience.It is a good technical beginning to study,build upon,and improvise with the wide variety of sailboat hardware and rigging methods detailed in dinghy Chapter H,and cabin sailboats Chapter J.

We also recommend spending an evening locating the parts listed below in one or more marine hardware catalogs.The **Block Series** and **General Hardware** parts listed were chosen from the excellent **Schaefer Marine Catalog.**

Can you locate and describe the following marine hardware parts—

Block Series—*list safe working loads*

1985 Schaefer Marine Catalog

Series 1—	________ *pounds*
Series 2—	________ *pounds*
Series 300—	________ *pounds*
Series 3,303—	________ *pounds*
Series 404,401—	________ *pounds*
Series 500—	________ *pounds*
Series 5,501—	________ *pounds*
Series 700—	________ *pounds*
Series 7,701—	________ *pounds*
Series 8,9—	________ *pounds*
Series 10,11—	________ *pounds*
Series 12,120—	________ *pounds*

______ **exit block**
______ **turning block**
______ **cheek block**
______ **snatch block**
______ **fiddle block**
______ **twin sheet lead block**
______ **spreacher block**
______ **traveler control block**
______ **multi-line cheek block**
______ **fairlead block**
______ **foot block**
______ **traveler block**
______ **snap shackle**
______ **upset shackle**

______ **swivel shackle**
______ **fairlead**
______ **halyard stoppers**
______ **backstay adjuster**
______ **roller chock on slide**
______ **cam cleats**
______ **cam stopper**
______ **midstay release lever**
______ **vertical halyard stopper**
______ **front/side shackle**
______ **turnbuckle**
______ **triple sheave cheek block**
______ **sheet stopper**
______ **cleat on slide**

Why is marine hardware expensive?

ocean-going corrosion resistant metals are seldom found in neighborhood hardware stores

Safe working load?

Tremendous differences exist between the **quality** and **use** of local home improvement hardware store metals,and marine hardware metal requirements.The local hardware store sells mass produced inexpensive metals for the protected home environment.

The first mate refers to the local marine store as the **male jewelry store** with marine hardware made to high precision standards becoming beautiful jewels in their own world.The metal parts are made in limited runs...to tremendously high standards. They must carry high continuous loads under tension and high impact loads while withstanding the continuous rigors of the ocean elements for many years of service.

***Schaefer** lists block strength at a safe working load in pounds.**Forespar** uses the same term for some blocks,and maximum working load for other blocks.**Harken** lists bullet blocks from 2000 lbs.recommended working loads with a breaking strength of 12,000 lbs.,to big block sheave diameters to 8.00" with a maximum free rolling load of 19,000 lbs and a breaking strength of 61,500 lbs.

For the person asking what can be used as a substitute,we recommend he take a walk on various docks where ocean-going commercial fishing boats are tied up.He can find many substitute metals on them,the parts having a short life span as they rust profusely...also consider how much of a continuous working load many of the corroding shackles can take,and for how long.

elliptical or round rod rigging

NAVTEC—
525 Great Road
Littleton,MA 01460

hydraulic backstay adjusters

Why choose rod rigging?

Rod rigging is a single strand of thick wire with approx. 35% less stretch than stranded rigging.A smaller diameter,round or elliptical shape rod rigging is sufficient to replace stranded rigging,due to increased rod rigging strength.Rod rigging attach methods were solved in 1970 by NAVTEC to become standard for 12 meter competitors.

Rod rigging has found considerable success on IOR and ULDB racing machines using hydraulic backstay adjusters,mast pullers,and other tensioning methods,pages 35, 114, carrying 3000 to 5000 pounds pressure.Cruising sailboats are finding increasing use for rod rigging to replace stranded rigging.While rod rigging may cost more initially it may last longer under identical sailing conditions with the price of both becoming similar.Send for the latest NAVTEC catalog if you desire more rod rigging information.

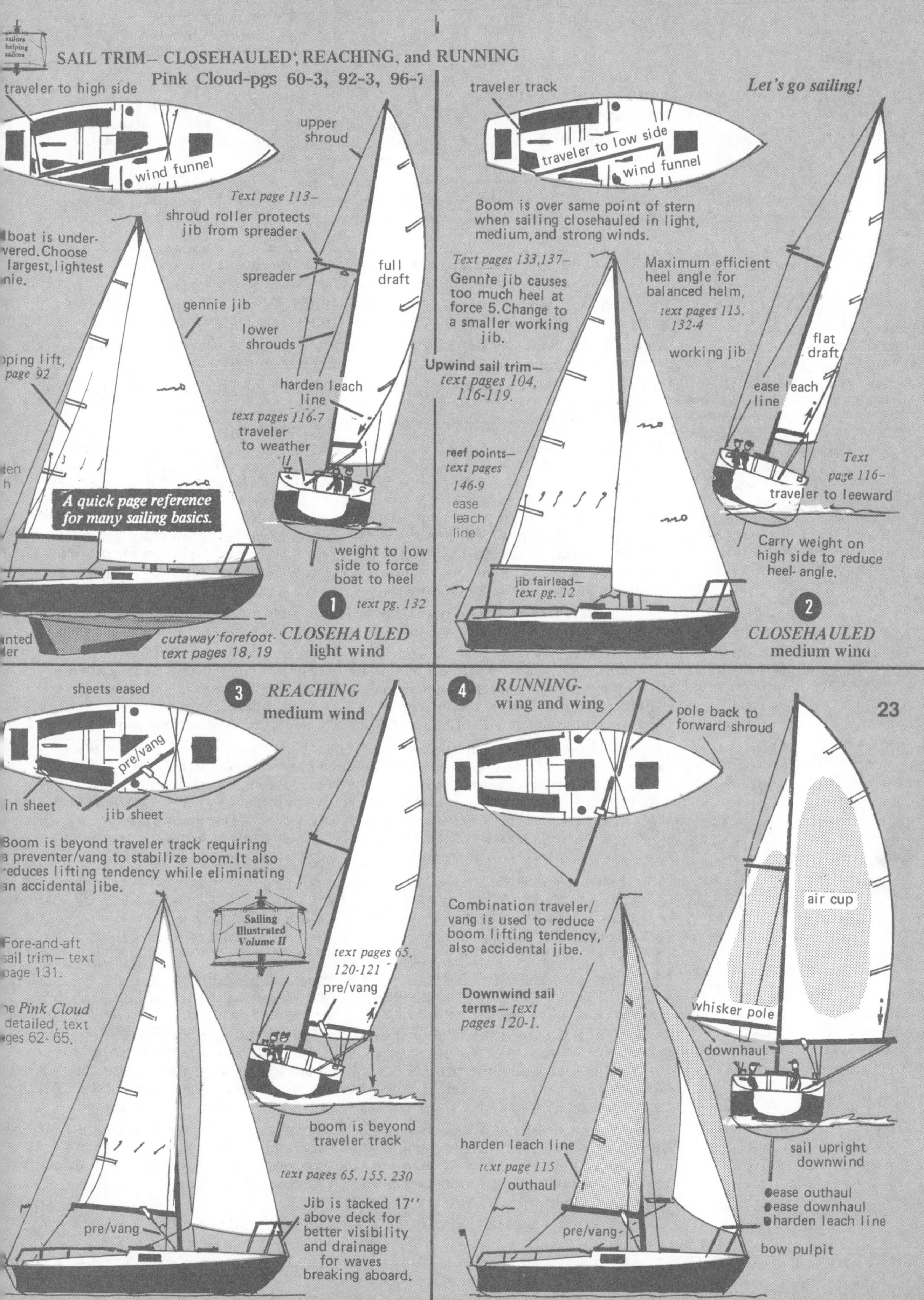
sailors helping sailors
SAIL TRIM– CLOSEHAULED, REACHING, and RUNNING
Pink Cloud-pgs 60-3, 92-3, 96-7
traveler to high side
wind funnel
upper shroud
Text page 113–
shroud roller protects jib from spreader
boat is under-
vered. Choose
largest, lightest
nie.
spreader
full draft
gennie jib
lower shrouds
pping lift,
page 92
harden leach line
text pages 116-7
traveler to weather
A quick page reference for many sailing basics.
weight to low side to force boat to heel
text pg. 132
cutaway forefoot-
text pages 18, 19
CLOSEHAULED
light wind
traveler track
Let's go sailing!
traveler to low side
wind funnel
Boom is over same point of stern when sailing closehauled in light, medium, and strong winds.
Text pages 133,137–
Gennie jib causes too much heel at force 5. Change to a smaller working jib.
Maximum efficient heel angle for balanced helm,
text pages 115, 132-4
working jib
flat draft
Upwind sail trim–
text pages 104, 116-119.
ease leach line
reef points–
text pages 146-9
ease leach line
Text page 116–
traveler to leeward
Carry weight on high side to reduce heel-angle.
jib fairlead–
text pg. 12
CLOSEHAULED
medium wind
sheets eased
REACHING
medium wind
pre/vang
in sheet
jib sheet
Boom is beyond traveler track requiring a preventer/vang to stabilize boom. It also reduces lifting tendency while eliminating an accidental jibe.
Sailing Illustrated Volume II
Fore-and-aft sail trim– text page 131.
he Pink Cloud detailed, text ges 62-65.
text pages 65, 120-121
pre/vang
boom is beyond traveler track
text pages 65, 155, 230
pre/vang
Jib is tacked 17'' above deck for better visibility and drainage for waves breaking aboard.
RUNNING-
wing and wing
pole back to forward shroud
Combination traveler/vang is used to reduce boom lifting tendency, also accidental jibe.
air cup
Downwind sail terms– text pages 120-1.
whisker pole
downhaul
harden leach line
text page 115
outhaul
sail upright downwind
ease outhaul
ease downhaul
harden leach line
pre/vang
bow pulpit

IALA MARITIME BUOY SYSTEMS A and B.

*International Association of Lighthouse Authorities

IALA* Worldwide Buoyage Systems

There were 30 major buoy systems used worldwide in 1976 often in complete contradiction with each other.

The 17 major systems found in heavily trafficked waters of Northern Europe from Lisbon to Leningrad produced confusion defying all logical attempts for analysis.After many wrecks and collisions in the Dover Straights separation lane....major changes had to be made.

The 30 systems had two basic patterns——

- European cardinal system–***red buoys to port***–emphasizing hazards such as shoals and sunken vessels to be avoided...letting you choose the safe course for your vessel.
- U.S. lateral system–***red buoys to starboard***–used port and starboard buoys to indicate a safe water route for a vessel staying within a channel...ignoring hazard buoys for isolated danger areas.

The IALA attempted to standardize buoy systems worldwide by composing them into two subsystems,Region A,and Region B,as following

Region A buoy system

Region A–***red buoys to port***–has been used since 1977 for Europe,Australia,New Zealand,the Persian Gulf, as well as a few African and Asian countries.

Region B buoy system

Region B–***red buoys to starboard***–has been adopted since 1980 by the Western Hemisphere nations,plus Japan,Korea,and the Phillippines.

2/3 of U.S buoys comply with the Region B system while the final 1/3 will be converted by the USCG from 1983 to 1989 to be in full compliance with the new **RRR (Red Right Returning)** safe water channel system.

GREEN to port, RED to starboard

GREEN–*a warning for sailors if evergreen trees are in the background... plus green grass,bushes, and trees in spring and summer.*

While inland waterway marks have been completed,port side cans and structures will be painted dark green.Junction and obstruction buoys (black and red horizontal bands) will have black bands painted green,the color of the top band indicating the preferred passing side.***WARNING***–on June 1982 we sailed and powered the 68' **Argus** thru the vast Sacramento delta finding the newly painted green spar buoys blending in and often disappearing with the green foliage background.Commercial fishermen trained to spot tiny swordfish fins prefer black buoy markers for maximum visibility.We find the black buoys have considerably better visibility especially in storm conditions...though our black can and spar buoys are changed to dark green.

red/white spherical buoy

80 unlighted **mid-channel buoys**...black and white vertical stripes,will be changed to red and white vertical stripes in the time period listed above.

GREEN lights to port
RED lights to starboard

While 4100 buoys presently use white lights,all **port buoys** will carry **green lights** and **starboard buoys red lights. Junction buoy lights** will match the red or green of the **top band** indicating the preferred passage side. Intensity of red and green lights will be increased to meet the intensity of the white lights being replaced. Around 150 **special marks**,yellow with yellow lights will mark non-navigational cables,pipes,etc.

the missing KEEP CLEAR buoy

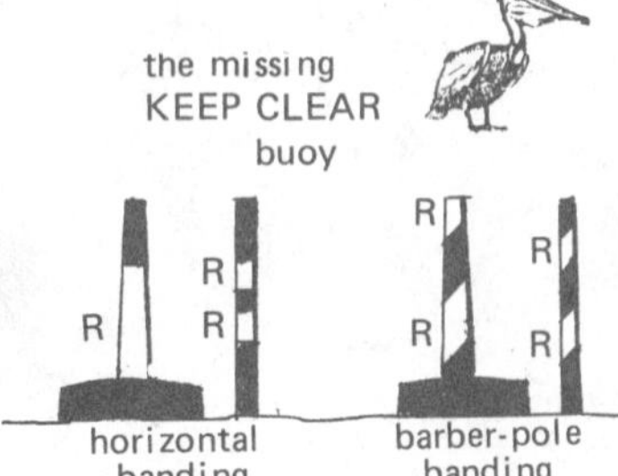
R
R
R
R
R
R
R
R

horizontal banding — barber-pole banding

Which warning method would you prefer even on a super tanker?

Isolated danger marks for hazards surrounded by navigable water ***may be placed only AFTER all other systems detailed have been completed.*** This may continue to be the weakness in our U.S. system with unmarked hazard potentials such as–
❶ the extremity of fish traps where submerged pilings may exist (Chart 1210 Tr),
❷ an unmarked hazard between two buoyage systems, ❸ a hazard where two buoyage systems meet and terminate,and ❹ an underwater obstruction or sunken vessel not visible on the water surface.

*NOTE–IALA *isolated danger marks* (keep clear buoys) with red and black horizontal bands could be confused with our older junction marks.May we recommend a *barber-pole marking* with a 45 degree red stripe on a black buoy for this mark for both IALA Region A and B which would make it distinctive,yet with no additional painting cost.

USCG at time of printing seems to have little interest with this mark feeling the situation is adequately covered under our present system,also the *barber-pole marking* could conflict with IALA systems.If our disagreement causes you to look for such hazards on your charts though possibly few in number,the curiosity may please *all* parties involved in the issue.

color in the buoys

Use marking pens to color the buoys on the IALA Region B system on the opposite page with R indicating the color red,and G,for green.

primary channel

Our system B shown ***begins with numbers entering from seaward.*** Proceed between buoys A and B,then go between buoys C and D.When going across the crossing channel turn to port for the shallow channel..or to starboard for the deeper channel.If the latter primary channel is preferred,proceed between buoys E and F,L and G,then to the correct sides of J and K.Finally pass close to P as you go onward to the dock..

secondary channel

If you desire to take the secondary channel when entering–go between spar buoys BB and CC,Z and AA,X and W,U and T,then to the anchorage or dock.Sequence and buoy colors ***are reversed when proceeding to seaward.*** Chart catalogs and nautical charts may be obtained from Regional offices or from main offices–

- National Ocean Survey,NOOA, Rockville,MD 20852
- Defense Mapping Agency Hydrographic Center,Washington,D.C.20390

IALA address–
13 Rue Yvon Villarceau
75116 Paris,France

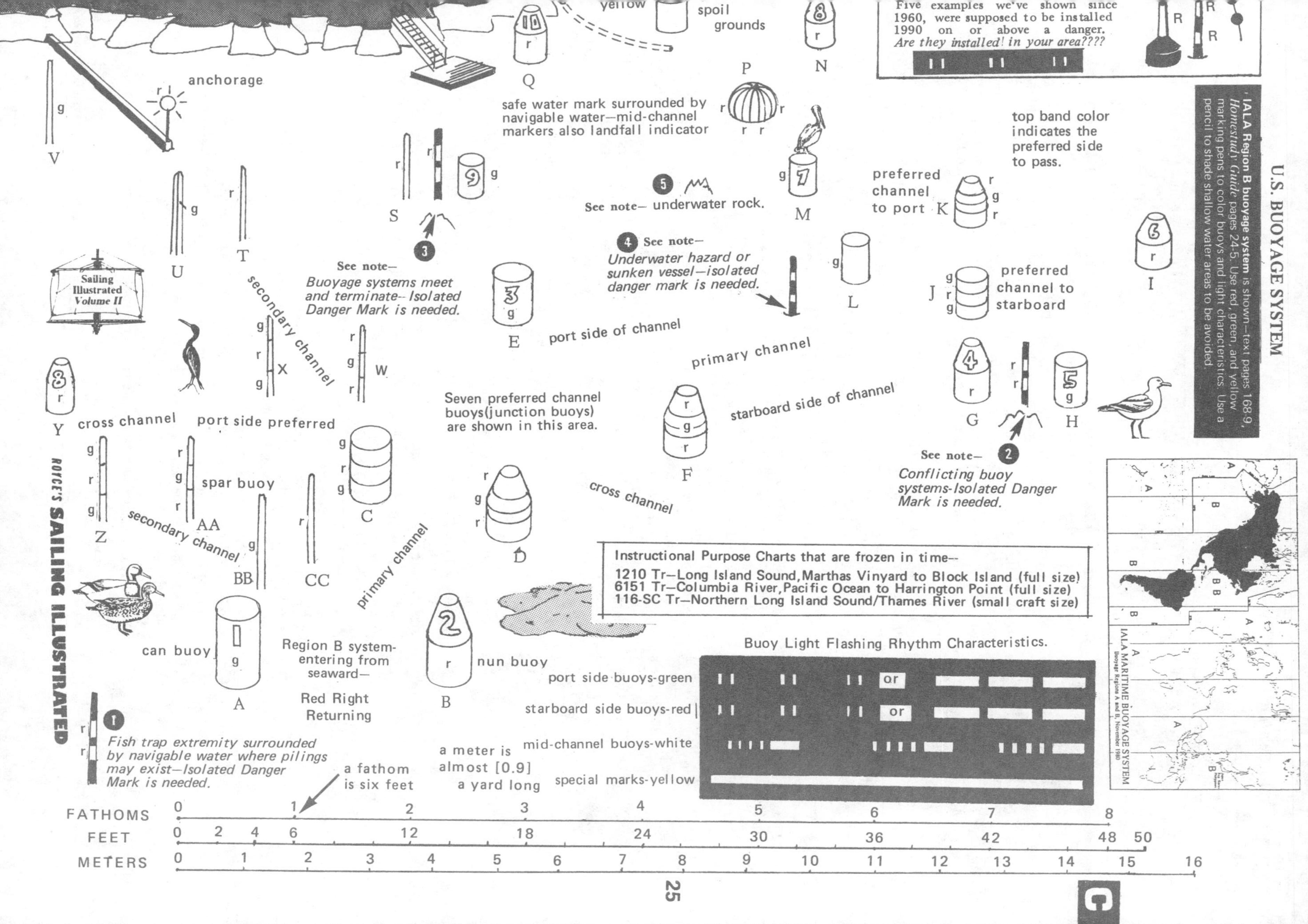
U.S. BUOYAGE SYSTEM
IALA Region B buoyage system is shown—text pages 168-9, Homestudy Guide pages 24-5. Use red, green, and yellow marking pens to color buoys and light characteristics. Use a pencil to shade shallow water areas to be avoided.
Five examples we've shown since 1960, were supposed to be installed 1990 on or above a danger. Are they installed! in your area????
anchorage
spoil grounds
yellow
safe water mark surrounded by navigable water—mid-channel markers also landfall indicator
top band color indicates the preferred side to pass.
preferred channel to port
preferred channel to starboard
See note— underwater rock.
See note— Underwater hazard or sunken vessel—isolated danger mark is needed.
See note— Buoyage systems meet and terminate—Isolated Danger Mark is needed.
See note— Conflicting buoy systems-Isolated Danger Mark is needed.
Fish trap extremity surrounded by navigable water where pilings may exist—Isolated Danger Mark is needed.
secondary channel
port side of channel
primary channel
starboard side of channel
Seven preferred channel buoys(junction buoys) are shown in this area.
cross channel
port side preferred
spar buoy
can buoy
nun buoy
Region B system-entering from seaward—
Red Right Returning
Sailing Illustrated Volume II
Instructional Purpose Charts that are frozen in time—
1210 Tr—Long Island Sound, Marthas Vinyard to Block Island (full size)
6151 Tr—Columbia River, Pacific Ocean to Harrington Point (full size)
116-SC Tr—Northern Long Island Sound/Thames River (small craft size)
Buoy Light Flashing Rhythm Characteristics.
port side buoys-green
starboard side buoys-red
mid-channel buoys-white
special marks-yellow
or
IALA MARITIME BUOYAGE SYSTEM
Buoyage Regions A and B, November 1980
a fathom is six feet
a meter is almost [0.9] a yard long
FATHOMS
FEET
METERS
ROYCE'S SAILING ILLUSTRATED
C

YOUR SAILBOAT...IS A POWERBOAT.

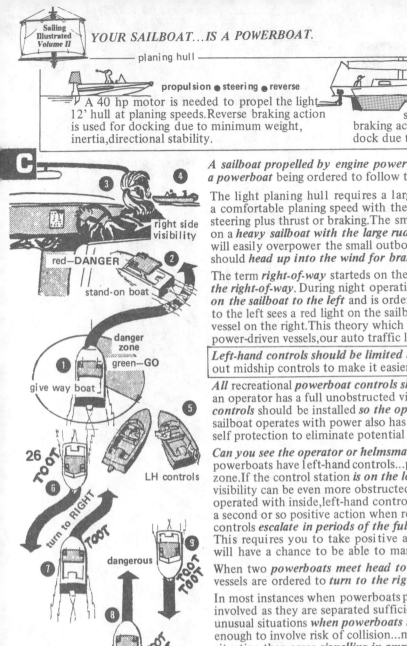

planing hull — propulsion ● steering ● reverse

A 40 hp motor is needed to propel the light 12' hull at planing speeds. Reverse braking action is used for docking due to minimum weight, inertia, directional stability.

displacement hull — rudder wind — propulsion ● ~~steering~~ ● ~~reverse~~

A 7½ hp motor pushes the heavy 24' sailboat at displacement hull speeds, Reverse braking action is nullified for stopping at a downwind dock due to tremendous weight and inertia.

C

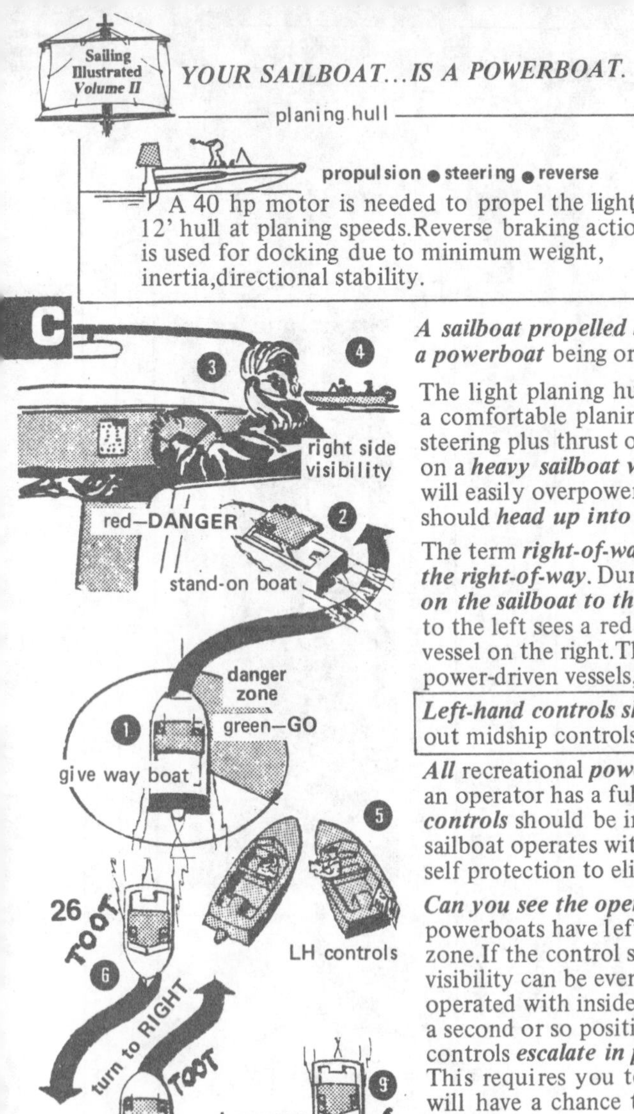
3
4
right side visibility
red—DANGER
2
stand-on boat
danger zone
green—GO
1
give way boat
5
LH controls
TOOT
6
turn to RIGHT
TOOT
7
dangerous
9
TOOT TOOT
8
TOOT TOOT

A sailboat propelled by engine power whether the sails are up or down, ***becomes a powerboat*** being ordered to follow the powerboat rules we detail.

The light planing hull requires a large horsepower outboard motor to push it at a comfortable planing speed with the lower unit and prop providing rudder-like steering plus thrust or braking. The small outboard motor is locked into fixed position on a *heavy sailboat with the large rudder providing steering.* Since weight and inertia will easily overpower the small outboard prop in reverse, the *sailboat* under power should *head up into the wind for braking action to stop* with minimum reverse.

The term *right-of-way* starteds on the ocean with the *sailboat on the right having the right-of-way.* During night operation the *sailboat on the right* sees a *green light on the sailboat to the left* and is ordered *to hold course and speed...* while the vessel to the left sees a red light on the sailboat to the right, ordering it to give way to the vessel on the right. This theory which started under sail on the ocean was adapted to power-driven vessels, our auto traffic lights...and to aircraft in the air.

Left-hand controls should be limited to USCG harbor patrol, and rescue boats without midship controls to make it easier to speak to operators of other powerboats.

All recreational *powerboat controls should be* from amidship *to the right side* so that an operator has a full unobstructed view of the right side of the boat. *Sailboat engine controls* should be installed *so the operator normally sits on the right side* when a sailboat operates with power also has full unobstructed sight of *the danger zone* for self protection to eliminate potential of collision with powerboats.

Can you see the operator or helmsman of an approaching powerboat? Many older powerboats have left-hand controls...partially blocking the visibility of their danger zone. If the control station *is on the left side of a powerboat inside the cabin,* operator's visibility can be even more obstructed. This is only part of it as powerboats I have operated with inside, left-hand controls are confusing in tight situations that delay a second or so positive action when required. The *hazards* of left-hand powerboat controls *escalate in periods of the full moon/high positive ion content* phase pg. 68. This requires you to take positive action earlier durring this time so both boats will have a chance to be able to maneuver out of a misunderstanding.

When two *powerboats meet head to head,* or head-on in normal operation, both vessels are ordered to *turn to the right* or port to port...to avoid a collision.

In most instances when powerboats pass starboard side to starboard, no signals are involved as they are separated sufficiently to avoid risk potentials of a collision. In unusual situations *when powerboats must pass starboard to starboard* that are close enough to involve risk of collision...make darn sure that both vessels know the situation then agree *signalling in ample time to maneuver out of a misunderstanding.*

O

TOOT TOOT
overtaken boats hold course
13
15
TOOT
TOOT TOOT
TOOT
overtaking boats
12
14

An overtaking boat, whether power or sail, should if any risk of collision exists *signal in ample time whether the passing* will be to the *port or starboard side* of the vessel being overtaken. The overtaken vessel should return the same signal if the course is clear, indicating it will hold course and speed until after passing when the risk of a collision no longer exists.

Admiralty laws governing power and sailboat operation seem strict and unbending when you start applying them. After you become familiar enough to apply them normally you soon begin to appreciate their no-nonsense approach.

The USCG Navigation Rules Booklet regulations are only part of the story since they can be considerably modified by Admiralty Court cases and interpretations.

For right-of-way regulations expanded with Admiralty Court interpretations—

- *Farwell's Rules of the Nautical Road*—the second half of the book covers Admiralty Court decisions and interpretations we've used for 30 years.
- *A Mariner's Guide to Rules of the Road*—William H. Tate discusses Admiralty Court cases to define and amplify the nautical rules—
Book Order Dep't, U.S. Naval Institute, General's Highway, Annapolis, MD 21401
P.S., also request the excellent Naval Institute Press Catalog.

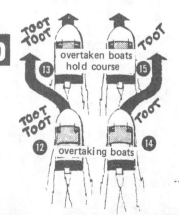

Signals, *Rule 34 (a)*... vessels in sight within a ½ mile.. *Rule 34 (b) may supplement... by* light signals.

Navigation Rules, International–Inland are covered in COMDTINST M16672.2A. Obtain publication from U.S. Gov't Printing Office, Washington, DC 20402.

olor R/G unning lights ith felt-tip pens.

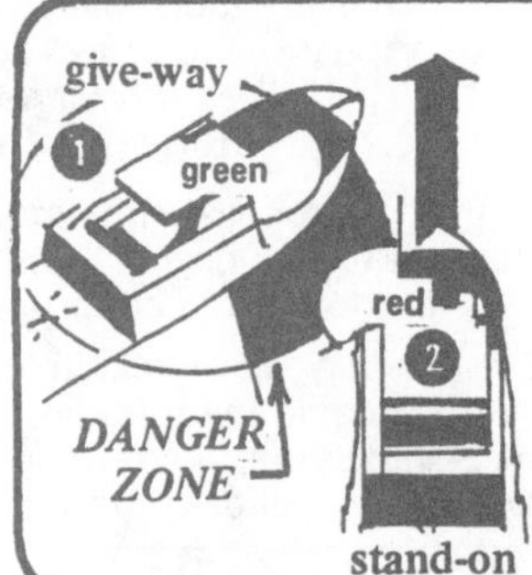
give-way
green
red
DANGER ZONE
stand-on

Crossing Situation, Rule 15–

When two power-driven vessels are crossing *so as* to involve risk of collision, the vessel which has the other on her starboard side shall keep out of the way and *shall...* avoid crossing ahead of the other vessel.

Rule 16. Give-Way Vessel..shall.. keep well clear..*R.17(a)(i) Stand on Vessel*–keep course and speed.

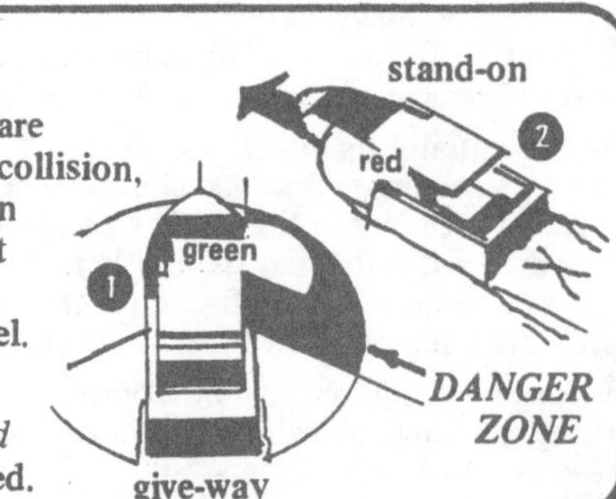
stand-on
red
green
DANGER ZONE
give-way

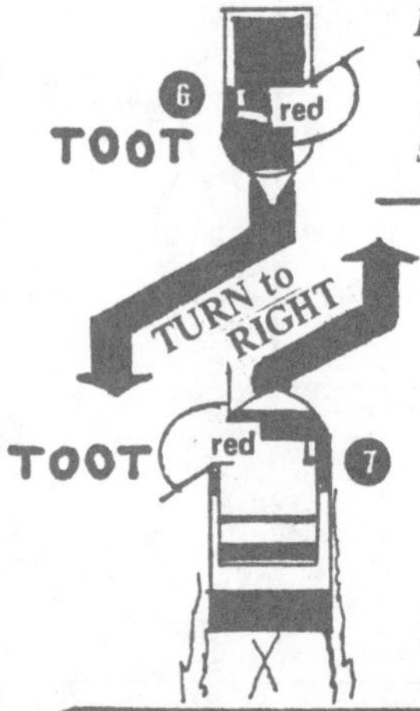

Head-on Situation, Rule 14 (a). When two power-driven vessels are meeting...*so as* to involve risk of collision, each shall alter her course to starboard *so that each shall pass on the port side of each other.*

TOOT
red
TURN to RIGHT
TOOT
red

TOOT TOOT
green

River/Tidal CURRENTS

Exceptions *to above rule: Inland Rule 9 (a)(ii)– a* power-driven vessel...with a following current shall have the right-of-way over an upbound vessel, *shall...initate...the signals...It is applied under International with Rule 18 (a)(ii).*

*Inland Rule 15 (b)...*a vessel crossing a river shall keep out of the way of a power-driven vessel ascending or descending the river.

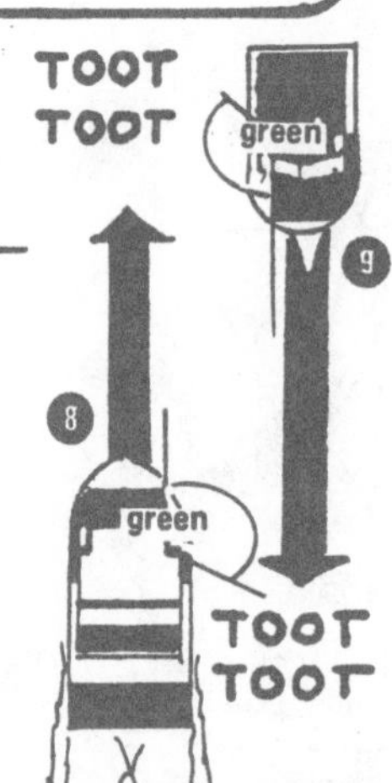
green
TOOT TOOT

Rule 32 (b).. short blast..*about* 1 *second duration. R.32 9c)..* prolonged blast..*4 to 6 second's duration.*

Maneuvering and Warning Signals– Rule 34 (g). When a power-driven vessel is leaving a dock *or berth, she shall sound* one prolonged blast.

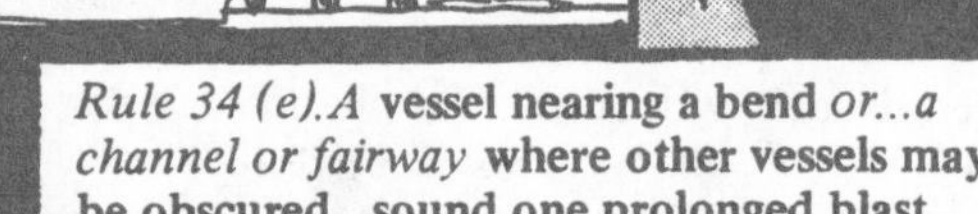
TOOT
sailing illustrated

Narrow Channels, Rule 9 (a)(i)– A vessel proceeding along...a narrow channel...shall keep *as near* to the outer limit...*as is safe and practical. Sound Signal–Rule 34 (e).*

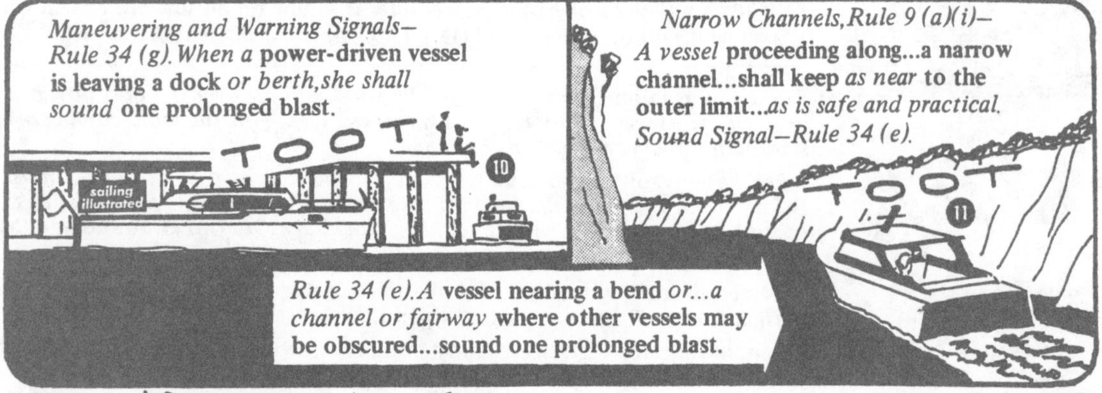

TOOT

Rule 34 (e). A vessel nearing a bend *or...a channel or fairway* where other vessels may be obscured...sound one prolonged blast.

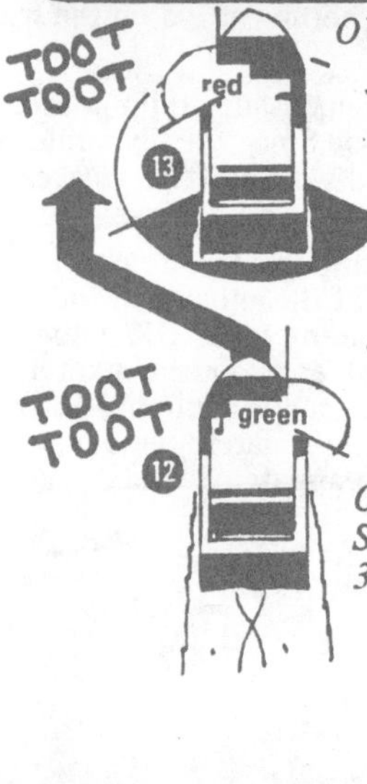

OVERTAKING Rule 13 (a).

any vessel overtaking.. shall keep out of the way *of the vessel being overtaken.*

TOOT TOOT
red
green
TOOT
TOOT TOOT
green
red
TOOT

Overtaking Signals–Rule 34 (c(i)(ii)

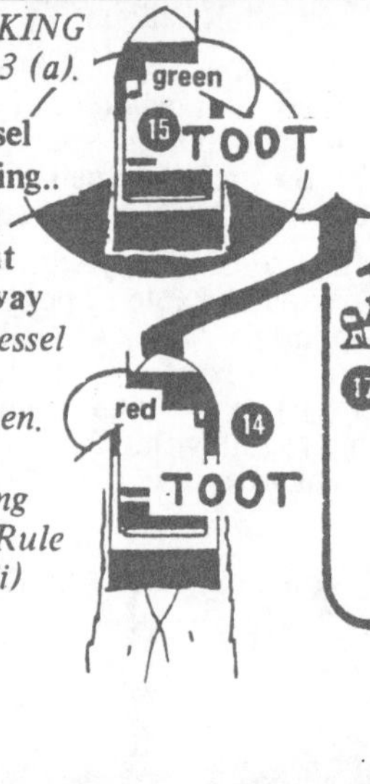

Rule 34 (a)(i)– three short blasts ..*"I am operating* astern propulsion".

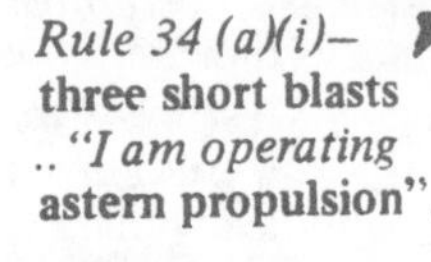
TOOT TOOT TOOT

TOOT TOOT TOOT TOOT TOOT

Warning Signals, Rule 34 (d). When vessels ...in doubt...to avoid collision...the vessel in doubt...giving at least five short *and* rapid blasts *on the whistle... may be supplemented by a* light signal *of at least five short and rapid flashes.*

PORT TACK,STARBOARD TACK definition

The sailing language—1000 B.C. to 2000 A.D.

Square riggers that were going opposite directions met in the Indian Ocean on a lazy,sunny afternoon.They exchanged sailors wanting to go other directions.

A vicious squall hits in the inky black at 0200 requiring all crew members on deck and aloft to work as a team to reduce sail area.Yet in their fo'c'sle below the same sailors:the East Indiaman,the Upsala Swede,the County Cork Irishman,and others found it difficult to communicate with each other in their home tongues.

These seamen required instant communication in their working sail language which was developed from slang terms started by Phoenician sailors.Many terms disappeared,some were compromised,and others accepted to become a part of this specialized ***international language*** undergoing a slow evolving heritage of over 3000 years.

Another major consideration was standardization of the location of all lines on square riggers to minimize language problems in noisy storm conditions.

Working square riggers have disappeared,leaving their language heritage to become the foundation for our modern sailing.It is undergoing a continuous,yet slow change to improve instant sailor communications.

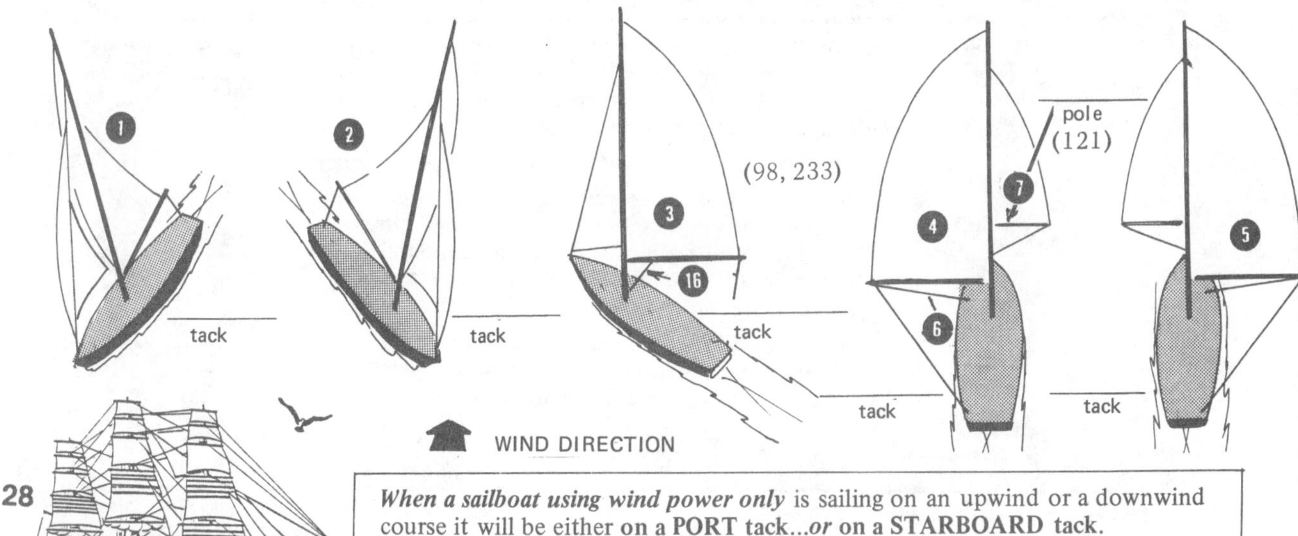

1
2
3
16
(98, 233)
pole
(121)
7
4
5
6
tack
tack
tack
tack
tack
WIND DIRECTION

Port Tack!

> ***When a sailboat using wind power only*** is sailing on an upwind or a downwind course it will be either **on a PORT tack...*or* on a STARBOARD tack.**

Sailboat ❶ is on a ***port tack with the wind coming over the port bow,beam,quarter, or stern...*** while sailboat ❷ is on a ***starboard tack with the wind coming over the starboard bow,beam,quarter,or stern.***

tack—boom vs boat side wind

After we agree on this idea,let us take a second look at the port tack/starboard tack theory.*When the wind hits the port side of a sailboat,it blows the boom to the starboard side of the boat...with the* ***sailboat on a tack OPPOSITE to the side that the boom is carried.***

broad reach—boom and tack

We test this idea with sailboat ❸ on a ***broad reach,****with the boom carried to the starboard side of the boat* putting the sailboat on a ***port tack.***

running—port or starboard tack

We apply this idea with two sailboats running downwind that are able to carry their booms on either side of the sailboat.Sailboat ❹ with the boom carried on the ***port side*** is on a ***starboard tack,*** while sailboat ❺ with the boom carried on the ***starboard side*** is on a ***port tack.***

preventer whisker pole

Sailboats ❹ and ❺ that are running downwind under mainsail and jib normally use a ❻ ***preventer*** to prevent an accidental mainsail jibe.Since the jib would be periodically blanked by the mainsail due to rolling and wind shifts,a ***whisker pole*** ❼ is used to hold out the jib clew to keep the jib full and pulling.

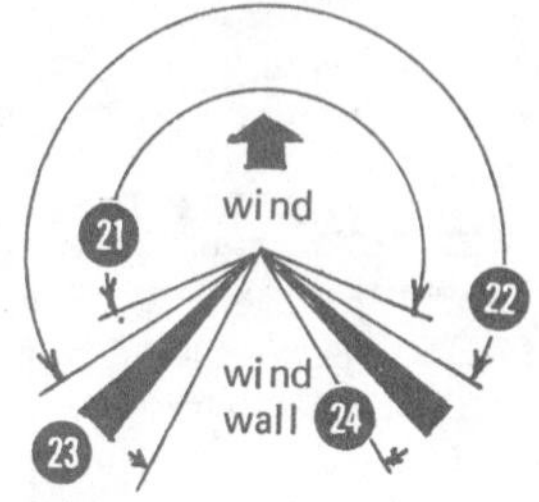

wind
21
22
wind wall
23
24

POINTING ability differs considerably with various sailboats.***Square riggers*** ㉑ that have clean bottoms may be able to point to *70* °of the apparent wind.While an average sloop may point to *40* °*or 45* ° of the apparent wind,IOR sailboats ㉔ may point up to *32*° *to 35* ° of the apparent wind.Older two masted ketches such as the ***Newporter*** ㉒ page J 19,were primarily designed for running down the trades may only be able to sail within *50*° *to 55* ° of the apparent wind.Yawls such as ***Finisterre*** ㉓ may sail within *40* ° *to 45* ° of the apparent wind.

SAIL COURSES UPWIND and DOWNWIND

What tacks are the sailboats on?

Sailing Illustrated Volume II

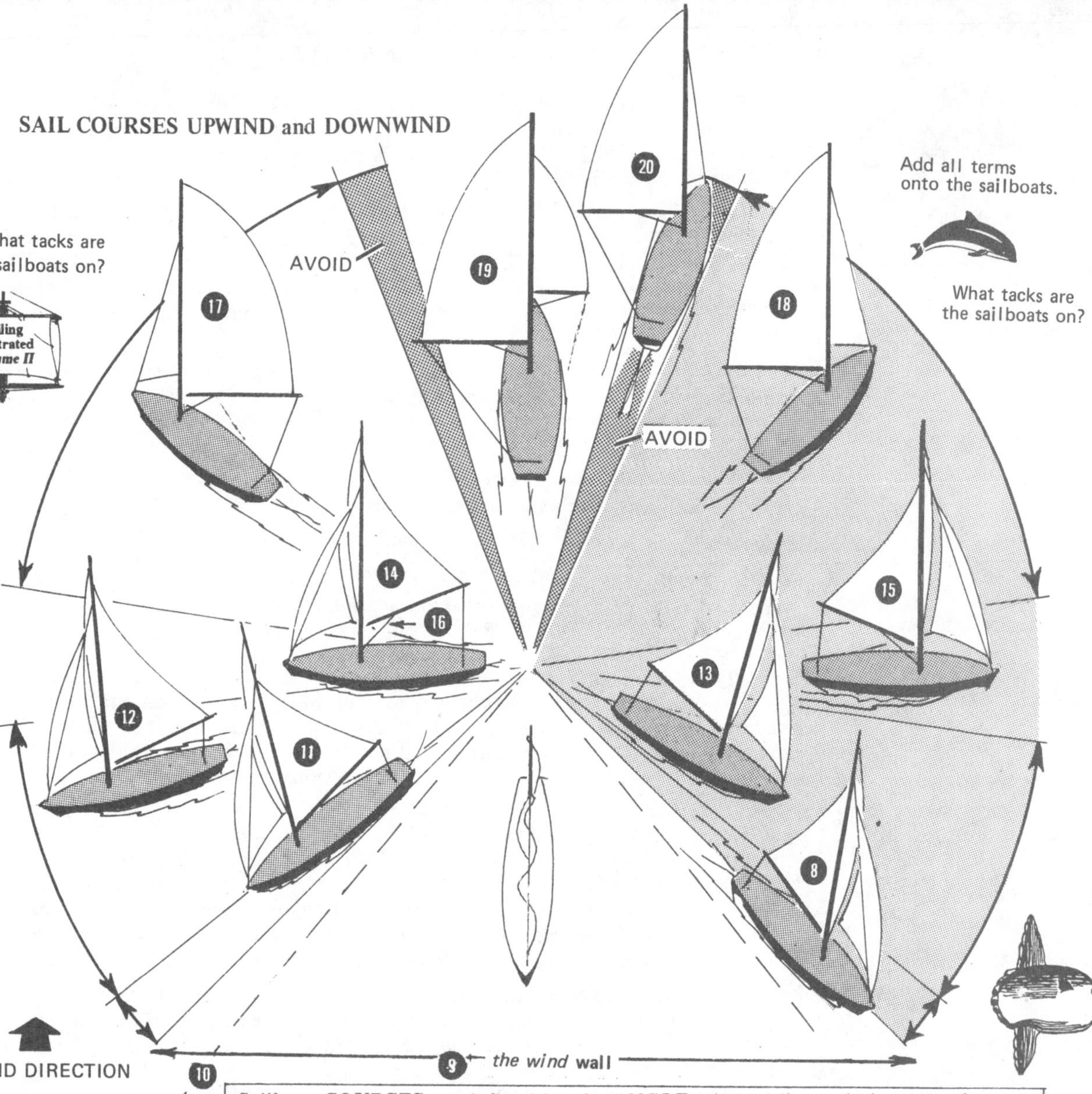

AVOID

20

19

17

18

Add all terms onto the sailboats.

What tacks are the sailboats on?

C

AVOID

14

16

15

13

12

11

8

WIND DIRECTION

10

9 ← the wind wall →

Sailboat *COURSES are* defined by *the ANGLE* a boat sails upwind or *into the wind* **CLOSEHAULED (or beating)...RUNNING downwind...or REACHING** which covers all other courses between the extremes of closehauled and running.

the three sailboat courses

closehauled—close-hauled

Sailboat 8 is sailing **CLOSEHAULED** when it sails as ***CLOSE to or as high into the wind*** as efficiency permits...with the ***sheets HAULED as tight*** as efficiency permits. A closehauled sailboat cannot hold a compass course as it may ***point higher as the wind increases,and point lower as the wind eases*** while holding a closehauled course.

upwind wall

A sailboat reaches an **UPWIND limit or WALL** 9 when the sail **airfoils STALL, then LIFT and BREAK**,changing the airfoils from **air LIFT to air BRAKES.**

pinching—a temporary measure

Sailboat 10 is **PINCHING with sails beginning to stall out** as they are on the edge of the wind wall.Pinching is a temporary method in strong winds to reduce excess heel and pressure until the sailboat can again resume a closehauled course.

reach
beam reach
broad reach

boom VANG

running wing and wing

Sailboat 11 is sailing a **compass course** with sheets eased **on a close reach**,while sailboats 12 13 are on a **reach**,with sailboats 14 15 on a **beam reach** that requires a **BOOM VANG** 16 **to minimize boom lift.**Sailboats 17 18 are on a **broad reach,with** sailboat 19 **running wing and wing.**Sailboat 20 is on a questionable course with the jib partially blanketed requiring the boat to sail higher to a broad reach,or to run wing and wing so both sails are full and pulling to balance the sailboat.

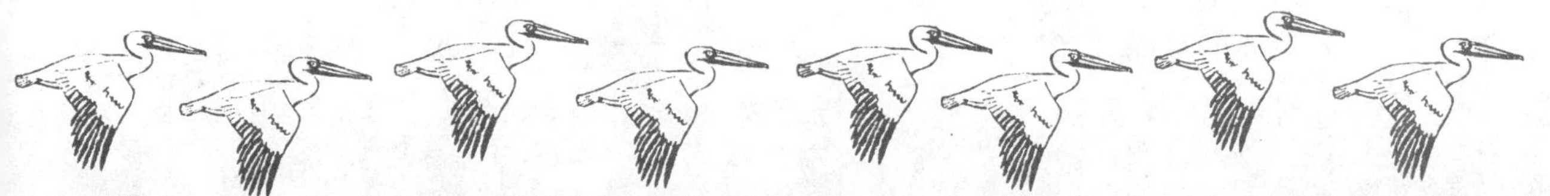

Sailing Illustrated Volume II

C

"I suppose youse gentlemen know the rules regarding the sailing vessel right-of-way!"

Complex Admiralty Law has a single purpose...*PREVENT* collisions.

ADMIRALTY LAW has a long history going back into common law over 2000 years ago to protect merchants involved in commerce between nations.The International Rules were first introduced in 1863 by France and England,with similar rules adopted the following year by the U.S.

Our present **"72 COLREGS"** refer to the International Regulations for Preventing Collisions at Sea,finalized in London,Oct.20,1972.These rules went into force tor International on 7/15/1977 in the U.S.,and for Inland Waters 12/24/81.The simplification was long overdue to cut thru the endless confusing redundancy of the previous rules deserving a special ***purple pickle award*** for those who developed the bureaucratic snafu.

sailboats on collision courses

sailboat rules summarized

Pages 28 and 29 cover basic port and starboard tacks and courses for a single sailboat underway. The next step is to define ***right-of-way procedures*** for sailboats on collision courses...sailboats on collision courses with powerboats.

*Different tack sailboats-**port tack keep clear.***

*Same tack sailboats–**windward boat keep clear.***

*Sailboat vs powerboat under 67.5 feet long–**powerboat keep clear.***

*Sailboat overtaking–**overtaking sailboat keep clear.***

Admiralty law orders the ***stand-on vessel*** to ***hold course and speed*** while the ***give-away vessel takes evasive action.***

Admiralty Law sets its own standards

Admiralty Law ***sets standards to follow*** to prevent collisions.*Rule 8 (a)–Any action taken to avoid collision shall...be positive,made in ample time and with due regard to the observance of good seamanship.* The rules are mandatory and must be obeyed ***with action taken in time*** to be corrected if misunderstood...in time ***to maneuver out of a misunderstanding.*** The reason becomes obvious when over 90% of court cases involving collisions are operator caused.

when the standards aren't sufficient–

When the standards fall apart... *Rule 2 (b)–"...due regard shall be had to all dangers of navigation and collision and to any **special circumstances**,including the limitations of the vessels involved,which may make a departure from these Rules necessary to avoid immediate danger.* When an occasional situation develops when the standards aren't sufficient,you are ***ordered to come up with new ideas to prevent the collision. even if it breaks part or all of the regulations.***

The mandatory rules MUST be followed.

You have the right-of-way... but you want to be a nice guy so out of good nature, convenience,or courtesy, you give the right-of way to the other boat on a collision course which OOOPS,***ends in a collision.*** *Rule 2 (a)–Nothing in these Rules...shall exonorate any...master or crew...from the consequence of the neglect to comply with these Rules.* Mister Good Guy suddenly has another look at his expensive goof... exit stage left Mr. Nice Guy.

How many boat owner's maintain adequate lookouts?

*Rule 5–Every vessel shall at all times **maintain a proper lookout** by sight and hearing... to make a full appraisal of the situation and the risk of collision.* Due to heavy local power and sailboat traffic I ask students at the first opportunity if they can see the operator on a converging sailboat or powerboat.The reason...if we can't see the operator of the other boat...how can we expect him to see our boat.

Initiate the first action–in time to maneuver out of a misunderstanding.

It is unfortunate that ***most visibility problems repeat themselves such as decksweeping gennies*** on sailboats without a bow lookout.The major problem on older powerboats is often a predictable problem with inside mounted,left-hand controls restricting the operator's visibility...with examples shown on the boats below.

Try to initiate the first action in a developing collision situation.One operator waiting too long,expecting the other operator to initiate the first action,may find as he fumbles to explain his problem to the judge... that the other boat operator had the same excuse.Always remember ***Rule 5*** if you want to enjoy sailing.

deadheads?

Visibility problems?

decksweeping jennie

"Enemy sighted– launch torpedoes!"

Sailing
Illustrated
Volume II

Newport Harbor on a peaceful Sunday afternoon.

Rule 12 (a). ***When two sailing vessels are approaching*** *one another,so as* **to involve risk of collision,one** *of them* ***shall keep out of the way*** *of the other as follows:–*

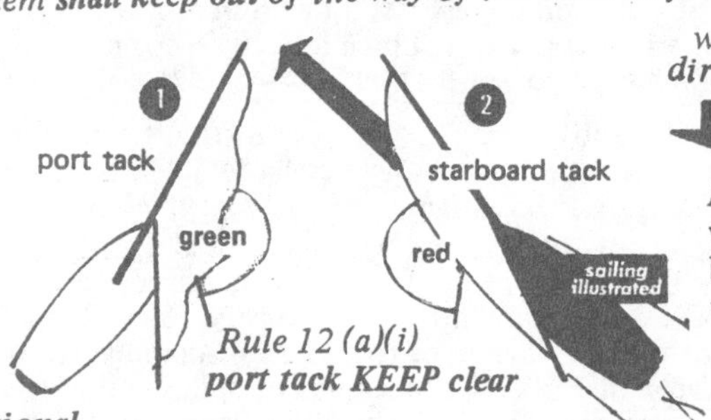
port tack
starboard tack
green
red
sailing illustrated
1
2

wind direction

Rule 12 (b) ...the **windward side shall be...***the side* **opposite to...***which* **the mainsail is carried.**

port tack
starboard tack

Rule 12 (a)(i)
port tack KEEP clear

Sailboat International AND Inland right-of-way Rules are identical.

When **each has the wind on a different side,** *the vessel which has the wind on the* **port side shall keep out of the way** *of the other.*

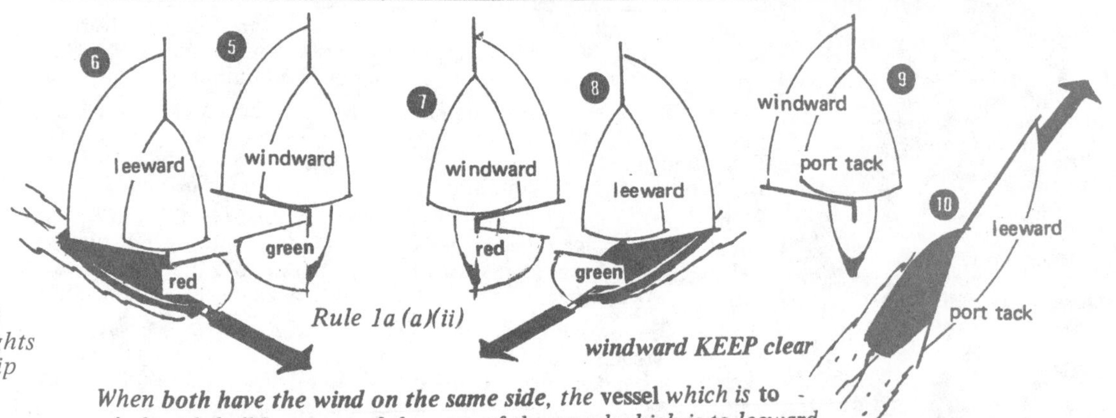
6
5
7
8
9
10
leeward
windward
windward
leeward
windward
port tack
leeward
port tack
green
red
red
green

Rule 1a (a)(ii)

windward KEEP clear

Color R/G running lights with felt-tip pens.

When ***both have the wind on the same side,*** *the* **vessel** *which* **is to windward shall keep out of the way** *of the vessel which is to leeward.*

Responsibilities Between Vessels–Rule 18 (a): **A power-driven vessel underway shall keep out of the way of:** *(iv)* **a sailing vessel.***Exceptions are–*

Rule 9–Narrow Channels? Rule 10–Traffic Separation Schemes? Rule 13–Overtaking.

Overtaking,Rule 13 (b). **A vessel shall be** *deemed* **to be overtaking when coming up...** *from a direction more than 22.5 degrees* **abaft her beam...to the vessel she is overtaking.**

*Rule 13 (d)...***keeping clear** *of the overtaken vessel* **until she is finally past and clear.**

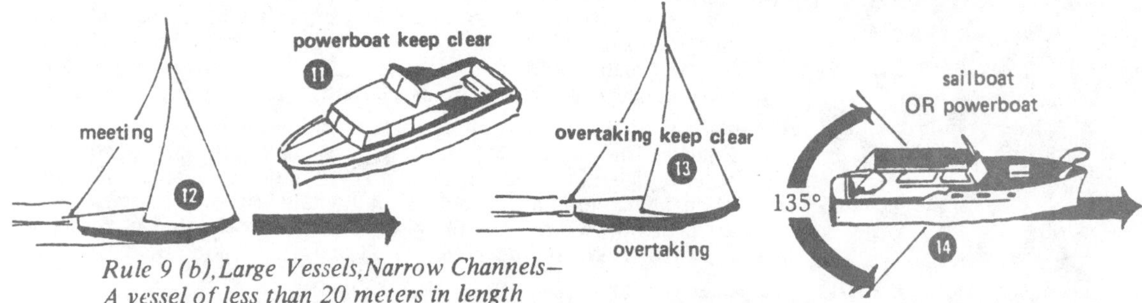
powerboat keep clear
11
meeting
12
overtaking keep clear
13
overtaking
sailboat
OR powerboat
135°
14

Rule 9 (b),Large Vessels,Narrow Channels– A vessel of less than 20 meters in length (65.7 feet) or **a sailboat shall not impede the passage** *of a vessel that can safely navigate only within a narrow channel.*

*Overtaking,Rule 13 (a).Nonwithstanding anything contained in the Rules...***any vessel overtaking... shall keep out of the way** *of the vessel being overtaken.*

C

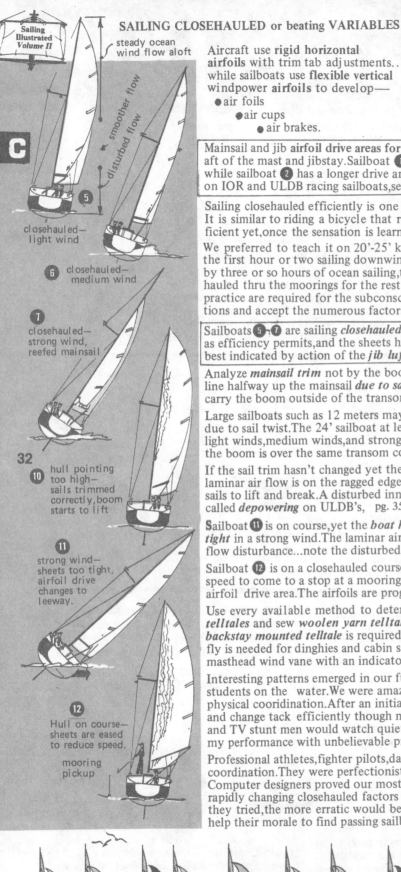

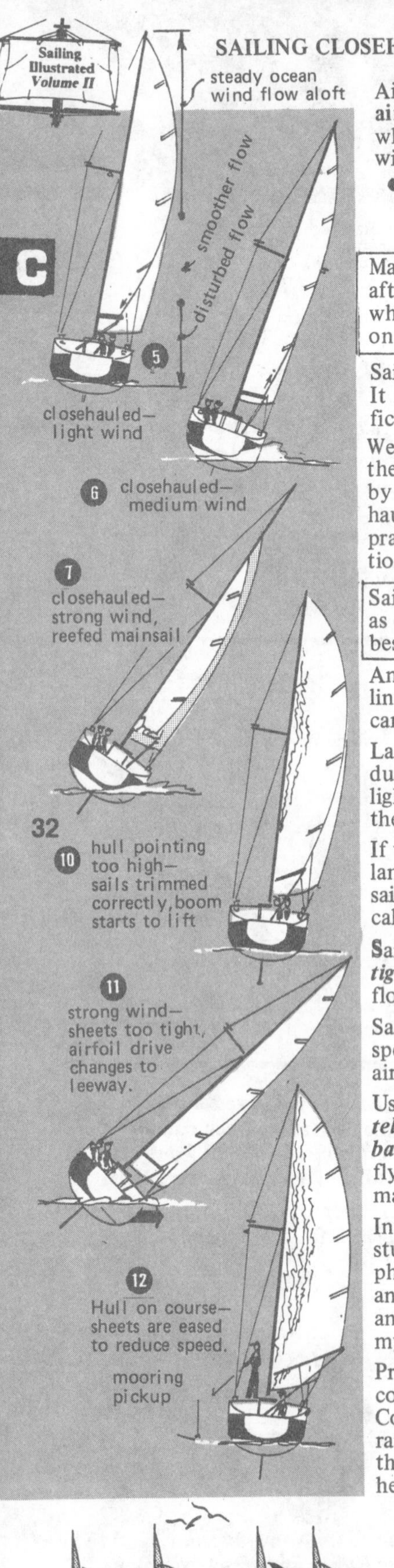
Sailing Illustrated Volume II
steady ocean wind flow aloft
smoother flow
disturbed flow
C
5
closehauled— light wind
6 closehauled— medium wind
7
closehauled— strong wind, reefed mainsail
10 hull pointing too high— sails trimmed correctly, boom starts to lift
11
strong wind— sheets too tight, airfoil drive changes to leeway.
12
Hull on course— sheets are eased to reduce speed.
mooring pickup

SAILING CLOSEHAULED or beating VARIABLES

Aircraft use **rigid horizontal airfoils** with trim tab adjustments.. while sailboats use **flexible vertical** windpower **airfoils** to develop—

- air foils
  - air cups
    - air brakes.

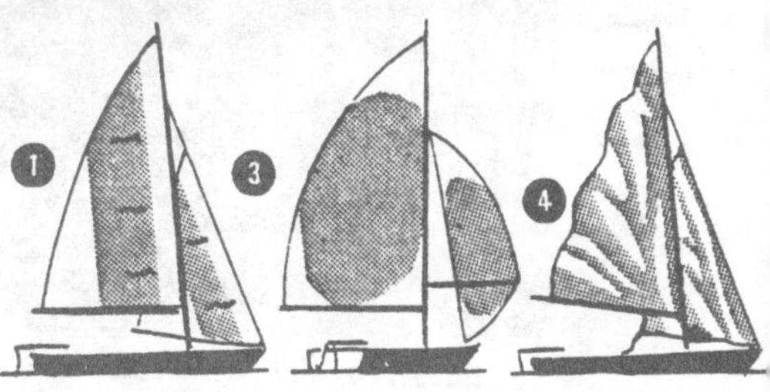
1
3
4

Mainsail and jib **airfoil drive areas for upwind lift** begin about 1/5 of the distance aft of the mast and jibstay. Sailboat (1) has a **medium aspect sail rig** for cruising, while sailboat (2) has a longer drive area, **high aspect rig** for upwind performance on IOR and ULDB racing sailboats, see pages 112 thru 117..

Sailing closehauled efficiently is one of the most difficult tasks facing a new sailor. It is similar to riding a bicycle that requires considerable practice to become proficient yet, once the sensation is learned, it will stay with a person for a lifetime.

We preferred to teach it on 20'-25' keel boats, in day-long sailing lessons with the the first hour or two sailing downwind to gain exposure to the tiller. This was followed by three or so hours of ocean sailing, then we returned to the harbor to sail closehauled thru the moorings for the rest of the day. Considerable exposure time and practice are required for the subconscious mind to pull together the many new sensations and accept the numerous factors involved in closehauled sailing.

Sailboats (5)-(7) are sailing ***closehauled*** with the bow pointing as high into the wind as efficiency permits, and the sheets hauled in as tight as efficiency permits. This is best indicated by action of the ***jib luff telltales*** as shown on the facing page.

Analyze ***mainsail trim*** not by the boom but by an imaginary horizontal sail trim line halfway up the mainsail ***due to sail twist.*** A small dinghy (8) see facing page, will carry the boom outside of the transom due to minimum sail twist.

Large sailboats such as 12 meters may have the boom (9) sheeted almost amidship due to sail twist. The 24' sailboat at left shows the boom position closehauled with light winds, medium winds, and strong winds use varied sail adjustments so the end of the boom is over the same transom corner area in various wind strengths.

If the sail trim hasn't changed yet the hull is ***pinching*** or pointing too high (10), the laminar air flow is on the ragged edge called ***luffing*** but is not high enough for the sails to lift and break. A disturbed inner jib telltale is the first indication of pinching called ***depowering*** on ULDB's, pg. 35, with a slow speed loss becoming apparent.

Sailboat (11) is on course, yet the ***boat heels excessively as the sails are sheeted in too tight*** in a strong wind. The laminar air flow on the leeward side changes into a vertical flow disturbance...note the disturbed outer or leeward jib telltale action.

Sailboat (12) is on a closehauled course, yet the sheets are slacked considerably to reduc speed to come to a stop at a mooring or dock. The sails are luffing over half of their airfoil drive area. The airfoils are progressively changing into ***air brakes.***

Use every available method to determine heel angle and wind direction. Use ***shrou telltales*** and sew ***woolen yarn telltales*** to the jib luff for upwind sailing, while a ***backstay mounted telltale*** is required in clean air for downwind sailing. A masthead fly is needed for dinghies and cabin sailboats to 30', while larger sailboats will require a masthead wind vane with an indicator dial easy to read by the helmsman.

Interesting patterns emerged in our full day sailing lessons after teaching over 1600 students on the water. We were amazed to find seven students had perfect mental and physical cooridination. After an initial exposure they could hold a closehauled course and change tack efficiently though none realized they had perfect coordination. Movie and TV stunt men would watch quietly for an hour or so asking no questions, then rep my performance with unbelievable precision.

Professional athletes, fighter pilots, dancers, and choreographers often showed poor coordination. They were perfectionists practicing continually to soon outperform me. Computer designers proved our most difficult students. Instead of analyzing the rapidly changing closehauled factors they would try to computerize them. The harder they tried, the more erratic would become their closehauled performance. It didn't help their morale to find passing sailboat operators asking if we had lost our rudder.

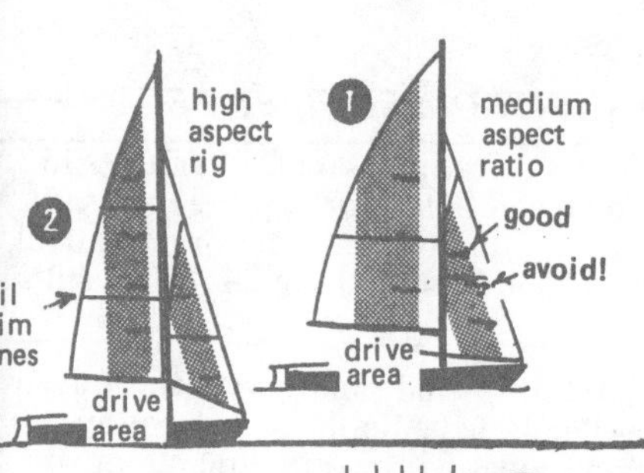
high
aspect
rig
2
1
medium
aspect
ratio
good
avoid!
drive
area
drive
area

REVIEW– *SAILING CLOSEHAULED...* fill in the blanks.

Sailing Illustrated Volume II

Location of jib luff telltales is critical. *They should be just inside of the leading edge of the shaded areas on the sails at left, with a window between, so it is easy to see the different colored telltales. We sailed on an IOR boat while completing this page with the jib telltales ahead of the shaded area. The sailmakers mistake can be an excellent way to lose a race as the telltale signals were disturbed and confusing.*

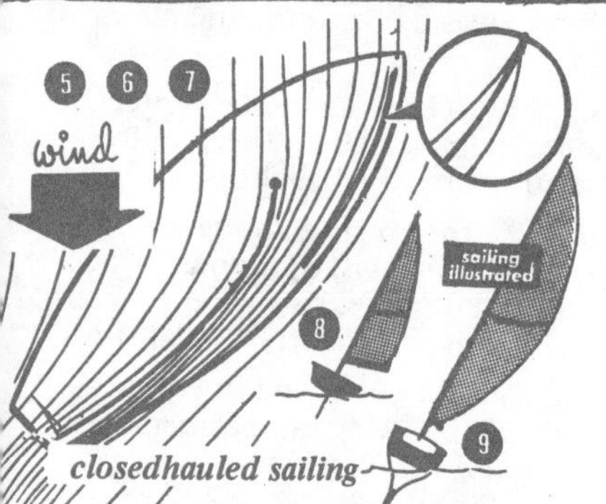
5 6 7
wind
sailing illustrated
8
9
closedhauled sailing

5 6 7 *Both jib telltales stream aft.*

These three examples are boats ***sailing as_____ to the wind as efficiency permits, with the sheets_________ as tight as efficiency permits, with the combined terms called______ ______ sailing.***

Mainsail boom trim is by ***an imaginary horizontal line half way up the mainsail.*** The end of the boom on a small dinghy 8 for example, will be______ the transom, lined up with the____ of the transom on the 24' keel boat, left page, while it may appear to be almost _________ on 12 meter sailboats 9 ***due to the twist of the large sail area.***

> Approximately 50% of todays sailing is upwind with pointing ability varying widely from meter and IOR boats able to point to 30° of the apparent wind...while some cruising boats for sailing down the trades may be limited to 50° of the apparent wind, see page 32.

pinching

bear off

10

10 *The inner jib telltale indicator shows an air flow breakdown... with the air flow streaming normally on the outer side of the jib.*

Sail trim hasn't changed, yet the hull is_______ or_______ too high with the speed dropping which is called ***depowering*** on a ULDB.

Pinching is difficult to feel on a heavy, narrow beam meter boat. The sails seem to be full and pulling. Except for a slow speed loss the only obvious sign is the disturbed inner jib telltale.

Pinching is more obvious on our wide beam 24' sailboat shown on the left page as it has a wide jib-sheeting base, page 12, with the boom starting to lift 10, and the luff just beginning to break.

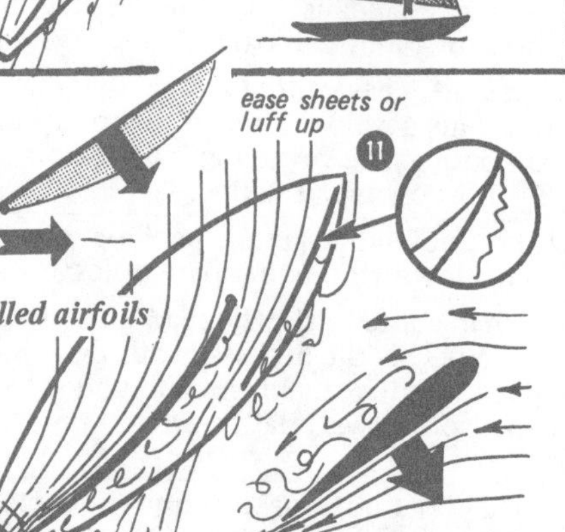
ease sheets or
luff up
11
stalled airfoils

11 *The outer jib telltale indicates the horizontal air flow has stalled as it flows upward... with the inner telltale flowing normally.*

The hull is on course, yet the sheets are hauled too______, which is normal for a new sailor in a light wind as the boat slowly drifts to a halt...as the forward drive changes to leeway drift.

We show an extreme example 11 of ***stalled airfoils*** in a strong wind. The hull is on course but it is ***drifting sideways*** as the ***excess heel*** causes the hull ***forward drive*** to change to ***leeway drift.***

The wing at left stalls out and the airplane loses altitude as air flow cannot follow the upper wing because of an excess wing-attack angle.

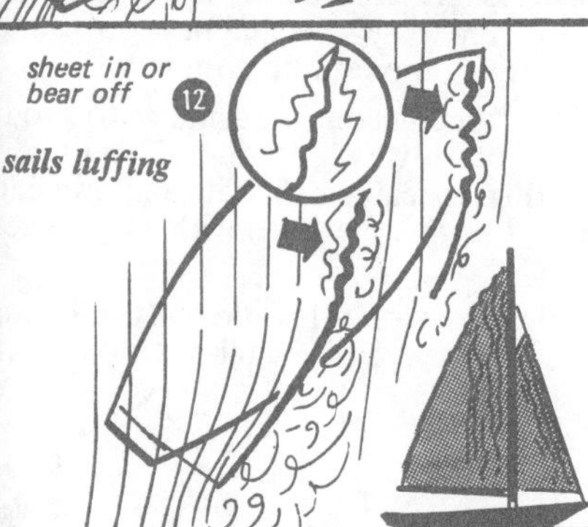
sheet in or
bear off
12
sails luffing

12 *The air flow has broken down as both jib telltales are disturbed.*

The hull is on course, ***yet the sheets are eased too______*** so that the ***boom begins to lift and the airfoil breaks.*** This is an excellent way to reduce spped to stop at a dock or mooring by ***changing airfoil lift 1 into 4 air brakes.***

13

luff ← x → stall
best setting — airfoil extremes

Trim your sails just above a luff 13 for maximum drive to produce maximum pointing and driving ability for closehauled sailing upwind.

Mainsail draft controls–upwind AIRFOIL to downwind CUP variables.

RIGID MAST SAIL CONTROLS ● CONTROLLED MAST BEND

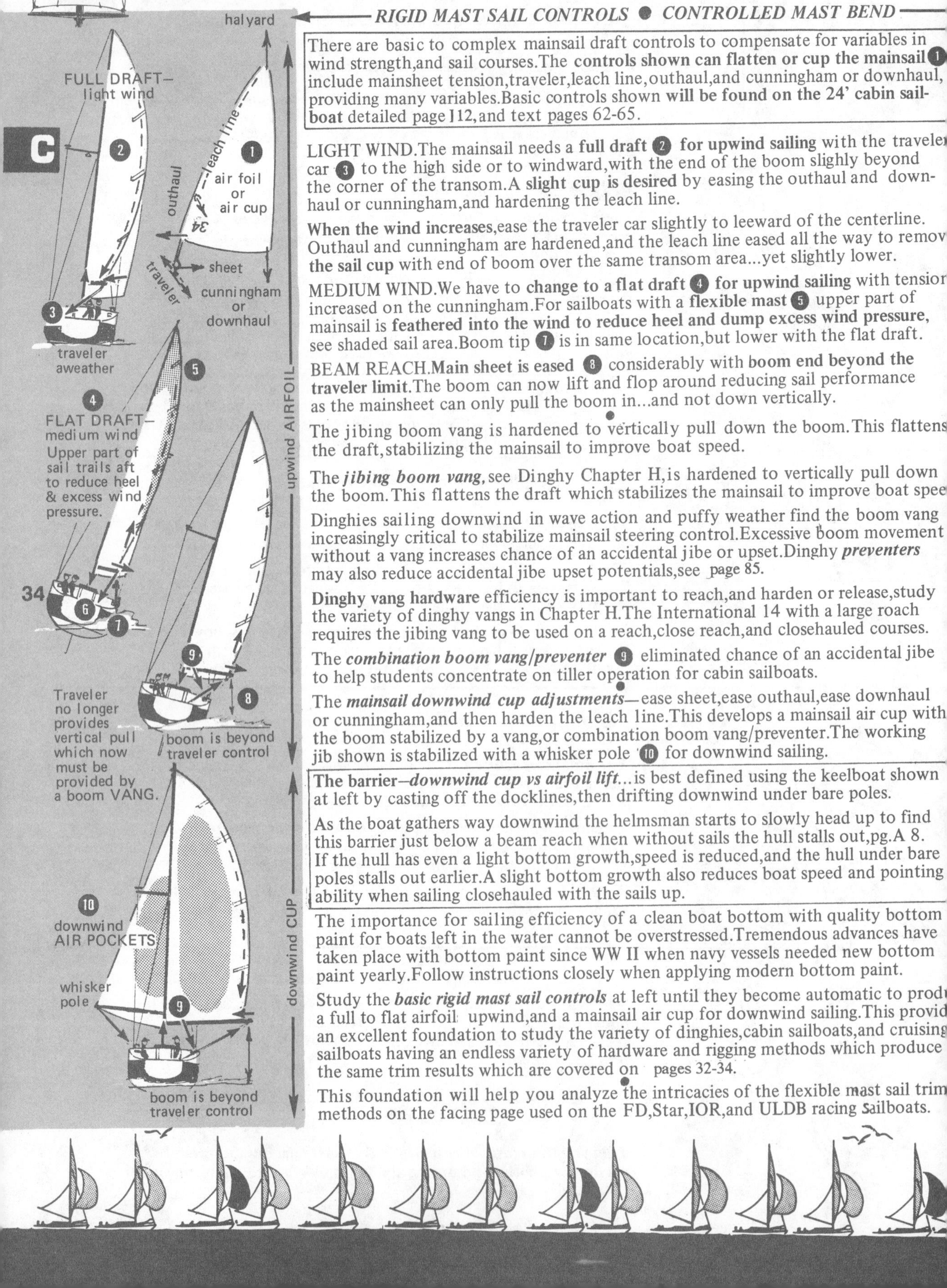
C
halyard
FULL DRAFT– light wind
2
1
leach line
outhaul
air foil or air cup
34
traveler
sheet
cunningham or downhaul
3
traveler aweather
5
4
FLAT DRAFT– medium wind
Upper part of sail trails aft to reduce heel & excess wind pressure.
6
7
9
8
Traveler no longer provides vertical pull which now must be provided by a boom VANG.
boom is beyond traveler control
upwind AIRFOIL
10
downwind AIR POCKETS
whisker pole
9
boom is beyond traveler control
downwind CUP

There are basic to complex mainsail draft controls to compensate for variables in wind strength,and sail courses.The **controls shown can flatten or cup the mainsail** (1) include mainsheet tension,traveler,leach line,outhaul,and cunningham or downhaul, providing many variables.Basic controls shown **will be found on the 24' cabin sailboat** detailed page J12,and text pages 62-65.

LIGHT WIND.The mainsail needs a **full draft** (2) **for upwind sailing** with the traveler car (3) to the high side or to windward,with the end of the boom slighly beyond the corner of the transom.A **slight cup is desired** by easing the outhaul and downhaul or cunningham,and hardening the leach line.

When the wind increases,ease the traveler car slightly to leeward of the centerline. Outhaul and cunningham are hardened,and the leach line eased all the way to remove **the sail cup** with end of boom over the same transom area...yet slightly lower.

MEDIUM WIND.We have to **change to a flat draft** (4) **for upwind sailing** with tension increased on the cunningham.For sailboats with a **flexible mast** (5) upper part of mainsail is **feathered into the wind to reduce heel and dump excess wind pressure**, see shaded sail area.Boom tip (7) is in same location,but lower with the flat draft.

BEAM REACH.**Main sheet is eased** (8) considerably with **boom end beyond the traveler limit**.The boom can now lift and flop around reducing sail performance as the mainsheet can only pull the boom in...and not down vertically.

The jibing boom vang is hardened to vertically pull down the boom.This flattens the draft,stabilizing the mainsail to improve boat speed.

The ***jibing boom vang***, see Dinghy Chapter H,is hardened to vertically pull down the boom.This flattens the draft which stabilizes the mainsail to improve boat speed.

Dinghies sailing downwind in wave action and puffy weather find the boom vang increasingly critical to stabilize mainsail steering control.Excessive boom movement without a vang increases chance of an accidental jibe or upset.Dinghy ***preventers*** may also reduce accidental jibe upset potentials,see page 85.

Dinghy vang hardware efficiency is important to reach,and harden or release,study the variety of dinghy vangs in Chapter H.The International 14 with a large roach requires the jibing vang to be used on a reach,close reach,and closehauled courses.

The ***combination boom vang/preventer*** (9) eliminated chance of an accidental jibe to help students concentrate on tiller operation for cabin sailboats.

The ***mainsail downwind cup adjustments***— ease sheet,ease outhaul,ease downhaul or cunningham,and then harden the leach line.This develops a mainsail air cup with the boom stabilized by a vang,or combination boom vang/preventer.The working jib shown is stabilized with a whisker pole (10) for downwind sailing.

The barrier–*downwind cup vs airfoil lift*...is best defined using the keelboat shown at left by casting off the docklines,then drifting downwind under bare poles.

As the boat gathers way downwind the helmsman starts to slowly head up to find this barrier just below a beam reach when without sails the hull stalls out,pg.A 8. If the hull has even a light bottom growth,speed is reduced,and the hull under bare poles stalls out earlier.A slight bottom growth also reduces boat speed and pointing ability when sailing closehauled with the sails up.

The importance for sailing efficiency of a clean boat bottom with quality bottom paint for boats left in the water cannot be overstressed.Tremendous advances have taken place with bottom paint since WW II when navy vessels needed new bottom paint yearly.Follow instructions closely when applying modern bottom paint.

Study the ***basic rigid mast sail controls*** at left until they become automatic to produce a full to flat airfoil upwind,and a mainsail air cup for downwind sailing.This provides an excellent foundation to study the variety of dinghies,cabin sailboats,and cruising sailboats having an endless variety of hardware and rigging methods which produce the same trim results which are covered on pages 32-34.

This foundation will help you analyze the intricacies of the flexible mast sail trim methods on the facing page used on the FD,Star,IOR,and ULDB racing sailboats.

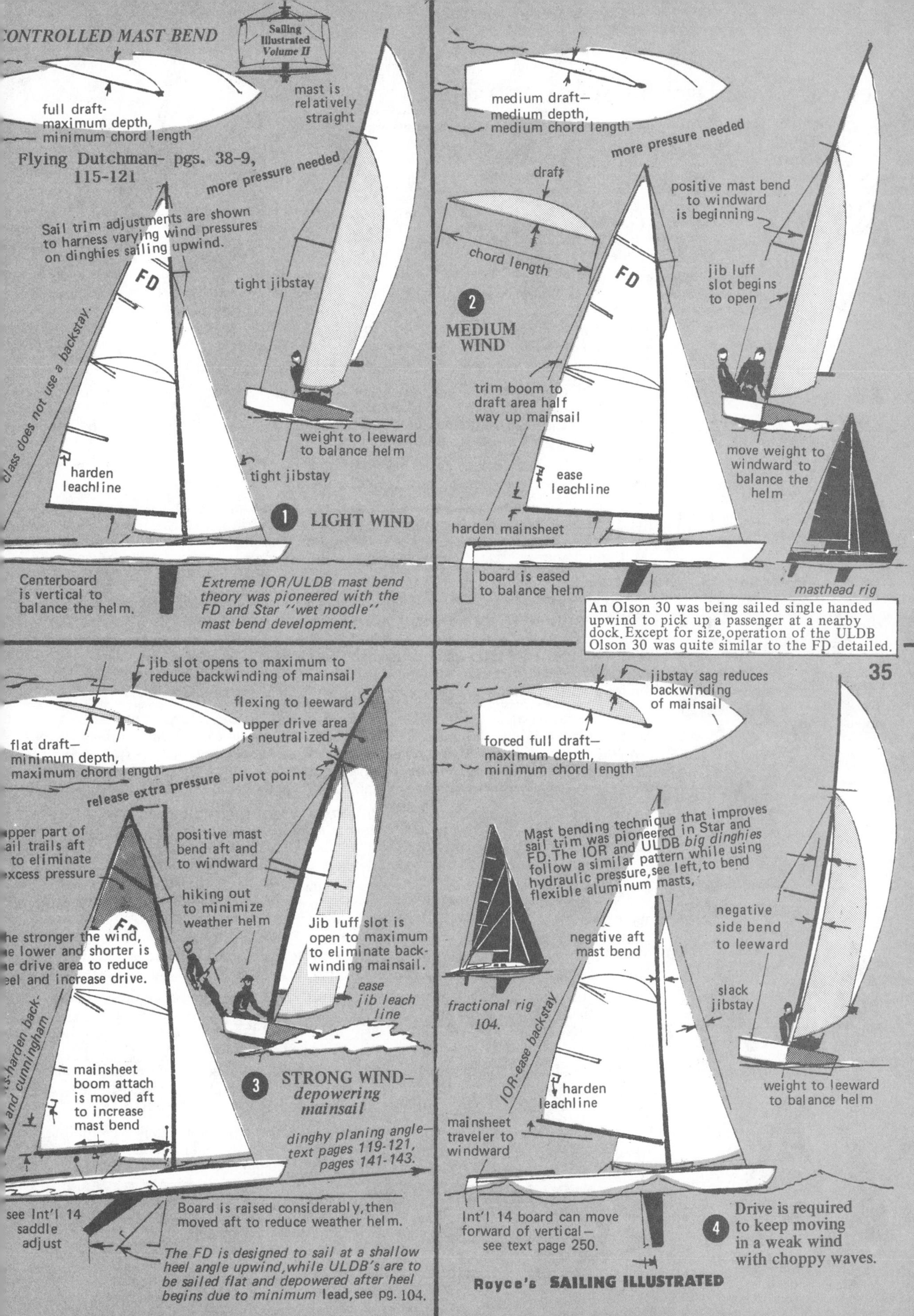

CONTROLLED MAST BEND
Sailing Illustrated Volume II
full draft-
maximum depth,
minimum chord length
mast is
relatively
straight
Flying Dutchman- pgs. 38-9,
115-121
more pressure needed
Sail trim adjustments are shown
to harness varying wind pressures
on dinghies sailing upwind.
FD
tight jibstay
class does not use a backstay.
weight to leeward
to balance helm
harden
leachline
tight jibstay
1 LIGHT WIND
Centerboard
is vertical to
balance the helm.
Extreme IOR/ULDB mast bend
theory was pioneered with the
FD and Star "wet noodle"
mast bend development.
medium draft—
medium depth,
medium chord length
more pressure needed
draft
positive mast bend
to windward
is beginning
chord length
FD
jib luff
slot begins
to open
2
MEDIUM
WIND
trim boom to
draft area half
way up mainsail
move weight to
windward to
balance the
helm
ease
leachline
harden mainsheet
board is eased
to balance helm
masthead rig
An Olson 30 was being sailed single handed
upwind to pick up a passenger at a nearby
dock. Except for size, operation of the ULDB
Olson 30 was quite similar to the FD detailed.
jib slot opens to maximum to
reduce backwinding of mainsail
flexing to leeward
upper drive area
is neutralized
flat draft—
minimum depth,
maximum chord length
release extra pressure
pivot point
upper part of
sail trails aft
to eliminate
excess pressure
positive mast
bend aft and
to windward
hiking out
to minimize
weather helm
The stronger the wind,
the lower and shorter is
the drive area to reduce
heel and increase drive.
Jib luff slot is
open to maximum
to eliminate back-
winding mainsail.
ease
jib leach
line
FD
...s-harden back-
... and cunningham
mainsheet
boom attach
is moved aft
to increase
mast bend
3 STRONG WIND—
depowering
mainsail
dinghy planing angle
text pages 119-121,
pages 141-143.
see Int'l 14
saddle
adjust
Board is raised considerably, then
moved aft to reduce weather helm.
The FD is designed to sail at a shallow
heel angle upwind, while ULDB's are to
be sailed flat and depowered after heel
begins due to minimum lead, see pg. 104.
jibstay sag reduces
backwinding
of mainsail
forced full draft—
maximum depth,
minimum chord length
Mast bending technique that improves
sail trim was pioneered in Star and
FD. The IOR and ULDB big dinghies
follow a similar pattern while using
hydraulic pressure, see left, to bend
flexible aluminum masts,
negative
side bend
to leeward
negative aft
mast bend
fractional rig
104.
IOR-ease backstay
slack
jibstay
harden
leachline
weight to leeward
to balance helm
mainsheet
traveler to
windward
Int'l 14 board can move
forward of vertical—
see text page 250.
4 Drive is required
to keep moving
in a weak wind
with choppy waves.

CHANGING TACK UPWIND HAS MANY VARIABLES.

READY ABOUT!
HELMS ALEE!
sailing illustrated
CUT!
wind
1
2
3
4
5
6
7
8
9

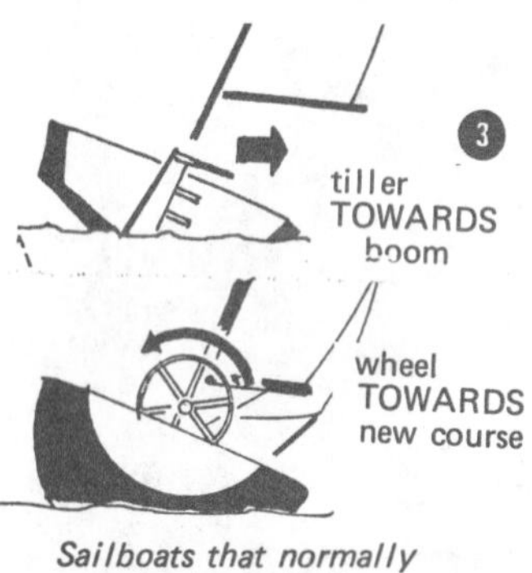
3
tiller TOWARDS boom
wheel TOWARDS new course

Coming about *is the method used to change from one upwind tack to the other upwind tack which may require* ***backing the jib*** *due to hull variables of directional stability, length,beam,weight,and inertia,plus efficiency of its airfoils and waterfoils.*

We taught on the 40' *Nimbus* which had a heavy,narrow beam hull similar to *Iris,* page 121. When changing tack upwind we would let the boat drift a considerable distance with the sails luffing due to its tremendous inertia and directional stability before changing to the new upwind tack.

The Newporter ketch,text pg.75,has a 105◦ course change when coming about required the jib to be continually backed in harbor sailing to maintain control.

When our 24' sailboat was new we found it had minimum but sufficient inertia realizing that due to its wide beam and cutaway forefoot,pg. 12,the jib has to be continually backed when coming about.We soon found this was an excellent asset as it could change tack in one boat length while maneuvering in tight moorings.

Command ***ready about*** (1) is given as an initial warning,while ***helms alee*** (2) indicates the **tiller is pushed *TOWARDS the boom*** (3). As the bow peads into the wind the **mainsail lifts and breaks** (4) then the tiller (5) is pulled amidship.

The **wind** is on the ***BACK SIDE of the jib*** (6) which spins the bow to the new tack. When the ***mainsail fills*** (7) and its sheet becomes taut, the final order of ***CUT*** (8) ***is given to release the jib sheet*** and cleat it on the other side of the boat (9) which is underway on its new tack without being **caught in irons.**

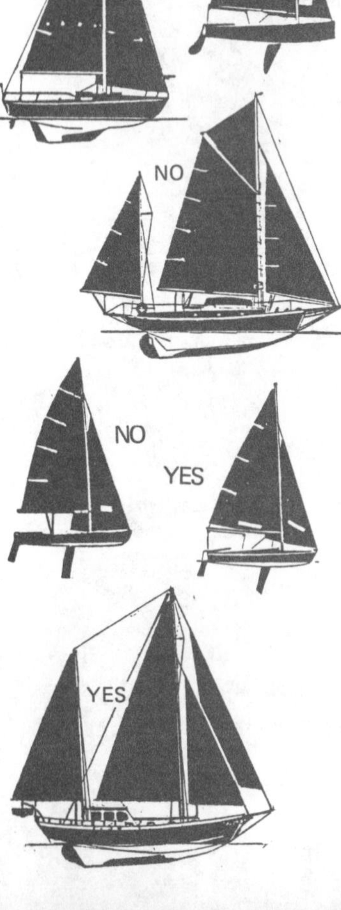
Sailboats that normally require backwinding—
YES
YES
NO
NO
YES
YES

After five hours of leisurely ocean sailing,pg. 13, we would return to our harbor with our boat sailing closehauled thru the moorings while we continually backed the jib when coming about.After being dropped off for a short recovery period at a local bar,they would return to begin enjoying the new sensation of closehauled sailing on a boat with considerable maneuverability by backing the jib.

I taught on many Lido 14's page 89, equiring the jib to be continually backed to maintain control,especially in strong winds.We had to spin the hull to the new tack so it would be underway with the sails pulling before the boat ran out of inertia. A capsize is assured if you try to sail a dinghy at a safe slow speed in a strong wind. The boat will run out of inertia,go into irons and stop.When it starts to drift backwards it will trip over its board and rudder waterfoils,pg. 70, with a rapid capsize following.

We found the Thistle page 88, with a long waterline had excellent directional stability,requiring the jib to be continually backed so it wouldn't be caught in irons. The C 15 however, page 91,spins so easily with its high aspect waterfoils and airfoils that backing the jib is normally an overcompensation that may cause a capsize.

Backing the jib is an excellent practice for most keel boats such as the 30' Catalina to provide maneuverability in tight moorings.*Except for light winds,* larger sailboats such as the Catalina 38 find backing the jib unnecessary in normal operation due to the tremendous weight and inertia...with exceptions such as the 48' *Taku.*

We sailed it for many hours with light winds in the San Diego Harbor changing tack by continually backing the jib.The *Taku* would then be on its new tack with all sails full and pulling though requiring a minute or more to start moving.

A word of caution—since the crew member releasing the jib sheet when backing the jib will have restricted visibility,he should wait for the command, ***"CUT!"*** to be given by the helmsman having full visibility of his sails,passing boats,wind shifts etc.

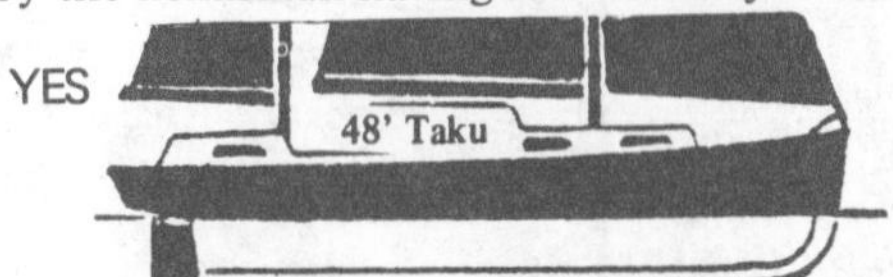
YES
48' Taku

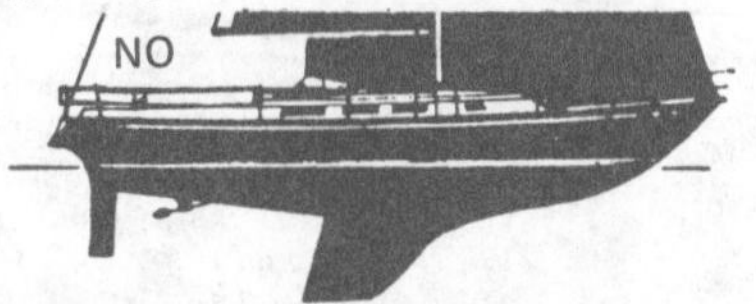
NO

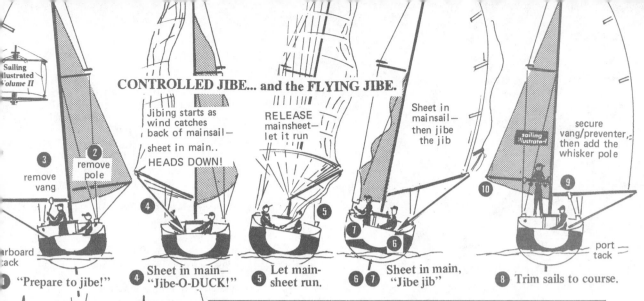

Sailing Illustrated Volume II

CONTROLLED JIBE... and the FLYING JIBE.

3 remove vang

2 remove pole

Jibing starts as wind catches back of mainsail– sheet in main.. HEADS DOWN!

RELEASE mainsheet– let it run

Sheet in mainsail– then jibe the jib

secure vang/preventer, then add the whisker pole

4 5 6 7 9 10

…rboard tack

port tack

1 "Prepare to jibe!"

4 Sheet in main– "Jibe-O-DUCK!"

5 Let main-sheet run.

6 7 Sheet in main, "Jibe jib"

8 Trim sails to course.

…ller AWAY
…rom boom
wheel TOWARDS
the boom

*Jibing is the term for a maneuver to change from one downwind tack to the other **by changing the wind direction** and the side the boom is carried **over the stern of a sailboat.** Jibing can also be used to change from one upwind tack to another in light winds, and it may also be useful to return a sailboat to an upwind dock with damaged rigging.*

Jibing is as common a practice as coming about.

Jibing is as common a method to change tack by changing the wind over the stern, as it is to change the wind and tack over the bow called *coming about.* It helps to have ideal conditions for your first jibing exposure to gain familiarity and coordination with the sequence so this maneuver becomes second nature.

five kinds of jibing

The five kinds of jibes are the ***controlled jibe*** above, the ***North River or flying jibe*** the ***Chicken Jibe,*** the ***Goosewing Jibe,*** and the uncontrolled or ***accidental jibe.***

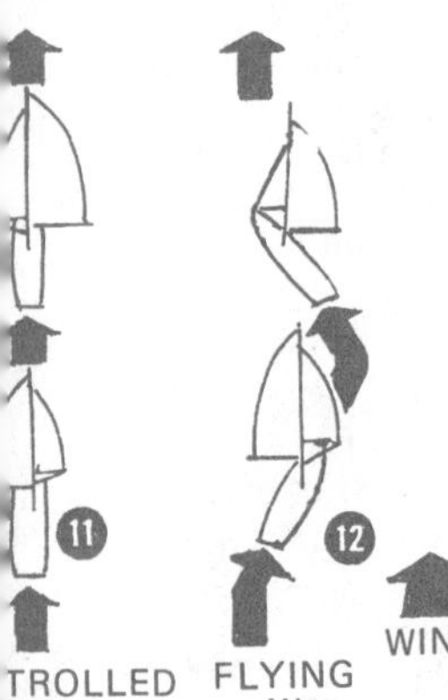

11
12
WIND
…TROLLED
…ibe
FLYING
jibe

After exposing students to thousands of jibes on the water thru the years from Lido 14 to 50 footers, it is ironic that the first time we define the basic sequences from the cockpit perspective is in the illustrations above. 37

The ***controlled jibe*** above and at left 11, is for light winds with normal jibing forces on sails, rigging, traveler, and boom gooseneck. Little course change is required for these conditions with jibing started by hauling in the mainsheet 4.

When the **wind increases** the forces involved in jibing increase, which must be compensated for with a ***flying jibe*** 12. ***When the boom begins to jibe, a course change*** of a of a few to several degrees ***is required*** so that when the boom reaches the end of its jibing arc ***to dissipate most of the energy*** without damage to traveler, gooseneck, sails, or rigging. Considerable variables exist such as sailboat size, wind strength, the maneuvering room, etc., as to whether the flying jibe is started with hauling in the mainsail...or letting it fly across the stern with nature's wind pressure helping.

The ***flying jibe is excellent*** for cb and db ***dinghies*** as it reduces upset potentials with minimal forces involved when the boom hits the end of its jibing arc. Our flying jibe dinghy exposure is excellent in force 5 winds. No upsets resulted in these spirited conditions that often required considerable bailing with endless FUN.

BANG
tremendous
inertia forces
boom
backstay

We have taught on three sailboats with the boom too long, ***the booms were stopped by the backstay in a flying jibe,*** a unnecessary hazard that can cause a dismasting.

We've had the end of the boom hang up on 20 or more sailboats with poorly engineered boom lift hardware. These were temporarily taped out of the way during the lessons which required replacement to eliminate an unnecessary hazard.

If the downhaul is too slack the boom will ride higher than normal. This increases the chance of end fittings catching the backstay. This can also become a hazard that might lead to a dismasting in a strong wind jibe.

"NOW THAT'S WHAT I CALL A JIBE."
ROYCE

Our favorite jibing cartoon at left has been in our text for every revision since 1956. We have been asked many times by new sailors...if that were what they should expect in a normal jibe.

If the situation were reversed and you were the artist, how would you answer their questions?

C

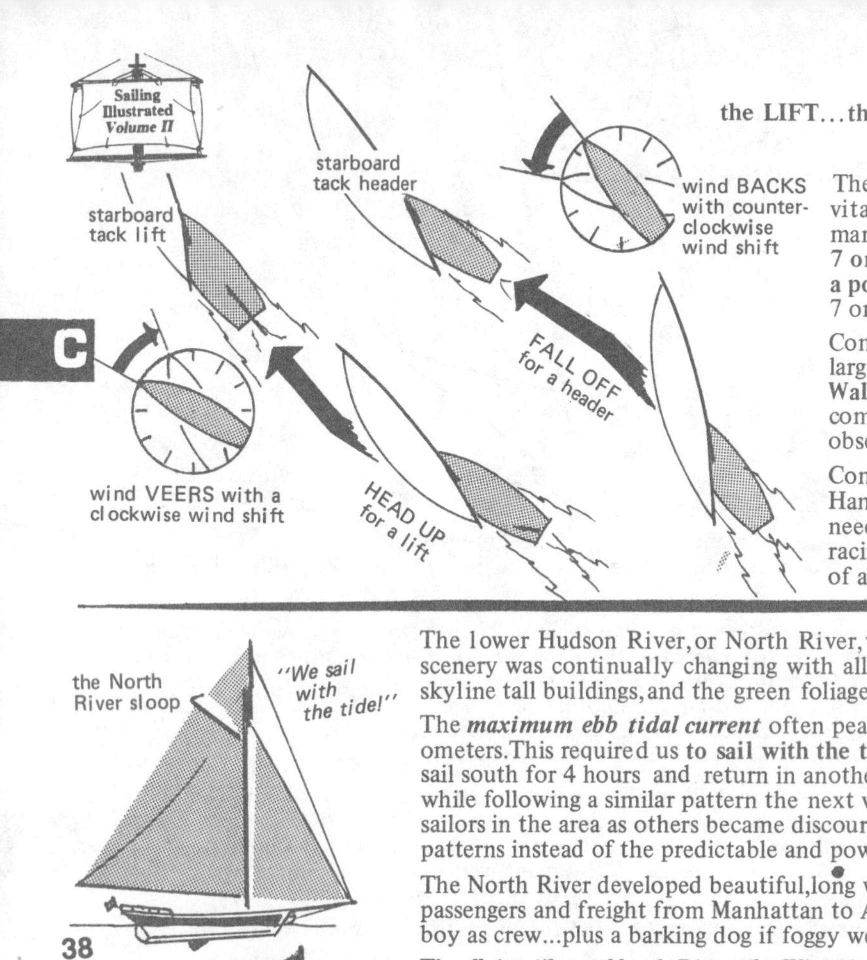

Sailing Illustrated Volume II
starboard tack header
starboard tack lift
wind BACKS with counter-clockwise wind shift
FALL OFF for a header
wind VEERS with a clockwise wind shift
HEAD UP for a lift
C

the LIFT...the HEADER...more FLYING JIBES.

The terms **head up** and **fall off** are of vital performance to all racing craft.**If a** mark is dead ahead and the **wind backs 7 or more degrees...flop** immediately **for a port tack lift** that will carry your boat 7 or more degrees higher on the new tack.

Communication problems can develop on larger sailboats,especially when racing. **Walkie talkies** should be considered for communication of lookout/jib telltale observer,to help the helmsman.

Communication on 40 footers is marginal. Hand signals and walkie talkies may be needed to avoid misunderstandings when racing in heavy traffic...or to take advantage of a sudden opening in a race.

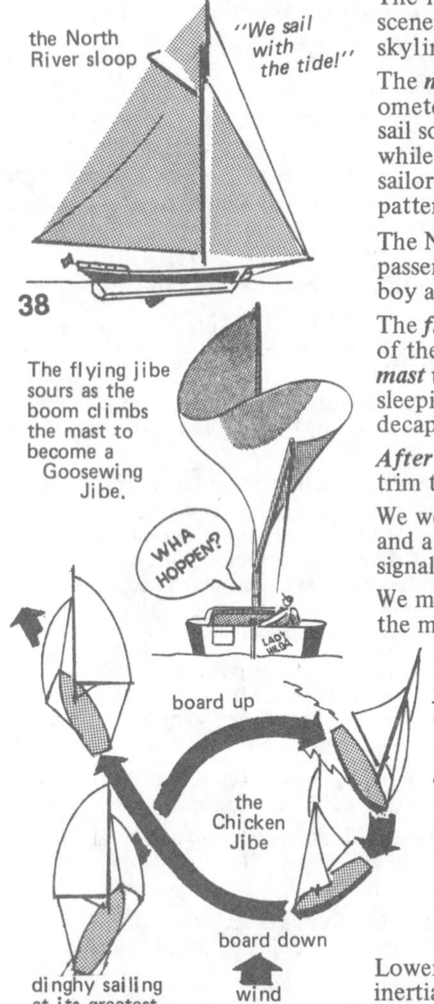

the North River sloop
"We sail with the tide!"
The flying jibe sours as the boom climbs the mast to become a Goosewing Jibe.
WHA HOPPEN?
LADY HILDA
board up
the Chicken Jibe
board down
wind
dinghy sailing at its greatest—can you swim?

The lower Hudson River,or North River,was our favorite early sailing area.The scenery was continually changing with all kinds of water traffic,the Manhattan skyline tall buildings,and the green foliage of the New Jersey shore.

The ***maximum ebb tidal current*** often peaked at ***5½ knots*** on nearby boat speed-ometers.This required us **to sail with the tidal current...NOT the wind.**We would sail south for 4 hours and return in another 4 hours on one weekend,then go north while following a similar pattern the next weekend.We seemed to be the only active sailors in the area as others became discouraged of following the unpredictable wind patterns instead of the predictable and powerful Hudson River tidal current patterns.

The North River developed beautiful,long waterline 80' to 100' sloops for carrying passengers and freight from Manhattan to Albany and return,with a skipper and boy as crew...plus a barking dog if foggy weather was anticipated.

The ***flying jibe or North River jibe.***When it was necessary to jibe in the upper reaches of the river the skipper would ***put the tiller up*** (to weather) ***then run forward of the mast*** to dodge the flying boom in a wild jibe.This noise awakened a Dutch merchant sleeping below who stuck his head out of a hatch to find what was happening.He was decapitated by the jibing mainsail sheet...his head was never recovered.

After the boom jibed the skipper would return to the side opposite of the boom to trim the sheets and handle the tiller with the North River sloop on its new tack.

We were sailing the channel into Freeport,Long Island,with a strong following wind and a peak flood current taking us with a speed over the bottom of 10 knots. We signalled a bridge to open on the sunny Sunday afternoon,that didn't open in time.

We made a furious flying jibe which turned into a ***goosewing jibe.***The boom climbed the mast as ***only the bottom half of the main jibed. REJIBE*** the boom and jibe again!

It is important to recognize when a flying jibe is changing to a goosewing jibe to have a quick recovery to minimize equipment damage.

The flying jibe is excellent for Lido 14,C 15,Thistle,Lightning,and similar dinghies in a spirited force 5.***A considerable change of course is required to absorb the jibing forces on hardware*** and to reduce upset potentials.Practice in lighter winds to gain the timing and coordination which is so essential for sail boards,catboats,and open dinghies in spirited winds, pages 78 thru 85.

If the wind increases,the flying jibe forces also increase with coordination and timing becoming increasingly critical.The time may soon arrive to consider the ***chicken jibe*** to change the wind over the bow from one downwind tack to the other...as the mechanics of jibing are becoming too hazardous.

Lower the board and back the jib as you spin thru the eye of the wind with sufficient inertia ...to be underway on the new tack without going into irons,see page 70.No physical thrill can be compared to force 5 to lower force 6 dinghy planing thrills with spray flying,plus every instinct and muscle ready for instant response.

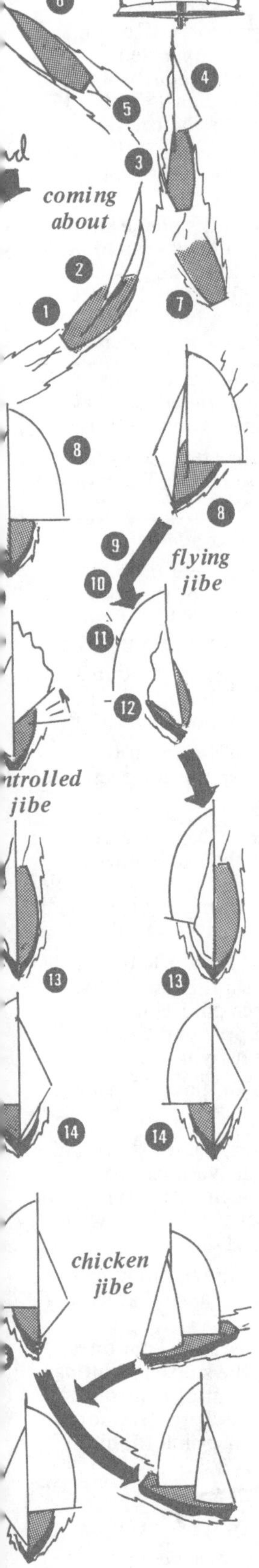

Sailing Illustrated Volume II

coming about

flying jibe

controlled jibe

chicken jibe

REVIEW–*CHANGING TACK over the bow... and over the stern.*

A sailboat** under sail only **is on a port tack or starboard tack** (several students have invented the stern tack). When it comes time to change to the other tack... **the wind must be changed over the bow...or over the stern.

COMING ABOUT* is** the method ***used to change the winds direction over the bow of a sailboat ***going to windward.*** Preparatory term ❶ ***"ready about"*** is given to alert the crew. The command ❷ ***"helm's alee"*** is given when the tiller is turned.

The boom lifts and the mainsail luffs ❸ until it fills on the new tack. The jib sheet is released ❺ on the order ***"CUT"***, so it is ❻ sheeted to the new tack.

When a sailboat comes about upwind the ***tiller is turned*** ❷ ***towards the boom.***

The jib is often backed or not released to insure the wind on the wrong side of the jib will spin the bow to the new tack without the boat being ***caught in irons.***

> ***Backing the jib*** ❹ *has many variables in light, medium, and strong winds, also is it a narrow, medium, or wide beam hull. If all factors are reasonably equal, backing the jib may be normal on a 30' sailboat, while a boat 4' to 6' longer may have double the inertia when coming about with backing the jib often becoming an overcorrection.*

Many dinghy capsizes in strong winds occur when the boat comes about too slowly without ❹ backing the jib, the boat ***runs out of inertia and is caught in irons.*** The boat starts to drift backwards out of control ❼ with the wind suddenly filling the sails. The wind pressure then flips the boat using the board as a lever, page 70.

IF the wind is very light all large sailboats may have to back the jib ❹ to insure a successful change of tack upwind.

Sailboats with long waterlines such as the ***17' Thistle*** and the ***48' Taku*** have so much extra directional stability or resistance to changing tack that backing the jib may be normal practice in light, medium, and strong winds.

Wide to medium ***sailboats to 30' long*** may find it advantageous to back the jib when going thru crowded moorings as it greatly aids their turning maneuverability.

While considerable individuality exists in single masted boats over 34', their ***excess inertia*** due to weight usually makes backing the jib an overcorrection, as also on most yawls. Backing the jib on some ***large cruising ketches*** may be very practical in light winds and in heavy winds to insure the successful upwind changes of tacks.

JIBING* is** the method ***used to change the winds direction over the stern of a sailboat ***from one downwind tack to the other.*** Three types of jibes are the ***controlled jibe,*** the ***flying jibe,*** and the ***chicken jibe...*** while the ***goosewing jibe,*** and the ***accidental jibes*** are to be avoided when possible.

> *Most sailing books provide a warning about jibing to the new sailor* **though jibing is as common a method to changing tack as coming about.** *A risk factor exists until the new sailor knows when, and how, to dodge the jibing boom and mainsheet while he develops his understanding of the variables involved in jibing.*

When a sailboat jibes from one downwind tack to the other ***the tiller is turned*** ❾ ***away from the boom.***

Terms used to jibe the 24' sailboat are ❽ ***"prepare to jibe".*** The mainsail sheet is taken in with the command ❿ ***"Jibe-O-Duck"*** given as the boom jibes from one side of the boat to the other. While the helmsman sets the mainsheet, the crew resets ⓭ preventer/vang, jibes the jib, resets the whisker pole and resets the jib sheet.

The ***flying jibe*** is used on the keel sailboat in a stronger wind. While the same sequence is followed, the course is changed sufficiently to take excess inertia ⓫ out of the jibing boom ⓬ to protect the sails, sheets, and hardware involved in the jibe.

It is a good practice to have a slight change of course when jibing dinghies in light to moderate winds. A point is reached, however, in an increasing wind when the timing, coordination, and crew cooperation may not be adequate. It becomes time to consider ***the chicken jibe*** ...which is the method to change from one downwind tack ⓯ to the other ⓱, by changing the wind over the bow ⓰. While it is a common procedure on dinghies, we occasionally find the ***chicken jibe*** is also preferred on cabin sailboats up to 40' or more in storm conditions particularly if the wind is puffy.

C

IF ANYTHING *CAN* GO WRONG...enjoy spinnaker operation.

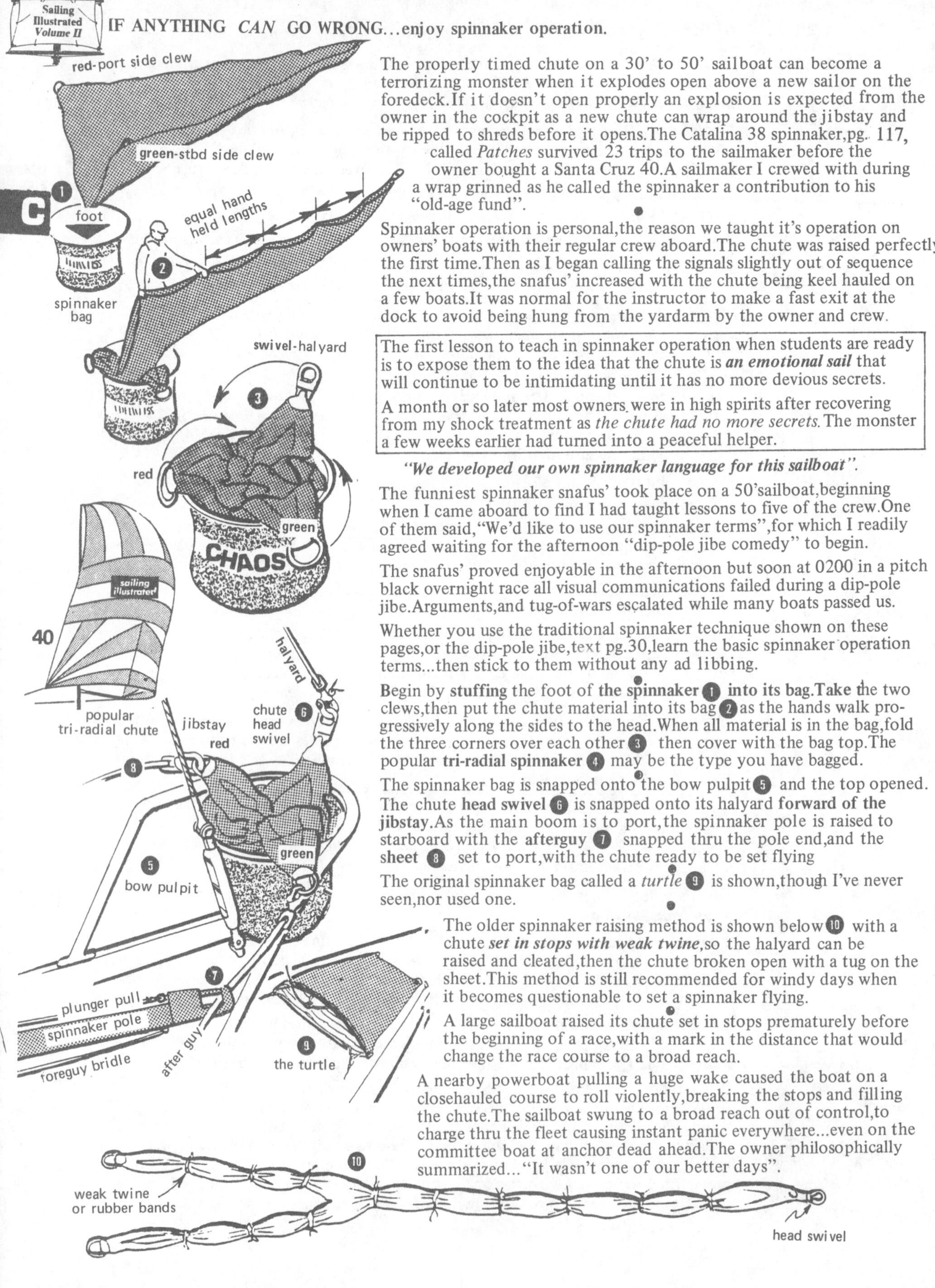

red-port side clew
green-stbd side clew
C
1
foot
equal hand held lengths
2
spinnaker bag
swivel-halyard
3
red
green
CHAOS
sailing illustrated
40
popular tri-radial chute
halyard
jibstay
chute head swivel
6
red
8
green
5
bow pulpit
7
plunger pull
spinnaker pole
foreguy bridle
after guy
9
the turtle
10
weak twine or rubber bands
head swivel

The properly timed chute on a 30' to 50' sailboat can become a terrorizing monster when it explodes open above a new sailor on the foredeck. If it doesn't open properly an explosion is expected from the owner in the cockpit as a new chute can wrap around the jibstay and be ripped to shreds before it opens. The Catalina 38 spinnaker, pg. 117, called *Patches* survived 23 trips to the sailmaker before the owner bought a Santa Cruz 40. A sailmaker I crewed with during a wrap grinned as he called the spinnaker a contribution to his "old-age fund".

Spinnaker operation is personal, the reason we taught it's operation on owners' boats with their regular crew aboard. The chute was raised perfectly the first time. Then as I began calling the signals slightly out of sequence the next times, the snafus' increased with the chute being keel hauled on a few boats. It was normal for the instructor to make a fast exit at the dock to avoid being hung from the yardarm by the owner and crew.

The first lesson to teach in spinnaker operation when students are ready is to expose them to the idea that the chute is ***an emotional sail*** that will continue to be intimidating until it has no more devious secrets.

A month or so later most owners were in high spirits after recovering from my shock treatment as *the chute had no more secrets.* The monster a few weeks earlier had turned into a peaceful helper.

"We developed our own spinnaker language for this sailboat".

The funniest spinnaker snafus' took place on a 50' sailboat, beginning when I came aboard to find I had taught lessons to five of the crew. One of them said, "We'd like to use our spinnaker terms", for which I readily agreed waiting for the afternoon "dip-pole jibe comedy" to begin.

The snafus' proved enjoyable in the afternoon but soon at 0200 in a pitch black overnight race all visual communications failed during a dip-pole jibe. Arguments, and tug-of-wars escalated while many boats passed us.

Whether you use the traditional spinnaker technique shown on these pages, or the dip-pole jibe, text pg. 30, learn the basic spinnaker operation terms...then stick to them without any ad libbing.

Begin by **stuffing** the foot of **the spinnaker 1 into its bag. Take** the two clews, then put the chute material into its bag 2 as the hands walk progressively along the sides to the head. When all material is in the bag, fold the three corners over each other 3 then cover with the bag top. The popular **tri-radial spinnaker 4** may be the type you have bagged.

The spinnaker bag is snapped onto the bow pulpit 5 and the top opened. The chute **head swivel 6** is snapped onto its halyard **forward of the jibstay.** As the main boom is to port, the spinnaker pole is raised to starboard with the **afterguy 7** snapped thru the pole end, and the **sheet 8** set to port, with the chute ready to be set flying

The original spinnaker bag called a *turtle* 9 is shown, though I've never seen, nor used one.

The older spinnaker raising method is shown below 10 with a chute ***set in stops with weak twine,*** so the halyard can be raised and cleated, then the chute broken open with a tug on the sheet. This method is still recommended for windy days when it becomes questionable to set a spinnaker flying.

A large sailboat raised its chute set in stops prematurely before the beginning of a race, with a mark in the distance that would change the race course to a broad reach.

A nearby powerboat pulling a huge wake caused the boat on a closehauled course to roll violently, breaking the stops and filling the chute. The sailboat swung to a broad reach out of control, to charge thru the fleet causing instant panic everywhere...even on the committee boat at anchor dead ahead. The owner philosophically summarized..."It wasn't one of our better days".

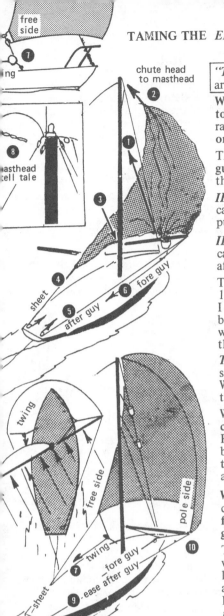

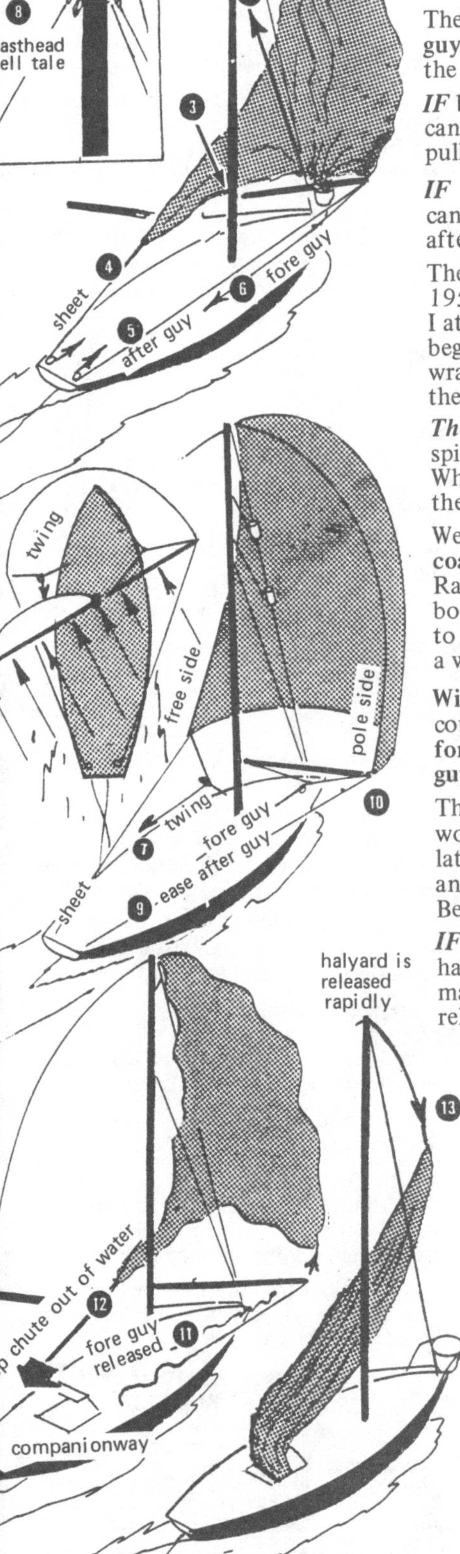
free side
chute head to masthead
sheet
after guy
fore guy
twing
free side
pole side
twing
fore guy
ease after guy
sheet
halyard is released rapidly
chute out of water
fore guy released
companionway

"That wasn't the way we did it on old ......", or, "But I thought......', are the excuses for most wraps, torn sails, and assorted spinnaker disasters.

When the turn mark is coming up the pole is rigged and supported by its **topping lift** (1) .All chute lines must be rigged so as the mark is turned the raising sequence is followed systematically with **one person only giving orders** who can see the **chute reach masthead** (2) and it's **halyard cleated** (3)

The order is given to **haul in the sheet** (4) 2 seconds later, then the **after guy set** (5) an additional 2 seconds later so the chute will pop open, then the jib is dropped. ***Adjust sheet, after guy, fore guy*** (6) ***and topping lift.***

***IF* before the halyard is cleated** the sheet or guy is pulled too soon, the chute can pop open early in a strong wind. The crew tailing the halyard may be pulled 10' to 20' off the deck, or let it go...out it's masthead pulley.

***IF* sheet or afterguy are hauled too late,..after the chute halyard is cleated,** can produce an instant wrap around the jibstay...or a wrap can also occur after the chute is up and set correctly–

The chute began to wrap on the 36' **Sunda** in a deteriorating wind in the 1959 Ensenada Race. Since pulling the sheet pulled the chute out of trim, I attached a second line to the free end of the chute so when the chute began to lift, a tug down on the new line we called a ***twing*** stopped the wrap. A block was added (7) ,the twing reeved thru it which returned to the cockpit so the ***twing or vang*** could reduce the wrap potentials.

The wrap begins in the upper ½ of the chute, then the lower half lifts and spins the opposite direction producing a tight hourglass wrap around the stay. When the upper wrap begins, the **twing** (7) **is hardened** so the lower half of the chute cannot lift or wrap around the stay to eliminate the problem.

We found the rest of our answer on a 26' sailboat with a masthead mounted **coat hanger using a 16" telltale** (8) that eliminated wraps in 3 Ensenada Races. ***When the wind shift begins aloft*** the telltale flows aft indicating the boat is going faster than the wind. This warning provides a 3 second notice to harden the free side of the chute with a twing to avoid the potentials of a wrap. Though it outperformed any instrument... it also produces a stiff neck.

With the turn mark coming up, raise the jib. After the boat starts to change course, one person again calls all signals. The afterguy is eased so (9) **the foreguy** can be released, then the pole plunger pulled (10) ,so the **after guy** (11) is released to run freely.

The **sheet becomes limp which must be hauled rapidly** (12) so the chute won't touch the water. The chute **halyard** (13) **is rapidly released** a second later with the chute coming down the companionway to keep the deck and cockpit clear. Unsnap halyard, ease topping lift, remove and store pole . Begin repacking the chute if another downwind course is anticipated.

***IF* the tail end of the afterguy** isn't fully released or catches on a cleat... it happened on a 38 footer in a force 6. The halyard jumped its pulley at masthead, wedging between the pulley and mast, with the stuck chute released seconds before going into the breaker line, with $800 damage.

- ***"I couldn't stop the knockdown...the tiller overpowered me!"***

Was the helmsman wet and tired with responses too slow to anticipate the knockdown...or didn't he have sufficient experience to anticipate and avoid the knockdown by **KEEPING the sailboat on its downwind course when it wants to head up.**

If the bow turning tendency isn't immediately stopped pressures rapidly increase on the rudder with all forces moving sideways when the boat goes up to a beam reach to produce a spectacular knockdown.

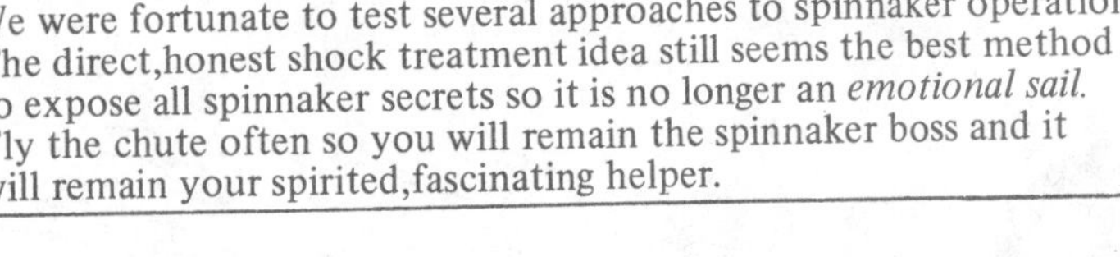
We were fortunate to test several approaches to spinnaker operation The direct, honest shock treatment idea still seems the best method to expose all spinnaker secrets so it is no longer an *emotional sail.* Fly the chute often so you will remain the spinnaker boss and it will remain your spirited, fascinating helper.

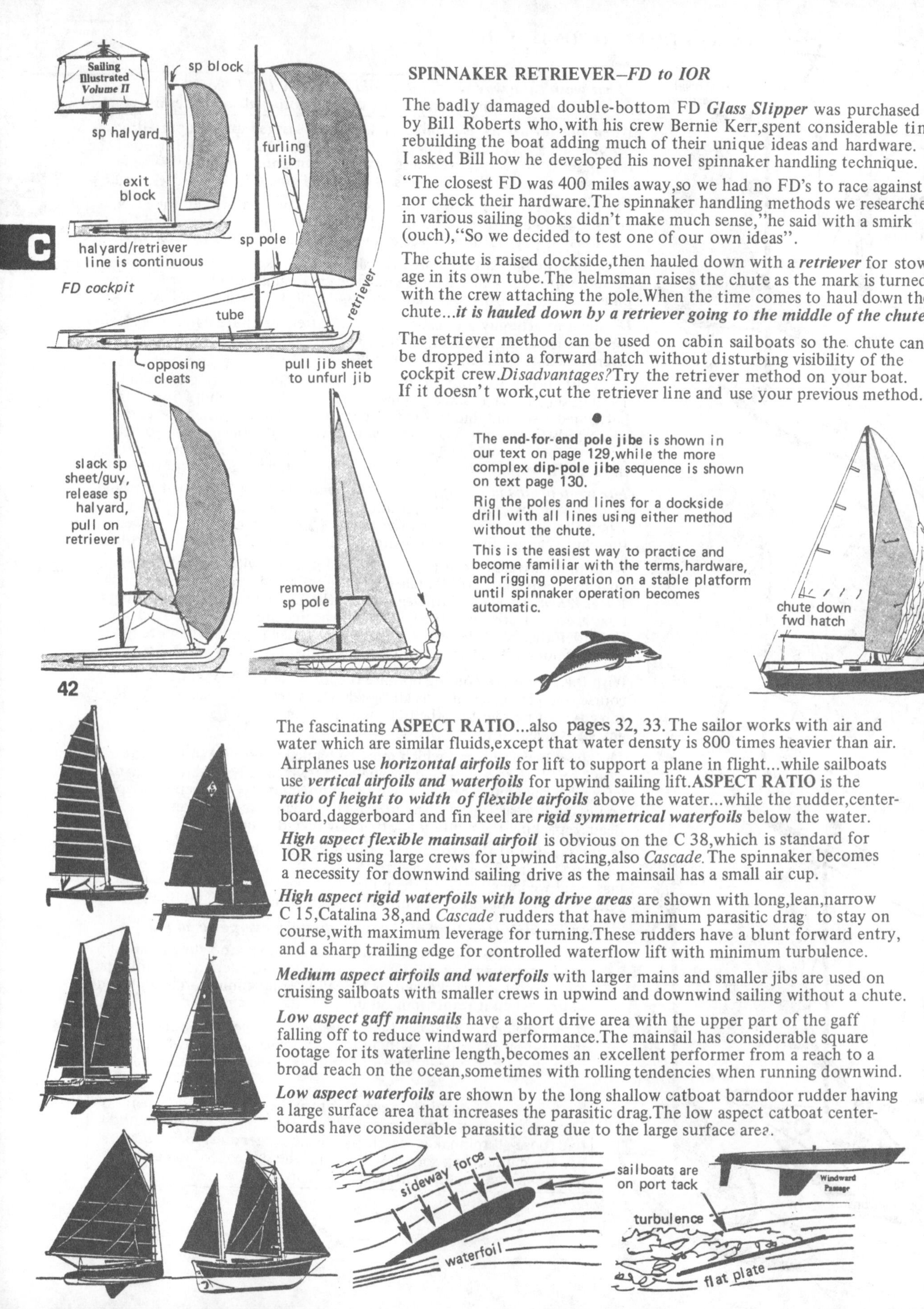
Sailing Illustrated Volume II
sp block
sp halyard
furling jib
exit block
C
halyard/retriever line is continuous
sp pole
FD cockpit
tube
retriever
opposing cleats
pull jib sheet to unfurl jib
slack sp sheet/guy, release sp halyard, pull on retriever
remove sp pole
chute down fwd hatch
sideway force
waterfoil
sailboats are on port tack
turbulence
flat plate
Windward Passage

SPINNAKER RETRIEVER–*FD to IOR*

The badly damaged double-bottom FD *Glass Slipper* was purchased by Bill Roberts who, with his crew Bernie Kerr, spent considerable time rebuilding the boat adding much of their unique ideas and hardware. I asked Bill how he developed his novel spinnaker handling technique.

"The closest FD was 400 miles away, so we had no FD's to race against nor check their hardware. The spinnaker handling methods we researched in various sailing books didn't make much sense," he said with a smirk (ouch), "So we decided to test one of our own ideas".

The chute is raised dockside, then hauled down with a ***retriever*** for stowage in its own tube. The helmsman raises the chute as the mark is turned, with the crew attaching the pole. When the time comes to haul down the chute...***it is hauled down by a retriever going to the middle of the chute.***

The retriever method can be used on cabin sailboats so the chute can be dropped into a forward hatch without disturbing visibility of the cockpit crew. *Disadvantages?* Try the retriever method on your boat. If it doesn't work, cut the retriever line and use your previous method.

•

The **end-for-end pole jibe** is shown in our text on page 129, while the more complex **dip-pole jibe** sequence is shown on text page 130.

Rig the poles and lines for a dockside drill with all lines using either method without the chute.

This is the easiest way to practice and become familiar with the terms, hardware, and rigging operation on a stable platform until spinnaker operation becomes automatic.

The fascinating **ASPECT RATIO**...also pages 32, 33. The sailor works with air and water which are similar fluids, except that water density is 800 times heavier than air. Airplanes use ***horizontal airfoils*** for lift to support a plane in flight...while sailboats use ***vertical airfoils and waterfoils*** for upwind sailing lift. **ASPECT RATIO** is the ***ratio of height to width of flexible airfoils*** above the water...while the rudder, centerboard, daggerboard and fin keel are ***rigid symmetrical waterfoils*** below the water.

High aspect flexible mainsail airfoil is obvious on the C 38, which is standard for IOR rigs using large crews for upwind racing, also *Cascade*. The spinnaker becomes a necessity for downwind sailing drive as the mainsail has a small air cup.

High aspect rigid waterfoils with long drive areas are shown with long, lean, narrow C 15, Catalina 38, and *Cascade* rudders that have minimum parasitic drag to stay on course, with maximum leverage for turning. These rudders have a blunt forward entry, and a sharp trailing edge for controlled waterflow lift with minimum turbulence.

Medium aspect airfoils and waterfoils with larger mains and smaller jibs are used on cruising sailboats with smaller crews in upwind and downwind sailing without a chute.

Low aspect gaff mainsails have a short drive area with the upper part of the gaff falling off to reduce windward performance. The mainsail has considerable square footage for its waterline length, becomes an excellent performer from a reach to a broad reach on the ocean, sometimes with rolling tendencies when running downwind.

Low aspect waterfoils are shown by the long shallow catboat barndoor rudder having a large surface area that increases the parasitic drag. The low aspect catboat centerboards have considerable parasitic drag due to the large surface area.

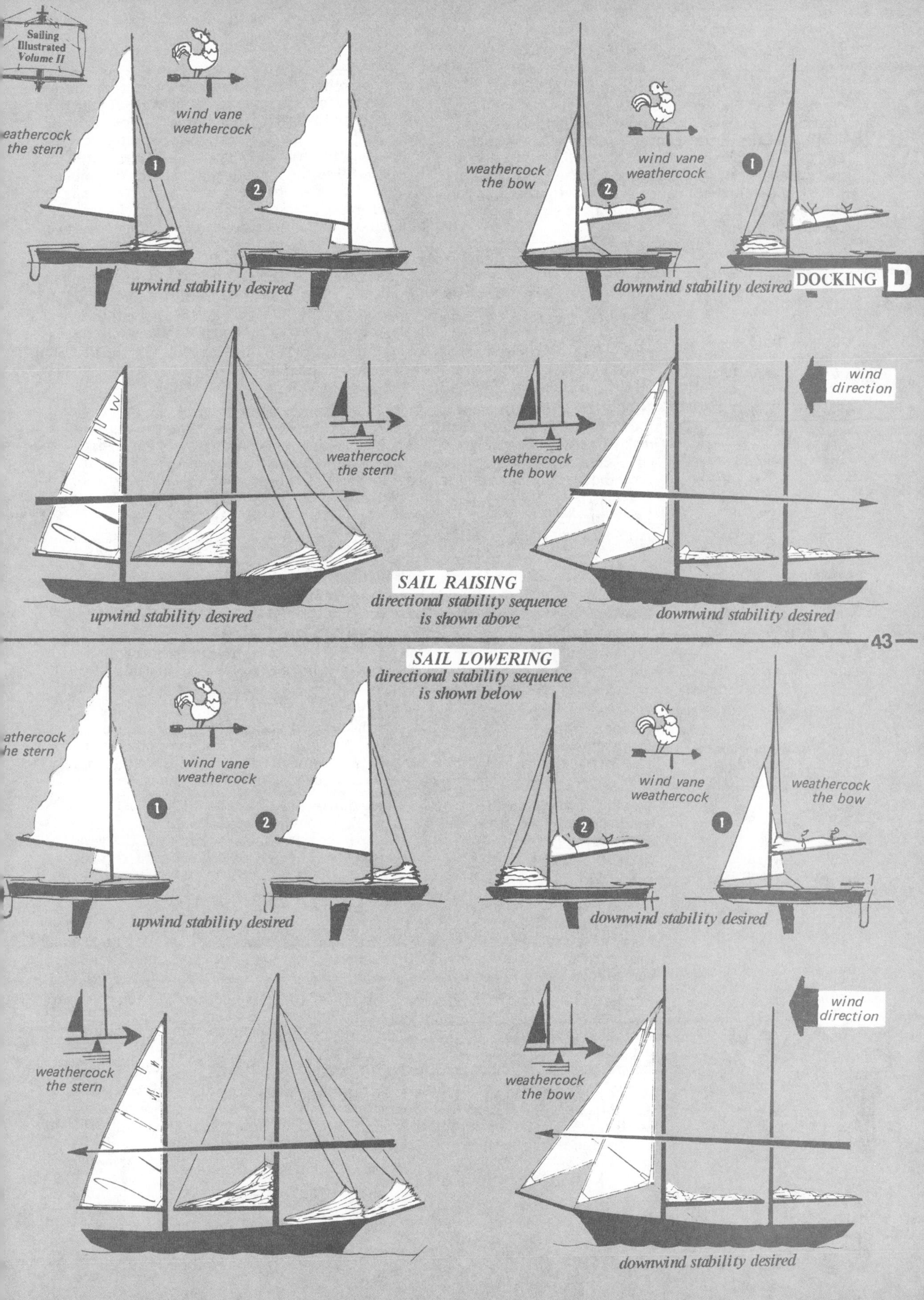

eathercock
the stern
wind vane
weathercock
1
2
weathercock
the bow
wind vane
weathercock
2
1
upwind stability desired
downwind stability desired
wind
direction
weathercock
the stern
weathercock
the bow
upwind stability desired
downwind stability desired
athercock
he stern
wind vane
weathercock
1
2
2
wind vane
weathercock
weathercock
the bow
1
upwind stability desired
downwind stability desired
weathercock
the stern
weathercock
the bow
wind
direction
downwind stability desired

SAIL RAISING
directional stability sequence
is shown above

SAIL LOWERING
directional stability sequence
is shown below

Sailing
Illustrated
Volume II

The basics–LEAVING & RETURNING

the self appointed oracle

Every club seems to have a self-appointed non-boat owner expert.We were tied between shad poles on the Hudson River above the George Washington Bridge in 1949.The current was going downstream at 5 knots, and our 20' sailboat was pointed downstream.I began raising sails when our local expert began to loudly tell his friends we were doing everything wrong...while he recounted his last square rigger trip around the horn for the umpteenth time.

I dropped sails,lowered the weighted centerboard,cast off,then drifted 120 or so feet downstream under full control with the water going faster than our boat.As our boat started moving and the speed difference was minimized,we turned to a beam reach,raising the jib, to sail out thru the remaining shad poles.The raucous laughter from the observers was music to our ears.This chapter will help to prepare you for the chance meeting of a self-appointed member of the rocking chair fleet.

D

centerboard Lido 14

When you take the Lido 14 ❶ for a sail your first consideration is the location of the boat.If it is sailed from the present cleat,the Lido will hit the downwind dock on its port before the sails are pulling and the boat is under control.

move to OUTER cleat

Backing the jib, page 36.

Tow boat to **cleat V** ❷,then lower the centerboard for stability. Raise the mainsail to weathercock the bow into the wind,then raise the jib.**BACKWIND the jib,then release bow dockline.**After the bow swings to port and the mainsail fills,the jib sheet is released,then pulled in on the port side.The boat is underway and under control on the port tack, *Backing the jib, page 36.*

stopping a centerboarder

180 degree water brake with sails up

MINIMUM INERTIA stop. The Lido 14 will be tied up in position ❸.**Pull centerboard** all the way up on the final downwind leg...then as you enter the slip area, make a **180 degree turn** next to the dock aiming for upper cleat ❼ releasing both sheets. The 180 degree turn slams on the water brakes as the hull with the **centerboard up,stalls out.**Turn bow to port,drift to position ❸ ,drop,stow sails.

the 14' keel Capri

move to outer cleat

MAXIMUM INERTIA stop. You next take a 14' Capri sailboat which has a fixed keel,otherwise it is identical to the Lido 14.Tow the Capri ❹ to outer cleat V ❺ raise mainsail,then jib. Backwind jib,then release bow dockline.The mainsail fills, the jib sheet is pulled to port with the sails pulling so the boat is under contro[.

stopping a keel boat

deadstick landing

180 degree water brake with sails down

On the final upwind approach drop mainsail ❻,then turn downwind heading for the slip.When the boat is on course,drop the jib for a dead stick landing to reduce speed and inertia.Make a **180 degree turn** next to the dock to apply the water brakes,the minimum inertia taking the **Capri** with a keel to the cleat ❼.

leave on broad reach

You next take out a 20' keel sloop ❽ with the wind on its quarter.Raise jib to sail out under jib only for downwind helm.After the boat has enough inertia and speed, momentarily head up to raise the mainsail,then fall back to the closehauled course until both sails are full and pulling...then enjoy a spirited sail.

upwind docking may be questionable

After a sail the boat is to be left tied to the dock at position ❿.You can make a **beam approach** ⓫ releasing jib sheet,then the main sheet so your boat will drift to a stop in the desired dock position.This approach has a hazard since the boom is beyond the hull,the **mainsheet can snag a dock cleat,with the mainsail filling.**

the downwind deadstick landing

You are on the same 20' sloop making a **downwind approach** with a dead stick ⓬ landing,dropping the mainsail just before turning downwind.The jib may,or may not be dropped on the downwind leg depending on the boat characteristics,wind strength,and your reflexes.After boat speed has been considerably reduced,make a 180 degree water brakes turn to stall out the hull,turn bow to starboard,then tie the boat up to the dock in the desired position.

Review the situations covered on the facing page for leaving and returning to a dock until the sail raising and lowering sequence becomes automatic...and you understand the inertia differences involved with sloops that are identical except one has a keel while the other uses a centerboard.

the author goofs

After teaching on many centerboard Lido 14's I delivered one of the first Capri keel versions to the Newport Harbor Yacht Club for an adult student.With 60 or more juniors looking on I made a 180° turn to apply the water brakes without dropping the sails.I can still hear the laughter of the juniors who were using our sail course material watching me sail out of the slip without slowing down,on the other tack.

a hand push... and a foot push

A 747 pilot received a 25' sailboat as a birthday present...the first sail was a disaster. The following day aboard their boat with a hand push one place,a foot push in another,we sailed out without hitting any boats.He grinned,summarizing,"I still can't understand how I bumped seven boats...with only five boats in the slip".

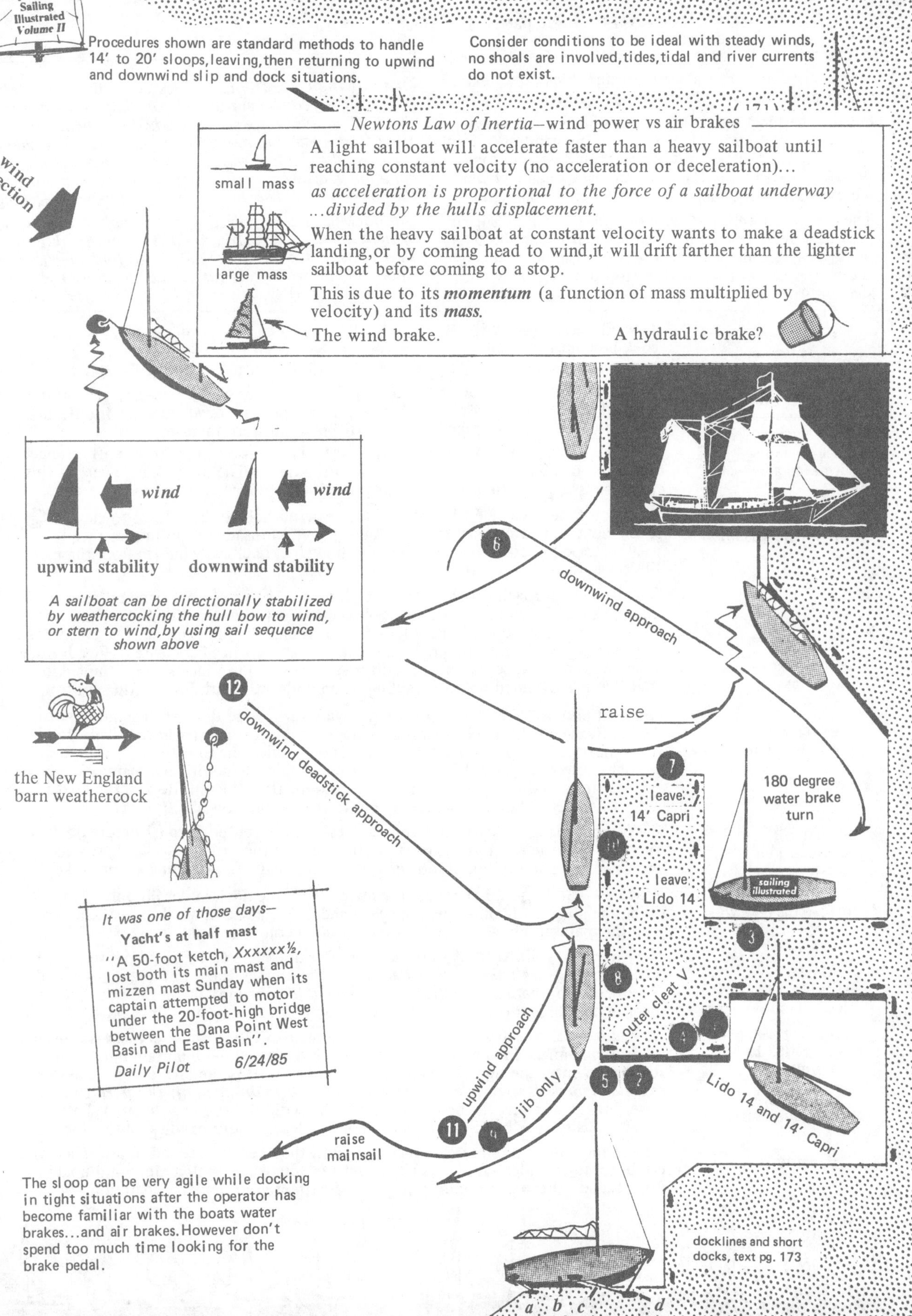

Sailing Illustrated Volume II
Procedures shown are standard methods to handle 14′ to 20′ sloops, leaving, then returning to upwind and downwind slip and dock situations.
Consider conditions to be ideal with steady winds, no shoals are involved, tides, tidal and river currents do not exist.
Newtons Law of Inertia—wind power vs air brakes
A light sailboat will accelerate faster than a heavy sailboat until reaching constant velocity (no acceleration or deceleration)...
as acceleration is proportional to the force of a sailboat underway ...divided by the hulls displacement.
When the heavy sailboat at constant velocity wants to make a deadstick landing, or by coming head to wind, it will drift farther than the lighter sailboat before coming to a stop.
This is due to its momentum (a function of mass multiplied by velocity) and its mass.
The wind brake.
A hydraulic brake?
small mass
large mass
wind direction
wind
wind
upwind stability
downwind stability
A sailboat can be directionally stabilized by weathercocking the hull bow to wind, or stern to wind, by using sail sequence shown above
the New England barn weathercock
downwind approach
downwind deadstick approach
raise
leave 14′ Capri
leave Lido 14
180 degree water brake turn
sailing illustrated
outer cleat V
upwind approach
jib only
raise mainsail
Lido 14 and 14′ Capri
It was one of those days—
Yacht's at half mast
"A 50-foot ketch, Xxxxxx½, lost both its main mast and mizzen mast Sunday when its captain attempted to motor under the 20-foot-high bridge between the Dana Point West Basin and East Basin".
Daily Pilot 6/24/85
The sloop can be very agile while docking in tight situations after the operator has become familiar with the boats water brakes...and air brakes. However don't spend too much time looking for the brake pedal.
docklines and short docks, text pg. 173
a
b
c
d

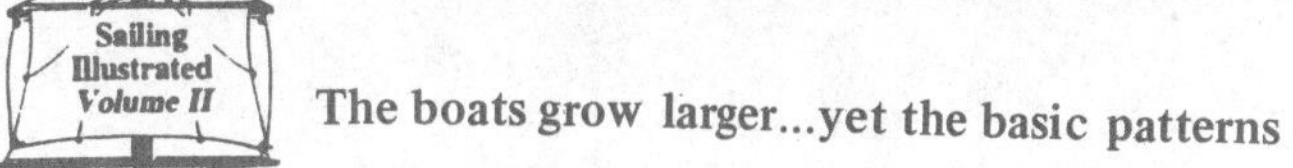
Sailing
Illustrated
Volume II

The boats grow larger...yet the basic patterns continue.

The most stimulating part of sailing—

More collision damages occur around docks than elsewhere due to lack of observation,and/or lack of training.

One of the most self-fulfilling parts of sailing is leaving and returning to your dock or slip using wind power only. The sailor with sufficient training should be able to dock most sailboats to 50' long without using engine power which is becoming a lost art for most cabin sailboats.

The exception we found with our boat,was a 20' slip on a port tack beam reach with another boat in the slip to starboard.A 4" clearance existed between the boats.When the mainsheet was released to stop our boat it would snag onto the other boat filling our mainsail...*oops!*

Many of the ideas in our Homestudy Guide *were tested in our sailing course evening classes that were open to the local public in the sixties.We had excellent cooperation from local racing and cruising sailors,sailmakers, designers,etc.,to test various ideas in these lectures,Our common goals were to find the questions,then provide the answers and ideas that the new sailors were seeking.*

Our docking charts evolved systematically for the variety of tight docks in our harbor which are even tighter today Two years of testing were required to find a lecturer who could dock the catboat on the facing page.He grinned "The answer is easy,I owned a 25' catboat for 2 years".

D

tow cutter to OUTER cleat

Tow cutter to cleat W (14) .Raise mainsail,inner jib,and outer jib in sequence to weathercock bow into the wind.Slip dockline,then **backwind outer jib** to pull the bow to starboard tack.When mainsail fills,trim outer jib sheet to port side of sailboat.

double mooring—upwind approach

Normal approach to a double mooring is into the wind (15) releasing jib sheet, staysail sheet,and mainsail sheet in sequence with the bow next to the tie line using the sails as **air brakes**.Secure boat bow and stern,then stow sails.

double mooring—downwind approach

A secondary approach (16) with a very light wind or torn sail,is to ease off all sheets on a beam reach,then head up to **drift into the tieline**.The questionable part of this approach is that the tieline may wrap around the rudder,keel,or prop.

let wind move your yawl

Next you take a **yawl** (17) for a sail.Let the wind help it drift down to cleat W (18), so the boat will swing bow to wind.Raise jigger,mainsail,and jib in sequence to weathercock the bow into the wind.Slip bow dockline,**backwind jib** until the main fills on starboard tack...then sheet jib to port.

head to wind—air brake stop

Traditional approach for the yawl to pick up a mooring (19) is to **head up**,release jib sheet,mainsail sheet,and jigger sheet to **weathercock the bow**.The luffing sails will provide air brakes so the boat will drift to a stop at the mooring can.The ***close reach*** approach (20) with the same upwind sheet release sequence is repeated.The advantage, if something unexpected occurs (a diver surfaces,etc.),the sheets can be pulled in, and the sails trimmed with the sailboat soon underway with full steering control.

close reach—air brakes

the CATBOAT—use a heaving line

You next take a 25' catboat (21) for a sail.Walk to upwind dock,then stand next to **cleat X.Heave a light line downwind** to the catboat,tie a heavier line to it then pull end of heavier line to you.Attach other end of heavier line to catboat bow,then pull catboat to cleat X (22) .**LOWER centerboard** and raise mainsail.**Back main boom** to starboard so bow swings to port.Release boom after the sail fills and the boat is underway. OOOOPS...did you remember to release the bow slip line????????

the stall out, centerboard up docking

The catboat makes a downwind approach **raising the centerboard** (23) before docking. Aim bow into the wind so the boat inertia will help the catboat drift sideway (24) into dock in its **stalled condition** with the luffing mainsail providing an air brake.

KETCH-leaving downwind

Heavy 40' ketch (26) can be sailed downwind from the dock under **jib only** (27) by jibing the jib.After it gains enough speed and inertia,head upwind to raise the mizzen, then the mainsail.Finally fall off to your desired course and enjoy a good sail.

KETCH-leaving upwind

The same heavy 40' ketch (28) can cast off after dock line and spring lines so that the bow will ***pivot on the heavy bow line*** secured to cleat Y.Raise mizzen,mainsail,and jib in sequence to weathercock the bow.***Backwind jib***,slip and take in the bow line, sheet in mizzen and main until they begin to pull,then sheet the jib to port.

downwind steering control MUST be maintained!

We had to dock a heavy 40' ketch in a slip similar to (30) .Downwind helm was needed by dropping mizzen,mainsail and jib to reduce the speed,yet maintain minimum steerage to enter the slip as the engine was inoperative.As the bow entered the slip, ***five metal buckets*** each tied to heavy docklines,***were dropped off the stern*** to become water brakes stopping the boat dead in the slip without touching the dock.Total damage was to four buckets which disappeared leaving four handles on the dock lines.

coffin corner water brakes

summary—

Repeat these docking situations mentally until they become second nature.Then you can begin to consider variables such as short or long keels,keel/centerboard boats, wind funnels,and other vessels underway that may affect your docking operation.

Procedures shown are standard methods to handle a variety of larger sailboats leaving, then returning to a variety of docking and mooring situations.

Consider conditions to be ideal with steady winds no shoals are involved, tides, tidal and river currents do not exist.

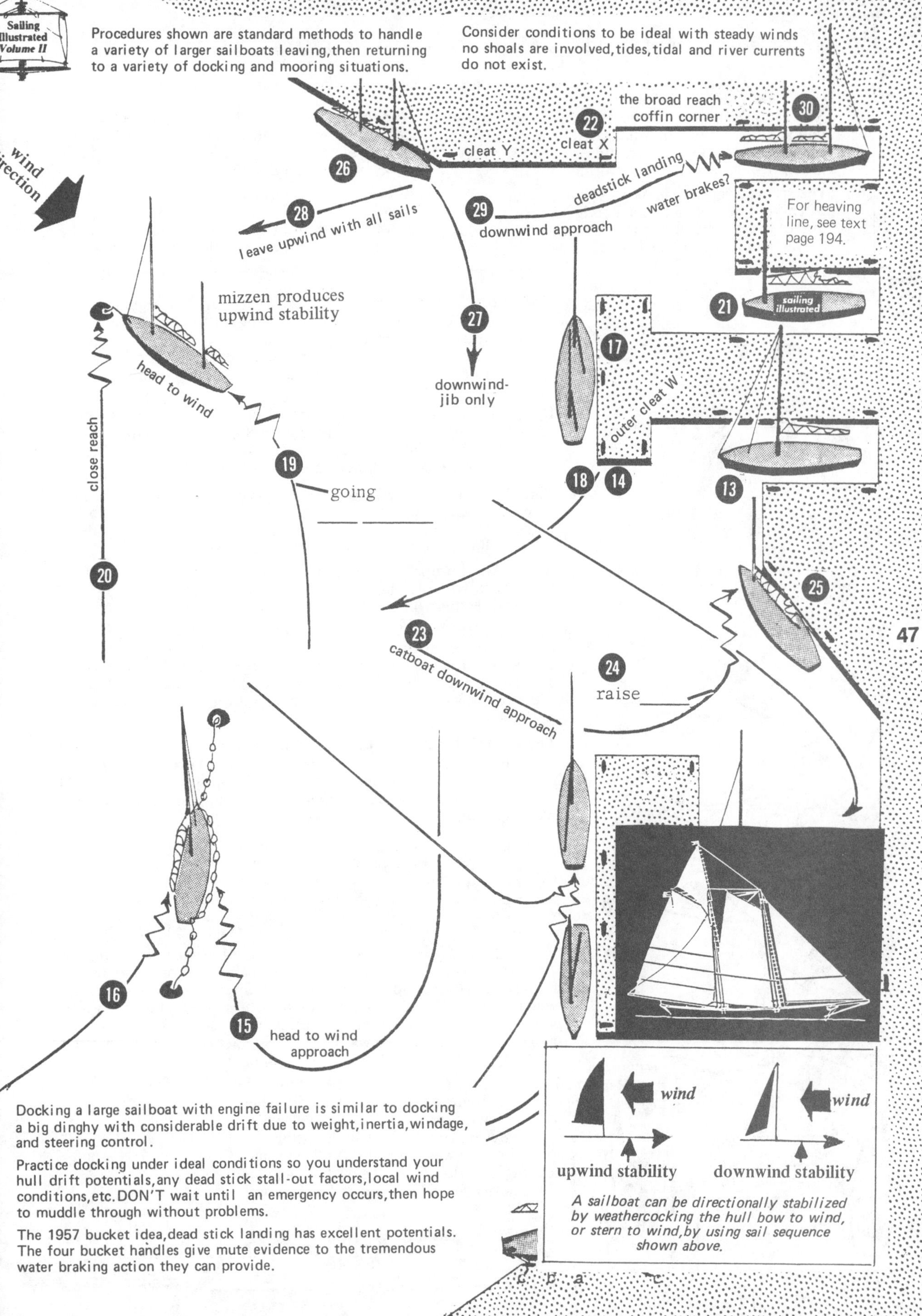

wind direction
the broad reach coffin corner
30
22
cleat X
cleat Y
26
deadstick landing
water brakes?
28
leave upwind with all sails
29
downwind approach
For heaving line, see text page 194.
mizzen produces upwind stability
27
sailing illustrated
21
17
downwind-jib only
head to wind
close reach
outer cleat W
19
going ___ ___
18
14
13
20
25
23
catboat downwind approach
24
raise ___
16
15
head to wind approach
wind
wind
upwind stability
downwind stability

A sailboat can be directionally stabilized by weathercocking the hull bow to wind, or stern to wind, by using sail sequence shown above.

Docking a large sailboat with engine failure is similar to docking a big dinghy with considerable drift due to weight, inertia, windage, and steering control.

Practice docking under ideal conditions so you understand your hull drift potentials, any dead stick stall-out factors, local wind conditions, etc. DON'T wait until an emergency occurs, then hope to muddle through without problems.

The 1957 bucket idea, dead stick landing has excellent potentials. The four bucket handles give mute evidence to the tremendous water braking action they can provide.

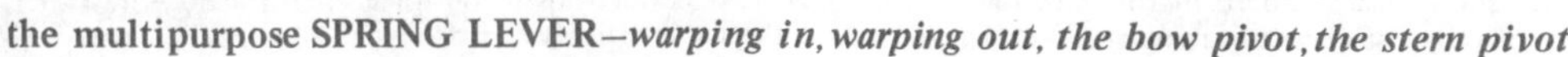

the multipurpose SPRING LEVER–*warping in, warping out, the bow pivot, the stern pivot*

the all-purpose spring–a puller, a pivot, a dock brake...and a dock line.

Small to medium-size sailboats often provide entertainment for onlookers when with little planning they are muscled alongside, into, or out of slips or docks with minimum maneuvering room.

The spring lever may be needed under sail or power when your boat is short handed in adverse winds or currents, though it becomes a standard procedure for large sailboats in ideal conditions.

The ***spring line is a lever*** holding one end of a boat that provides a ***pivot*** around which the other end is able to swing on or maneuver when leaving an awkward or tight docking situation.

It can help a sailboat ***warp in or warp out*** of a tight slip. It can provide a wide-beam sailboat with a ***stern in, stern out*** adjustment. The spring can be a ***dock brake*** to stop a boat in a limited area.

D

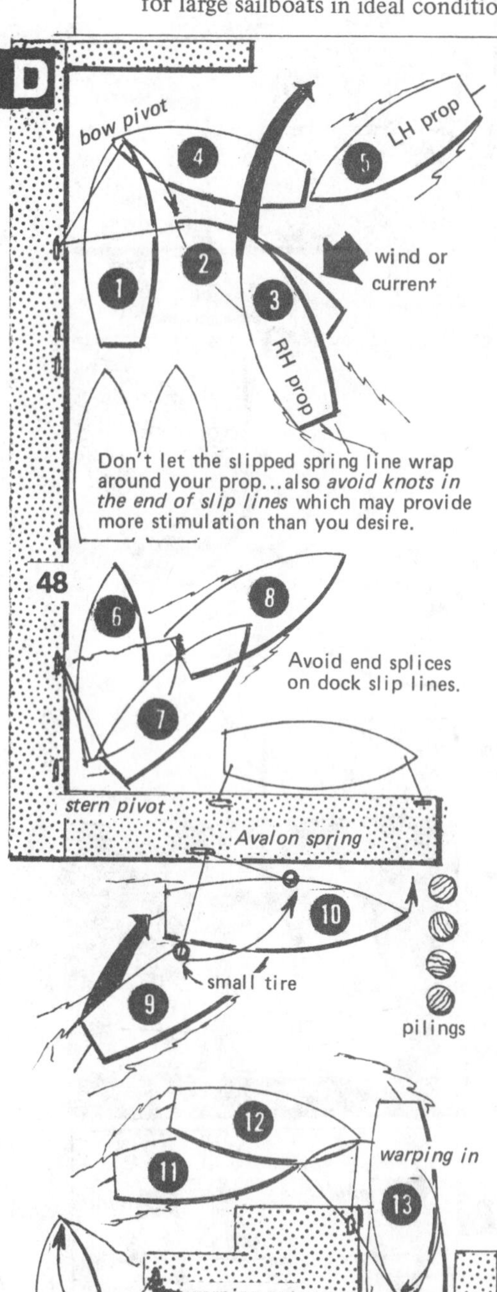

bow pivot
LH prop
wind or current
RH prop
1
2
3
4
5
6
7
8
9
10
11
12
13
14
15
16
Avoid end splices on dock slip lines.
stern pivot
Avalon spring
small tire
pilings
warping in
warping out

Don't let the slipped spring line wrap around your prop...also *avoid knots in the end of slip lines* which may provide more stimulation than you desire.

The automobile tires track or follow when driving around a corner due to tire friction...the exception, turning on an unexpected patch of ice. The sailboat which uses a keel as a pivot point to turn, can steer from either end. **The rudder turns the stern** of a sailboat as it starts to come about, with the **backed jib** taking over, **pulling the bow** to the new tack.

If standard docking procedures don't provide the answers you desire, consider using the spring as a maneuvering pivot to make one end of your sailboat go in an opposite direction from the other end such as with the wind and/or currents shown at left.

The **BOW SPRING ❶** is used to pivot the stern out with a little forward power, rudder towards the dock, sometimes requiring a bow fender. After the boat with a LH prop is at right angles to the dock, the bow line is slipped...with the engine in reverse.

A right hand prop ❸ will tend to pull the stern to port, permitting the bow to swing to starboard. The boat with a **left hand prop ❺ is slipped earlier,** with reverse applied with the stern still swinging.

The **STERN SPRING ❼** is used with engine in a slow reverse, a stern fender is required, The rudder is towards the dock until the bow is almost into the wind, then the spring is slipped and the boat powers directly into the wind. If the spring is slipped a few seconds late... the pivot and wind forces may push it into the docked boat on its right or to starboard

The **AVALON SPRING ❿** is used by shoreboat water taxi's. When a taxi is coming into its dock to discharge passengers, the taxi makes a power-on landing picking up a **short midship spring line brake** that pulls the boat alongside its dock often in surge or choppy water with tall pilings a few feet ahead which support a pier.

When leaving the dock the taxi engine is put into forward with the spring line providing a pivot for the stern to swing away from the dock. Reverse is applied and the spring line is cast off. Forward power is applied when the taxi is far enough from the dock.

6/10/85. The 150 ton, 3 masted, 90 schooner *Resolution* was built as a fisherman in 1926. She had been launched at the boat yard across our bay preparatory to leaving for the Mediterranean. We watched the crew turn it 180° with springs and docklines using pilings as pivot points against a force 3 breeze. Warping in or out, or turning large sailing vessels with levers was a common practice a century ago. It was a thrill to see this art still practiced by modern sailors.

The *Argus, pg.104,* built for the Northern European trade was over 30 years old when it's first engine was installed by the Nazi's. It operates up to 300 days a year using spring lines to warp in and out of unusual docking situations with the enthusiastic help of it's active Sea Scout boy and girl crew.

Sailing
Illustrated
Volume II

We enjoy sailing our sailboat into its slip which is shorter than the boat. Living however in an imperfect world,it is necessary to provide for unexpected variables when a sheet snags,a surprise puff fills the sails... or the skipper makes a miscalculation.A ***short midship spring line*** ❶ provides an excellent ***dock brake snubber*** to stop our sailboat before it plows into the end of its slip.

After we leave the dock our docklines are secured topside on their cleats When docking,sew-in **marline dockline markers** ❷ permit a variety of crew members to cleat the boat in its slip with little wasted effort as it is no longer necessary to adjust the docklines.

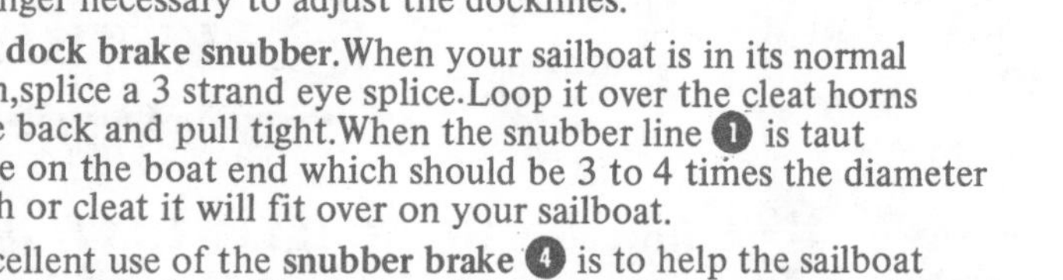

Splice your dock brake snubber. When your sailboat is in its normal slip position,splice a 3 strand eye splice.Loop it over the cleat horns then double back and pull tight.When the snubber line ❶ is taut splice an eye on the boat end which should be 3 to 4 times the diameter of the winch or cleat it will fit over on your sailboat.

Another excellent use of the **snubber brake** ❹ is to help the sailboat shown stop before its bow hits the varnished powerboat stern dead ahead. We prefer 3 strand Dacron for dock-mounted snubbers on sailboats under 30' long,and 3 strand nylon,for larger sailboats.

As the **size and inertia increases** with sailboats and motorsailers to 50' and longer,engine power is normally used for docking ...but how can the boat be stopped accurately without hitting the end of the slip?

The helmsman should have a toe rail or cap rail marker on his boat he can easily see from his normal steering position ❻ that will line up with a mark on the dock for **precision landings.** A **snubber dock line** ❼ can be helpful to hold the boat while the dock lines are being secured.Many owners of these large boats may prefer to leave their dock lines on the cleats of their permanent slip,with permanent adjustment markings to position them on the sailboat cleats with little effort.

Large sailboats NEED an emergency snubber when the best of plans fail. We were helping test the heavy 97' schooner *Estrilita** made of Australian ironwood which hadn't been operated for a long time.

When coming in for a landing in it's San Diego slip the throttle handle caught in the steering wheel spokes with the throttle stuck in forward A 2" manila midship spring line that was secured to a deck cleat was rapidly lashed to a dock cleat.While this line stopped the 97' sailboat witnesses reported it pulled that part of the dock over 3' out of the water.If the line which was close to its breaking strength had broken it would have reduced damage to the boat and dock ***but a major hazard would have occurred to crew members if either cleat had broken loose.***

Narrow beam sailboats in the 1950's were easily secured with bow and stern lines in their slips making it easy to step onto the dock.As taxes zoomed in the sixties,sailboats became shorter AND wider ..also lighter and more comfortable.The older bow and stern dockline were too limiting for the new generation of sailboats.

Add ***midship cleats*** to wide beam sailboats so that a midship dock line ❽ can be used as a spring line to pull the stern to the dock (bow out) to make it easy to step aboard in the cockpit area...or bow in (stern out) ❾ if desired.The midship dock line will also permit more variables in the fore and aft positioning of your sailboat in a tight docking situation.

Our sailboat is 25' long including its bow pulpit.We use a 32',¼" ***nylon turning line*** ❿ with eye splices on both ends.A loop is secured to the stern cleat,the other end to a dock cleat.The boat is slowly pushed ⓫ to drift backward out of the slip.After the bow clears the slip,the stern line pulls the stern ⓮ back into the slip where the docklines are secured with the bow pointing out of the slip.The turning line permits a boat to 30' long to be turned 180° in light conditions within little more than its own length.

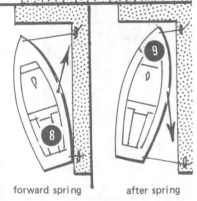

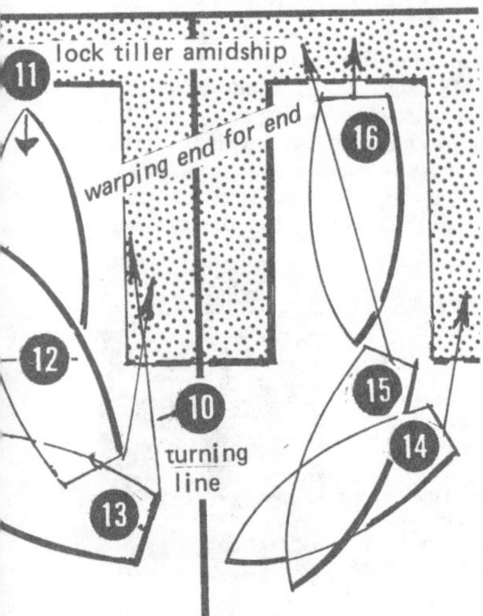
lock tiller amidship
warping end for end
11
12
13
10
turning
line
14
15
16

*The last time we saw *Estrilita* a new owner had rebuilt it with the rigging changed to a yawl.Two years later it was reported to have hit a reef sinking the boat a mile off Tasmania...it's draft was ten feet.

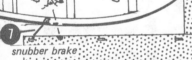

ROYCE'S
sailing illustrated
the SAILOR'S BIBLE since '56

Royce's
Sailing Illustrated
ISBN 0-911284-00-1
368 pages 5 1/4 x 7 1/2
paperback
~~$12.00 retail, U.S.~~

$ 15.00 **retail,** USA

plus $2.25 mailing
"The Sailors Bible since 1956".

Royce Publications
The best of all sailing worlds, and the best of all powerboating worlds.
Box 1967, Newport Beach
CA 92663, USA
(714) 642-4430
FAX (714) 646-SAIL

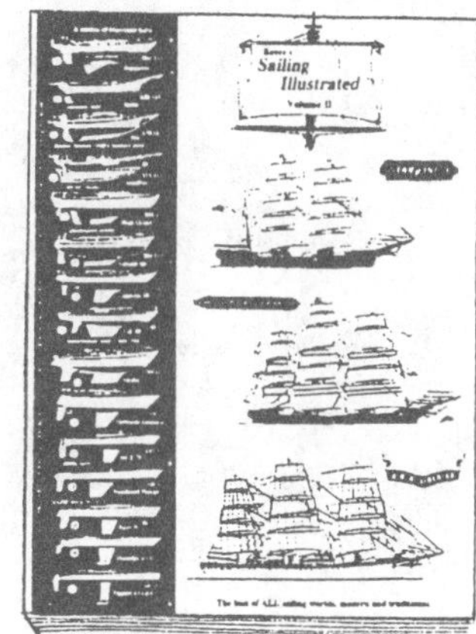
Sailing Illustrated

Royce's *SAILING ILLUSTRATED* Series

The best of ALL sailing worlds.

Royce's Sailing Illustrated, Patrick M. Royce, PB 5 1/4 x 7 1/2, 368pp., index, 1993. Truly a classic. Dense with information on all aspects of sailing, fully illustrated by the artist/author. 38 pages of Glossary definitions. A trusted classroom learning text, as well as onboard look-it-up book. A favorite since1956.

Royce's Sailing Illustrated, Vol. II, P.M. Royce, PB, 7 1/2 x 10, 162 pp.,index,1996. A companion to Vol. I with larger detailed illustrations of dinghies, cabin sailboats, plus square riggers **Cutty Sark, Star of India, Libertad, U.S.S. Constitution.** 30 difficult docking sequences illustrated, marine metals.
0-911284-07-9 $15.00

Learn to sail with an artist providing 40 years testing, research, then publishing his findings. Pat talks direct to you in his first-hand exposure as each student/reader has his individual drive, and learning patterns. Pat provides flexibility with humor in the privacy of your home, or classroom with neighbors interested in sailing.

Royce's Sailing Illustrated Workbook, PB, 7 1/2 x 10, 48 pgs. Testing has been continuous since 1960, finally printed in 1994. It is excellent for evening dry-land lectures, plus dockside with instructors able to assign homework for individual student needs.

It is also a self-testing format equally useful for readers wanting to learn sailing on their own, and when time requirements are important with answers provided in *Sailing Illustrated,* **Volumes I and II.**

Royce's Instructors Manual, 96 pages. It includes the 48 page **Sailing Illustrated Workbook,** plus ***25 Workbook lecture pages word-for-word,*** and methods to help sailing students.

$12.00 retail, now **$7.00.** Due to a printing size goof, we have a major price reduction to instructors and students... with no compromise in technical accuracy. It is your bargain.

Royce's
Sailing Illustrated
Workbook
ISBN 0-911284-05-2
48 pages 7 1/2 x 10
FULLY illustrated
$5.00 retail $1.50 mailing

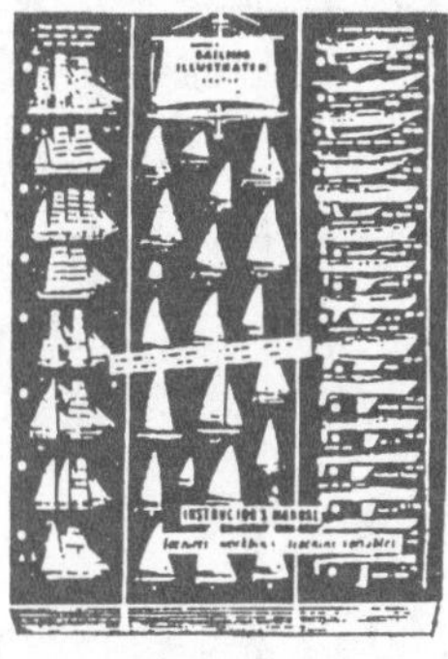

Royce's
Instructor's Manual
ISBN 0-911284-01-X
96 pages plus cover

$7.00 retail $1.75 mailing
48 pages lecture material
***plus* 48 page Worbook**

ROYCE'S
Powerboating Illustrated
The Best of All Powerboating Worlds
6th Edition
Trailerboating Illustrated
FUEL
35 years of basic powerboating concepts
27 easy ways to enter powerboating.

Royce's Powerboating Illustrated, Patrick Royce, PB 5 1/4 x 7 1/2, 416pp.,index, 1996. A compact, illustrated manual with 27 ways for new mechanics and operators to learn the basics of the portable powerboat field. Full coverage of hulls, trailers, 2 & 4 cycle engines, propellers, wiring, fiberglass repairs.

Royce's Powerboating Illustrated Workbook, PB, 7 1/2 x 10, 48 pages, contents index, 1996. *27 easy ways to enter powerboating* are listed. A new owner or mechanic can start with any basic concept, filling in the Workbook questions, then systematically filling in the rest of the concepts in any sequence desired for a broad foundation.

Royce's *POWERBOATING ILLUSTRATED* Series

27 easy ways to enter powerboating.

Royce's
Powerboating Illustrated
ISBN 0-911284-02-8
416 pages 5 1/4 x 7 1/2
paperback
$15.00 retail, U.S.,
plus $2.50 mailing
"The best of ALL Powerboating Worlds".

Royce's **Powerboating Illustrated Workbook**
ISBN 0-911284-03-6
48 pages 7 1/2 x 10
$5.00 retail $1.50 mailing
Volume discounts?
The most efficient teaching method for industry & owners

Powerboating Illustrated

PRIDE OF BALTIMORE II
ling
rated
me II

Pride of Baltimore, Inc.
100 Light Street
Baltimore, Maryland 21202
(301) 625-5460

Pride II	*Pride*
185.5 long tons	121 long tons
LOA 157'3"	LOA 137'
deck length 100'	deck length 86'
beam 26'	beam 23'
LWL 91'	LWL 77'
draft 12' 4"	draft 9'9"
sail area-10,442 sq. ft.	sail area-9523 sq. ft.

Mayor William Donald Schaefer,
City of Baltimore—

"*Pride* is one way that we share our maritime heritage with others, She is one of the world's unique goodwill ambassadores".

the first *Pride*

Architect—Thomas Gillmer
Builder—Melbourne Smith
Building—1976
Commissioning—5/1/1977

MARINE ROPE* E

The *Pride* is so large we show a 6 foot tall sailor for comparison on the main deck

The American clipper boom, starting with the *Rainbow*, and *Sea Witch*, both under 1000 tons, lasted from 1848 to 1858.

The *Sovereign of the Seas* was launched June, 1852 with a tonnage of almost 2500 tons...the first vessel to sail more than 400 miles in 24 hours, *page 154*. She was lost 1859 on Pyramid Shoals in the Malacca Straits.

3/16"

1/4"

51

It was the prototype for the 2096 ton *Lightning*, the 2525 ton *James Braines*, and others. A second 1226 ton vessel *Sovereign of the Seas* proved to be a poor performer. She was burned in 1861 in Sydney, Australia, by an unhappy crew member.

5/16"

3/8"

*While we use the term MARINE ROPE... the subject is better known as *marlinespike seamanship*. It is the mark of an able seaman to handle, care for, plus being able to splice a variety of kinds and sizes of ropes.

overeign of the Seas

LOA 258' 2"
keel 245'0"
beam 44'7"
draft 20'0"

disp. 2403 long ton
hold depth-23'
canvas-12,000 yds.
crew-105 men, boys

7/16"

OPE QUALITIES to consider—

- trength
- tretch
- ildew resistance
- UV ray resistance
- chafe resistance
- abrasion resistance

VORKING STRENGTH—some experts ecommend 10% to 15%, others to 20% or a safe, continuous working load of rope breaking strength table, see right.

OIL LAY TWIST of 3 strand rope is eversed from yarn, to strands, to rope... stabilize the rope by reducing its endencies to unwind. It also increases ope strength due to internal friction mong the fibers, yarns, strands, and rope.

ope LAY depends on the amount of vist in the strands...with a hard laid ope having more twists in the strands an a soft laid rope.

BREAKING STRENGTH table is for new rope in laboratory test conditions.

diameter	mm-metric	traditional 3 strand manila	impact absorption—controlled stretch 3 strand nylon	impact absorption—controlled stretch braided Gold-N-Braid	minimum stretch—for control lines 3 strand Dacron & polypro	minimum stretch—for control lines braided Yacht Braid	galvanized chain
1/4	6	600	1850	2100	1750	2300	2700
5/16	8	1000	2850	3500	2650	3450	3700
3/8	9	1350	4000	4800	3600	4950	4600
7/16	10½	1750	5500	6500	4800	6600	6200
1/2	12	2650	7100	8300	6100	8600	8200
9/16	14	3400	8350	11200	7400	11700	10200
5/8	16	4400	10500	14500	9000	15200	12500
3/4	18	5400	14200	18000	12500	19100	17700
7/8	22	7700	19000	26500	16000	28300	24000
1	24	9000	24600	31300	20000	33600	31000

Braided rope strength is provided by Samson Ocean Systems, Inc.
Many variables exist with 3 strand specifications.

1/2"

5/8"

3/4"

ROPE,BLOCK,and TACKLE HAVE A LONG HISTORY.

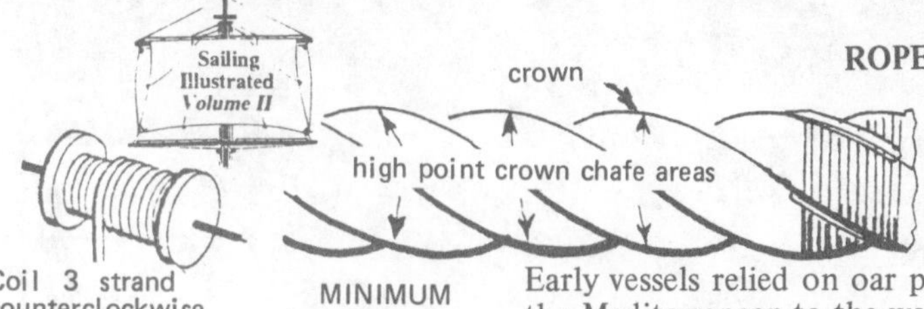
Sailing
Illustrated
Volume II
crown
high point crown chafe areas
MINIMUM
bearing surfaces

Coil 3 strand counterclockwise when it comes off the spool.

The development from rafts to open boats to ocean sailing craft required thousands of years development opening many technical fields beginning with rope.

Early vessels relied on oar power which had too many limitations. Sailcrs on the Mediterranean to the west...and on the Yangtze to the east,began exploring a cheaper resource called wind power.Rope was needed to hold up the mast and trim the sail starting with locally obtained hides,organic materials,etc.

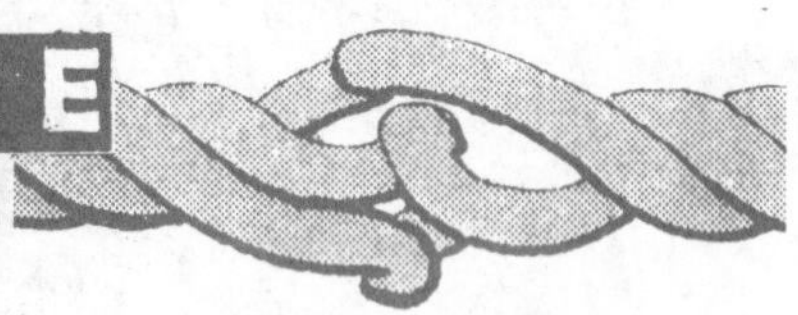

3 strand TWISTED LAY
3 strand is RIGHT lay
spliceable
rotational,will unwind always under stress with itself

Vikings began weaving rope out of leather which had too much shrink due to humidity.They found it more practical to periodically invade Germany for flax to replentish their rope supply... plus their dark beer.

Three strand rope weaving design with opposed twisting and tensioning which goes from yarn,to strands,to rope to improve its balance or resistance to unwinding has changed little from Egypt 7000 years ago...except for rope materials

E

We sailed for ten years using yacht quality manila for halyards,sheets,dock, and anchor lines...regular quality manila has a rougher surface.Manila is woven from 4' to 8' strands of the abaca plant that is related to the banana tree.

the hockle–3 strand rope out of balance

Manila rope has to be prestretched or broken in before normal use.Manila rope has a short life as it weathers fast.The oil added to reduce mildew growth is lost as it becomes dry and limp.Manila halyards have to be slacked as humidity increases as *moisture absorption increases its diameter while shortening the halyard length.* Moisture collecting inside the manila fibers and yarns start organic rot decomposition.This weakens the strands as they start breaking under normal use.This will progressively reduce the life and strength of manila rope.

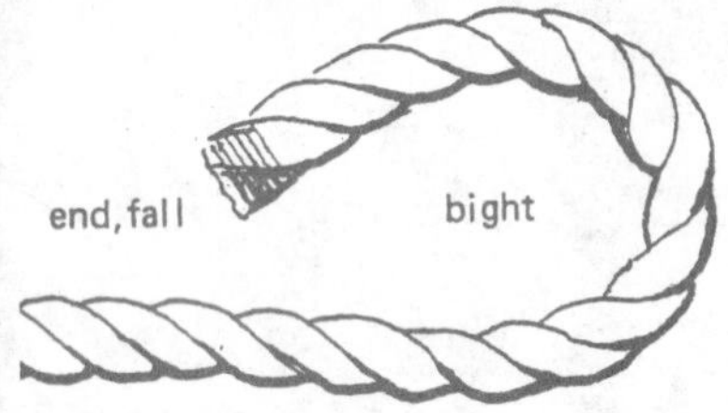
end,fall
bight
standing part

Hygroscopic salts,pg. *133,* have to be washed out of manila anchor lines used in salt water.After the line is dry it must be stored in a well-ventilated compartment to reduce mildew potentials,pg. *134*. ***Manila rope needs chafe protection.*** We towed a ski boat behind a 40' sailboat using a manila painter that chafed thru twice in three days at the chock.The third splice was wrapped with exterior electrical tape having no further evidence of chafe after ten days of vacation sailing.

Transition from 3 strand organic rope to 3 strand synthetic rope was usually a ho-hum situation,with a few exceptions.We crewed on a new backyard built 36' yawl in the 1959 race to Ensenada,Mexico.After leaving we found all sheets and halyards were made of 3 strand nylon which proved most fortunate as it was a downwind race.The flexing helped us win 1st place in Class C,missing first overall by 8 minutes...and we didn't even have a spinnaker.The return sail upwind after the race found us in a force 6 only able to sail on a beam reach on one tack to a beam reach on the other tack with our stretchy halyards and sheets.It also needed more gravel ballast as its lead keel hadn't been installed.

overhand loop

overhand knot

underhand loop

figure 8 knot

Synthetic rope quality? We prefer oversize braided dock lines exposed year around for five years that still seem to be in good condition,while adding 3 strand nylon spring lines for storm conditions.We've seen imported rope used for dock lines with an unknown background in similar conditions which became brittle with broken interior and exterior fibers that required replacement in two years.

Nylon docklines and mooring lines may look good on visual examination,yet due to the ***ultraviolet sun's rays*** they can fail considerably below their rated breaking strength when tested on laboratory equipment.We feel this is a good reason to retire docklines early before the stormy season begins in your area.

Nylon anchor line with little chafe that has not been overstressed,may be used for many years due to minimum exposure to the sun's rays,and then only with short lengths exposed above deck since the rest of the line is in the water.

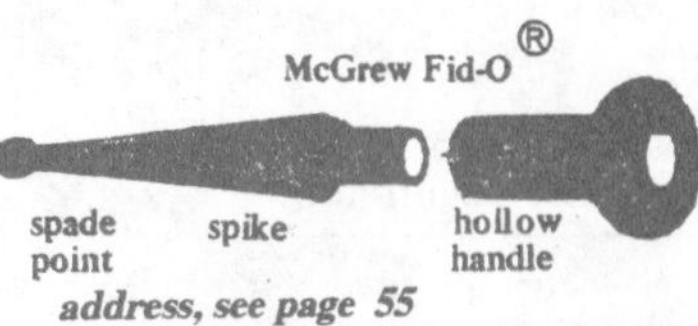
McGrew Fid-O®
spade point
spike
hollow handle

address, see page 55

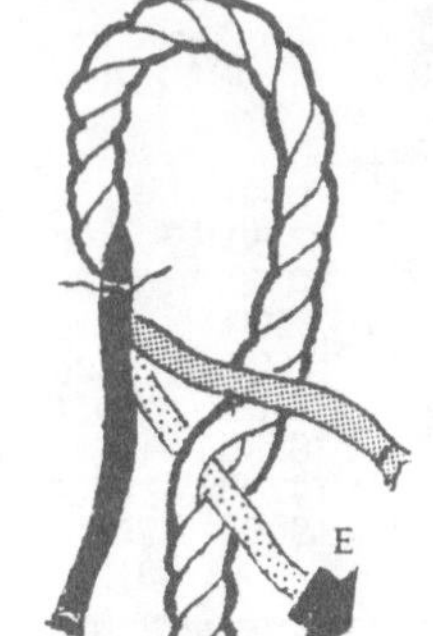
D

We've handled a variety of fids thru the years for splicing,using a screwdriver when nothing else was available.The fid at left should be carried on all cabin sailboats as it is the best fid we've used for splicing soft,medium,and its specialty, hard lay rope.The problem,friends are continually borrowing the fid so keep a record of all the borrowers.I forgot to the last time–

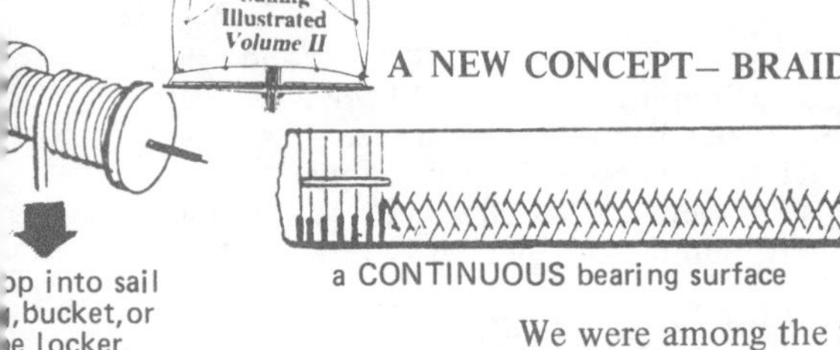
Sailing
Illustrated
Volume II

A NEW CONCEPT– BRAIDED ROPE

a CONTINUOUS bearing surface

Double braid synthetic rope was introduced in 1960 by **Samson Ocean Systems, Inc.**, the present company name. Splicing methods required a new education for sailors, AND my bewildered professional skipper friends.

op into sail
,bucket,or
e locker.

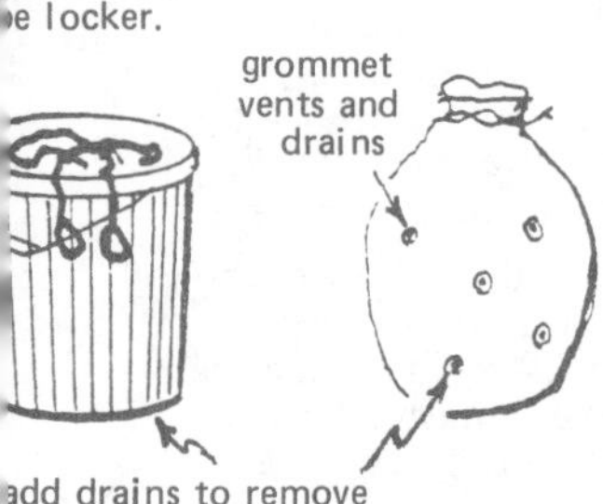
grommet
vents and
drains

add drains to remove
water and reduce humidity

We were among the first to test and report the new double braid world to our readers. The first question was how it compared with 3 strand anchor lines. The testing started in Goat Harbor on Catalina Island when we were anchored bow and stern during a three day period with full moon and maximum tides. The surge was strong for three days becoming intolerable the fourth day.

When we examined the 3 strand anchor line several of the high point crowns had chafed thru on the barnacles and sharp rocks. Many crown fibers and yarns were cut considerably reducing the the 3 strand anchor line strength.

The braided anchor line showed exposure without broken strands nor noticeable chafe....due to its ***continuous bearing surface*** instead of the 3 strand crown areas where the chafe was considerable.

Further testing found the bearing surface also provided up to 50% contact areas with better grip and less slippage on winches and cleats.

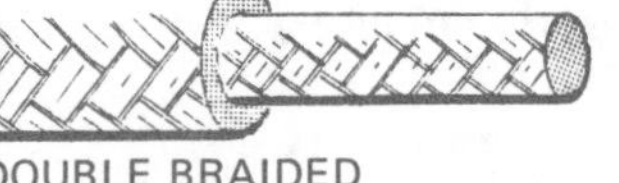

DOUBLE BRAIDED
- inner & outer core
- makes excellent splices
- non-rotational
- neutral lay
- not under stress with itself
- excellent for halyards, sheets, anchor lines

Double braid resistance to coiling, twisting, and torquing, is due to equal numbers of yarns going opposite directions to produce a **neutral lay**. This eliminates the 3 strand kinking and hockling potentials shown on the facing page which over stresses the fibers and yarns which weaken and breaks them in the kinked area. ***Discourage 3 strand anchor line hockling potentials by periodically trolling the line behind your boat underway.*** This helps to unwind any extra twists.. or to add twists to return the 3 strand line to its normal twist balance.

We found the double braid **neutral lay** proved ideal for use as a ***heaving line*** while 3 strand heaving lines proved questionable for recreational use especially in an emergency. The braided line dropped neatly into its container though resembling a rat's nest while maintaining its neutral lay, page 21. Over 500 students could heave the line a full 50' to 60' after one or two attempts without any kinking.

HOLLOW BRAIDED
- hollow center, no core
- non-rotational
- neutral lay
- not under stress with itself
- less efficient splice
- usually polypropolene
- a floater, good for towing

Double braid rope provided many happy surprises...except for the ***new braided splicing method.*** We tried a new approach by doing everything wrong to run out of mistakes after 43 unsuccessful splices. After testing and detailing our new double braid splicing sequence, text pages 195 to 199, we tested it on seven people who had never made such a splice. All of their first splices were successful though all of those involved were quite puzzled with steps 21 to 26. After pulling out the ***core at step D,*** they began pulling as shown in steps 28 and 29. Smiles suddenly began to appear as the braided eye splices suddenly popped into place.

Important double braid splicing factors—start with ***new*** double braid rope that has not been under tension. ***Correct fid size*** is important. Stainless fids work better than plastic fids especially when making difficult ¼" double braid splices. The most difficult hand operation for most men was to hold the pusher and fid correctly for which women adapted to more easily.

SOLID BRAIDED
- non-rotational
- neutral lay
- not under stress with itself
- has a solid core
- seldom used for boating

Rope strength variables??? American rope tables normally list the *average rope breaking strength...* while European rope tables list the *minimum rope breaking strength.* Both rope table ratings are listed for ***new rope being tested under laboratory conditions.*** Because of these differences some experts recommend 10% to 15% of the breaking strength be used for a continuous load...while others may move it up to a 20% load. This percentage is a theoretical loading number using friesh new rope without chafe, made of synthetic fibers.

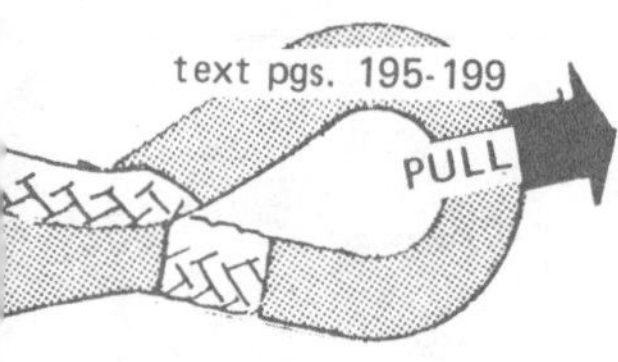
text pgs. 195-199
PULL

a NEW splicing concept

Consider oversize halyards AND double braid halyards at replacement time. .. after larger masthead sheaves have been added. Rope halyards are easier on the hands, they are easier to grip onto when leverage is needed in storm conditions. If you forget to tie off the halyards at the dock or at anchor the pounding will become a dull thud instead of a metallic clang that is chafing the mast anodizing. **Double braid chafe or stress damage becomes obvious** while it is difficult to find a stainless halyard fish hook indicating it is time for replacement. as it has been overstressed. A broken or lost halyard can result in storm conditions.

E

Sailing
Illustrated
Volume II

WHIPPING, the BLOCK, CHAFE, the END SPLICE

Whip against the lay of three strand rope. Whipping length should be roughly equal to the diameter of the rope.

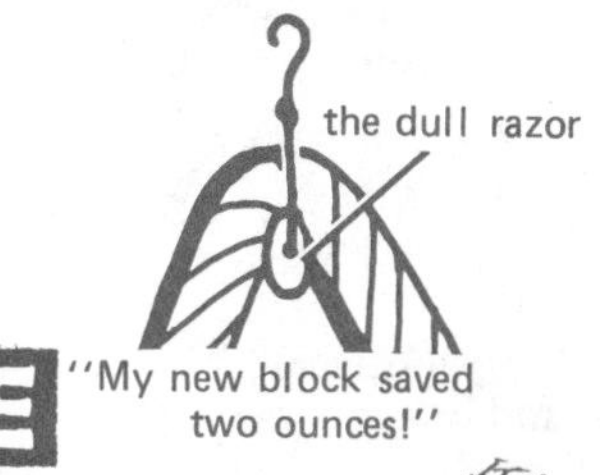
the dull razor

"My new block saved two ounces!"

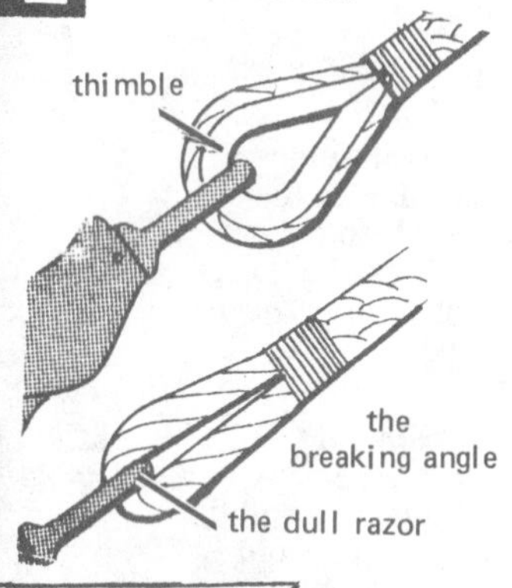
thimble
the breaking angle
the dull razor

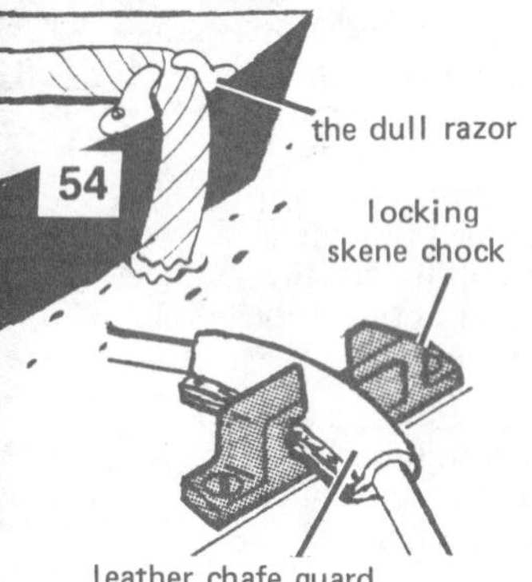
the dull razor
locking skene chock
leather chafe guard

E

The most permanent method to prevent the ends of all synthetic 3 strand and braided rope from unwinding is the palm and needle whipping, text page 200, while the plain whipping may be sufficient for manila rope which has a rougher surface. Decorative knots, plus the end or back splice shown below avoid whipping, while doubling the diameter of the rope end. The back space should be avoided on running rigging and dock slip lines, **page 48**, as the larger diameter slipped end may lock in the cleat.

Synthetic rope fibers unravel rapidly- the reason marine stores cut the rope with a hot knife to seal the ends. If you don't have a cutting heat tool, tape the area, then cut the rope thru the middle of the tape with a razor or sharp knife, then ***fuse or heat seal*** the ends with a butane lighter or soldering iron. You can use foot long fireplace matches to fuse synthetic rope ends which leaves the melted ends black. *Avoid using short matches* as they can't generate sufficient heat for this purpose.

After the fused ends have cooled remove the tape to begin the needle/palm whipping shown above, text pg. 200, for ALL synthetic braided and 3 strand rope. Whether organic marline, or nylon whipping twine are used they seem to last a similar length of time until new whipping is needed. Manila rope has a somewhat abrasive surface which may only require a regular whipping in normal use without using a needle.

Chafe is the major enemy of rope which is the reason hardware catalog list the **maximum line diameter for blocks.** While the lead must be fair to reduce chafe, if a slightly larger diameter rope goes thru the block, it will be too tight for the sheave due to the radius of the rope. This extremely short radius will produce a tight bend which will chafe and weaken the internal fibers of the rope.

All sailboats in long distance races require a thorough periodic check every 24 to 48 hours. It includes sails, sheets, halyards, shrouds, stays and metal fittings on deck as well as aloft where violent motion is continuous. Only with such checking can you anticipate, then take care of chafe and metal fatigue before failure can take place.

The 1969 Transpac Race to Hawaii was a gear buster with, 1. metal fatigue, 2. spinnaker cloth failure, and 3. ***eye splices without metal or plastic thimbles.*** It was reported to me by Jeff Reuger who checked most of the boats for damage patterns.

Metal rope thimbles had been used on ocean racers for many decades. Many new crew members involved in this race had *a dinghy racing background.* They were responsible for reducing weight aloft such as eliminating metal thimbles. Many eye splices had no chafe protection, while some used leather. The idea may be commendable and practical for afternoon racing around the buoys. The philosophy fell far short of its objective however in the continuous day after day rigors of ocean racing. The sharp bend angle of eye splices and the endless chafe were the cause of many unnecessary equipment failures.

Take a walk down various boat docks to examine bow and stern line chocks... Many of them will have ***sharp edges,*** they are ***undersize,*** with ***a straight lead.*** The sharp edges can cause a sawing action against the dock lines in stormy conditions while the lines may jump out of the chocks to chafe against screw heads, gennie tracks..etc.

Replace with **locking skene chocks** which will contain dock lines in a wave action. They should preferably be large enough to contain a ***one inch tow line*** for ocean use. Also add oversize ***leather sleeves for chafe protection*** to protect dock lines and anchor lines where the lead takes them thru the chocks. Rope sleeves made of synthetic materials tend to self destruct more rapidly in severe storm conditions.

Readers interested in rope and rigging practices of the previous century should add the 1819 collectors item...**Lever's Young Sea Officer's Sheet Anchor** to their library. It begins with weaving hemp yarns into 3 strand, 4 strand, and hawser-laid rope, to rigging and operating sailing vessels of that period. This text was used to teach sailors and officers of the British Navy, and the East India Company Service.

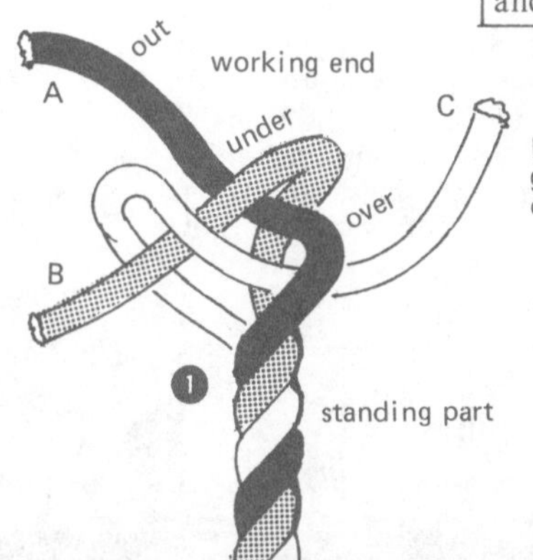
out
working end
A
under
C
over
B
1
standing part

The end splice or back splice.

If you want to stop a line from going thru a block, use a backsplice or stopper knot instead of whipping.

❶ Begin with a crown knot taking the strands over—under—and out.

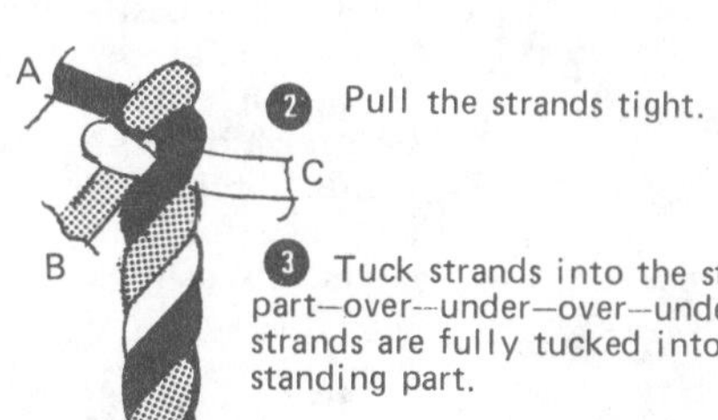
A
C
B

❷ Pull the strands tight.

❸ Tuck strands into the standing part—over—under—over—under until strands are fully tucked into the standing part.

Sailing
llustrated
Volume II

knots, bends, hitches, coiling, splicing, whipping-- text pages 184-203

McGrew Splicing Tool Co.
8120 Rio Linda Blvd.
Elverta, CA 95626

the *Minka*, a Contest 31
LOA 31' 4''
LWL 24' 11'' D/L 239
beam 9' 4''
draft 4' 1''
ballast 3530 lbs.
disp. 8380 lbs.
total sail 480 sq.ft.

TEST and EXPAND your marlinspike seamanship knowledge.

Good rope is expensive and perishable. Our goal is to provide readers an understanding of variables involved in handling, caring for, and splicing rope so your investment will be able to maintain normal operational strength for a maximum number of hours.

____ **figure 8 knot**	____ **rolling hitch**	____ **3 strand eye splice**
____ **square knot**	____ **tugboat hitch**	____ **double braid eye splice**
____ **bowline**	____ **sheepshank**	____ **short splice**
____ **slippery hitch**	____ **carrick bend**	____ **end splice**
____ **adjustable hitch**	____ **sheet bend**	____ **whipping**
____ **clove hitch**	____ **double sheet bend**	____ **coiling for storage**
____ **jam hitch**	____ **fisherman's bend**	____ **halyard coiling**

Rope information covered in our text and *Guide* is what we wished were available when we learned to sail, plus coverage we wanted to provide to sailing students.

E

Jim McGrew is our favorite splicing expert who developed his **FID-O®AWL** in 1972, page 52, to make difficult hard-laid splices. Sailors soon found his new tool made splicing easier and faster, which could also be used for macrame and leather.

We had an interesting discussion of knot tying between left and right handers. Jim complained of an article written by a left hander, as the knot fell apart when made by a right hander. He also recommended redoing my backsplice illustration made to verbal instructions by a right hander. Jim suddenly answered a personal problem since as a left hander I find it almost impossible to understand verbal knot instructions. Our answer was to illustrate knots and splices with minimum word instructions.

Jim has developed many new splicing tools and methods for 3 strand and double-braid rope, he doesn't sell rope. Contact Jim for better, faster splicing methods and tools.

Many thanks go to the **Minka** which served a special part while preparing this material as its 747 senior pilot Bill Schulz operates his boat more as an airplane ready to move on short notice. It operates year-round when his time permits, providing excellent heavy weather exposure, pages 55 and 77, when other sailboats stay dockside.

The **Minka** carries a 25 pound plow anchor, 100' of ¼" chain, and 300' of ½" double braid for most anchoring. It is a *complex, compact 31' cruiser for coastal hopping* with a tremendous equipment inventory for living aboard, all-weather operation, and diving. A 35' cruiser with double the cubic capacity, pages 110, 118, may be preferred for a *minimum size long distance cruiser.* ***Storage will be a continuous problem for both cruisers requiring a place for everything... with everything stored in its correct place.***

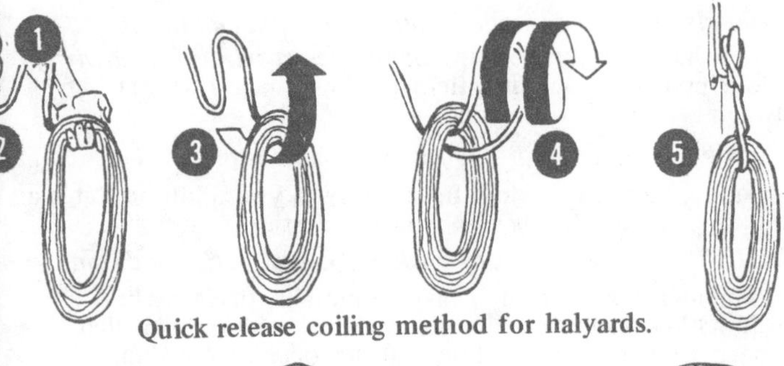
1
2
3
4
5
Quick release coiling method for halyards.

Coiling halyards. Cleat, coil, pull loop thru, add twists, then loop eye over cleat.

Coiling for storage. Coil, pull loop thru, then up and over top, then down other side... pull end to lock loop. Coiling braided lines has variables, see text pg. 193.

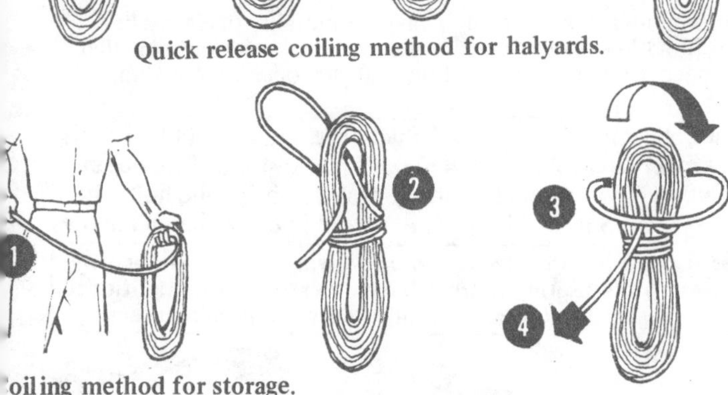
1
2
3
4
Coiling method for storage.

● send for marine rope catalogs—
SAMSON OCEAN SYSTEMS—99 High St., Boston, MA 02110
WALL ROPE WORKS—Railroad Ave., Beverly, NJ 08010
COLUMBIA ROPE CO.—Columbian Drive, Auburn, NY 13021
YALE CORDAGE—Old Sparhawk Mill, Yarmouth, ME 04096
NEW ENGLAND ROPES—Popes Island, New Bedford, MA 02740
FORESPAR—wire to rope halyards, 2672 Dow Ave., Tustin, CA 92680

Sovereign of the Seas

Sailing
Illustrated
Volume II

First came PROVERBS*...then BAROMETERS...then TV SATELLITE pictures.

*short,pithy weather wisdom sayings by seamen...a mixture of superstition,local color...plus science.

Our continually changing weather is the product of collisions and tug-of-wars with complex worldwide air mass patterns eternally on the move from our earth to the stratosphere. Add terms at right to *water clouds* and *frozen clouds,* text pages 204-5

Man has gone down to the ocean in small sailing vessels long before recorded history. Seamen had to develop a primitive,practical weather wisdom foundation to survive, then use these wind forces to drive their sailing vessels for periods of weeks and months.

Ancient sailors had to live with natures wind power to drive their vessels...and be able to survive its temperament.

Ancient sailors had to be continually alert to changing weather with many ideas still applicable today in proverb form before the barometer was introduced.Factors are temperature changes,different colors of the rising and setting sun,the moon with its halo,changing cloud patterns,plus the action of porpoises,fish...and sea birds.

- *Mackerel sky and mare's tails...make lofty ships carry low sails* (and go like h...!).

Northern Hemisphere only—

- *When the wind shifts against the sun...trust it not,for back it will run*—a backing wind.

science vs ancient proverbs—seamen,farmers,gardeners...

- *When clouds appear like rocks and towers,the earth is refreshed by frequent showers (???).*
- *If clouds look as though scratched by a hen,get ready to reef your topsails then (!!!!).*

a long predicted major storm is moving in!

the barometer starts to drop..

Mares'tails develop,followed by the scratchy mackerel sky,and a white cirrostratus film producing a ***lunar halo*** with a ***backing wind*** to soon follow. It can indicate a storm moving in,in 12,24,to 48 hours.As the barometer drops,wind blowing from the W and SW may ease,then blow hard...text pages 208-9.

F

The glass—a glass tube was our first barometer.

- *At sea with low and falling glass,the greenhorn sleeps like a careless jackass.*
- *But when the glass is high and rising...May soundly sleep the careful wise one.*
- *Short warning,soon past.* Shorter the warning and change,shorter will be the disturbance.

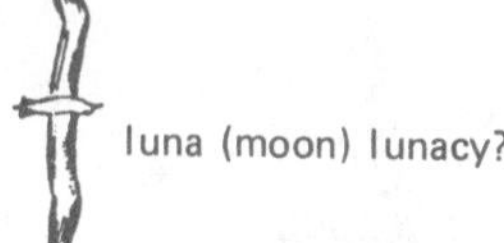

rapid barometer drop...

- *Long foretold,long last!* The longer the warning,the longer the disturbance will last as duration and intensity of bad weather depends on size and speed of the advancing low pressure cyclonic storm in our westerly belt.

DON.T relax just because the barometer is rising...

A rapid barometer drop indicates stormy weather and rain.Severe N and NW gales often occur AFTER the barometer is very low-29.0 (?)...then begins to rise.with—

local weather bureau phone—

- *Quick rise after a low...fortells a stronger blow.*
- *While rise begins after a low...squalls expect and a clear blow.*

barometer rises rapidly...

If the barometer is erratic or rises rapidly,it indicates unsettled weather.A barometer that rises slowly and steadily can indicate fair weather...with a few exceptions.

- *A red sky in the morning is a sailor's warning;But a red sky at night is a sailors delight.*

soft colors,soft cloud forms vs ragged clouds with hard shapes,strong colors

- *A light bright blue sky clap on all sails,yet think twice with a dark,gloomy blue sky.*
- *A pale yellow sky brings rain... while a bright yellow sky at sunset presages wind.*

Light color tints with soft,delicate cloud forms indicate light winds...while ragged oily to greasy looking clouds with hard edges and/or bright colors indicate strong winds

- *The moon,governess of the floods (high tides)...pale in her anger washes all the air.*

luna (moon) lunacy?

A cirrus ***lunar halo*** predicts behavioral changes...*when the desert winds are howling...* as positive ions move into our bodies causing unanticipated brawls and riots that increase with intensity with our worldwide devil winds,see page F 13.

- *Wooly fleeces deck the heavenly way...make sure no rain will mar a summers day.*

wooly fleece can rapidly grow to ugly monsters

BEWARE of a hot,humid,inland afternoon if wooly fleeces grow skyward into unstable air masses... providing short duration thunderstorms with winds of hurricane intensity.

- *Seagull,seagull,sit on the land...it's never good weather when you are on the land (sand).*

local color????? trust seagulls IF they aren't civilized...

A low pressure area grounds many birds especially heavy cormorants that may be barely able to take off and fly.Other reasons are that no minnows are around,or that the seagulls have a full stomach after their gourmet feast at the local garbage dump.

- *When the sea hog jumps...stand by your pumps.*

*How could seamen evaluate an ocean going crazy 100 years before we recognized it as the freak worldwide **El Nino?***

Lin Pardey spent three hours checking these proverbs with me, drawing a blank with the *sea hogs.* A delivery skipper later told me of a major Pacific storm."The ocean was wild. Noise was deafening below with all kinds of sea life hitting the hull, plus scores of birds hitting the topside. Survival in the water would be less than a minute".

science weather predictions still more art than science

The science of weather prediction is a few decades old,involving interaction of large air masses covering large areas.While useful,sailors still have to rely on the traditional methods to predict rapidly changing local weather conditions with more accuracy.

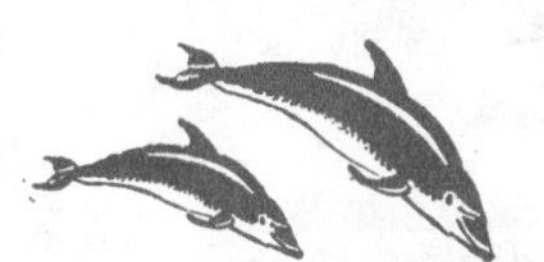

13
12
11
9
the WEATHER FACTORY
8
F
7
57
3
Sailing Illustrated Volume II
5
4
sailing illustrated
1

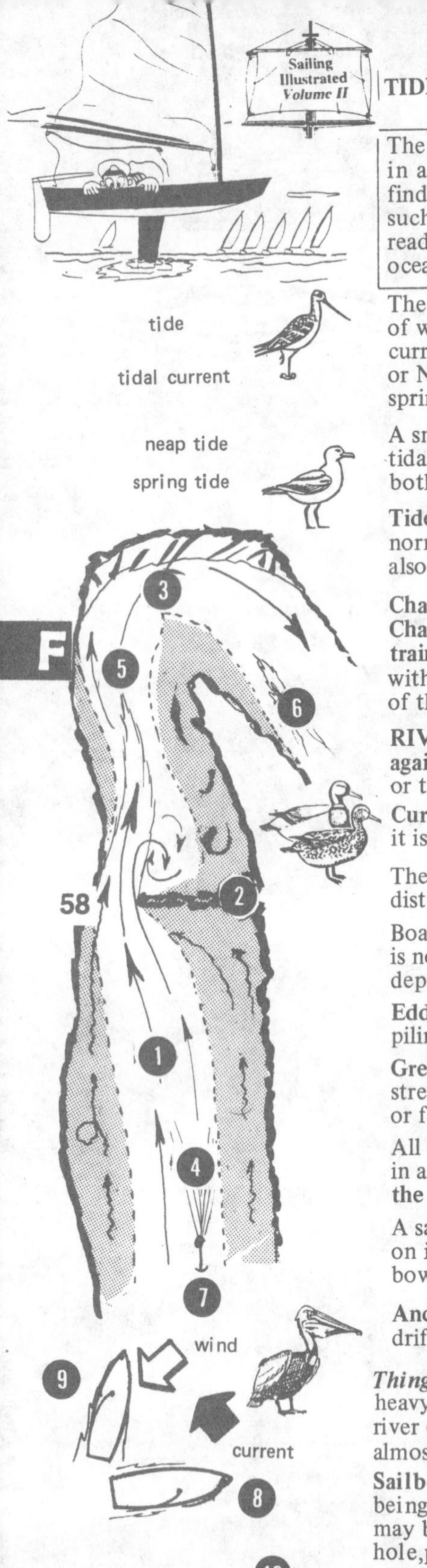
Sailing Illustrated Volume II
tide
tidal current
neap tide
spring tide
F
wind
current
deadhead
current

TIDES, TIDAL CURRENTS, RIVER CURRENTS...and TRAINING CHARTS.

The purpose of our *Guide* is to provide a good foundation for the new sailor in a variety of his specialized fields. We concentrate on information difficult to find in organized patterns elsewhere, while only providing a brief coverage on subjects such as tides for which other publications provide much technical information. For readers also desiring an excellent non-technical book on tides and a variety of other ocean subjects we recommend *the Sea Around Us* by Rachel Carson.

The vertical rise and fall of a body of water is called **tide**...while the horizontal flow of water is called a **current**. When a tide change causes a directional change in the current, reversing with the next tidal change, it becomes a **tidal current**. The Hudson or North River tidal current can affect it almost as far north as Albany during the spring thaw, and only half as far during the fall dry season.

A smaller than average tidal range is called a **neap tide**...while a greater than average tidal range is called a **spring tide** with the position of the moon a major factor in both situations as maximum tides often occur during the full moon period.

•

Tide Tables, Current Tables, and Tidal Current Charts if not available through your normal sources, contact the **National Ocean Survey, Rockville, MD 20852. You** can also order standard size *training charts* from N.O.S., that are frozen in time.

Chart 1210 Tr covers the New England Coast from Martha's Vineyard to Block Island; **Chart 6151 Tr**, Columbia River, Pacific Ocean to Harrington Point; and **small craft training charts** folded, and easy to roll into a small size, with a sample **chart 116-SC Tr** with the coastal New England area on one side, plus detail charts on the other side of the Niantic River, Thames River, New London Harbor, and the Connecticut River.

•

RIVER and TIDAL CURRENTS. Maximum wave action occurs when the wind blows **against** the current...and the **least wave action** when the wind blows **with** the river or tidal current, **page 72.**

Current flow is normally smoother and faster ❶ in the center of the stream, while it is slower and more disturbed in shallower water next to the river bank.

The **dike** ❷ should be given sufficient room when passing due to eddies and disturbed currents on the downstream side of the dike.

Boats should **avoid cutting the corners** ❸ in a river or tidal estuary since deep water is normally found on the outside bend, with the maximum current and greatest depth next to the higher river bank.

Eddies and current swirls ❹ will be found on the downstream side of a mooring, piling, or aid to navigation.

Greatest depth ❺ is found in the center of a V pointing downstream in a straight stretch of river...while an **upstream V** ❻ may indicate an underwater obstruction or funnel.

All vessels should **give considerable room when passing above a fixed object** ❼ in a stream such as a buoy, anchored boat, etc., to allow for ample drift to **clear the obstruction.**

A sailboat normally makes ***better headway*** towards its destination with the current on its **lee bow** ❽ **called leebowing,** while a sailboat with the wind on its windward bow ❾ will have ***minimum headway*** towards its destination.

Anchor a sailboat that capsizes in a current ❿ as it might otherwise turn turtle, drift into shallow water, and be dismasted.

•

Things that go bump in the night. A continual hazard faced by boat owners in heavy rains and spring thaws, is floating driftwood in river and tidal currents, river outlets and jetty entrances. ***Deadheads*** are vertical logs or timbers that are almost waterlogged, barely afloat, and difficult to see.

Sailboat first aid??? Every sailboat owner should consider the chance of his craft being holed when hitting a solid object or floating debris. Temporary measures may be sufficient if you have a ***tapered wooden plug*** carried aboard to plug the hole, plus an adequate ***bilge pump installation*** that is in good operational condition.

BLUB

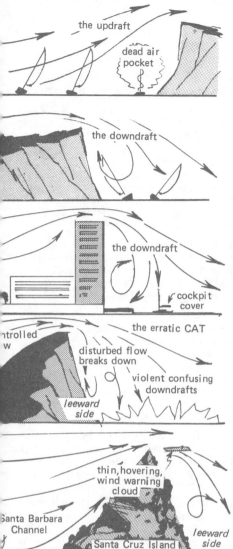

STIMULATING DOWNDRAFTS and WIND FUNNELS

the updraft
dead air pocket
the downdraft
the downdraft
cockpit cover
the erratic CAT
disturbed flow breaks down
violent confusing downdrafts
leeward side
thin, hovering, wind warning cloud
Santa Barbara Channel
Santa Cruz Island
leeward side

those wonderful westerlies

Local ocean sailing can be simple in the early afternoon when the westerlies are moving in. After the boat is a mile or so past the jetty, undisturbed ocean winds coming over long distances often permit shock cord steering. Sailing becomes stimulating after returning to the harbor due to natural and man-made obstacles disturbing the wind flow– beginning with **wind funnels** flowing down local streets.

It is fun racing near the edge of an **updraft** where the wind is the strongest, to be able to lure the competitor further inside where he will be trapped in a dead air pocket. What wonderful memories.....

Vertical whirlpool downdrafts provided a San Francisco Bay photo with two sailboats racing on opposite tacks on the same course **beneath a bluff** handled by sailors knowing local conditions. If a third sailboat tried to sail between the two it would be trapped in the middle of a **downdraft**...as it heels excessively coming to a screeching halt.

Remove a cockpit sunshade before taking a sailboat under power into a dock beneath a building more than three stories tall with wind flowing off the top of the building at left. The first time we powered into a new slip such as that, our cockpit sunshade became a square sail causing rapid acceleration at the dock due to **vertical downdrafts.**

California listed 9 high mountain drownings in 1973, cause unknown, in **high altitude lakes** that had recently been opened to boating. When I was contacted, none of the reports made sense except for violent winds and confused waves.

We checked to find one basic element involved in all drownings. It proved to be a high sloping hill facing the wind, with a steep lee side. the erratic patterns indicated a ***CAT (clear air turbulence)*** as the wind flowing over the top of the hill became confused to spill down vertically onto the lakes with tremendous violence lasting a few minutes.

We've enjoyed a few sailing lessons on owner's sailboats, pg..**101, wanting** exposure to heavy weather operation...with the Santa Barbara Channel usually being most cooperative in August and September westerlies.

Santa Cruz Island develops a thin, hovering ***lenticular wind warning cloud*** that can be seen from the mainland. It indicates that strong winds exist in the Santa Barbara Channel north of the island.

As the strong wind reaches the island it rises, cools, and condenses to rapidly tumble down the lee side of the island. This continuous process produces a ***small wind warning cloud*** for sailors to soon tie in a reef, and for powerboat owners to head for a protected harbor.

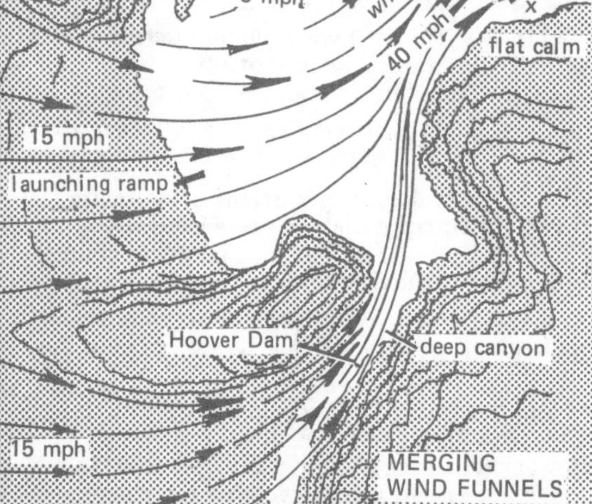
north
5 mph
wind accelerates
40 mph
x
flat calm
15 mph
launching ramp
Hoover Dam
deep canyon
15 mph
MERGING WIND FUNNELS

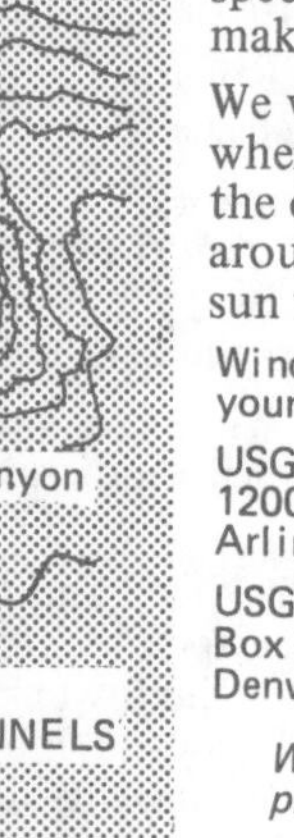

It is important to be able to anticipate **merging wind funnels** if your sailing is in western canyons, or lakes and reservoirs surrounded by high, steep hills usually in mountain areas.

A wide valley narrows down to the launching ramp on Lake Mead, outside of Las Vegas, Nevada. Another funnel comes up the Colorado River, being squeezed with the flow speed increasing as it goes over the top of the dam, while making a controlled turn flow of almost 70 degrees.

We were involved in making a rescue in our outboard boat where these two funnels merged together, easily doubling the original 15 mph wind speed. After both boats made it around the point marked X, we were suddenly in a hot desert sun without any wind with whitecaps 200' away from us.

Wind funnels can be predicted on USGS Topographic Maps of your inland sailing area. which are topographic charts. Contact–

USGS Survey
1200 South Eads St.
Arlington, VA 22202

USGS Survey
Box 25286, Fedeaal Center
Denver, CO 80225

Wind funnels can provide stimulating surprises.

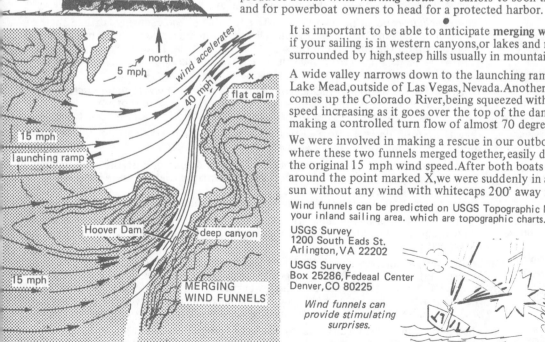

F

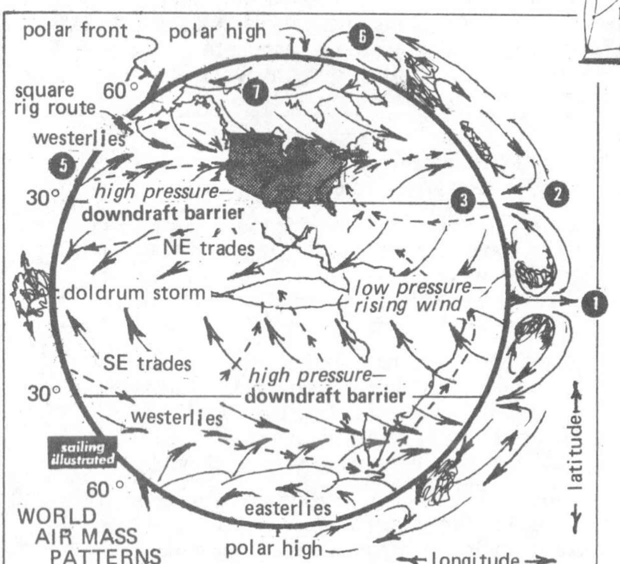
polar front
polar high
square rig route
60°
westerlies
30°
high pressure–
downdraft barrier
NE trades
doldrum storm
low pressure–
rising wind
SE trades
30°
high pressure–
downdraft barrier
westerlies
sailing illustrated
60°
latitude
WORLD AIR MASS PATTERNS
easterlies
polar high
longitude

Sailing Illustrated Volume II

Wind basics start with heat & earth rotation.

Wind direction is reported as the direction it comes from. The westerlies for example,flow toward the east.

Air flow and water flow fluid basics respond to similar forces of nature...except water has 800 times the density and can't be compressed.Warm air and warm water rises, while cold air and water descends or sinks.An exception– **air can be compressed**...then it flows outward from a higher pressure area,to a lower pressure area,where it rises,cools,and condenses...the start of a storm.

Water and air flow **frictional retardation** is governed by their boundary surfaces.A river flows faster in the center of a straight stream with a smooth bottom,but slower along the shallow sides.Flow speed decreases with rough and irregular bottoms and/or irregular sides.

Ocean storm winds exceed those experienced on land. Frictional retardation due to irregular land surfaces, hills,canyons,mountains,and heat thermals effect wind flow to 2000' above the land.

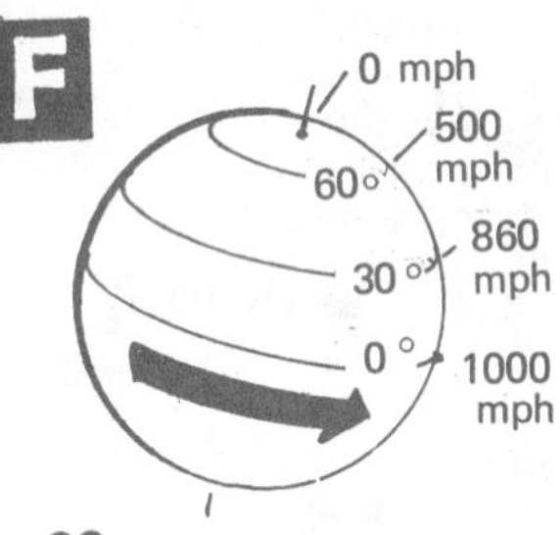
0 mph
500 mph
60°
860 mph
30°
0°
1000 mph

60 Earth rotational speeds differ according to the latitude.

basic weather ideas–

- continued fair weather — wind from W or NW barometer high and rising sunset sky red & yellow dew or frost forms at night
- change to unsettled weather– winds backing & increasing barometer falling high clouds thicken & lower clouds move two directions at different levels mild temperature at night
- change to clearing– wind shift to W or NW barometer levels,begins to rise clouds lighten & break heavy rain changes to intermittent drizzle temperature suddenly drops with wind shift
- warmer weather coming — wind from south increases sun or moon bright red when near horizon
- cooler weather coming– wind from the north distant hills clear & sharp clear evening,weakening wind

Wind flow begins with ***thermal heat currents*** from our Suns' rays.Uneven heating is maximum at the equator which theoretically rises,flows to the cold poles and descends to return to the equator.We add to this the Coriolis Force or ***earth rotation flow patterns*** with 1000 mile speed at the equator to zero speed at the poles.

Weather at the equator ❶ is clear with warm air rising,then arcing ❷ to the north and east.These winds pile up in the horse latitudes ❸ where some descends to earth,turning west for the ***steady*** ❹ NE Trades.Some of this flow goes further to the north to be deflected to the east,where it descends in the 30° to 60° temperate middle latitudes to become the ***continually changing*** ❺ **prevailing westerlies.**

A part of this air flow from the equator continues to the North Pole ❻ where it contract and descends.As the pressure builds,a southward **polar front flow** begins on the surface, turning to the west.At latitude 60° the polar front ❼ collides with,forcing itself under the warm westerlies.These westerlies rise and cool to produce unsettled weather conditions with winter cold waves that may go as far south as Florida and Mexico.

Seasonal changes occur in our yearly earth cycle due to the changing latitude angle of the earth to the sun.Our seasonal change in the spring increases the heat ray absorption from the sun on the land and in the sea...pushing the polar front storm tracks northward.When the heat rays from the sun are reduced in the fall,the land and water surfaces start to cool...with the polar front starting its annual trek southward.

When the land is warm and the ocean cool in the summer,two stationary ***permanent highs*** develop in the northern hemisphere which produce weak,spotty winds sailors try to avoid.One is in the eastern Atlantic,the other is in the eastern Pacific, page 67,

Prevailing storm paths ❽ flow eastward as we are in the ***prevailing westerly patterns*** of our northern hemisphere which we show on the facing page.

Wind flow patterns follow the pattern of a different drummer with the cyclonic,typical middle latitude weather circulation north of the equator.**High pressure areas** with ***heavier air*** provide an outward flow ❾ in a clockwise rotation...changing to a counterclockwise rotation as it flows into the center ❿ of the ***lighter air*** low pressure area.

The resulting **lighter air spiraling wind flow** on the surface has no place to go but upward where it cools and condenses ⓫ ,with moisture droplets starting to fall the reason low pressure areas produce storms.

Storm intensity increases as to the speed and the amount a barometer drops...with the lowest readings recorded on the eastern seaboard as a hurricane moves in.When a barometer starts to rise,it indicates the lower pressure is moving out of the area.This rise can indicate strong N and NW gales after a severe drop,good weather with weak winds or the prevailing westerlies are again moving in to predominate your area.

The interaction of the resulting highs and lows provided the wind power to move older square riggers to their advantage,which we can also study,adapt,then make the most of these wind patterns to move the wind machines we enjoy sailing today and in the future.

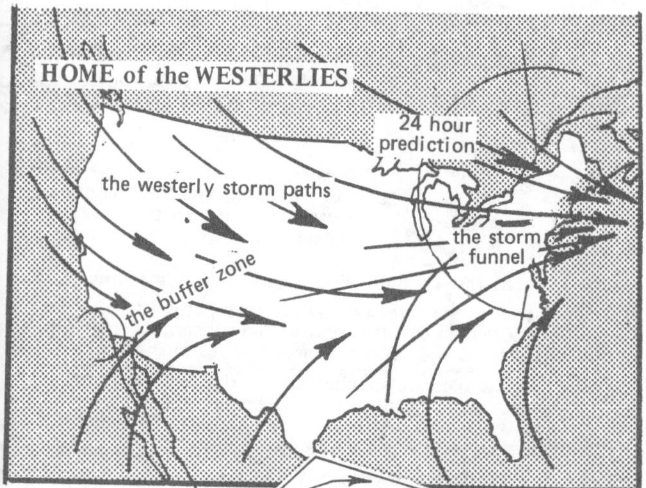

HOME of the WESTERLIES

24 hour prediction

the westerly storm paths

the storm funnel

the buffer zone

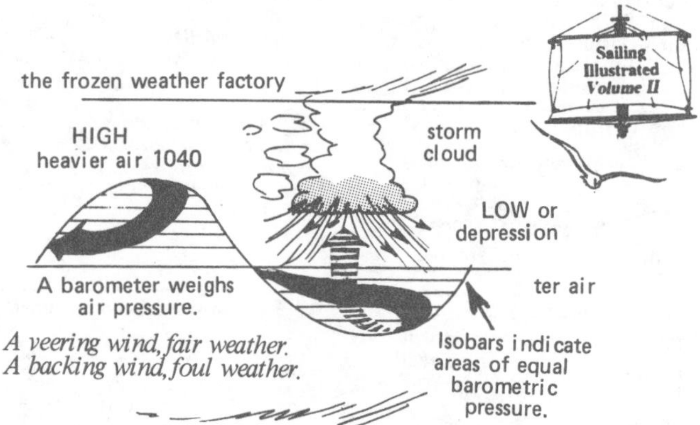

the frozen weather factory

HIGH heavier air 1040

storm cloud

LOW or depression

A barometer weighs air pressure.

A veering wind, fair weather.
A backing wind, foul weather.

Isobars indicate areas of equal barometric pressure.

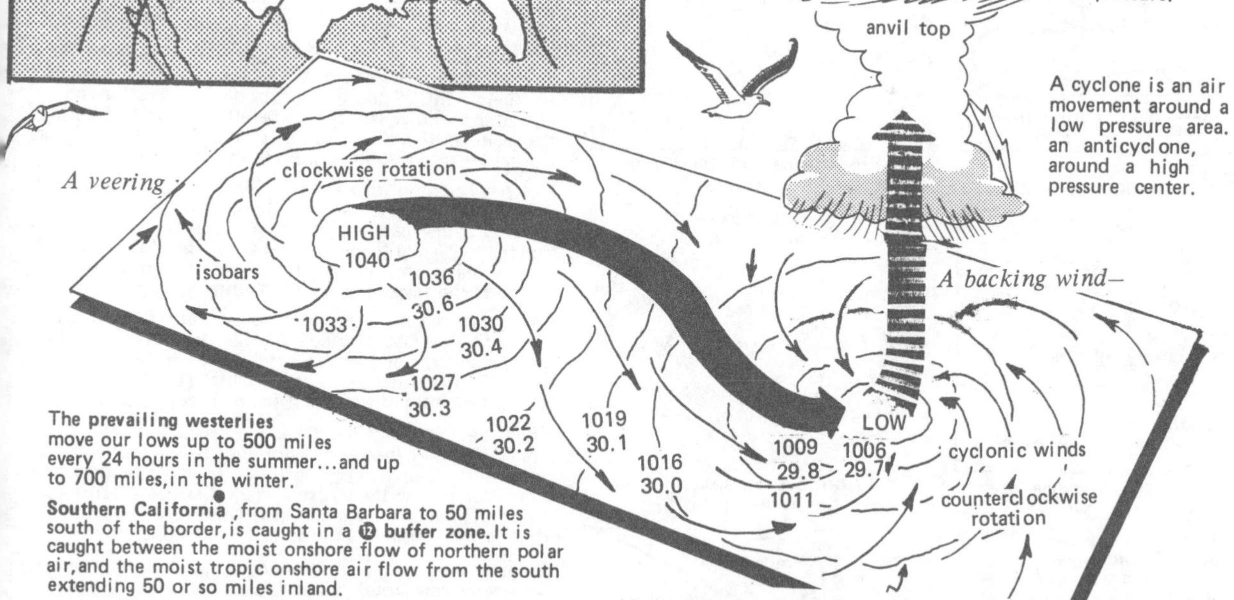

anvil top

A cyclone is an air movement around a low pressure area. an anticyclone, around a high pressure center.

A veering clockwise rotation

HIGH 1040 isobars 1036 30.6 1033 1030 30.4 1027 30.3 1022 30.2 1019 30.1 1016 30.0

A backing wind—

LOW 1009 29.8 1006 29.7 1011 cyclonic winds counterclockwise rotation

The **prevailing westerlies** move our lows up to **500** miles every 24 hours in the summer...and up to **700** miles, in the winter.

Southern California, from Santa Barbara to 50 miles south of the border, is caught in a (12) **buffer zone.** It is caught between the moist onshore flow of northern polar air, and the moist tropic onshore air flow from the south extending 50 or so miles inland.

Our buffer zone helps to moderate local coastal weather to provide mild winters, and cool, comfortable summers. Very **sensitive barometers are required** to register our weak local pressures that vary little which still need a **thumping** to produce an accurate reading.

The **east coast wind funnel...** is the opposite extreme with the Chesapeake Bay to the south, up thru New England to the north. Storm fronts (13) from the northwest, west, and the southwest flow thru this storm funnel. Storm fronts also flow up the Mississippi Valley and southeast states, taking a right turn to flow out to sea thru the storm funnel area.

Weather reporting is excellent today in the storm funnel area with a nation-wide communication system, plus tv satellite coverage. Weather reporting was rather primitive there when we learned sailing in the late 1940's with much of our learning done the hard way, from mistakes.

After a couple of bad scares we began studying Chicago weather which provided a clue. Draw a 500 mile radius west of your funnel area home (14), with an arc of 160° from the Chesapeake Bay to the south and up thru Canada to the north. Any storm in this sector **may go thru your sailing area 24 hours later** due to our prevailing westerlies shown above (8), while New England weather does not flow to Chicago.

Little did we realize how fortunate we were in our early east coast sailing days to have exposure to these rapidly moving storms from Staten Island to the North River and the south side of Long Island to Freeport to analyze the storm funnel theory when developing this book.

July 4, 1948 found us paddling a Folbot Kayak on the Hudson or North River while I was studying the beautiful clouds in an approaching thunderstorm to detail in an illustration.

The storm hit with a vengeance. The wind was still increasing after the last of the Manhattan weather instruments disintegrated above 114 knots. We landed at a Yonkers boat club dock with a German *beer bust* underway. Most of the customers enjoyed such an early start that they were well past the point of being aware that a major storm though brief, was howling outside.

A couple of years later, also on the 4th of July, our 20' cb V-bottom sailboat was one of 54 boats anchored bow and stern in a tiny harbor near Jones Beach Inlet, plus a Tahiti ketch using 8 anchors in the middle of the shallow pond.

A thunderstorm hit at 0230 causing the greatest anchor foulup in local history with only five boats left at dawn. We were all high and dry as the wind which peaked at 84 knots at the nearby USCG base had blown all water out of the shallow pond. Hordes of gnats next moved in to provide an encore that were so small our mosquito netting provided no barrier.

confusing meteorology terms

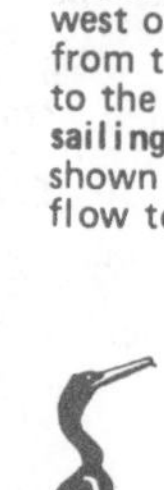

Though some of these terms sound archaic...prevailing westerly wind systems are known as cyclones and anticyclones. The counterclockwise flow of wind in the Northern Hemisphere going into an overcast low-pressure area is called cyclonic circulation. **Extratropical cyclones** are mid-latitude lows surrounded by combating air masses with warm and cold fronts between. Cyclonic flow will have clockwise circulation into a low in the Southern Hemisphere.

Tropical cyclones are unstable air mass storms with winds above 64 knots of hurricane strength from the Equator to latitude 30 degrees north and south. They are a single-mass, small and intense without fronts, with water warmer than 80 degrees. They are called **hurricanes** in the U.S. **typhoons** in the western North Pacific, **baguios** in the Philippines, **willy-willies** in Australia and **cyclones** in the Indian Ocean.

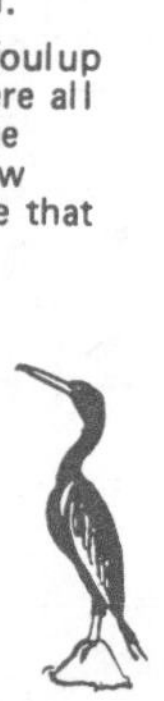

The low...a backing wind,foul weather.

A-Arctic—low temperature,low humidity
cP-Polar continental—low temp.,low humidity
mP-Polar maritime—low temp.,high humidity
mT-Tropical maritime—warm temp.,high humidity
cT-Tropical continental—high temp.,low humidity
E-Equatorial—high temp.,high humidity

Major air masses affecting our weather.

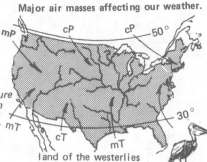

mP
cP
cP
50°
mT
cT
mT
30°
land of the westerlies

Sailing
Illustrated
Volume

Type of front—

Warm front
Cold front
Stationary front
Occluded front
Upper warm front
Upper cold front

Become your own forecaster to anticipate changes in a major storm that can take two days or longer to pass your sailing area.

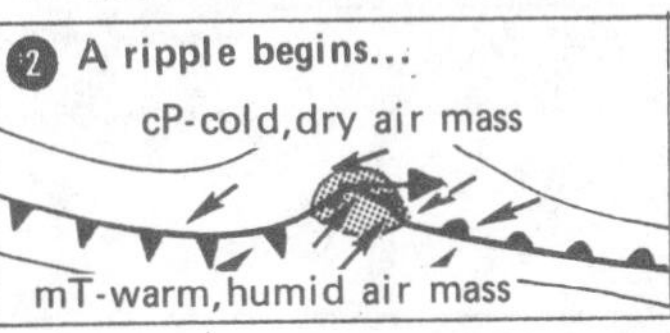

❷ A ripple begins...
cP-cold,dry air mass
mT-warm,humid air mass

❶ A low pressure area begins when polar air bumps into tropical air on the frontal surface at left.

❸ **To become a wavelet...**
the faster cold front
storm direction
the slower warm front
7

Disturbance is more intense as circulation increases around apex.

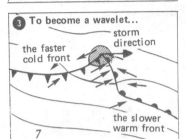

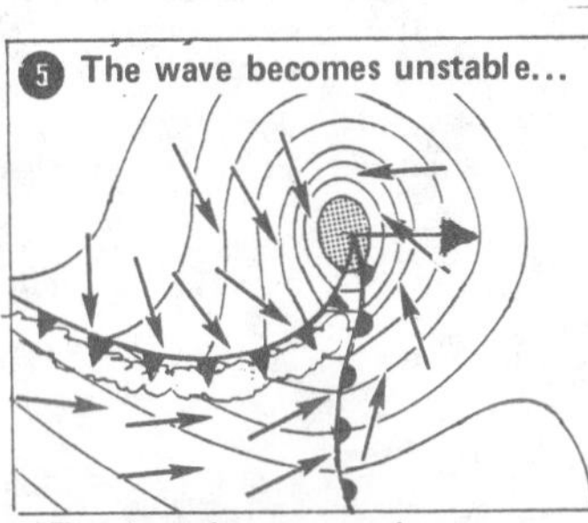

❺ The wave becomes unstable...

The low deepens as the warm sector shrinks in size.

❹ **To grow to a mature wave.**
❶

see enlargement below

A mature cyclone has developed around an intense low.

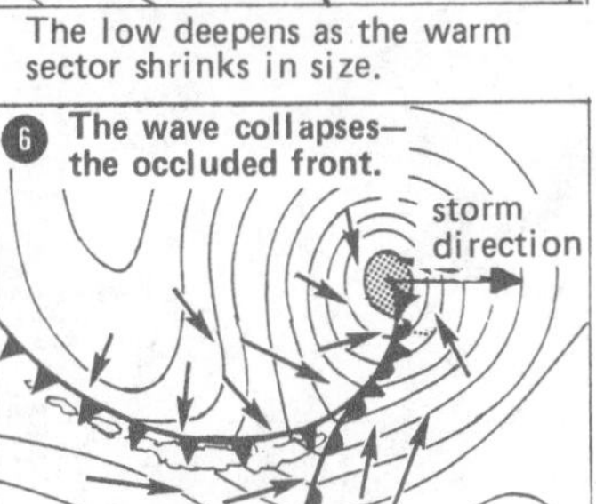
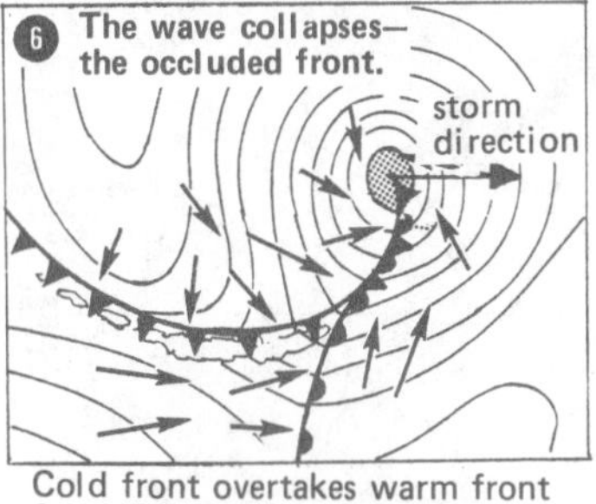

❻ The wave collapses— the occluded front.
storm direction

Cold front overtakes warm front forcing the warm air aloft.

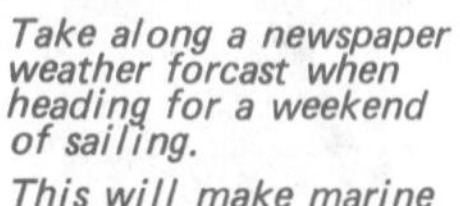

Take along a newspaper weather forcast when heading for a weekend of sailing.

This will make marine weather forecasts more coherent as they are too basic.

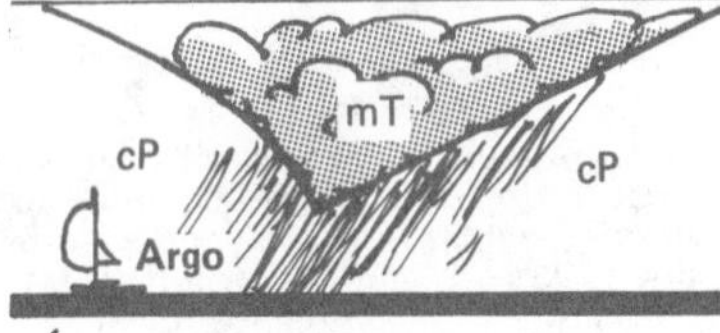

mT
cP
cP
Argo

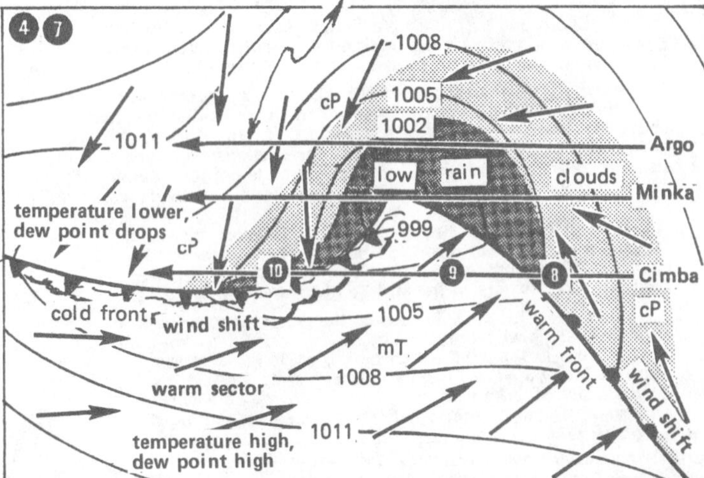

❹ ❼
1008
1005
1002
cP
1011
Argo
low
rain
clouds
Minka
temperature lower, dew point drops
999
cP
❿
❾
❽
Cimba
cold front
wind shift
1005
cP
mT
warm front
1008
wind shift
warm sector
1011
temperature high, dew point high

The low-pressure,wind-factory energy machine.

Page F 6 shows theoretical air flow pattern from a high pressure area to a low pressure area,where its moisture rises,cools and condenses,as a new storm is born.

The low pressure area begins as a ripple on a frontal surface,growing to a wavelet,then to a mature wave. The wave continues like an ocean wave as it becomes unstable,then breaks as the low dissipates.

A front develops when cold and warm air masses collide, and being unlike do not mix,producing drizzles and unsettled weather. Isobars are parallel on both sides of the front until a distortion or ripple ❷ develops on the **frontal surface,** the humble birth of a **frontal wave.**

The ripple grows into a wavelet ❸ as its self-perpetuating wind flow increases around the developing apex,its low flowing in the path of the prevailing westerlies. Two parts emerge with the **leading warm front,the slower part of the frontal wave...and the trailing cold front behind, which is the faster part of the frontal wave.**

Development time from birth to a mature wave ❹ along the frontal surface may be 12 to 24 hours. Then the faster moving cold front starts to catch up with the warm front as the frontal wave becomes unstable ❺. The low meanwhile deepens and the warm sector becomes smaller.

When the cold front overtakes the warm front,the two similar cool air masses mix,forcing the warmer air aloft to become an upper ❺❻ **occluded front.** As the warm air continues to rise the entire system dissipates. Barometer pressure gradually rises called **filling** for a few days after formation of the upper occluded front.

We must analyze all wind factory signs—weather reports, barometer,and clouds,to anticipate and make the most use of its variable wind power to our advantage on our wind machines. We must be alert to maintain our advantage so it doesn't suddenly overpower us.

What can be more exciting than a spirited,romping sail in the rain with wind forces 5,6,and lower 7. We go down to the surface to see how three sailboats fare as a mature low-pressure frontal wave moves over their area.

Thru the CENTER—the many faces of a storm.

2/18/84. We were aboard **Minka** heading for Catalina. The cloud wedge had been dropping for 30 hours with more shower activity. The boat eased after we changed to a working jib,course broad reach,port tack,force 5 wind.

The rain suddenly stopped as the warm front moved thru with an **abrupt wind change.**.We flopped to port tack, closehauled,with similar wind strength. One of my companions went below for a nap.

20 minutes later I saw a long line of large whitecapped waves a mile away on the starboard bow,calling everyone topside. A cold front nearing occlusion hit with a weak force 7 as we flopped to starboard tack closehauled with **an abrupt wind shift.** After a fishermans reef on the main for two minutes,the wind dropped to a spirited force 5.

The wind held with steady rain for two hours to our anchorage,followed by intermittant showers till 2300. We awoke at 0800 to find a clear,beautiful sunny morning.

Simplifying our national weather patterns proved an interesting challenge...but how can readers put this information into practice? The first mate collected two months of daily weather forecasts from our local newspaper. It is a simple,practical method to follow as a brushup to anticipate changing weather patterns when the spring sailing time nears.

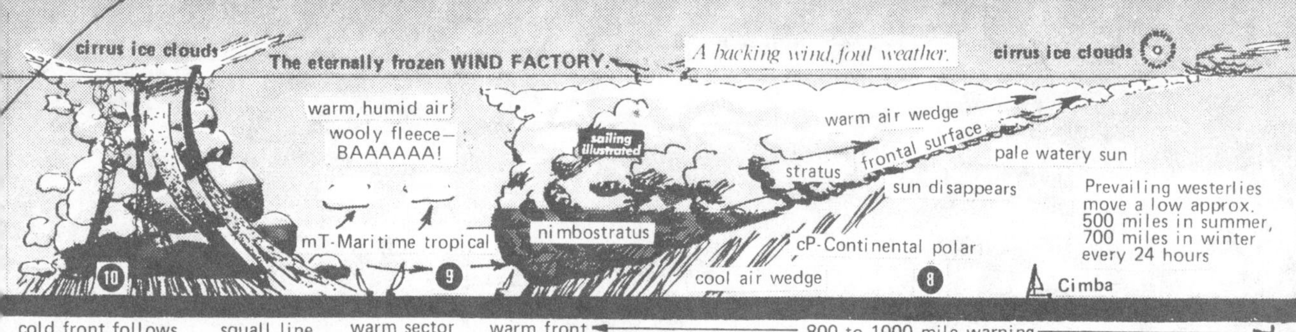

cirrus ice clouds
The eternally frozen WIND FACTORY.
A backing wind, foul weather.
cirrus ice clouds
warm, humid air
wooly fleece—
BAAAAAA!
sailing illustrated
warm air wedge
frontal surface
pale watery sun
stratus
sun disappears
Prevailing westerlies move a low approx. 500 miles in summer, 700 miles in winter every 24 hours
mT-Maritime tropical
nimbostratus
cP-Continental polar
cool air wedge
10
9
8
Cimba
cold front follows
squall line
warm sector
warm front
800 to 1000 mile warning

Strong upper westerlies flatten the anvil top.

illibars	inches
050	31.0
047	30.9
044	30.8
041	30.7
038	30.6
035	30.5
032	
029	30.4
026	30.3
023	30.2
020	30.1
017	30.0
014	29.9
011	
008	29.8
005	29.7
002	29.6
999	29.5
996	29.4
993	29.3
990	29.2
987	
984	29.1
981	29.0
978	28.9
975	28.8
972	28.7
969	28.6
966	28.5
963	28.4
960	28.3
957	28.2
954	28.1
951	28.0
948	

Mackerel sky and mare's tails-

Check GLASS continually!

At sea with low and falling glass-

Clouds scratched by a hen-

When clouds appear like rocks and towers???

Too dang busy to pray!

Long foretold, long last-

A moving warm front can range from mild to severe, text pages 208-9. Its intensity is indicated by the amount a barometer drops plus increasing static from an inexpensive portable AM radio.

To the NORTH—we are aboard **Argo** sighting thin mare's tails moving towards us from the west changing to the hen scratches mackerel sky, with a halo around the moon at night. As the warm cloud bank wedge moves closer and lower, the sun changes to a pale, waterly look, weakens, and disappears ❽ behind a thick stratus cloud bank, followed with spotty showers.

The cloud layer darkens to nimbostratus with showers changing to heavy rain, not often with rapid wind shifts. Rain eventually eases, with spotty showers that eventually stop. The clouds become lighter as you break out into sunshine with a clean blue sky and beautiful ocean.

We began on a port tack run, force 4, as the clouds moved in. The wind changes to force 5, then upper force 5 as the boom jibes to starboard tack, wind now on a broad reach. When the rain stops it is abeam, force 4...perfect for a spinnaker reach after a wet, refreshing sail.

OOPS—we faced a similar force 4 to 6 wet sail on **Minka** 11/11/83 for two spirited days. The low must have changed course rapidly, increasing to force 8 in the last 90 minutes before entering Oxnard harbor, page 72. Fronts can shift...**watch your barometer for local changes.**

To the SOUTH—we are aboard **Cimba** off the New England coast in the early fall. A strong low front went thru Chicago the previous day, the barometer had been dropping steadily (slowly or rapidly?) and a warning has been issued. The same wedge pattern warm front occurs except the front has a large peasoup fog, text 222-3, due to high relative humidity.

The warm front moves past in the morning, as the warm sector moves in. The weather is clear, hot and humid. Mare's tails, long evident, are dwarfed behind a towering black wall in the late afternoon moving towards you. The sun disappears behind a dark purple to black wall to the NW.

Cimba is too far from a protected harbor so you prepare to ride it out expecting rapid, severe wind shifts. Advancing squall line cloud colors can be brilliant in the afternoon sunshine. **ALWAYS prepare for the squall line...reef down, lash loose objects, and prepare for lightning.**

Inky darkness swallows your boat as the water becomes black with sparkling white-capped waves. **An abrupt wind shift momentarily blows the water flat.** Large waves develop rapidly with stinging spray blown off their tops. A solid stream of wind-driven rain pours off the triple-reefed mainsail producing a waterfall that pours into the cockpit. The black ocean turns to a luminescent green or purple in deep water...or a coppery hue in shallow, muddy water.

You may be in the middle of a squall system with several short, violent squalls, with light shifting winds until another squall hits...or it can be a thunderstorm moving thru with considerable violence though lasting less than half an hour. After the cold front moves thru and the air clears, you are lucky finding good, steady winds for sailing. Stay alert for storm-related debris such as deadheads...and for boats not so lucky that may require help.

4 to 5 days later—occluded front aloft.

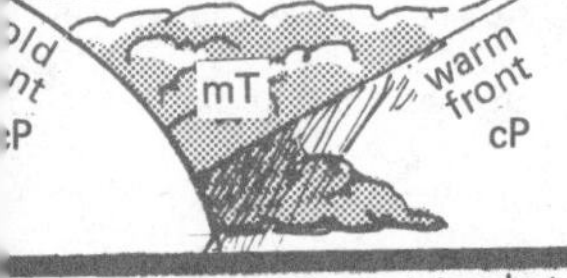

old
nt
mT
warm front
cP
P

The cold front overtakes the warm front.

The occluded front begins at the apex ❺ as the frontal wave becomes too steep and unstable. The cold front overtakes the warm front forcing the warm sector moist warm air aloft ❻ which eventually loses its moisture while the two cold air masses mingle across the front to become one air mass again. The fully occluded cyclone may cause a major weather disturbance as a parting shot up to 100 miles north of the apex, and then it will dissipate.

❻ The warmer part tends to rise over the colder part, continuing to rise until the system dissipates.

Will that first trip south be the experience of a lifetime, or become a nightmare.

New England sailing provides spirited, spring, summer, and early fall sailing. Then it becomes necessary for the decision, will the boat be drydocked, stay in a well-protected marina..or head south to winter in Florida or the Caribbean (dream on) page 125.

September and October weather records list many hurricanes with extreme high tides and extreme low tides, plus fierce winds...while December is too late to head south as the frigid arctic northers knife down from Canada to well south of the warm Gulf Stream.

November is the questionable compromise with late hurricanes and gales...with sailboats heading south increasing ten fold in ten years. Sinkings and assists have increased considerably with new owners and crew unprepared for the weather potentials they may face. It is a specialized seamanship challenge, **NOT a survival situation**, a well-found boat with a trained crew should be able to face to share a wonderful experience...and the problem seems a growing one.

New England yacht clubs can provide simple, workable answers with weekend seminars inviting owners and crews before their first trip south, that can be in charge of many competent sailors with first-hand experience on previous trips from New England to Florida...and return.

New England sailing...

pirited spring, summer, and arly fall sailing in the wind unnel area with lobster pots, olonial architecture, forests, ovely harbors, etc.

When autumn arrives and the eaves change colors...

A lifetime memory—half elated/ half scared.

F

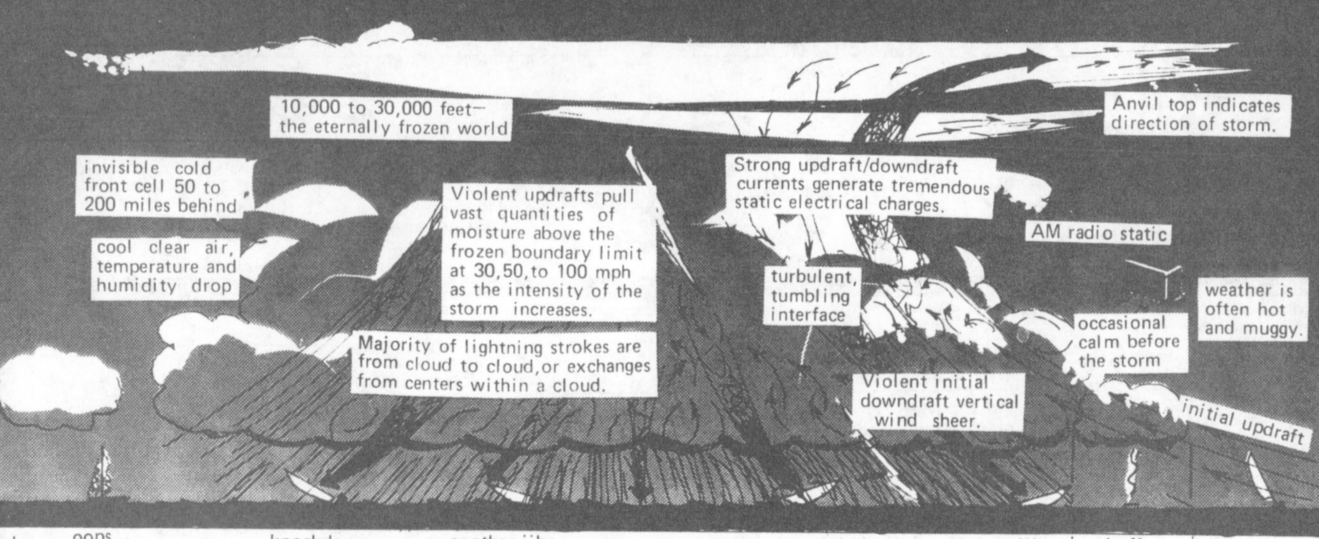
10,000 to 30,000 feet—
the eternally frozen world
Anvil top indicates
direction of storm.
invisible cold
front cell 50 to
200 miles behind
Strong updraft/downdraft
currents generate tremendous
static electrical charges.
Violent updrafts pull
vast quantities of
moisture above the
frozen boundary limit
at 30,50,to 100 mph
as the intensity of the
storm increases.
cool clear air,
temperature and
humidity drop
AM radio static
turbulent,
tumbling
interface
weather is
often hot
and muggy.
occasional
calm before
the storm
Majority of lightning strokes are
from cloud to cloud,or exchanges
from centers within a cloud.
Violent initial
downdraft vertical
wind sheer.
initial updraft
oops...
knockdown
another jibe
knockdown
violent jibe
buffer
cool updraft

F

64

The freezing level may be as high as 30,000' in the summer,and descend as low as the surface of the earth during the winter.

the average U.S. thunderstorm count variables

Clear weather visual sighting can be many miles away

recommended reading—
"Weather for the Great Lakes Sailor",Commercial Weather Services,
2107 Davidson Rd.,
Flint,MI 48506

When will it hit?

It is over ONLY if the air is clear!

The unstable air mass thunderstorm follows NO patterns.

Inexpensive AM radio warming for hilly,mountainous storm predictability.

Blue sky DUSTERS can be predicted.

Sailing
Illustrated
Volume II

Tropical thunderstorms make their own rules.

A mile away....less than two minutes to reef!!!!

Considerable artistic license was used to shrink the vertical growth of a towering thunderstorm to 70,000 feet high,and to expand the time frame of a sailboat with minimum steering control exposed to strong updrafts,and violent downdrafts hitting the water at an angle.

A squall line of **frontal thunderstorms may generate winds of hurricane intensity for short periods...**while a **hurricane** is a storm covering a much larger area for a longer period of time,with winds of force 12 or stronger.

Yearly thunderstorms average 20 in New England,35 on the Chesapeake Bay,90 on the west coast of Florida,with one in 3 years in our west coast buffer zone.It is necessary to reef way down as one of these wind bombs*move thru,with momentary loss of controls due to downdrafts on vertical airfoils...while a horizontal cockpit sunshade becomes an erratic square sail.

Low pressure,cold-front LINE SQUALLS usually sweep across the U.S. following the prevailing westerlies from the SW,W,to NW quadrant.If the air is clear,mare'stails from the anvil top can be seen great distances which also indicates direction of travel of the storm.

The **FRONTAL THUNDERSTORM** is part of a squall line with the cold front aloft 20 to 200 miles ahead of the surface cold front cell retarded by friction.The stable,dense cold air aloft is displaced by warm unstable surface air flowing upwards to increase the violent and unstable air currents.The incoming cold front thunderstorm is reported by the weather service.The barometer is dropping,**STATIC intensity is increasing on an inexpensive AM radio.** If the air is clear the anvil top mare's tails will be visible above the towering storm cloud.

If LIGHTNING is visible with the sound of thunder traveling a mile in 5 seconds,it helps to indicate how far the storm is from you. Time is running out...if the storm is one mile from you that is traveling 30 mph you have TWO MINUTES to make a major reef.

The typical cold-front thunderstorm is often over and out in 20 minutes *IF the sky becomes cool and clear.* On a hot and humid June afternoon off Staten Island a vicious thunderstorm moved thru,yet the sky still remained hazy.A second squall line moved thru which was followed an hour later by a third vicious squall line until the sky became clear and the humidity dropped.

An UNSTABLE loner AIR MASS *(rogue thunderstorm)* develops from individual cells wherever convection heating conditions exist in an unstable atmosphere.Heated land or water on a hot, humid summer afternoon will cause air to rise rapidly to generate air currents in cumulus clouds which explode upward into the frozen air factory.

Updraft speeds in this frozen world become violent pulling the anvil tops from 35,000 to 70,000 or more feet high with rain drops and snow flakes below producing a radar echo.It develops static on a AM radio with the storm violence indicated by the static intensity as it moves in.The **rogue loner is unpredictable and highly dangerous** as it may suddenly expand and make a major course change,move rapidly,stop,or suddenly dissipate **following NO pattern**.

Hilly mountainous areas can restrict visibility to hide thunderstorms until a few minutes away. The most practical warning method may be an AM radio softly playing in the background.

The Plains states have strong,violent **DUSTERS** on hot summer afternoons with clear blue skies. *They can be predicted by AM radio static.* Visibility is usually excellent.Use a distant landmark in the western quadrant to estimate the time the violent dust clouds will arrive.

Tropical ocean thunderstorms **occur from midnight to dawn.** Warm air rises from the water surface to a stationary cold front aloft.The updraft cools,condenses,and triggers the 0200 tropical storm which is smaller,and with less intensity than frontal squalls or unstable air mass thunderstorms.The inexpensive,portable AM radio again provides early warning *IF it is playing!*

The *BOMB...birthplace of ROGUE WAVES?????

Long after this page was completed we found the term *bomb* becoming accepted as an intense storm dropping one or more millibars per hour for 24 hours or longer.While waves build moderately in **short duration squalls...**a long duration storm of force 8 or more can produce 20 to 30 foot waves,*while individual waves may be expected twice as high.*

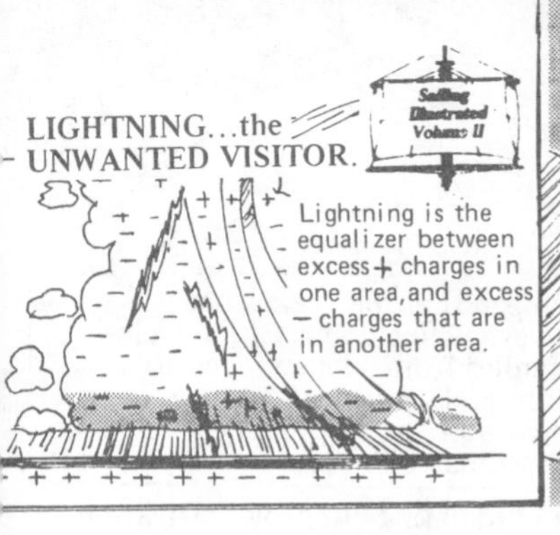

LIGHTNING...the UNWANTED VISITOR.
Sailing Illustrated Volume II
Lightning is the equalizer between excess + charges in one area, and excess – charges that are in another area.

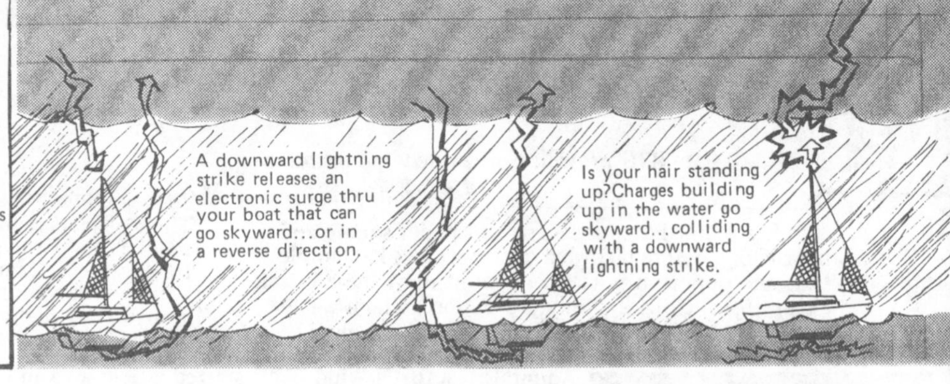

A downward lightning strike releases an electronic surge thru your boat that can go skyward...or in a reverse direction.
Is your hair standing up? Charges building up in the water go skyward...colliding with a downward lightning strike.

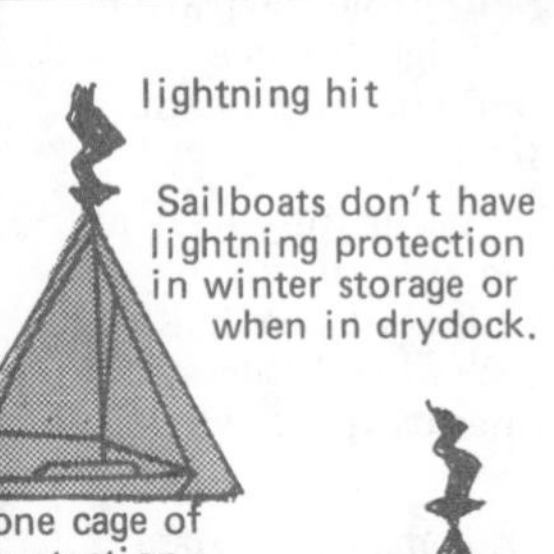

lightning hit

Sailboats don't have lightning protection in winter storage or when in drydock.

one cage of protection

tection is ded for both ts at right.

If lightning follows corrosion bonding system with prop shaft discharge, flashovers may result.

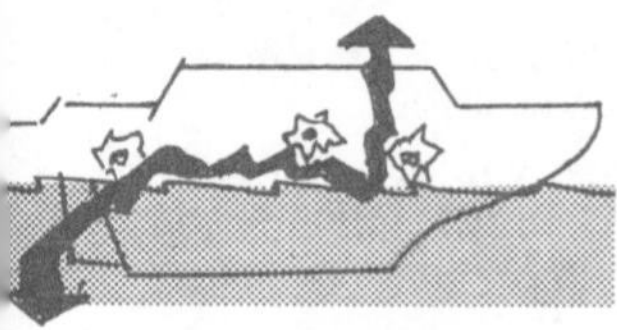

The straight vertical path discharge has minimum resistance.

Temporary protection–

bolt grounding cable to mast with minimum turn angle avoiding metal objects on boat.

Tiedowns are required.

DON'T secure grounding cable to stainless stays or shrouds to avoid erratic side flashes.

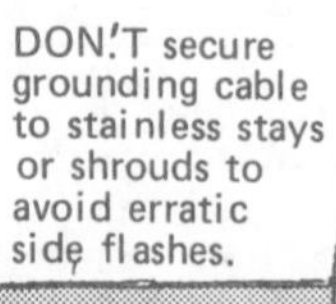

A thunderstorm awakens as it grows past the frozen boundary. The greater the vertical development from 40,000 to 80,000 feet, the more the increase occurs proportionally due to the tumbling friction of updrafts and downdrafts. It produces an excess of negative charges in one area, and a deficiency of positive charges in another, or visa versa. Lightning is the sparkplug tension equalizer between the charges with your sailboat hopefully not caught in the middle.

The traditional protection method for a sailboat is a *lightning rod.* It starts at the masthead with a well-bolted metallic spike having a sharp tip pointed upward to provide an *easily controlled path down the mast, and thru the boat with the charges released harmlessly into the water.* The masthead spike tip must be at least 6'' above all masthead equipment to draw the charge to provide a 60° cage cone of protection for a lightning discharge. Radio equipment requires additional protection with an antenna lead-in cable lightning arrester.

While the idea sounds commendable the flow may have two turns in many installations. In the millionth part of a second when this unwanted visitor is aboard as it goes thru the cabin and engine compartments it may flow close to many metal objects. In a storm-tossed pitching boat where everyone is trying to stay away from metal parts to avoid electrocution... flashovers may occur. **The problem is the traditional boat bonding method** with all metal objects wired or bonded together to reduce corrosion potentials, *page 133.*

A simplistic analysis—*Because of lightning protection in modern sailboats most metallic parts are bonded together to create a low resistance path for lightning strikes to reach the water. These strikes exit thru the keel, prop shaft, and thru-hull fittings with little or no harm to crew or equipment.*

A second approach— **Do you bond a lightning rod to your home plumbing...***or does your building code to protect your home and plumbing, require a separate lightning rod going straight to its own ground.* The mast is a lightning rod which should also be installed without turns...and the rod should be separated from the sailboat's metal bonding system to avoid flashovers. Research indicates that a blunt upper lightning rod tip may be twice as efficient as a sharp rod tip...but can you live with the extra ounces of masthead weight?

Maximum conductivity should be considered which follows a straight path to permit a controlled lightning surge without bends to reduce flashover potentials.

Square riggers with wooden hulls and wooden masts without lightning rod protection often suffered lightning damage...as each mast requires its own cone cage for protection.

Wooden masts require a copper lightning rod spike with a flat braided copper grounding wire, or a 6 or 8 gage stranded copper lead bolted to a metal keel, centerboard, or keel plate underwater. If aluminum cable is substituted, double the cross section to equalize its conductivity to that of copper. The deck mounted aluminum mast becomes its own conductor from the masthead spike, with a 20 gage ½'' copper strap leading from the mast base, bolted to the keel.

The sudden 25,000 degree heat generated by a lightning strike will *instantly incinerate solder and insulation...* requiring crimp-on fittings and a bare grounding cable. **Copper-bottom paint should be considered** for lightning conductivity since some bottom paint formulas may instead become insulators causing flashover potentials.

Temporary lightning protection for a boat NOT underway—bolt a grounding cable to the metal mast base, the other to a 1/16 inch thick, square foot copper sheet, add a lead weight so it will stay at least two feet below the water in wave action. Secure with fore and aft lines so the plate weight isn't carried by the bonding cable. The cable **MUST be far enough away** from metal toerails, lifelines, stanchions, cleats, metal vents, etc., to reduce flashover potentials.

Only copper, or aluminum with 2/3 the conductivity of copper, is able to contain the huge lightning surge. **Avoid attaching a grounding cable to stainless stays or shrouds** as 18-8 stainless has 1/50 the conductivity of copper. *Stainless resistance can cause* erratic current surges with *confused lightning flashovers* that may wipe out batteries, electrical systems, etc.

Traditional lightning rod theory is necessary to evaluate new lightning concepts. One approach, lightning can come down the mast then return 300 times faster to the clouds...or it can hit the water and return to the clouds up the mast. If your hair begins to stand up when swimming, or sailing a trampoline cat, head for land. An excessive charge is developing in the water to produce a blue masthead glow called **St. Elmo's fire.** This charge can leap skyward to meet a downward strike ABOVE the mast to produce a huge thunderclap, which will protect your boat. Expect a sudden hearing loss for a half hour or so.

A few parts of the lightning protection jigsaw puzzle still seem missing. Tremendous lightning research progress has taken place in recent years to protect munition depots, factories, etc. We hope some of the new scientists in this field could join the sailing fraternity to help us put together the final pieces in this fascinating puzzle.

Sailing
Illustrated
Volume II

PILOT CHARTS provide worldwide wind patterns.

Mutiny insurance—the officers only protection.

Man has roamed the restless oceans under square and lug rig long before recorded history.Crews had ample time and opportunity to take command of these vessels except for the officers only protection...which was to keep all of their navigational secrets to themselves.

Their officers realized that the oceans had predictable pathways which could take vessels for thousands of miles from a beam reach to a run...with a completely different return course.They had to wait for a Lt.Maury who changed their guesstimates to predictability.

Lt. Maury, wind and current charts-----1847

Admiral Beaufort's Wind Scale started a new idea in eliminating blindfold navigation by recording wind direction and strength on the ocean voyages of English naval vessels.Another 50 years passed until an obscure stagecoach accident started a chain of events which made worldwide ocean weather predictions practical.

The accident broke the leg of line officer Lt.Matthew Maury which never fully healed. His new assignment in 1842 was to the Depot of Charts and Instruments,storing thousands of ship logs going back to the birth of our navy.He and his staff began a systematic study of weather,sea,and wind conditions published as Wind and Current Charts in 1847.The purpose...reduce sailing time around South America from one port to another,and from our east coast to the west coast.

The resulting *Pilot Charts* were produced monthly for many generations,now issued every four months.While they were simplified beginning in 1983,we show their older concept for a typical July at the start of the L.A.Transpac Race to Hawaii.

PILOT CHARTS of the ocean

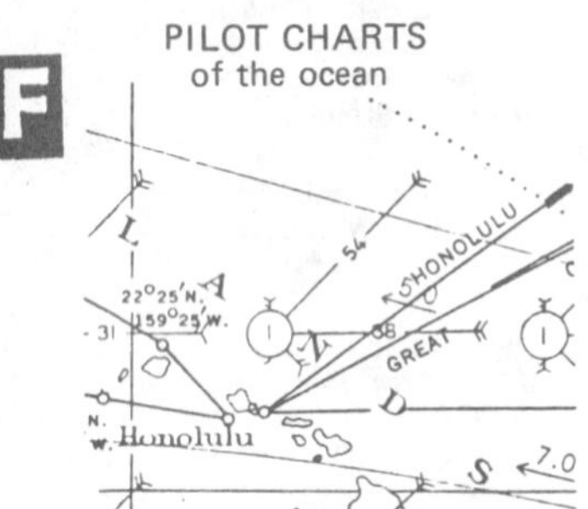
HONOLULU
GREAT
54
38
22°25'N.
159°25'W.
Honolulu
7.0

The ***wind rose,*** shown at left,which is located north of Honolulu indicates the prevailing winds predicted for that area of the ocean.

The ***arrows*** indicate the ***wind direction,*** while their ***length*** indicates the ***percentage of time it blows from that direction.*** The influence of the northeast trades becomes obvious with over 95% of the winds coming from a 90° easterly arc...without any westerly winds anticipated.

The number of ***feathers*** indicate the ***average Beaufort Wind Scale*** predicted.A force 4 is expected from the northeast 54% of the time,with a force 3 from the east 38% of the time.The 1% in the wind rose center indicates the ***percentage of recorded calms,*** light airs,and variables...with probably one day in three months.

downhill romp to Hawaii 14-25 days

Daily current drift and endless other details are included.At right you can see a couple of days after the L.A.Transpac Race begins the wind moves abeam,to a broad reach, then to a downhill sleigh ride romp with the NE Trades on the stern.You now learn the reason that the long waterline **ULDB surfing grayhounds** are in their home element to come in first.Since ULDB's are not designed by traditionalist's rules they make the Transpac Race Committee members job an uncomfortable one.

NE trade wind trap 20-25 day return.

You will face another sailing world when returning to the mainland as it is necessary to sail over 1000 miles closehauled due north...to break out of the NE Trades wind trap.After that it is easy to sail to Alaska as it is to Victoria,the Puget Sound,San Francisco,Los Angeles,Long Beach,San Diego,or Acapulco.

Poor performing ***sailboats not able to break out of this trap*** drift back to Hawaii, then to downwind islands such as Tahiti where the questionable bargains are for sale. A heavy-displacement 43' ketch didn't quite break out of the return trap when it turned east running into 5 hurricanes with the boat,sails,and rigging deteriorating daily. The boat was lifted to the deck level of a rescuing freighter so the crew could jump aboard.It was abandoned 100 miles off Mazatlan,all sails gone,a helpless derelict with no water and little food.I was stunned to find the owner next bought a 40' ULDB.

Pilot Chart source—

Pilot Charts of the **North Atlantic Ocean**,and **Pilot Charts** of the **Northern Pacific Ocean** are published three times a year.**Pilot Chart Atlases** are available for the South Pacific and Indian Oceans,and the South Atlantic and Central American Waters.Order charts of foreign waters,and the Pilot Charts desired from the—**DMAHC Topographic Center,Washington,D.C. 20315.**

Fogs ARE predictable.

"Hello,foggy isn't it!"

Fog potentials can be predicted when the humidity increases to the dew point.The questions are...will the fog be light or a peasouper and when will it arrive and when will it leave.Study text pages 218-219 to analyze fog predictability.

Eighteen months of continuous testing were required to understand the time-lag patterns to predict an approaching fog.Finally if we were on the ocean with students aboard as a peasoup fog moved in,we were there of my choice.

The pattern proved so successful it required seven years for a fog to move in so rapidly it wasn't anticipated on the indicator.The humidity needle rose so rapidly in the next minute it broke the indicator.A humidity/fog indicator is needed which is specifically designed for the sailboat and powerboat environment.

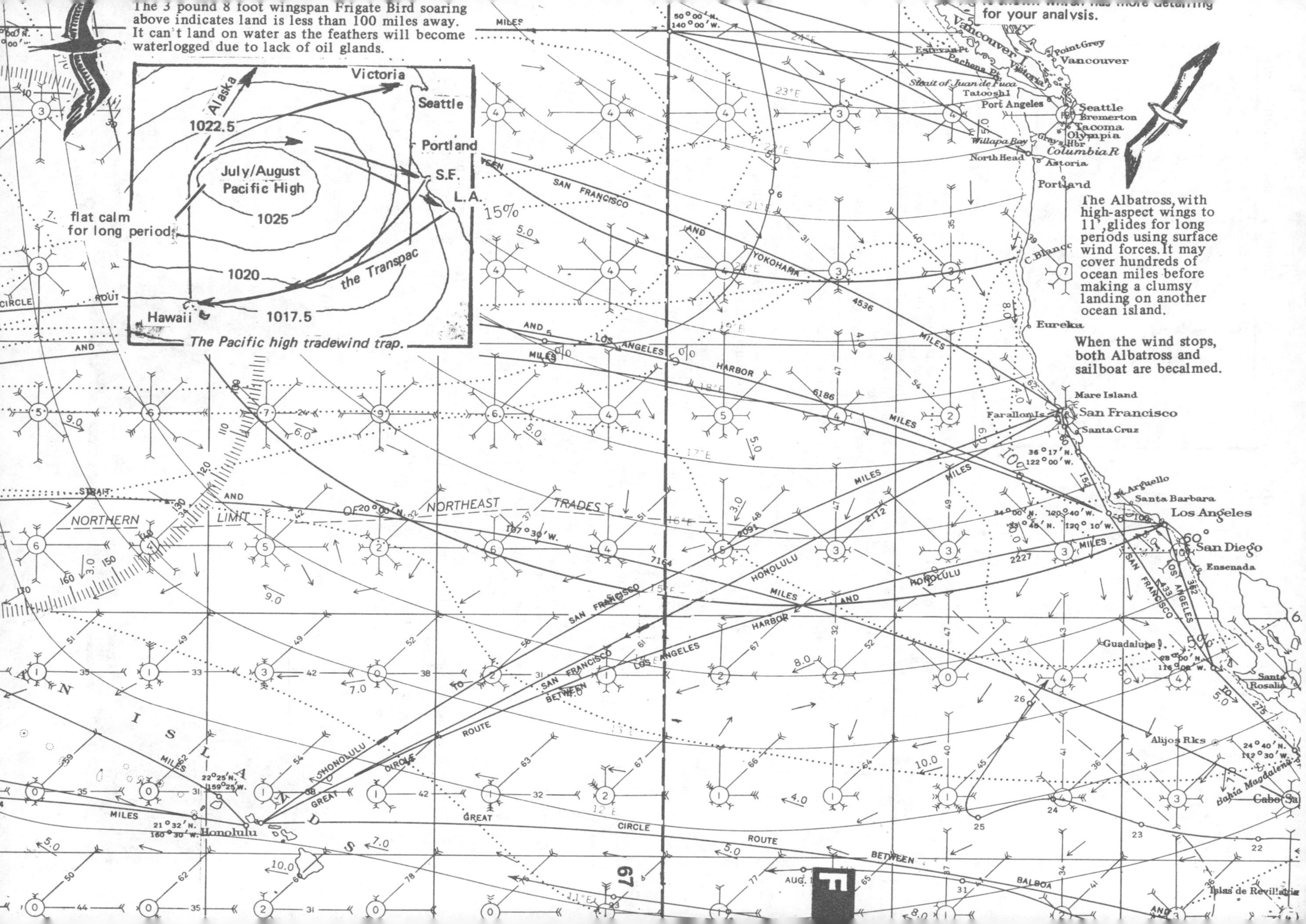

for your analysis.
The 3 pound 8 foot wingspan Frigate Bird soaring above indicates land is less than 100 miles away. It can't land on water as the feathers will become waterlogged due to lack of oil glands.
Victoria
Alaska
Seattle
Portland
S.F.
L.A.
1022.5
July/August
Pacific High
1025
1020
1017.5
the Transpac
flat calm
for long period
Hawaii
The Pacific high tradewind trap.
The Albatross, with high-aspect wings to 11', glides for long periods using surface wind forces. It may cover hundreds of ocean miles before making a clumsy landing on another ocean island.
When the wind stops, both Albatross and sailboat are becalmed.
Vancouver I.
Point Grey
Vancouver
Estevan Pt
Pachena Pt.
Victoria
Strait of Juan de Fuca
Tatoosh I
Port Angeles
Seattle
Bremerton
Tacoma
Olympia
Grays Hbr
Willapa Bay
North Head
Columbia R
Astoria
Portland
C. Blanco
Eureka
Mare Island
San Francisco
Farallon Is.
Santa Cruz
Pt. Arguello
Santa Barbara
Los Angeles
San Diego
Ensenada
Guadalupe I.
Santa Rosalia
Alijos Rks
Bahia Magdalena
Cabo San
Islas de Revillagigedo
Honolulu
50°00'N. 140°00'W.
36°17'N. 122°00'W.
34°00'N. 120°40'W.
33°49'N. 120°10'W.
28°00'N. 116°00'W.
24°40'N. 112°30'W.
22°25'N. 159°25'W.
21°32'N. 160°30'W.
20°00'N. 157°30'W.
NORTHERN LIMIT OF NORTHEAST TRADES
SAN FRANCISCO AND YOKOHAMA 4536 MILES
LOS ANGELES HARBOR 6186 MILES
SAN FRANCISCO HONOLULU 2112 MILES
LOS ANGELES AND HONOLULU 2227 MILES
SAN FRANCISCO HARBOR
LOS ANGELES
HONOLULU GREAT CIRCLE ROUTE
GREAT CIRCLE ROUTE BETWEEN
BALBOA AND
SAN FRANCISCO 433 LOS ANGELES 362
I S L A N D S
F

The WORLDWIDE DEVIL WINDS—when the desert winds are howling, and the moon is full...

The devil winds dance to a different wind god tune.
the high plateau
HIGH
LOW
Ventura
Santa Clara River
El Cajon Pass funnel
Los Angeles
Riverside
San Gorgonio Pass funnel
San Nicholas Island
Catalina Island

Devil winds have many local terms worldwide.

American Practical Navigator by Bowditch defines ***foehn*** as a dry wind with a downward component while a ***fall wind*** is a cold wind blowing down an incline. Local foehns are called ***Santa Anas*** or ***santanas*** (santanta-indian,***devil wind***), while the early Spanish called it ***devil winds from the north.*** The term is ***foehn*** in Switzerland,***pampero*** in Argentina,***mistral*** in the western Mediterranean,***chinook*** by the Rocky Mountain Indians,***tehuantepecer*** in Mexico and Central America,***williwa*** in Alaska,and by other local terms worldwide.The most descriptive common term we've found after facing it's wrath for over 35 years,often under sail...is the ***devil wind.***

Hot devil wind activities are often well reported on police blotters.

It's birth starts with a high pressure area in Nevada and nearby high desert areas from late September thru April. Prevailing westerlies in our area temporarily stop. A westward air flow begins thru the mountain passes down to the ocean. The early ***hot devil winds*** have a low 10% humidity,developing a buffer between the devil winds and the westerlies. Auto collisions increase,and friendly discussions may become fights. With no wind it is time to go fishing.

Cold devil winds cause considerable destruction to boats, trees, houses, campers, & trailers.

When the storm tracks move south later in November,the ***cold devil winds*** that average 30% humidity will overpower the buffer zone trying to uproot all trees and houses on its way to the ocean. It can be puffy ranging from weak to strong,it can last a few hours or a few days.

It is time to avoid making important decisions.

Major factors involved with the ***vicious,cold devil winds***—the high plateau temperature may be below zero,intense differences may exist between the high and low pressure areas,and it may follow on the heels of a major storm system moving thru. Weak moist air currents begin to trickle across the high plateau. They lose moisture as they go uphill to funnel thru mountain passes. They gain speed tumbling down these passes which compresses and warms the air* 20-30 °.

A Catalina Island devil wind warning is needed.

It is time for boats to leave the eastern side of Catalina Island which may become a ***vicious windward shore IF the cold devil winds hit.*** Clues—30% humidity,the weather is cold,and visibility due to strong winds is so clear you can see snow on the mountains surrounding the LA Basin.

the Alaskan devil wind

Alaska has violent 60-100 knot ***cold devil winds*** as they increase in speed when their masses pour down the mountainsides,especially canyon mouths. Dig anchors deep on shore, AVOID tying to trees which can be uprooted with the winds blowing your boat and tree out to sea.

positive ions are bad guys

negative ions are good guys

The compression rapidly warms these winds as the humidity drops to build a **high positive ion content** which causes rapid chemical and electrical impulse changes in the brain as they replace the **negative ion.** This intensifies itself when the full moon peaks at the same time as both diminish the brain's analytical ability for 8 to 40 hours. This is the time to postpone critical decisions until the brain adapts to the positive ion charge. Watch dogs,cats,and horses for diminished coordination. This is the time suicides escalate and friendly parties can change to brawls. Personality changes are interesting to watch when the full moon and/or devil winds move in.

Our continuous testing over several years found that a good quality relative-humidity indicator is the best tool to predict that either a ***warm or cold devil wind*** is moving in following wind warnings that alert camper and trailer owners to avoid windy canyon passes.

**Air is a gas that is warmed 1° F for each 185' of descent due to compression.*

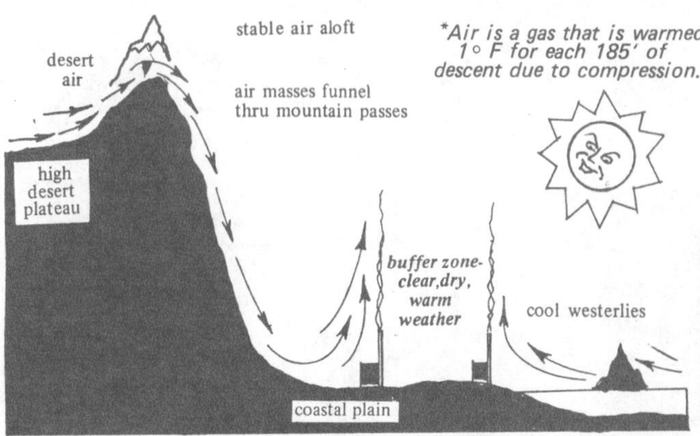

desert air
stable air aloft
air masses funnel thru mountain passes
high desert plateau
buffer zone-clear,dry, warm weather
cool westerlies
coastal plain

Weak ***warm devil winds*** with a buffer.

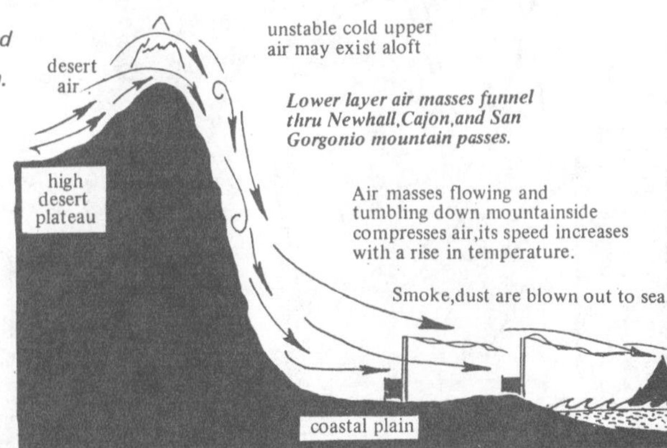

desert air
unstable cold upper air may exist aloft
Lower layer air masses funnel thru Newhall,Cajon,and San Gorgonio mountain passes.
high desert plateau
Air masses flowing and tumbling down mountainside compresses air,its speed increases with a rise in temperature.
Smoke,dust are blown out to sea.
coastal plain

The cold vicious devil winds.

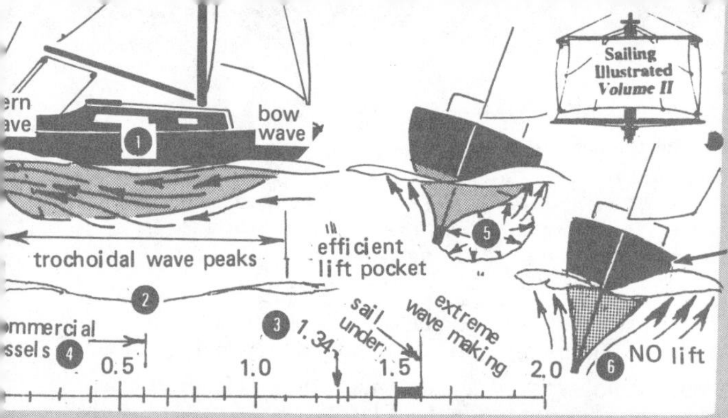
Sailing Illustrated Volume II
ern
ave
bow
wave
1
trochoidal wave peaks
efficient
lift pocket
5
2
sail under
extreme wave making
mmercial
ssels 4
3 1.34
0.5
1.0
1.5
2.0
6 NO lift

Displacement HULL SPEED Theory.

The HULL SPEED RATIO of large heavy displacement hulls is based on the *dynamic moving* WATERLINE LENGTH distance ① between bow and stern wave peaks. These coincide with SPEED of the length ② between equal peaks of ocean TROCHOIDAL WAVES.

Trochoidal theoretical wave peak speeds coinciding with the $1.34\sqrt{WL}$ heavy displacement hull speed–

20.0 feet–6 knots	45.0 feet–9 knots
27.2 feet–7 knots	55.6 feet–10 knots
35.6 feet–8 knots	67.3 feet–11 knots

The MAXIMUM efficient speed a heavy hull can push itself effortlessly and efficiently thru the water with a ③ $1.34\sqrt{WL}$ SPEED-LENGTH ratio.

It can go a little faster up to $1.5\sqrt{WL}$ at which the hull can't go faster. If the wind still increases, it will blow a spinnaker, or the mast, sails, and rigging will go faster than the hull...called dismasting.

The large square rigger wanted to maintain the $1.34\sqrt{WL}$ speed with bow and stern wave trap. It will begin to sink at $1.5\sqrt{WL}$ as the wave peaks spread, while at $1.6\sqrt{WL}$ it may be sailed under if sail can't be reduced to slow the vessel.

FRICTIONAL RESISTANCE is the other side of the story. Water hardens as a vessel goes faster, the reason supertankers, **page140**, travel under 15 knots, $0.6\sqrt{WL}$ with minimum resistance ④ to save fuel. A small planing powerboat starts to rise bodily after $2.5\sqrt{WL}$ climbing onto a full plane due to lift provided by the water hardening from $3.5\sqrt{WL}$ to $4.0\sqrt{WL}$.

The MEDIUM displacement Cal 40 page 11, introduced downwind surfing for short periods on the Hawaiian Transpac due to good bottom lifting action to reduce water friction which increased surfing speed. Sailors began to extend these surfing periods and speeds with experience.

ULDB's may not point quite as high as IOR boats, pg. J 15, but with light, lean, long-waterline hulls they can turn to a reach or run in a force 5 and above to surf or lift for long periods, pg. 133, as they are designed to make the most of water resistance/ lift.

Light dinghies, page14, have hulls narrowing forward for weatherliness, broadening aft of the chain plates to a wide stable bottom with a sharp transom chine for planing lift. They are light, rising easily as the water hardens for a speed increase, text pgs. 140-143.

There are considerable variables with LIGHT and MEDIUM displacement hulls. My experience is with the Cal 25, page 16, which surfs easily, page 77, with good bottom designed for lift, plus the trapped pressure pocket ⑤ shown above.

the heavy displacement hull
speed/length ratio: 0, 0.5, 1.0, 1.34, 1.5, 1.6, 2.0, 2.5, 3.0, 3.5, 4.0
frictional resistance: 3-4 lbs., 10-15 lbs., 30-40 lbs.
water resistance doubles
heavy wave making / frictional resistance–lbs. per ton of disp.
surfing begins
all-out planing / water lb. pressure 14 times that of 1.0

● SMALL heavy displacement SAILBOATS–MAYBE group.

We report on *page 77*, our heavy 24 footer surfing for 14 miles with speedometer hard on the 10 knot peg while reaching due to a ⑤ trapped water lift pocket. A heavy narrow-beam hull without this lift nor speed increase may have had torn sails or a dismasting.

On the same page we report the heavy MINKA peaking up to 10 knots on a run with the stern wave cresting way aft of the stern while the bow was almost sailed under.

The most critical situation was a 30' wooden gaff rigger sailing downwind being caught on an all-out plane with stresses that can never be computed which could have exploded the hull if it had maintained that speed.

Analyze the variables in the MAYBE group so you have an educated guess when to REEF...or when to let it ROMP on a reach to a broad reach. It is easier to shake out an unneeded reef than to make one too late.

PATTY CAT I

WIND POWER vs HULL SPEED

Smaller day catamarans gain their speed from hull/water lift to reduce friction...plus twin hull leverage.

⑦ WATER PRESSURE RELEASE ...$4.0\sqrt{WL}$?

The Rudy Choy designed big cats have long, slim displacement hulls designed to RELEASE pressure from under the hulls...also eliminating the monohull bow and stern ① wave trap.

The big cats depend on beam length-ratio LEVERAGE stability, permitting weight reduction. The twin hulls float higher on the water with minimum displacement, minimum water pressure, minimal frontal area, and less parasitic drag.

The SOFT WATER SUPPORT produces a comfortable ride under ocean conditions. Handling is easy at upper speeds to 20 knots with minimum wake...except the 65' SEASMOKE had a roostertail at 24 knots.

Patty Cat I below, came to an untimely end at 20 knots or so when port tacked by a submerged coral reef.

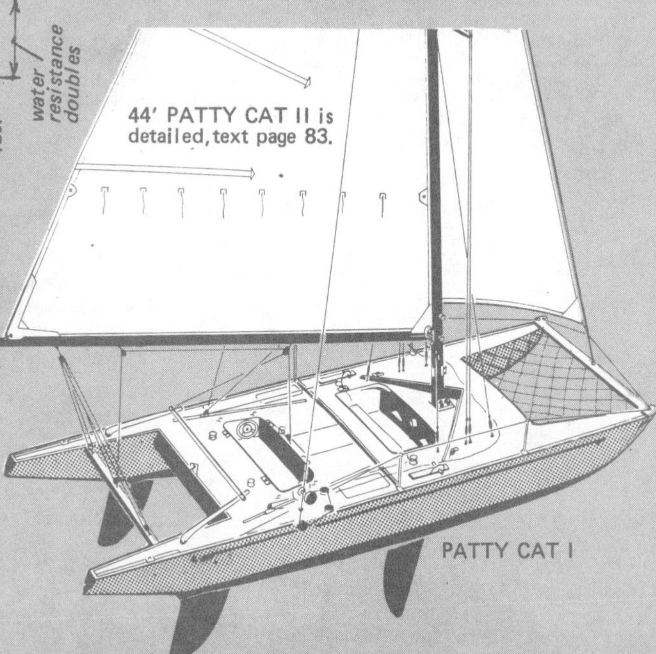
44' PATTY CAT II is detailed, text page 83.
PATTY CAT I

G

Sailing
Illustrated
Volume II

A MEMORY to LAST a LIFETIME...that *FIRST BIG SPLASH.*

Don't let a dinghy intimidate you.

the wind machine hot rods

The ultimate sailing thrill is a dinghy with spray flying in a strong gusty wind, with everything on the ragged edge. The sailor has to know his boat, and its equipment must be in good condition. He must know the capabilities and limitations of his craft, to adequately reach and hold its maximum performance potentials. This is not the world for a sailor with a heavy hand...or the weak of heart.

There are a variety of daggerboard and centerboard performance levels differing from Optimist to Flying Dutchman. Their common denominator, they can capsize.

self-rescuing, sail-out potentials

Several of our recovery patterns follow that of a Lido 14, a good, steady performer that doesn't have the ***self-rescuing, sail-out capabilities*** of later classes. I haven't been involved in a capsize though teaching on over 40 Lido's. Almost all of them had considerable water taken aboard during their sailing lessons to expose students to the capabilities and limitations of the Lido in a spirited breeze.

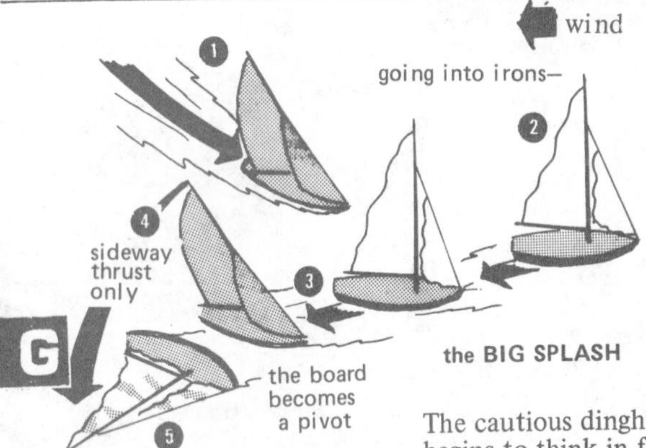

wind
going into irons—
1
2
3
4
sideway thrust only
5
the board becomes a pivot
the BIG SPLASH

one more time-

Majority of dinghy upsets occur in a good wind when the operator is scared, cautious and confused as his boat changes tack too slowly (1) then ***goes into irons.*** Rudder and steering controls disappear (2) as the boat drifts backwards. When the sails fill suddenly, ***a sideway thrust develops*** instead of a forward lift (4), ***as the hull trips over the cb or db, causing a rapid capsize*** (5) ***Maximum speed with minimum rudder drag must be maintained at all times when coming about in a spirited wind.*** The board boat has to change tack rapidly by ***backing the jib*** continually when coming about so the boat is underway on the new tack before it comes to a screeching halt. If this happens and the boat runs out of momentum it will go into irons. As it starts to drift backward the sails fill and the boat trips over its board. Backing the jib is an overcorrection on the C 15, ***page 36.***

The cautious dinghy sailor faces an unexpected swim in a spirited wind until he begins to think in flying terms that it is necessary to maintain speed for control and for maneuverability...you don't fly low and slow if you want to be safe.

other upset causes

Other upset causes are a boat heeling excessively, equipment failure, and/or the operator is not paying enough attention to changing wind conditions. ***Dinghy sailors beware—*** a large sailboat upwind can momentarily block your wind, then as it passes you are hit with its wind funnel in a strong wind that can rapidly flip your boat. *Was it intentional????*

•

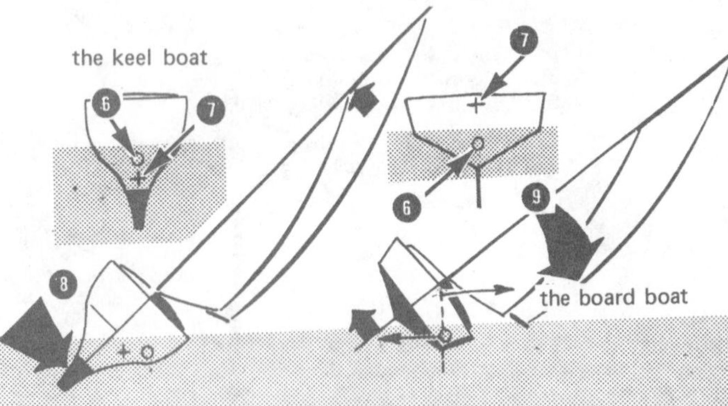

the keel boat
6
7
8
9
the board boat

(6) C of B—*Center of Buoyancy*
(7) C of G—*Center of Gravity*

A keelboat C of G is below the C of B so that in a knockdown the C of G hardens to help the boat right itself...or have a 360° roll to become stable.

This is reversed in a daggerboard or centerboard boat as the righting force weakens then disappears around 45° with the changing C of B and C of G making the boat more stable in an upset.

This is hardly the time to ask a new crew member if he can swim. He must be comfortable in the water to help you recover your sailboat so the both of you can continue the sail.

•

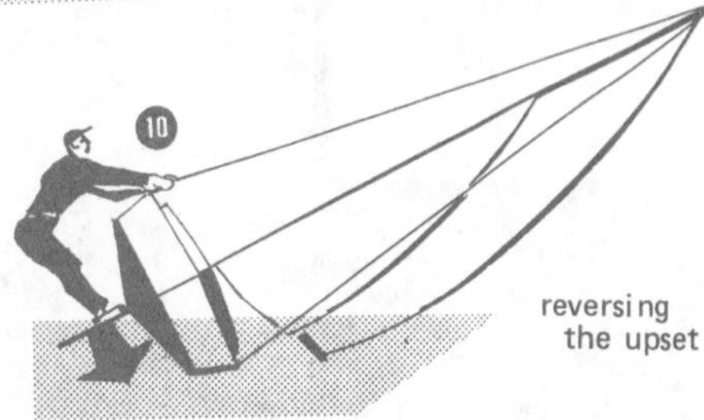

10
reversing the upset

Some sailboats upset slowly in a knockdown wanting to stop at 90°, while others such as the local Lehman 12, an open catboat, rolls so fast it doesn't stop until it turns turtle, or 180°.

If a dinghy exceeds its optimum heel angle underway when a strong puff hits with a rapidly disappearing righting force...reverse the process with a nimble crew member jumping out on the board (10) to reverse the procedure, helping the righting force. He should jump back in the boat before the force is overcompensated with the boat rolling to capsize on its other side...*this is REAL sailing!*

TILT
Humbug!

RECOVERY FROM a KNOCKDOWN...and TURNING TURTLE

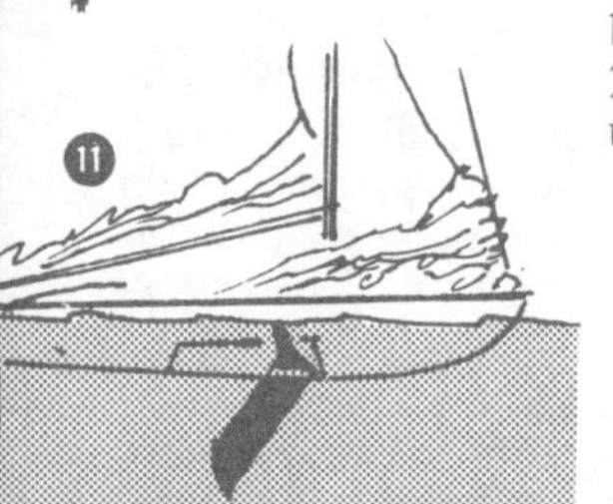
11

The March harbor water was cold when a Lido flipped.The sails were dropped,the boat was righted,and three spirited bailers were soon at work.The boat was still awash 20 minutes later...with water pouring out of the top of the centerboard trunk still under water,so ***plug the db or cb trunk top opening before bailing begins.***

It was one of those days- three new sailors launched a catboat that promptly flipped. A nearby harbor patrol boat towed it back to the dock where after righting,bailing, and sail raising,the boat left the dock...to flip again.The patient harbor patrol crew towed it back to the dock a second time for righting,bailing,and sail raising.The catboat left the dock a third time with a 180° capsize a few seconds later the metal dagger-board sinking to the bottom in 20' of water.***Secure daggerboards with lanyards.***

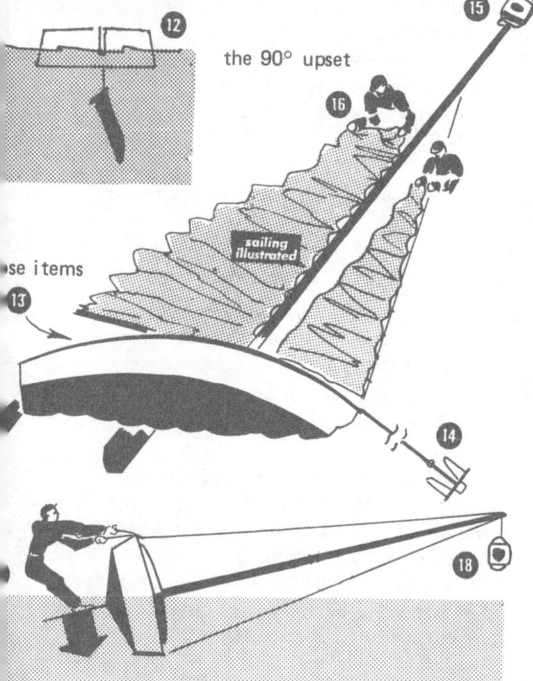
12
the 90° upset
15
16
sailing illustrated
se items
13
14

The dinghy at left has taken a 90° knockdown.The first job is to check the condition of crew members,then lash all objects to the boat that can sink or float away.The next job is to ease the main halyard.

Swim to the top of the mast,unshackle the main halyard then ***secure a cushion or dock fender to the halyard snap.*** With the cushion or fender at masthead to reduce chances of a 180° upset,drop the sails,right the boat,begin bailing,then drop and retrieve the cushion or fender,secure halyard to mainsail.

Other considerations...drop an anchor especially in a current, **page 58,** to avoid being dismasted if the boat drifts into shallow water.Again,plug cb or db trunk before bailing begins.

When a 180° upset or ***turtle*** occurs,the first job is to check the condition of crew members,the second,***release main sheet and jib sheet all the way*** on a sloop,or the mainsheet on a catboat,an excellent reason for easy to release jam cleats.

If the sheets aren't released all the way,the tremendous water pressure against the sails during a 180° upset recovery can often cause a dismasting.

Rig a line across the bottom of a boat (20) ***so your weight can be used as a righting lever.*** After releasing the sheets the boat should be easy to right,then lower the sails,plug the db or cb trunk,and commence bailing.

Fresh water weight averages 8.3 lbs. per gallon,regular gasoline, 6.6 lbs. per gallon,and diesel oil,7.3 lbs. per gallon.

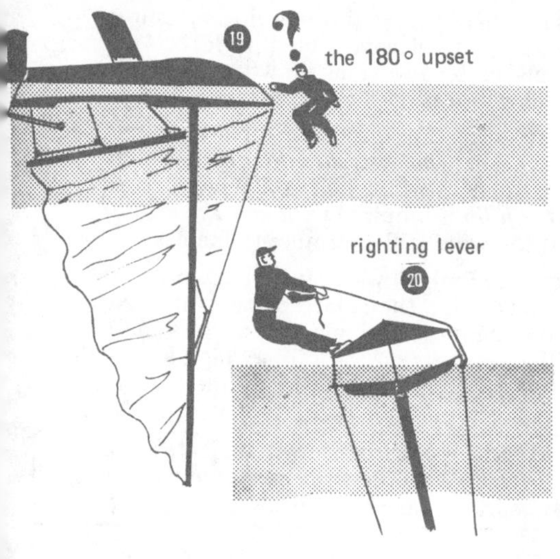
18
19
the 180° upset
righting lever
20

The sailing lesson on an open 17' dinghy had been stimulating to help its owner recover from a broach and dismasting on his previous sail.He was preparing to lift his boat out of the water as I left to walk to my car...which was interrupted with a loud crash.He had forgotten to bail the five or so gallons of water aboard,becoming movable ballast as the boat was raised.This snapped a lifting line with the boat crashing to the dock below. ***How many pounds of movable ballast were involved?***

Open dinghies. Classes such as Sabot,Penguin,and Thistle in an upset usually need to be taken to shallow water,or alongside a dock or larger craft for righting,bailing,and sail raising. Their sailing as a result should be limited to protected areas.

Decked-over dinghies. The Lido 14,older Finn,Lightning and Snipe classes in moderate weather may be righted in deeper water after an upset.They may be bailed,boarded,and the sails raised to continue your sail.

Self-rescuing dinghies. Newer Finn,Snipe,and Lightning classes plus the 420,470,505,and C 15 have built-in sealed flotation. *Consider a dinghy with sail-out capabilities* that can be righted and sailed with water draining out the stern openings.

WIND FORCE produces WAVE ACTION...and SAIL LOADING.

wind force vs sail loading

Nature has organized visual patterns that you can apply to sailing. *Wind is an invisible ACTION force that creates an opposing REACTION force* which is visible on the water surface.

Study wave pressure patterns until they become second nature *to anticipate when to reef or reduce sail area...and when to increase sail area.*

The patterns at right were developed by Admiral Beaufort in the late 1700's to be reported continuously in the log of every British Admiralty vessel. These recorded wind patterns provided predictable lengths of time required for voyages in British naval vessels, plus monthly changing variables, page 66.

Water surface disturbance becomes a visual wind force when the pressure has a chance to develop patterns over a large area or fetch of open ocean.

The visual water patterns are next calibrated into approximate pounds of pressure per square foot on page 75..We have slightly altered the wave patterns, especially forces 5 and 6, so they are easier to apply to your sailing from dinghies to large sailboats.→

The wind force scale is easy to learn. Some students create problems when taking a shortcut trying to substitute land terms of miles or knots. Wind force numbers should also be added to wind speed dial indicators...see scale at left.

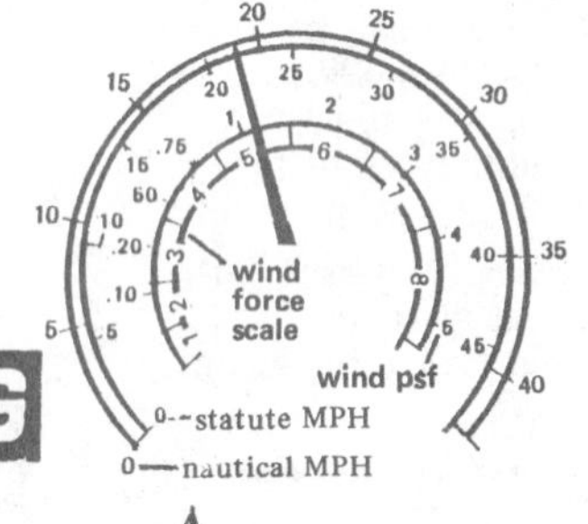
wind force scale
wind psf
statute MPH
nautical MPH

The wind pressure patterns an ocean sailor will be putting to use are shown on the facing page. The patterns are easy to remember–***wind forces 1 and 2–RIPPLES... wind forces 3 and 4–WAVES...wind forces 5 and 6–WHITECAPS...and for force 7 we face WHITECAPS and LARGE WAVES.***

Force 1 is indicated *by spotty ripple patches,* while a weak, slightly stronger force 2 will show *an overall pattern of light ripples.*

As wind strength continues to increase, ripples begin to stretch out into small waves indicating a force 3, while more wind produces *longer waves.* indicating a force 4.

A *few whitecaps develop* from a weak to a mid force 5. ***The white cap count will increase considerably*** in an upper force 5 to a mid force 6...though the vertical wave ***height*** is usually not much more than an upper force 5.

Wave patterns ***spread out as the waves grow much taller with many whitecaps*** in a force 7. If the wind still increases, the wave spread and vertical height become increasingly difficult to visually evaluate, for example–

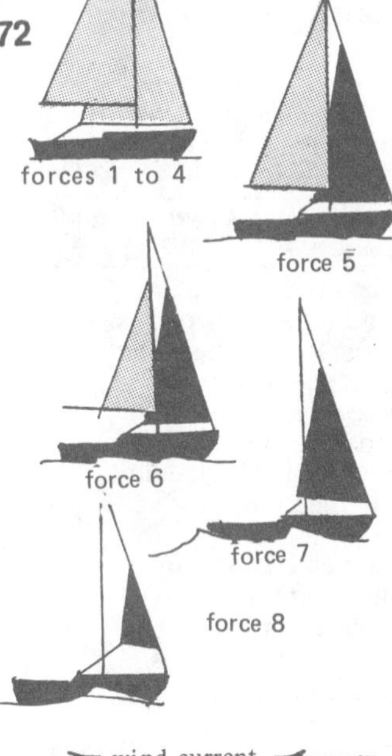
forces 1 to 4
force 5
force 6
force 7
force 8

11/13/83. We witnessed the change to force 8 on the 31' *Minka,* pages 55 and 77, with the wind indicator the last hour averaging 35-43 knots. Rudder loading increased with ***heavy spray continually breaking aboard...hitting hard as buckshot.*** During the last mile before entering Oxnard Harbor we paralleled the coast with surf breaking 30' to 40' high a couple of boat lengths to starboard.

The Oxnard jetty was a seething cauldron of white wave action as we entered under diesel and small main steadying sail. Our other choice, head for sea for a beating under bare poles. Since all of our clothes had been soaked in three days of cold stormy weather, a laundromat and dry martinis overruled the risks of a wild breaking jetty.

After you can visualize the wave patterns, translate the wind forces into pressures per square foot. It will be normal to carry as much sail as possible thru force 4... while at mid force 5, the gennie is often replaced by a working jib when the wind pressure averaging *one pound per square foot* is reached.

The ***wind pressure doubles at mid force 6,*** requiring the force 5 sail area to be reduced by half to stay in the normal operating range. The ***wind pressure doubles again at mid force 7*** with a sloop operating under a strong working jib. If the wind increases to double the pressure or force...***a stout storm jib*** is required ***with half the area of the working jib.*** All sail must be dropped if the wind still continues to increase.

Add 1, 2, or 3 additional wind forces on protected inland waters which are not large enough to develop wave patterns of the open ocean...though the same wind pressures exist. *ALSO*–stand on a nearby hill overlooking protected inland reservoirs and lakes to analyze varied wind/wave patterns. Sailing students on 11,000 feet high Lake Dillon in Colorado, were soon able to recognize five different wind forces on the reservoir, then analyze the causes and locations due to canyon funnels and protecting hills.

→ wind current ←

→ wind current →

When ***a CURRENT opposes the wind,*** wave surface disturbance will indicate a higher wind force than exists. When ***WIND and CURRENT go the same direction,*** the wind will be considerably stronger than the wave surface patterns indicate.

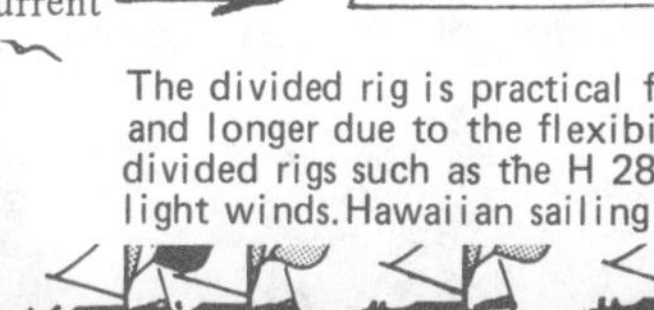

The divided rig is practical for sailboats over 36', becoming excellent for those 40' and longer due to the flexibility of sail combinations. While I've enjoyed sailing on divided rigs such as the H 28 yawl,, the performance seemed questionable in our light winds. Hawaiian sailing friends recommend the H 28 for their strong winds.

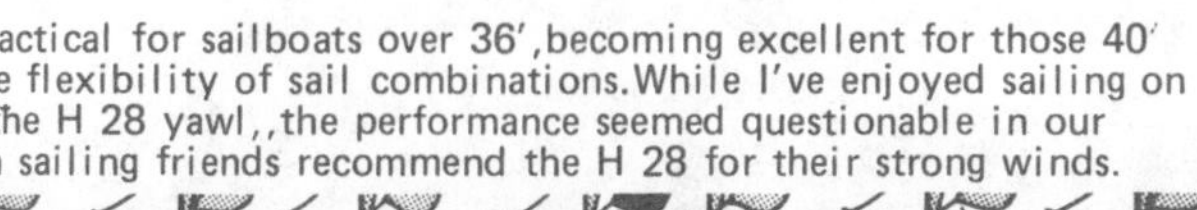

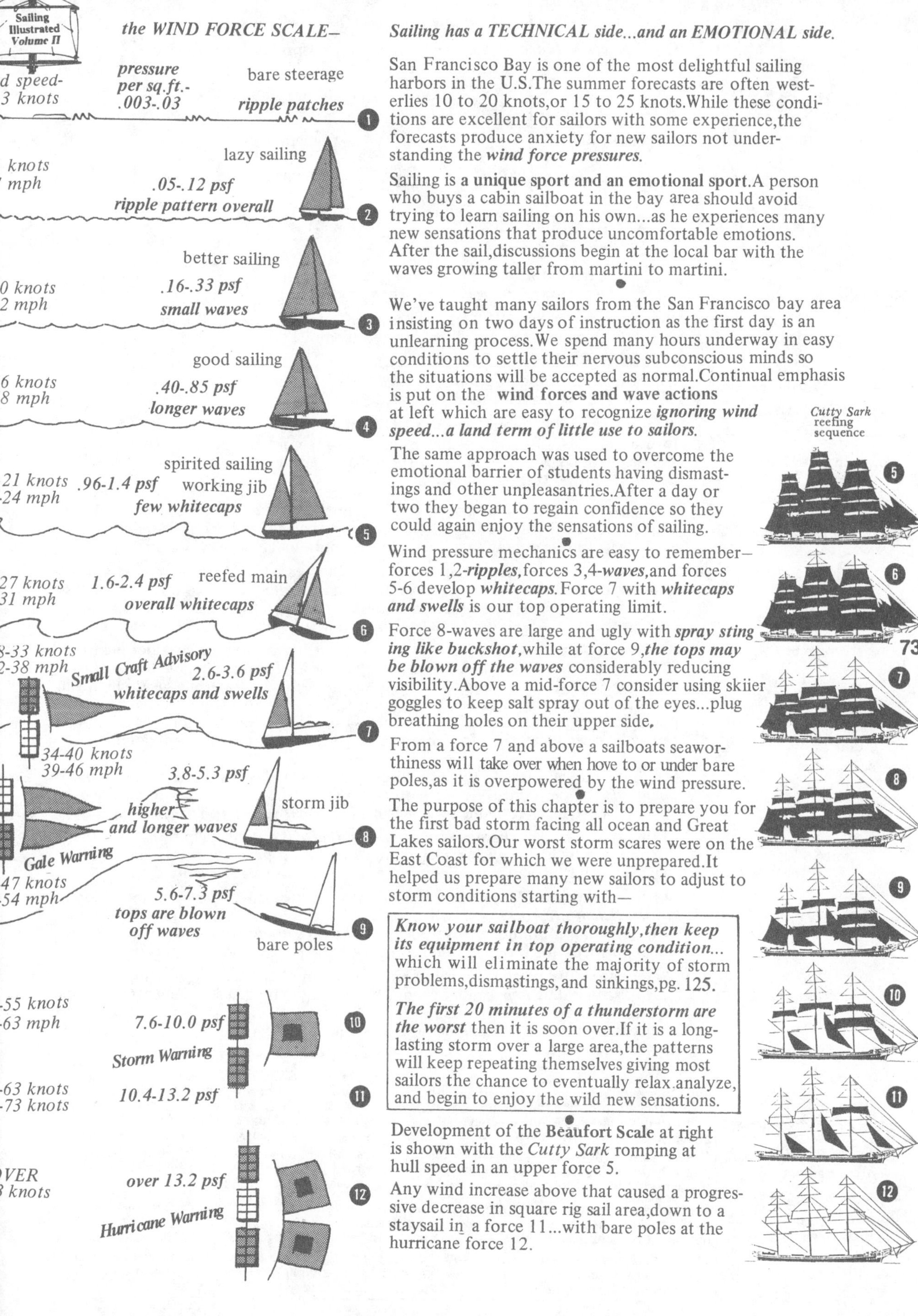

Sailing Illustrated Volume II
the WIND FORCE SCALE–
d speed-
3 knots
pressure per sq.ft.-
.003-.03
bare steerage
ripple patches
1
knots
mph
lazy sailing
.05-.12 psf
ripple pattern overall
2
0 knots
2 mph
better sailing
.16-.33 psf
small waves
3
6 knots
8 mph
good sailing
.40-.85 psf
longer waves
4
-21 knots
-24 mph
.96-1.4 psf
spirited sailing
working jib
few whitecaps
5
27 knots
31 mph
1.6-2.4 psf
reefed main
overall whitecaps
6
8-33 knots
2-38 mph
Small Craft Advisory
2.6-3.6 psf
whitecaps and swells
7
34-40 knots
39-46 mph
3.8-5.3 psf
higher and longer waves
storm jib
8
Gale Warning
-47 knots
-54 mph
5.6-7.3 psf
tops are blown off waves
bare poles
9
-55 knots
-63 mph
7.6-10.0 psf
Storm Warning
10
-63 knots
-73 knots
10.4-13.2 psf
11
VER
3 knots
over 13.2 psf
Hurricane Warning
12
Cutty Sark reefing sequence
5
6
7
8
9
10
11
12

Sailing has a TECHNICAL side...and an EMOTIONAL side.

San Francisco Bay is one of the most delightful sailing harbors in the U.S.The summer forecasts are often westerlies 10 to 20 knots,or 15 to 25 knots.While these conditions are excellent for sailors with some experience,the forecasts produce anxiety for new sailors not understanding the ***wind force pressures.***

Sailing is **a unique sport and an emotional sport.**A person who buys a cabin sailboat in the bay area should avoid trying to learn sailing on his own...as he experiences many new sensations that produce uncomfortable emotions. After the sail,discussions begin at the local bar with the waves growing taller from martini to martini.

•

We've taught many sailors from the San Francisco bay area insisting on two days of instruction as the first day is an unlearning process. We spend many hours underway in easy conditions to settle their nervous subconscious minds so the situations will be accepted as normal.Continual emphasis is put on the **wind forces and wave actions** at left which are easy to recognize ***ignoring wind speed...a land term of little use to sailors.***

The same approach was used to overcome the emotional barrier of students having dismastings and other unpleasantries.After a day or two they began to regain confidence so they could again enjoy the sensations of sailing.

•

Wind pressure mechanics are easy to remember–forces 1,2-***ripples,***forces 3,4-***waves,***and forces 5-6 develop ***whitecaps.*** Force 7 with ***whitecaps and swells*** is our top operating limit.

Force 8-waves are large and ugly with ***spray stinging like buckshot,***while at force 9,***the tops may be blown off the waves*** considerably reducing visibility.Above a mid-force 7 consider using skiier goggles to keep salt spray out of the eyes...plug breathing holes on their upper side.

From a force 7 and above a sailboats seaworthiness will take over when hove to or under bare poles,as it is overpowered by the wind pressure.

•

The purpose of this chapter is to prepare you for the first bad storm facing all ocean and Great Lakes sailors.Our worst storm scares were on the East Coast for which we were unprepared.It helped us prepare many new sailors to adjust to storm conditions starting with–

Know your sailboat thoroughly,then keep its equipment in top operating condition... which will eliminate the majority of storm problems,dismastings,and sinkings,pg. 125.

The first 20 minutes of a thunderstorm are the worst then it is soon over.If it is a long-lasting storm over a large area,the patterns will keep repeating themselves giving most sailors the chance to eventually relax.analyze, and begin to enjoy the wild new sensations.

•

Development of the **Beaufort Scale** at right is shown with the *Cutty Sark* romping at hull speed in an upper force 5.

Any wind increase above that caused a progressive decrease in square rig sail area,down to a staysail in a force 11...with bare poles at the hurricane force 12.

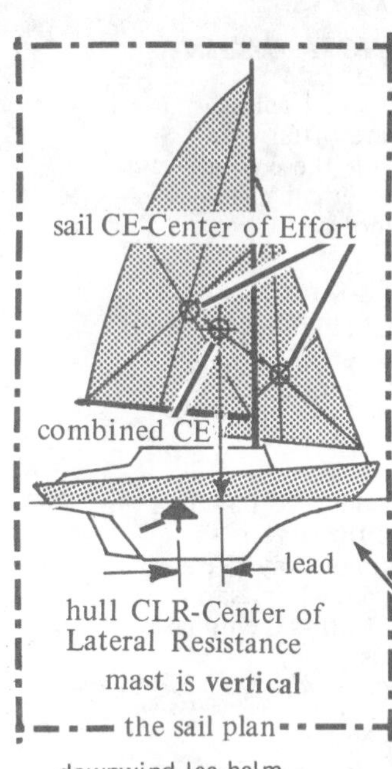
sail CE-Center of Effort
combined CE
lead
hull CLR-Center of Lateral Resistance
mast is vertical
the sail plan

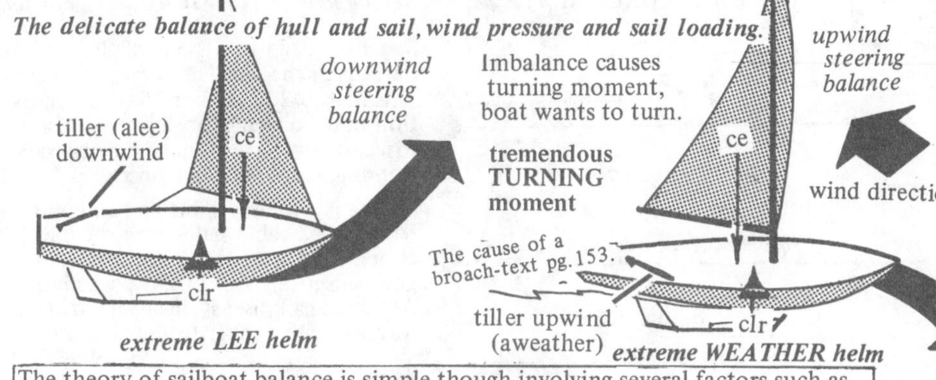
The delicate balance of hull and sail, wind pressure and sail loading.
downwind steering balance
Imbalance causes turning moment, boat wants to turn.
upwind steering balance
tiller (alee) downwind
ce
tremendous TURNING moment
wind direction
The cause of a broach-text pg.153.
clr
tiller upwind (aweather)
extreme LEE helm
extreme WEATHER helm

The theory of sailboat balance is simple,though involving several factors such as... **trim the sails** (Center of Effort),and **trim the moveable weight** (Center of Lateral Resistance), to **balance the rudder** so a sailboat is theoretically able to sail itself on various courses...and in a variety of wind conditions.

Sailboat plans *show a sailboat vertical with the boom amidship.* As a result the CE and CLR will not be in alignment,the difference between the two is called the ***lead.***

downwind lee helm
upwind weather helm

A sailboat under jib alone develops **DOWNWIND helm** steering since the CE is forward of the CLR. A sloop under mainsail only normally develops **UPWIND helm** steering with CE aft of the CLR as the unbalanced rudder wants to steer the sailboat up into the wind,then go into irons.

•

wind,hull,heel factor variables

The wind force or pressure coverage of the previous page is expanded in depth to add the **CE/ CLR balance factors** with the **heel angle/lee bow pressure wave** for a 24' keel sailboat operating with a 300 psf optimum efficient wind pressure.

torces 1–4

Carry as much sail area as possible from wind forces 1 thru 4 as the boat sail area is **underpowered.** Moveable weight on this kind of sailboat should be on the low side with a 4-5 degree heel to help balance the CE/CLR. As the wind increases,move the crew to the high side to limit the heel angle under 18 degrees for self steering.

force 5

normal heel limits

At wind force 5 the wind pressure heel angle begins to produce **weather helm/ rudder drag** ...which is compensated for by changing from the gennie to the working jib.The heel angle is now producing considerable **lee bow wave pressure** which will require the crew weight to be carried on the high side...to again keep the heel angle under 18 degrees.An adequately balanced sloop or two master under these conditions can often steer themselves for considerable periods with a shock cord dampener.

•

fishermans reef—backwinding mainsail

As the wind increases to a lower force 6 the ***main sheet is eased to backwind the mainsail....*** or periodically released,then sheeted back immediately to release excess wind pressure loads to reduce weather helm.This is called a ***fishermans reef.***

force 6—mainsail reef

If the wind increases ***the mainsail should be reefed.*** This will help to balance the CE and CLR,reducing excess heel,minimizing the strong lee bow wave pressure. This will help to balance the helm by reducing excess weather helm drag.

force 7—working jib

We found that the CE and CLR move somewhat forward of the mast on a sloop in a force 7.A ***stout working jib*** will carry all the wind pressure a sloop can carry without being continuously overpowered.***The jib should be tacked 12" to 18" above the deck*** for waves to drain overboard that protects the jib and its rigging.

•

water density vs air density

Water has 800 times the density of air with a foot of rudder drag is comparable to 800 feet of sail air drag.Any rudder change beyond a temporary steering correction,such as a constant weather helm drag loading,will reduce boat speed as well as causing unnecessary strain on the rudder and its support,comparable to driving a car with the hand brake on.

Heavy weather operation...wheel,tiller,transom

steering wheel vs the tiller

Pooped—a heavy wave breaks aboard over the stern when sailing downwind in a storm.

April 1979,time 1700,we were aboard a heavy displacement 32' IOR boat sailing downwind from San Francisco under bare poles with engine on,the lower force 9 producing huge waves The sky was blue and the sun bright shining on the tall rocky cliffs of the Ship's Graveyard two miles on our port beam.We faced five unexpected and unusual equipment failures so far on this new boat,it had broached once,and with Vern Withun now on the wheel we were being pooped for the third time. **"Duck Vern"**, I hollered.He started to turn sideways to look up at the green wave just beginning to break three feet above his head.He fortunately turned just enough to avoid being slammed into the wheel which without such a warning would have been a bone crusher.

vertical transom

the reverse transom in heavy weather-

The waves were continually going faster downwind than the boat. We constantly pumped water out of the cockpit though it had a narrow,vertical transom.If it had a reverse transom,waves would have bounced off the transom into the cockpit with continual flooding and erratic steering.

the tiller-a personal preference

The tiller is preferred with waves going faster downwind than the boat. The helmsman can look aft as easily as forward to anticipate waves coming aboard,reducing the chance of broken bones.The tiller has less steering failure potentials than the wheel...especially in heavy weather sailing.

Square riggers with small rudders steered mostly with sails, pages 51, 154-- so ***balance your sailboat airfoils and waterfoils... to balance your helm.***

200 sq.ft mainsail

180 sq.ft. gennie

induce a lee bow wave

ce

ower Force 5

tiller amidship

crew weight amidsh

clr

carry maximum sail area

balanced rudder-a happy sailboat

Balance of deep keel monohulls and large multihulls can be very delicate. **Tuning** is require so when **variables** of **sail trim, weight trim,** and **lee bow pressure** come together the **result** is a **balanced rudder** with the boat able to sail itself in a **variety of wind conditions.** If momentarily overpowered from a beam reach to closehauled...temporary weather helm protects the sailboat until a correction is made,or the wind eases.

sail area	balance	heel angle
wind pressure	▲	lee bow wave

Hull balance steering forces are shown on a 24' full keel sailboat operating at its best or optimum efficiency of approximately 300 pounds of continuous wind pressure.

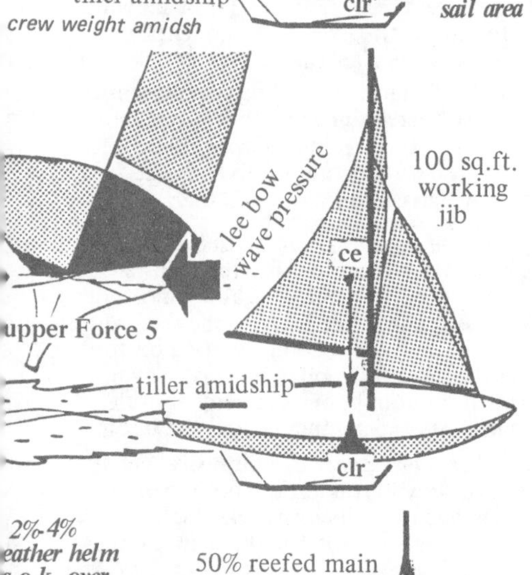

lee bow wave pressure
100 sq.ft. working jib
ce
upper Force 5
tiller amidship
clr

- **Force 2** (.05-.12 psf) .10 psf x 380 sq.ft.--38 lbs.pressure

The sailboat is underpowered in forces 1 and 2,use the largest gennie upwind...and downwind,the largest drifter.

An upright keel sailboat will have to heel first before it can start moving. Keep **weight on the low side** to induce **heel** so when a **puff moves in**,the wind **pressure is immediately translated into forward drive.**

- **Force 3** (.16-.33)sf) .30 psf x 380 sq.ft.--114 lbs.pressure
- **Force 4** (.40-.85 psf) .70 psf x 380 sq.ft.--266 lbs. pressure
- **Force 5** (.96-1.4 psf) 1.0 psf x 380 sq.ft.--300 lbs. pressure

The large **gennie** is used in a lower force 5.In a wind increase the excess **heel/lee bow wave pressure** produces a constant **weather helm** acting as a brake to reduce hull speed.

At some point within a force 5,optimum hull speed will be reached by **putting as much weight on the high side as possible to minimize weather helm.**When this is no longer sufficient--

The excess tiller weather helm pressure indicates **it is time to change from a gennie to a working jib.**

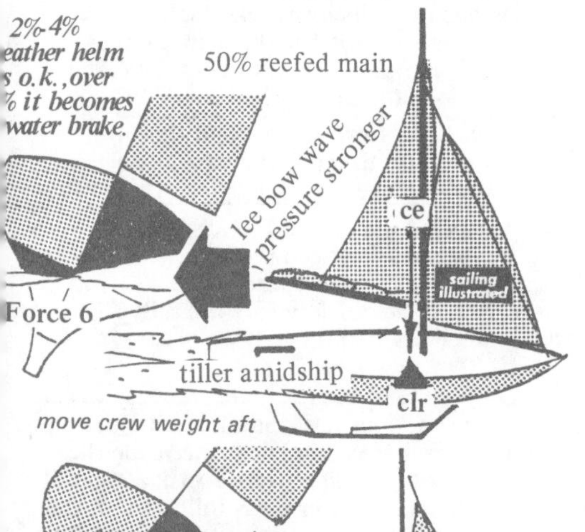

2%-4% eather helm s o.k.,over % it becomes water brake.
50% reefed main
lee bow wave pressure stronger
ce
sailing illustrated
Force 6
tiller amidship
clr
move crew weight aft

- **Force 6** (1.6-2.4 psf) 1.6 psf x 200 sq.ft.--320 lbs. pressure

The ***fishermans reef*** which backwinds the mainsail,see pg. 76, temporarily reduces excess wind pressure from upper force 5 to a lower force 6.This action reduces the weather helm by ***reducing the*** heel induced ***lee bow wave pressure.***

A 50% mainsail reef is shown at left,carrying a very ample total of 200 sq.ft of combined mainsail and working jib.

- **Force 7** (2.6-3.6 psf) 3.0 psf x 100 sq.ft.--300 lbs. pressure

Working jib alone provides the total 300 lbs. pressure to **counteract the heel force/lee bow wave pressure**...compensated for by the **CE and CLR moving forward** to provide balanced steering helm if the wave actions are in a normal sequence. After a storm the waves fall out of sequence with erratic steering often required to hold a course.

When the meeting point of CE and CLR moves **forward of the mast...expect the stern to swing in a wider arc** because of unusual location of the CE and CLR in a force 7.

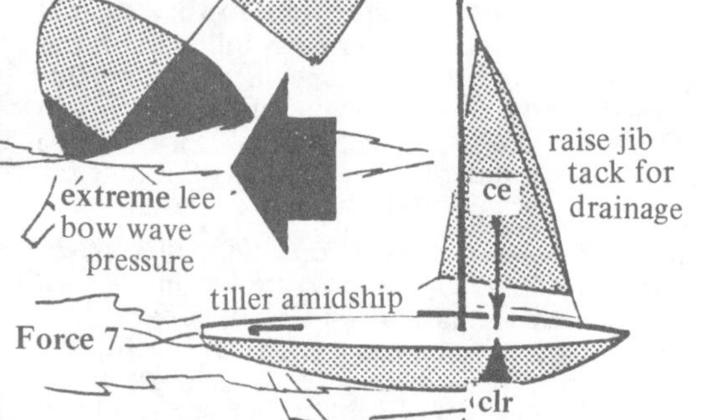

raise jib tack for drainage
ce
extreme lee bow wave pressure
tiller amidship
Force 7
clr

The next step is to simplify the math by concentrating on the wind force scale with continually changing pressures to balance the helm...or have a slight weather helm for most cabin/keel sailboats. Variables exist such as an under-rigged motorsailer carrying full sails up to a force 6 before reefing becomes necessary.

Traditional reefing sequence is shown above. An IOR or ULDB racer is overpowered when excess heel and weather helm reduces speed and increases leeway. **Depowering mainsail** is necessary for light sailboats with a 20° heel and 30° for heavier ones to reduce weather helm rudder drag to an acceptable 3° to 4°. Page 35, shows depowering method to open jib slot and flatten the mainsail for racing sailboats with a flexible mast starting with a Flying Dutchman dinghy.

overpowered

depowered–under 20°

AFTER YOU CAN PREDICT A STORM MOVING IN...

mainsail temporarily luffing

text pg.147

tight jib

the fishermans reef

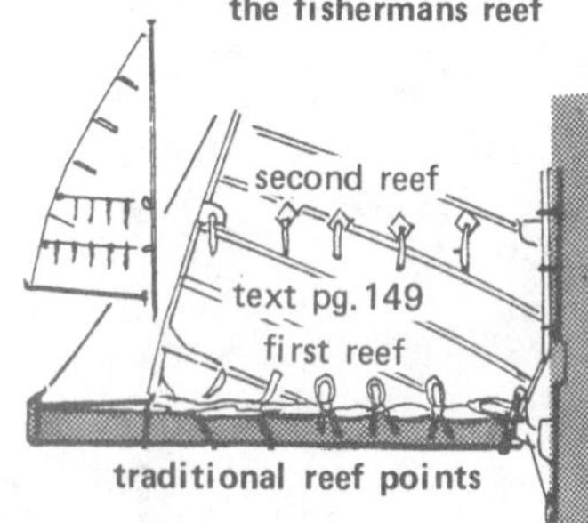

second reef
text pg.149
first reef

traditional reef points

G

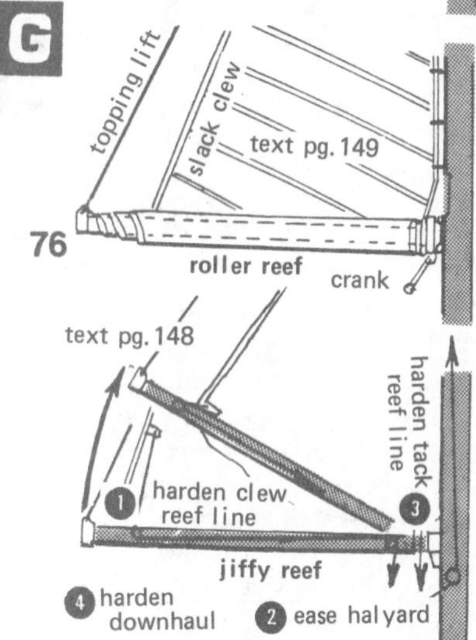

topping lift
slack clew
text pg.149
crank
text pg.148
harden tack reef line
harden clew reef line

roller reef

jiffy reef

4 harden downhaul

2 ease halyard

We provide a brief exposure to the mechanics of reefing on this page. They are detailed on pages 146 to 155 in our text which should be carried aboard your sailboat so you can practice reefing while underway.

Whether your sailing interest is racing or cruising the wind force scale is simple to understand and apply. You can then anticipate a storm moving in with your sails reefed to the correct amount *before* the storm hits. You can then enjoy the antics of your racing competitors losing precious minutes as they try to reef *after* the storm hits in the worst possible conditions that greatly increase the chances of personal injuries which could have been avoided.

• The ***fishermans reef*** is practical while sailing a sloop in rather steady winds if the boat is momentarily overpowered in a sudden puff.

The main sheet is rapidly eased to dump excess wind pressure. This backwinds the mainsail moving the CE forward to reduce the excessive momentary weather helm. The main sheet is hauled in again after the puff eases off.

The ***big cats*** have a critical need for the fishermans reef ***with the mainsheet released rapidly to five feet...then rapidly sheeted in again.*** We've had catamaran students practice this method for 5 to 10 minutes until it becomes automatic. It is also an excellent idea to use on dinghies up to Star size which keeps them upright and moving efficiently in puffy weather.

• Advantage of the ***traditional reefing method*** is that it can be tied in at the dock or at anchor *before* raising the sails. If a second reef is later required, the mainsail must be dropped, to tie the reef in, then raised again while under way...*the main disadvantage.* Standard reefing practice is to tie the reef points under the sail instead of around the boom, with the second reef tied on top of the first reef. This practice began in the days of wooden booms to avoid chafing the varnish. If your boat has an aluminum boom you may consider having the first reef tied under the sail... and the second around the boom.

• A mainsail using the original type of ***roller reefing gear*** can be easily reefed underway with the sail up as it is cranked down around the boom (avoid sharp objects on the boom that may damage the sail cloth). *The disadvantage* if you are dockside or at anchor in puffy storm conditions, the mainsail must be raised fully, then rolled down the desired amount. The lack of *leach tiedowns* with this method produces abnormal strains on the sail cloth.

We operated our boat for over ten years using both roller reef and the standard reef methods. It was a good compromise to make the best use of both methods...while avoiding their disadvantages.

The ***jiffy reef*** (it has a variety of names) started in the San Francisco area for racing with a mainsail reefed and pulling in a few seconds later when operated by trained crew members and the leads were well designed. We presently use the jiffy reef which can be tied at the dock before the sails are raised, or at anchor, as well as when underway with little fuss.

• ***Cruising reefing methods*** are shown on page 119.

leftover seas?

The ***windless storm*** is a monster seldom discussed, even our term is original. It was one of the most severe tests facing square riggers when the wind suddenly quits... yet the storm wave action continues. This phenomenon, though rare, caused dismastings and split decks open.

Our first experience with this monster was at dusk in 1957 during an overnight race on a 28' ketch. The boat had been sailing easily until the wind stopped...followed by the ugly remnants coming from the NW of an old storm where the waves had fallen out of sequence.

The boat pitched and rolled like a bronco in these huge, steep waves. Two of us stayed topside alternately changing places every 10 to 15 minutes with one of us lashed to the mast as a lookout, the other on the wheel trying to follow a wildly spinning compass as we powered to nearby Catalina Island. The remaining three crew members were on the main cabin floor to help the hull stability.

Our second exposure was in an Ensenada Race running head-on into a blown-out Mexican hurricane. While the large waves had fallen out of sequence, it fortunately still had a light breeze. The same pattern was followed on this 28' sloop with the five remaining crew members spending much time stretched out on the main cabin floor to help the stability, also reducing rolling potentials. Ensenada was quiet that year with under half of the boats finishing the race after it had become a nasty survival contest.

The windless storm is a monster that can't be predicted. The only way we could help you prepare for one was with the two examples above. Lash down all loose objects, keep chafe potentials to a minimum, and while topside rope yourself to the boat. Wear jackets, sweaters, and preservers for body protection as you may still find black and blue bruise souvenirs a month after your exposure to a windless storm monster, fortunately a rare phenomenon.

HEAVY WEATHER WIND...WAVE... MAYBE Group VARIABLES

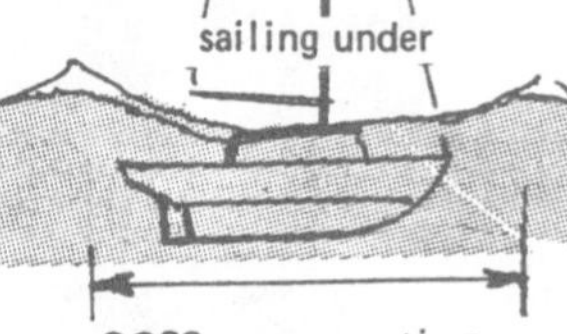
Maximum efficient speed for heavy displacement hulls.

Storm conditions have many variables.

Sailing upwind—if you aren't ready for a storm the rapidly changing *heel angle safety factor* is a warning to make sail changes. Sails may be blown out, dismastings may occur due to rigging failure, and a large heavy-displacement sailboat may be temporarily sailed under.

Downwind sailing has no safety factor. Rapidly building stress loads may cause dismastings and/or torn sails. If a sloop carries a working jib and a mainsail it can have a broach followed by a roll, and a knockdown...this situation isn't quite as critical on a headsail sloop.

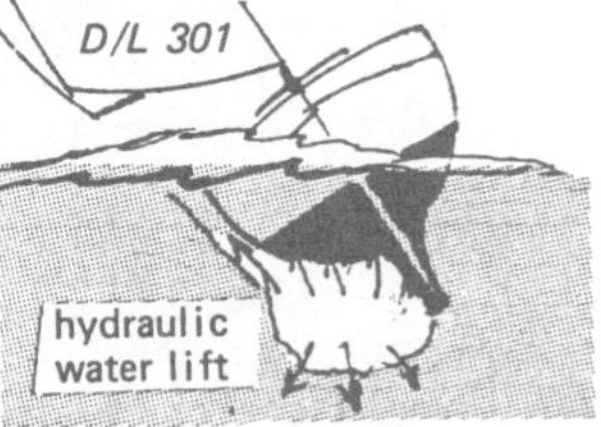
sailing under
OOPS, one more time...

Before the 1960's the traditional efficient hull speed of 1.34 √WL was important for heavy displacement sailboats. Above this waterline speed limit the excess loading on hull, rigging, and sails increased rapidly as the bow pushed a huge wave forward, pulling a big stern wave aft...with a growing hole between the bow and stern waves.

Many large sailboats of that period were heavy displacement with narrow beam. When a sudden storm hit when sailing upwind increasing the waterline speed to over 1.6√WL...if excessive rigging loads didn't cause a dismasting, the boat may fall into this hole and be sailed under. It would suddenly stop due to the 800:1 water/air density factor, then hopefully pop to the surface to drop or reef the sails.

Under similar conditions—
The Cal 25 went faster than the waves—
Our *Pink Cloud* matched the wave speed—
The Pearson 28 *Viva* was slower than the waves.

BUT DOWNWIND...a white squall suddenly blew the water flat on the Chesapeake Bay putting a heavy, cranky, old wooden 30' gaff-rigged cutter on a careening plane (20 knots?) with loads beyond belief until the sails were dropped and drags used to reduce the speed and hull loading before it could explode and sink.

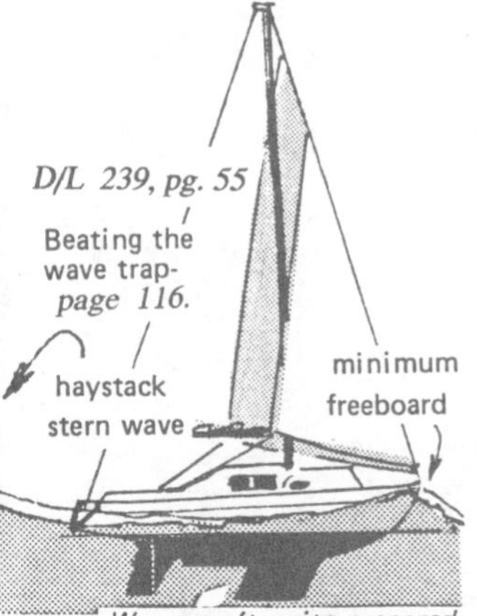
D/L 301
hydraulic water lift
the reach pressure pocket

Small heavy displacement sailboats with fiberglass hulls seem to avoid this waterline hull speed "sailing under" potential. We powered half the way back from Catalina in Oct. 1972 with sails up, when a force 6 wind hit so fast on a beam reach we couldn't reef, nor add a preventer, just use a "fishermans reef". The speedometer was hard on the 10 knot speedometer peg for most of the next 14 miles (maximum theoretical hull speed about 5 knots) as a pressure pocket developed under the hull which must have caused the boat to lift bodily...reducing hull drag. Steering was easy on this wild scary ride producing excessive loads on hull, rigging, and sails.

G

77

I was on the "Minka" on 5/5/83 as we left Santa Cruz Island with owner Bill Schulz, and Ted Stupak a friend, both commercial pilots. We were flying twin jibs with home port dead downwind (max. efficient hull speed approx. 6.2 knots).

At 1800 in a force 6, speed was 7.5 to 8.3 knots. As it moved to an upper force 6, speed was 8.3 to 8.9 knots with tremendous loading on hull, rigging and sails. The hull was pushing a huge bow wave with little freeboard forward, while the stern was riding level producing a haystack stern wave 20' to 30' aft of the stern. The small jib was jibed behind the jennie reducing speed to average 7.8 knots. An upper force 7 moved in with speeds 9.5 to 10.7 knots, the minimum freeboard becoming critical, dropping sails at 2000 hours after 44 wild nautical miles. Next—

D/L 239, pg. 55

Beating the wave trap-*page 116.*

haystack stern wave

minimum freeboard

We weren't quite prepared.

Bare pole sailing averaged 3.7-5.7 knots downwind with numerous 20-20 to 40-40 degree rolls, being pooped once. After 26 miles of bare pole dead downwind sailing, we raised a working jib near Point Vincente to help reduce the miserable rolling motion, as the boat speed increased to 7.5 knots at 0530.

The medium displacement "Minka" exceeded it's hull-speed barrier without lift nor surfing tendencies causing extreme stress loading on hull, rigging, and sails. The choice of twin jibs was excellent for downwind helm, while running above force 6 with a reefed mainsail and working jib could cause a broach, a violent roll, and a knockdown.

We were teaching in the Santa Barbara Channel, August, when the wind increased to force 6 with excessive weather helm. The Cal 25's main was dropped after which the boat on a beam to broad reach surfed easily at 10-15 knots for the next hour. The pressure pocket provided better lift on the lighter Cal 25, pg.101, with more efficient hull lines. Such a wild and wonderful sensation with fingertip control takes at least 20 minutes for a new sailor to adjust to, it can't be explained with words.

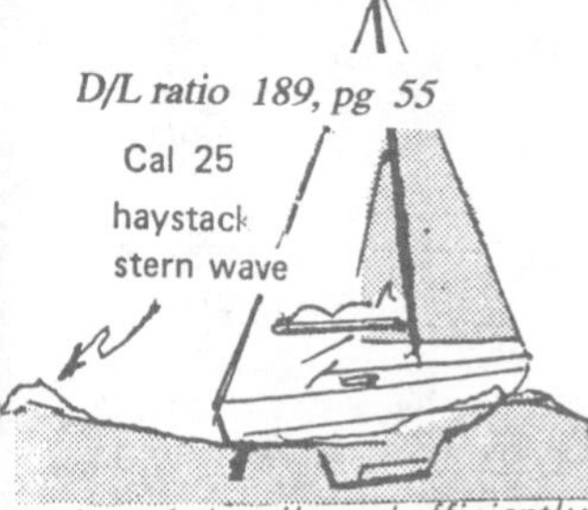
D/L ratio 189, pg 55
Cal 25
haystack stern wave
it surfed easily and efficiently

Light displacement hulls, and ULDB ocean greyhounds with large sail rigs, lean and easily-driven hulls come alive in their designed element at force 5, to upper 5 and 6, as they romp easily while reaching, then surf downwind for long periods with a finger-tip touch. This chapter is designed to provide a foundation in heavy-weather operation so you will find it easy to analyze additional information of a very complex subject.

The RUDDERLESS SAILING SURFBOARD.

climbing aboard wind

uphaul

We have enjoyed the antics of local sailing surfboarders for several years since less than 100 yards across the bay from our slip is a sandy beach which is ideal for their purposes...especially for windsurfing schools. We enjoy swapping ideas with them hoping not too many will hit our boat.

The SPLAAT of novices continually hitting the water can become teeth chattering. We are amazed how most take this continuous punishment sometimes even coming up with a smile. The only exception thru the years was a muscular guy around 30 who started cussing his board after several SPLAAATS. The board fought back with an increased cunning as his swearing became louder and more definitive. If he could have seen the hysterical laughter he provided for onlookers...

I asked a gent around 60 between his splashes why he didn't buy a real sailboat. "I have a 38' IOR sailboat and a Hobie 16...SPLAAT...but my son says this is the real challenge, and I want to show him I can do just as good a job....SPLAAT.... as he can!" Love the guy.

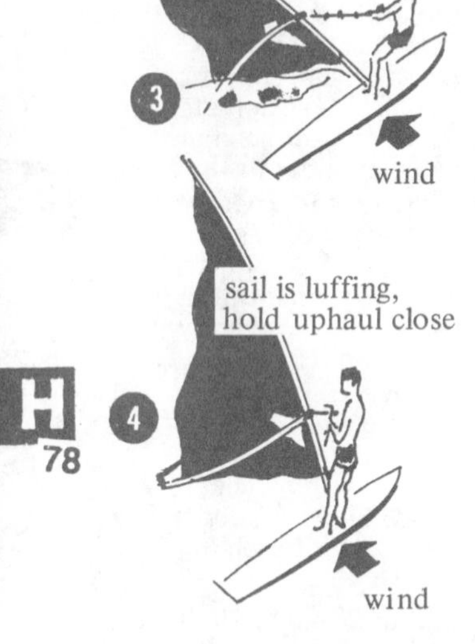
pull slowly and
steadily to
dump
water
wind
sail is luffing,
hold uphaul close
wind

The sailing surfboard requires balance, coordination...and practice. Begin by adding all terms to the illustration on the facing page for familiarity.

Choose a sandy beach to launch your board so you will be in smooth, waist-deep water, making it easier to climb aboard...are the outhaul and downhaul medium tight?

(1) **Climb aboard** from the windward side. When you are on the board rise to your knees, then grab the uphaul line. (2) **Now stand up** and rock your ankles, keeping your hips and knees flexible to get the feel of the board with one foot forward of the mast, the other aft of the mast or on the daggerboard.

The board must stay on a beam reach while raising the sail (3) which has to be pulled straight towards you. If it is raised aft the board will head up...if slightly forward, it will start to turn downwind.

Relax hips, knees, and ankles, then bend your knees slightly so your body will flow with the board as you are on an unstable platform. If your legs become tense, the overcompensation can cause an uspet.

Squat slightly, tip your body backward then (3) **lift the sail slowly to let the water drain**...then rapidly pull the uphaul line until the boom end is out of the water. If you yank the uphaul too hard while the sail is still full of water to offset the initial resistance...when it does come out the overcompensation will cause you to fall backwards off the board.

You have pulled in the uphaul with both hands close to the boom. Stand straight with arms bent, holding (4) **the luffing sail** somewhat below vertical with the boom and the clew out of the water. The board, still beam to wind, starts to gain leeway.

(5) **Move your forward hand** to the boom 6 to 10 inches aft of the mast...then move your other hand a shoulder length aft of the first hand. Pull the mast slightly forward and to windward holding the sail until the board starts to move.

The hand on the boom closer to the mast **becomes the shroud**...while the after hand **becomes the sheet**. Both hands and arms have to work as a team to support the mast in its proper position for steering and propulsion...in absence of a rudder.

When you (6) **start to sheet in the boom** to fill the sail, lean the mast slightly aft to head up...or slightly forward to sail downwind. After the board is on course, bring the mast approximately 90° to the board so it will hold the desired course with no further turning.

Underway–in light winds keep your knees slightly bent and your back straight with your feet on the centerline, pulling just enough to fill the sail without overtrimming.

When the wind pressure increases in the sail...the surfer must lean backwards more to exert an equal and opposing pressure. Since wind pressure is seldom steady, the surfer has to continually harden in or ease the wishbone boom to compensate and balance the continually changing wind pressures.

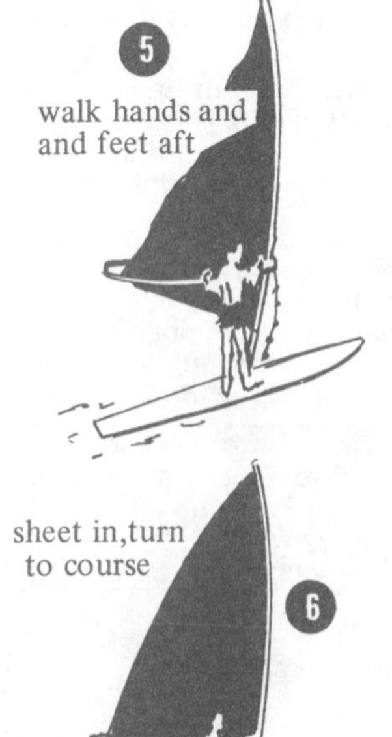
walk hands and
and feet aft
sheet in,turn
to course
sheet is
after arm
stand on centerline
shroud is
forward arm

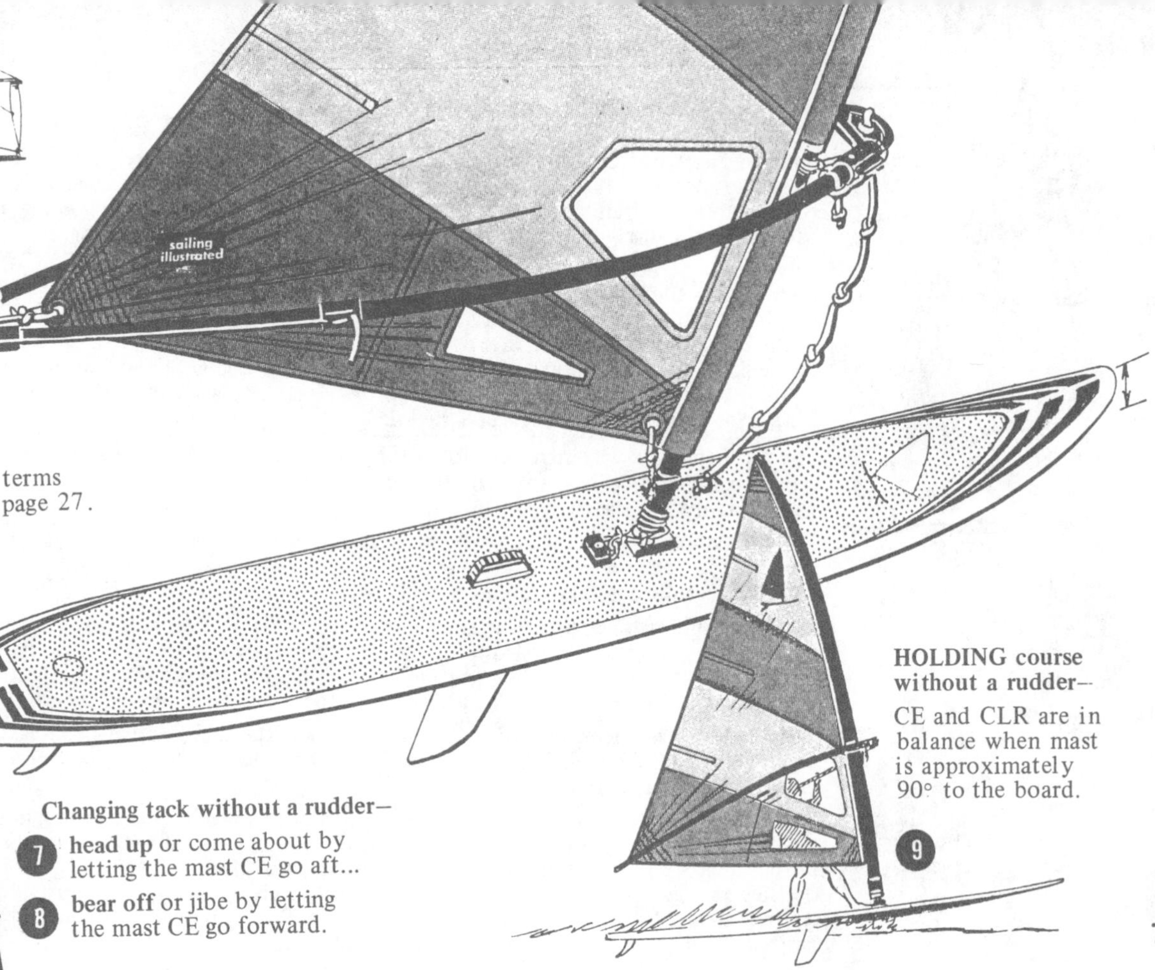

Add terms text page 27.

HOLDING course without a rudder–

CE and CLR are in balance when mast is approximately 90° to the board.

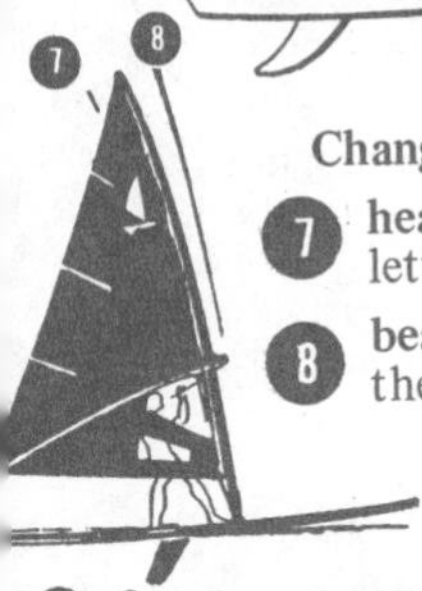

Changing tack without a rudder–

7 **head up** or come about by letting the mast CE go aft...

8 **bear off** or jibe by letting the mast CE go forward.

9

CE and CLR definitions–pg. G 6.

7 **Coming about** begins when the rig is eased a few inches aft of vertical,so the board can come up into the wind with the sail luffing.

In the meantime you walk around the forward side of the sail shown below transferring hands from the boom, to the mast,to.the other side of the wishboom.The board meanwhile has changed to the other tack,going down to a beam reach.

Then using the forward hand as a shroud and the aft hand as a sheet,sheet in to start moving,while moving the mast a little forward or aft for the new course.

8 **Jibing** begins when the rig is pulled a few inches forward of vertical,so the stern of the board comes up into the wind with the sail luffing.

In the meantime walk around the forward side of the mast as shown below transferring hands from the boom, to the mast,to the other side of the wishboom.The board meanwhile has changed to the other tack with the bow coming up to a beam reach.

Then using the forward hand as a shroud and the aft hand as a sheet,sheet in to start moving,while moving the mast a little forward or aft for the new course.

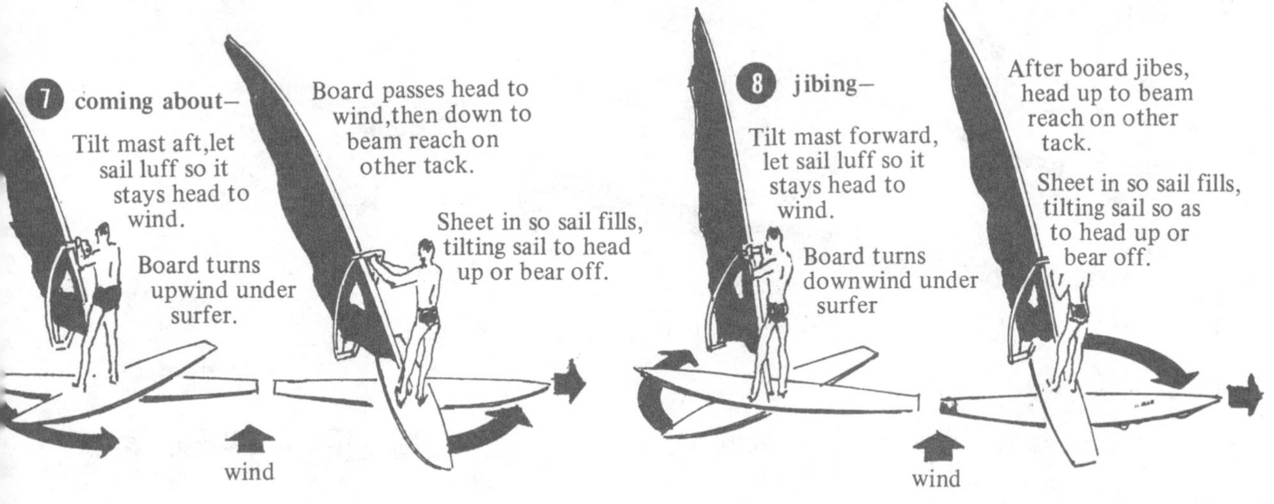
7 coming about–
Tilt mast aft,let sail luff so it stays head to wind.
Board turns upwind under surfer.
Board passes head to wind,then down to beam reach on other tack.
Sheet in so sail fills, tilting sail to head up or bear off.
wind
8 jibing–
Tilt mast forward, let sail luff so it stays head to wind.
Board turns downwind under surfer
After board jibes, head up to beam reach on other tack.
Sheet in so sail fills, tilting sail so as to head up or bear off.
wind

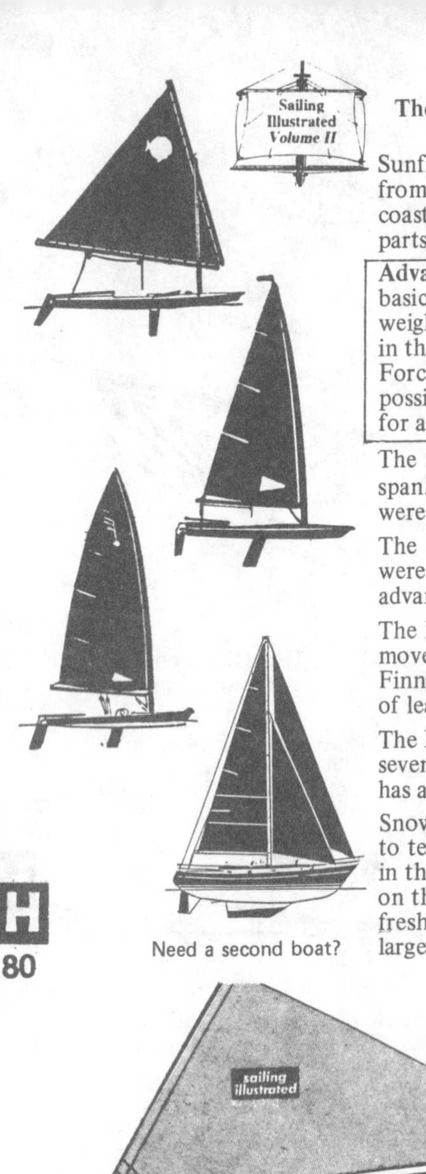
Sailing
Illustrated
Volume II

Need a second boat?

The sporty, no fuss, car-topper BEACH BOAT.

Sunfish, Laser, Force 5, and similar craft are **beach boats** that are easy to launch from the shores of lakes, reservoirs, or rivers, and protected ocean beaches and coastal areas. Add all terms to these three boats, then compare their rigging and parts so you can rig the boats, raise the sails, add rudders and daggerboards.

Advantages of beach boats are popularity, minimum cost, minimum weight, and basic rigging thoug[illegible]rce 5 has a couple of extra lines. They are excellent car toppers weighing in at 125 to 145 pounds to join you on that next vacation...with the Sunfish in the background on many vacation folders. Or you can sail in a different Sunfish, Force 5, or Laser regatta every weekend somewhere in the U.S. and Hawaii with the possible exception of December. Write to the class associations listed in our text for a copy of their **Race Regatta Schedule**.

The **Sunfish** Class was introduced in 1958, being made of fiberglass during its life-span. It can be found in many remote corners of the world with 170,000 craft that were produced in the first 25 years of the Sunfish Class.

The **Laser** was introduced in 1970, spawning a new generation of junior sailors. They were able to test their racing skills and rule applications more rapidly, and in more advanced conditions than juniors starting with less efficient catboat dinghies.

The Laser juniors developed the **fluid movement skills** to new levels using body movement. After graduating from the junior circuit they entered the single-handed Finn Class with their new skills, sending its older, highly competitive and athletic core of leaders to other classes. Their only competition...new emerging junior competitors.

The **Force 5** was introduced in 1973, listed as the 10th most popular U.S. class only seven years later. Though Laser and Force 5 are both 13' 10½" long, the Force 5 has a larger sail area and more sail trim adjustments.

Snow belt sailors owning large sailboats often choose a beach boat as their second to test their racing ability in October in the sun belt area when their big boats are in their cradles. They often repeat the process again in March or April to brush up on their racing skills against the highly competitive class leaders. It also provides a fresh exposure to the complex racing rules that will become handy when racing his large sailboat the following spring, summer, and fall.

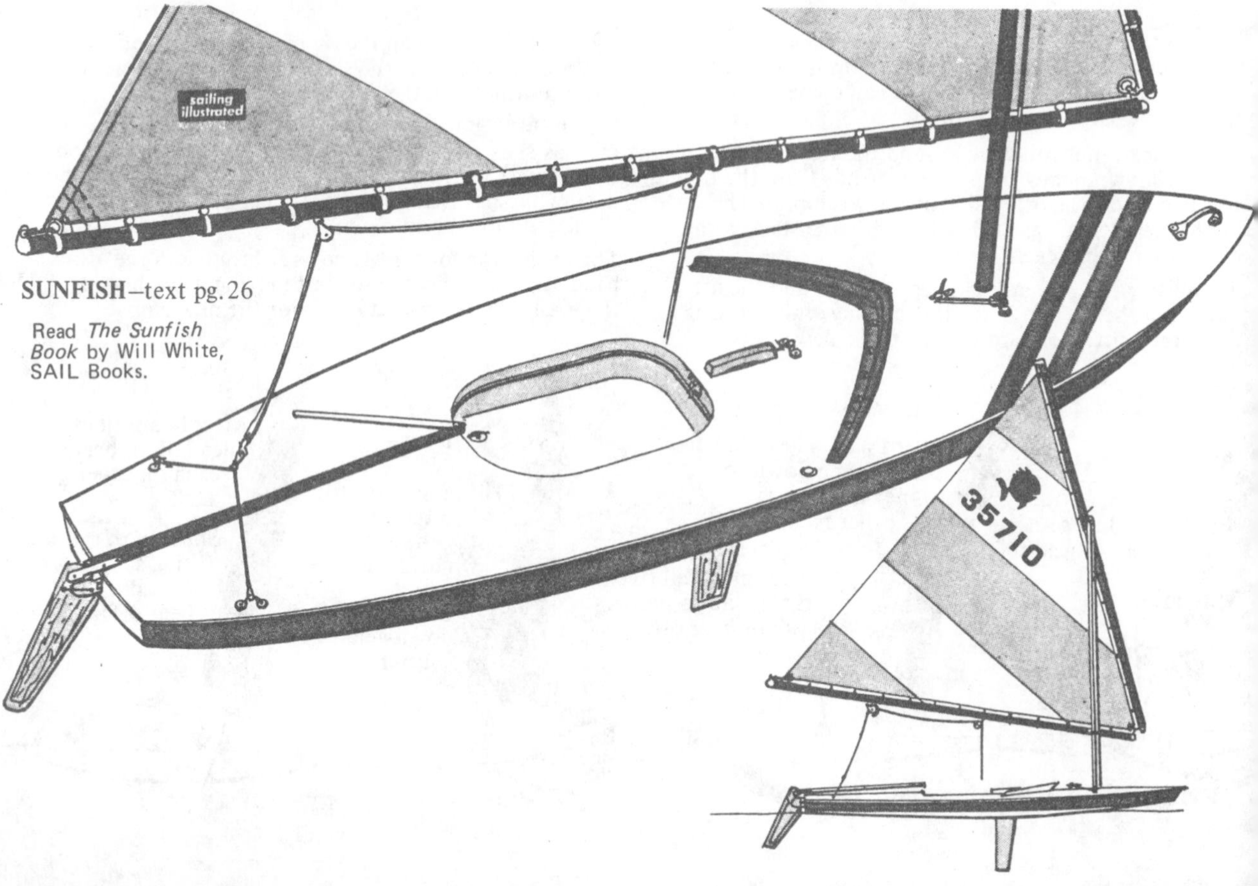

SUNFISH–text pg. 26

Read *The Sunfish Book* by Will White, SAIL Books.

mast bending. Olympic Star Gold Medal winner Lowell North's 43' *Sleeper* has the smallest mast section in the fleet plus other Star tested ideas.

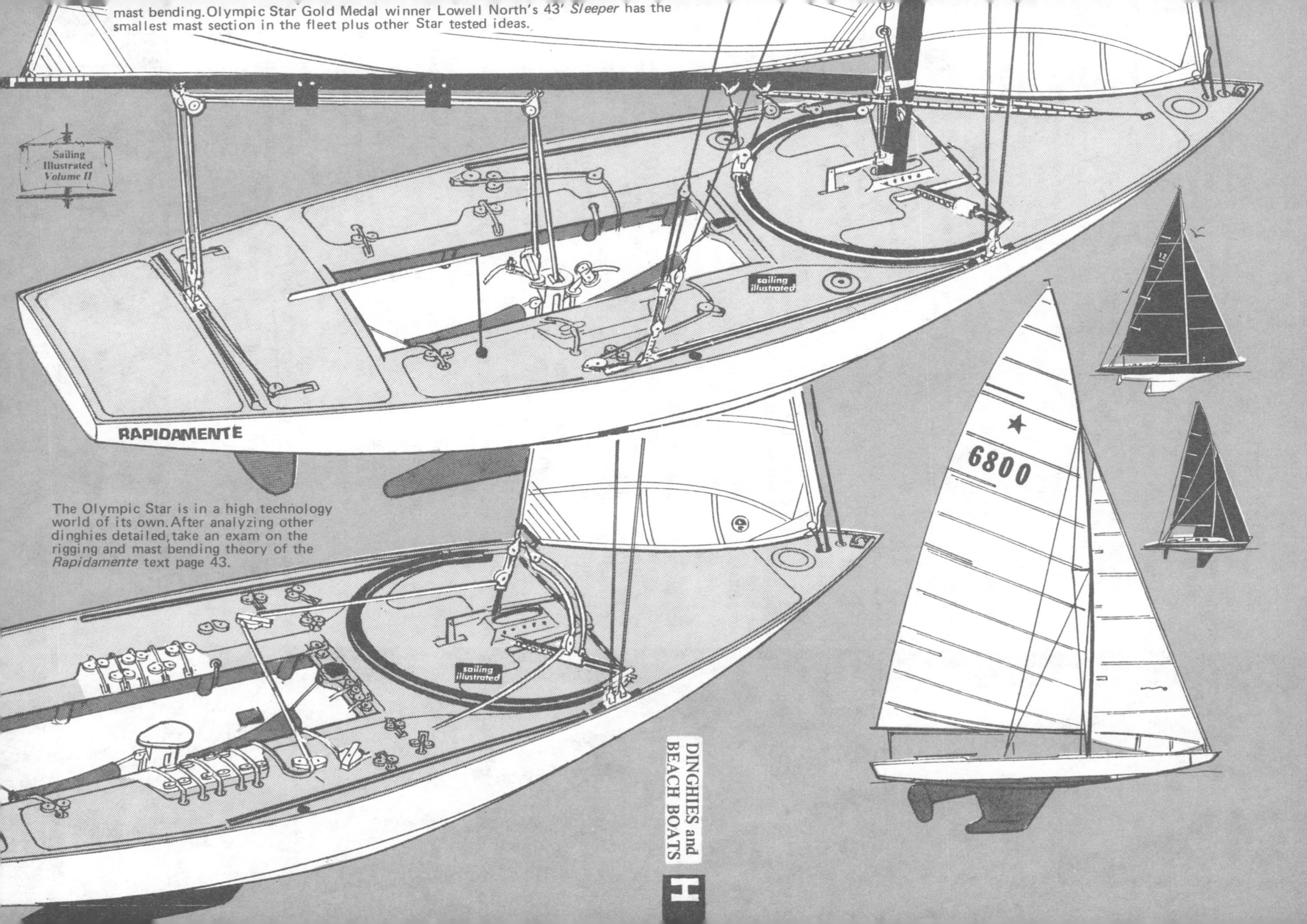

Sailing Illustrated Volume II
RAPIDAMENTE
sailing illustrated
6800
12
sailing illustrated

The Olympic Star is in a high technology world of its own. After analyzing other dinghies detailed, take an exam on the rigging and mast bending theory of the *Rapidamente* text page 43.

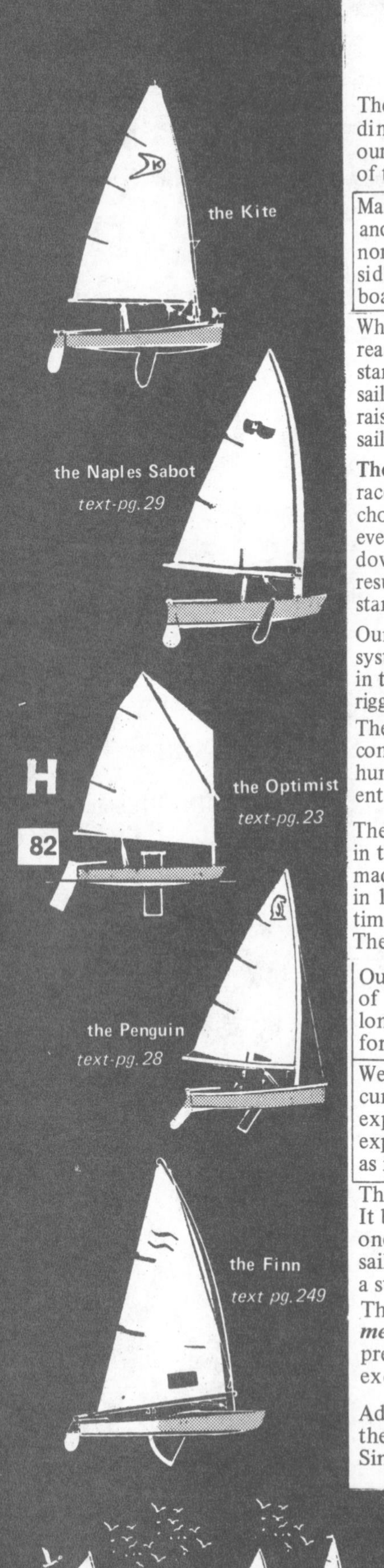
the Kite
the Naples Sabot
text-pg.29
H
82
the Optimist
text-pg.23
the Penguin
text-pg.28
the Finn
text pg.249

NOT BECAUSE...BUT OFTEN IN SPITE OF...

The first solo command of many yacht club juniors ages 9 thru 12,is a catboat dinghy chosen for yacht club teaching programs that vary considerably across our country due to local preferences.That dinghy,often a clunker,will become one of the most cherished memories a new sailor will have in his lifetime.

Many catboat dinghies appear with little to offer.Somehow they start to grow and improve if the class has good leadership,and the rules are neither too strict nor too flexible thus permitting steady class improvement and growth.On the other side is the Kite,a strict one-design fiberglass boat designed to be a junior training boat for the Finn class.Though it had excellent potentials it had a brief life span.

While many of the small catboat dinghy classes flourish for their own unorthodox reasons,we provide the story of the Sabot with which we have more familiarity that started as a ship to shore rowing pram.A local owner revised it by adding a mast and sail,plus a leeboard so nearby Naples juniors could sail it up on their sandy beach... raising the leeboard at the last moment.A San Francisco owner added a mast and sail,plus a daggerboard so it could point higher,becoming the El Toro.

The Sabot is a low performance dinghy,it's main advantage. If you want to win Sabot races,good dry-land instruction,and lots of sailing practice are required.While builder choice,weight and good rigging controls are required for boat speed...it must be sailed every moment while you try to out think the competition...otherwise it will slow down,and the rest of the fleet pass you.Since the Sabot is slow,more short races result with more races during the same time period.A major Sabot plus is more critical starts...which is a major weakness for better performing classes with fewer starts.

Our Sabots *Tilt* and *Stormy Nite* belonging to our twins began with basic rigging systems which can be installed with a drill,screw driver,and wrenches,putting them in the middle of the Sabot Class.Competitors prefer wooden hulls with complex rigging systems for Class A racing Sabots,costing five times as much as one of ours. The names of ex-junior Sabot racers with international recognition are endless with competitive one-design classes,12 meters,the Hawaiian Transpac,and others.It was humorous to find Congressional Cup winners for many years were too young to enter the clubhouse bar...due to an excellent Sabot racing background.

The **Clearwater Optimist** was designed in 1949 by Clark Mills for juniors to age 15 in the Clearwater,Florida area.A major interest developed in Europe where it was made a little longer and a little faster,starting the International Optimist Association in 1965 with reputed fleets in 38 countries.We hadn't seen an Optimist at detailing time requesting help from U.S. and European sources as rigging varies considerably. The Vanguard Optmiist was chosen instead due to standardization.

Our search for the **ideal catboat with single rigging controls** led us to a short run of fiberglass **Penguins** which must have been a financial disaster for the builder.It has a long history of being built at home by individuals out of wood,or a group project for club and college sailing programs...so expect considerable rigging differences.

We added the latest single rigging adjustments to our Penguin in 1982 such as outhaul, cunningham,and preventer.We mailed a copy of our illustration to the Penguin Class expert who replied that all of our adjustments were legal under their rules...but don't expect to find such a Penguin.We recommend you study the Penguin layout closely as it might have rigging ideas you are looking for in other classes.

The **Finn** was designed by Rickard Sarby for a 1949 Finland Single-hander contest. It became the Olympic Single hander in 1952,an honor it still holds.The Finn is a one-man torture rack,an impersonal boat that enjoys rolling to windward with a new sailor aboard.It was designed by a hair dresser who cut the end off a canoe,adding a stern,mast,sail,and centerboard.Its simplicity soon changed.

The new generation Vanguard Finn ***with double port and starboard control adjustments*** using an aluminum mast was chosen for the 1984 Olympics.We detail the previous generation Finn with a wooden mast for your analysis.Controls are similar except for different location of the hand adjustment double controls.

Add all terms to the five catboat classes,and analyze each class separately,then compare the hull and rigging variables against each other to understand todays catboat classes. Since they are close to the water...it helps to be a good,confident swimmer.

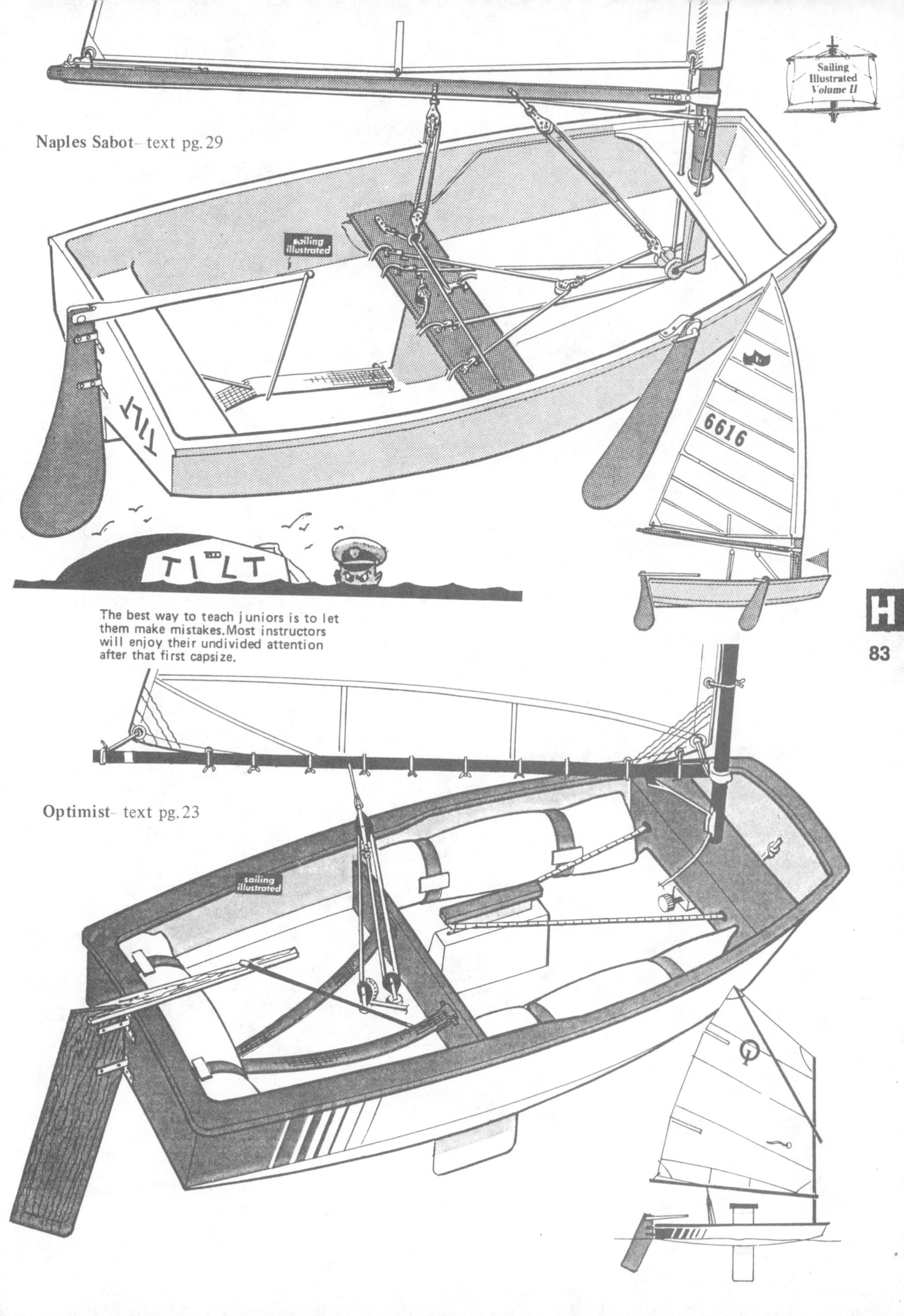
Sailing
Illustrated
Volume II
Naples Sabot—text pg. 29
sailing
illustrated
TILT
6616
TI LT
The best way to teach juniors is to let them make mistakes. Most instructors will enjoy their undivided attention after that first capsize.
Optimist—text pg. 23
sailing
illustrated

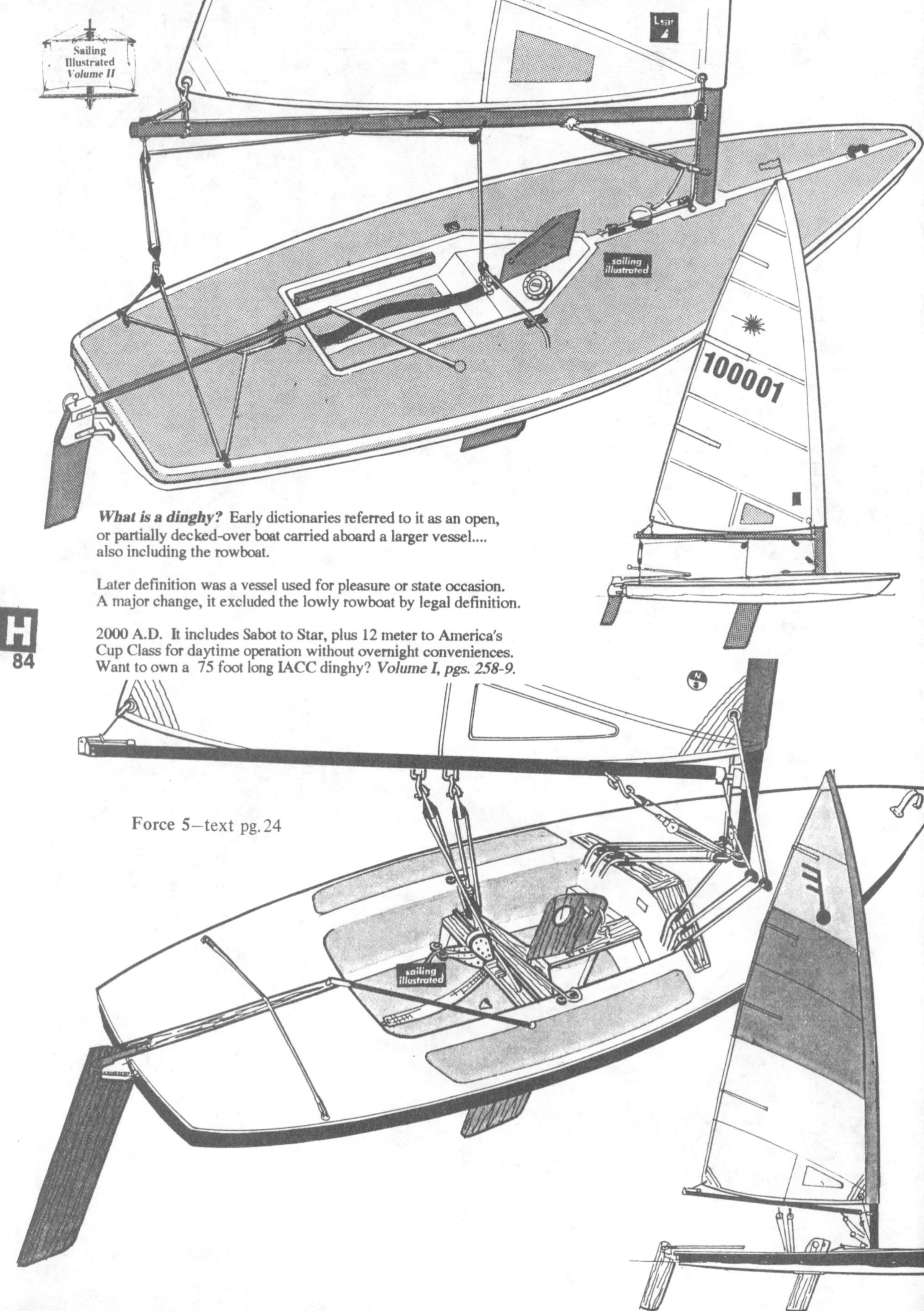
Sailing
Illustrated
Volume II
sailing
illustrated
100001
sailing
illustrated

What is a dinghy? Early dictionaries referred to it as an open, or partially decked-over boat carried aboard a larger vessel.... also including the rowboat.

Later definition was a vessel used for pleasure or state occasion. A major change, it excluded the lowly rowboat by legal definition.

2000 A.D. It includes Sabot to Star, plus 12 meter to America's Cup Class for daytime operation without overnight conveniences. Want to own a 75 foot long IACC dinghy? *Volume I, pgs. 258-9.*

Force 5–text pg. 24

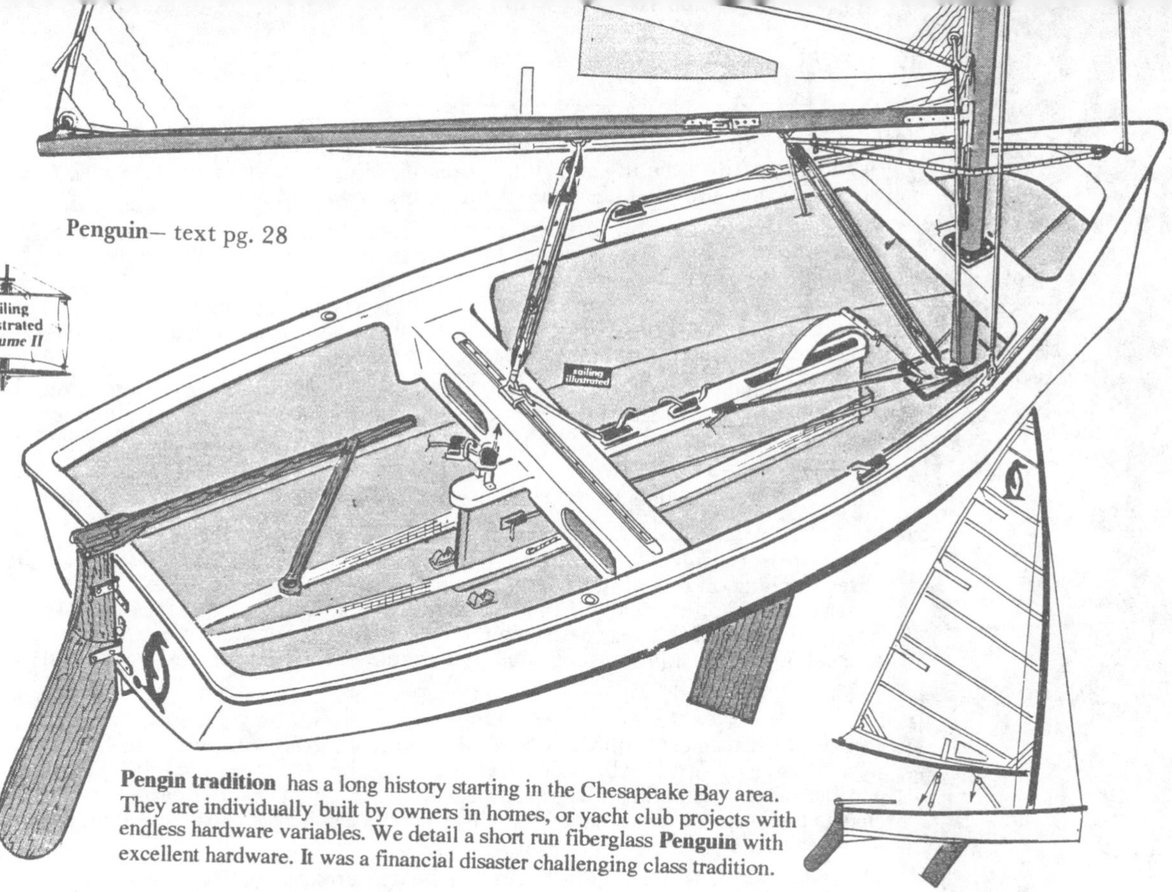

Penguin— text pg. 28

Sailing Illustrated Volume II

Pengin tradition has a long history starting in the Chesapeake Bay area. They are individually built by owners in homes, or yacht club projects with endless hardware variables. We detail a short run fiberglass **Penguin** with excellent hardware. It was a financial disaster challenging class tradition.

The author's admiration and thanks go to Carter Pyle, designer and builder of the first fully, self-rescuing dinghy with a short run. What I enjoyed, its zero tolerance was intimidating to the best racer.

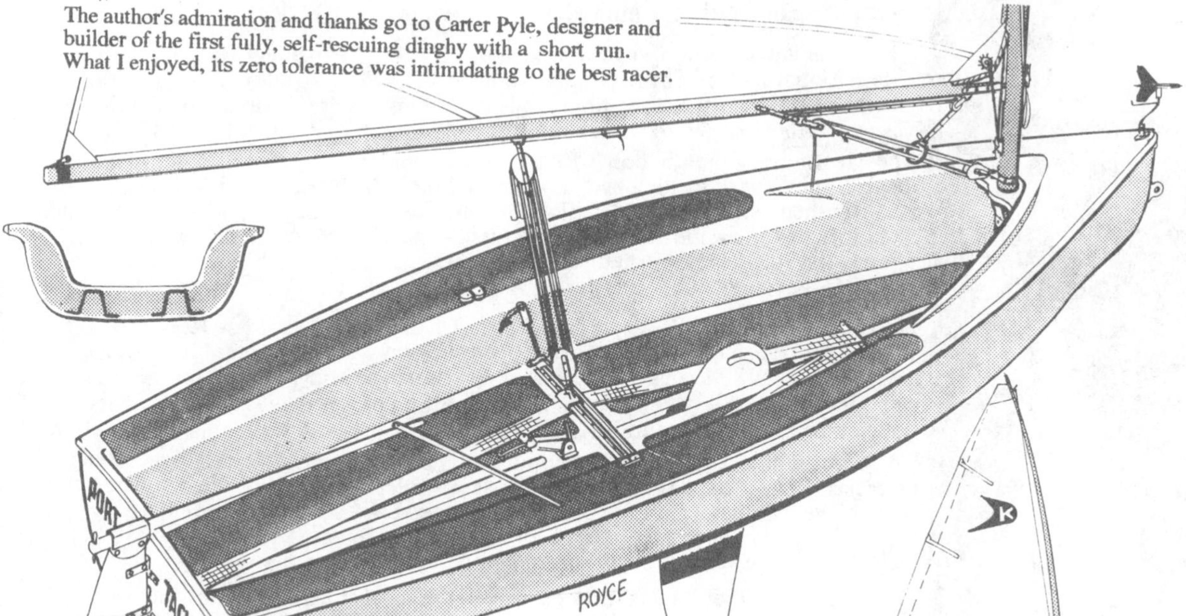

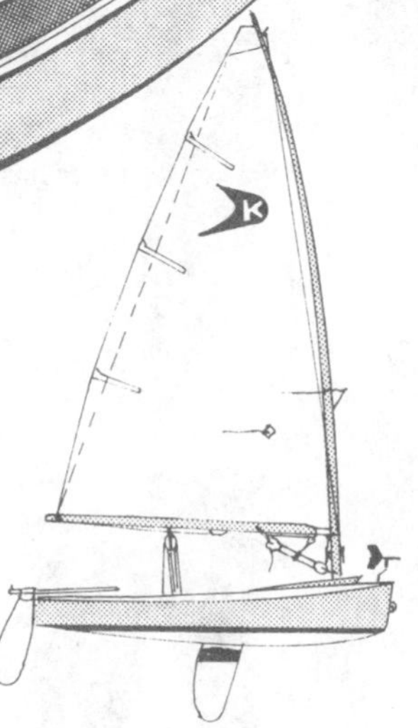

How I enjoyed sailing a Kite for a week in crowded Avalon Harbor on Catalina. I'd sail it twice a day with a drink in hand. looking bored. I could sail higher, or lower moving an arm, shoulder, or posterior an inch or so. Heavy-handed owners of larger sailboats wiped out by the Kite, just stared. My secret, none knew the darn Kite almost sank seven times while towing it to Catalina.

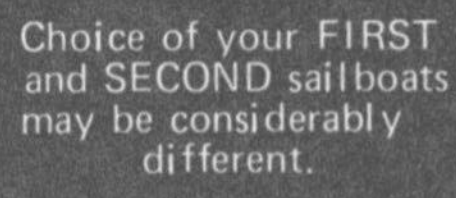

Choice of your FIRST and SECOND sailboats may be considerably different.

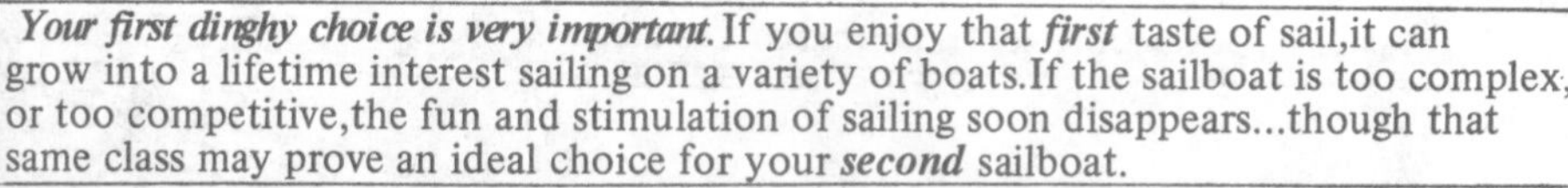

Your first dinghy choice is very important. If you enjoy that ***first*** taste of sail,it can grow into a lifetime interest sailing on a variety of boats.If the sailboat is too complex, or too competitive,the fun and stimulation of sailing soon disappears...though that same class may prove an ideal choice for your ***second*** sailboat.

We detail six considerably different popular sloop dinghies which have grown and succeeded in their own class worlds for your analysis.Systematically study each sailboat until you can mentally climb aboard,raise,and trim sails,knowing where to reach all of the specific controls.The next step is to begin comparing the differences in hulls and rigging with the wide variety of rigging adjustments that accomplish the same purposes due to hull shape and class rules.

The **traditional dinghy term** when we began sailing referred to a small,undecked sailboat.The popular use of the term expanded to include decked over sailboats without a cabin including,Snipe,Lightning,and Star.When we jokingly called the **Windward Passage** a big dinghy...the term rapidly caught on.

While 12 meter sailboats fit the basic pattern of a decked over sailboat without a cabin...can you call a two to five million dollar investment a dinghy?

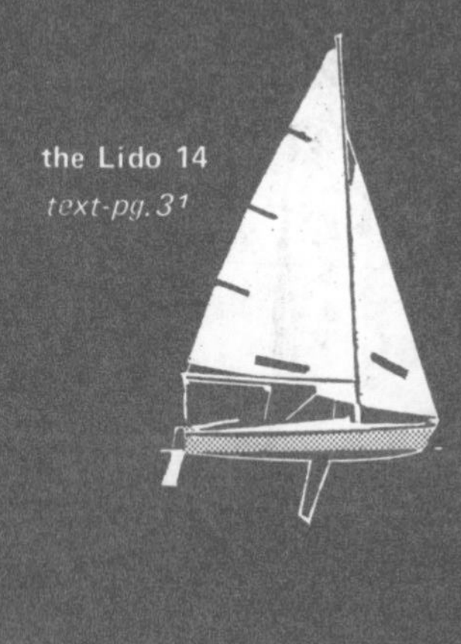

the Lido 14

text-pg. 31

The **Lido 14**,introduced in 1958,was we feel the first quality fiberglass sloop dinghy. After teaching on probably 45 Lido's we rank the Lido 14 as the #1 sloop dinghy for the new sailor,especially if they want to buy a larger cabin sailboat.I taught on one Lido when after a year of sailing the present owner felt competent to move up to a cabinsailboat,a process repeated by two more families with minimum cost.

The Lido 14 is a fully worked out,strict one-design sailboat ready to sail as it comes from the factory.After our morning homework,we can show its sensitivity to heel and weight placement with the afternoon winds.By the end of the day the students were hanging on for dear life as we were charging thru the moorings,relying on its excellent maneuverability.The high aspect centerboard and rudder permits it to change tack rapidly (always back the jib),so it can again accelerate before running out of inertia.

the Thistle

text-pg. 32

The Lido 14 is sensitive,responsive,and well engineered,the perfect boat for family participation.It is also the choice of many intercollegiate sailing instruction and racing programs with 20 Lidos at the nearby university sailing center.

•

The **classic open Thistle** was the traditional big dinghy,the next size up after the International 14.The Thistle,which can be made of 5 ply cold-molded wood,or fiberglass is a class frozen in time.While class numbers aren't large,probably half the fleet is still supposed to be competitive including *Paukie* which is hull #1.

The Thistle has a plumb bow with a long waterline for directional stability and displacement speed tacking performance upwind...the jib has to be continually backed when coming about.The flat bottom allows the Thistle to plane easily down-wind carrying the same sail area as the Lightning...though the Thistle weighs 200 pounds less.A discussion whether the Lightning or Thistle was faster started the first **OOAK (One Of A Kind) Series**...with the lighter Thistle the winner.

•

the International Snipe

text-pg. 33

The **Snipe**,a 1931 design,has its first Worlds Championship listed as 1934.It is still difficult to realize a class with such a long tradition underwent more improvements from 1965 to 1980 than any other class we studied to stimulate self improvement and interest.After detailing ***five*** generations of Snipes,we hope it has reached its engineering saturation point (dream on),but not with worldwide Snipe competition.

We expect rebuttals believing the popular Snipe should only be considered after a racer has reached the upper level of a less known,less competitive dinghy class.Only at that level will he begin to understand,enjoy,and put the full potentials of the Snipe to use.He must expect to be a tail ender for his rookie year and longer due to the high competitive spirit that also draws top competitive racers from other classes.

The Snipe is a rather impersonal boat where the mechanics of sail must be mastered so you can concentrate on outmaneuvering the competition,compared to playing a huge game of chess on the water that also pulls in offshore racers.If a new sailor chooses the Snipe for his first boat,he may soon be discouraged due to the high level of competition even with the local level ***home folk racers*** for which he isn't prepared.

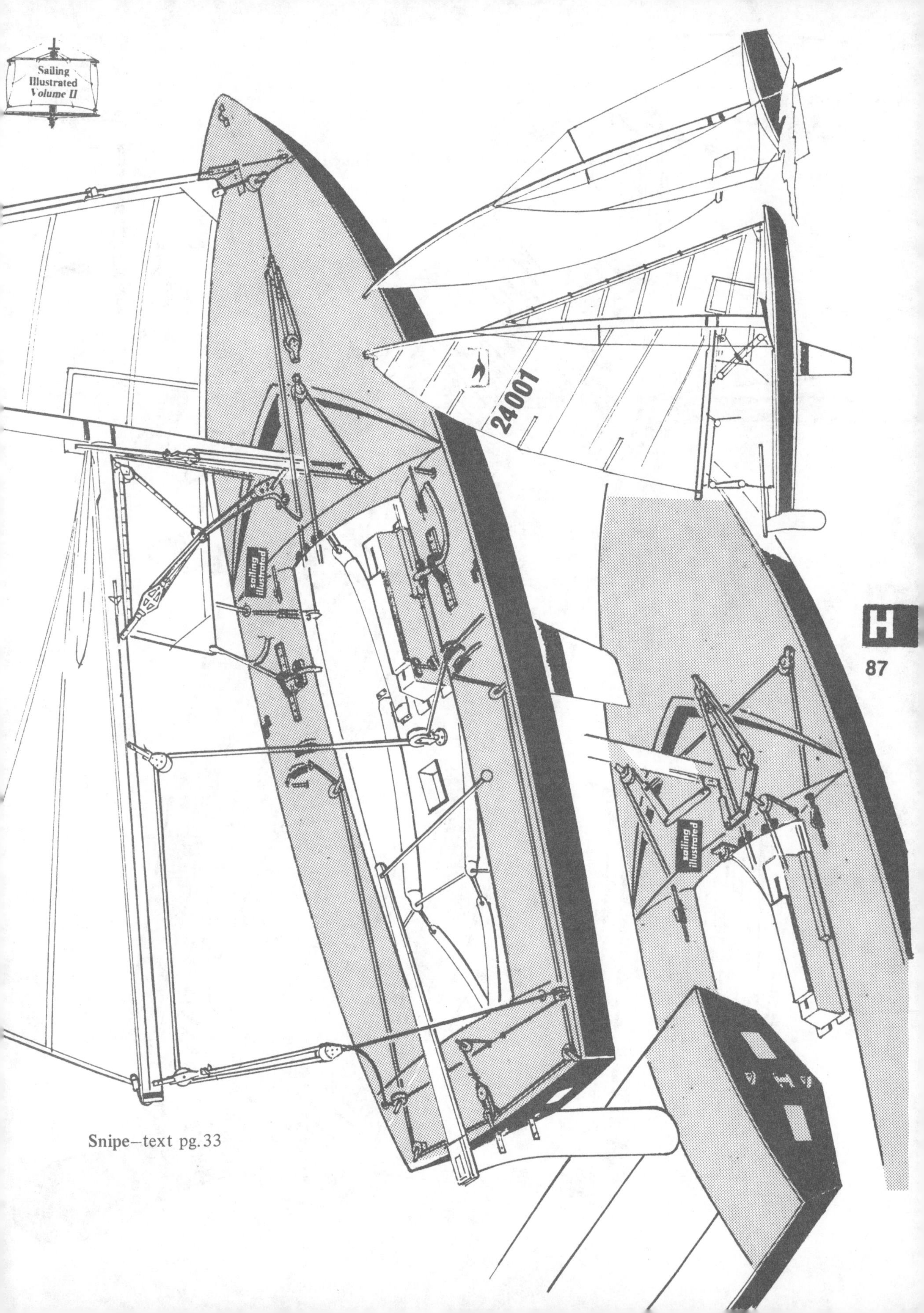
24001
sailing illustrated
sailing illustrated

Snipe—text pg. 33

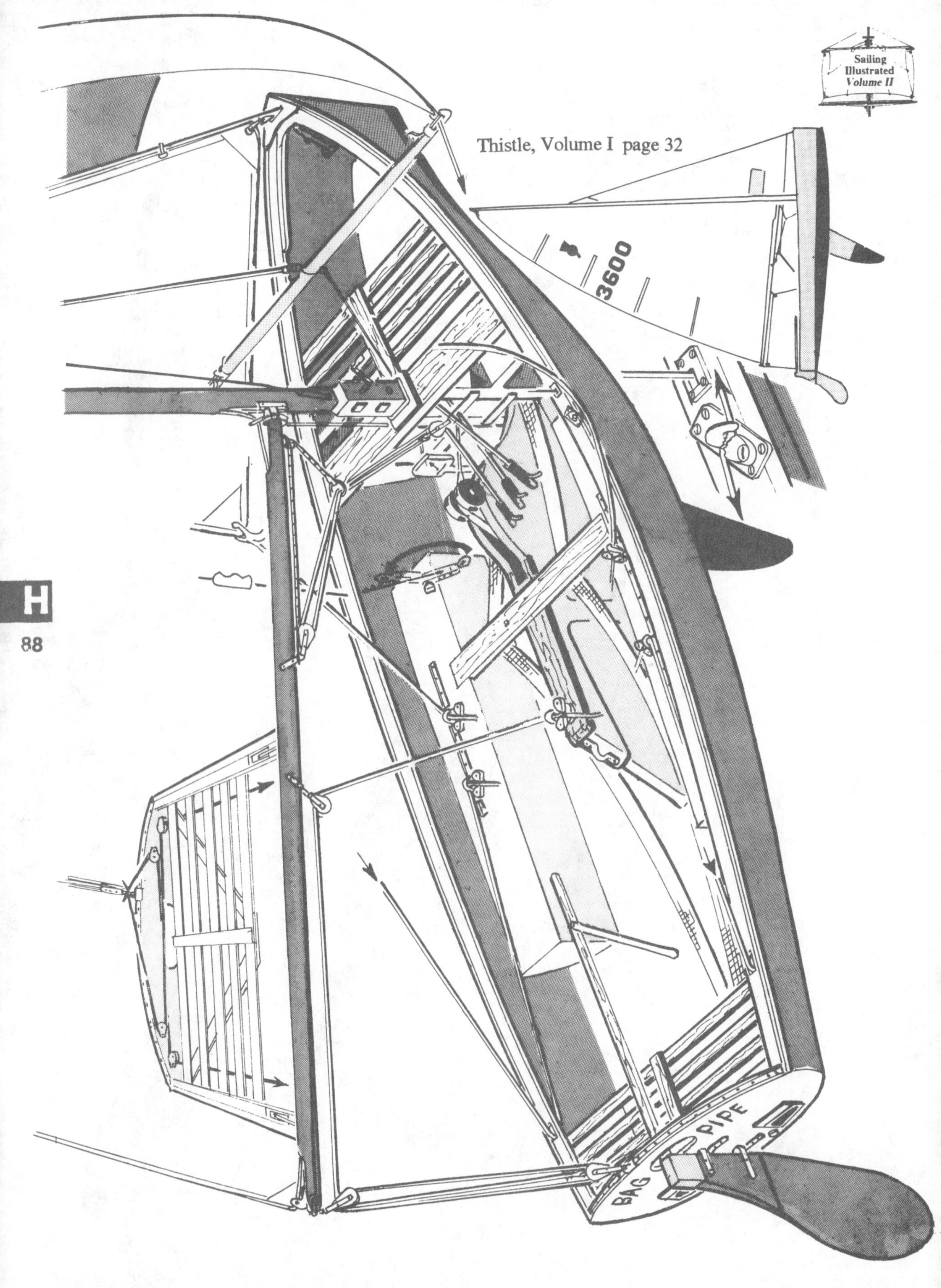
Sailing Illustrated Volume II
Thistle, Volume I page 32
3600
BAG PIPE
H

Lido 14—text pg. 31

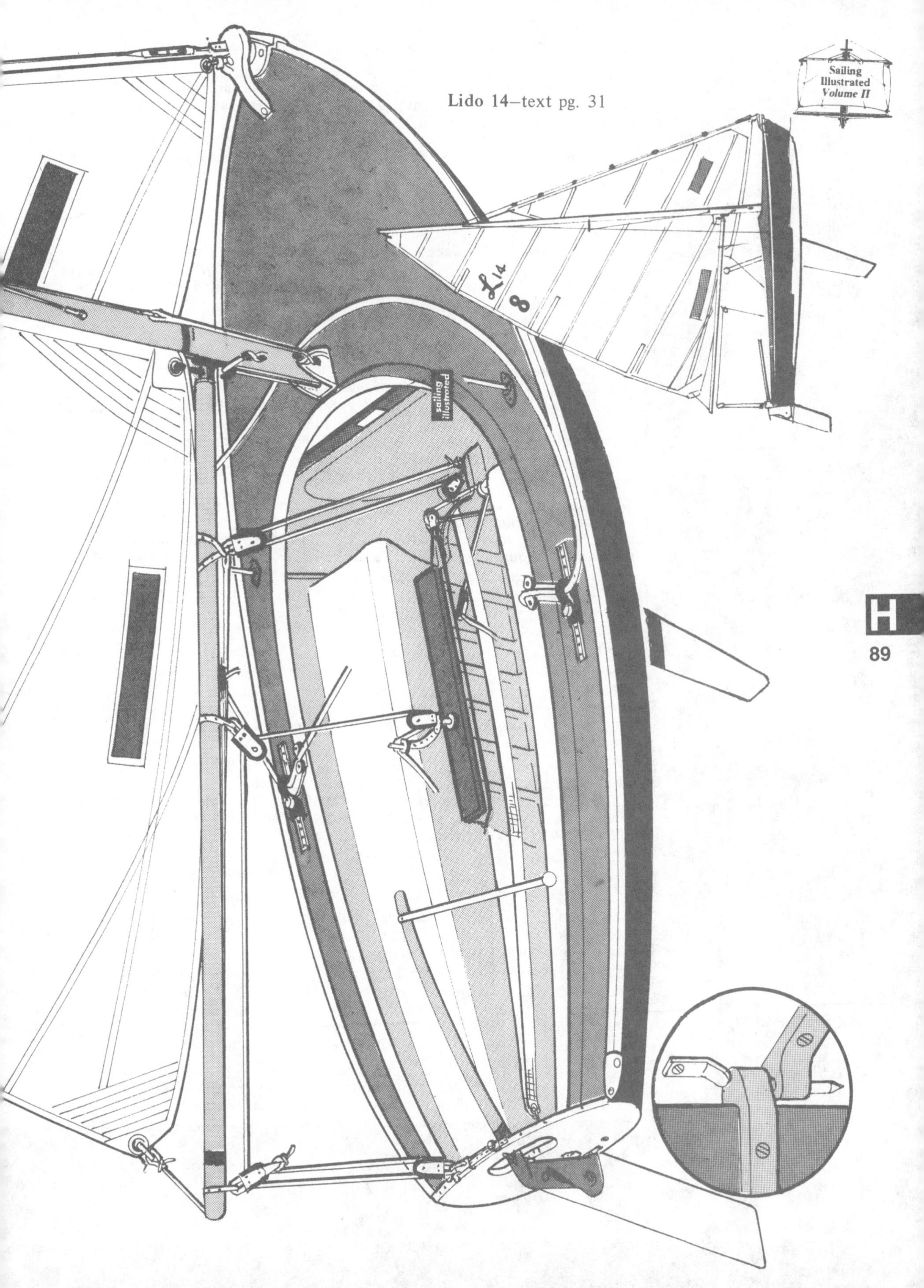
Sailing
Illustrated
Volume II
L 14
8
sailing
illustrated

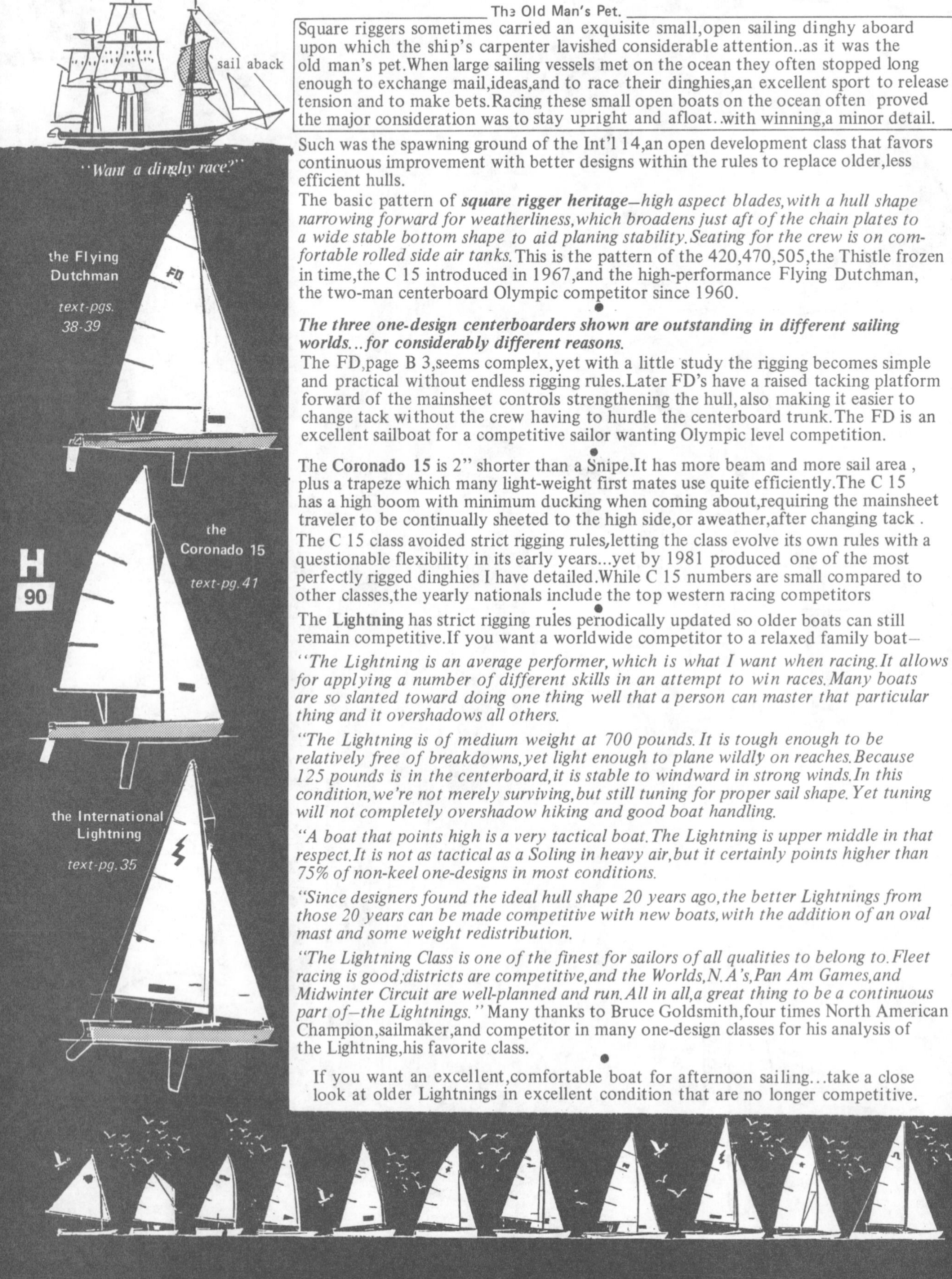
sail aback
"Want a dinghy race?"
the Flying Dutchman
text-pgs. 38-39
the Coronado 15
text-pg. 41
the International Lightning
text-pg. 35

Some high-performance racers enjoy a square-rigger heritage.

The Old Man's Pet.

Square riggers sometimes carried an exquisite small, open sailing dinghy aboard upon which the ship's carpenter lavished considerable attention..as it was the old man's pet. When large sailing vessels met on the ocean they often stopped long enough to exchange mail, ideas, and to race their dinghies, an excellent sport to release tension and to make bets. Racing these small open boats on the ocean often proved the major consideration was to stay upright and afloat. .with winning, a minor detail.

Such was the spawning ground of the Int'l 14, an open development class that favors continuous improvement with better designs within the rules to replace older, less efficient hulls.

The basic pattern of ***square rigger heritage****—high aspect blades, with a hull shape narrowing forward for weatherliness, which broadens just aft of the chain plates to a wide stable bottom shape to aid planing stability. Seating for the crew is on comfortable rolled side air tanks.* This is the pattern of the 420, 470, 505, the Thistle frozen in time, the C 15 introduced in 1967, and the high-performance Flying Dutchman, the two-man centerboard Olympic competitor since 1960.

•

The three one-design centerboarders shown are outstanding in different sailing worlds... for considerably different reasons.

The FD, page B 3, seems complex, yet with a little study the rigging becomes simple and practical without endless rigging rules. Later FD's have a raised tacking platform forward of the mainsheet controls strengthening the hull, also making it easier to change tack without the crew having to hurdle the centerboard trunk. The FD is an excellent sailboat for a competitive sailor wanting Olympic level competition.

•

The **Coronado 15** is 2" shorter than a Snipe. It has more beam and more sail area, plus a trapeze which many light-weight first mates use quite efficiently. The C 15 has a high boom with minimum ducking when coming about, requiring the mainsheet traveler to be continually sheeted to the high side, or aweather, after changing tack. The C 15 class avoided strict rigging rules, letting the class evolve its own rules with a questionable flexibility in its early years...yet by 1981 produced one of the most perfectly rigged dinghies I have detailed. While C 15 numbers are small compared to other classes, the yearly nationals include the top western racing competitors

•

The **Lightning** has strict rigging rules periodically updated so older boats can still remain competitive. If you want a worldwide competitor to a relaxed family boat—

"The Lightning is an average performer, which is what I want when racing. It allows for applying a number of different skills in an attempt to win races. Many boats are so slanted toward doing one thing well that a person can master that particular thing and it overshadows all others.

"The Lightning is of medium weight at 700 pounds. It is tough enough to be relatively free of breakdowns, yet light enough to plane wildly on reaches. Because 125 pounds is in the centerboard, it is stable to windward in strong winds. In this condition, we're not merely surviving, but still tuning for proper sail shape. Yet tuning will not completely overshadow hiking and good boat handling.

"A boat that points high is a very tactical boat. The Lightning is upper middle in that respect. It is not as tactical as a Soling in heavy air, but it certainly points higher than 75% of non-keel one-designs in most conditions.

"Since designers found the ideal hull shape 20 years ago, the better Lightnings from those 20 years can be made competitive with new boats, with the addition of an oval mast and some weight redistribution.

"The Lightning Class is one of the finest for sailors of all qualities to belong to. Fleet racing is good; districts are competitive, and the Worlds, N.A's, Pan Am Games, and Midwinter Circuit are well-planned and run. All in all, a great thing to be a continuous part of—the Lightnings." Many thanks to Bruce Goldsmith, four times North American Champion, sailmaker, and competitor in many one-design classes for his analysis of the Lightning, his favorite class.

•

If you want an excellent, comfortable boat for afternoon sailing...take a close look at older Lightnings in excellent condition that are no longer competitive.

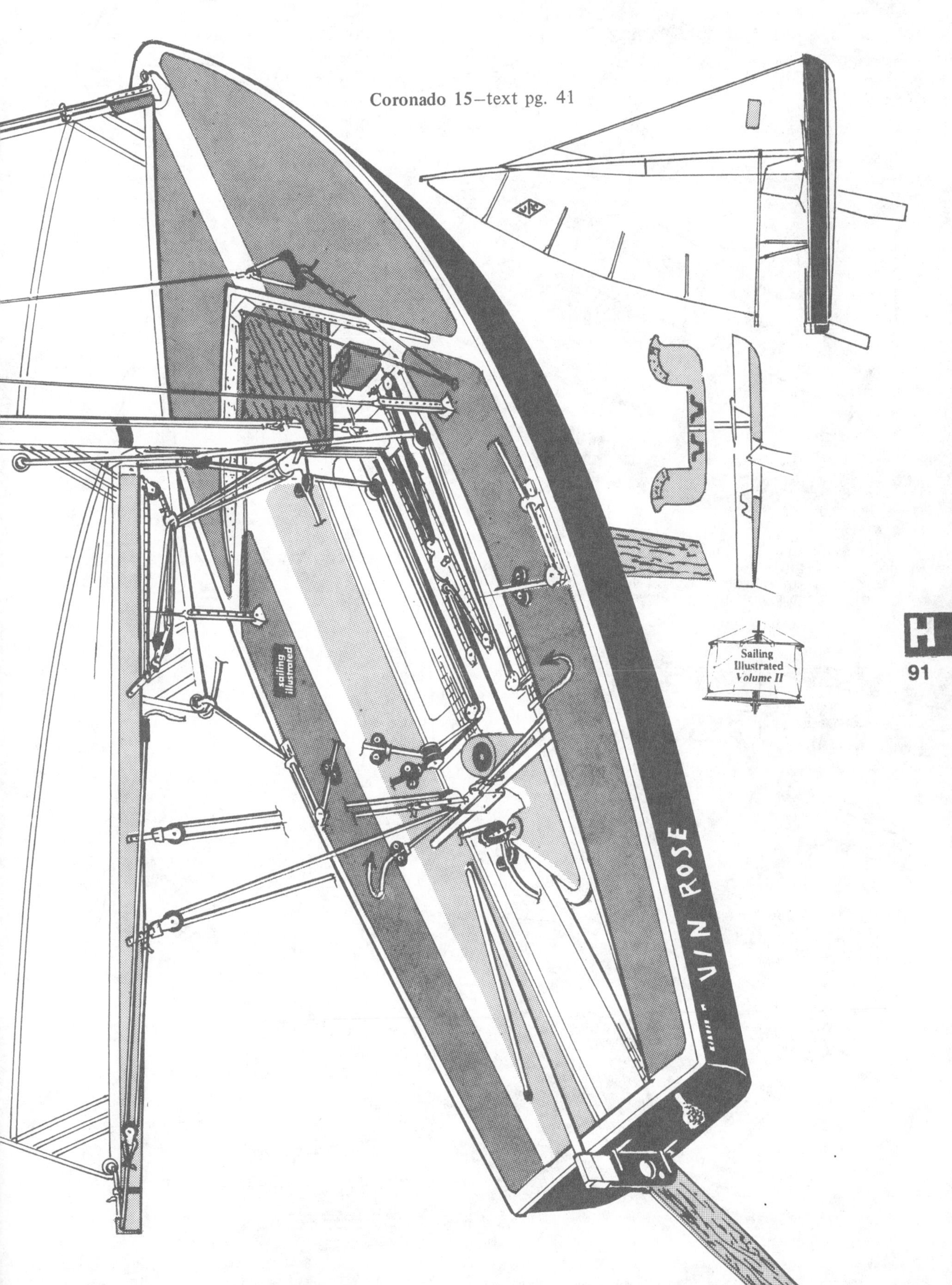
Coronado 15–text pg. 41
sailing illustrated
V/N ROSE
Sailing Illustrated Volume II

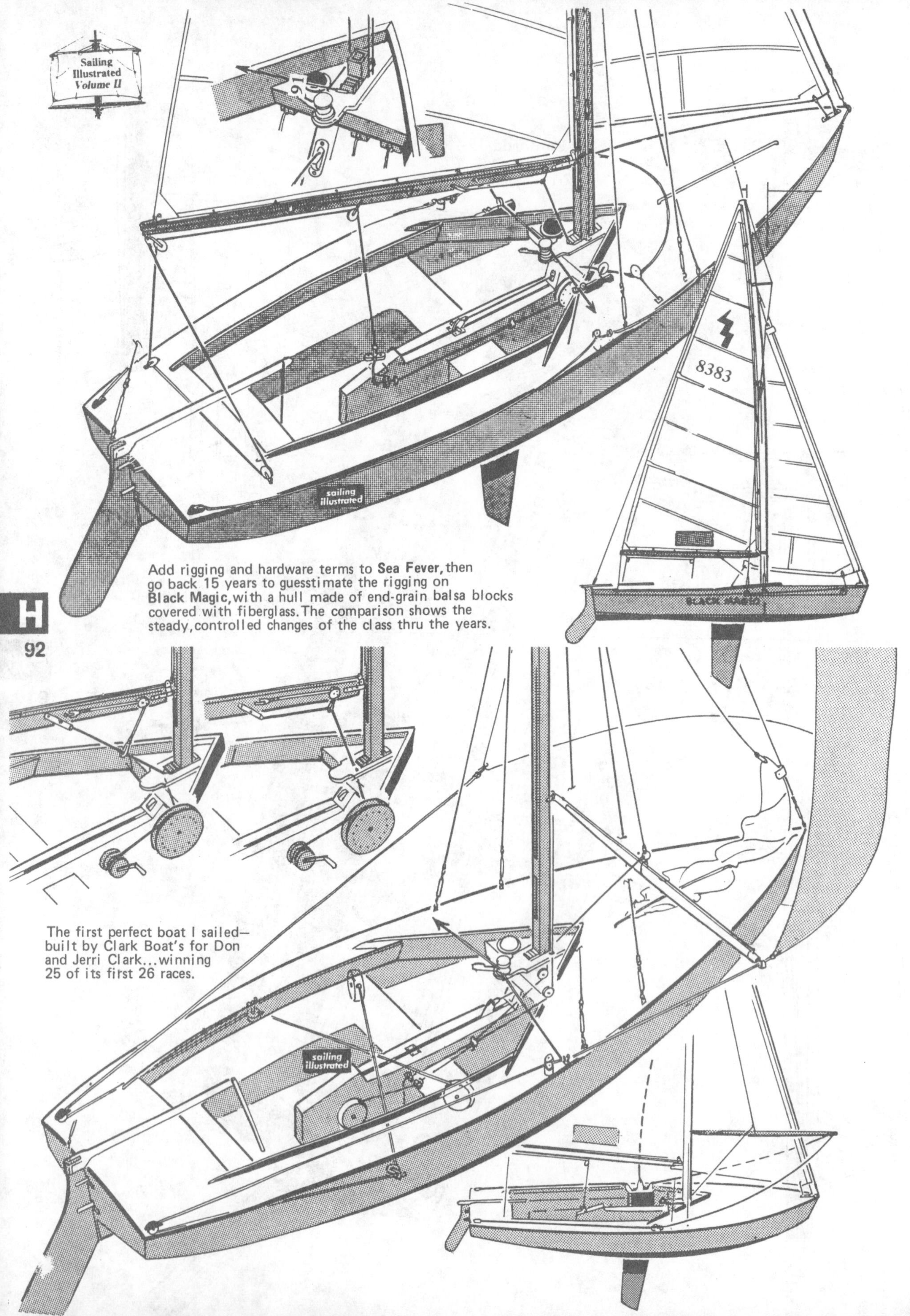
Sailing Illustrated Volume II
8383
sailing illustrated
sailing illustrated

Add rigging and hardware terms to **Sea Fever,** then go back 15 years to guesstimate the rigging on **Black Magic,** with a hull made of end-grain balsa blocks covered with fiberglass. The comparison shows the steady, controlled changes of the class thru the years.

The first perfect boat I sailed—built by Clark Boat's for Don and Jerri Clark...winning 25 of its first 26 races.

Sailing Illustrated Volume II
sailing illustrated
13191
Lightning--text pgs.34-37
SEA FEVER
H

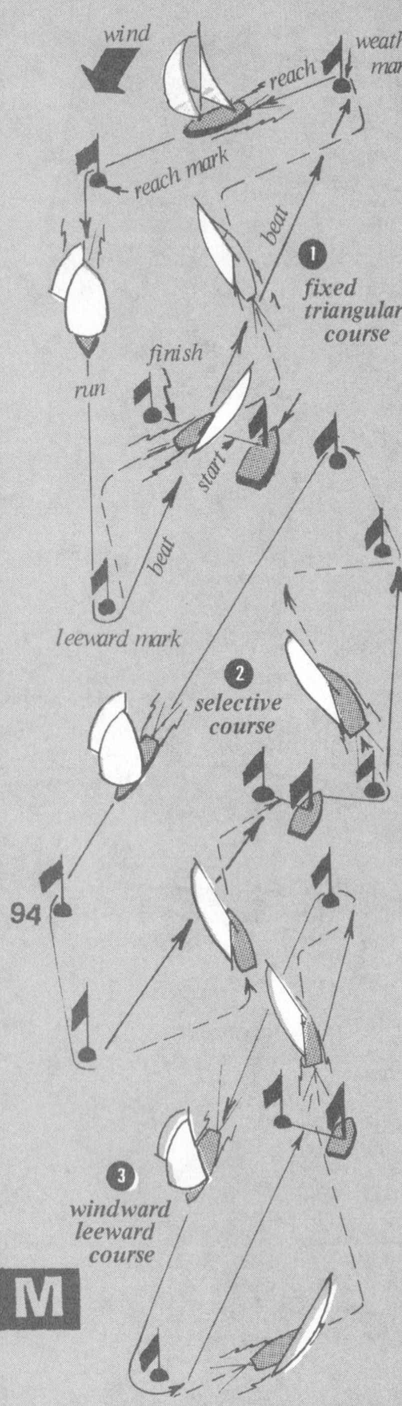

wind
weather mark
reach
reach mark
beat
fixed triangular course
finish
run
start
beat
leeward mark
selective course
windward leeward course

M

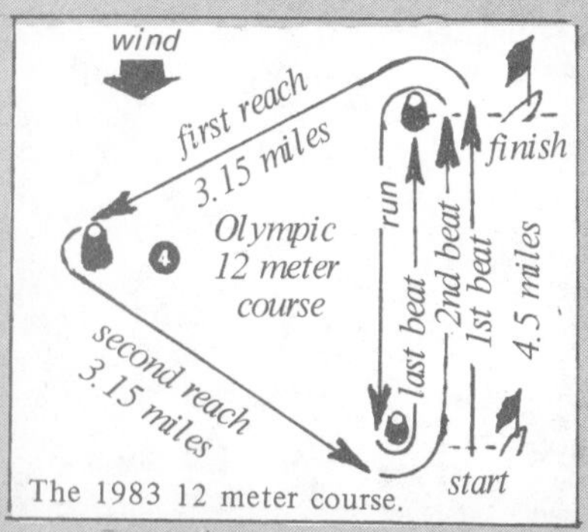

wind
first reach 3.15 miles
Olympic 12 meter course
run
last beat
2nd beat
1st beat
4.5 miles
finish
second reach 3.15 miles
start

The 1983 12 meter course.

Welcome to sailboat racing!

Luck may contribute 5% to winning a sailboat race.

Sailing has more challenges to those wanting active competition from ages 9 thru 80 than any other competitive sport.

80% of a race is won by preparation by boat, skipper, and crew before the start of a race. IF you hope to reach the upper level of c[ass competition you must have the best prepared hull, the best waterfoils below, the best rigging layout and hardware, and the best airfoils above that you can afford.

15% depends on race course gamesmanship. If you are relaxed and prepared, you are able to lean back, relax, and enjoy trading tack for tack with contestants... looking for that little opening so you are able to outthink your competition.

5 % involves luck as defined by top-level competitors of Lightning, Star, Snipe, Hobie, and FD classes involved in regional, national, and international competition.

"Five to seven of us are equal at the top level regardless of class. Near the end it takes a slight wind change, a wind hole, or small equipment failure for one of us to move in to take that first place. We also know the following year our first place leader will face an identical, fragile, competitive situation".

Sailing the Course, 51-1 (a). A yacht shall—

START and FINISH only as prescribed in the starting and finishing definitions even if the committee boat is anchored on the side of the starting or finishing MARK opposite to that prescribed in the sailing instructions.

A fixed triangular course ❶ usually has marks passed to port or counterclockwise. The first leg is normally a beat, followed by a reach, a run, and a beat to the finish.

A selective course ❷ may be used in areas having a variety of markers. Just before the race the course to be sailed is given. Race instructions then provide the sequence of the markers to be followed.

A windward leeward course ❸ may be specified used either once or twice around.

The Olympic 12 meter course ❹ covers a total distance of 24.3 nautical miles. It begins with a beat, a first reach, a second reach, a beat, a run, and finally a beat to the finish.

Starting Signals, 4-4 (a).

Unless otherwise prescribed in the sailing instructions, signals for starting... many be made at 5-minute intervals exactly and shall be either——

❺ *white warning signal*

❻ *blue preparatory signal*

❼ *red starting signal.*

Sailing Illustrated Volume II

In system (ii) each signal shall be lowered 30 seconds before hoisting of the next, and in starting yachts by classes, the starting signal for each class shall be the preparatory signal for the next class.

Color in the ***International Flag Code Signals*** at right so they will be easy to remember.

Our 3 day Midwinter Regatta in early March has storms before and after the event. It was fortunate due to a heavy work load I had to cancel out of one Midwinter Race.

The race committee boat was flying the reverse course signal near the stern seen only by part of the racers...so some raced the course clockwise, others, counterclockwise. Large fleet confrontations took place at turn marks when meeting headon with others going an opposite direction.

How did the race committee let it get so far out of hand with protests underway three days later? This example seems an excellent idea for you to memorize those signals.

Color in signals

Lima — yellow, black, black, yellow

come within ha
or follow me

Mike — blue, blue, blue, blue

blue — *mark signal*

November

abandonment sig

Papa — blue

preparatory sign

Sierra — blue, white

shorted course sig

X-ray — blue

reverse course sig

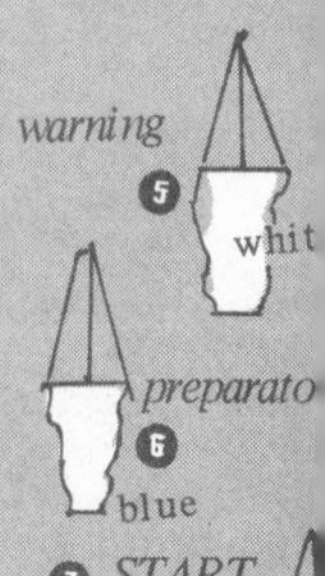

warning
❺
whit
preparato
❻
blue

❼ *START*

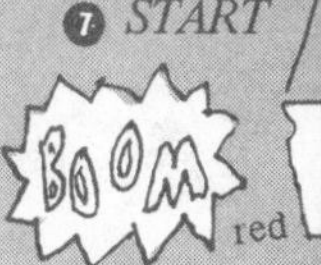

BOOM
red

BOOM
START
BOINK
Eight ways NOT to win races..
TILT
TILT
POP
BLUB
Sailing Illustrated Volume II
RTC
FINISH
ROYCE
FD
Flying Dutchman
1984, 1988 Olympic dinghy competitors
470
the 470
Finn
Tornado cat
Star
text-pg. 43
151
Soling
the America Cup Challenge
1851 to ??????
12
RACING BASICS
M

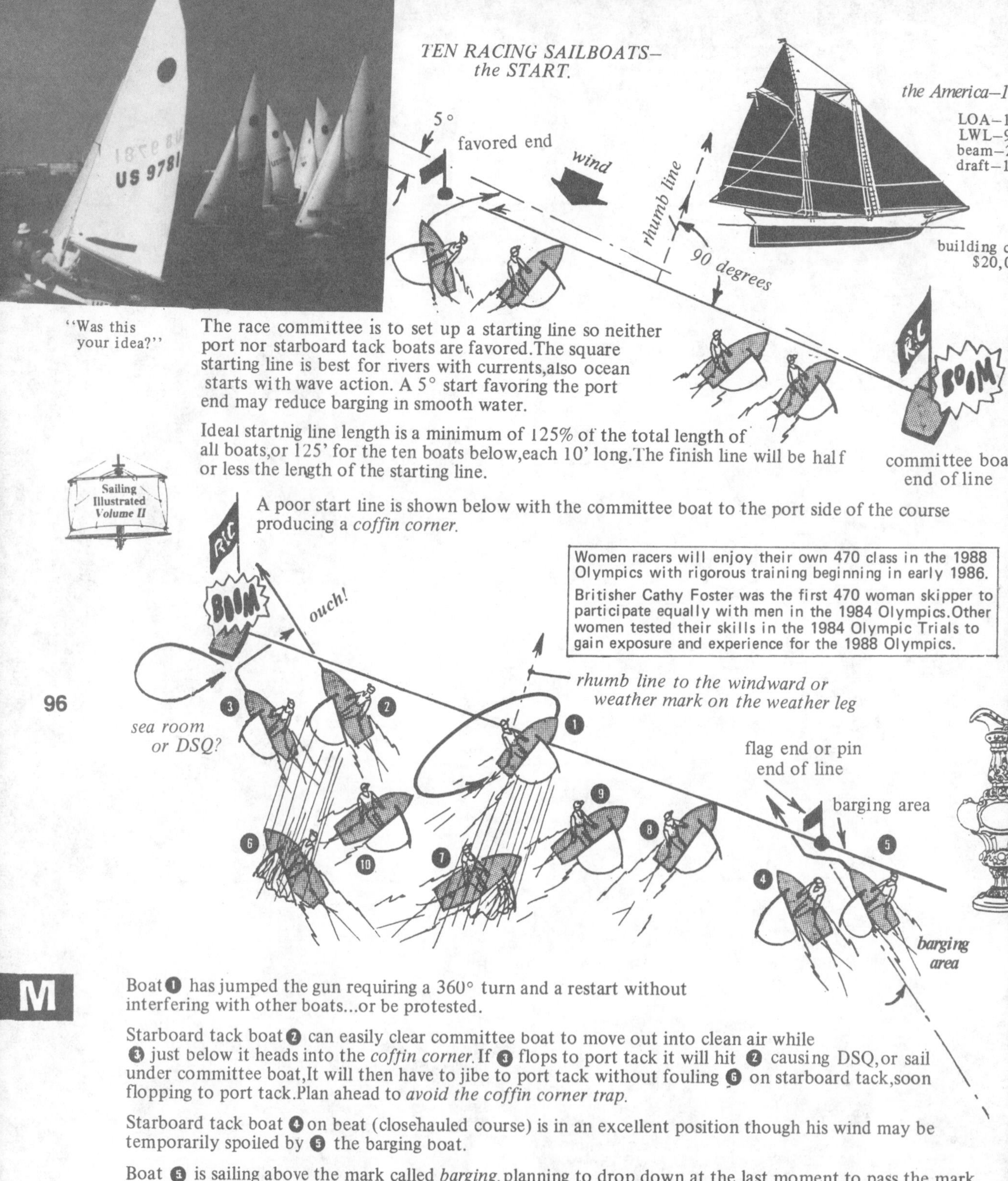
US 9781
TEN RACING SAILBOATS–
the START.
5°
favored end
wind
rhumb line
90 degrees
R/C
BOOM
the America–1
LOA–1
LWL–9
beam–2
draft–1
building c
$20,0
committee boat
end of line
Sailing Illustrated Volume II
R/C
BOOM
ouch!
rhumb line to the windward or
weather mark on the weather leg
sea room
or DSQ?
flag end or pin
end of line
barging area
barging
area
1
2
3
4
5
6
7
8
9
10

"Was this your idea?"

The race committee is to set up a starting line so neither port nor starboard tack boats are favored.The square starting line is best for rivers with currents,also ocean starts with wave action. A 5° start favoring the port end may reduce barging in smooth water.

Ideal startnig line length is a minimum of 125% of the total length of all boats,or 125' for the ten boats below,each 10' long.The finish line will be half or less the length of the starting line.

A poor start line is shown below with the committee boat to the port side of the course producing a *coffin corner.*

Women racers will enjoy their own 470 class in the 1988 Olympics with rigorous training beginning in early 1986.

Britisher Cathy Foster was the first 470 woman skipper to participate equally with men in the 1984 Olympics.Other women tested their skills in the 1984 Olympic Trials to gain exposure and experience for the 1988 Olympics.

Boat ❶ has jumped the gun requiring a 360° turn and a restart without interfering with other boats...or be protested.

Starboard tack boat ❷ can easily clear committee boat to move out into clean air while ❸ just below it heads into the *coffin corner.* If ❸ flops to port tack it will hit ❷ causing DSQ,or sail under committee boat,It will then have to jibe to port tack without fouling ❻ on starboard tack,soon flopping to port tack.Plan ahead to *avoid the coffin corner trap.*

Starboard tack boat ❹ on beat (closehauled course) is in an excellent position though his wind may be temporarily spoiled by ❺ the barging boat.

Boat ❺ is sailing above the mark called *barging,* planning to drop down at the last moment to pass the mark on the correct side.One approach is to avoid barging as it has too many risks.On the other boat ❹ is the class leader with the barging boat ❺ coming out when clear... to stick near the leaders stern to duplicate his movements.Near the end of the race ❺ will try to capitalize on any mistake and try to outsail the leaaer.

Sailboats ❼ , ❽ ,and ❾ on port tack,must rapidly shift to starboard tack to avoid ❹ and ❺ and each other,without bunching up on the new tack.

Boats ❻ and ❼ are *in the tank* with wind shadows and wakes from upwind boats due to poor planning, insufficient experience,or both...with boat ❻ headed for a jam-up at the committee boat.

Sailing
Illustrated
Volume II

TEN RACING SAILBOATS–the REACH, the RUN, the BEAT, and the FINISH.

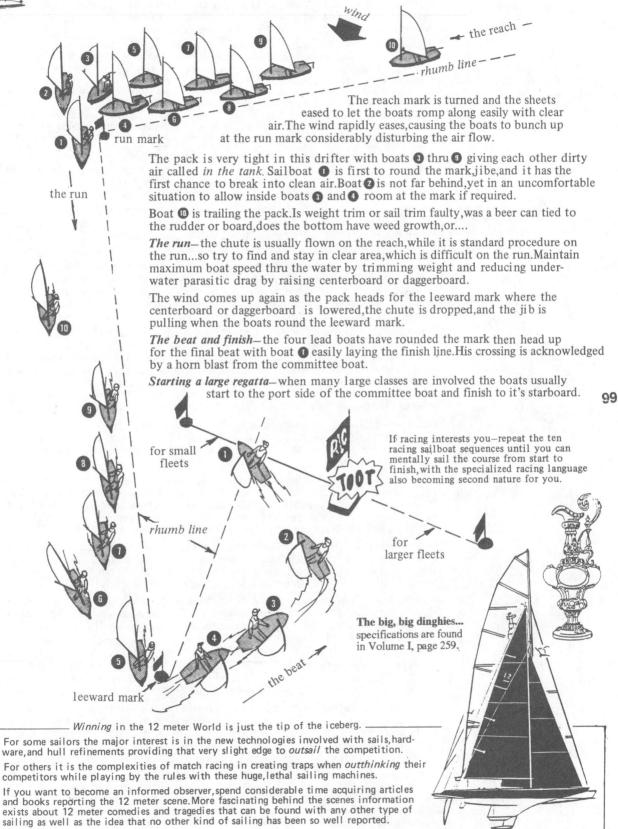

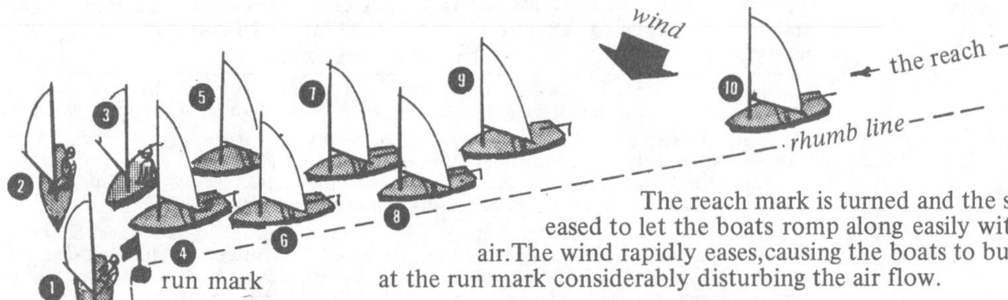

wind
the reach
rhumb line
run mark
the run
rhumb line
for small fleets
for larger fleets
leeward mark
the beat
TOOT
R/C

The reach mark is turned and the sheets eased to let the boats romp along easily with clear air. The wind rapidly eases, causing the boats to bunch up at the run mark considerably disturbing the air flow.

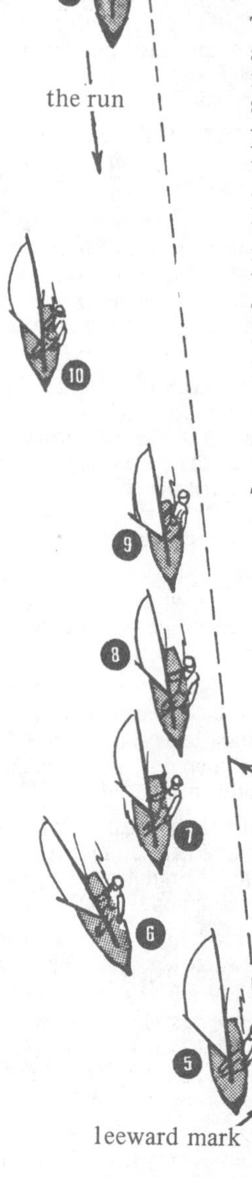

The pack is very tight in this drifter with boats ❸ thru ❾ giving each other dirty air called *in the tank*. Sailboat ❶ is first to round the mark, jibe, and it has the first chance to break into clean air. Boat ❷ is not far behind, yet in an uncomfortable situation to allow inside boats ❸ and ❹ room at the mark if required.

Boat ❿ is trailing the pack. Is weight trim or sail trim faulty, was a beer can tied to the rudder or board, does the bottom have weed growth, or....

The run– the chute is usually flown on the reach, while it is standard procedure on the run...so try to find and stay in clear area, which is difficult on the run. Maintain maximum boat speed thru the water by trimming weight and reducing underwater parasitic drag by raising centerboard or daggerboard.

The wind comes up again as the pack heads for the leeward mark where the centerboard or daggerboard is lowered, the chute is dropped, and the jib is pulling when the boats round the leeward mark.

The beat and finish– the four lead boats have rounded the mark then head up for the final beat with boat ❶ easily laying the finish line. His crossing is acknowledged by a horn blast from the committee boat.

Starting a large regatta– when many large classes are involved the boats usually start to the port side of the committee boat and finish to it's starboard.

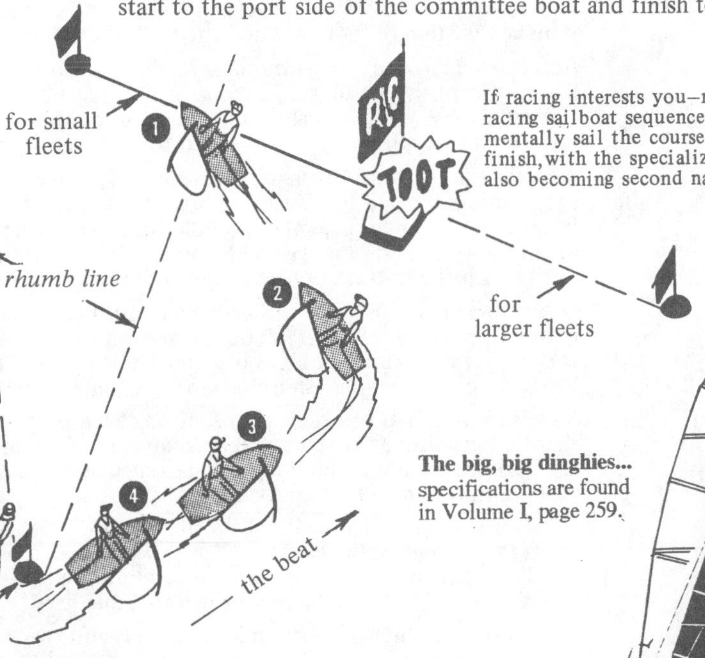

If racing interests you–repeat the ten racing sailboat sequences until you can mentally sail the course from start to finish, with the specialized racing language also becoming second nature for you.

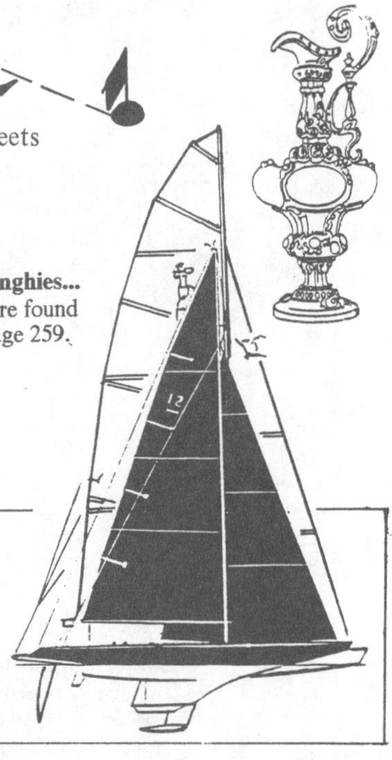

The big, big dinghies... specifications are found in Volume I, page 259.

Winning in the 12 meter World is just the tip of the iceberg.

For some sailors the major interest is in the new technologies involved with sails, hardware, and hull refinements providing that very slight edge to *outsail* the competition.

For others it is the complexities of match racing in creating traps when *outthinking* their competitors while playing by the rules with these huge, lethal sailing machines.

If you want to become an informed observer, spend considerable time acquiring articles and books reporting the 12 meter scene. More fascinating behind the scenes information exists about 12 meter comedies and tragedies that can be found with any other type of sailing as well as the idea that no other kind of sailing has been so well reported.

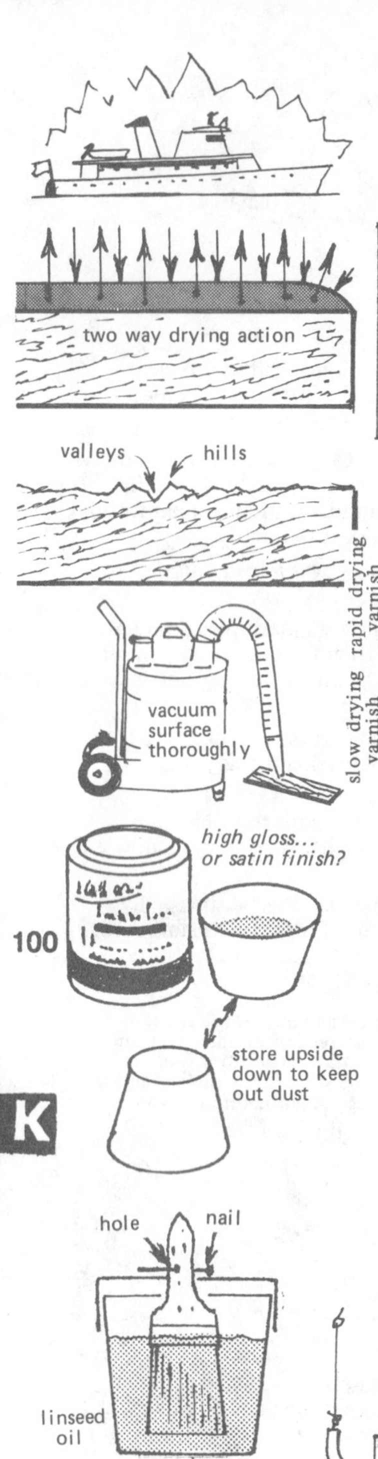

two way drying action
valleys
hills
rapid drying varnish
slow drying varnish
vacuum surface thoroughly
high gloss... or satin finish?
100
store upside down to keep out dust
K
hole
nail
linseed oil
container
board of nails
Burma teak— varnish may NOT be your answer.

"Why does my varnish hate me?????"

A good varnish job requires time and patience.Professional skippers have confided that when competing for a new job,the first factor to consider is to have a pleasing personality... followed closely by varnishing expertise.

> Varnish dries from the inside out by chemical action.Inner volatiles are escaping while non-volatiles are hardening or polymerizing with both actions taking place at the same time.
>
> The major enemy of varnish is the Ultra Violet rays of the sun,a good reason to cover the brightwork when leaving your boat.Dust is an ever present enemy while varnishing the reason you should avoid sanding and varnishing in the same area.Avoid varnishing outdoors if even a light drizzle may be expected as it will damage the drying varnish.
>
> The humidity dropped rapidly from 55° to 3° on our indicator as a warm Santana moved in while varnishing several boat parts in our backyard.The outer skin dried immediately sealing the surface while retarding the drying action beneath.Ten days drying action was required.

Sand new wood with the grain using coarse 60 waterproof (wet/dry) paper to remove hills from the wood surface.Clean wood surface and surrounding area with a vacuum cleaner.Next rub the wood surface with a ***tack rag*** to break static electricity which would otherwise hold an invisible layer of sawdust.

Float on a rapid drying foundation of ***jet speed*** or similar varnish.*Drying time may be reduced by cooling the varnish below the wood surface temperature before applying.* After varnish surface is dry,sand with 60 to 100 paper until wood grain hills disappear. If varnish balls develop while sanding,the varnish isn't dry...sand later.

Vacuum,use tack rag,then flow on the 3rd coat of rapid drying varnish by ***brushing across the grain*** to fill the pores.After the surface is dry sand lightly with 220 to 230 fine waterproof paper to just ***remove the shine*** so that the next layer of varnish has a surface to adhere to.Vacuum,use a tack rag,then flow on a coat (the 4th) of ***Polyurethane,Durathane,*** or similar layer of slow drying varnish.

Professionals often added up to 17 coats of varnish in the fifties.Some owners favor 5 layers of modern varnish which we tested on our name boards that were exposed to the year-round elements that developed small cracks in the varnish.Moisture seeped thru the cracks into the wood causing a discoloration stain.The boards were removed, sanded to the wood in the stained area and stored inside until dry.The stained area was sanded,then several varnish layers added.*If aging* or character is desired,partially remove the stain,or let new wood age first to develop waterstains...then varnish.

Revarnish BEFORE cracks develop in the varnish surface.When we tested 7 to 10 layers of varnish,the surface lasted a year without cracks nor water stains...though the surface becomes dull.The name boards should be sanded lightly,then two or three coats of slow drying varnish are added for another year of service.

A quality 1½" bristol brush will provide a lifetime of varnishing as it improves with age if properly cared for.Clean the brush with turpentine after varnishing,then brush it out on an old newspaper.Drill a hole thru the brush handle as shown so that the brush can be stored in a plastic container with the top adjusted so the brush hairs can't touch the bottom or side of the container...then add linseed oil.

Pour sufficient varnish into a clean paper cup,then replace the varnish can top snugly before a chemical action starts on the varnish surface inside the can.***Don't shake or stir varnish*** as harmful bubbles develop.These bubbles must be removed by pouring the varnish thru small mesh nylon stocking material which traps the bubbles.

Varnish several flat pieces at a time,storing each piece on a bed of nails (remove the sharp points with a file) thus catching any varnish running down the sides.When you are varnishing parts with unusual shapes such as a tiller,add small screw eyes to the parts so they can be tied up for drying. ***The reason a new elixar appears monthly—***

> Exterior mahogany trim will take a rich varnish finish...while varnish is difficult to adhere to expensive ***Burma teak (Tectona grandis)*** due to it's high natural oil content slowly seeping out to provide long life and durability.If your teak trim is left alone... its color will fade from the rich brown to a dull gray.
>
> An oiling every month on outside teak trims,and twice a year on teak floorboards below is sufficient for teak to maintain its natural golden brown color.Exterior teak decks require continual care to be eye appealing,or let it weather to become gray and improve its non-skid footing.***Avoid***— food with an oil base falling on teak such as butter,peanut butter,mayonnaise,fried chicken,etc.,that cause long-lasting stains.

Sailing Illustrated Volume II

Epoxy? While driving past the diamond plater slips in our anchorge, a worker was varnishing an expensive nameplate. When walking down the dock, it was obvious he was varnishing teak. I asked how he sealed the oil inside. " If Catalina Yachts uses ***Epoxy*** with a five year sealant protection from blisters, why can't epoxy seal the teak oil inside just as efficiently?" ***After 40 years varnishing...***

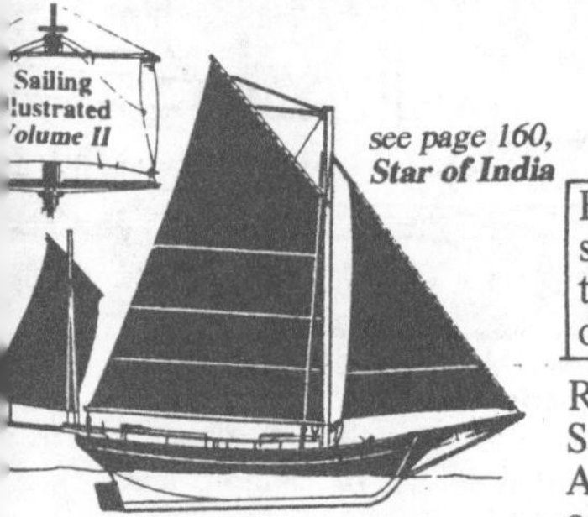
Sailing
Illustrated
Volume II

see page 160, **Star of India**

THE FIRST SAILBOAT MAY OFTEN BE CHOSEN FOR THE WRONG REASONS

Buying your first *dream boat* is one of the most emotional decisions in your life,the second...selling the boat.Our exposure indicated one in four first-time buyers chose the right cabin sailboat for their ***personality*** ,experience,and kind of sailing.We hope our *Homestudy Guide* may help turn these odds in your favor.

Joshua Slocum's SPRAY
36'9'' LOA
14'2'' beam
4'2'' draft
rebuilding cost-
13 months labor
$556.63 total cost

Retired USN Admiral Ed King bought the **Igdrasil** which was an identical replica of Slocum's **Spray**.It had sailed around the world twice under its first owner,while the Admiral was preparing it for another circumnavigation,rebuilding it below with a lot of stainless steel resembling the inside of a battlewagon.

Ed received a hurried call from a broker to survey a large schooner.After an hour of checking,Ed came topside to report the craft was in such poor condition that he would not charge for his services.The bristling customer shoved a check for the full amount into the brokers hand.It was the only sailboat they had seen about which his wife had made a favorable comment.She liked the *blue curtains.*

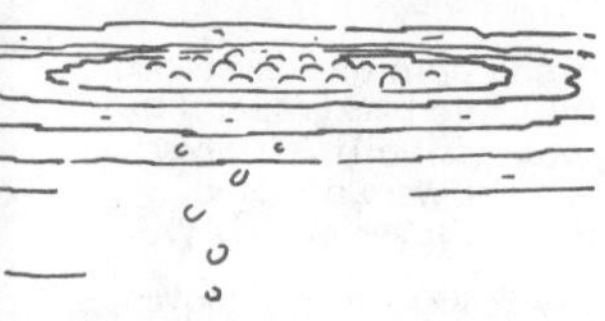

Farewell blue curtains!

The issue disturbed Ed,yet the sail to Hawaii was uneventful.It was again provisioned for a long trip,the destination,Tahiti.A slight problem developed after it headed out from the dock,sinking like a rock before reaching the harbor jetty.Ed had a big grin as he handed me a mug of coffee,"The latest information...the owner wants to sue me for not stopping him buying his *blue curtain dream boat". If we had more surveyors...*

Aavertising keeps the wheels of American business turning. Advertising provides exposure so readers can compare competitive products...such as a new car to replace the old one.The person seeking his first sailboat without such a foundation for analysis may be in *a captive situation.* Some salesmen try to sell the customer what he needs,which develops confidence and a good relationship so the owner returns to buy his second...and third sailboat. A salesman taking advantage of the situation by selling the largest,most expensive sailboat for the largest commission which is beyond the owners competency may cause hard feelings discouraging repeat sales.

The loner,competitive fighter pilot personality type needs competitive boats with small crews.

Our sailing lessons provided many surprises. Several highly competitive corporation officers wanted to buy big cruising sailboats for relaxation.By the end of the day I helped convince them to buy a competitive Cal 25,and to be active in racing and yacht club activities.After a race they can meet similar officers of other companies on a first name basis in the yacht club bar to make deals.Both could then make end runs up their corporate ladders to bypass officers above them.

The large sailboat,bomber pilot type personality is deceptive.Sailors want to join his team as he is a good leader,easy and relaxed to be with in tight quarters.

Salesmen goofed on three students..."The salesman said I shouldn't buy a boat over 20 feet".They were tall,relaxed,and action oriented with little interest in small talk. At the end of the day I recommended they buy 40' or larger sailboats as their easy-going personalities would insure an endless list of excellent crew members.I wish I were present when their salesmen found their deceptive and unimpressive customers...had unlimited bank accounts and lots of leisure time.

sailboats are out of their element,and deceptive to analyze at boat shows

Sailboat shows provide an exposure to boats and dealers for comparison...yet the sailboats are out of their element with too much emphasis on the downstairs apartment. ***Used sailboats deserve consideration*** as loose ends may be worked out and extra equipment installed.If the boats are in the water,go for a sail,but *only buy a boat you are interested in after it is fully checked by a marine surveyor.* Some sailors want a second opinion feeling new sailboats should also be surveyed before buying.

used sailboats may be better buys than realized

Your age and personality are major factors to consider when buying a sailboat,the reason we provide a wide coverage from the load-carrying cruising sailboats to the long,lean ULDB racers.If you intend to borrow heavily to finance a sailboat,it will seldom work out...while a smaller boat may be a better choice than realized.

age,personality,and bank account...are major factors to analyze

If you desire a large cruising sailboat,***consider chartering*** 2 or 3 cruising boats of the size you desire to analyze the compromises you are looking for.

No man will be a sailor who has contrivance enough to get himself into a jail,for being in a ship is being in jail with the chance of being drowned...a man in a jail has more room,better food,and commonly better company—
Samuel Johnson,1759

A few random ideas have been provided to consider before buying that first sailboat plus a couple of pitfalls...so when you hire a surveyor you hope he will have the standards of EdKing.The happiest boat owner I remember,moved to Newport Beach to retire at age 70.Though Mel Keim had a butler,and a chauffeur,and he could probably buy the largest sailboat in the harbor,his choice was Lido 14 #80,on which we enjoyed many sails together.Mel was the first WW 1 officer appointed to the Signal Corps to start what would grow into our Airforce..After his assignment Mel wandered out of the office in shock muttering..."But what is an aeroplane?"

SOLD— subject to survey.

A sailboat is for sale... buyer and seller agree to terms. A marine surveyor is chosen to examine the boat, basically checking items listed by the seller needing work. If the boat passes survey, you own your sailboat, and you pay the surveyor for his expertise. **Add a clause to the sale agreement, *If the sailboat can't pass survey,*** the seller will instead pay the surveyor.

Santa Maria

A 3 to 1 length to width hull ratio was common in the 1700's...increasing to 5.7 to 1 with the extreme 1850 early clippers.

*Admiralty and other precious historical model information—

National Maritime Museum—London SE10 9NF01-858 4422

Our favorite—*Ships of the Western Tradition to 1815, by A.H.Waite*

EVOLUTION of the SAILBOAT HULL

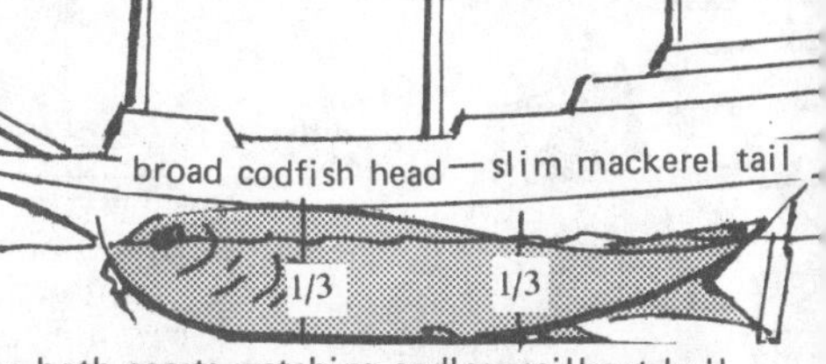

broad codfish head — slim mackerel tail
1/3
1/3

Our friends the ducks, seagulls, and pelicans, have displacement hull bodies designed by nature. Their waterlines or *waterplanes* are similar to sailboat monohull waterplanes.

For four decades I've enjoyed exploring boatyards on both coasts, watching endless sailboat hull designs supported by tired blocks of wood, and partially corroded nails Where did each design idea begin, how did it grow to reach the present state of the art, and how can it be improved.

Present day sailing designs started and grew with the practical idea that goods *or* cannons may be moved in volume with more cost effectiveness than horse, mule, oxcart...or camel*.

Traditional European hull design had a *bluff codfish bow entry* and maximum beam well forward, narrowing to slim *mackerel stern lines.* Typical vessels were the *Santa Maria* and the *Mayflower* that were cranky downwind with a maximum 6 knot speed, while the flexible hemp rigging reduced practical windward performance, see *page 146.*

Admiralty models* began to be submitted for important proposed naval and merchant vessels in the 1600's, often taking 3 to 5 years to build. They were made scale size plank by plank with frames, bulkheads, and interiors below which could be taken apart for analysis...with masts, sails, and rigging functional topside for critical evaluation. The investment was well spent for the winning shipyard which could support it for a few years. The choice was made by European Admiralty naval officers long on practical experience who had worked their way thru the ranks,

Though naval architects began making line plan drawings by the 1700's Admiralty officers still short on hull design theory, preferred making their choice with these beautiful models.

The Revolutionary War was a disaster for our small, novice sailing fleet. The next century was to be the testing ground for faster, more efficient, and more seaworthy sailing vessels such as the **Pride of Baltimore** we can use as a benchmark as it is alive and sailing today.

Sovereign of the Seas

A middle ground communications method was needed to analyze the strong opinions developed by naval architects short on sea duty, and captains and mates without academic backgrounds but with tremendous practical experience. The seamen, while often on long voyages, built *lift-layer half models* with alternate slab layers of dark and light wood. After the slabs were doweled together the side view, top view, and maximum width were carved on the slab layer assembly.

The final whittling began until it was down to the desired lines. The dowels were then removed, with hull measurements made of the slab layer waterlines...which were enlarged to full size on the shipyard loft floor to which full sections, diagonals, and buttocks were added.

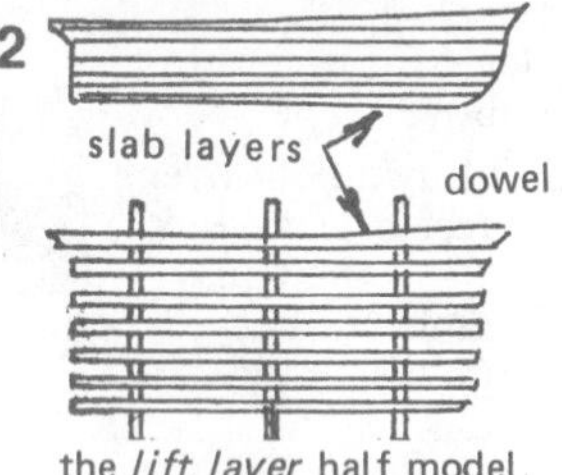

slab layers
dowel

the *lift layer* half model

The evolving *duck waterplane theory* began. The wide, bluff codfish bow above developed a disturbance and **lift action. The reaction** on the other end of the hull tetter totter, text pg. 115, was for the slim mackerel tail to begin sinking, dragging its tail without aft hull support.

The bow entry was slimmed down, and the beam increased from midship to the stern to provide an aft waterplane to resist tail dragging. The new concept worked well but required improvement for the bow entry to reduce lift tendencies as the wind increased. The *Baltimore Clippers* then could sail on their fore and aft lines carrying tremendous canvas loads to break all speed records.

Our naval architects adopted the new waterplane theory around 1870 developing new math formulas to take the lead with accurate, precise hull line drawings. This technology has been fine-tuned thru the century with the 1938 **Iris** lines shown at right, *page 121.*

The line plans show regularly spaced sections defining the accurate hull section in three dimensions. It shows a hull form from the side, bottom, bow and stern, with each view detailing three sets of lines, two being straight, the third, curved.

Chinese junk lug rig

The *North Sea double-ender design* developed from Viking long boats to Norwegian rescue lifeboats designed to row out from...and return to the beach thru heavy surf, with sail used only as auxiliary power. Double enders today have reduced hull capacity, with more rolling tendencies downwind, and are more active at anchor than wide transom sailboats.

Chinese sailing history which has been a way of life for 2000 years has been ignored by their historians. It required Marco Polo in 1298 while in a Chinese prison to make a report of fleets of 4 masted junks used by merchants. The large ones had 13 watertight compartments and a single deck with 60 cabins, more or less, for merchants plus pepper, cloth, etc. The larger vessels required crews of up to 300 for handling under sail with four to handle a sweep or oar.

Chinese hull design theory...*it should ride the water like a duck with a wider beam aft, becoming narrower at the bow.* If you ordered a traditionally-built junk, the length would be governed by how many compartments were desired...without any line drawings. The bottom would be built first, the watertight bulkheads added, planking is added to the sides, followed by adding the decking and masts. The Chinese introduced the daggerboard, centerboard and stern rudders. The balanced lug sail operation is covered on page J 23, introduced by Blondie Hasler to the western world.

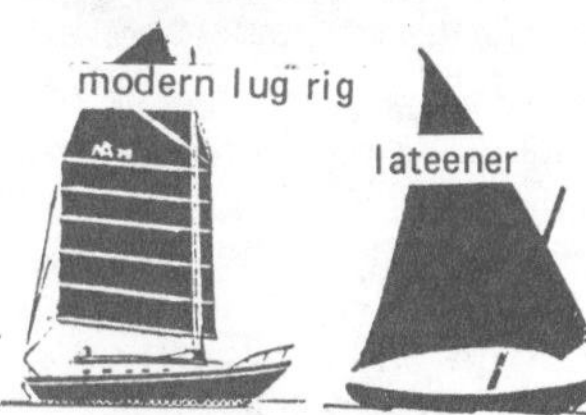

modern lug rig
lateener

Only two books we feel have recorded the great sailing days of the Arab lateener which have gone forever. One is the *Periplus* in Arabic...the other, the **Sons of Sinbad,** was written by Alan Villers, published by Charles Scribner's Sons.

Villiers spent a year sailing Arab lateeners starting in late 1938. He reported the darndest combination of boatbuilding, operation, and sailing procedures governed by religion and tradition. Their hulls also used the *duck waterplane theory.* This is one of the most outstanding sailing books ever published which should be placed on your must read list.

Ship of the Desert

*Islam used the oxcart to the 5th century requiring straighter, wider streets with gentle grades. The sure-footed camel able to carry ¼ ton, replaced the wheeled oxcart. Streets using camel and donkey delivery became narrow and winding, with steep, changing angles. Gulf oil fortunes after 1965 sent camels to the stew pot, to be replaced by new cities, cadillacs...and the 747.

Present hull score—mackerel tail 1...duck 3. Tomorrow...????

Ship Models to 1815, A.H.Waite—Bookshop, National Maritime Museum, Greenwich, London, SE10 9NF

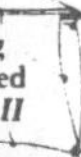

The LINES DRAWING *shows a hull shape from three views—profile, plan, and sections.*

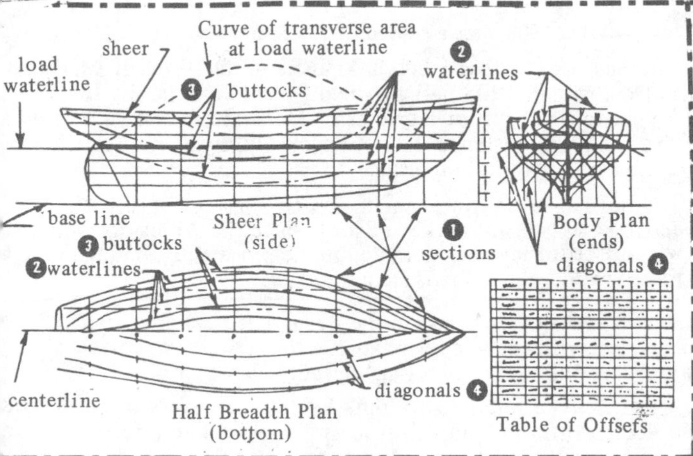

Curve of transverse area at load waterline
sheer
load waterline
2 waterlines
3 buttocks
base line
Sheer Plan (side)
3 buttocks
2 waterlines
1 sections
Body Plan (ends)
diagonals 4
centerline
Half Breadth Plan (bottom)
diagonals 4
Table of Offsets

The **SHEER PLAN** details the *side view* of a hull, will it be graceful, pudgy, or long and lean. It also shows deck height above the water called the *freeboard* in relation to its length, the gentle *sheer* of its deck line...and the *rake* of its bow and stern.

The **HALF BREADTH PLAN** shows the *beam*, how wide it is, and how the hull width is distributed along its length.

The **BODY PLAN** *(end views)* provide exact shape with accurate offset measurements on the hull shape at each station...or at each point of its width.

After the hull line plans have been approved, the line plans are laid out full size on the mold loft floor using measurements provided in the **TABLE of OFFSETS.**

The drawings at left and the line plans on the mold loft floor should be identical, except the lines on the floor are *full size...hopefully within an 1/8'' of measurements in offset table.*

1 ***Sections***, cross sections, or stations, are athwartship (beam) sections of the hull.

2 **Waterlines** are horizontal planes parallel to the load waterline in feet and inches.

3 *Buttock* lines are vertical planes at regular intervals parallel to the keel.

4 Diagonals are lines crossing frames close to right angles to develop hull lines.

5 A ***rabbet*** is a groove cut into a keel, etc., to receive edges or ends of planking.

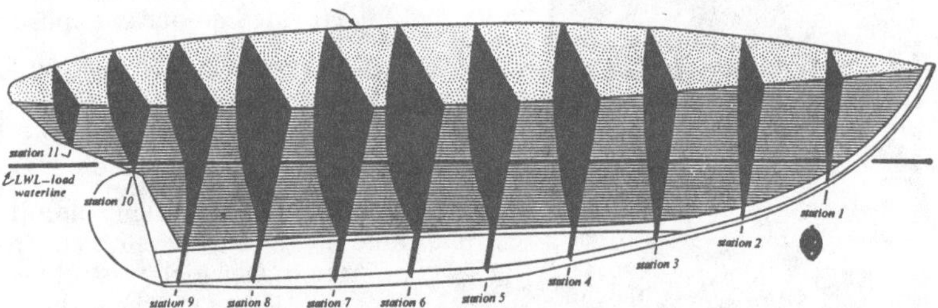

station 11
LWL-load waterline
station 10
station 9
station 8
station 7
station 6
station 5
station 4
station 3
station 2
station 1

The naval architect *lines drawing* above...and our perspective interpretations of them at right are of the lovely *Iris*, a 1938 design *pg. 121, text pages 71-2.*

/e hope to work with a lines drawing when we etail a new sailboat. It becomes an easy though 'me-consuming task to translate these plans into erspective which you see in our Homestudy Guide.

/e are often limited to a side view and a top view. /e have to mark stations on the boat, then draw ections with much measuring. The Pacific Cat was nolded by hand without plans nor measurements. /e had to mark stations on a hull, then cut card- oard templates to develop the lines in perspective.

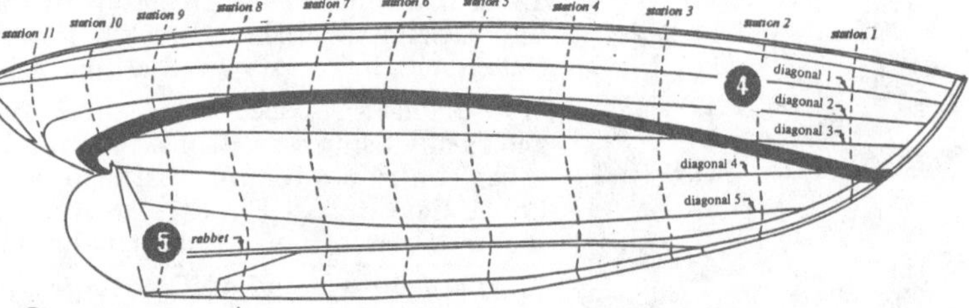

station 11
station 10
station 9
station 8
station 7
station 6
station 5
station 4
station 3
station 2
station 1
4
diagonal 1
diagonal 2
diagonal 3
diagonal 4
diagonal 5
5
rabbet

The lines of an 83 foot IOR maxi.

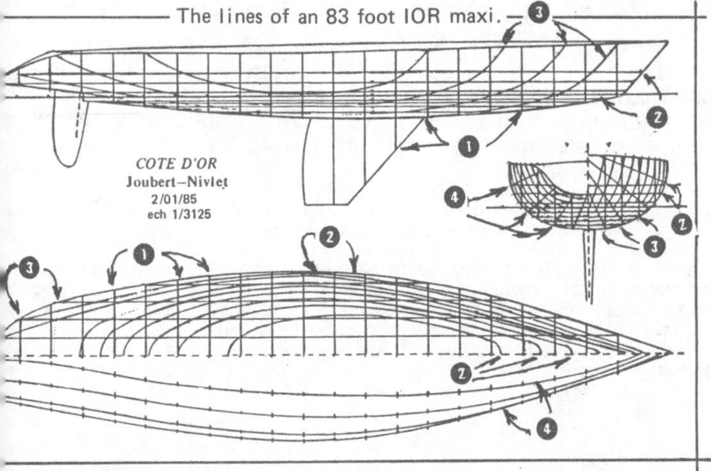

COTE D'OR
Joubert–Nivlet
2/01/85
ech 1/3125

After you understand the lines of the 1938 cruiser above...take an exam to apply this knowledge to the 1985 maxi lines shown at left.

Our responsibility in this *Guide* was to show a full and balanced story of sailing. This posed many interesting problems especially when we wanted to show the latest state-of-the-art set of IOR maxi lines for comparison with *Iris*.

Just before press time we received permission from Joubert-Nivelt* to show the lines of their 1985 maxi. It is a highly qualified team of designers for which we give thanks for helping our readers.

*Michel Joubert-L. Aubrecay-St.-Xandre, 17138 Puilboreau, France

*Bernard Nivelt-15 Main St., Stonington, CT 06378 USA

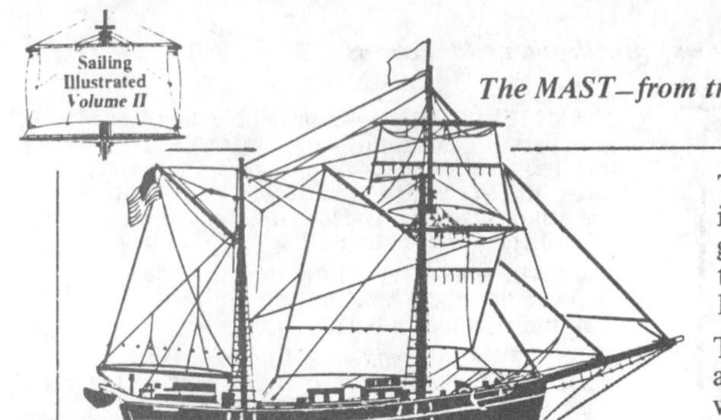
Sailing
Illustrated
Volume II

The MAST–from tree trunk...to the wet noodle...to the laminated tree trunk.

the 1908 classic crewed by Sea Scouts

The Sea Scout topsail ketch **Argus** is 68 feet long.It was built in Denmark in 1908,being owned by the same family for many generations except in World War II when it was taken over by the Nazis who installed its first engine.Our local Sea Scout Base has been the **Argus** home since 1970.*

The normal crew complement as a training vessel is five adults and fifteen boy and girl Sea Scouts since the **Argus** doesn't have winches requiring considerable muscle power.It uses much manila line even though most sails are made of Dacron.

Girl Sea Scouts working aloft.

I flew to Oakland in June 1982 to spend a week on the **Argus.**The next day we had a sail thru the Sacramento Delta with the wind force 6 due to the westerlies.While it is underrigged,it held hull speed on a run for a long period...what a thrill!

It was fun to be probably the first afterguard to bunk with the Sea Scouts in the hold finding they were very tolerant with no complaints of my snoring.The traditional rigging required considerable amounts of *Svedish Steam* from it's Sea Scout crew.

Who can predict the contributions the aging **Argus** will have for the future of sailing as by 1982 it provided an ocean exposure for over 20,000 boy and girl scouts.

When **Argus** needs a new mast a search begins for a tree trunk with the right dimensions. After WW II the hollow wooden mast gained favor ,but by 1960 the aluminum mast had become standard for many reasons.The strength requirements of aluminum masts ordered today by boatbuilders will average a safety factor of 2.5:1.

the popular
ARGUS mascot
ARGUS
wet
noodle
rig
backstay
runners
midstay
vang
babystay
the Chinese junk
Freedom 40
BE PREPARED
BSA

Eagle Award

Quartermaster Award

Mast requirements for the racing circuit are considerably different.The desire is to use hydraulic pressure to develop controlled mast bend to utilize maximum fractional rig sail trim potentials,which was pioneered in Star and FD classes,see page C 13.

The mast bending technique of the small dinghies has been adapted to the big dinghy IOR grand prix racers.The small section racing masts are lighter with less windage making them more aerodynamically efficient.Their bend can be changed precisely to provide the most efficient sail shape for varied conditions by tensioning the mast bending controls at left...sometimes with a mast safety factor of 1.1:1.

Hydraulic adjusters on backstay,babystay,midstay,and vang,can bend the center of the mast forward...with 4500 to 5500 psi pressure on just an IOR racer backstay. *For every action, nature provides an opposite reaction...* with these extreme mast pressures having to be absorbed by the hull.

Grand prix dismastings are common. Star sailor Lowell North provided a novel answer on his fractional rig 43' *Sleeper* with the smallest mast section in the fleet.It has a thin backstay planned to break before the upper mast if the runners are not taken in fast enough in a heavy weather jibe which may also include a broach.

Most dismastings occur after spreaders,tangs,or rigging fails,crew mistakes, collisions, and finally using a small mast section.If a spinnaker pole digs in during a wild run, it can contribute to a dismasting,or a weakness leading to a later mast failure. **Police Car**,dismasted in the Pan Am Race,was also in the 1979 Fastnet Race using the same mast when few mast failures occurred.Is an age factor potential also involved?

The need for seasonal AND periodic maintenance checks seem important to reduce the chance of dismastings,plus a continual awareness for problems in the developing stage.

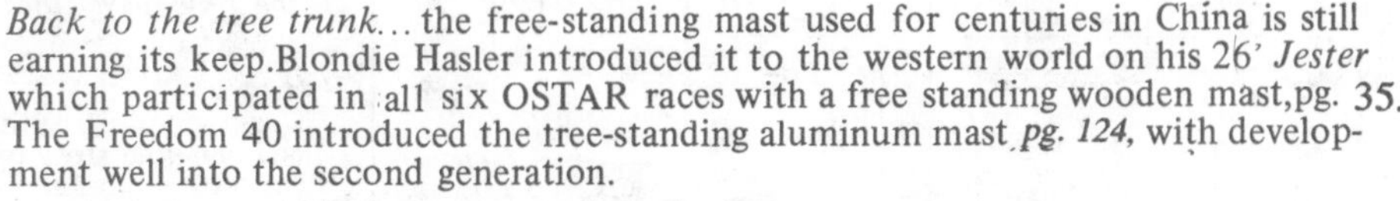

Back to the tree trunk... the free-standing mast used for centuries in China is still earning its keep.Blondie Hasler introduced it to the western world on his 26' *Jester* which participated in all six OSTAR races with a free standing wooden mast,pg. 35. The Freedom 40 introduced the tree-standing aluminum mast *pg. 124,* with development well into the second generation.

*Any person or business wanting to contribute to the coed Sea Explorer *Argus,* write to–SHIP 1069,Sea Scout Base,1931 Pacific Coast Highway,Newport Beach CA 92663.

The greatest potential any nation has is its future generation.The goal of Scouting is to help provide leaders for future generations in industry,government,and the armed services.The purpose of Sea Scouting is to develop leaders for ocean-oriented services from boatbuilding,to hardware manufacturing,and for our Navy.If you have a sailboat would you like to become involved with your local Sea Scout program to enjoy the friendship and challenge of active teenagers.It can be an investment in which everyone gains.

MAST RAISING METHODS

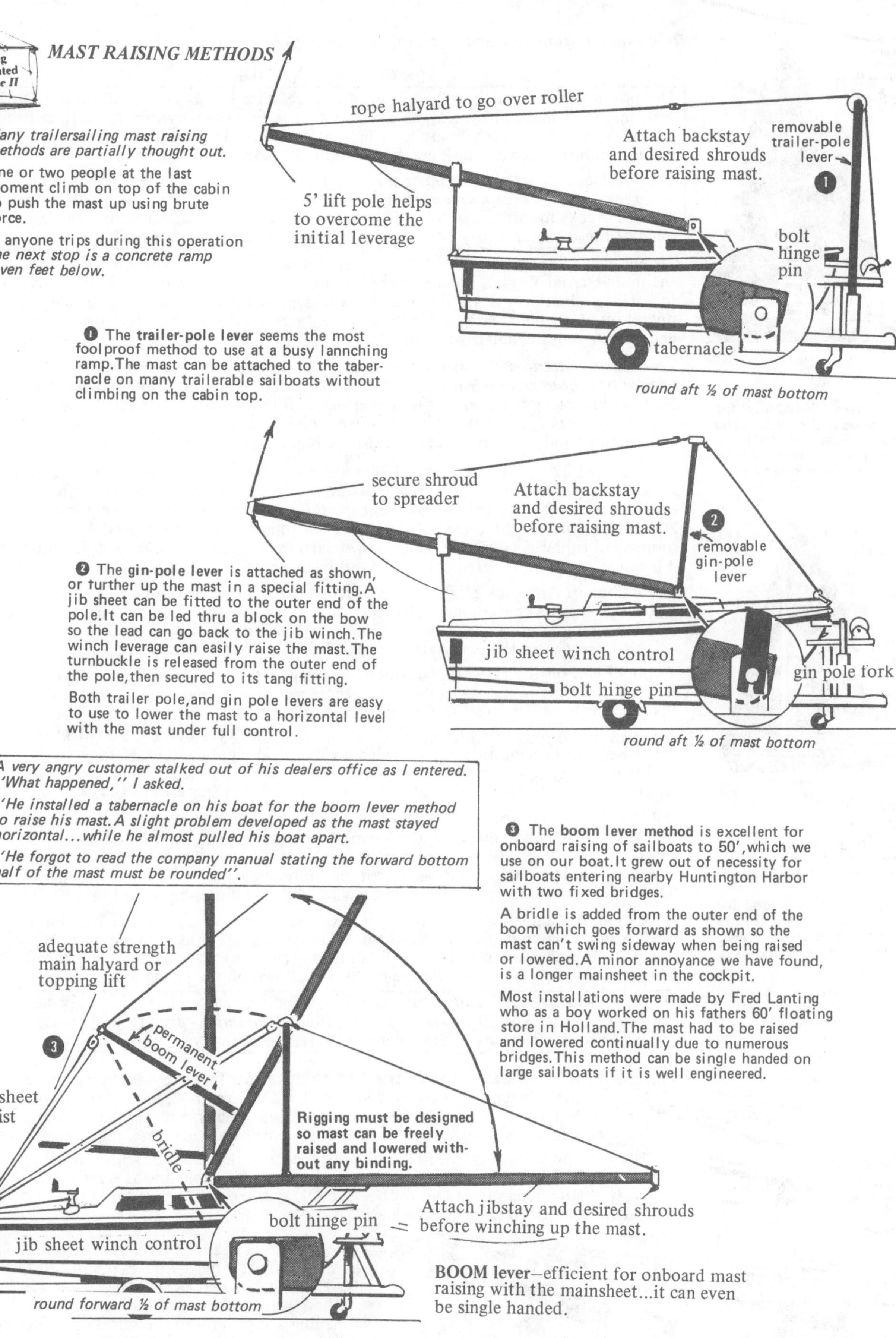
rope halyard to go over roller
Attach backstay
and desired shrouds
before raising mast.
removable
trailer-pole
lever
1
5' lift pole helps
to overcome the
initial leverage
bolt
hinge
pin
tabernacle
round aft ½ of mast bottom
secure shroud
to spreader
Attach backstay
and desired shrouds
before raising mast.
2
removable
gin-pole
lever
jib sheet winch control
gin pole fork
bolt hinge pin
round aft ½ of mast bottom
adequate strength
main halyard or
topping lift
3
permanent
boom lever
ain sheet
hoist
bridle
Rigging must be designed
so mast can be freely
raised and lowered with-
out any binding.
bolt hinge pin
Attach jibstay and desired shrouds
before winching up the mast.
jib sheet winch control
round forward ½ of mast bottom

Many trailersailing mast raising methods are partially thought out.

One or two people at the last moment climb on top of the cabin to push the mast up using brute force.

If anyone trips during this operation *the next stop is a concrete ramp seven feet below.*

❶ The **trailer-pole lever** seems the most foolproof method to use at a busy lannching ramp. The mast can be attached to the tabernacle on many trailerable sailboats without climbing on the cabin top.

❷ The **gin-pole lever** is attached as shown, or turther up the mast in a special fitting. A jib sheet can be fitted to the outer end of the pole. It can be led thru a block on the bow so the lead can go back to the jib winch. The winch leverage can easily raise the mast. The turnbuckle is released from the outer end of the pole, then secured to its tang fitting.

Both trailer pole, and gin pole levers are easy to use to lower the mast to a horizontal level with the mast under full control.

A very angry customer stalked out of his dealers office as I entered. ''What happened,'' I asked.

''He installed a tabernacle on his boat for the boom lever method to raise his mast. A slight problem developed as the mast stayed horizontal...while he almost pulled his boat apart.

''He forgot to read the company manual stating the forward bottom half of the mast must be rounded''.

❸ The **boom lever method** is excellent for onboard raising of sailboats to 50', which we use on our boat. It grew out of necessity for sailboats entering nearby Huntington Harbor with two fixed bridges.

A bridle is added from the outer end of the boom which goes forward as shown so the mast can't swing sideway when being raised or lowered. A minor annoyance we have found, is a longer mainsheet in the cockpit.

Most installations were made by Fred Lanting who as a boy worked on his fathers 60' floating store in Holland. The mast had to be raised and lowered continually due to numerous bridges. This method can be single handed on large sailboats if it is well engineered.

BOOM lever—efficient for onboard mast raising with the mainsheet...it can even be single handed.

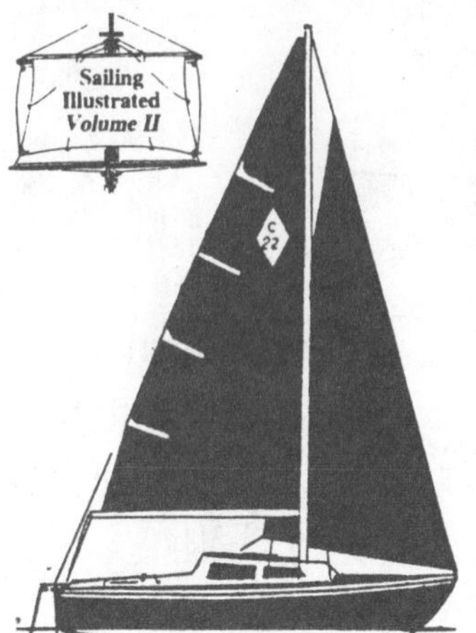
Sailing Illustrated Volume II
C 22

The excellent Mini-Cruiser for coastal areas and bays is found worldwide. Beaching, trailer loading and launching potentials may not be the strong point.

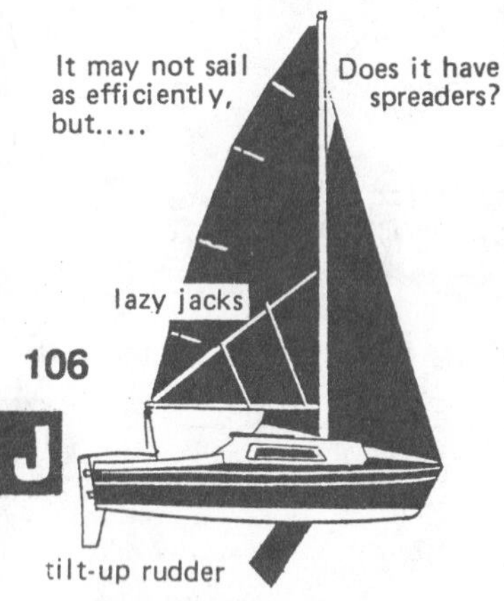
It may not sail as efficiently, but.....
Does it have spreaders?
lazy jacks
tilt-up rudder

The cabin sailboat is a beach boat with its fully retractible centerboard.... excellent for inland waters.

The 21' length is ideal for beaching, launching, loading and trailering. Weight and capacity increases rapidly with size.

The trailer choice is as important as the choice of a trailersailer!

How much portability and beaching do you desire?

sailboats without a tradition

The portable cabin sailboat had a questionable start. It was launched around 1967 with major promotion campaigns, the target...the first owner without a sailing background. Many of the early boats were light as possible, hardware and rigging were absolute minimum, with stark creature comforts below.

The *overloaded, partially engineered trailer* that was clumsy at the launching ramp, compounded the ***bargain dream.*** Many bargains were soon up for sale, or collecting dust for weeks, months...and years. If you have time, patience, and a sailing background, some of these bargains may be a blessing in disguise...after much rebuilding.

We enjoyed a variety of trailer-sailing students from Washington, Oregon, Lake Tahoe, the midwest, and Virginia. Most had unpleasant experiences with rigging limitations in a strong wind. Most of the day was spent underway understanding the normal operation of a sailboat's rigging requirements. the rest with creature comforts below and storage requirements, *pages 101-111.*

The heavy centerboard, also called a swing keel, ***requires a locking pin or preventer in case of a knockdown.*** Without such a locking mechanism in a knockdown, *the board could swing back into its well insuring a 180° capsize...* yet the lock should *be able to break if the board hits an underwater obstacle.* Check pivot pin for wear and chafe periodically, to be replaced if required..do you have extra pins?

The **Catalina 22**, detailed text pg. 51, is one of the ***ten breakthrough sailboats*** chosen by ***SAIL*** magazine, Jan. 1980. It is adequately designed topside and below, with an excellent Parts Catalog. It is an excellent *small bay and coastal sailboat* requiring 20" draft as the weighted centerboard does not fully retract into its well. A fully submerged trailer is needed at the launching ramp for launching and recovery...while it is much easier to be lifted off and be put back on its trailer with a hoist.

The **Balboa or Aquarius 21** ***Felix*** *is an excellent beach boat.* It can be run up on a sandy beach as its centerboard fully retracts into its well, and it can be easy to handle on a launching ramp *if it has an adequately engineered tilt trailer. Our first* exposure to this class was on the ocean finding the 21 didn't like ocean wave action.

We met ***Felix*** on the Hood Canal which has extreme tidal ranges in Washington. It was the first time returning to the Canal where my first sailing exposure had taken place 38 years earlier on a Flattie, now called a Geary 18.

We measured a foot of water at the dock *at low tide...* yet ***Felix*** was still afloat. We tossed our heaving line to our twins on the nearby public dock so they could pull it into deeper water. ***The centerboard was lowered,*** the rudder and sails added, and the comedy began as sailboats under sail were rare in this area of the canal.

While the force 5 is normal for local Newport Beach sailing, restaurant customers, commercial fishermen, mechanics and marina operators, stared in disbelief as we ***Felix*** headed into the whitecaps where it romped happily and spirited for eight hours. The boat was in its natural element with the short steep chop that was a considerably different motion from longer ocean wave patterns it didn't seem to like.

If we lived in a similar area, the choice of a Balboa 21 or similar would be high on our list. ***It would have to be fully rerigged for singlehanding*** as it was extremely hazardous to raise sails underway in a force 5. All sail raising and lowering, docklines, and anchor lines must be single handed from the cockpit as shown on the facing page.

Size compromises are involved for efficient handling with 21' to 23' trailerables the most popular. The 24 footer ***may have double the cubic capacity, weight. etc.*** compared to the 20 footer...the seemingly outer limits for normal, practical handling.

Start with the tilt-bed trailer!

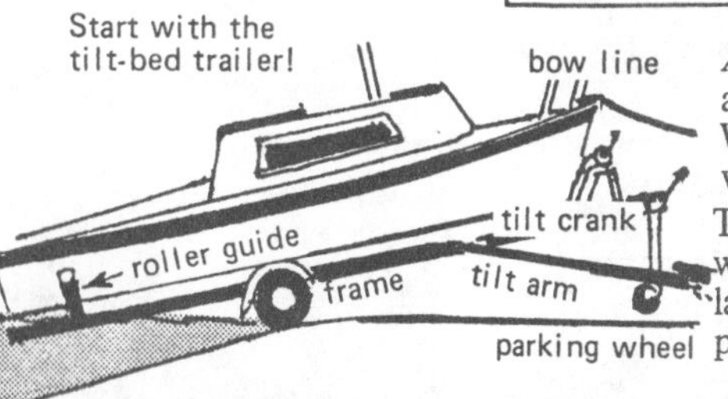
bow line
tilt crank
roller guide
frame
tilt arm
parking wheel

An overloaded trailer is a hazardous trailer. Its gross weight, capacity, axles, hitch, etc., may be adequate for an empty boat leaving the factory. Will the trailer safely carry your fully loaded boat plus fuel and water when it is ready to roll...or will it become overloaded and dangerous?

The ***controlled tilt-bed trailer*** is excellent for the 21' beachboat above, which can be easily launched and recovered nationwide at a variety of launching ramps. Our outboard book *Trailerboating Illustrated* was first published in 1960 also has ideas of use to the trailer sailor.

Our first choice trailer for a keel sailboat is the ***trolley/trailer design*** by E.B. van de Stadt, also FD designer, text pg. 61. The trailer does not have to be submerged for loading nor launching, and the boat can be stored on its trolley.

Rigging for single handling—text pg. 59

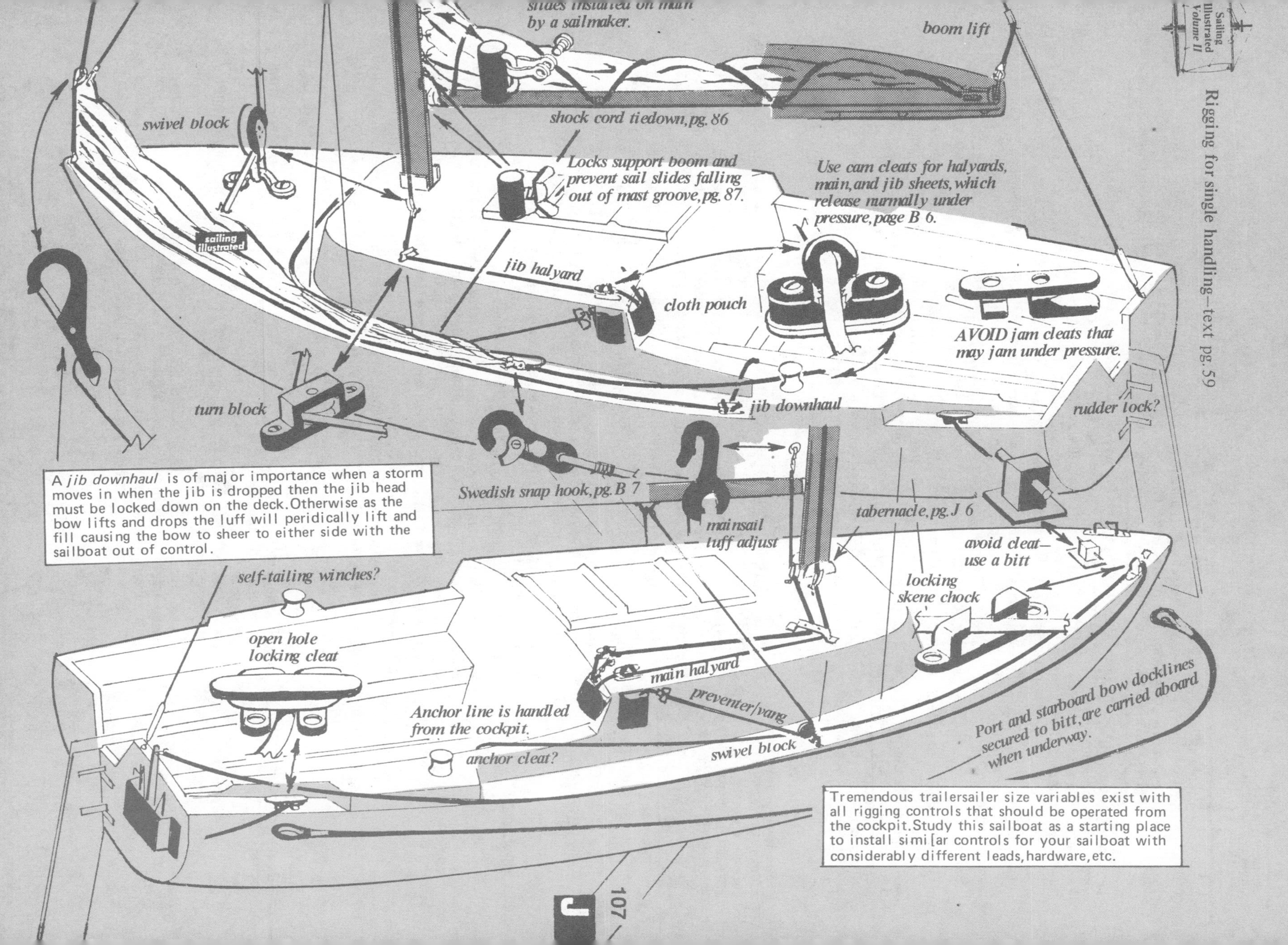

slides installed on main by a sailmaker.
boom lift
swivel block
shock cord tiedown, pg. 86
Locks support boom and prevent sail slides falling out of mast groove, pg. 87.
Use cam cleats for halyards, main, and jib sheets, which release nurmally under pressure, page B 6.
sailing illustrated
jib halyard
cloth pouch
AVOID jam cleats that may jam under pressure.
turn block
jib downhaul
rudder lock?
A *jib downhaul* is of major importance when a storm moves in when the jib is dropped then the jib head must be locked down on the deck. Otherwise as the bow lifts and drops the luff will peridically lift and fill causing the bow to sheer to either side with the sailboat out of control.
Swedish snap hook, pg. B 7
mainsail luff adjust
tabernacle, pg. J 6
avoid cleat—use a bitt
locking skene chock
self-tailing winches?
open hole locking cleat
main halyard
preventer/vang
Anchor line is handled from the cockpit.
anchor cleat?
swivel block
Port and starboard bow docklines secured to bitt, are carried aboard when underway.
Tremendous trailersailer size variables exist with all rigging controls that should be operated from the cockpit. Study this sailboat as a starting place to install simi[ar controls for your sailboat with considerably different leads, hardware, etc.

Sailing
Illustrated
Volume II

Careful choice and planning are required to be comfortable for long periods aboard.

the traditional pocket cruiser world

The dream of many restless sailors during the past century was the early blue-water pocket cruiser, proving a continuous seamanship challenge. These small boats close to the ocean surface with wooden hulls, canvas sails, manila rope, and poor quality metals, required continuous maintenance. They were operated by rugged sailors with few creature comforts as many compromises were required in early pocket cruisers.

cargo carrying capacity— water and food requirements for medium and heavy displacement sailboats

Load carrying capacity for weight and storage are major factors to analyze for the distance you want to cruise. A person averages a gallon of potable water a day at 8.3 lbs. per gallon, 60 lbs. per week, *salt water may be used for cooking and washing, use salt water soap,* plus 25 lbs. of food per week. The total is 85 lbs. per person of food and water a week under normal, NOT survival conditions.

weight and storage needs— for self sufficiency with two persons aboard for two weeks

Two persons aboard for two weeks would require a carrying capacity of 340 pounds. If a 50% safety factor is added due to adverse winds or lack of wind, etc., the weight increases to 510 pounds. To this add an additional 100 pounds per person for books, clothing, foul weather gear, plus a few bottles of beer and wine ...the total is 710 pounds.

choose pocket cruisers carefully

We enjoy all kinds of sailing though our favorite is the pocket cruiser. We checked endless boats up to 25' which are adequate for afternoon sailing or single operation for long periods. Wooden designs lacked comfort and privacy below for two persons with limited storage area...while most fiberglass hulls needed better planning.

Spend considerable time on various mini-cruisers to find their weaknesses...before you begin to recognize the right choice that will be comfortable.

The first practical pocket cruiser we found was the Columbia Challenger buying hull 223. We ordered it with basic standing rigging and some running rigging, yet minimum installations below. It was the beginning of a new, specialized sailing world we wanted to explore on our own with answers of possible use to readers.

CUSTOMIZING—

Due to small size you can't afford that first mistake— Take time to make ALL installations as accurately as you possibly can.

Our boat was operational in six weeks though it took three years to work out the loose ends until we were happy with the boat as *minaturization* was the challenge. Autopilot, depth sounder, and other installations were made later.

We averaged over 100 days yearly for familiarization on the water for the first three years while teaching or vacationing. This concentrated exposure to sailing proved ideal to analyze the variables in the pocket cruiser sailboats.

REPLACE lower single shrouds

We soon found in considerable wave action that the mast would go one way and the hull the other because of the single lower shrouds. This reverse motion ceased when the single lower shrouds were replaced with **double lower shrouds**.

visibility under jib

The working jib was raised 17" above the deck to improve student visibility when sailing through tight moorings. It proved a blessing in heavy weather as waves drained overboard easily under the jib, protecting the sail, sheets, and rigging.

lifelines???????????

Several owners installed **lifelines** we detailed in an early Challenger illustration. We had second thoughts for our 24' sailboat feeling that the low lifelines would increase the chance of tripping and falling overboard..

cockpit railing

We installed a stainless cockpit railing to reduce the chance of students falling overboat. It soon proved excellent to secure our safety harnesses to in heavy weather sailing. We added a high bow pulpit to protect the crew forward when anchoring or mooring in bad weather, also to install our large running lights.

also the floating bungalow

Another feature of the pocket cruiser is as a **floating bungalow** for that lazy summer weekend when you want to loaf, swim, fish, gossip with dockside neighbors, or invite friends aboard for a barbecue supper with changing scenery. During the winter our boat often becomes a second office for analyzing new material and proof reading... with the wind and rain whistling in the rigging.

How much food and water for two persons to Hawaii, ...to Tahiti?

weekend cruising vs tradewind cruising

The 24' Challenger *Fille,* owned by Don and Colleen Brolin, made two round trips between California and Hawaii. Our builder Dick Valdez told us, "The last time we were in Hawaii we saw seven of our 24's, both flush deck and cabin models, recent arrivals in Waikiki's Ala Wai Yacht Harbor. After owners found the high shipping cost they decided it was more fun and more practical to sail their 24's to Hawaii.

with sufficient planning....

"We built over 2600 flush-deck Challengers. One of our most enjoyable moments was to find a Challenger from Canada in Papeete, tied stern to the quay. It had been sailed across the Pacific by a husband and wife crew". Pocket cruisers have limitations, yet with sufficient planning they have been sailed long distances.

Cloud
24'4"
18' 0"
3' 4"
t 1850 lbs.
3930 lbs

rea–
5 sq.ft.

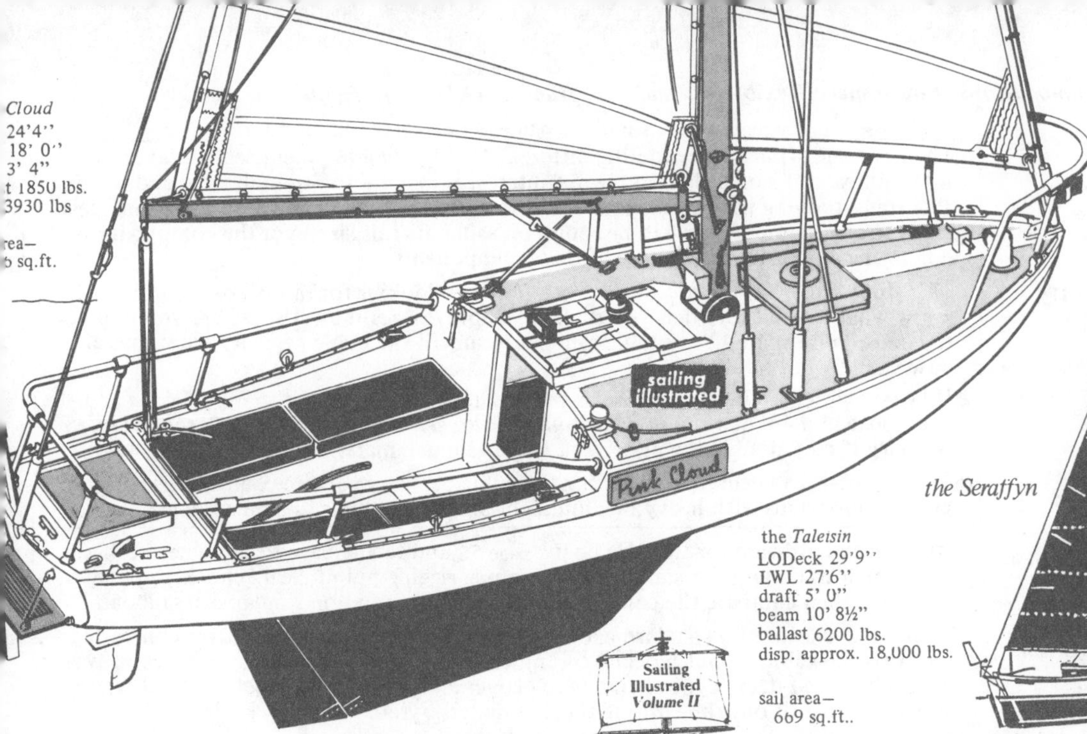

the *Seraffyn*
LODeck 24'7"
LWL 22'2"
draft 4'8"
ballast 2720 lbs.
disp. 10,686 lbs.

sail area–
461 sq.ft.

sailing illustrated

Pink Cloud

the *Seraffyn*

the *Taleisin*
LODeck 29'9"
LWL 27'6"
draft 5' 0"
beam 10' 8½"
ballast 6200 lbs.
disp. approx. 18,000 lbs.

sail area–
669 sq.ft..

Sailing Illustrated Volume II

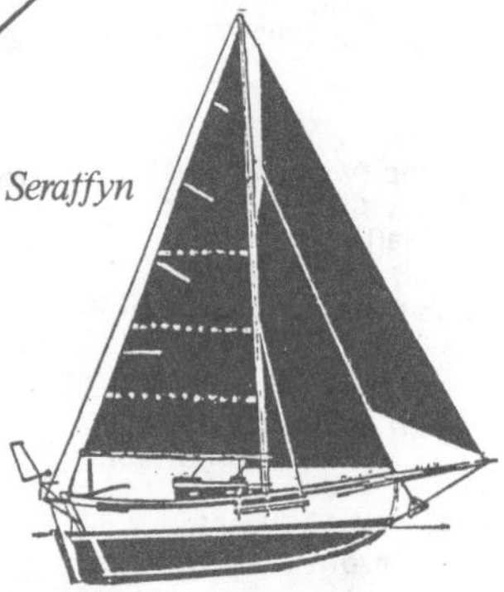

While most of us sit, dream, and procrastinate as we grow older each day, Lin and Larry Pardey spent ten years sailing around the world in their engineless 24' *Seraffyn*. They are provisioning their new engineless 30' *Taleisin* for departure nearby as this page is being prepared. Good Luck Lin and Larry...we will follow your worldwide adventures in your excellent books and magazine articles!

A summary follows of 25 years of the rapidly changing fiberglass boatbuilding technology terms. It will be interesting to watch the changing state-of-the-art techniques for the next decade with many new fiberglass ideas in the research and development stages.

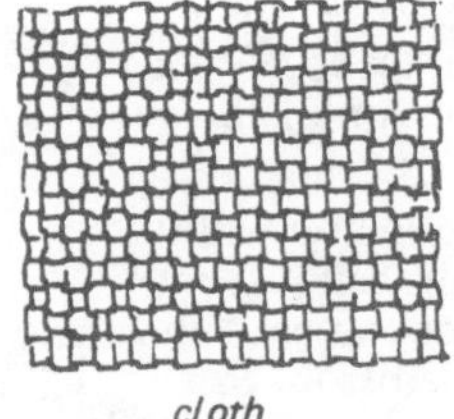

cloth

- The common fiberglass hull is a sandwich laminate made of layers of cloth, roving, and mat spun from glass fibers. These fibers are saturated with a resin compound. After the resin sets or polymerizes, the layers of the sandwich fuse together into one piece. This structural method eliminates the need in smaller glass boats for a permanent frame required for wooden boats.

  Fiberglass **cloth** has a fine weave, woven from fiberglass yarns of various plies and twists. **Roving** is a coarse weave fabric, the strands woven together without a twist. **Mat** is made of equal length fibers cut in a random pattern bonded with a powdered resin binder.

- **Polyester resin** is used on most production boats, while the more expensive **vinylester resin** is used with custom-built boats. **Epoxy resin** is used on hulls made of laminated wood strips, *pg. 137*, custom, and semi-custom hulls. Military boats use fire-retardant resins.

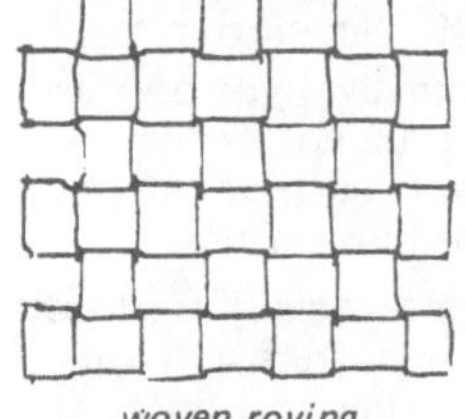

woven roving

- **Hand layup.** A layer of gel coat is sprayed into the female hull mold. This is followed with alternate layers of cloth, roving, and mat with a sufficient build up until the desired strength or thickness is reached. This is an expensive labor process as each laminate layer must be squeegeed to remove excess resin before it sets up. The glass to resin ratio is the key to the strength to weight ratio.

- The **chopper gun** was a questionable process when first used on outboard hulls. Sailboat builders watched and waited for it to be perfected. After the gel coat has been sprayed onto the female mold, the operator requires considerable training to avoid spraying on excess resin content which is indicated by the fiberglass color. A strand of colored filament goes into the gun with several strands of white, the resulting color hue indicating the glass content. The chopper gun advantage is less labor intensive, and the method isn't as expensive.

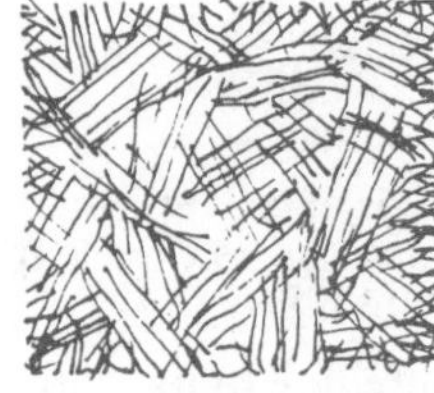

mat

- **Sandwich construction** uses a layer of wood or foam between two layers of fiberglass, with balsa the most common type core to produce strong, light hulls. The balsa grain is laid parallel to the fiberglass so if the skin is punctured, water damage will be minimized. An early balsa core, fiberglass hull was the Lightning *Black Magic, page 92*, with an outstanding racing record.

- **Vacuum bagging**– all laminates have been placed in the mold before the resin has been cured. A plastic sheet covers the full laminate, the sheet is sealed, and the air withdrawn. Atmospheric pressure compresses the laminates for a lighter, high glass to resin ratio.

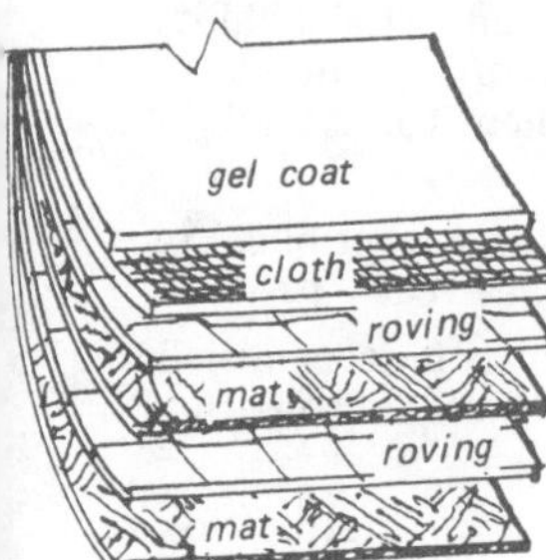
gel coat
cloth
roving
mat
roving
mat

- **Nomex** is a nylon fiber core material that is lighter than balsa blocks for sandwich construction. It is an excellent core for bulkheads, etc.

- **S-glass** is a structural glass cloth with less short strands of better quality. **Unidirectional biaxial, and triaxial fibers** are stitched together, not weaved together, which eliminates pockets for the resin to collect. While the method is more expensive to build high glass content laminations for light hulls, less material is required making it cost competitive with other methods.

- Any of the latter materials can be **pre- impregnated** fiberglass, with partially cured resin added by the manufacturer, which is kept frozen until it will be used. The final cure can be in an oven for an hour at 200 °F.

Accommodations,storage,space,flexibility—make it efficient AND comfortable.

Components are similar...with endless arrangement patterns.

Add callouts listed on text page 65 to the facing page.

The new sailor finds a bewildering difference in rigging,equipment,seating layout,etc., with sailboats of similar length.If your interest is in a 24' to 30' sailboat,spend considerable time studying the topside,and below deck arrangement shown on the facing page.

- **Many similar components will be found on sailboats this size...yet the complexity is due to the endless arrangements of these components.**

ADD ON,SUBTRACT or ELIMINATE

This study time will prove to be a great aid when looking for a sailboat as you will **know what to look for,what you'd like to improve or add on.Also,where you'd like to compromise** on a 22' portable sailboat with half the cubic capacity,**what to scale down...and what to eliminate.**

A sailboat four feet longer—

- If beam and length ratios are similar when comparing a 20' boat to a 24' boat...and a 40' boat to a 44' boat...***a sailboat four feet longer may have DOUBLE the cubic capacity.*** It may double the price with twice as much material,heavier rigging,etc.

tremendous cubic capacity differences—heavy disp.to ULDB sailboats.

- This is a basis to begin understanding the cubic capacity,volume of materials,and price comparisons with heavy,medium,light,and ULDB hulls of similar length.

human engineering topside—make it efficient

Study **deck hardware** for this size boat, page 56 and facing page to analyze the basic hardware installations for standing and running rigging,pulpit,cleats,chocks,running lights,etc.,then compare the components with those found on similar size sailboats.

human engineering below—make it comfortable

raised deck or cabin tradeoffs

We had the choice of **a standard cabin,or a raised deck** on a 24' hull.After comparing tradeoffs,the cabin layout blocked too much visibility underway,and the cockpit was small.The raised-deck layout had a much larger and more comfortable cockpit where we spend most of our time during the day underway...or when dockside.

What is standing headroom... and is it necessary?

Standing room is overstressed.It is very comfortable to sit below,read for long periods and to cook in our raised-deck hull though I am 6'6",and our boat is the *Model T* of pocket cruisers.I find the overhead of many cabin sailboats even up to 30' long which are uncomfortable for me when sitting below due to the junction of the deck and cabin which hits me in the back of the head or neck.

home sweet home afloat

Analyze a sailboat below at night.

Spend a night aboard a new or used sailboat before signing the check.You will find the new world below to influence your buying...or turning down the sale.I spent a night aboard a 25' boat I liked,to find the layout poor,the cushions too hard and the bunks too short...with a similar experience on a new 32' boat I sailed from San Francisco.The complaints continue with a lovely 54' schooner I checked for friends that was excellent topside.Layout,accommodations,and stowage planning were so poor it's practical capacity was considerably less than found in a 40' Newporter.

Poorly planned bunks are torture racks on boats 20,30,40,50, and 60 feet long.

Sleeping bags, pillow bolsters, soft cushions, and bunk straps

Our three bunks are 6.6" long with 5" thick cushions covered with naugahyde on the bottom and cloth on the top...as naugahyde will stick to bare skin on a hot night. Sleeping bags are excellent at night which during the day become soft cushions after being stuffed into pillow bolsters..Seat belt webbing is excellent for bunk straps.

bulkhead duffel bags page K 13

Every item needs its own place...and needs to be stowed in its place especially for loose items such as clothing.Our five duffel bulkhead bags are excellent organizers with one per person for all but a heavy jacket or sweater,and one for foul weather gear,boots,etc. Grommet drains provide excellent ventilation eliminating mildew potentials.

instrumentation

Depth sounder,heel indicator,and speedometer/odometer are mounted below for protection though are easy to see from the cockpit.The speedometer/odometer is very important to record speed and distance in low visibility ocean sailing.

Auto pilot vs wind vane?

The automatic pilot using battery power to follow compass headings is excellent for coastal sailing under wind power,engine power,or both.While the wind vane is excellent for offshore trade winds for long periods,it is questionable for coastal sailing.

Colored cockpit awnings are needed for summer use...AVOID white,due to its glare.

Midship sections of similar length hulls.

the hard chine

the hard bilge

The compromise—performance vs ride. The ***hard-chine*** hull with high-initial stability and greater keel depth,can have a quick motion underway.The ***hard-bilge*** hull has a slightly softer ride with a little less speed.While the hull is excellent for coastal racing,its motion may be too active for long-distance cruising.

the round bilge

The ***round bilge*** hull heels easier initially as it is more tender,with a deeper bilge for a lower cabin sole.It has a softer ride with a pressure-pocket lift on a reach page 77.

the slack bilge

The ***slack-bilge section*** (high-deadrise,or wine-glass section) for larger hulls is initially the most tender hull when you step aboard. It provides the stiffest hull section after it heels,to provide the softest ride for long-distance cruising.

extreme slack bilge

beam/length ratio

The ***extreme slack bilge,***heavy-displacement 1875 cutter has a 7 beam/length ratio-as for example a 70' long hull with a 7' beam,which was very tender and easy to sail under,see pages 69 to 77. Most sailboats in this chapter have a 3 to 4 beam/length ratio while extreme ULDB *Meridian,* page 177, has an approx. 4.8 beam/length ratio.

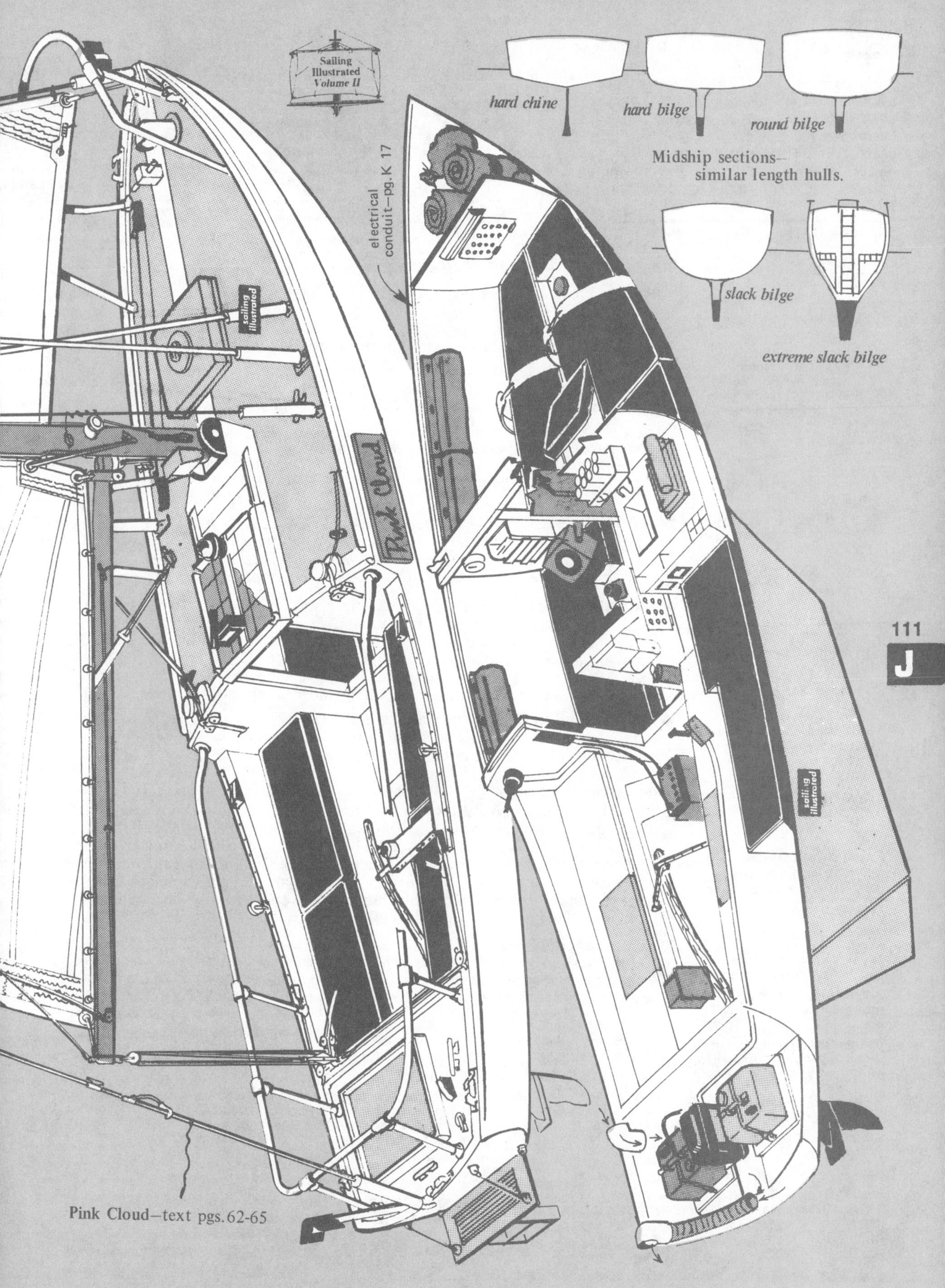
Sailing Illustrated Volume II
hard chine
hard bilge
round bilge
Midship sections–
similar length hulls.
slack bilge
extreme slack bilge
electrical conduit–pg. K 17
sailing illustrated
Pink Cloud
sailing illustrated
Pink Cloud–text pgs. 62-65

ANALYZE the D/L RATIO–heavy to ULDB.

sailboats	Chall.	Cal 25	J24	M24
LOA	24'4"	25'3"	24'0"	23'9"
LWL	18'0"	20'0"	20'0"	21'9"
beam	8'0"	8'0"	8'11"	7'2"
draft	3'4"	4'0"	4'0"	4'3"
ballast	1850	1700	950	2000 lbs.
disp.	3930	4000	2600	2000 lbs.
sail area	306	362	261	313 sq.ft.
disp.ratio -	301	189	145	86

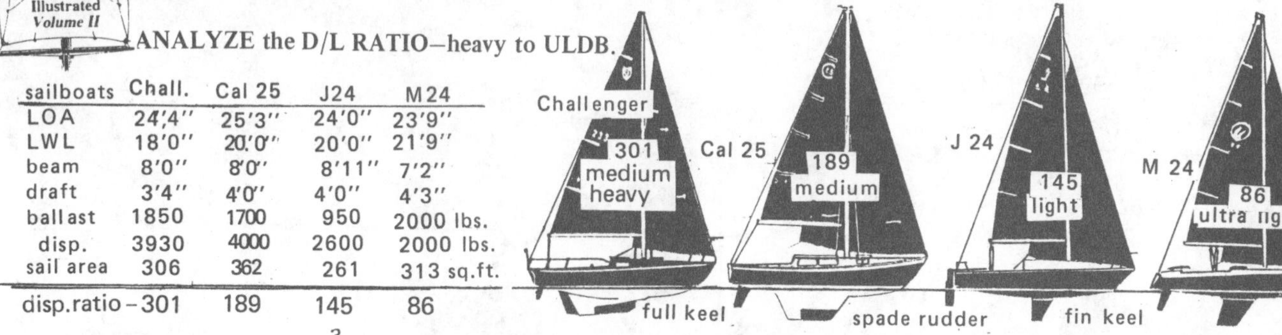

Challenger
301 medium heavy
Cal 25
189 medium
J 24
145 light
M 24
86 ultra ligh
full keel
spade rudder
fin keel
load carrying capacity
all out racing mach

$\frac{\text{Displacement}}{2240} \div (.01 \times \text{LWL})^3 = \text{D/L ratio}$

2240 lbs. = one long ton

What basic factors separate the four pocket cruisers 24' to 25' long into different groups?

We found it easy to verbally compare specific sailboats in similar size ranges. When we tried to find *one common pattern* involving monohulls of similar length that may interest you, the answer was missing except that they were sloop rigged. When friends wanted us to buy a J 24, we began checking into hull size...or capacity.

The J 24 is excellent, though small, and not suited to our personality. Our search developed for four similar sailboats with different cubic capacities and sailing efficiency. The missing answer proved to be the ***Displacement to Length ratio.***

Choose the D/L ratio according to your personality.

The deceptive *displacement to length* **or D/L ratio** becomes a major factor to analyze when buying a 25, 30, 35, 40, 50, or 60 foot cabin sailboat for cruising, racing, or a combination of both. The best way to begin this analysis which includes a bewildering variety of sailboats is with the examples above of popular pocket cruisers having a similar length.

If all sailboats are well designed and well built–

The D/L factors predicts performance characteristics.

*"The **D/L ratio** is one of several factors, a good place to start, that is relatively accurate in predicting performance characteristics. The problem is the classification and terminology breakdown between the ratios...that does change, with a ULDB of yesterday becoming a conservative medium-displacement boat tomorrow", –Robert H. Perry.*

compare pocket size cruisers to hot rod pocket size racers–

maximum cubic capacity for cargo/live aboard

STRICT speed limits

excellent for commercial use in larger size craft

● The **full keel medium-heavy disp. Challenger** was made to the 1964 state of the art before builders knew how to reduce weight when building a fiberglass hull. The extra weight and wetted surface limits racing potentials against later, lighter classes. Though our boat has considerably exceeded hull speed on a reach under ideal conditions, see page 77. other heavies a couple of feet longer bog down as loads on hulls, rigging, and sails **become overpowering** with sailing under potentials, see **Minka**, page 77.

Still excellent, with less cubic capacity for cargo/live aboard...for formula racing, AND cruising.

May surf easily on a reach but AVOID overloading.

● The **spade rudder, medium-displacement Cal 25** is a later, lighter design with less wetted surface. **Loads on hull, sails, and rigging are considerably reduced when surfing** after hull speed is exceeded on a reach with a flatter run aft for lift, page 77. Load-carrying capacity may be slightly less than with the Challenger. Medium displacement sailboats are **excellent for cruising AND racing**...with many articles written on the subject.

Excellent MORC racer with trailer portability. good for camp-out cruising

● The **light displacement J 24** is excellent for round-the-buoy racing and overnight ocean racing using ***hot bunks*** due to its small size. The Jan., issue of **Sail** listed the J 24 as one of the breakthrough boats. The 2600 pounds makes it trailerable from yacht club crane to anywhere nationwide. It is excellent for younger, competitive racing sailors as it is easy to sail, surf, and track. If you want to camp out it will be adaptible since most of the daytime hours will be spent topside. The majority of larger IOR designs also favor light displacement sailboats.

All-out racing machine-spirited tall-rig performer.

A spartan coastal racer with minimum cubic capacity.

Stand-up room–over 37', limited storage for cruising, requires good planning, with minimum port to port time.

● The rocket cruiser **ULDB Moore 24** carries approx. 50 more square feet of sail, with 600 pounds less displacement than the similar length J 24. The M 24 planes easily without pounding to provide a dry deck due to a fine entry with hollow bows, a 15° deadrise forward, and a flat run aft. It is an all-out racing machine, excellent for windy areas from Monterey north to and including the San Francisco Bay area.

The M 24 **ballast to displacement ratio** makes it stiff with a good keel and rudder for upwind pointing...and downwind tracking. The better a ULDB is at carrying a large rig, the faster it will accelerate.

Note–D/L numbers define basic ratios with flexible numerical boundaries.

Thanks- go to Naval Architects Claude McKernan for help with the basic D/L coverage on these pages...and to Bob Perry for his excellent analysis of the complexities of the D/L ratio with boundaries in a continuous state of change. The ratios may seem complex initially yet with a little study the patterns will become obvious while the complexity disappears.

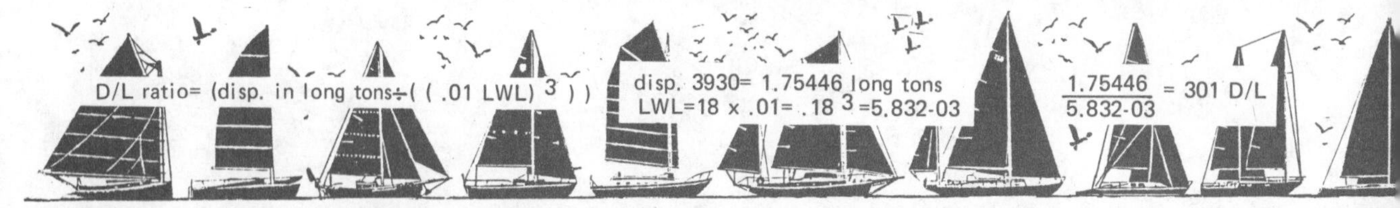

D/L ratio= (disp. in long tons÷((.01 LWL) 3))
disp. 3930= 1.75446 long tons
LWL=18 x .01= .18 3 =5.832-03
1.75446 / 5.832-03 = 301 D/L

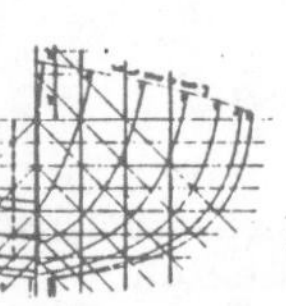

the BIG DINGHY RACING GREYHOUNDS

Windward Passage *International 14 Dinghy*

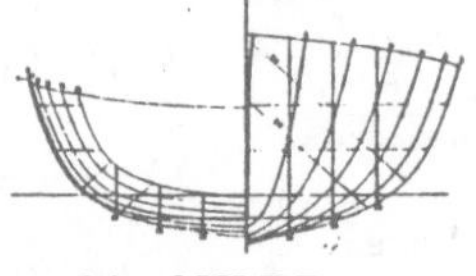

text pg.250

Forget the rulebook AND formula racing to enter the specialized world of ULDB sailboats.Bob Johnson,builder and first owner of the 73' **Windward Passage** defined his objectives–*to hell with corrected time prizes... sail fast and finish first.*

Windward Passage has the distinction of being the first big ULDB with a D/L ratio of 100.It was designed by Alan Gurney to be extremely strong and light with a plywood deck,and triple diagonal planked spruce hull that was launched in 1968 with endless dire predictions.Yet after 15 years as a worldwide competitor.........

the brotherhood of sharing,craftsmanship,and excellence

Birthplace of the ULDB world however is the sleepy rural town of Santa Cruz,California,next to the Pacific with brisk westerlies and long rolling waves for sailboat surfing.It was the ideal place to hold the 1970 505 dinghy world championship.

Considerable interest developed among a small group of counter culturists who wanted to do something different...and better.The brotherhood began building unique sailboats following the light 505 concept.Their unusual approach for sharing their ideas instead of competing,pushed the Santa Cruzian standards to the high levels they maintain today.BEWARE of quick buck artists producing flimsy bargains passed off as ULDB's.They can be hazardous clunkers that may produce a long, long,and very cold swim back to shore for owner and crew.

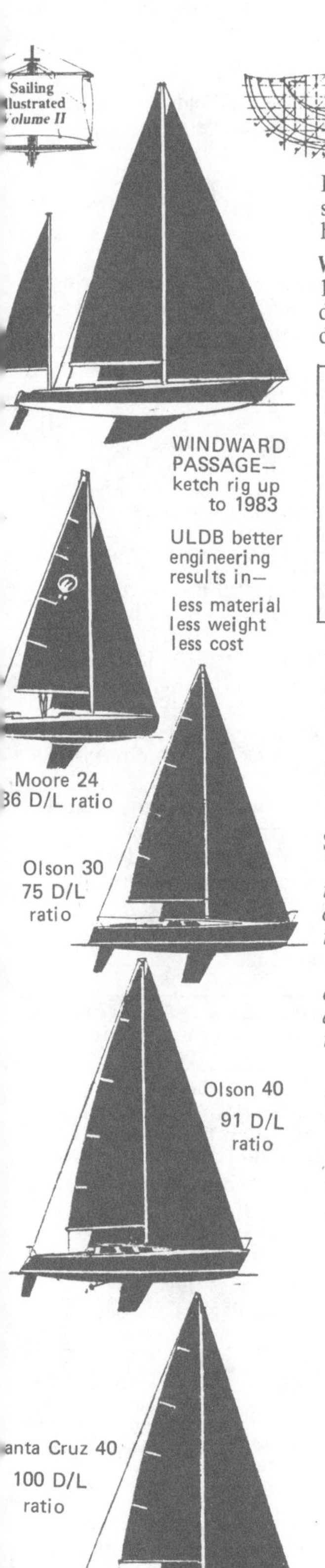

Sailing Illustrated Volume II
WINDWARD PASSAGE– ketch rig up to 1983
ULDB better engineering results in–
less material
less weight
less cost
Moore 24
36 D/L ratio
Olson 30
75 D/L ratio
Olson 40
91 D/L ratio
Santa Cruz 40
100 D/L ratio

Lean,strong ULDB ocean greyhounds romp along surfing and planing while they enjoy wind forces 5,6,and 7,when heavy hulls have to reef down or face dismasting. .but what is a ULDB?Designer/columnist Robert H. Perry graciously consented to help by defining ***the ULDB ratio***–*"If you have to draw the lines I would suggest zero to 110 for ULDB's,110 to 160 for light displacement boats,160 to 220 for medium-light displacement boats,220 to 280 for medium displacement,280 to 320 for medium-heavy,and 320 and up for heavy displacement...at this time (4/18/84)".*The Cal 40 considered light displacement during the 1960's had a 250 D/L ratio.

Sailing friend Carl Schumacher,designer of Express 27,37,and others,told us... *"ULDB's have to be well engineered,but the loads on the boats and people are lower than with conventional boats.Sail area/displacement ratios are important in ULDB design...if you can reduce this displacement,you are going to help this ratio.Among the ultra-lights,the better a boat is at carrying a large rig,the faster it will accelerate.*

"An absence of weight-increasing clutter gives a person more room to move around down below.Their interiors may be simpler than the traditional cruising boat,yet they are quite habitable.They are also better for cruising than many realize since the Olson 40, the Santa Cruz 40,and the Express 37 I designed...have standing headroom."

For more ULDB information contact–

- Moore 24–Moore Brothers,1650 Commercial Way,Santa Cruz,CA 95065.
- Express 27 and 37–Alsberg Brothers,953-A Tower Place,Santa Cruz,CA 95062
- Olson 30 and 40–Pacific Boats,1041 17th Ave.,Santa Cruz,CA 95062.
- Santa Cruz 27,33,50–Bill Lee Yachts,3700 B Hilltop Road,Soquel,CA 95073.

The Moore Brothers provide excellent information for pocket cruisers,while the Olson 40 brochures cover a broad range of ULDB construction,philosophy,etc.

•

The lean,all-muscle ULDB grayhounds are designed for maximum function,strength and material content with each component carefully studied to remove every unnecessary pound of displacement with no compromise in durability or safety. Yes,Virginia,potted palms are seldom found as standard ULDB equipment.

Whole interior sections such as bunks/settes,etc.,are assembled as a unit,varnished then bonded directly onto the hull laminate,with excellent joinerwork.The Olson 40 has accommodations for two after "quarterdoubles",upper and lower P & S settee berths,and six seabags on mounting tracks for clothing stowage.For much of this information I.d like to give thanks to new ULDB designer Claude McKernan,USCG,who spent a week with us checking our book,providing much new ULDB information.

•

Consider the ULDB's with 20 knot speedometers as **big dinghies to be sailed flat,** and **depowered** to avoid heel by changing to a smaller jib...or pinching up for short periods.Rod rigging is often standard equipment such as on the Olson 40 with Navtec hydraulic adjust for backstay,babystay,and vang.Designer/builder George Olson summarizes,"It is a lot more fun to sail past a 40 foot sailboat competitor when you know your whole boat costs as much as their winches".

The big dinghy bendy rig–

The modern *IOR and ULDB bendy rigs* bend the mast to reduce excess wind pressure by flattening the mainsail and opening the jib slot,pages C 13,G 7. Older masthead rigs have 2" to 3" bend,newer masthead rigs,6" to 8" bend. Fractional rigs may bend 12" to 15",see hydraulic control forces *page 104.*

Sailing Illustrated Volume II

Fact or fantasy...the IOR grand prix custom racing sailboat.

40% mainsail area

60% jib area

extreme IOR fractional rig

Competitive sailors have been trying to develop a method for sailboats which are not identical to compete equally against each other using a handicap formula starting with the English 1790 Custom House Rule.

As each new rule emerges to fulfill *the impossible dream*...sharpshooters appear wondering if the new answer is worse than the old problem.Will the rule be too restrictive producing dull,multipurpose sailboats devoid of outstanding features... or will the rule develop extreme,limited single-purpose designs?

Americans have enjoyed racing ***dual-purpose boats*** with the CCA* as a base favoring the 50%/50% sail plan.It is implemented under MORC**,PHRF***,and other rules which are *easy to apply and inexpensive to maintain handicap rules.*

European sailors raced or cruised...the racer couldn't imagine going for a cruise. From this European racing interest developed a goal for a worldwide organization of fleets of *grand prix custom racing sailboats.*

American peers adopted the International Offshore Rule (IOR) in 1970. Publicized goals of this *development rule* was to develop a sixth Olympic Offshore Racing Class. It would provide an *international rating system* with one certificate to race worldwide avoiding endless local country rules.The IOR opened a new market for expensive medium to light,one off or a few custom hulls from an original mold.

displacement by formula, NOT by weighing

Designers had to design IOR boats to new formulas as the hull displacement is made by measurement...not by weighing.The overgenerous sail plan (Sail Hull Ratio) requires well-trained crews to handle large sails and mast-bending techniques.The IOR headsail/spinnaker rig encouraged extreme sail plans with the *proper IOR yacht* often requiring up to 15 sails,sometimes causing storage problems below for the crew.

Brethern...you must have faith in the IOR leadership.

The new ***tall IOR rigs...limited to sloops***,were under considerable standing rigging tension at all times.They could outpoint and outfoot similar length CCA rigs upwind as the ***headsail sloops carried a 60% jib fore triangle.The spinnaker became a necessity*** due to the small mainsail after the buoy was turned for a run.A CCA rig might pass the IOR boat downwind without a chute...due to the larger CCA mainsail.

*CCA-Cruising Club of American
**MORC–Midget Ocean Racing Class
*** PHRF–Performance Handicap Rating Formula

"My boat should be competitive for the next 14 months,then..."was sometimes heard as IOR rules changed very rapidly in the first ten years.Some grand prix racers soon became obsolete while others continued to stay competitive.We seem to find locally some of the IOR racers spending lots of time dockside as overspecialization limits other usage.What will be their resale potentials after retiring from IOR racing?

A development rule... **not** a handicapping rule.

To ease the financial pain, the *good old boy* rule.

To ease the disaster the....*good old boy rule*...called IOR IIIa was adopted to provide an old-age rating formula limited to older marconi-rigged masthead sloops.. the rules still haven't made any openings however for split rigs.

The real IOR winner,the ULDB, was kicked out of the grand prix club!

The IOR unexpectedly spawned the new breed of competitive ***ULDB lightweights*** by designers following the IOR rules.The IOR in its wisdom changed the math factor in 1979 to eliminate the ULDB's...which began winning too much hardware.

An IOR exception– the Catalina 38.

The ***Catalina 38*** detailed is an excellent,conservative IOR design.Instead of over specialization found in many IOR designs,it can race under a variety of rules such as PHRF to insure the investment and class longetivity for owners.It also races as a one-design in the Congressional Cup Series,replacing the Cal 40 no longer in production.

The Catalina 38 *Defiance* proved one of the rare,perfectly tuned,and perfectly balanced sailboats I've handled the few times aboard.While it was sensitive in a light breeze, in a force 6 upwind it pointed and tracked excellently with a light two finger touch of the wheel.Leeway became noticeable after reaching a 30° heel angle.

Sloops only apply– ketches,yawls and schooners are not welcomed by IOR.

Page 116, provides more of the interesting IOR philosophy briefly as the development rule goes thru a series of changes...causing many emotions for boat owners trying to remain competitive within the rules.

CREWING COST?

Crewing on IOR sailboats such as *Defiance* may be as expensive as playing golf.. join the club and buy the equipment.Join a yacht club to meet potential owners,then make an investment in sailing togs,foul weather gear,etc.

Does crewing fit your sailing interest? Owners of competitive boats and cruising boats are always looking for reliable,competitive,compatible,and well-trained crew members for racing,cruising,and chartering...which is a major purpose of this *Guide.*

The blue aluminum 81' *Boomerang* was born Feb.1984.In the short period before going to press,it had a slight edge to become the fastest maxi in the world.Skipper Whitmore stresses,"Competition is nice but the only real fun is winning",*Sailing,Apr.1985.*

26 regular crew members?

He states a major factor in its success is competent crew work.All 26 are regular key,and important contributing crew members.Would you like to join such an elite team...do you have the experience,time and bank account to crew on the big dinghies. It may be a shorter step up for leading dinghy sailors than realized who know the operational theory,yet with considerably heavier rigging systems.

The *blooper*—IOR boats on a run had rolling tendencies with a large chute on one side, and a small main on the other. This was dampened by adding a full-bellied jib opposite to the chute.

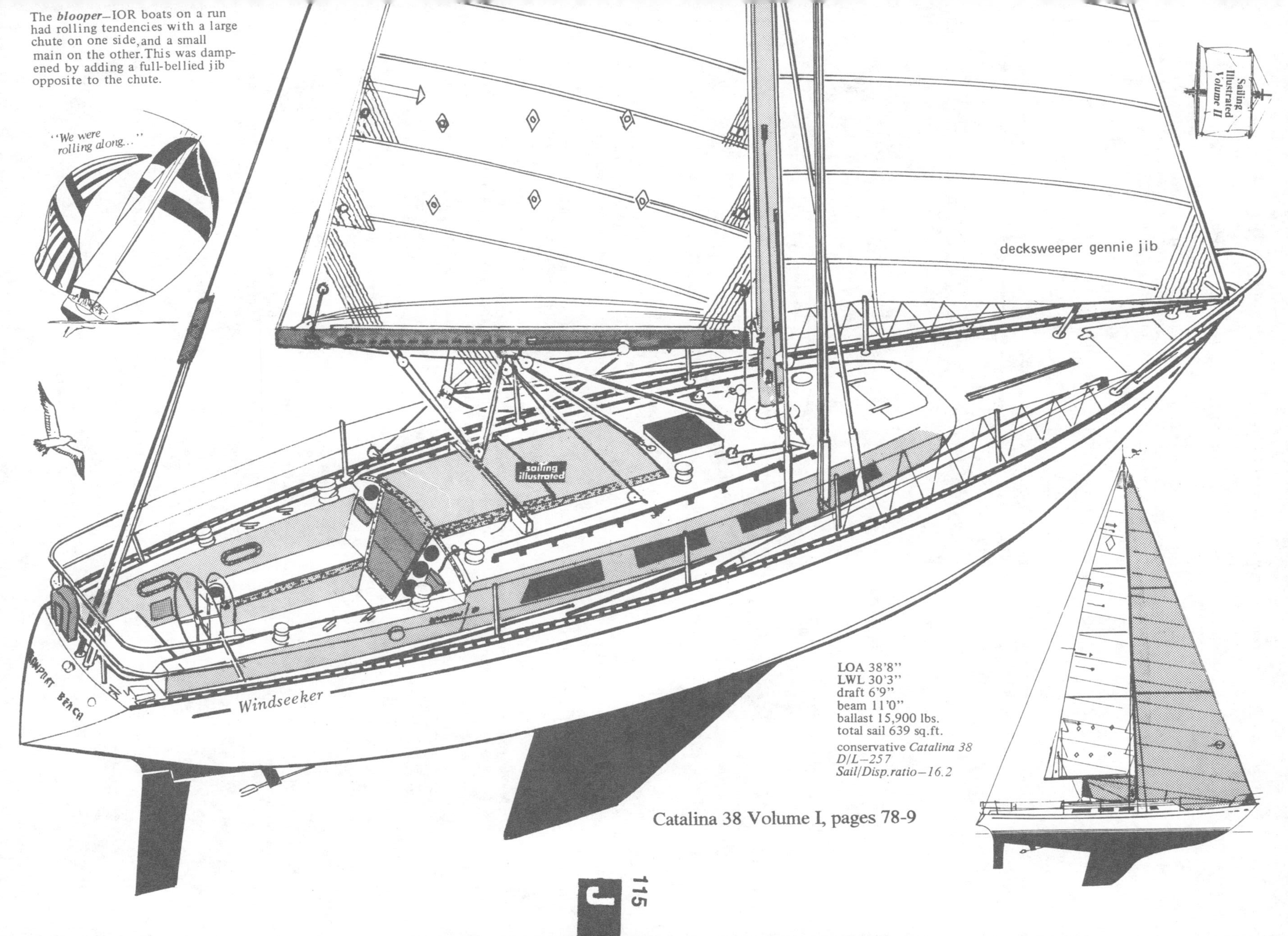
"We were rolling along..."
Sailing Illustrated Volume II
decksweeper gennie jib
sailing illustrated
Windseeker
NEWPORT BEACH

LOA 38'8"
LWL 30'3"
draft 6'9"
beam 11'0"
ballast 15,900 lbs.
total sail 639 sq.ft.
conservative *Catalina 38*
D/L—257
Sail/Disp.ratio—16.2

Catalina 38 Volume I, pages 78-9

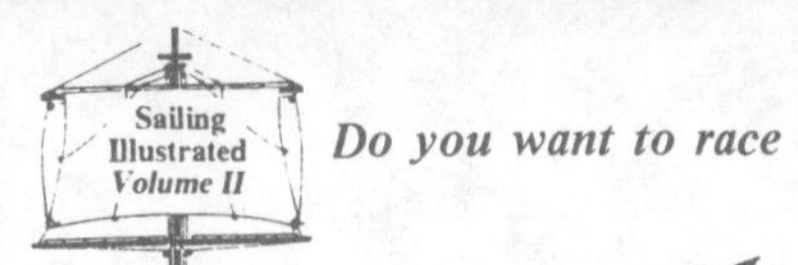
Sailing
Illustrated
Volume II

Do you want to race around-the-world singlehanded... or as a crew member?

LOA 82'00"
LWL 65'
draft 12'95"
beam 19'52"
ballast 37,475 lbs.
disp. 74,950 lbs.
main 1,292 sq.ft.
gennie 2,100 sq.ft.
spi 4,360 sq.ft.

Cape D'Or—an 82' maxi (maxis rate above 70')
D/L— 121.8

designers—Michael Joubert and Bernard Nivelt

The Joubert-Nivelt IOR maxi;a Whitbread around-the-world racer.

The English Whitbread Brewery sponsors a round-the-world race every four years with the Whitbread Trophy awarded for the best corrected time.It will start in Portsmouth, England on Sept.28,1985,with stopovers in Capetown,South Africa;Aukland,New Zealand; and Puntal del Este,Uruguay...with the finish line at Portsmouth,England.

Van Rietschoten's *Flyer* won the 1891 Whitbread Trophy while also delivering the fastest circumnavigation that required 120 days and 6 hours for the four leg course.

Twenty sailboats of which seven may be IOR maxi's hope to be on the 1985 starting line. We show the excellent 83' maxi Joubert—Nivelt design with a maximum IOR 70 foot rating.The skipper will be the well-known French competitor Eric Tabarly.

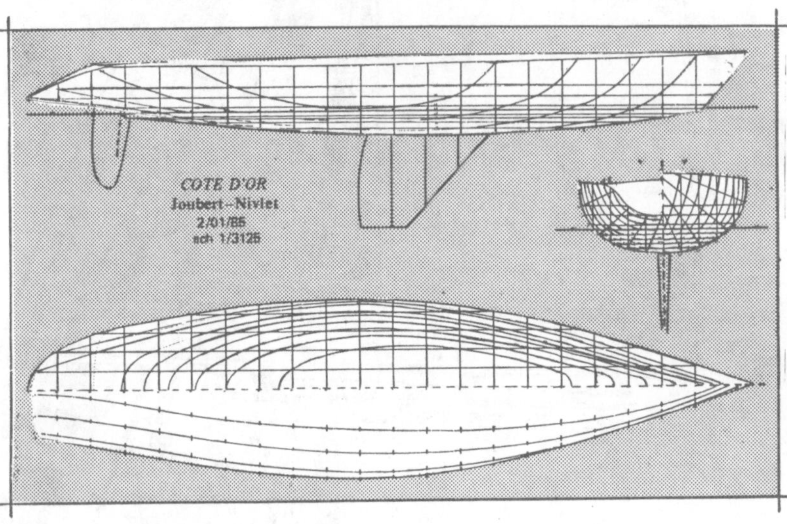
COTE D'OR
Joubert-Nivlet
2/01/85
ech 1/3125

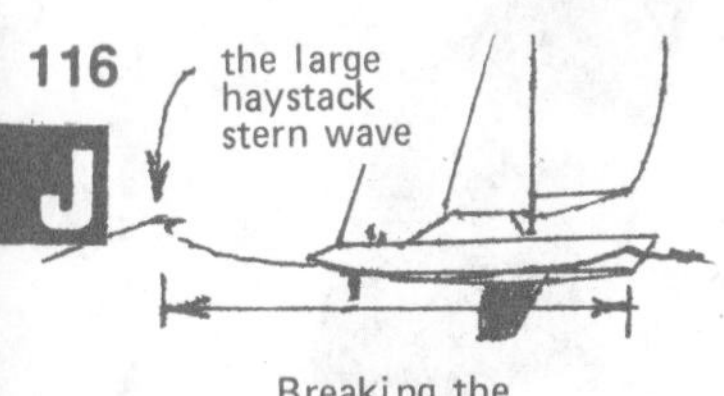
the large
haystack
stern wave

Breaking the $1.34\sqrt{WL}$ wave trap.

sharp transom chine

lift pocket

rocker

A sailboat *hollow or lift pocket* prevents stern drag after exceeding hull speed.

Poweboats use a hook or wedge to provide stern lift to level out the hull for lower planing speeds.

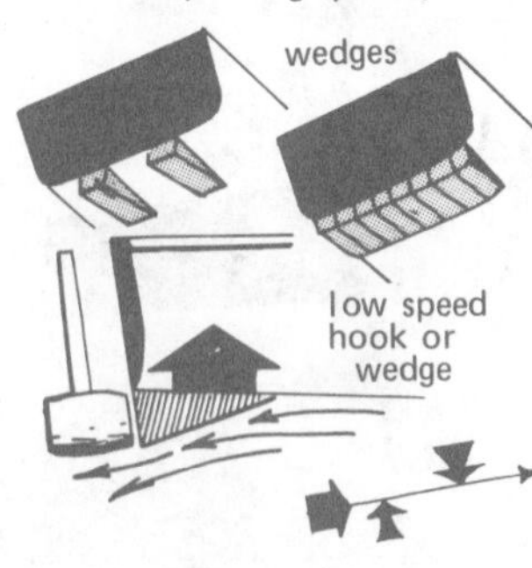
wedges
low speed
hook or
wedge

The Whitbread Round the World Race.

Any sailboat designed to compete in an all-out 27,000 mile race around the world needs tremendous planning and excellent construction with no details left to chance.The deck layout has to be workable in all conditions...and the mast has to stay upright and remain on deck to operate in storm conditions thousands of miles from available help.

Designs for the Whitbread marathon broke nearly even in opposing concepts.Some contestants have *larger sailplans and shorter waterlines* to power thru the light winds of the doldrums. Others such as the *Cote D'Or* is designed to sail at its IOR rating or better...with *less sail area and a longer waterline* to carry it thru the Southern Ocean's heavy weather conditions.

Weather forecasting interpretations will play a major contribution in the race which may favor either of these concepts...also any boat that ends on the wrong side of a high or low pressure area at any time will move out of the winners circle.

The *Cote D'Or* has a soft,wide-beam IOR design.The hull has big radiuses,minimum wetted surfaces,and a powerful stern planned more for off-the-wind than on-the-wind conditions.The forefoot is softer without a flat bottom to provide a softer ride than found in many IOR designs. The freeboard is low producing a sleek sheer line finished off by a strongly raked stern.

The IOR stern hollow concept for lift is shown between stations 17 and 19 with the water flow cut sharply at the transom chine.This combination provides a smooth flow of water to increase the distance between the bow and stern waves to increase the waterline length hu[l speed.

The single-handed BOC Challenge Race.

It began 8/28/82 with 16 single handers starting the first such race around the world which was sponsored by the British Oxygen,Corporation,a London based holding company.It was limited to two monohull classes only...Class I—45 to 56 feet long;Class II—32 to 44 feet.

The rules were to sail from Newport,RI clockwise around the world.Stops were 7100 miles from Newport to Cape Town,South Africa;then 6900 miles to Sydney,Australia;7800 miles to Rio;and 5300 miles to return to Newport,Rhode Island.

Philip Jeantot from Le Havre,France was the Class I winner—27,500 miles on 5/9/83 taking 159 days,2 hours,51 minutes on *Credit Agricole.* Yukoh Tada of Japan was the Class II winner in his 44' *Koden Okera V* in 207 days,13 hours,13 minutes.

A second single hander BOC Challenge Race is planned for 1986.Since the only person aboard will have his hours of operation limited to the time awake to anticipate the actions of icebergs, supertankers,whales,deadheads,etc.,your author plans to sit this race out dockside.

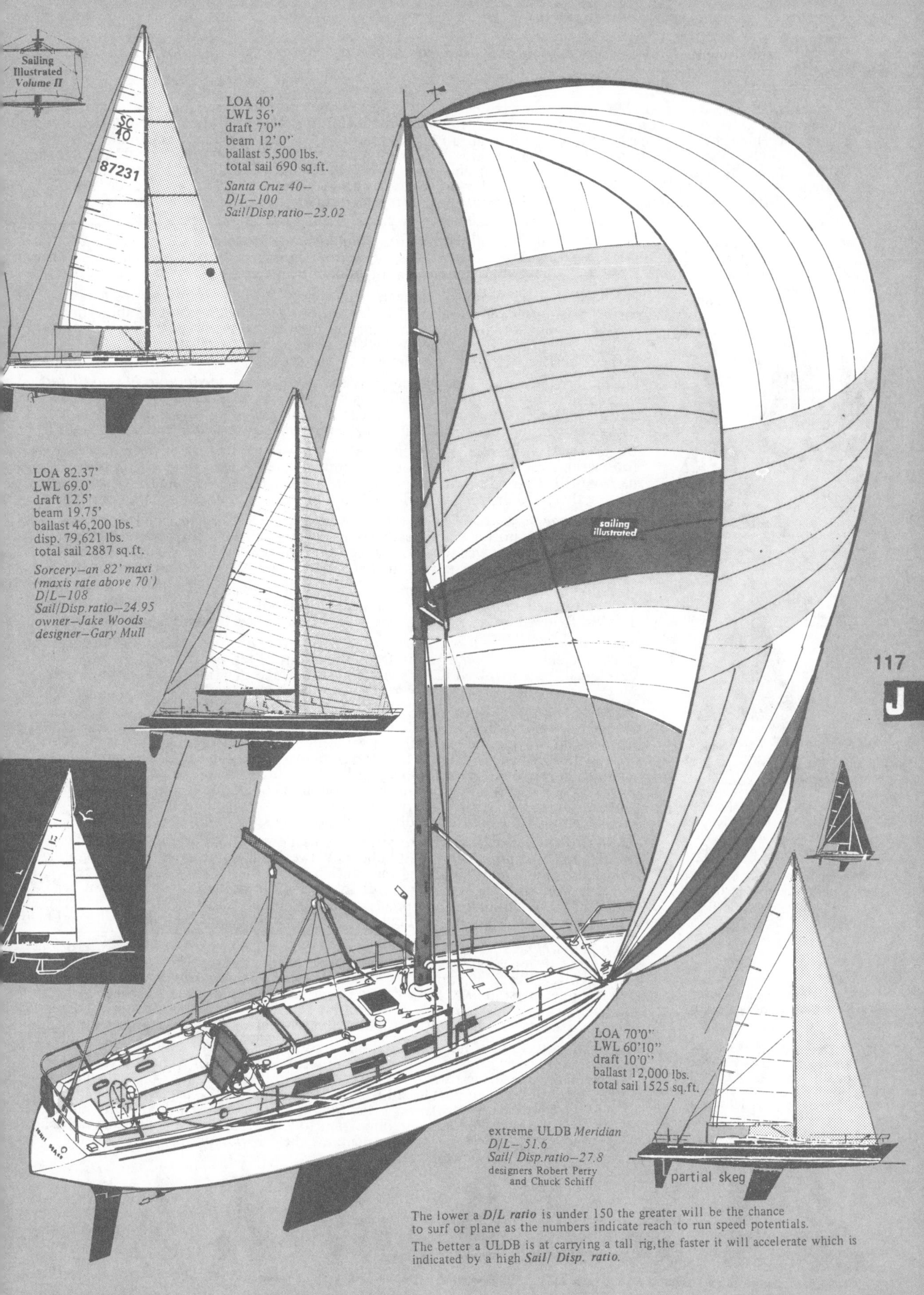
Sailing
Illustrated
Volume II
SC
40
87231
LOA 40'
LWL 36'
draft 7'0"
beam 12' 0"
ballast 5,500 lbs.
total sail 690 sq.ft.
Santa Cruz 40–
D/L–100
Sail/Disp.ratio–23.02
LOA 82.37'
LWL 69.0'
draft 12.5'
beam 19.75'
ballast 46,200 lbs.
disp. 79,621 lbs.
total sail 2887 sq.ft.
Sorcery–an 82' maxi
(maxis rate above 70')
D/L–108
Sail/Disp.ratio–24.95
owner–Jake Woods
designer–Gary Mull
sailing
illustrated
LOA 70'0"
LWL 60'10"
draft 10'0"
ballast 12,000 lbs.
total sail 1525 sq.ft.
extreme ULDB Meridian
D/L– 51.6
Sail/ Disp.ratio–27.8
designers Robert Perry
and Chuck Schiff
partial skeg
The lower a D/L ratio is under 150 the greater will be the chance
to surf or plane as the numbers indicate reach to run speed potentials.
The better a ULDB is at carrying a tall rig, the faster it will accelerate which is
indicated by a high Sail/ Disp. ratio.

The deceptive BLUE WATER CRUISER...*capacity..comfort...congeniality...in a floating bungalow.*

The majority of sailors by middle age often prefer a comfortable cruising sailboat.

Man was born to be competitive though his methods often change as he grows older. *Younger aggressive sailors* gain self measurement by competing against each other in group activities such as racing. *Older goal-oriented sailors* are often competitive within themselves who enjoy cruising at their own pace with little interest in group activities. A happy cruising sailboat, also requires, *emotional planning.*

Several sailing students were interested in large cruising sailboats but by the end of the day found that a competitive racer fitted their personalities. Others convinced by salesmen to buy smaller sailboats found their personaliti bank accounts and time schedules ideal for larger cruising sailboats. Personality, age, money and ample sp time for cruising are major factors involved.

OH--Operator Hostile
OU--Operator Unfriendly
OF--Operator Friendly
OVF Operator Very Friendly

40' Newporter ketch rig—text pg.75

40' Newporter—cutter rig

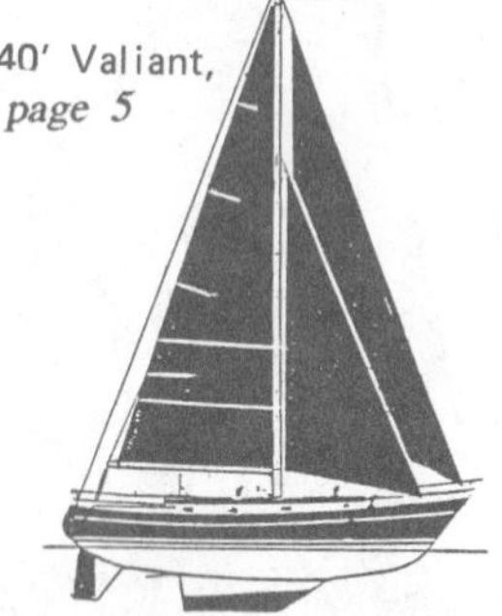

40' Valiant, *page 5*

A satisfactory weekend cruiser may be inadequate as a live aboard blue-water cruiser for long periods.

charter a cruising boat before buying to find the human engineering topside AND below

land of enchantment AND mutiny—Tahiti

The moment of truth—We leave it to Sam Johnson to ably define the Operator Hostile Boat 225 years ago, see page J 1.

The active cruising sailboat requires a full keel or a stout skeg to protect its rudder in a grounding. Avoid the naked spade rudder which can be severely damaged during grounding on an uninhabited island reef, or hitting deadheads, porpoises, or whales.

The 40' ketch was popular 20 years ago, **page 72,** when leisurely cruising was normal. The ***cutter rig*** is preferred today with better upwind pointing ability, plus self-tailing winches, improved hardware and running rigging for ***single-handed operation.*** Hand steering time will be minimal with autopilot for coastal steering and the wind vane used further offshore for steadier wind patterns.

The preferred cruising sailboat length is 35' to 40' with a ***medium to heavy d/l ratio*** with considerable cargo storage capacity for 2 to 3 persons aboard for long periods. Human engineering becomes the major factor since over half the time will be spent dockside or at anchor...for which we have improvised computer terms at left.

OU—a small 40 footer. We sailed a lovely 40' wooden boat taking the new owners for a week's vacation to enter sailing. Tempers flared the 2nd day out as the boat was narrow with four adults and two children walking on each others feet. It was built during the 1930 depression period when human engineering was unknown.

OVF—a large 40 footer. We feel the first sailboat specifically designed for cruising was the 40' Newporter ketch. I sailed one to Catalina Island for a four day filming session. The purpose was to shoot background footage for a movie of the steamship **Sacramento** which was sunk on the Sacramento reef off Baja, Mexico in 1849.

Vast diving and movie equipment poured aboard. It was followed by food, sleeping bags, and varied equipment that disappeared into bottomless storage compartments. This was followed by eleven of the most diverse personalities I've ever seen on a sailboat.

118

J

The real surprise was its excellent room as feet weren't trampled on in the cockpit, doghouse, below, or forward topside. If even a hint of temper or *campfire sickness* developed, those involved had a swim, snorkel, or take the dinghy ashore for a walk on the beach. I was amazed how well it was designed with eleven persons maintaining such harmony on a 40' sailboat...however the cutter rig is still our first choice.

Human engineering developed slowly in cruising sailboats with the 1958 Newporter ketch above proving the exception as we found loose ends on many other sailboats. Around 1970 when the charter business began to expand in the Caribbean, human engineering started to become a way of life for efficiency and comfort. Topside it involved hardware, running rigging, and a common complaint, the location of engine controls. The living area engineering improved below for galley layout, storage, eating, sleeping, and loafing areas...goodby old floating locker rooms.

Spend two to three nights aboard your potential dream-boat cruiser, an idea that doesn't make me popular with all builders. We've found some cabin layouts, lighting, storage, etc., much more practical than anticipated. Other boats had unexpected problems—cabins becoming saunas due to ventilation problems, layout and/or head ventilation problems, engines impractical to work on, etc. Cruising sailboats are very deceptive so charter before buying to understand human engineering topside and below.

Camp fire sickness? Tahiti, Panama, and Cape Town, South Africa lead in cruising sailboat mutinies. We helped cool two major mutinies in our short stay in Papeete. They involved likeable people *not chosen for a congenial personality mix.* Balance crew member personalities for a happy, convivial mix...since even a novice having a good personality can learn underway, and may prove more cooperative or productive than an experienced sailor with a slightly abrasive personality, or one that snores.

These sailors were confined in tight quarters for more than 60 days in poorly designed ***operator hostile boats*** bought either on impulse, a bargain, or for romanticism with little human engineering. I was sitting under a palm tree with an ex-crew member watching new crew members board for the second half of the trip. While I wanted to ask why he flew to New Zealand for the first half of the cruise not knowing the personalities involved, it was more important to let him unwind his emotions which were stored too long. P.S., also enjoy planning the *emotional aspects* of cruising.

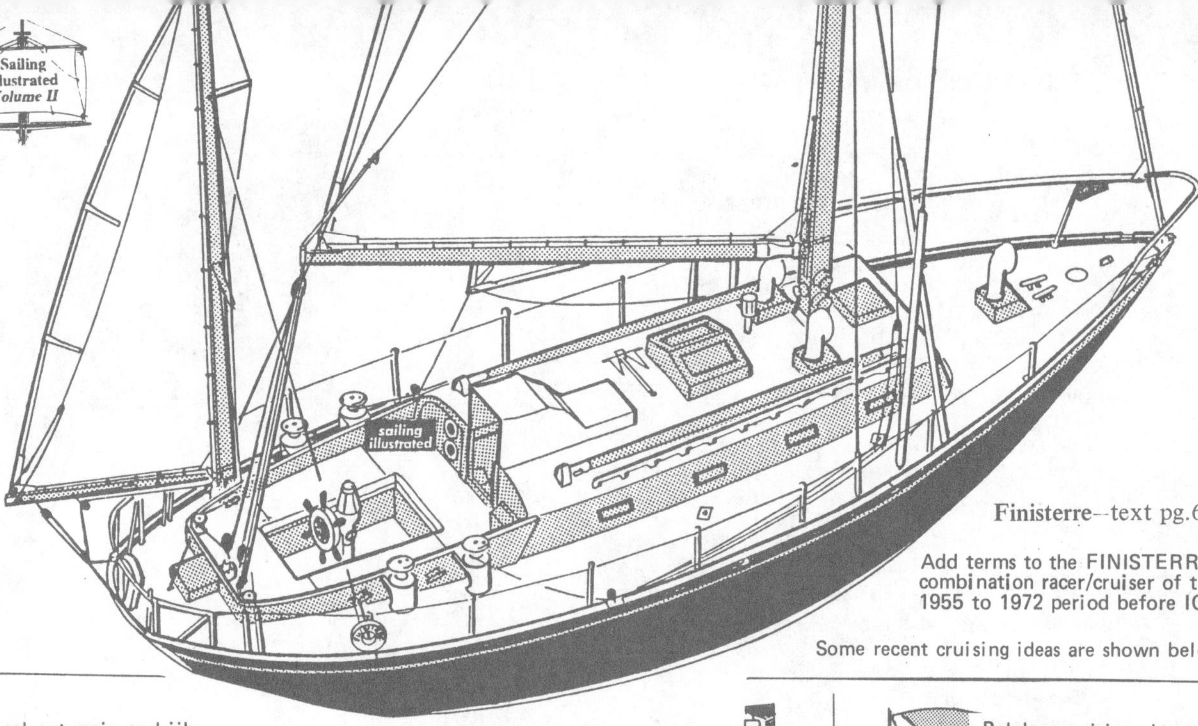

sailing illustrated

Finisterre—text pg.67

Add terms to the FINISTERRE, combination racer/cruiser of the 1955 to 1972 period before IOR.

Some recent cruising ideas are shown below.

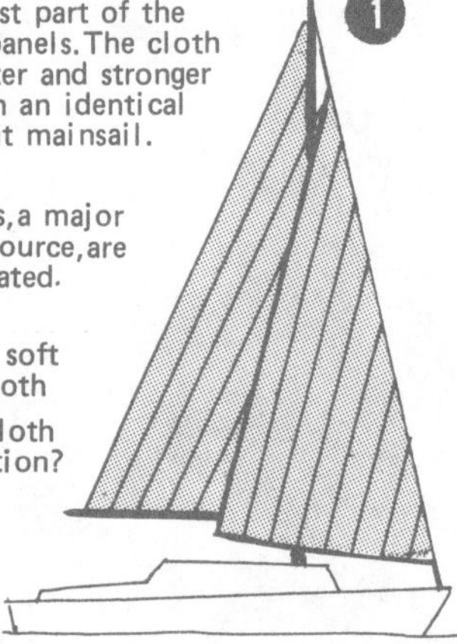

1

rtical cut main and jib ry their load on the ongest part of the th panels. The cloth ighter and stronger n on an identical sscut mainsail.

ttens, a major afe source, are minated.

oose soft il cloth

V. cloth otection?

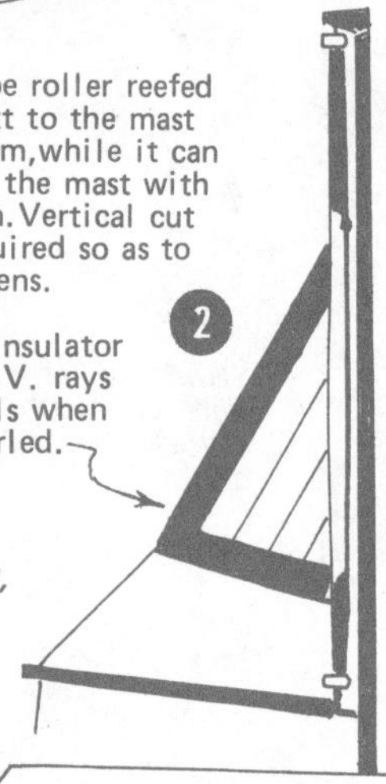

2

Mainsail can be roller reefed and furled next to the mast with one system, while it can be furled into the mast with another system. Vertical cut panels are required so as to eliminate battens.

Outer acrylic insulator panels keep U.V. rays off inner panels when the main is furled.

Seven Seas Cruising Association—box 2190, Covington, LA 70434

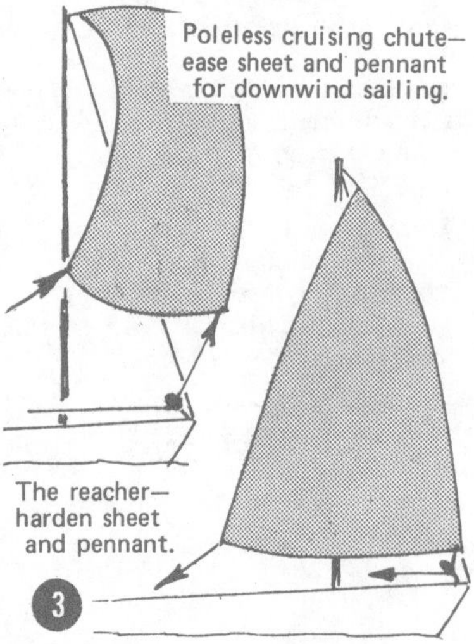

3

Poleless cruising chute—ease sheet and pennant for downwind sailing.

The reacher—harden sheet and pennant.

J

4

Modern lug and stayless rigs use lazy jacks so the main can drop between the jacks like a venetian blind without the sail spilling off the boom... eliminating the topping lift.

lazy jacks

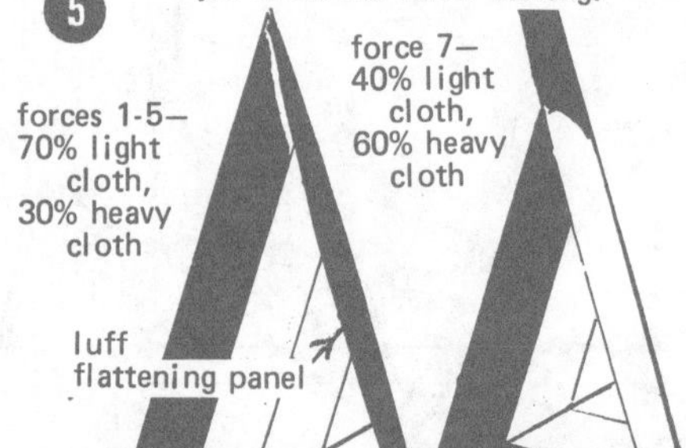

5

Multi-purpose, variable weight jib cloth for roller reefing.

forces 1-5—70% light cloth, 30% heavy cloth

force 7—40% light cloth, 60% heavy cloth

luff flattening panel

4-6 oz. panels

U.V. acrylic insulator

6-8 oz. panels

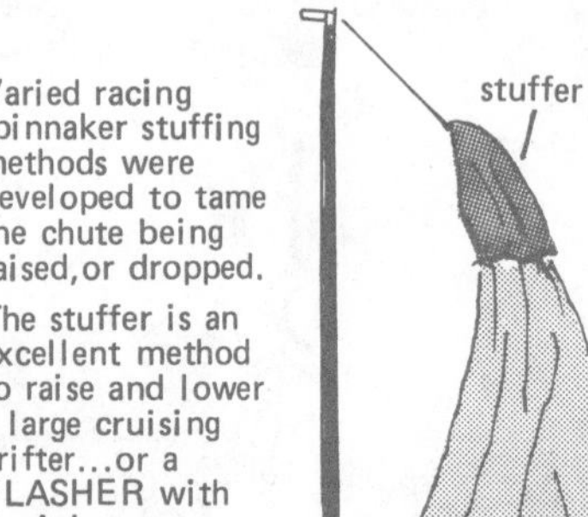

6

Varied racing spinnaker stuffing methods were developed to tame the chute being raised, or dropped.

The stuffer is an excellent method to raise and lower a large cruising drifter...or a FLASHER with a minimum cruising crew.

stuffer

New sail material, hardware, and rigging methods were developed in the late 1970's that were specifically designed for cruising sailboats with small crews.

Look for fully tested running rigging ideas, methods, etc., that are simple to operate. Study new methods being used in cruising sail cloth and Ultra Violet ray protection.

The FINISTERRE spawned look alikes worldwide.

Add terms to **Finisterre** so you can analyze the sails and rigging of its 1955 rig. What changes would you consider if you wanted to rerig it to modern cruising standards?

"There may not be a *perfect* cruising boat as people's individual requirements differ...people often set out in whatever boat they happen to own". This excellent observation was made by Jim Cornwell who interviewed 62 blue water sailors passing thru Suva, Fiji in a two month period.

"The happiest lot seemed to be people on board in the 35' to 40' range, with a ratio of crew per boat of 2.5". Anyone planning to buy a long range cruising sailboat should obtain a copy of this article in the March 1979 issue of **Motor Boating & Sailing**.

Wind power isn't free but is a bargain with good sails. Eliminate battens and roaches when ordering cruising sails as battens cause chafe failure.

Dacron panels chafe against each other while stitching faces early failure due to the sun's Ultra-Violet rays. Use triple stitching to extend your sails useful life. Keep your sails fully covered when not in use in the tropics where Ultra-Violet ray intensity is maximum. 5000 hours of use may be expected with two years of continuous tropical exposure, or ten year weekend uses with periodic seam stitching.

Extend your useful sail life with U.V. protected cloth, or have it chemically treated...or use an Acrylic insulator for roller-reefed sails when furled.

Collect articles on cruising sails and rigging to keep up with this changing field.

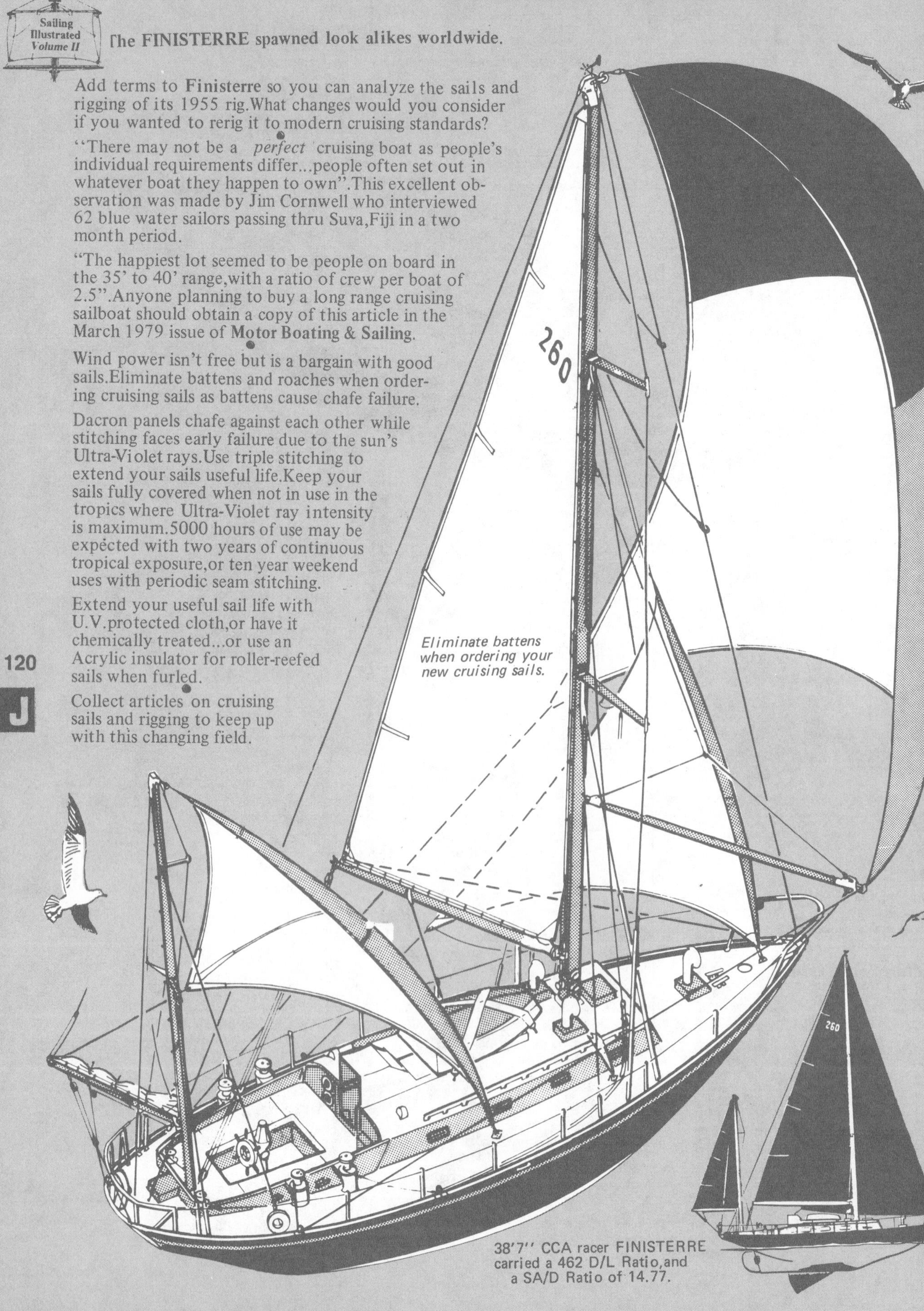
260
Eliminate battens when ordering your new cruising sails.
260

38'7" CCA racer FINISTERRE carried a 462 D/L Ratio, and a SA/D Ratio of 14.77.

The Mystic Museum Seaport Museum Model of 1930 Yachting.

We receive many letters thru the years from cruising sailors in out of the way ports throughout the world. Several of them owned wooden sailboats often gaff rigged which require a lot of tender loving care. Some of these sailboats were older than their owners.

Their popularity was obvious when we counted 54 sailboats stern to the quay in Paleete in 1974 with many gaff rigged. There were a few metal hulls, an excellent cement boat, but NO fiberglass sailboats and NO multihulls.

The majority were wooden world travelers from Africa, England, France, Australia, and New Zealand as a sample of our international sailing fraternity.

Most of these wooden boats were tired, yet still darn proud in fulfilling their destiny after sailing thousands of miles to reach Tahiti. They were having a well-deserved rest to be followed by lots of attention and care...before sailing to another distant horizon. Many were changing crews in midocean for the next part of the cruise.

If you know sailing and the gaff-rig language it would be easy to find a berth on a sailboat heading any direction you may want to crew. Add all terms to *Iris* in its 1938 rig for gaff rig familiarity.

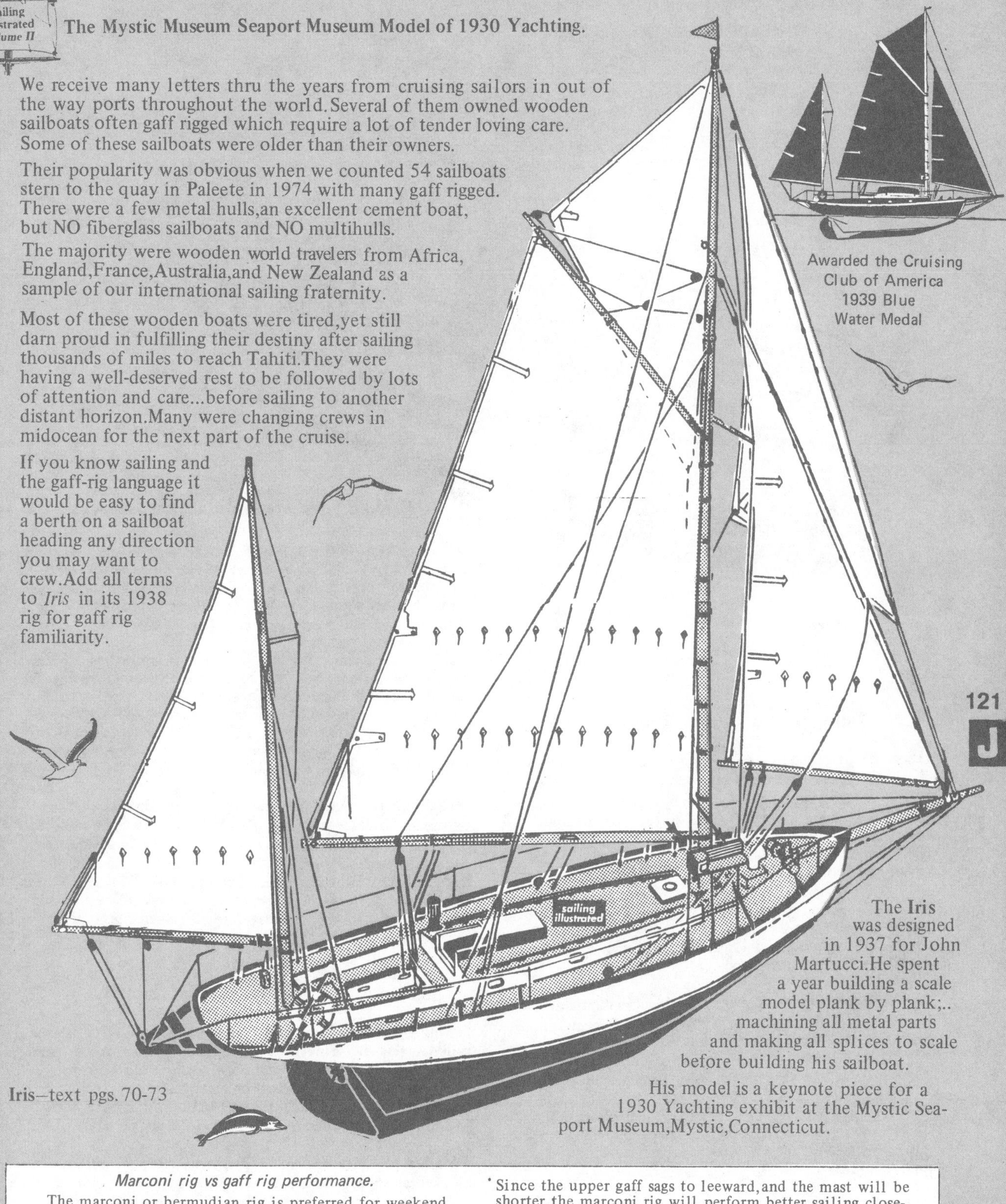
sailing
illustrated

Awarded the Cruising Club of America 1939 Blue Water Medal

The **Iris** was designed in 1937 for John Martucci. He spent a year building a scale model plank by plank;.. machining all metal parts and making all splices to scale before building his sailboat.

Iris—text pgs. 70-73

His model is a keynote piece for a 1930 Yachting exhibit at the Mystic Seaport Museum, Mystic, Connecticut.

Marconi rig vs gaff rig performance.

The marconi or bermudian rig is preferred for weekend cruising and racing in light breezes along our coasts, and for sailing on inland lakes. Lug rigs and gaff rigs using modern materials for hulls, metals, and sails are excellent for long distance blue-water cruising boats.

Gaff-rigged boats produce minimum advertising revenues so resulting magazine articles are seldom complementary. Let us consider identical hulls with similar total sail areas operating with identical wind and water conditions.

Since the upper gaff sags to leeward, and the mast will be shorter, the marconi rig will perform better sailing close-hauled. When the sheets are eased for a reach the gaff rig may begin to pull ahead. The gaff rig may be the better performer downwind if neither vessel uses a spinnaker.

The stayless rig may be the commercial sailing work-horse of the future. Small crews can operate large, deep water cargo carrying sailing vessels. Fishing vessels can make longer offshore trips with minimum crews which considerably reduce their operational expenses.

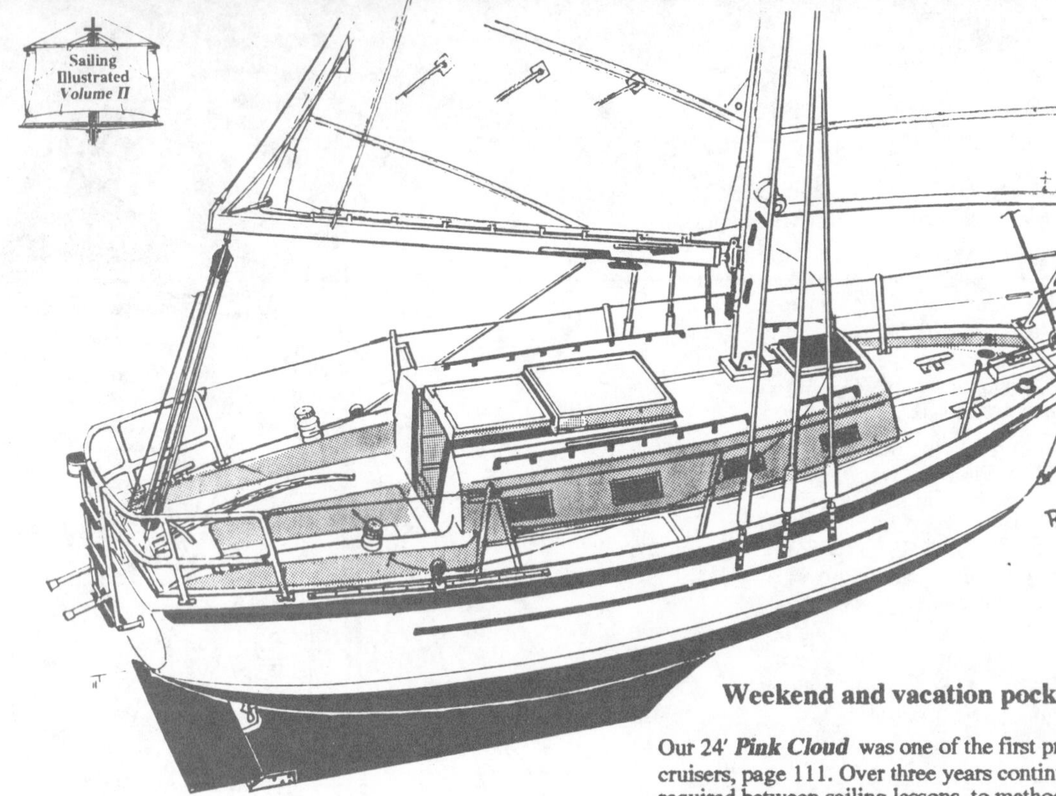
ROYCE

Weekend and vacation pocket cruisers.

Our 24' ***Pink Cloud*** was one of the first practical pocket cruisers, page 111. Over three years continuous effort were required between sailing lessons to methodically search for ideas, then test them. Over **50%** of all items bought had to be returned. The next sailing lesson tested our new ideas..

Our continuous operation provided an advantage few owners have to make their cruisers comfortable below and topside. We provide detailed illustrations for readers to examine. Balancing her for self steering with shock cord, required much effort with sail trim and weight sensitivity. Then we added an autopilot for cruising to Catalina. We enjoyed fishing underway, often filling our icebox when reaching the island.

Many ideas we started are just as practical today such as the bulkhead duffel storage bags. **Bunk straps** should be installed on all cruising sailboats for a good sleep in rough weather. Adjustable seat belts proved the best answer, stowed out of the way below bunk cushions when not in use. *Pink Cloud* was retired after 32 years, high and dry outside my office window. We often share a "wee nip" together as the sun goes down, trying to outdo each other with our *"almost true sea stories"*.

LOA	27' 3"	Draft	3'10"
LOD	24' 2"	Displacement (lbs.	8,000
LWL	21' 5"	Ballast (lbs.)	3,200
Beam	8' 7"	Sail Area (sq. ft.)	358

Long distance pocket cruisers.

Dana 24, designed in 1985 by W.J.B. "Bill" Crealock, is built by **Pacific Seacraft** Corporation in Fullerton, CA. The *Dana 24* is designed and hand built for long distance offshore cruising. Over 200 *Dana 24's* are cruising the oceans of the world. The factory is continually receiving postcards from tropical islands detailing their wonderful memories.

With 8000 pounds displacement and 6' 1" headroom, she is not your average 24 footer, LOA is 27' with bowsprit. She's able to be trailered. Owners have portaged her across the U.S., Mexico, and Canada.

Pacific Seacraft craftsmanship is evident in the meticulous joiner teak work from the butterfly joints in the cap rail, to the individual hand fit of each bulkhead. Deck hardware is almost exclusively bronze (polished or chrome plated), with the portlights, hand polished in New Zealand to our spec's.

Equipped standard as a sloop, many owners chose the flexibility of a cutter rig. Spars and deck layout can be set up to exact standard owner spec's as each sailboat is individually built.

She is quite spacious below decks.. The V-berth forward is a wide double.The main salon has two single berth settees, plus enclosed head. The galley has a propane two burner stove and oven. The 18 hp Yanmar diesel is standard.

Pacific Seacraft has been building offshore cruising sail-boats since 1976 from their baby *20' Flicka* to their 44 footer.

Submitted by Jeff Merrill, **Pacific Seacraft** Corporation.
FAX (714) 879--5454

The popular all-purpose Catalina 30.

During the past 20 years I've spent many hours on a variety of sailboats this size, cruising, teaching, and helping deliver from port to port. Variables are endless wirh questionable testing before being sold. If east coast builders tested new prototypes for a month or two in Long Beach Harbor with predictable winds and full- year operation, many ***loose ends*** would be eliminated.

Catalina 30, introduced in 1970, is the largest of the 30 footer classes sailing worldwide. Whether weekend cruising with five aboard, or overnight racing to Ensenada, Mexico, her design with many generation improvements, is the sailboat I'd prefer in this size. Her 257 D/L with broad beam, is the excellent combination for force 2 to upper 6 west coast sailing.

New owners and charterers may be critical of the deceptive Catalina 30. It is a big dingy, very sensitive to weight with crew changing sides tacking upwind...while able to change tack upwind in its own length. See the options a new owner has to choose from on a 30 footer. Also pages 76-7, Volume I.

CATALINA 30... REACHING UPWIND

Volume I, page 77

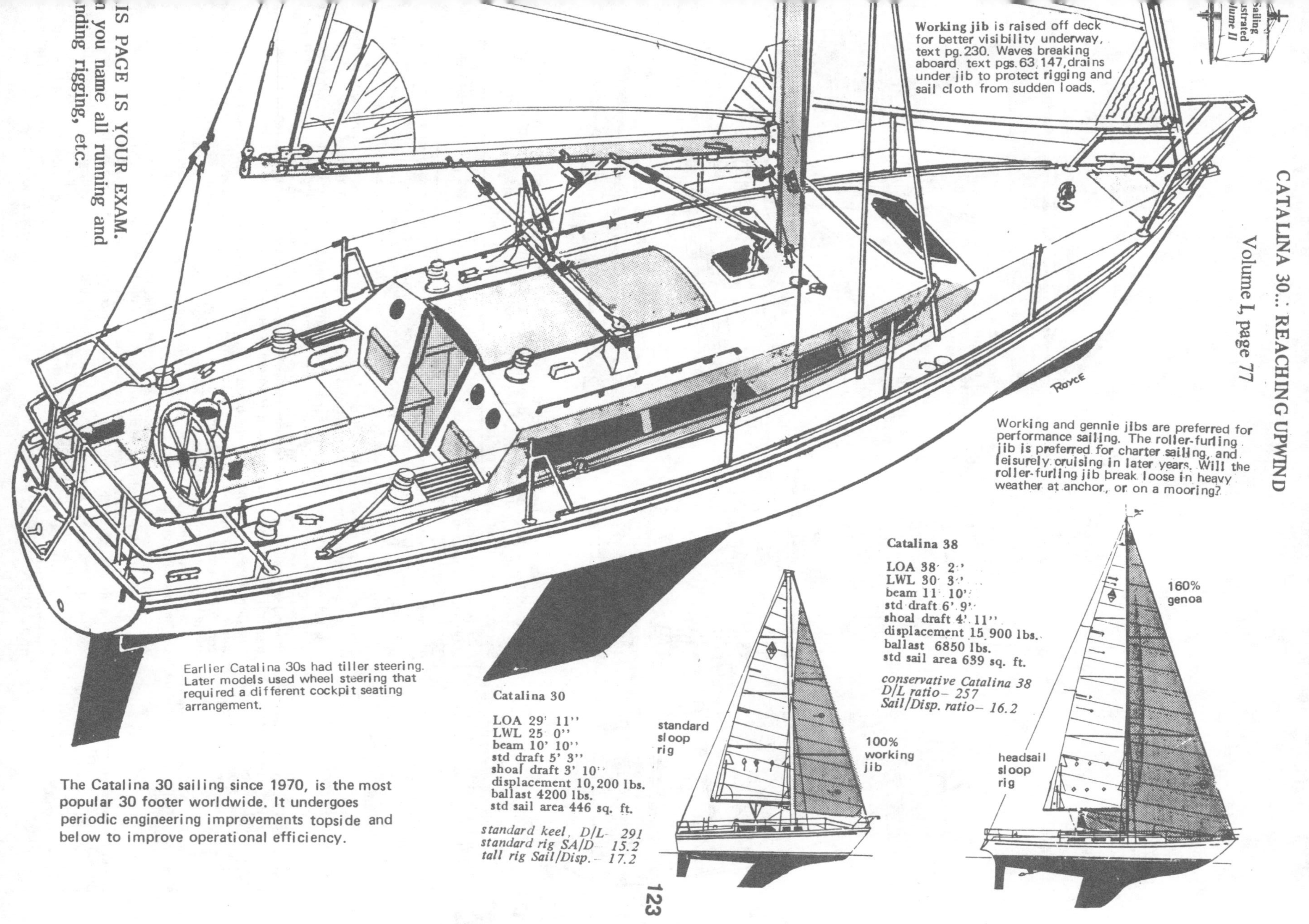

Sailing
ROYCE
160% genoa
headsail sloop rig
100% working jib
standard sloop rig

Working jib is raised off deck for better visibility underway, text pg. 230. Waves breaking aboard text pgs. 63 147, drains under jib to protect rigging and sail cloth from sudden loads.

Working and gennie jibs are preferred for performance sailing. The roller-furling jib is preferred for charter sailing, and leisurely cruising in later years. Will the roller-furling jib break loose in heavy weather at anchor, or on a mooring?

Catalina 38

LOA 38' 2''
LWL 30' 3''
beam 11' 10''
std draft 6' 9''
shoal draft 4' 11''
displacement 15,900 lbs.
ballast 6850 lbs.
std sail area 639 sq. ft.

conservative Catalina 38
D/L ratio– 257
Sail/Disp. ratio– 16.2

Catalina 30

LOA 29' 11''
LWL 25' 0''
beam 10' 10''
std draft 5' 3''
shoal draft 3' 10''
displacement 10,200 lbs.
ballast 4200 lbs.
std sail area 446 sq. ft.

standard keel, D/L 291
standard rig SA/D 15.2
tall rig Sail/Disp. 17.2

Earlier Catalina 30s had tiller steering. Later models used wheel steering that required a different cockpit seating arrangement.

The Catalina 30 sailing since 1970, is the most popular 30 footer worldwide. It undergoes periodic engineering improvements topside and below to improve operational efficiency.

IS PAGE IS YOUR EXAM.
n you name all running and
nding rigging, etc.

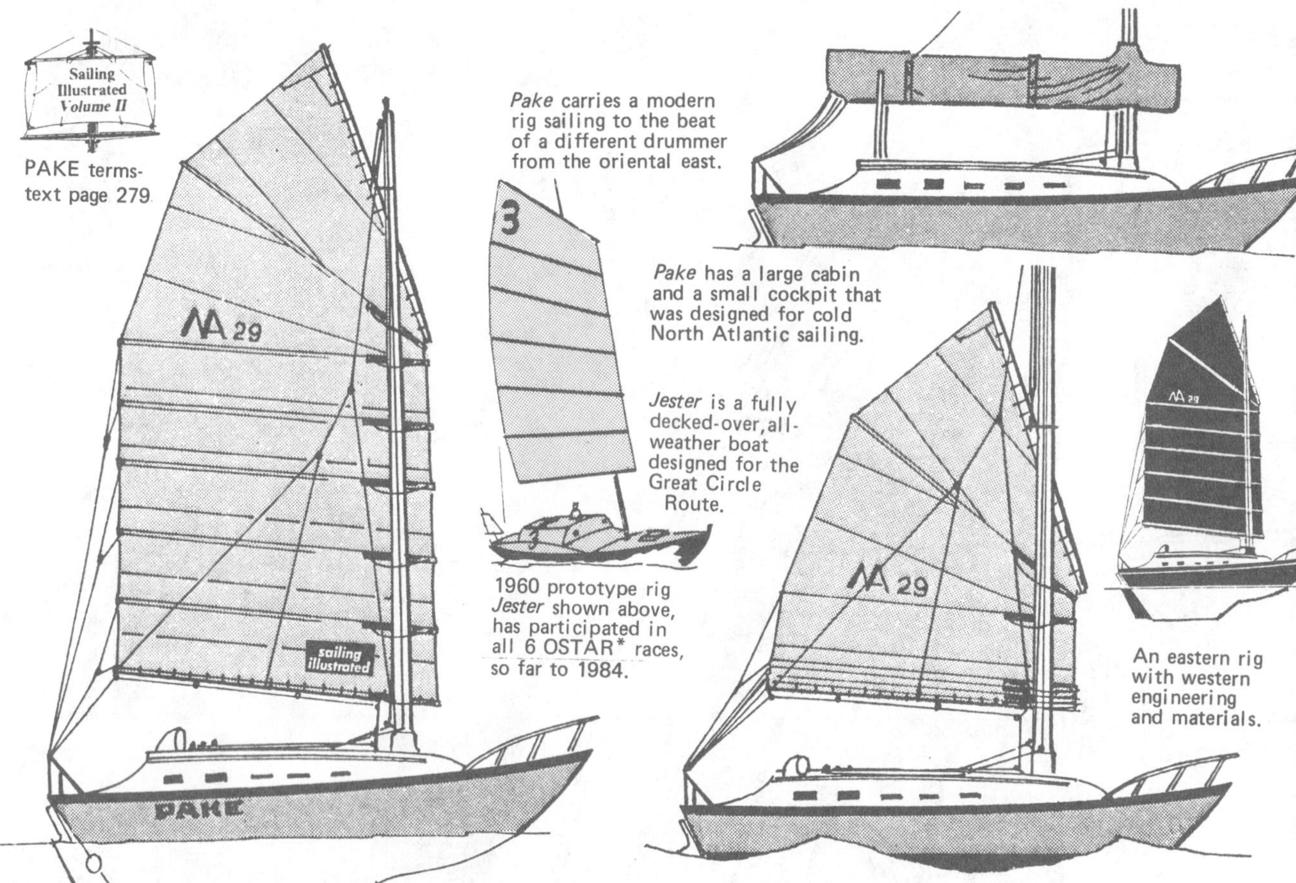
Sailing Illustrated Volume II
PAKE terms-
text page 279
Pake carries a modern rig sailing to the beat of a different drummer from the oriental east.
Pake has a large cabin and a small cockpit that was designed for cold North Atlantic sailing.
Jester is a fully decked-over, all-weather boat designed for the Great Circle Route.
1960 prototype rig Jester shown above, has participated in all 6 OSTAR* races, so far to 1984.
An eastern rig with western engineering and materials.
PAKE

J

Potentials of the modern, stayless lug rig has to be one of the best kept secrets in sailing...but why?

*Observer Single Handed Transatlantic Race

For more lug rig information—

Contact author Thomas Colvin, a naval architect who designed commercial sailing vessels with lug rigs, also writing books on this subject—Seven Seas Press, 524 Thames St., Newport, RI 02840

Write to Jack McCleod—Hawk Hill Rosmarkie, By Fortress, Ross-Shire, Scotland

If you are fortunate enough to see the movie *Cockleshell Heroes* on late TV, this is the same Colonel Blondie Hasler leading a WW II commando raid on Bordeau, France.

The marconi and gaff rig standards of the western world are well adapted to active crews in warm weather sailing. *Pake* is designed for a different concept that is an efficient rig for long distance solo sloppy, cold-weather sailing using a non-complaining wind vane for steering. Sail trim adjustments can be easily made below without going topside.

Pake is an interesting hybrid using a free-standing mast on a full-batten lug rig that has over 2000 years of **eastern oriental customer testing...** using the latest **western materials and technology** for sails, mast, and hull.

The best known western example is the 26' folkboat *Jester* which was rerigged as a modern lugger for the 1960 OSTAR*. The owner/designer Colonel Blondie Hasler also introduce the first self-steering van in the 1960 race. Hasler made 9 transatlantic crossings in *Jester* while the new owner Michael Richey had made four transatlantic crossings on *Jester* as of 1984.

The *balanced lug rig* shown is excellent for cruising. It has good upwind performance without the last couple of degrees of weatherliness for racing...or in very light airs.

The balanced self-tending lug rig changes tack easily downwind. Since part of the sail is forward of the mast it acts as a brake on the sail area aft of the mast, permitting the sail to jibe softly. This is in contrast to a jibe on marconi and gaff rigs. Tremendous torque forces develop on the end of the boom, producing large thrust forces on the boom jaws when jibing to release the mainsail wind pressure as it changes from one tack to the other.

The Chinese philosophy behind the balanced lug rig is to *deliver maximum results with minimum wasted energy.* The full-batten sail provides a rather flat curve with sheetlets controlling the shape for sailing upwind and downwind. The wind force is easily absorbed by the hull thru the mast which does not have stays nor shrouds. Sail force stresses and loads are spread over the entire sail resulting in cloth damage limited to a localized area...so sail repairs can be made at your convenience.

When you want to get underway, ease the sheetlets, raise the halyard the number of panels you desire, release dock lines, sheet the sheetlets, and then the boat is underway. When the wind is too strong, drop one or two panels by easing the halyard. If a white squall hits, release the halyard all the way so the panels will be down in seconds to be contained by the lazy jacks.

If I had the chance to choose a sailboat to leisurely cruise the Pacific singlehanded, the balanced-lug rig would be my first choice. A different hull would be chosen with a roomier cockpit and a larger wine cellar...dream on. Many thanks go to Colonel Blondie Hasler from a long time admirer for his excellent contributions to the western sailing world. He was the originator of the 1960 OSTAR....the modern lug rig...and the popular silent wind-vane helmsman.

Your SNOW-BELT SAILING SCHEDULE—WEATHER .... SEASONS.........MAINTENANCE.

Caribbean charter?
Christmas

blizzards, gales, freezing weather

NY Boat Show

Prepare list of products to check at boat shows.

other boat shows

Dec

Jan

Feb

major electrical engine, hull, and rigging maintenance

preparation maintenance time

brush up on swimming, scuba diving

Sun Belt regatta?

WARNING!!!

finish the details to prepare for launching

Western U.S.— long early spring

Eastern U.S.— what spring?

flooding begins

Time is running out!

Mar

Apr

heavy spring storms, flooding

launching

spring showers

yacht clubs open

Memorial Day

May

June

Prolonged lack of use is the greatest destroyer of sailboats...and sailboat equipment.

4th of July

July

enjoy every moment of sailing!

hurricane potentials

Happy Sailing!

Aug

add notes to maintenance records

Labor Day

Sept

MAXIMUM hurricane risk

Western U.S.— a very short fall

Eastern U.S.— long, lovely fall

an Indian summer with warm lovely days until—

storm tracks move south with arctic air behind the *northers* as they head south.

yacht clubs close

haul out time

MAINTENANCE

prepare work list

Sun Belt regatta?

Time to tell almost-true sea stories.

Oct

outboard motor maintenance?

decommission boat ashore

off-season sail repair discount?

Nov

Thanksgiving

inflatable repairs?

Dry martini sailing begins... as the almost true sea stories of the exciting spring to fall grow with each fond retelling.

Finalize maintenance list in most efficient sequence.

RECORDS

The memory has limitations!

We wish we had started such a record book 20 years ago. This spring as an example, we bought two gallons of bottom paint...instead of two quarts.

Keep a simple record of installations such as wiring diagram with its color coding. Also part changes, company addresses of difficult parts to obtain such as gooseneck, outhaul, etc.

List parts with periodic maintenance such as the head joker valve, outboard motor water pump, inflatable dinghy parts, lubrication periods for overboard valves, engine oil changes, etc.

Start a file of articles, new product announcements, etc., to analyze and refer to for future use.

Is your tool kit adequate?
Check periodically to eliminate unnecessary tool duplication.

HEADING SOUTH can be the experience of a lifetime...or a nightmare, see *page 63.*

K

Good seamanship begins with normal periodic maintenance practices.

Buy a quality sailboat, install quality equipment, then stay within the operating limits of your equipment. *If your boat is maintained normally it will protect and treat you right.* If maintenance is below par, any airplane, auto, or sailboat will become dangerous.

We wish we could assign 200 pages to sailboat maintenance...yet we were limited to 19 pages. We have tried to choose the most important and most basic answers facing the new sailor. We begin with corrosion which has so many twists, turns, and variables it is little reported since smarter writers often stick to easier, more popular subjects

Any sailor with a small, medium, or large cabin sailboat can handle a variety of basic maintenance chores turning the rest to the boatyard or to the mechanic of your choice. Ask endless questions while expanding your maintenance knowledge by observation and collecting magazine articles. Have a buttermilk, beer, or martini handy when you have the opportunity to exchange ideas (bribery ?) with a good marine mechanic. You may soon find many other applications for the basic ideas covered in our maintenance chapter.

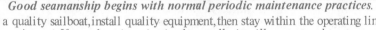

Prolonged lack of use is the greatest destroyer of sailboats and equipment.

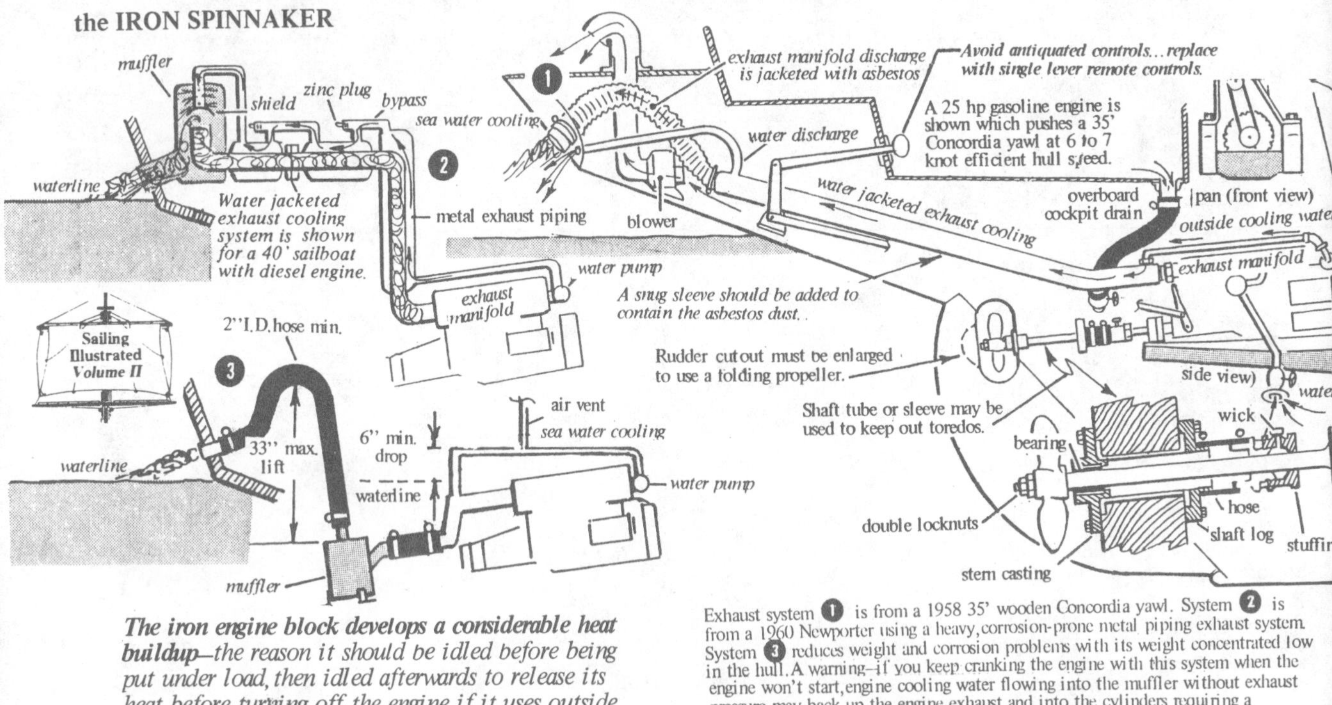
muffler
shield
zinc plug
bypass
sea water cooling
waterline
Water jacketed exhaust cooling system is shown for a 40' sailboat with diesel engine.
metal exhaust piping
exhaust manifold
water pump
Sailing Illustrated Volume II
2" I.D. hose min.
33" max. lift
6" min. drop
waterline
air vent
sea water cooling
water pump
muffler
exhaust manifold discharge is jacketed with asbestos
water discharge
blower
A snug sleeve should be added to contain the asbestos dust.
Avoid antiquated controls... replace with single lever remote controls.
A 25 hp gasoline engine is shown which pushes a 35' Concordia yawl at 6 to 7 knot efficient hull speed.
water jacketed exhaust cooling
overboard cockpit drain
pan (front view)
outside cooling wate
exhaust manifold
Rudder cutout must be enlarged to use a folding propeller.
Shaft tube or sleeve may be used to keep out toredos.
side view)
wick
bearing
hose
shaft log
stuffir
double locknuts
stem casting

The iron engine block develops a considerable heat buildup*—the reason it should be idled before being put under load, then idled afterwards to release its heat before turning off the engine if it uses outside cooling water*.*

Exhaust system ❶ is from a 1958 35' wooden Concordia yawl. System ❷ is from a 1960 Newporter using a heavy, corrosion-prone metal piping exhaust system. System ❸ reduces weight and corrosion problems with its weight concentrated low in the hull. A warning—if you keep cranking the engine with this system when the engine won't start, engine cooling water flowing into the muffler without exhaust pressure may back up the engine exhaust and into the cylinders requiring a major engine overhaul to repair the compression/corrosion damages.

Are you able to hand crank a sailboat gasoline or diesel engine?

The ignored, overlooked engine has its final chance to fight back.

"Most sailboat sinkings in the Pacific occur after reaching a protected area... due to a sudden unexpected engine failure", said local GM diesel distributor Tom Kelly, deceased, a close friend and adviser for 20 years.

most engine failures follow predictable patterns

The number of engine failures I've witnessed while teaching or crewing on sailboats seems average with many more occurring on powerboats. The factors involved—***thoroughly know how all of your engine components operate....keep your equipmen adequately maintained...then OPERATE the engine often.*** If any of these factors are overlooked it won't be a matter IF...but WHEN engine failure will occur.

operational manual and parts catalog

Whether it is a new or used sailboat obtain the *operational manual* and *parts catalog* of your engine from it's manufacturer, then become familiar with the names and functions of all it's components. Periodically check intake, manifold, and exhaust systems, the hoses and clamps of all exhaust systems which ***must go upward***... with an outer water jacket to cool the hot exhaust. This check is especially important with gasoline engines to ***avoid the danger of carbon monoxide leaks.*** *IF you smell any engine exhaust you are also smelling carbon monoxide gas.*

If you smell exhaust fumes— **you are ALSO smelling dangerous carbon monoxide fumes.**

problems of lower engine operating temperatures

Engine heat is important. Sulfur from incomplete combustion plus ***water*** from conde sation collecting in the lubricating oil produces weak but ***corrosive sulfuric acid.*** High auto engine temperatures help to boil out a large percentage of these contamina

Most gasoline sailboat engines use *a continuous flow of outside cooling water* . They operate in a maximum heat range with a 150° cooling system thermostat so minera and salts flowing thru the cooling system stay in suspension to be exhausted overboard

**Water temperature must stay below 150° in a continuous flow system.*

The reason is for the ocean water to keep flowing thru without the minerals and salts falling out of suspension.

Above this temperature the minerals and salts fall out of suspension to form *boiler scale* which will plug the cooling system passages.

An owner had his sportscar mechanic check his sailboat engine, replacing the 120° thermostat with a 180° thermostat plus some snide remarks. I helped sail the boat with its new owner soon afterwards to Long Beach Terminal Island. I turned on the engine while dropping the sails when entering the harbor due to heavy traffic. Engine temperature skyrocketed with the salts and minerals falling out of suspension. They plugged the cooling system with ***boiler scale.*** causing an expensive engine repair bill and a difficult sail for a heavy 40 footer in tight channels to its awkward dock.

Warm operating captive cooling systems **provide a long life yet add considerable to the system's complexity.**

Marine engines used in water-taxi service normally have *captive cooling systems* with 180° or higher cooling system thermostats. With normal maintenance they operate many more hours than auto engines before a major overhaul. The reason—marine inboard engine carburetors don't have to digest *abrasive concrete and asph dust particles* from pounding tires, a major destroyer of auto and truck engines.

The least understood technical field in sailing... is the outboard motor.

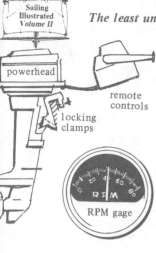

powerhead
remote controls
locking clamps
RPM gage

2 cycle & 4 cycle powerplants have different requirements.

Operational requirements differ considerably between the heavy iron-block 4 cycle inboard engine,and the lightweight aluminum portable 2 cycle outboard motor.Either may provide sufficient shaft horsepower to push a variety of sailboats to their displacement hull speed.

The specialized sailboat market for outboard powerplants *is limited to motors up to 10 hp.* More specialized engineering is needed as motor manufacturer's primary past interest has been larger,high hp motors on outboard hulls for planing speeds.

The *2 cycle engine* is the most versatile powerplant in the world,called a motor by traditional usage.It has approx.¼ the weight of a similar inboard engine prop shaft torque horsepower.Half as many cylinders are needed as every down piston is a power stroke...while a 4 cycle engine fires every 2nd downward stroke.

The *small,cold running* outboard motor *doesn't need a cooling system thermostat.* An aluminum block ***releases heat five times as rapidly*** as an iron 4 cycle block which eliminates the need for warmup and idle afterwards.The low operating temp.reduces the chance of boiler scale buildup,pg.K 7.Boiler scale problems are often caused by incorrect fuel which leaves cylinder deposits to become insulators that reduce heat transference.This causes cylinder heat buildup that rapidly develops a boiler-scale buildup.

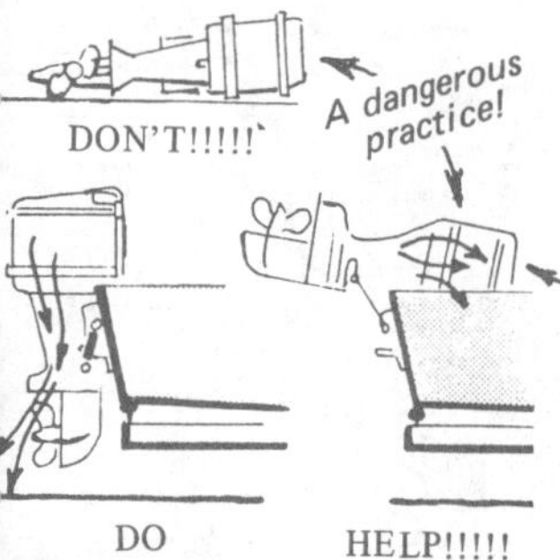
DON'T!!!!!
A dangerous practice!
DO
HELP!!!!!

RPM gages are needed. An outboard motor is designed to reach and maintain maximum rated rpm for long periods as the crankshaft is floating in bearings.The gage is equally important for 4 cycle with fewer bearings operating at lower rpm.

Battery started aluminum outboard motors face electrolysis hazards, pages 129,132. That is the reason we prefer a hand-cranked outboard motor for most sailboat use.

The outboard motor powerhead must always be carried and stored higher than the lower unit. If the lower unit is momentarily raised higher,cooling system water may drain into powerhead cylinders starting rapid metal-expansion corrosion, page 129.

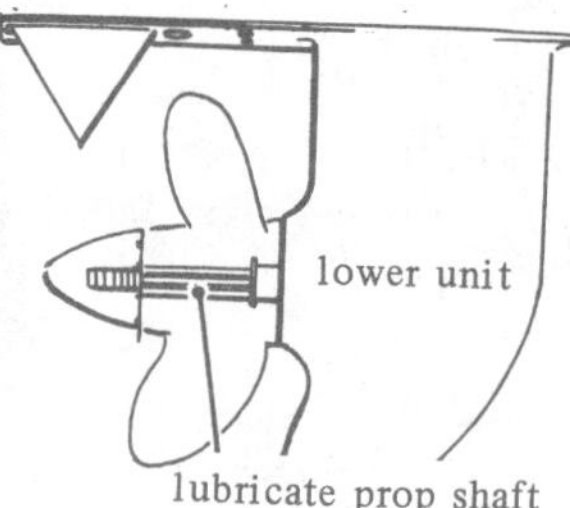
lower unit
lubricate prop shaft

Use aluminum slipclutch props with aluminum similar to the lower unit which reduces galvanic corrosion.The *2 blade stock prop* used on small motors for dinghies and rowboats will have too much bite,the prop slipping under load,momentarily exceeding the rated rpm.Replace it with a ***3 blade load prop*** which has less bite and more surface thrust so your outboard motor can operate at its rated top rpm to efficiently power your sailboat.

stock prop
load prop

The ***stainless locking clamps*** in an aluminum forging need periodic lubrication to avoid the different metals expanding and permanently locking together.Another type of locking method is needed to prevent the clamps from unwinding due to vibration and the motor falling overboard.Remove the prop and its nut periodically to grease the shaft which will prevent the dissimilar metal parts from permanently bonding together.

Copper bottom paint on outboard motor lower units reduce underwater growth... while speeding lower unit corrosion. If you install an outboard motor that cannot be tilted out of the water,paint the underwater metal surface with anodic zinc chromate primer, plus an outer TBTO tin compound paint to retard weed growth.When the paint surface breaks to expose metal,wash with distilled water,add zinc chromate,then paint with TBTO.

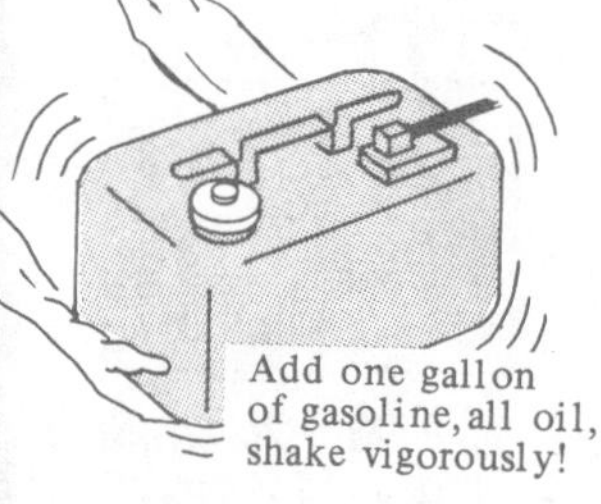
Add one gallon of gasoline, all oil, shake vigorously!

Follow manual recommended ***fuel mixture proportions closely.*** Pour a gallon of gasoline into a new 6 gallon tank,then add all oil.Shake rapidly so they will mix thoroughly. Add the rest of the gasoline rapidly so the oil doesn't cling to the inner surfaces of a fuel tank.

Condensation may collect in the bottom of a fuel tank requiring an additive if the motor isn't used often.Another method is to depress the hose connector ball valve with a screw driver to pump some of this bottom condensation overboard.

An advantage— most outboard motors can be taken yearly to a certified outboard mechanic who has all the needed tools and testers in his shop...while a mechanic has to go to the boat with an inboard engine whether it has a major problem or normal maintenance.

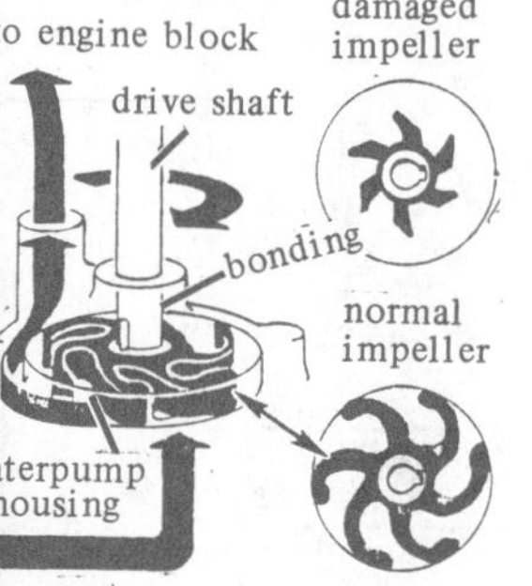
to engine block
damaged impeller
drive shaft
bonding
normal impeller
waterpump housing
water intake

Replace waterpump impellers yearly due to their limited useful lifespan...as waterpump failures are a major cause of expensive outboard motor and inboard engine repairs.We've seen impellers in fair condition after two years of active operation,with more damage in little used engines.The impeller failed in a motor operated 3 times in 4 months due to barnacles in the housing which acted like rough sandpaper.If you purchase a used sailboat with an inboard engine or outboard motor,replace the impellers before operating since the shaft bonding adhesive could fail during storage if the waterpump housing becomes dry.

Americans have been raised on 4 cycle auto engines.This background with minor changes is easy to apply to gasoline inboard engines on sailboats.Considerable misinformation exists with the outboard motor as few sailors have been raised with an exposure to 2 cycle engines. *Problems develop rapidly when 4 cycle operation ideas are applied to a 2 cycle engine.*

Seagoing metals–birth...life...death

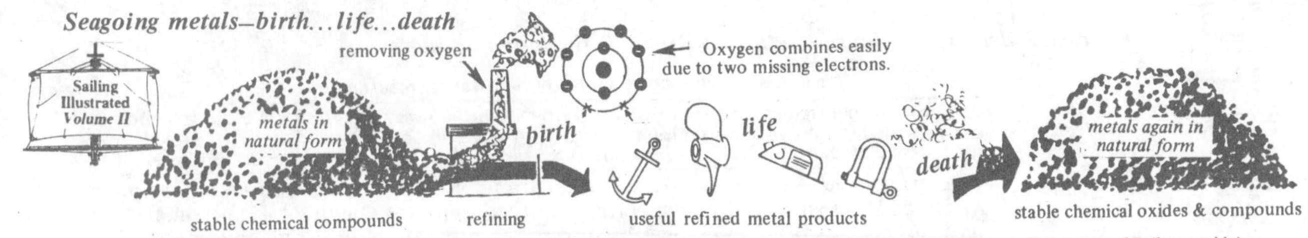
Sailing Illustrated Volume II
removing oxygen
Oxygen combines easily due to two missing electrons.
metals in natural form
birth
life
death
metals again in natural form
stable chemical compounds
refining
useful refined metal products
stable chemical oxides & compounds

HEMATITE (red iron-oxide ore) ...becomes pig iron...changes to iron,steel compounds & alloys...corrodes to a brown powder (iron oxide)

BAUXITE is refined to Alumina (aluminum oxide)..to become aluminum compounds and alloys...corrodes to a white powder (aluminum oxide)

OXIDATION occurs above water

METAL COMPOUNDS

Birth, life, and destruction of seagoing metals.
Most seagoing metals exist temporarily in their refined condition. They begin as stable compounds of nature. The oxygen is removed or "cooked out" at the refinery so that the raw products can be refined into compounds and alloys for our seagoing use. Our responsibility is to choose stable metals, then apply a wide variety of corrosion prevention methods to extend their useful life *before they return to more stable oxides* which we can no longer use.

METAL MIXTURES– AVOID!

AVOID metal mixtures such as home improvement store brasses and pot metals which are chemically unstable, corroding and failing rapidly in the salt water environment.

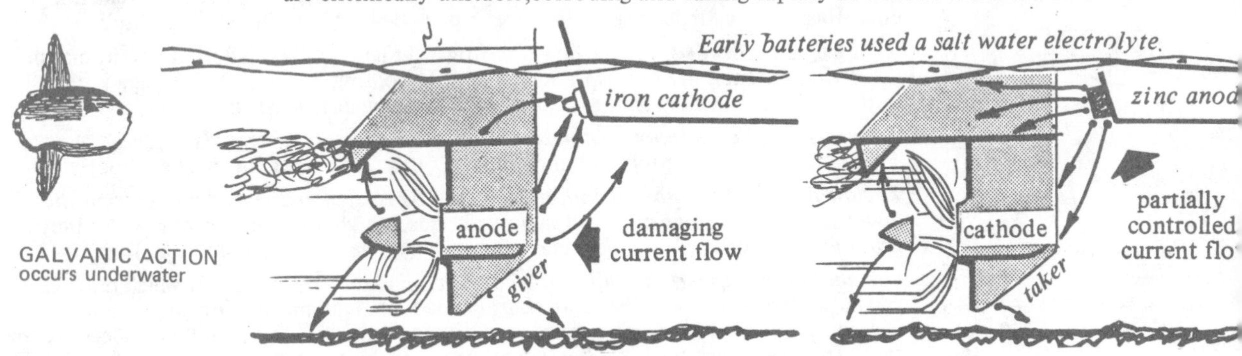
Early batteries used a salt water electrolyte.
iron cathode
anode
damaging current flow
giver
zinc anod
cathode
partially controlled current flo
taker

GALVANIC ACTION occurs underwater

An outward current flow carries molecules or flakes of metal away in the salt water electrolyte galvanic corrosion action with underwater metals reacting as *takers and givers.* ***Galvanic corrosion*** or galvanic action, is similar to electroplating as current flows thru an electrolyte...except flakes of iron, aluminum, or zinc go into solution instead of plating another metal. Zinc is used as a waster metal added to protect the surrounding metals as it has the higher EMF rating with the zinc flakes instead easily dissolving into the water.

K

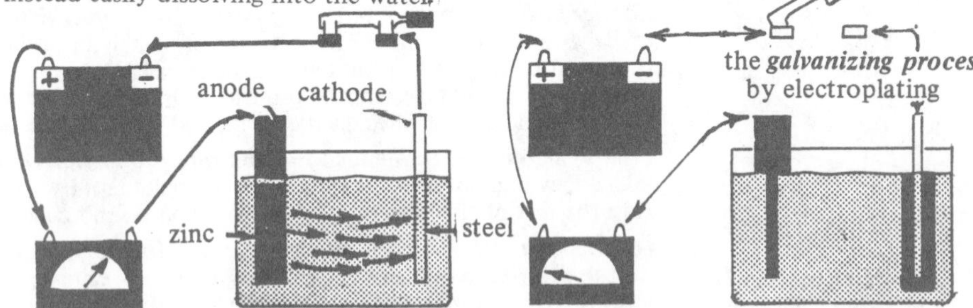
anode
cathode
zinc
steel
the galvanizing process
by electroplating

ELECTROPLATING– controlled electrolysis

An *ion* of one metal placed at the *positive anode* is carried thru an ***electrolyte solution*** where it is deposited on the *negative cathode* terminal. The amount deposited is directly proportional to the quantity of the charge carried thru the electrolyte...the stronger the charge the faster will be the plating action.

METAL FATIGUE– sharp corners, sharp edges

Pressures on boat parts under load tension such as lifting lugs tend to move to and concentrate in areas with *sharp corners and sharp edges*. This reduces the useful life of the part which is speeded by metal fatigue. U.S.Navy marine hardware parts have rounded edges to spread the pressure throughout the parts when under load. This not only increases the useful life of the part...but the ***rounded edges*** also protect sailors. *Does your sailboat have any unnecessary sharp corners and sharp edges below and topside that could prove a hazard to the crew in sloppy weather?*

SHARP CORNERS are hazardous!

Follow **standard USN practice**–*eliminate sharp corners and sharp edges topside and below that can be hazardous to skipper and crew in good and in bad weather.*

Will nuclear subs eventually use sail power? Dream on.

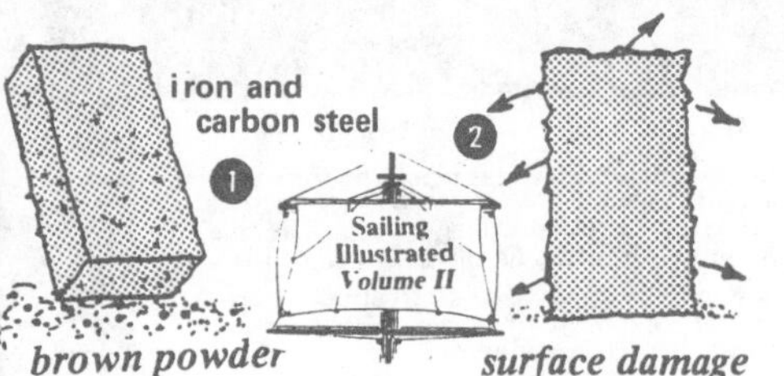
iron and
carbon steel
1
Sailing
Illustrated
Volume II
2
brown powder
surface damage

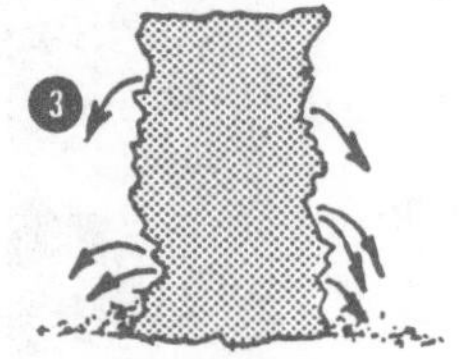
3
major damage

4
total damage

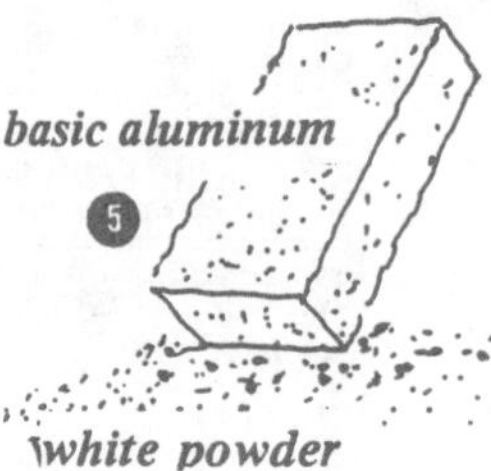
basic aluminum
5
white powder

iron and carbon steel corrosion

Iron and carbon steel parts *develop a brown oxide* ***surface coating*** leaving a brown rust powder as particles flake off. This corrosion process will go progressively deeper until the part fails if not stopped by a zinc coating, a continuous enamel paint film, or both. ***AVOID*** grinding iron or steel parts on your boat, or wash the area thoroughly afterwards, as the invisble metal particles soon oxidize developing deck stains difficult to remove.

aluminum corrosion

Unprotected *aluminum* surfaces start pitting *developing a fine white oxide* ***surface coating*** that may grow into a hard surface barrier retarding, then stopping further corrosion action... which is speeded by ***anodizing***, an electrochemical process of rapid, controlled corrosion.

brass and pot metal corrosion

Corrosion occurs ***throughout mixtures*** *of hardware-store brass and pot metal*...the term originating with linotype printing where metal scraps of unknown origin were continually added to, and mixed in a pot of molten metal to be cast into type.

carbon steel expands as it corrodes

Corrosion expansion—minimum protective carbon steel screws, bolts, and nuts, ***may expand 3 to 4 diameters***, with aluminum up to 6 diameters as the parts oxidize and/or corrode. A nut on a carbon steel bolt becomes difficult to remove when corrosion begins. The outer bolt surface and inner surface of the nut continue their corrosion expansion against each other until the crushing forces permanently lock the parts together...after a short useful life.

Light corrosion can sometimes be useful.

New metal hazards?

New metals may be hazardous. A 30' sailboat was launched Tuesday and dismasted Thursday in a force 5 as the unlocked turnbuckles began unwinding. The excuse was that the mechanic didn't have time to tune the rigging, *page 19.* After a month or so of operation the salt spray may help to develop enough minimum corrosion which may retard the turnbuckle unwinding potentials.

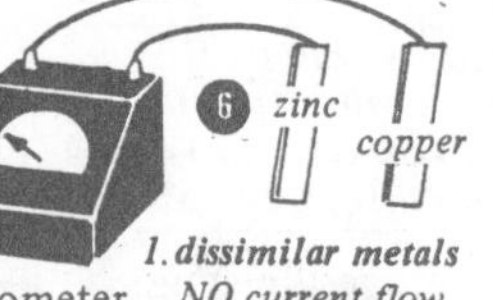
6
zinc
copper
anometer

1. *dissimilar metals NO current flow*

WD 40® was the first modern product to unlock stuck turnbuckles. It is a *penetrant* to remove moisture from metal surface pores providing smooth *clean metal surfaces.* ***TRIFLON***™ and similar products produce a micron-depth *sticky film* to reduce surface/locking corrosion potentials for bolts, nuts, machinery, etc. Both are excellent, considerably different products to carry aboard for your use with seagoing metals plus your protection for corrosion prone carbon steel drills, bitts, screwdrivers, etc.

Cold water vs warm water seagoing metals.

Seven large wooden trawlers were built in Sweden in the early 1960's with woods and metals used successfully for 50 years on traditional fishing trawlers in that area. Six months after arriving locally for use as yachts, metal problems and wood problems were developing, *pg. 137.* *as these trawlers were built for a completely different cold salt water environment.*

K

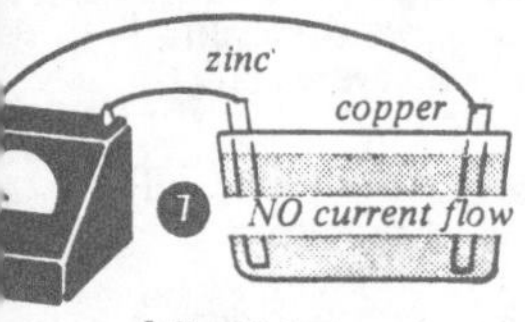
zinc
copper
7
NO current flow

2. *liquid (solvent)*

Dissimilar metals vs ***water temperature.*** The fishing waters of Sweden, Norway, and Iceland are close to freezing with iron and carbon-steel metals adequate, unaffected by ***underwater galvanic action*** for practical purposes. Galvanic action problems rapidly developed in local waters with 57° to 75° temperatures, rapidly escalating in Acapulco with engine intake water 80° to 82°. Replacement was required with much more expensive corrosion-resistant metals...a starting place to discuss galvanic corrosion.

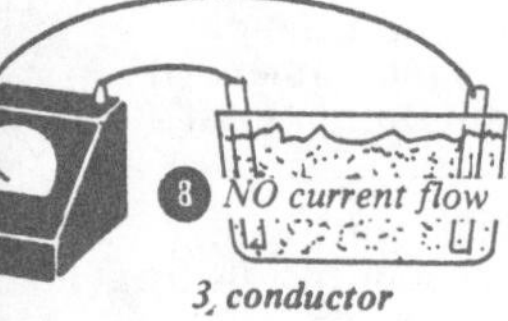
8
NO current flow

3. *conductor*

Galvanic action can't occur when— 6 metals are separated (oxidation may occur), 7 when dissimilar metals are submerged in distilled water with minerals removed, and 8 the metals are submerged in conductors (minerals, salt, etc) without oxygen or water.

Action begins in an electrolyte 9 composed of liquid and conductors (salts, minerals, soda, and/or alkali) capable of supporting a current (ionic flow). Metal atoms begin to flow from a giver metal with a higher EMF voltage...to a dissimilar taker metal with a lower EMF voltage listed on the following page.

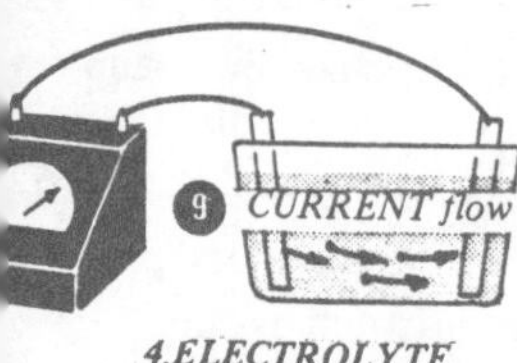
9
CURRENT flow

4. *ELECTROLYTE liquid and conductor*

Aluminum is an excellent electrical conductor in an electrolyte... a good reason to unhook an outboard motor battery harness before turning on a battery charger.

Add an AC current—a local boat owner intended to go fishing later in the day. He stopped by his boat to charge his 12v lead/acid batteries...forgetting to unhook his battery harness, and forgetting to raise the twin 35 hp outboard motor lower units out of the water. When returning after breakfast he was stunned to find his motor's lower units disappeared at the waterline with only the stainless drive shafts remaining, the props and gears had fallen to the bottom of the bay. The 115v AC current had gone thru the batteries and out the lower units to ground in the bay. It could have electrocuted nearby swimmers without tripping the dockside circuit breakers.

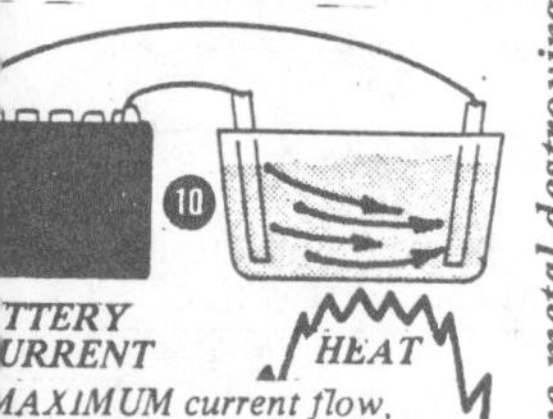
10
TTERY
URRENT
HEAT

AXIMUM current flow,
AXIMUM metal damage!

the metal destroying electrolyte gang

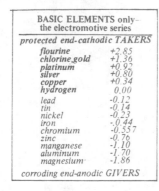

GALVANIC SERIES– compounds and alloys
protected end– cathodic TAKERS
platinum
gold
graphite
silver
*18-8-3 stainless***
*18-8 stainless***
*chromium-iron***
*Inconel***
*nickel***
silver solder
Monel
copper-nickel alloys
bronzes
copper
brasses
*Inconel**
*nickel**
tin
lead
lead-tin solders
*18-8-3 stainless**
*18-8 stainless**
Ni-Resist
aluminum-iron
cast iron
steel or iron
aluminum 17ST
cadmium
aluminum 2 S
zinc
magnesium alloys
magnesium
corroding end– anodic GIVERS
*active
**passive

BASIC ELEMENTS only– the electromotive series	
protected end-cathodic TAKERS	
flourine	+2.85
chlorine,gold	+1.36
platinum	+0.92
silver	+0.80
copper	+0.34
hydrogen	0.00
lead	-0.12
tin	-0.14
nickel	-0.23
iron	-.0.44
chromium	-0.557
zinc	-0.76
manganese	-1.10
aluminum	-1.70
magnesium	-1.86
corroding end-anodic GIVERS	

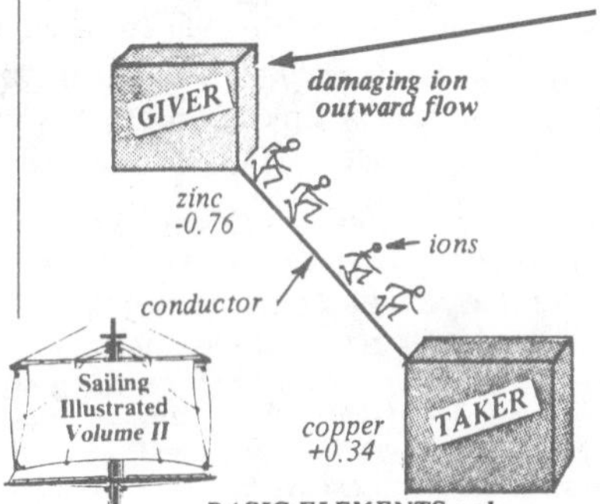

GIVER
damaging ion outward flow
zinc -0.76
ions
conductor
Sailing Illustrated Volume II
copper +0.34
TAKER

BASIC ELEMENTS only– the electromotive series

the EMF–Electromotive Force Series of Metals

The lower a metal element is placed on the ***giver end*** of the EMF scale,the greater becomes its electrical potential,instability and willingness...such as zinc, to combine with metals on the ***taker end*** of the scale.

This ion exchange and metal destruction process is speeded with exposure to oxygen,salt spray,heat, and escaping electrical currents.

The corrosion story introduction begins with the basic elements listed in the EMF series,and the seagoing metals of alloys or compounds listed in the Galvanic Series except for the elements zinc and copper.

We show the elements zinc and copper with identical size or volumes,as rigid bundles of electrical energy.

Zinc is the anodic GIVER while ***copper is the cathodic TAKER*** or energy gainer with the differing electrical contents listed on the EMF Series at left.

This ion energy exchange leading to metal destruction called corrosion, *needs oxygen, heat,and an electrolyte,* to change our refined seagoing metals...back to more stable oxides no longer of use to us.

The higher an alloy or compound is on the protected ***cathodic TAKER end***,the more corrosion resistant it becomes for sailing extremes such as warm tropical waters, as well as protection in freak circumstances.

Our friend *zinc,the corroding end anodic GIVER* of energy is a perpetual do-gooder committing suicide to protect your surrounding metals...a successful loser.

Seagoing metal families of steel,aluminum,and bronze (naval brass)react differently in ways to protect themselves,to react on nearby metals,or corrode rapidly in the harsh ocean water/air environment.Titanium is the highly expensive exception being an element without corrosion potentials... or react with nearby metals.

The toughest and most versatile metal is 1/3 the weight of iron... and the most expensive to manufacture.

AVOID–aircraft aluminum

Aluminum is the third largest element in the world,it was first produced in small amounts in 1852.The aircraft and aluminum industries started and expanded together as aluminum is light with a tremendous number of alloys to serve different purposes.A warning—***avoid surplus aircraft aluminum*** parts,bolts,and screws NOT designed for marine use as they can rapidly self-destruct.

normal corrosion vs light anodizing and heavy anodizing

Oxygen is the enemy...AND friend of aluminum. A corrosive oxide surface layer will develop on an aluminum mast or part if the correct alloy was chosen for marine use which may seal the surface from further corrosion.***Anodizing*** uses the electroplating process to build up a dense,hard,black-oxide surface to protect masts and fittings.

painting aluminum masts

If a new mast hasn't been anodized to seal its surface...don't let nature as the sails will rub against the mast collecting the gray aluminum oxide as a stain on the jib clew and mainsail luff.A hard LPG paint coating,any color desired,is recommended taking a month to dry.A second choice is a vinyl paint to seal the aluminum mast surface every two years to avoid the messy sail stains.

aluminum IOR sailboats

Aluminum seems preferred as the easiest and fastest method to build light,rigid, one-off IOR sailboat hulls.Care is required to separate and insulate other metals from the hull,also for hull protection from stray corrosive electrical currents.

outboard motor metal engineering

We are amazed at the excellent engineering we've found with corrosion-resistant aluminum and stainless parts in the 12 or 13 American built,light outboard motor powerplants we've owned thru the years.Aluminum powerheads have the excellent ability to dissipate heat from the combustion chambers to avoid limestone/boiler scale buildup in the cooling systems used in salt water.None of them used cooling system thermostats.

boiler scale is a problem for 2 and 4 cycle engines

Boiler scale buildup occurs in fresh water with a high mineral content such as the Southern California Aqueduct Svstem and Lake Mead in Nevada.If you sail on the Salton Sea or Great Salt Lake,choose an air-cooled outboard motor,or have a pure sailboat since the high mineral and alkali content will rapidly plug any outboard motor or inboard engine cooling systemwith boiler scale.

Why flush outboard motors..

Flushing outboard motors? We recommend it ***yearly*** to kill barnacles when our waterpump is periodically replaced.This is a practice we've followed while operating outboard motors for 30 years without boiler scale buildup.The high mineral content in fresh water used for flushing in many areas seems a greater hazard than salt water.

Oceangoing metal families have different corrosion protection methods.

What are two reasons why shroud covers should roll easily?*

stainless—a name that causes confusion

tight shroud rollers block oxygen flow

Stainless is a name for various steel alloys with minimum rust properties.The main advantage of stainless is that ***failure potentials are usually obvious with stress cracks*** in fittings and broken wire ***fish hooks*** on shrouds,stays,and halyards.Stainless needs a *continuous oxygen flow protection so it can corrode at its programmed rate.*

wrought iron has a long history

5000 year old wrought iron implements were found in Egyptian tombs.They were forged under a hammer from rigid form red hot sponge iron at 1470 °F,the process used to forge metal parts for **Pride of Baltimore.**Wrought iron is still used due to corrosion resistance on commercial vessels.Enough heat.2800 °F,was first developed in the 14th century to melt iron,yet bulk steel was not produced until 1856.

Haematite to pig iron

A *ferrous metal* indicates iron is it's major component,derived from *ferrum* (Latin for iron)is one of our most useful metals.Oxygen is cooked out of the red ore Haematite.The liquid cools and solidifys into ***pig iron*** or cast iron which is hard and brittle with over 2% carbon content.It is commonly used for engine blocks.

carbon steel—the tough workhorse for tools and industry...needs protection

Iron with less than a 2% carbon content when mixed with other elements becomes an ***alloy steel.*** Carbon steel is an important high stress metal used for building and for tools such as drills,bitts,screwdrivers,etc.It requires continuous protection as a part left on a deck overnight may corrode so rapidly it will leave a rust stain.

stainless—the glamorous toughie

Stress fatigue *(intergranular corrosion)* develops on undersize stainless steel shrouds, stays,and halyards.The first indication is broken strands called ***fish hooks.*** Also consider rapid replacement of turnbuckle jaw ends,chainplates,and masthead fittings when ***stress fatigue crack patterns*** develop on parts under stress.

stainless MUST breathe

A major stainless plus—developing failures can be obvious

Standing rigging—*1 x 19* (1 strand,19 wires),***types 302/304 stainless are alloys-*** (18% chrome,8% nickel) have minimum stretch,maximum strength,flexibility,resistance to fatigue,similar carbon content.*A continuous oxygen flow is needed to oxidize chromium ions at a programmed rate for protection,* with nickel added for easy working.***Crevice corrosion develops*** when the oxygen flow is disturbed,such as by taping a small shroud area blocking oxygen and salt-water drainage.Chromium ions panic,rushing to that area in overwhelming numbers to produce localized corrosion.

stress fatigue

Stainless water and fuel tanks are questionable as they require a continuous air flow on top,sides,bottom,and ends with crevice corrosion potentials in support areas.Underwater stainless fittings face ***oxygen starvation corrosion*** if the chromium ions panic.

different concepts for oxygen protection

Crevice corrosion may be eliminated if you avoid taping stainless turnbuckles by using ***oversize shroud covers*** that allow drainage and breathing.Fully-sealed horizontal stainless lifelines only develop panic crevice corrosion when a hole chafes into the lifeline.This permits salt spray to enter...clean,then seal the exposed area for protection.

How can you tell brass from bronze?

The terms brass and bronze provide a language problem.Ocean sailing requires stable ***bronze compounds with several corrosion steps*** before failure...the English naval brass may cause confusion as it belongs to the stable bronze family compounds.Consider *brass,a one-step corrosion zinc/copper mixture that rapidly dezincs* on the ocean though adequate for home decorations,ammunition cartridges,etc.Brass screws can be a shiny yellow,while bronze screws have a yellow,red color.

Decorative brass for home use will self destruct rapidly on the ocean.

The history of brass goes back around 3000 years.Copper is heated to its melting point of 1990°,then zinc is added with a lower 790° melting point to produce a mixture, not a compound,for use in protected home and office environments.***Brass rapidly dezincs*** in a salt water electrolyte leaving a weak,spongy,salmon-colored copper part behind.Brass screws sealed in wood for fastening wooden decks,or in a bulkhead below will also dezinc due to the moisture and resins in the wood.

Bronze,excellent for underwater and structural use...protects itself with a dirty,oxide face.

Bronze has a 5000 year history beginning with 25% tin added to copper.It includes numerous compounds using a wide variety of alloys.The more complex and expensive the bronze compound is,generally the more corrosive steps that are involved before replacement...though it doesn't have the beautiful appearance of stainless.

The large,non-glamorous bronze family is the choice **for underwater use and wooden boatbuilding**

Bronze metal family life may be extended by sealing to keep out oxygen. Bronze bolts and screws are excellent for wooden boatbuilding as they may be sealed inside the wood,while bronze turnbuckle life is extended by taping.Quality bronzes are excellent for underwater use due to minimum oxygen and galvanic action protection.

Quality bronzes are poor mixers..as they corrode nearby metals.

Monel and nickel bronzes are excellent ***soloists*** for overboard valves and underwater parts as ***cathodic takers.Avoid***—we bought several Monel washers at bargain prices which were used in our outboard boat...with many unexpected equipment failures a few months later.Monel parts will always be troublemakers when *used as a mixed team player* accidentally combined with other metals.

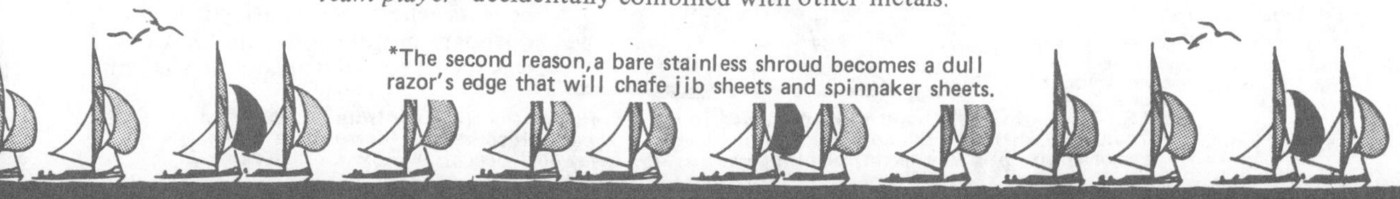

*The second reason,a bare stainless shroud becomes a dull razor's edge that will chafe jib sheets and spinnaker sheets.

Sailing
Illustrated
Volume II

screws have protection

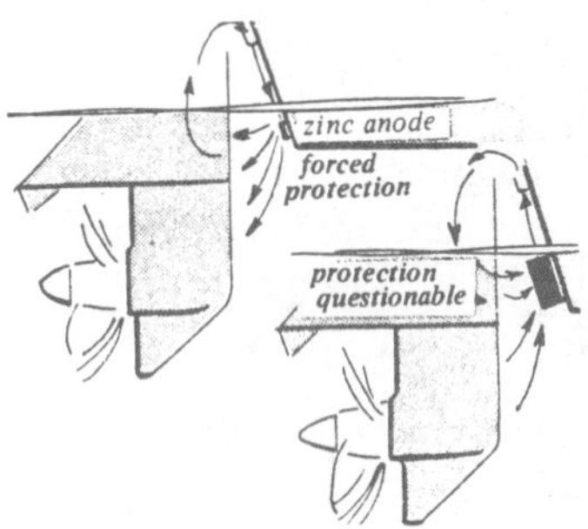
copper
balanced?
aluminum
giver
aluminum
copper taker
zinc anode
forced protection
protection questionable

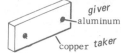

screws face FORCED corrosion

The zinc waster anode operates in a world of its own.

When you mix different metals in an electrolyte,will the mixture serve its purpose or will the mixture cause trouble?The first item to consider is their distance apart in the Galvanic Series.Chances for corrosion are minimal with copper,bronze, Monel,and copper-nickel alloys *if the parts are of similar size or volume.* Rapid corrosion may result when aluminum 2S and 18-8 stainless parts of equal size are mixed with *aluminum the giver,* while ***stainless becomes the taker.***

Use zinc anodes to FORCE corrosion protection.

Relative sizes of metal parts mixed in an electrolyte *are an important factor to cause...or to reduce the corrosion factor.* ***Except for zinc anodes*** avoid combinations where the larger part is on the ***taker end*** and the smaller part is on the *giver end.*

Copper screws used with an aluminum plate are on different sides of the galvanic series.Their energy bundle contents may balance out comfortably...while aluminum screws may corrode rapidly in a copper plate.

The *small zinc GIVER* uses the forced corrosion action theory so the zinc waster block will corrode it a problem develops in salt OR fresh water.*Replace a corroded zinc anode with one the same size or smaller...* until the problem is defined and taken care of.***If a larger zinc block is added,it's protective action may be reduced*** with a rapid corrosion increase of the surrounding parts that it was supposed to protect.

Current corrosion flow can be reversed.

.1.Flow direction due to *natural EMF* with different metals in an electrolyte.

.2. *Battery discharging,* outboard motor at low rpm,battery current leakage.

.3.*Battery charging* at higher rpm with battery current leakage stopped.

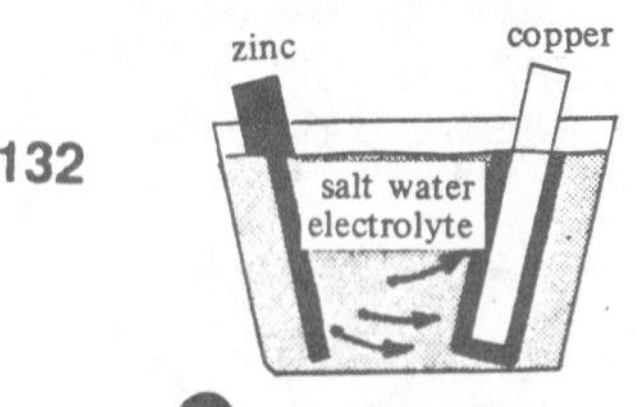
zinc
copper
salt water electrolyte

1 normal EMF flow

1.Corrosion current flow due to voltage difference (EMF) between metals.

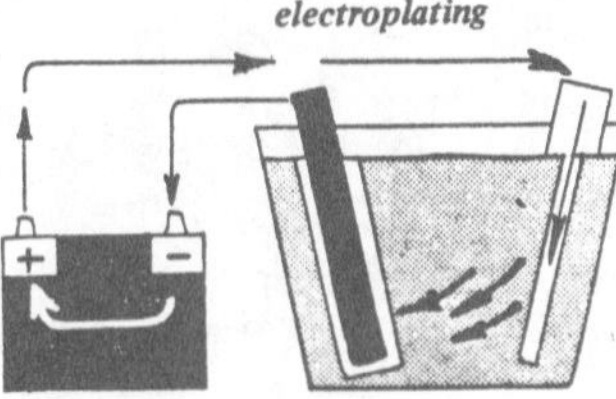
electroplating

2 *battery discharging— Franklin flow theory*

2.Battery leakage imposes stronger current than natural EMF with corrosion current flow reversed with lower unit damage.

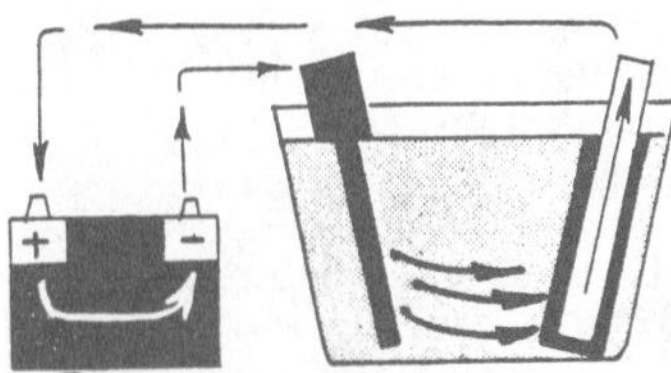

3 *battery charging*

3.Any battery leakage should speed the disintegration of the zinc anode *giver* instead of outboard motor lower unit

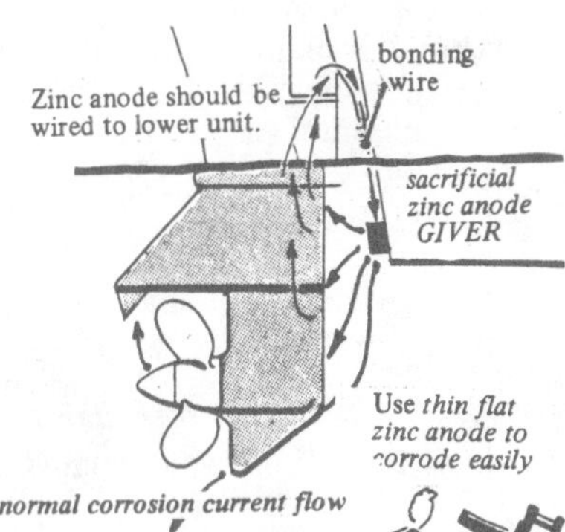
Zinc anode should be wired to lower unit.
bonding wire
sacrificial zinc anode GIVER
Use thin flat zinc anode to corrode easily

normal corrosion current flow

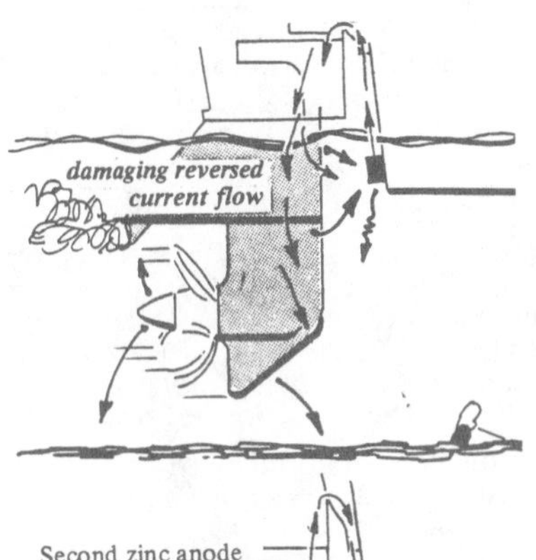
damaging reversed current flow

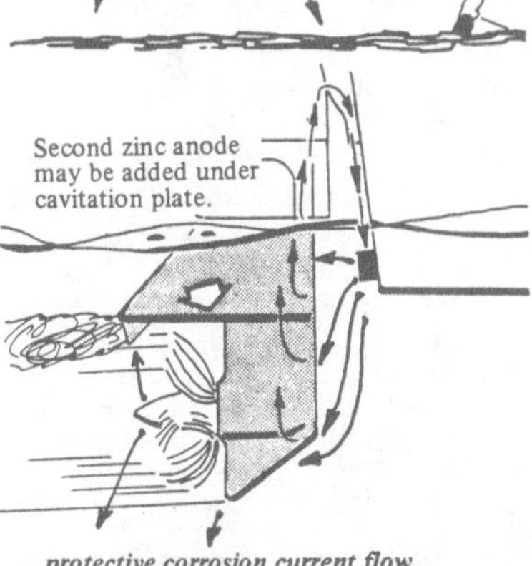
Second zinc anode may be added under cavitation plate.

protective corrosion current flow

Electrical wiring,bonding,and corrosion-resistant metals may be correctly installed on a sailboat for underwater protection,but→

A walk thru boatyards often finds many *zincs covered with copper bottom paint* eliminating zinc protection underwater.

Choose a ***hand-cranked outboard motor*** if the lower unit cannot be fully tilted out of the water to eliminate electrolysis from battery leakage problems.

The lower unit needs a zinc-chromate primer, with a TBTO outer coat of paint to reduce corrosion potentials.*AVOID copper bottom paint on outboard motor lower units which can rapidly corrode the aluminum housing.*

The quality outboard motor is a strong,high rpm engine which can be excellent to charge a lead/acid battery underway.However—

Outboard motors for sailboats with battery charging capabilities need close observation as rapid lower unit corrosion can occur due to the conductivity of aluminum.

Problems may develop at night with the cabin lights on with the same outboard motor at idle or operating at a low rpm for long periods with a ***discharging battery.*** If conditions are ideal the lower unit develops rapid electrolysis.

Before charging a battery—disconnect the electrical harness and/or tilt the lower unit out of the water before turning on the 115v battery charger,see example **page 129.**

Unusual situations—it is not just a salt water problem.Our worst lower unit corrosion in 30 years.occurred on Lake Mead with high mineral content fresh water.For two nights we were moored alongside a 25' steel power-boat,its generator operating continually.Our outboard motor's lower unit in the water was trying to electroplate the steel hull.

P.S.—The varied twists and turns discussed in the maintenance chapter are from our experiences. If yours are different, the combination of ideas will always prove helpful. Please write to the author if you find any technical bloopers—*Box 1967, Newport Beach, CA 92663...* thanks.

hygroscopic salts...overboard valves...hose clamps...bonding to zincs

heavy hygroscopic salts
16 to 17'

"I wiped the spray off my metals an hour ago... but they are moist again".

Water drainage over eons of time has carried mineral and salt deposits to the ocean where they will stay forever in suspension.The magnesium,calcium and iodine salts in suspension are responsible for most ***oxidation corrosion.***

These hygroscopic or water seeking salts are continually thirsty pulling moisture out of the air. The same old electrolyte gang is present in different proportions having ample amounts of ***heat*** and ***oxygen*** to speed oxidation corrosion.

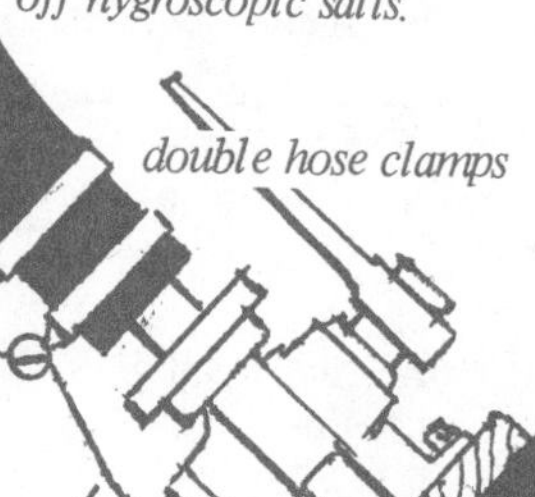
I'm thirsty!
Ahhhhhhhhh, that's better!

Use fresh water to hose off hygroscopic salts.

•

We were aboard the 54' cutter **Good News** in the early sixties shortly before it sailed around the world.The owner was telling us that it had one of the first four aluminum masts made around 1940 before anodizing for ocean use was fully understood.

When we examined the aluminum mast we found considerable corrosion up to 12' above the deck...while above that the oxide corrosion was minimal.The corrosion on the lower part of the mast was due to ***heavy hygroscopic ocean salts*** *which soon fall out of suspension after reaching land.* This is the reason the worst corrosion potentials are cars,and homes with exposed outside pipes near the surf...while half a mile inland with minimum heavy ocean salts in the air corrosion damage is minimal.

Sea Cock Valves*—traditionally the best bronzes,positive on/off. Problem, they need continuous lubrication as they stick easily due to maximum contact areas.*

Globe Valves*—less expensive, less sticking,less lubrication,you aren't always sure they are fully closed. What assurance do you have of corrosion resistant metals;read on...*

A 40' sailboat returned to it's home port four years after launching,enjoying ample cruising in warm Mexican waters.The owner was home with a tall brew enjoying tv when the phone rang..."Your boat is sinking at the dock!"

The owner had taken normal precautions when leaving his boat turning off all valves, but the globe valve had ***a bronze housing,an iron handle,and a brass gate*** inside. The gate crumbling in the mechanics hands when he took the shutoff valve apart. Why the shutoff valve zinc/copper mixture failure didn't occur earlier in wave action in warm Mexican seas...will forever remain a happy,happy mystery.

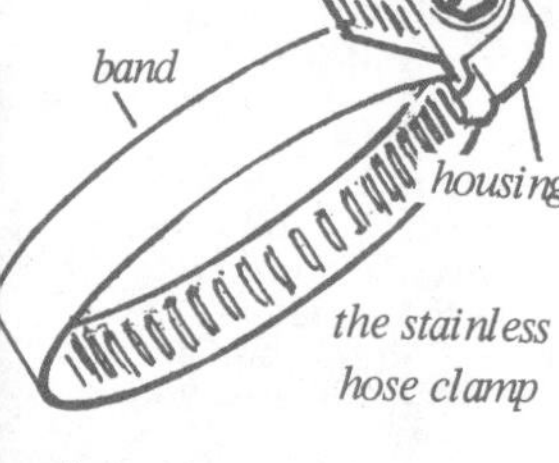
double hose clamps
bonding

Exercise ALL sea cock valves *each time you go aboard as they stick easily—lubricate with vegetable oil.*

•

While we stated earlier that most sailboats lost in the South Pacific seemed to be due to minor unexpected engine failures,your guess is as accurate as ours as to how many boats went to the bottom due to a ***failure of one hose clamp.*** The answer is to add *double clamps to all hose systems...* as double clamps seldom fail at the same time.

K

band

housing

the stainless hose clamp

•

Before buying hose clamps—check them with a sensitive Alnico magnet for use in the salt water environment.*300 series stainless alloys with minimum magnetism* should provide better corrosion resistance for hose clamp housing,band,and screw...while *400 series stainless alloys with more magnetism* and less protection should be limited to fresh water use.Again use the magnet to avoid hose clamp failure when a 400 series screw and housing are mixed with a 300 series band.

•

Expect confusing answers when you ask—***Why bond various metals together on sailboats and powerboats?.*** The best answer for bonding occurred in 1960 when it became evident that 60% of the 40' Newporter engine failures were caused by water jacket cooling system failures ***due to small isolated hose clamp failures.***

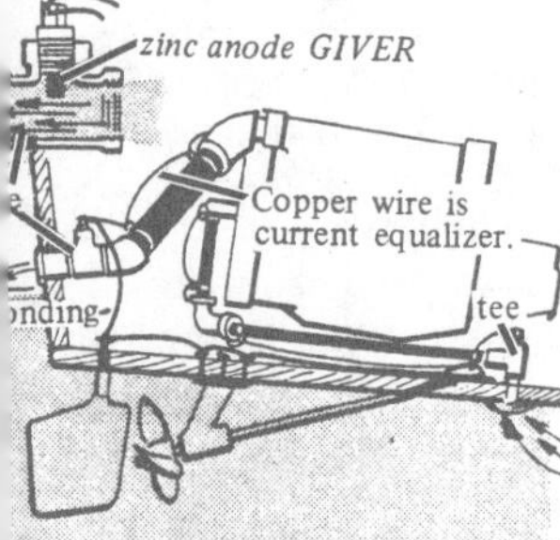
zinc anode GIVER
Copper wire is current equalizer.
tee
nding

Four months later we saw the results of hose clamp bonding on a trouble-prone Newporter.All hose clamps that had been bonded together looked new...while 40% of the water inlet and discharge zinc plugs had been destroyed,see detail.

The compact hotrod powerboat engine at left proved excellent to show the bonding theory.All hose clamps are bonded to the engine block to zincs on the water inlet and overboard discharges of inboard engines.The bonding eliminated the isolated hose clamp failures transferring the damage to our friends the zinc plugs.

eavily corroded zinc anodes

bonding may have variables

Bonding can be a friend...and an enemy.

Consider bonding a method to **combat developing corrosion problems.** For a rebuttal we know a few boats with above average **existing corrosion problems.** Their problems were reduced after much of the metal bonding was disconnected which produced complaints from their insurance companies...the boat owners had excellent electrical and commercial aircraft engineering backgrounds. More research may be indicated to **reduce lightning flashover potentials,** page 65, which may be partially caused by our present bonding theories.

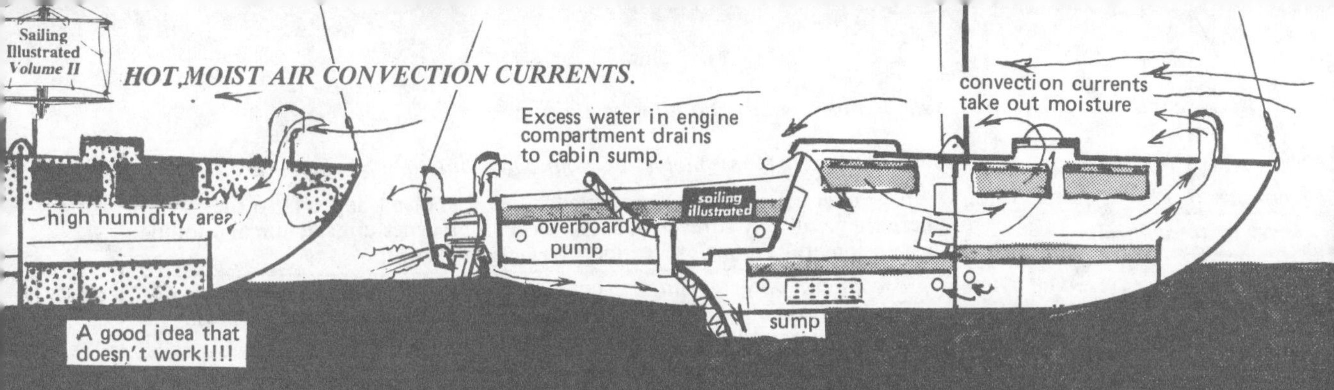
Sailing Illustrated Volume II
HOT,MOIST AIR CONVECTION CURRENTS.
convection currents take out moisture
Excess water in engine compartment drains to cabin sump.
high humidity area
sailing illustrated
overboard pump
sump
A good idea that doesn't work!!!!

human engineering factors continue–
hot air rises
Get rid of the nasty guys!
suction air flow
suction air rising

134

Release moisture...don't bottle it up!

Black mildew will grow on every organic and synthetic surface when the desired heat humidity and oxygen potentials are reached. A new fiberglass hull may look smooth though it has *small microscopic pores* that enlarge with time to provide a surface for mildew to attach to and grow...the major reason for waxing fiberglass hulls and topsides.

Mildew and fungi awaken and grow below in dark enclosed areas where humidity can rapidly build up. If a wooden or fiberglass boat has any mildew potentials below, open all cabinets and doors below, then turn seat cushions up to improve the air flow before leaving. Give your boat a good airing after a storm to remove any mildew potentials.

Our liberal education with mildew began in mid-July 1964 when our fiberglass boat had been in the water only two weeks. Mildew started growing under cushions, in cabinets, on bulkheads, and the overhead. We drilled 22 two inch vents plus a 4" dia. air scoop to start an air flow to reduce our humidity potentials.

The following year headers were introduced installed on sailboat cabin overheads. They proved an excellent idea to stabilize humidity by absorbing excess moisture... then providing a controlled moisture air release as the humidity goes down.

A storm was moving into our area so we pointed the forward air scoop into the prevailing westerlies to improve the air flow thru our boat. After three days of heavy rain followed by a hot summer day, we returned to find a healthy mildew farm below requiring hours of scrubbing to remove and a lot of ventilation to dry out.

A month or so later when leaving Catalina we turned the forward air scoop aft to prevent spray going below in a sloppy seaway. We forgot to turn the vent into the westerlies after returning to our dock as we were soaked and tired. After two days of heavy rain and two hot summer days we expected to find another mildew farm... finding only a few traces of mildew.

K

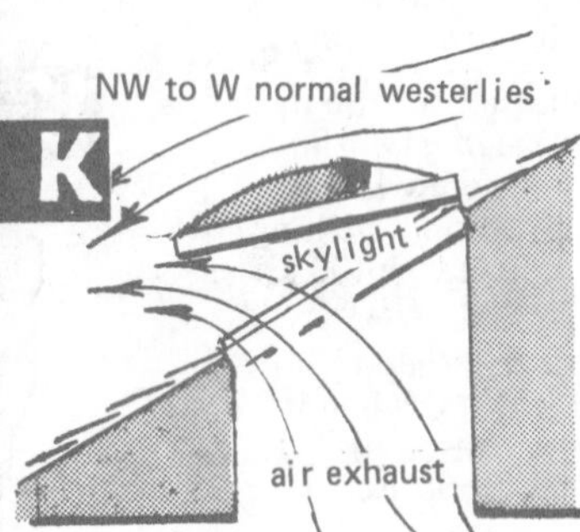
NW to W normal westerlies
skylight
air exhaust

Skylight updraft ceases when S to SSE winds arrive with high humidity and warm temperature after crossing thousands of miles of tropical ocean.

The friendly, helpful convection currents.

The forward air scoop facing away from the prevailing westerlies began a suction flow coming from the aft part of our boat with the moist humid air being pulled up and exhausted out the forward air vents. The idea proved so practical that we decided to use the same idea in our home which was rather warm in the summer. Westerlies can now flow thru our home with the hot moist air convection currents rising and going out the new skylight facing east which dropped the humidity and heat considerably.

The humidity fight continues–when the overpowering 1982-1983 *El Nino,* page 56. gave us the second heaviest rain in local recorded history, all boat owners we contacted had mildew problems. That spring we installed a ***suction vent*** which provided an immediate improvement in the forward cabin exhaust air flow. Mildew problems disappeared that fall and early 1984, yet results were inconclusive with very little rain.

12/20/84. We returned to our boat after three days of heavy rain and strong winds. 145 pumps by hand were required to empty our large sump, which if the water started to come over the floorboards, would require 270 pumps to empty *(IOR sumps, page 116).* We found light moisture below with no mildew of consequence.

A sailboat on a single mooring has excellent air flow potentials while slip-berthed boats often have less than ideal ventilation conditions requiring more care to avoid mildew formation below decks. The wooden boat in its cradle laid up for the winter requires special attention for ventilation to reduce humidity as the normal protective wind patterns are seldom observed.

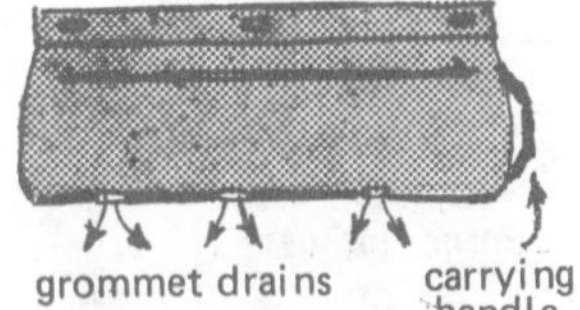
bulkhead bag
grommet drains
carrying handle

grommets, pg. 21

We've had excellent luck with our bulkhead storage bags after grommet drains were added. While they protected organic clothing from mildew, foul weather togs stored wet in the bags for a few days didn't develop any mildew...while mildew growth would have been rapid without the drains. *P.S.*–mildew grows rapidly on the outer surface of the plastic clothing or storage bags.

WOOD=*STABILIZED–dead and healthy*← 15% moisture content 20% →*active and sick–DETEORIATING*

performance of identical sailboats in fiberglass, and wood construction

A 5.5 meter one-design class?????

The battle for superiority of wood vs fiberglass was tested when Columbia Yachts built an excellent 5.5 meter fiberglass sailboat in 1967.Wooden open-design 5.5's *proved lighter with more rigidity* which could outperform the *heavier 5.5 fiberglass hulls which had less rigidity and more flexibility.* Present boatbuilding practice is to use the best features of both materials to make sailboat hulls,decks,and bulkheads lighter,stronger,and more rigid.

Wood becomes expensive as it's quantity and it's quality diminish.

Wood is our traditional boatbuilding material,still the favorite for a one-off boat built by an owner,or a carpenter with apprentices.Wood has a disadvantage in mass-production boatbuilding as many expensive wood scraps are left behind...while all fiberglass raw materials are used up when adequately engineered.

Keep your wood friends healthy and happy.

Some wooden boats 50 or more years old still operate with minimum wood problems. The successful pattern starts with wood choice having good resistance to rot,then to have it well seasoned.Ventilate as much as possible so it will be difficult for rot to begin,especially in problem areas such as chain lockers,icebox drains,lockers under bunks and sink,and the engine bed.Stay far as possible from wood disease contaminants such as run-down docks with rotting timbers,half-sunk derelicts,garden compost,etc.

Fungi are plant growths requiring fresh water to survive and grow.

Wood is an organic product of nature whose death returns the chemicals to nature to feed the next generation of forest vegitation.*Fungi are the agents of mother nature on her routine business,the scavengers of the plant world,* that return the dead organic chemicals back to the soil.Your job is to understand this procedure of nature and use all practical methods to eliminate fungi growth potentials.Then you can enjoy the wood on your boat that though dead...seems to mellow and improve with age.

dry rot vs wet rot?

wood content-
60% cellulose
28% lignum
12% organic compounds

The term ***dry rot*** probably originated with early sailors when they were able to crush wood in their hands ***after the damage was terminal*** and the moisture was no longer present.The major concern if you own a wooden boat *is to develop a continual awareness for the sweet smell of fungi converting wood cellulose into sugar...* as 60% of wood content is cellulose.Approximately 28% is *lignum* which cements the wood tubes together.The remaining 12% provide the *rot resistance and water absorption differences* among the various kinds of wood.

Take time to know the quiet enemy so he can't surprise you.

All boat owners should take periodic walks thru boatyards to study sailboats and powerboats with wood problems being repaired...how were the problems found,the cause,and the answer.This exposure should help so when rot problems appear on your boat,you are able to handle them easily and efficiently *in the beginning stages.* A favorite sailing writer,H.A.Calahan,was offered a five year old 50' schooner for free. The fungi problem had been ignored until the hull was *in the terminal stage of the disease thru all timbers,planks,and frames.* The hull had to be broken up a few days later,then the parts burned to avoid infecting nearby wooden boats.

The free 50' schooner...

natures stabilizers— density,natural oils, organic chemicals

Trees develop varying degrees of natural resistance to rot for survival instincts in their natural surroundings.Burma teak developed ***maximum*** resistance to survive in the harsh forests and jungles...with civilization the enemy that may exhaust the teak forests by 1995.The most resistant wood in our country is redwood yet it is too rigid for boatbuilding,also it has minimum sudden impact or shock resistance.

traditional drying and curing methods to stabilize wood

After a tree is cut down and hauled to the mill,it is cut into timbers and planks.This ***green wood has a sap and moisture content above 18%*** which has to be reduced below 15% to minimize warping and rot potentials.The traditional storage method was in outside sheds for 3 or more years to permit natural drying and curing...while thick timbers required additional curing time.

rapid kiln drying

Much wood used today is kiln dried in a small building with controlled temperature, humidity,and ventilation,to reduce excess moisture and sap content with a one week period of kiln drying,comparable to a year of natural outside curing.

Cold water protection... vs tropical heat,rain,and humidity,rapidly shorten the life of wood,metal, and other products.

Oregon grown ***douglas fir*** with moderate rot resistance proved it could last for long periods on commercial fishing trawlers in cold Scandinavian waters close to freezing, also protecting inexpensive metals.When similar vessels move to our area with higher temperatures and humidity,ventilation has to be improved to protect the boat.When the same boat is moved into hot tropical areas with rain and high humidity the survival problems of the same fir and inexpensive metals may increase three fold.

those nasty critters *unwelcome termites*

If sawdust trails indicate ***termites*** are enjoying a gourmet feast on your wooden boom,mast,or boat...consider a periodic fumigation every four years,the same pattern that is also recommended for home fumigation to eliminate termites.

BAD GUYS DON'T ALWAYS WEAR BLACK HATS.

Mildew—black surface spots inside boats; also decaying sawdust, leaves, on wood in storage..is it surface discoloration?

Dry rot—powdery and dry, white to light tan.

Wet rot—light brown to dark brown, moist and crumbling.

Surface rot—decay on outer wood layers becoming soft in tropics under very wet conditions.

Pocket rot—local pocket decay surrounded by apparently healthy wood.

Metal poisoning—black wood stains around keel bolts, chain plates, and hull fastenings that crush surrounding wood—*not* wood rot.

mycelium
Sailing
Illustrated
Volume II
hypha
"Now there is
a tasty morsel".

Fungi are microscopic plant life with a large and varied menu, plus an enormous appetite. How many contributions can your boat offer to this hungry horde?

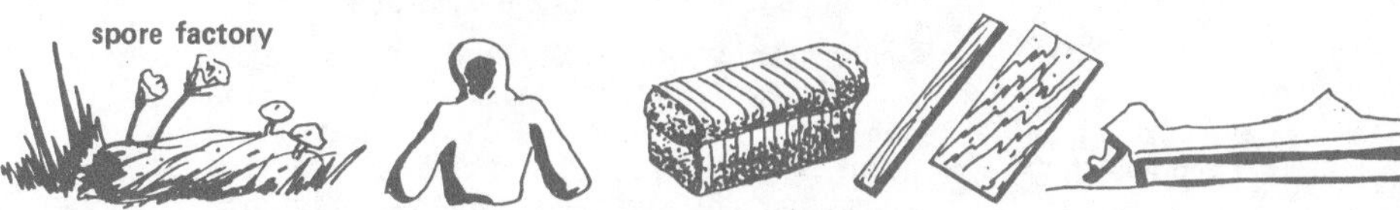
spore factory

There are many kinds of fungi with appetities for one or more of the products above. All species have the same basic needs...***1.food,2.oxygen,3.fresh water,and 4.favorable temperature*** to survive,grow,and reproduce. Remove any of these items and the fungi's growth will become dormant and go into hibernation...or be killed.

Tap every inch of a wooden boat with a hammer to check for rot. While healthy wood sounds may vary from a sharp to a softer deeper ***ping***, use chalk to mark every area that has a ***mushy sound.*** During an inspection use protective goggles and gloves, also protect your mouth and lungs as fungi spores may produce allergies.

Healthy wood fibers separated by a dull ice pick while probing will soon go back together.

Is splinter long and flexible or short and brittle?

1 End grain infection begins.

Soft, punky splinters—probe for soft spots.

136

surface discoloration?

2

Wood barely able to hold shape and support its weight.

K

3

Rot spreads along wood grain.

highly contagious to nearby wood

4

Earth to earth...dust to dust...

After wood is seasoned or cured with it's moisture down to 15% of its weight, the natural resistance depends on protective natural oils and resins, how water-tight the wood is, plus fungacidal protection chemicals added to retard decay. Hopefully nature has well plugged the pores of the wood, but—

The spores that seed a culture are everywhere in the air remaining inactive until the wood moisture content reaches 20% of its weight. A baby spore lands on damp, warm wood to enter the end grain where it starts an invisible invasion making itself at home. The ***mycelium*** sends out tiny ***hypa threads*** producing *that sweet smell* while eating the cellulose, their voracious appetite changing it to sugar. The splinter may be too flexible (1) if the wood isn't fully seasoned.

The ***hypa threads*** are becoming so numerous (2) that the ***mycelium plant*** causing the action and damage has become a visible mass. ***Most damage begins at the ends of planks...then follows a damp wet path thru the wood grain.*** The mycelium produc more hungry growing spores as the hypa threads push thru the wood to continually branch out. The fungi is now hard at work eating the cellulose and possibly other organic chemicals. The timber is an empty shape or shell (3) barely able to support its own weight at rest without movement.

After the cellulose has been eaten away, comprising 2/3 of the wood content, it will crumble (4) into small chunks with the least pressure or movement, the stage at whic early sailors discovered *dry rot.* Fungi scavengers have completed natures routine by returning the organic chemicals to what it thought was food for the next generation of forest vegetation...that can help your local garden.

Pocket rot can occur inside of what seems to be healthy wood. If the PING doesn't sound right...use a hand drill with an 1/8" bitt. When the normal wood resistant eases, this indicates you have reached the damaged area. Keep drilling until the normal wood resistance returns...indicating the depth of the rot area. Slowly remove the bitt to check sawdust, smell, color, and moisture. The next step is to find how large the pocket is, then treat the part...or have it replaced.

Is paint beneficial..or a hazard?

Did paint
cause this
damage?
Was wood
dry and well
seasoned
before
painting?
permeable paint
enamel paint

Light color ***permeable paints*** have small holes to aid breathing action, plus ventilation and drainage that maintain better temperature control, low moisture content, and better immunity to the ever-present contagious spores in the air.

Enamel produces a hard, glossy, waterproof coating reducing wood breathing to inside the boat. ***A thick outer paint layer*** increases the problem...especially if a ***dark, heat-absorption enamel*** was used. The heat expansion squeezes caulking out from between the planks, increasing humidity/moisture content inside the planks. If the wood was painted when damp, or before it was seasoned sealing moisture and oxygen inside the planks...the fungi will awaken after a long, cold, winter's hibernation with a ravenous appetite for a spring cellulose feast.

Sailing
Illustrated
Volume II
plastic top

temp 80° humidity 100%

CULTIVATING YOUR OWN FUNGI FARM...

Moisture and heat variables.

Wood moisture content—is the major factor. Fungi begins to awaken above 18% water content by weight with maximum growth potentials occurring between 20% and 35%. Above that fungi growth decreases, then becomes dormant at 75% due to insufficient oxygen. When wood is submerged or waterlogged with moisture content up to 150% of its weight, the lack of oxygen kills the fungi while marine borers move in for a gourmet underwater feast.

Heat sensitivity—growth ceases below 40° F as the fungi become dormant. Maximum fungi growth potentials are between temperatures of 70° to 90°...while decreasing above 100°. If sufficient temperature time above 150° is involved but below the ignition point, it can kill the fungi . though the wood can be reinfected later.

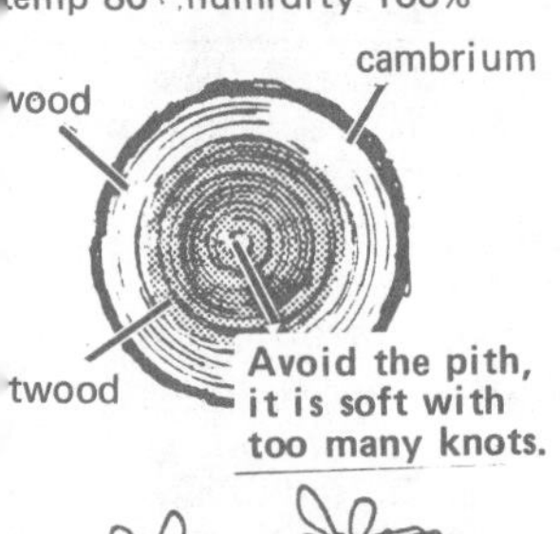
cambrium
wood
twood
Avoid the pith, it is soft with too many knots.

Wood must breathe continuously to keep the moisture content below 18% to 20% that requires continuous ventilation. If enamel is used on the hull outside, wood on the inside should remain bare, or permeable paint used to release the heat and moisture especially if darker colors are used. After fungacide protection has been added to wood in the bilges it is often left unpainted to aid its continuous breathing.

Choose ***heartwood*** for boatbuilding with it's low moisture and sap content. The only part of a tree alive and growing is the thin *cambrium layer* of cells beneath the bark, about 1% of a tree's bulk. This outer layer begins at the root tips, comes up the trunk, then goes out the branches to the leaves and buds. This layer has a high moisture and sap content called ***sapwood, a major cause of rot,*** which must be avoided.

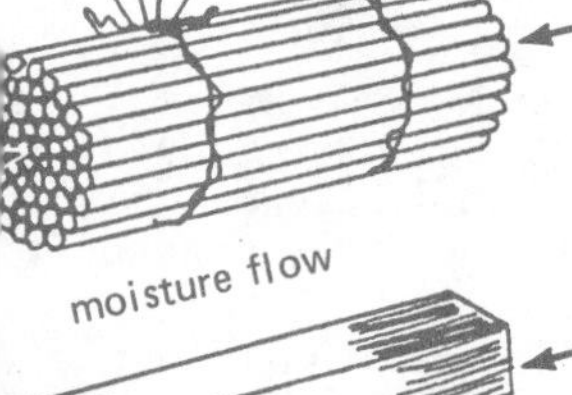

Consider wood a tightly-bound bundle of drinking straws. Condensation and fresh water can enter these pores running with the grain developed by nature...however minimum moisture absorption goes thru the sides of a plank against the grain.

moisture flow

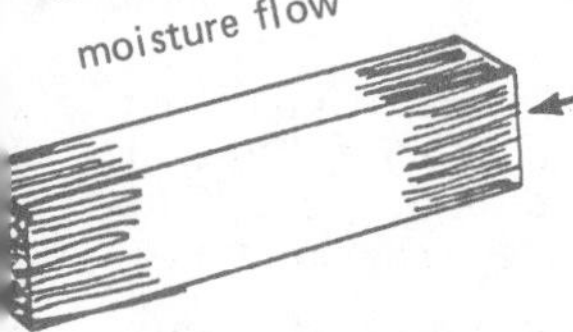

Short timbers or joints with end-cut angles have the greatest rot potentials. These are the areas in wooden boats that require continuous checking, especially with fresh water sailing due to the large areas of end grain exposed to humidity and rain.

Pickling—wooden fishing boats use ***rock salt in the bilges*** and areas above the water prone to rot that are difficult to check. Since melting ice to protect the fish is continuously present, fresh water drains into the bilge, changing to salt water which retards fungi growth in the wood...with mixed blessings. This increased the metal corrosion rate since the least corrosion resistant metals for ocean use are often found on wooden fishing vessels. Older wooden cargo vessels used tons of ***salt packing*** for critical areas such as between inner and outer planking.

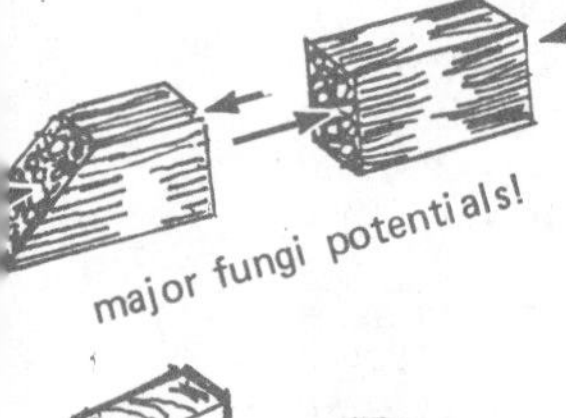
major fungi potentials!

Marine plywood has it's inner voids filled to provide maximum fungi resistance for exterior use which makes it quite expensive. Quality exterior grade plywood will have many boatbuilding uses as it is also temporarily sterilized by heat lamination bonding. Since it has voids the cost is considerably less.

Cold-molded, laminated veneer strips glued together are considerably lighter than planked wooden hulls. Laminated hulls have weight and structural strength equal to fiberglass and aluminum hulls. Hidden wood defects are prevented as veneers are not thick enough to hide a wood fault...and underwater borers don't like the epoxy glue.

K

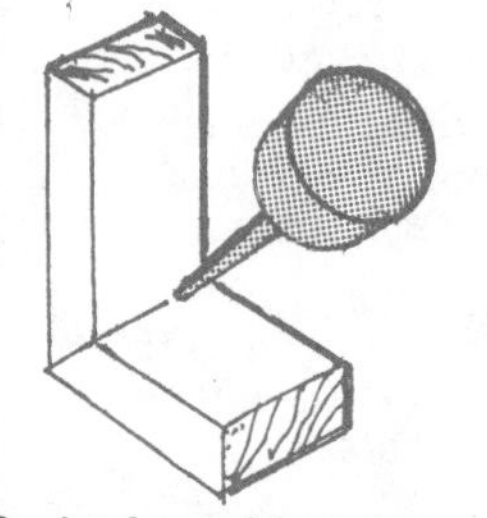

Epoxy glues create a water-vapor absorption barrier by penetrating 1/16" into the veneer surfaces isolating the inner plies. This stabilizes the wood's dimensional and mechanical characteristics, eliminating moisture absorption and rot potentials called the *Wood Epoxy Saturation Technique...or WEST.* The method is also excellent to build hot tubs, furniture, etc. Contact the Gougeon Brothers, Bay City, MI 48706.

Squirt fungacide twice yearly into all end joints.

We were washing a teak deck on a 40' sailboat with ocean water. Little did we realize that the owner of a new 34' production powerboat was watching to follow our procedure without protecting his metals (1958). His rapidly corroding topside metals had to be rechromed two years later.

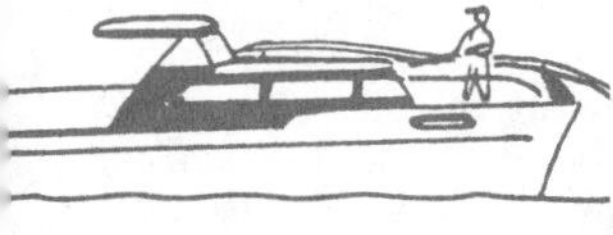

When we pulled into our slip we saw him washing his wooden boat with fresh water to protect his metals...his *sweet smelling* powerboat now facing a new problem. We wanted to warn him, yet his authoritative barking commands to his wife and three children changed our mind...also the wind was blowing his spores away from us. How would you have responded in this situation?

Protecting metals or irrigating fungi?????

Do you desire a year or two sailing vacation?

Does a wooden sailboat meet your requirements?

The long line of wooden cruising sailboats in Papeete, pg. 121, provides better recommendations for this type of craft than endless advertising. The wooden sailboat may be ideal for a year or two cruise after being subjected to a thorough survey by a wooden boat expert. Your initial investment is often returned when the boat is sold after the cruise.

If a dismasting occurs in the backwaters of nowhere a craftsman may often be found to chop down a tree to build your new mast, oops—*AVOID Iceland.* An aluminum mast by air freight may be prohibitively expensive. Also how long would it take to reach your sailboat when the last 87 miles is by dugout canoe thru hippos and crocodiles?

metal cancer...single wire economy...positive vs negative electrical ground

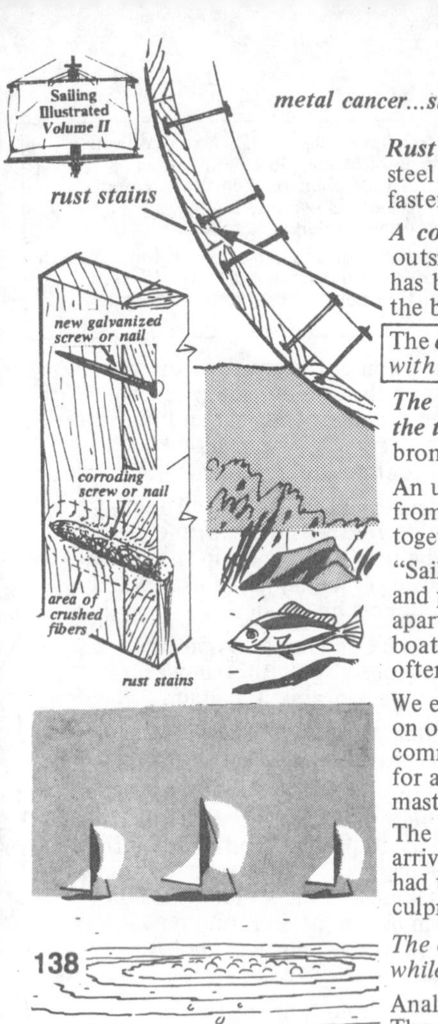
rust stains
new galvanized screw or nail
corroding screw or nail
area of crushed fibers
rust stains

Rust streaks down the sides of older wooden boats ***indicate metal cancer*** from steel products without zinc galvanizing protection such as screws,nuts,bolts,and fastenings...or the zinc has been used up thru the years.

A continuous film paint without breathing holes,often white enamel,is used on the outside of the hull while the inside wood may be bare or have ***permeable paint*** that has breathing holes.Condensation moisture will eventually enter the planks inside the boat to develop an electrolyte pocket *held by gravity* around the bolt head.

The ***diameter increases*** of a nongalvanized screw,bolt,and nut,*as the cancer progresses with age...while the growing pressures crush the surrounding wood fibers.*

The replacement bolt,screw,or nail must have a considerably larger diameter than the tired part being replaced. The first corrosion resistant metal to consider is in the bronze family,the second choice is galvanized steel with heavy zinc protection.

An unexpected rebuttal to this theory developed when chartering a 40' sailboat from a movie executive for an Ensenada Race.While we were checking the boat together for familiarity a discussion started about the many faces of corrosion.

"Sailing has been my hobby for many years.It is also my business as I buy sailboats and powerboats worldwide which are shipped to our studio where they are cut apart topside and below decks for our movie sets.We were surprised to find older boats that we cut apart which used galvanized bolts,screws,and fastenings,were often in better condition,while those with bronze parts had more corrosion".

We enjoy random discussions with acquaintances especially when we are working on our boat.Our double wiring for engine and masthead lights produced interesting comments such as,"*A single wire system* with a ground frame return is excellent for an auto.It should be even more practical for your sailboat if you use the aluminum mast as a return ground",the time was 1964.

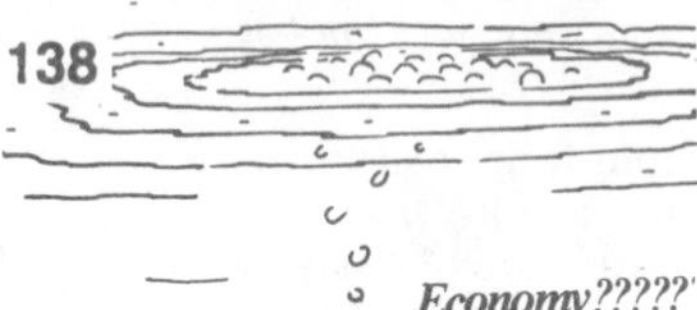

The owner of a new large diamond plater that had been in the water five months arrived to go sailing to find only the tips of the mast visible at it's mooring.The hull had to be sealed,pumped with air,raised,and towed to a shipyard for inspection.The culprit proved to be an overboard head valve that crumbled at the mechanics touch.

The electrician had installed a single wire system for the engine and masthead lights while using the mast as the electrical return to the battery ground.

Analysis indicated stray electrical currents came down the stays to the chainplates. Then by devious ways they went thru chain in the chain locker to the bilge,and finally to the overboard head valve where they exited to the watery ground.The single wire economy seems questionable...when compared to shipyard repairs.

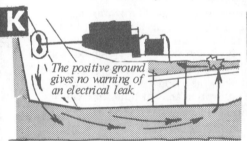

Economy?????

K

A wooden sailboat with ***a negative ground electrical system*** has a defective wire splice that has dropped into the bilge water.When the master switch and that circuit are turned on...a fuse should blow or a circuit breaker trip to alert the owner of a major problem.

The positive ground gives no warning of an electrical leak.

We next analyze an identical wooden boat that has *a positive ground electrical system* with an identical bad wire splice in its watery bilge.

The current now leaks from the battery to the engine,out the prop shaft,thru the water and up the keel bolts.The current continues into the bilge,thru the wire splice returning to the battery *without a warning of rapidly corroding keel bolts... except for it's battery not holding a charge.*

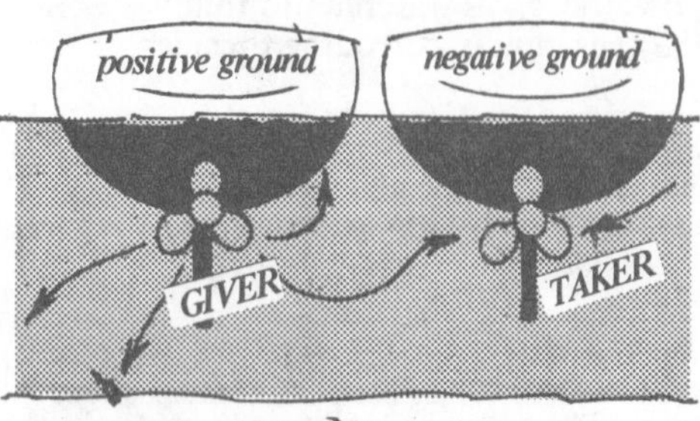
positive ground
negative ground
GIVER
TAKER

We've known several wooden sailboats with positive battery grounds that had sailed in cold European waters for many years without obvious electrolysis problems.Rapid electrolytic metal destruction developed shortly after they moved to our warm local waters.

If these sailboats intend to stay in warm local waters a major overhaul is required of the engine,electronic,and electrical wiring to fully change them to the protective negative electrical ground systems.Some owners, often with engineering backgrounds, took a simplistic look at the situation compounded the problem by only reversing the battery leads.Their excuses when they finally understood the idea provided fond memories such as...*"My wife must have done it while I was in London"*

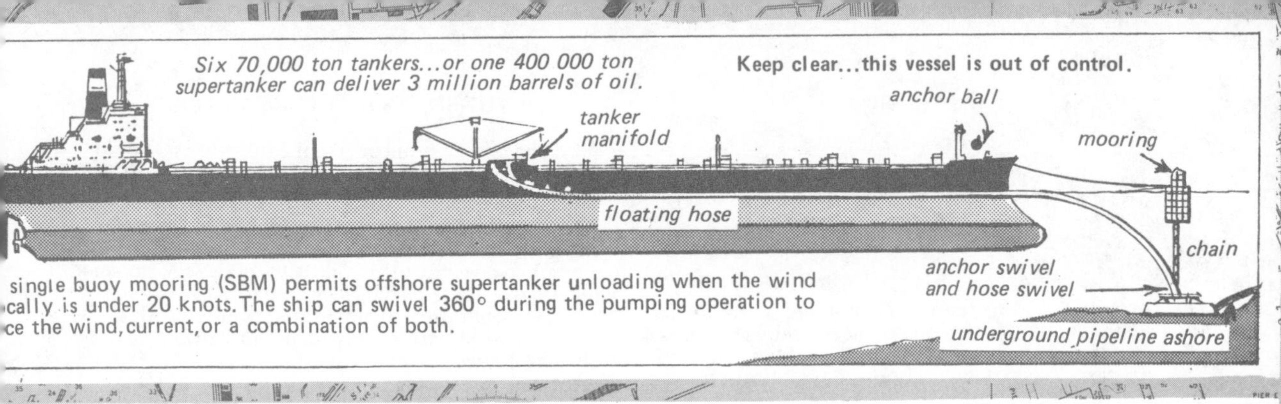
Six 70,000 ton tankers...or one 400 000 ton supertanker can deliver 3 million barrels of oil.
Keep clear...this vessel is out of control.
anchor ball
tanker manifold
mooring
floating hose
chain
anchor swivel and hose swivel
underground pipeline ashore

single buoy mooring (SBM) permits offshore supertanker unloading when the wind cally is under 20 knots. The ship can swivel 360° during the pumping operation to ce the wind, current, or a combination of both.

The harbor tug is the unglamorous workhorse of the fleet. Study the numerous lights and shapes. While they indicate the wide variety of tugboat services *they all carry the same* **survival warning to KEEP CLEAR** *due to no maneuverability...or to highly limited maneuverability.*

The tugboat is returning from a tow...or it is on its way to pick up a tow.

It pushes a bow wave and pulls a stern wave with a deep trough between. The tug is operating at its top displacement hull speed with power to spare.

If you have the good fortune to be invited aboard a tug ask to see the engine room. Those we've seen are spotless with metals polished to a super glow.

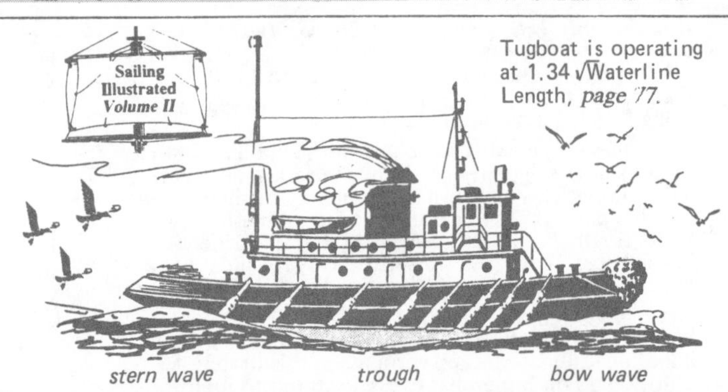
Sailing Illustrated Volume II
Tugboat is operating at 1.34 √Waterline Length, page 77.
stern wave
trough
bow wave

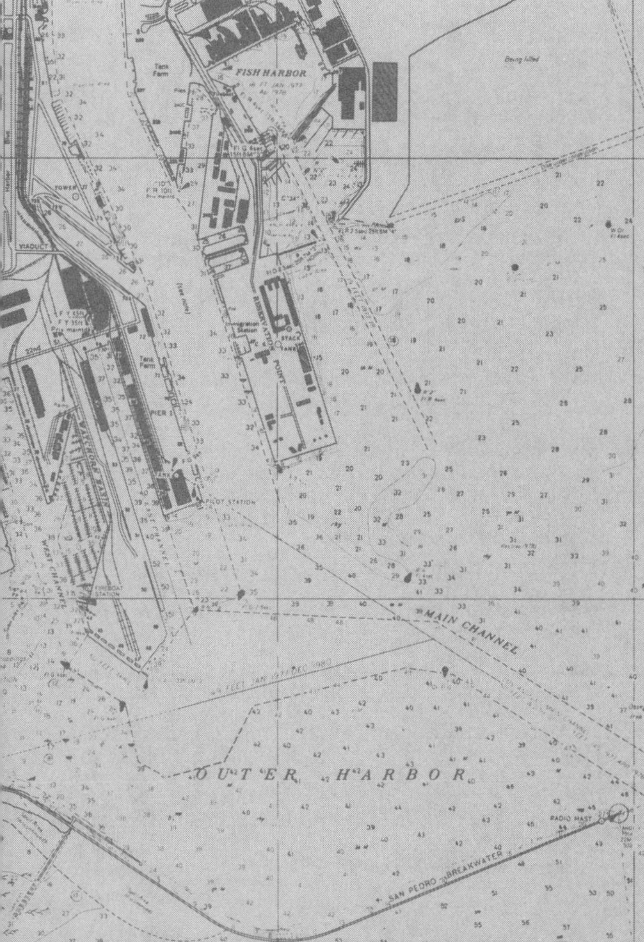
FISH HARBOR
OUTER HARBOR
MAIN CHANNEL
SAN PEDRO BREAKWATER

"What the H... class is he racing in?"

An official harbor greeter.

chart 18751–29th Edition 4/30/83

The ***Ports of Los Angeles(San Pedro), and Long Beach*** are a major marine crossroad of the world with ships of all kinds and ages representing all maritime nations. They will carry flags of origin, house flags, and funnel markings for identification.

It is ***the only U.S. port, one of 20 worldwide,*** that is able to handle the extreme draft of smaller supertankers. While this port has handled vessels up to 1150' long the draft is more important with 51' in L.A., and 65' in Long Beach, a maximum high tide draft.

It is a harbor we enjoy watching in the cooler winter months as the big ones go about their local and worldwide chores. This harbor handles merchant ships, small to large tankers, passenger liners, a large tuna fleet, work boats, floating drill rigs...as well as aircraft carriers, battleships, submarines, cruisers, destroyers, and a wide variety of other navy craft heading towards...or leaving the Long Beach Naval Shipyard.

We've had a variety of unusual experiences since 1957 handling sailboats and powerboats in this harbor. A sailor on a Polish merchant vessel wanted to jump overboard if we would pick him up as he couldn't swim, but we preferred to not be on the late TV news.

A fully loaded small super tanker was entering its dock as we passed by to look at other ships being repaired in a huge shipyard. When we passed the large tanker on our return 20 minutes later, it's bow line was being thrown to the waiting crew on the dock as it had finally run out of momentum to come to a stop.

I was enjoying the Midwinter Races on a committee boat when the races stopped for a half hour. The 700' container ship *Island Sky* riding high in ballast drifted thru our starting line to come to a halt and anchor, the stern 200' upwind of us. The *Angel's Pilot* came alongside to cool committee tempers, see photos. ***page 139.***

I had enjoyed teaching these harbor pilots sailing in 1971 when they wanted to learn to communicate with, and anticipate the action of sailboats. If the pilots had recognized me...my only protection would have been a long, cold swim, water temp. 56°, back to shore.

The ***harbor pilot flag*** is flown from the moment a harbor pilot comes aboard...until he leaves. While the pilot is in charge of handling vessels in his local waters, the captain can still take over anytime he desires.

Both ports have an administrative Chief Pilot* and 16 pilots of equal rank at time of writing who climb aboard commercial vessels at sea, conducting them to their anchorage or dock, then later back to sea where the pilots are picked up by their own pilot boats.

Before anyone can apply for a job as harbor pilot, if an opening exists, he has to have 20 year's experience with a captain's background in deep-sea tugs, cargo, or passenger vessels. A major requirement is a strong back to be able to climb a ladder up the steep side of a ship in ballast (no cargo) as it rolls in wave action.

**Our thanks to Chief Pilot, Captain Jackson Pearson, Port of Los Angeles, for his help with this chapter.*

TUGBOATS to SUPERTANKERS

Pilots have a 12 hour on, and 12 hour off schedule. They take a vessel when their number comes up without having a choice of vessels.

When a radical new type of vessel enters the harbor the pilot involved afterwards calls a meeting to pass along his ideas for other pilots to analyze. Many such meetings were required from 1967 to 1971 when the new generation of supertankers entered this harbor...often with widely different handling characteristics.

When a vessel with a pilot aboard leaves and crosses the ***demarkation line*** which makes the change from Inland to International Rules, the pilot is picked up. The vessel then begins operating in an international world with all maritime countries supposedly cooperating so these vessels may go about their global business without piracy, etc.

Boiler failure is serious. The best insurance is to have extra boilers so if one or two fail the third will take over. Older tankers had two to three boilers and merchantmen sometimes more. The *Queen Mary* had twenty-four boilers for her main engines with three more for her domestic uses.

VLCC**and ULCC*** supertankers are ***one-boiler*** ships to make their price more attractive. When the boiler fails the prop stops, the computers cease to work, and the lights go out. The monster then begins to drift to the whims of the winds and currents.

A VLCC over 214,000 deadweight tons is larger than the *Queen Mary*. ***Over 80% of the bulk*** of these huge floating oil cans, fully loaded to the Plimsol Line ***is underwater...*** which is similar to an iceberg.

Supertankers must operate at their most efficient displacement speed of 14 to 15 knots, $0.6\sqrt{WL}$, ***pg. 69,***, to conserve fuel. They try to follow ***traditional sailing routes, pg. 145,***, when practical whether in ballast or fully loaded to make the most use of ocean winds and currents and also to help conserve fuel.

A supertanker voyage from the U.S. or Europe to the Persian Gulf may average 2 ½ months. It may be loaded at deepwater offshore platforms in 12 to 18 hours...then without a stopover the return voyage begins.

The only stop on the return trip is 12 miles or so off Cape Town, South Africa where supplies are taken aboard from a launch or lowered to the deck by a helicopter.

Unloading may be in the remote port area of an offshore loading platform, or into smaller tankers out at sea since the ULCC's seldom go into port except to be drydocked. They are too large to go thru the Suez or Panama Canals.

These large tankers are too expensive to be idle so they are often underway up to 340 days a year. Crews may work 5 to 6 months which is followed by a 6 to 8 week shoreside vacation.

During a 7/83 sailing vacation we had to make major course changes four times to avoid the big ones underway. The worst was at 0300 in low visibility with an overtaking VLCC in ballast, a huge nondescript barge shape with an aft range light mounted near the bow. It is still a nightmare. *We recommend you study this chapter thoroughly if you sail near large vessels. Review it yearly due to the complexities and variables.*

**VLCC—Very Large Crude Carrier over 200,000 tons
***ULCC—Ultra Large Crude Carrier over 400,000 tons

stern light
aft range light
green starboard light
forward range light

"What are the credentials of the skipper operating that boat which is on a collision course with us?"

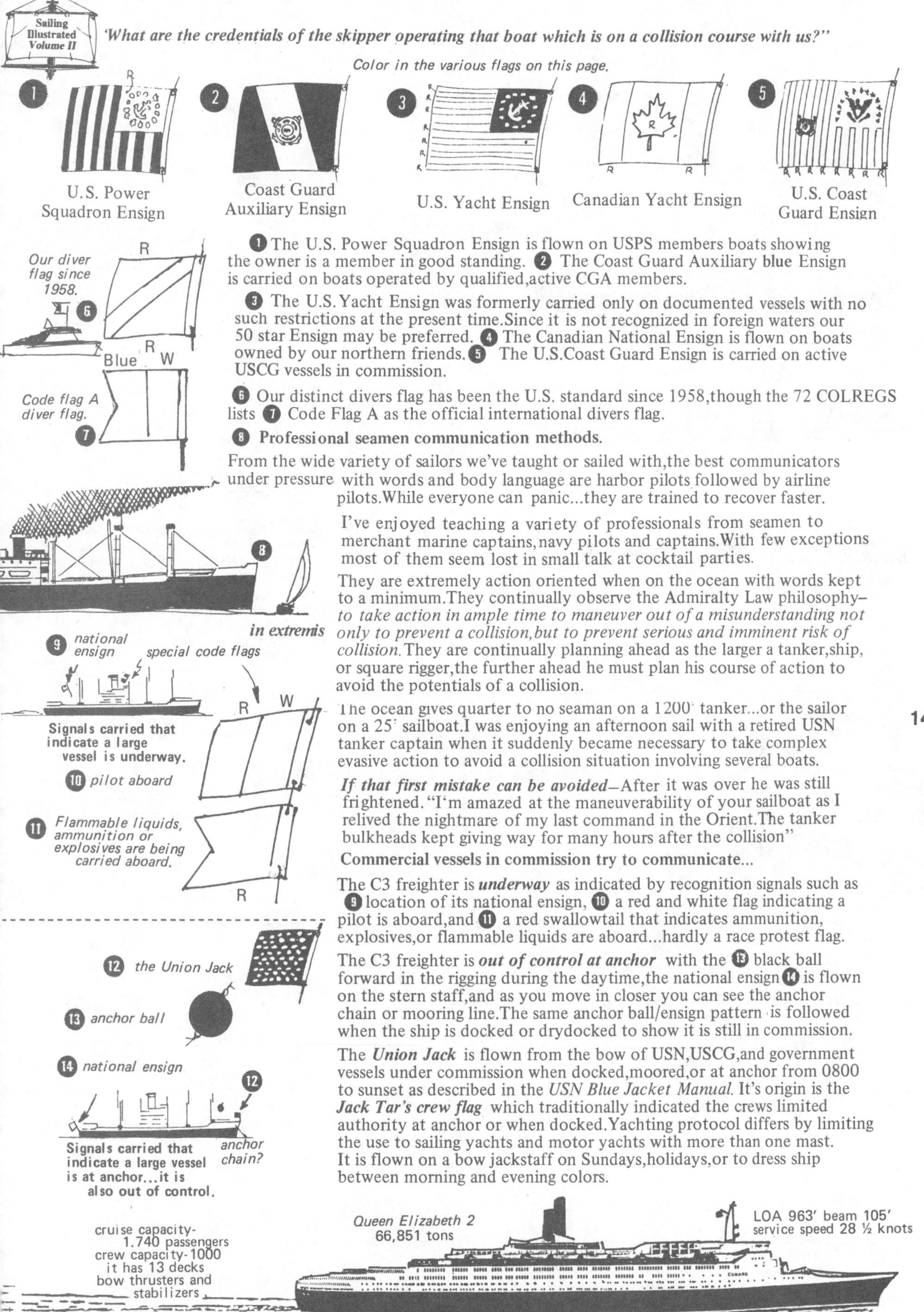
Color in the various flags on this page.
1
U.S. Power Squadron Ensign
2
Coast Guard Auxiliary Ensign
3
U.S. Yacht Ensign
4
Canadian Yacht Ensign
5
U.S. Coast Guard Ensign
Our diver flag since 1958.
6
R
Blue
W
Code flag A diver flag.
7
8
in extremis
9 national ensign
special code flags
Signals carried that indicate a large vessel is underway.
10 pilot aboard
11 Flammable liquids, ammunition or explosives are being carried aboard.
12 the Union Jack
13 anchor ball
14 national ensign
12
Signals carried that indicate a large vessel is at anchor...it is also out of control.
anchor chain?
cruise capacity- 1.740 passengers
crew capacity-1000
it has 13 decks
bow thrusters and stabilizers
Queen Elizabeth 2
66,851 tons
LOA 963′ beam 105′
service speed 28 ½ knots

❶ The U.S. Power Squadron Ensign is flown on USPS members boats showing the owner is a member in good standing. ❷ The Coast Guard Auxiliary **blue** Ensign is carried on boats operated by qualified,active CGA members.

❸ The U.S.Yacht Ensign was formerly carried only on documented vessels with no such restrictions at the present time.Since it is not recognized in foreign waters our 50 star Ensign may be preferred. ❹ The Canadian National Ensign is flown on boats owned by our northern friends. ❺ The U.S.Coast Guard Ensign is carried on active USCG vessels in commission.

❻ Our distinct divers flag has been the U.S. standard since 1958,though the 72 COLREGS lists ❼ Code Flag A as the official international divers flag.

❽ **Professional seamen communication methods.**

From the wide variety of sailors we've taught or sailed with,the best communicators under pressure with words and body language are harbor pilots followed by airline pilots.While everyone can panic...they are trained to recover faster.

I've enjoyed teaching a variety of professionals from seamen to merchant marine captains,navy pilots and captains.With few exceptions most of them seem lost in small talk at cocktail parties.

They are extremely action oriented when on the ocean with words kept to a minimum.They continually observe the Admiralty Law philosophy– *to take action in ample time to maneuver out of a misunderstanding not only to prevent a collision,but to prevent serious and imminent risk of collision.* They are continually planning ahead as the larger a tanker,ship, or square rigger,the further ahead he must plan his course of action to avoid the potentials of a collision.

The ocean gives quarter to no seaman on a 1200′ tanker...or the sailor on a 25′ sailboat.I was enjoying an afternoon sail with a retired USN tanker captain when it suddenly became necessary to take complex evasive action to avoid a collision situation involving several boats.

If that first mistake can be avoided–After it was over he was still frightened."I'm amazed at the maneuverability of your sailboat as I relived the nightmare of my last command in the Orient.The tanker bulkheads kept giving way for many hours after the collision"

Commercial vessels in commission try to communicate...

The C3 freighter is ***underway*** as indicated by recognition signals such as ❾ location of its national ensign, ❿ a red and white flag indicating a pilot is aboard,and ⓫ a red swallowtail that indicates ammunition, explosives,or flammable liquids are aboard...hardly a race protest flag.

The C3 freighter is ***out of control at anchor*** with the ⓭ black ball forward in the rigging during the daytime,the national ensign ⓮ is flown on the stern staff,and as you move in closer you can see the anchor chain or mooring line.The same anchor ball/ensign pattern is followed when the ship is docked or drydocked to show it is still in commission.

The ***Union Jack*** is flown from the bow of USN,USCG,and government vessels under commission when docked,moored,or at anchor from 0800 to sunset as described in the *USN Blue Jacket Manual.* It's origin is the ***Jack Tar's crew flag*** which traditionally indicated the crews limited authority at anchor or when docked.Yachting protocol differs by limiting the use to sailing yachts and motor yachts with more than one mast. It is flown on a bow jackstaff on Sundays,holidays,or to dress ship between morning and evening colors.

"Don't worry Henry. It is only a supertanker... and we are on starboard tack".

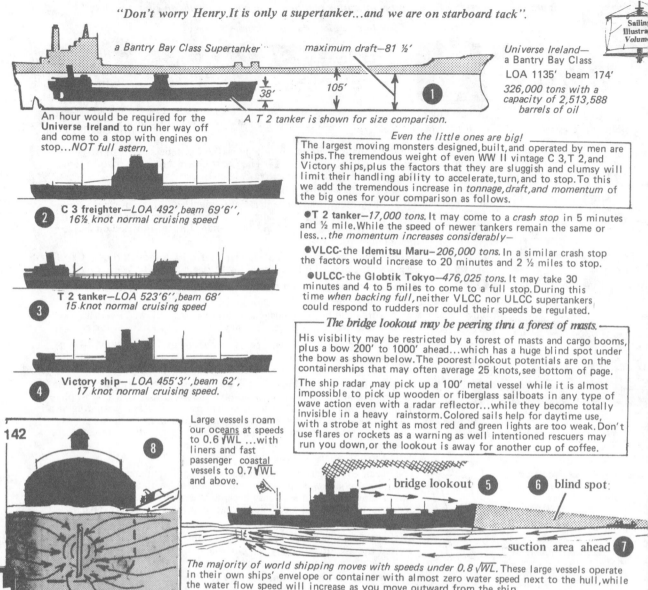

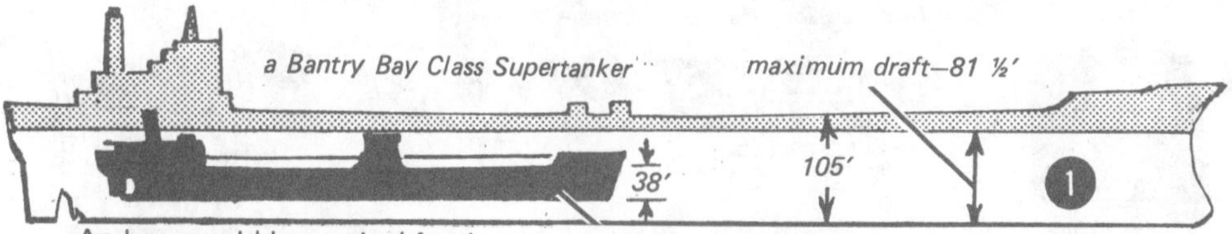

a Bantry Bay Class Supertanker

maximum draft—81 ½'

38'

105'

1

Universe Ireland—
a Bantry Bay Class
LOA 1135' beam 174'
326,000 tons with a capacity of 2,513,588 barrels of oil

An hour would be required for the **Universe Ireland** to run her way off and come to a stop with engines on stop... *NOT full astern.*

A T 2 tanker is shown for size comparison.

Even the little ones are big!

The largest moving monsters designed, built, and operated by men are ships. The tremendous weight of even WW II vintage C 3, T 2, and Victory ships, plus the factors that they are sluggish and clumsy will limit their handling ability to accelerate, turn, and to stop. To this we add the tremendous increase in *tonnage, draft, and momentum* of the big ones for your comparison as follows.

2 **C 3 freighter**—*LOA 492', beam 69'6'', 16½ knot normal cruising speed*

3 **T 2 tanker**—*LOA 523'6'', beam 68' 15 knot normal cruising speed*

4 **Victory ship**— *LOA 455'3'', beam 62', 17 knot normal cruising speed.*

- **T 2 tanker**—*17,000 tons.* It may come to a *crash stop* in 5 minutes and ½ mile. While the speed of newer tankers remain the same or less... *the momentum increases considerably—*
- **VLCC**-the **Idemitsu Maru**—*206,000 tons.* In a similar crash stop the factors would increase to 20 minutes and 2 ½ miles to stop.
- **ULCC**-the **Globtik Tokyo**—*476,025 tons.* It may take 30 minutes and 4 to 5 miles to come to a full stop. During this time *when backing full,* neither VLCC nor ULCC supertankers could respond to rudders nor could their speeds be regulated.

The bridge lookout may be peering thru a forest of masts.

His visibility may be restricted by a forest of masts and cargo booms, plus a bow 200' to 1000' ahead... which has a huge blind spot under the bow as shown below. The poorest lookout potentials are on the containerships that may often average 25 knots, see bottom of page.

The ship radar, may pick up a 100' metal vessel while it is almost impossible to pick up wooden or fiberglass sailboats in any type of wave action even with a radar reflector... while they become totally invisible in a heavy rainstorm. Colored sails help for daytime use, with a strobe at night as most red and green lights are too weak. Don't use flares or rockets as a warning as well intentioned rescuers may run you down, or the lookout is away for another cup of coffee.

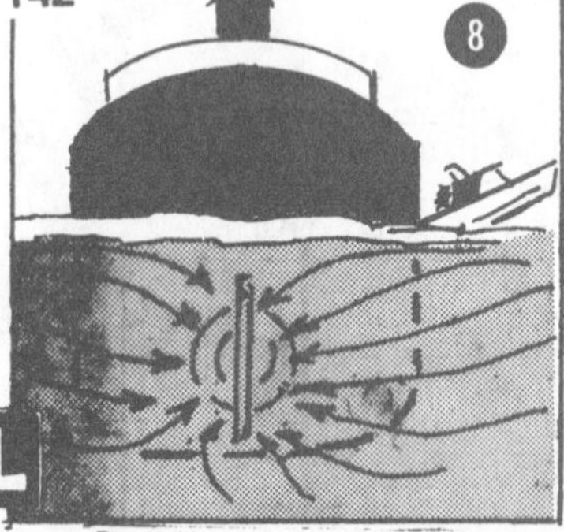

142

8

Large vessels roam our oceans at speeds to 0.6 $\sqrt{WL}$ ...with liners and fast passenger coastal vessels to 0.7 $\sqrt{WL}$ and above.

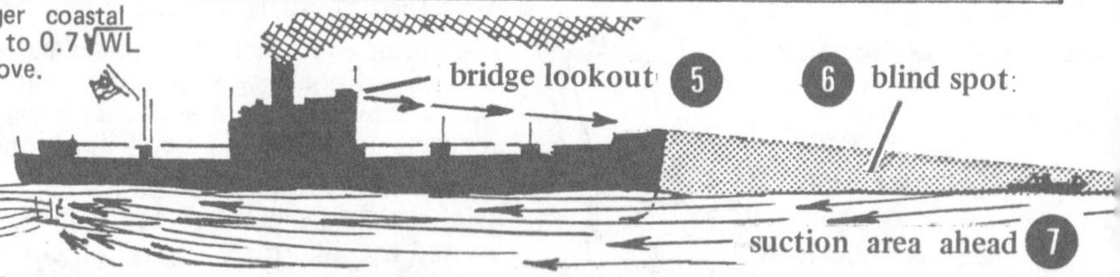

bridge lookout 5

6 blind spot

suction area ahead 7

Propeller suction is very dangerous near large vessels especially near the stern when they are accelerating.

The majority of world shipping moves with speeds under 0.8 $\sqrt{WL}$. These large vessels operate in their own ships' envelope or container with almost zero water speed next to the hull, while the water flow speed will increase as you move outward from the ship.

The movement of a ship displaces a tremendous volume of water around and under this moving container at hull speed. It produces a suction ½ to 3 lengths ahead to fill the void created by the propeller suction near the stern. *This propeller suction increases in all directions when accelerating. This suction increases considerably in shallow bays or rivers where the same total volume has to be pulled in from greater horizontal distances.*

The large vessel bow wave may tend to push your boat away... *but AVOID the stern.* For example—a ship stopped outside of L.A. Harbor to pick up a pilot with several small boats in the area. As the ship began to accelerate the prop suction pulled in and trapped several small boats under its stern counter. This was fortunately spotted by an off-duty crew member as the noise of the ship overpowered the honking horns on the trapped boats.

Keep clear of tugboats with tows particularly when they are going downstream. They will have stopping problems in an emergency.

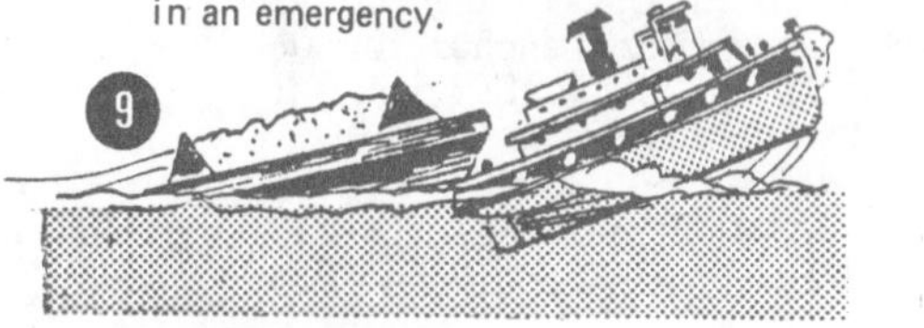

9

We've seen overpowered tugboats on the Hudson (North) River that were pointing upstream while towing barges. They were going backwards down stream in the strong tidal currents as the tugboat captains had either made a mistake with the current tables or they had forgotten to read them.

Any sailboat or powerboat that cuts in front of a tugboat with tows will cause a problem. The captain has the choice of going thru your boat... *OR if he hits the reverse* the momentum of the tow or barges will ride up and over his stern. If you were the tugboat captain... what would be your choice?

Super tanker information is difficult to find. We recommend SUPERSHIP by Noel Mostert (Alfred A. Knoff, Inc.)— a 1974 excellent coverage of this highly technical world.

Farrel Lines containership AUSTRAL PURITAN, 27,706 DWT, is shown below on the New York to Australia run, can carry 1708 containers of which 825 may be reefer units.

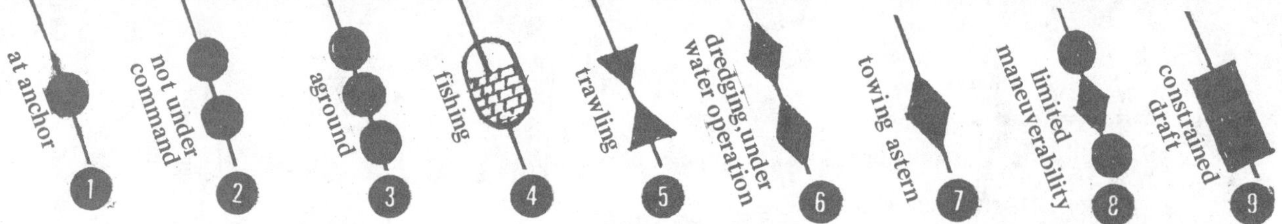
at anchor
1
not under command
2
aground
3
fishing
4
trawling
5
dredging, under water operation
6
towing astern
7
limited maneuverability
8
constrained draft
9

Commercial vessel daytime identification shapes carried in their rigging are shown above.

Conversion Table	
4.5 M	14.8 ft.
0.5 M	16.4 ft.
0.6 M	19.7 ft.
0.7 M	23.0 ft.
0.8 M	26.2 ft.
10 M	32.8 ft.
12 M	39.4 ft.
20 M	65.6 ft
25 M	82.0 ft.
50 M	164.0 ft.

Tugboats under 50 meters long may carry a second masthead light abaft of and higher than the forward one-Rule 23 (a)(ii).

Rule 22 defines light intensity for vessels–

- under 12 meters (39.4')
- 12 meters to under 50 meters (164')
- 50 meters and longer

Official source of **lights and day signals** detailed are found in the *USCG Navigational Rules-COMDTINST M16672.2A* International and Inland Rules. Order your copy from the Sup't of Documents, Government Printing Office, Wash., DC 20402...phone (202) 783-3238.

Commercial vessels ***indicate their purpose and type of work*** with a variety of signals shown in their rigging. All of these official signals carry the same message—***KEEP CLEAR due to limited maneuverability or NO maneuverability.***

It requires time and patience to find the location of the daytime signals shown above as their locations vary considerably due to numerous hull shapes, bridge locations, etc.

Color the lights below and on the following pages as indicated using felt tip pens. We feel such coloring is the easiest way to become familiar with the standard operational procedures of commercial vessels at work or underway at night from tugboats to supertankers.

Sunset to sunrise–the first warning you will see when a tugboat is coming towards your boat is the ***strong range lights*** which indicate the course of the tugboat.

You later see the weaker red light ⓫ if you are looking at its ***port side***, or the green light ⓾ ⓭ if you are looking at the ***starboard side*** of the tugboat. If you see both ***red and green*** running lights ⓬ the tugboat is heading ***directly towards your boat.***

If you see a ***single white light*** ⓮ the tugboat is going away from your vessel.

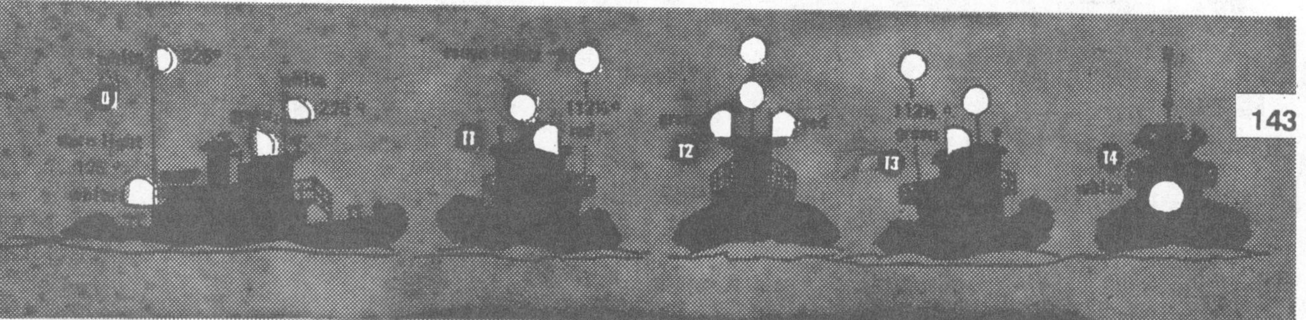
10
11
12
13
14

Your ability to operate and survive in commercial traffic depends on your recognition and interpretation of these lights, plus knowledge of and application of the specific rules involved.

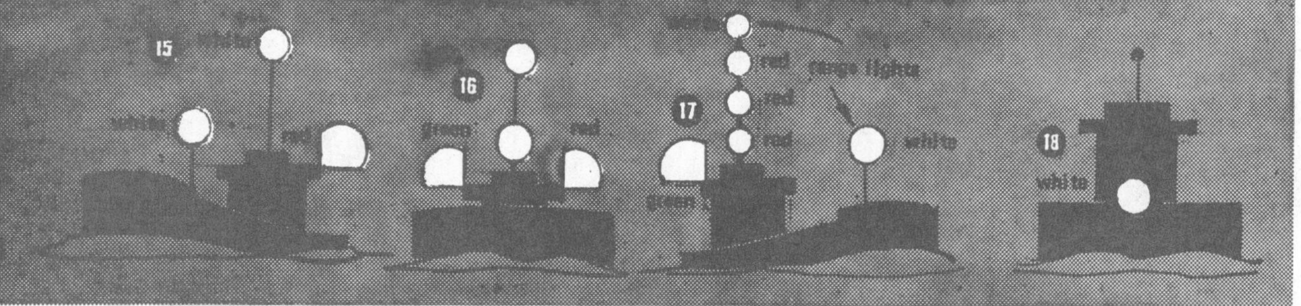
15
white
red
16
green
red
17
red
red
red
range lights
white
green
18
white

ote–though range lights re far apart on the tankers hown...range lights may e close together near the ow of some vessels due) their structure.

The supertanker ⓯ is passing your vessel on its port side, while ⓱ is passing your vessel on its starboard side. The three vertical red lights indicate that the vessel ***must stay in its channel due to constrained draft.***

If you see white range lights one above the other ⓰ followed by ***both red AND green*** running lights it is rather late to worry about additional insurance coverage.

Where will the daytime signals be displayed on this supertanker?

Sailing
Illustrated
Volume II

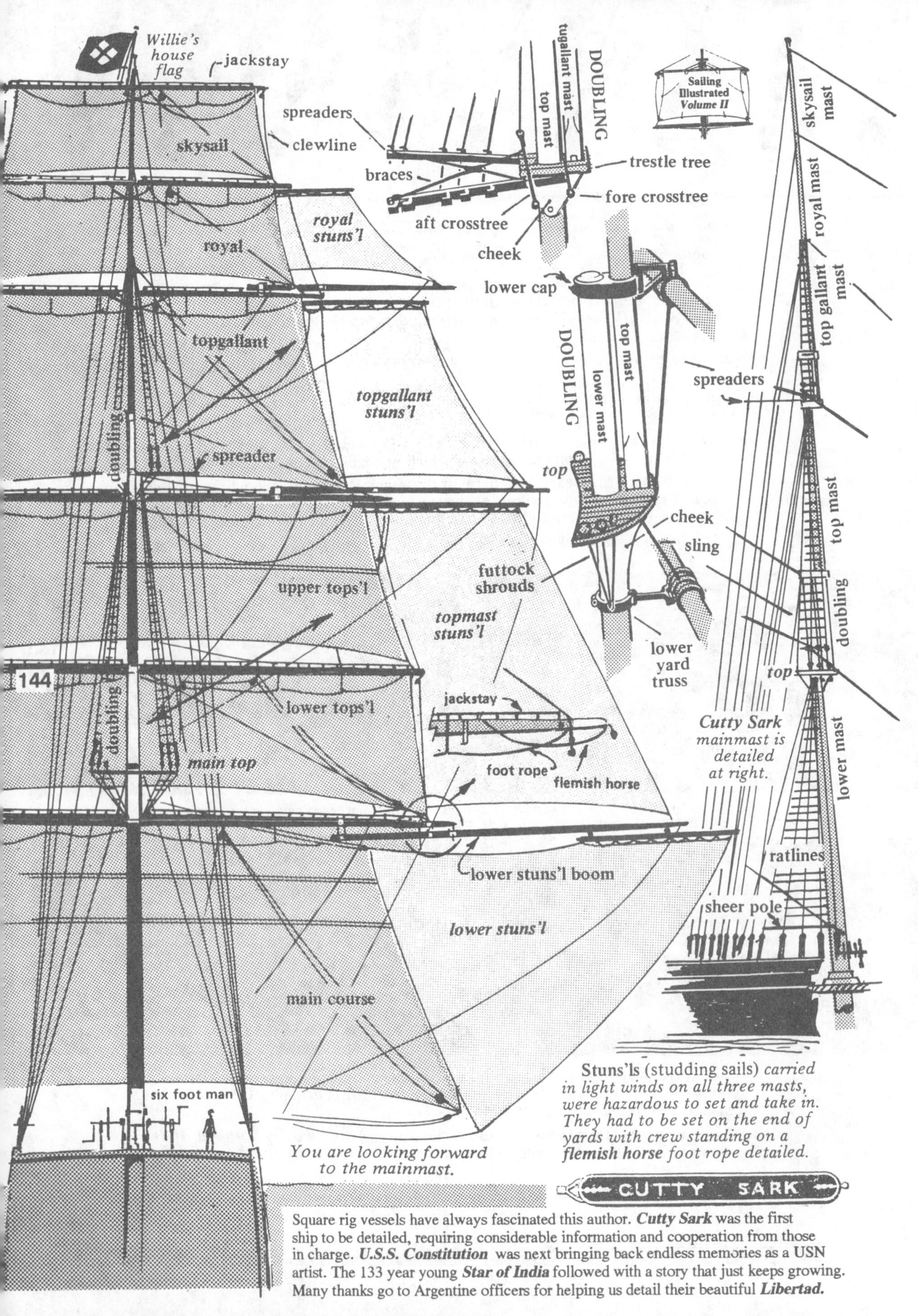
Willie's house flag
jackstay
skysail
clewline
spreaders
braces
aft crosstree
cheek
tugallant mast
top mast
DOUBLING
trestle tree
fore crosstree
Sailing Illustrated Volume II
skysail mast
royal mast
top gallant mast
royal
royal stuns'l
lower cap
topgallant
topgallant stuns'l
DOUBLING
top mast
lower mast
spreaders
doubling
spreader
top
cheek
sling
futtock shrouds
upper tops'l
topmast stuns'l
lower yard truss
top mast
doubling
top
144
doubling
lower tops'l
jackstay
main top
foot rope
flemish horse
Cutty Sark mainmast is detailed at right.
lower mast
lower stuns'l boom
ratlines
sheer pole
lower stuns'l
main course
six foot man
CUTTY SARK

Stuns'ls (studding sails) *carried in light winds on all three masts, were hazardous to set and take in. They had to be set on the end of yards with crew standing on a* ***flemish horse*** *foot rope detailed.*

You are looking forward to the mainmast.

Square rig vessels have always fascinated this author. ***Cutty Sark*** was the first ship to be detailed, requiring considerable information and cooperation from those in charge. ***U.S.S. Constitution*** was next bringing back endless memories as a USN artist. The 133 year young ***Star of India*** followed with a story that just keeps growing. Many thanks go to Argentine officers for helping us detail their beautiful ***Libertad.***

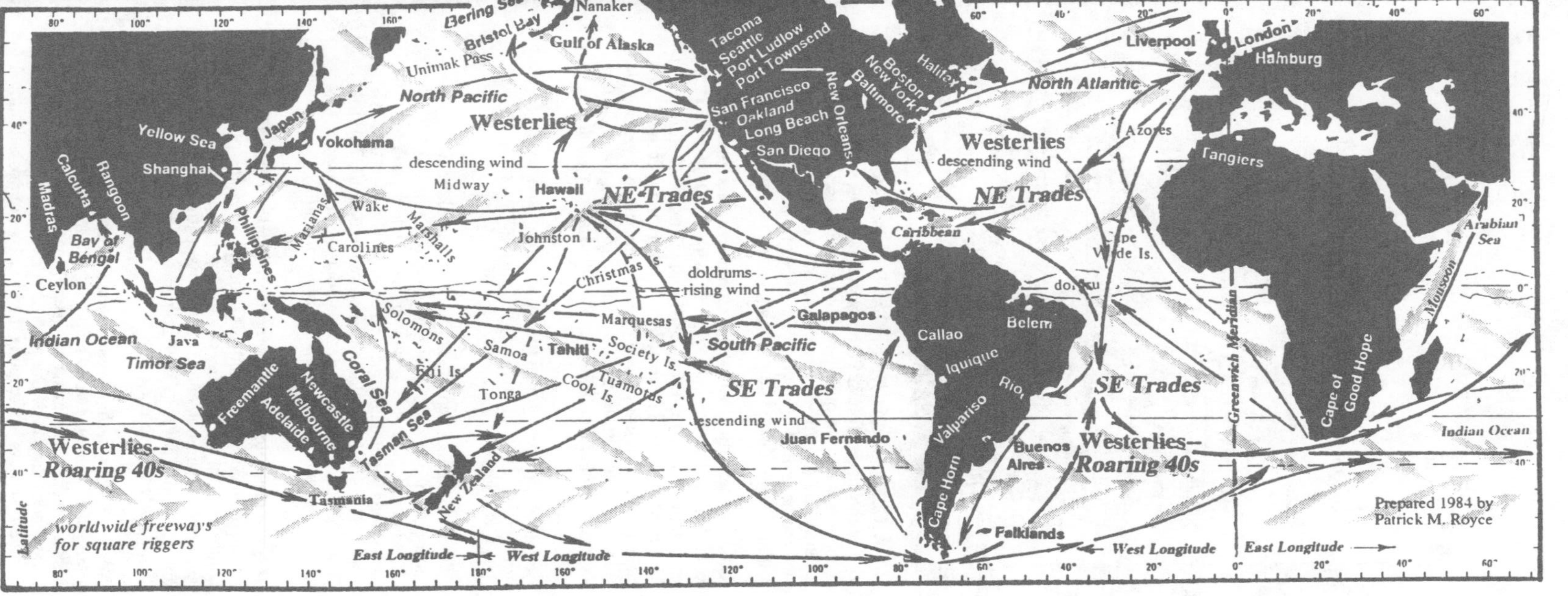

Bering Sea
Nanaker
Bristol Bay
Gulf of Alaska
Unimak Pass
North Pacific
Westerlies
Yellow Sea
Japan
Yokohama
Shanghai
Calcutta
Rangoon
Madras
descending wind
Midway
Hawaii
NE Trades
Wake
Marianas
Marshalls
Philippines
Carolines
Johnston I.
Bay of Bengal
Ceylon
Christmas Is.
doldrums-
rising wind
Marquesas
Solomons
Indian Ocean
Java
Samoa
Tahiti
Society Is.
Timor Sea
Coral Sea
Fiji Is.
Tonga
Cook Is.
Tuamotus
Freemantle
Newcastle
Melbourne
Adelaide
Tasman Sea
Westerlies--
Roaring 40s
Tasmania
New Zealand
worldwide freeways
for square riggers
Latitude
East Longitude
West Longitude
Tacoma
Seattle
Port Ludlow
Port Townsend
San Francisco
Oakland
Long Beach
San Diego
New Orleans
Boston
New York
Baltimore
Halifax
Galapagos
South Pacific
SE Trades
Juan Fernando
Caribbean
Callao
Iquique
Valpariso
Cape Horn
Belem
Rio
Buenos Aires
Falklands
North Atlantic
Liverpool
London
Hamburg
Azores
Tangiers
Greenwich Meridian
Monsoon
Arabian Sea
Cape of Good Hope
Indian Ocean
Prepared 1984 by
Patrick M. Royce
Sailing Illustrated Volume II
polar front
polar high
square rig route
westerlies
60°
30°
high pressure–
downdraft barrier
NE trades
doldrum storm
low pressure–
rising wind
SE trades
easterlies
sailing illustrated
WORLD AIR MASS PATTERNS
longitude
latitude

Beware-- *windless storm* page 76, **El Nino,** pg. 56.

Square rig downwind sailing routes follow worldwide wind patterns.

Thermal heat currents begin with wind flow caused by rays of the sun. Uneven heating is maximum at equator. It rises flowing to the cold poles, then descends to return to equator. To this we add a **coriolis force,** or earth flow pattern, *zero speed at poles, 1000 mile speed at equator.*

Weather at equator is clear, with warm air rising, then arcing to north and east. The winds pile up in the **horse latitudes,** producing minimum surface wind downdrafts.

Some of this flows farther north, to be deflected to the east. It descends in the 30 to 60 degree middle latitude surface flow prevailing ***westerlies.*** This pattern is best known in U.S., flows across Atlantic, thru Europe and China, across the North Pacific, to return to the U.S.

The remaining part of wind in descending horse latitudes, turns west to produce steady ***NE trades.*** Below equator descending winds turn SE to produce steady ***SE trades.***

Square rigger routes make the most of prevailing wind patterns. *New York to Rio*--time is saved traveling past mid Atlantic, turning south. If vessel followed shortest line between these ports... sailing time would be doubled.

After passing Cape Horn, vessel heads for Fairbanks, Alaska. At 30 degrees North, it turn east to deliver cargo to San Francisco. *The return route*--it is easy to sail to Hawaii, the Marquesas, and Tahiti. At 30 degrees South, a slow turn with sails reefed down for Cape Horn. The course afterwards is the Caribbean, New Orleans, our east coast,north to New York, Boston, and/or Halifax.

Australian wool trade. Windjammers left England with a stop in Rio. At 30 degrees South, it heads for ***Cape of Good Hope.*** with a straight east course thru the Indian Ocean for wool shearing ports Sept. thru Oct. The next course, sail ***east*** to pass **Cape Horn.** A northerly course takes windjammers or clippers to London in time for the January to March textile market.Timing is very critical to avoid warehouse charges if too early.

Sailing
Illustrated
Volume II
main skysail
main royal
main topgallant
main royal stays'l
main t'g't stays'l
main upper tops'l
main lower tops'l
main topmast stays'l
main course
fore royal
fore topgallant
fore upper tops'l
fore lower tops'l
fore course
fore topmast stays'l
inner jib
outer jib
flying jib
mizzen royal
mizzen topgallant
mizzen t'g't stays'l
mizzen upper tops'l
mizzen topmast stays'l
mizzen lower tops'l
cro'jack, crossjack
mizzen stays'l
spanker
bowsprit
jib boom
dolphin striker
ROYCE

CUTTY SARK

Cutty Sark required 7 miles of hemp running rigging, and 4 miles of iron wire standing rigging.

Early sailors used many local available rope materials. *Vikings used strips of leather and walrus hide with too much flexibility, plus inner tree bark. They made raids periodically to central Europe for flax and hemp with less shrink and stretch problems.*

Nile and Euphrates sailors *used weak papyrus, reeds, and coconut coir.* Chinese sailors *used silk, jute, and sisal. They imported manila as their junks traded on regular schedules 2000 years ago with the Phillippines.*

Preussen, page 148, *was the largest windjammer, 407′ LOA,* that carried 26 sails. Rope lengths are approximate.

Standing rigging 35,400′; hemp running rigging 56,600′; wire running rigging 43,300′; chain running rigging 2300′.

Total 138,000′ of rope, wire, and chain were carried aloft. Add to this weight the yards, masts, 2600 blocks, etc.

Hemp rope was the sailors best friend for many centuries.

Availability was excellent as hemp ***the happy weed*** can grow near boatyards and rope mills in most climates.

Sailors lives depended on hemp from our colonial days, and much earlier, for British sailors. It was the best available rope for ***standing rigging*** to support masts, and ***running rigging*** to raise, control, and trim sails on small harbor craft, to clipper ships, and large windjammers.

Hemp and Manila have similar strength. Around 1860 U.S. imported manila rope began to replace hemp on sailing vessels for stability, not strength. Hemp rigging was slack in dry weather. Length shrank excessively in high humidity as the diameter enlarged. Manila was more stable with less shrink and stretch. As both were organic, deterioration began after its oily content disappeared, becoming brittle and weak.

1849. Gold miners arriving in San Francisco soon found one of the largest forests in the world, was the real gold. Its lumber was used to build new homes and factories for our country. Builders made large fleets of wooden sailing vessels delivering lumber thruout the Pacific as far as Australia and China powered with hemp rigging grown next to shipyards.

U.S. is systematically destroying natures most fertile and useful crop. This forest has shrunk to under 10% with replacement trees requiring to 70 years to mature before becoming lumber. ***The problem is government caused.*** Print newspapers with fast growing hemp maturing in 3 years with minimum space, instead of daily destroying our forests. *Most bureaucrtic blunders begin slowly with naieve regulations.*

Tobacco. Congress found it easy to control and tax, as tobacco is a difficult crop to grow, then in limited areas in a few states.

Hemp. Congress then tried to tax hemp smokers with over-the-counter sales. Congress soon found it a *happy weed that could grow worldwide under endless* conditions beyond bureaucratic control. Their frustration changed to spoiled child vengeance with their 1937 Act. Their blind logic as their new tax source evaporated... *legislate hemp growing and smoking illegal!*

If hemp growing and smoking were legalized tomorrow, prison population could shrink to normal, releasing prisoners behind bars for only selling or smoking hemp. This could ***eliminate*** their goal, endless self-perpetuating police bureaucracies. *Town, city, and state police could return to their traditional responsibility... protect the public.*

Hemp powered sailing vessels worldwide for hundreds of years, plus replacing wood pulp today, a traditional medicine. Instead of three martinis, many people can relax with a hemp cigarette at days end. Our present bureaucratic hemp blunder esculating cost is bankrupting the U.S. ... as our constitutional rights erode & disappear without practical, justifiable reasons.

P.S., the author has always been a nonsmoker, neither "hemp" nor tobacco. Good bourbon needs no substitute.

Cutty Sark figurehead witch "Nannie" in a short chemise graced her bow.

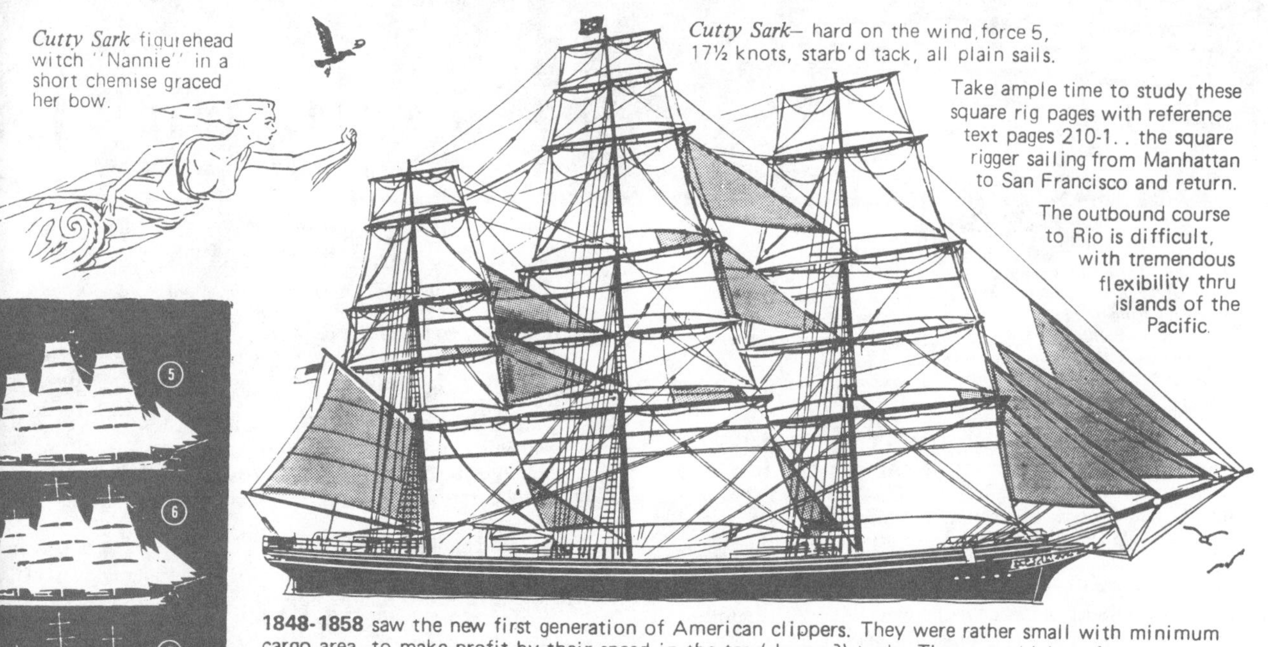

Cutty Sark– hard on the wind, force 5, 17½ knots, starb'd tack, all plain sails.

Take ample time to study these square rig pages with reference text pages 210-1. . the square rigger sailing from Manhattan to San Francisco and return.

The outbound course to Rio is difficult, with tremendous flexibility thru islands of the Pacific.

1848-1858 saw the new first generation of American clippers. They were rather small with minimum cargo area, to make profit by their speed in the tea (slavery?) trade They were high-performance racers with hard-driving captains pushing them to new limits never seen on the ocean.

1869– the second generation clipper *Cutty Sark* was launched. She was composite-built of wood using iron frames, beams, stringers, and diagonal plates added to stress areas. While outbound clippers had to sail around the tip of Africa to sail to China, the Suez Canal opened the same year reducing steamship distance from the British Isles to China by 4000 miles. Steam was just beginning to prove itself, and new coaling stations had to be opened before steamships slowly took over the tea trade.

Cutty Sark made good voyages, but not the tea trade records she was designed for. Her masts and yards were shortened, the skysail and stuns'ls were removed for better performance in the southern *roaring forties.* When outward bound she carried coal sailing down to the tip of Africa, heading east to Australia. She arrived during wool shearing from Sept., thru Oct. She loaded wool for the homeward passage to London for the Jan. to March textile market delivery avoiding expensive warehouse charges. She sailed east below New Zealand with the wind on her stern to round Cape Horn, turning NE for the channel. For ten years Captain Woodget who was a hard driver of men and ships made consistent records of 68, 69, and 70 days from Sydney to the English Channel.

After 26 years under the British flag she was sold to a Portugese owner. Her coal cargo shifted in heavy seas. While on beams end her masts were cut away for survival. She was towed to Capetown to be rerigged as a barkentine. After 53 years service she returned to the Red Ensign in 1922. She was restored to her original state as a full-rigged clipper ship, with her last sea passage in 1938.

We thank *THE "CUTTY SARK" MARITIME TRUST* for permission to detail her. Since records of her reefing sequence were missing, we contacted model sailboat builder Eric Christian. Over 2½ hours discussion was required to show beam reach steering stability to minimize rudder pressure, losing her rudder twice. She carried more sails forward and less sails aft to sail downwind. Detailing the *Cutty Sark* has been the dream of this artist from Wyoming who was drawing square riggers in grade school.

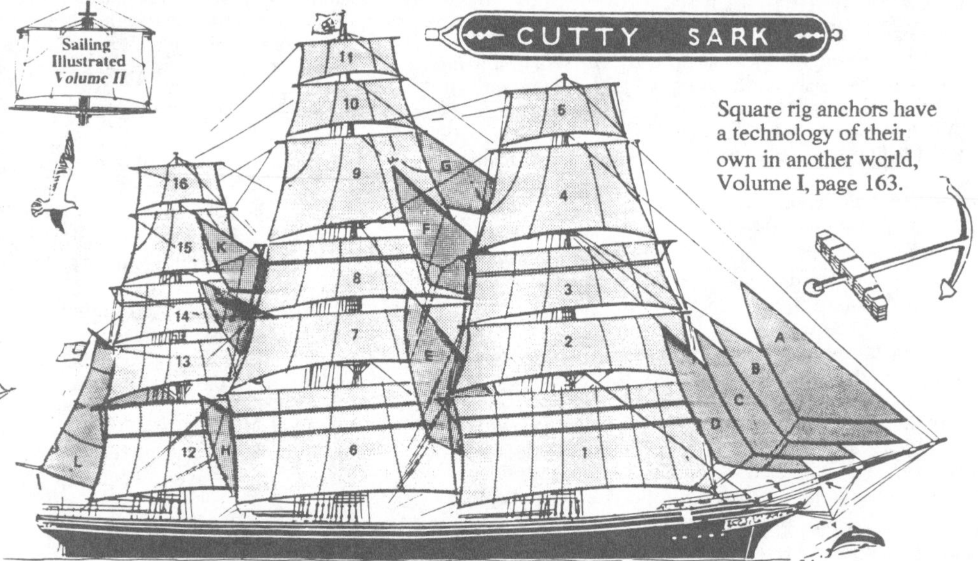
Sailing Illustrated Volume II
CUTTY SARK

Square rig anchors have a technology of their own in another world, Volume I, page 163.

1918-1922– her barkentine rig.

the *Preussen*
1902–1909
407' LOA
53' beam
8000 tons deadweight
42 crewmen

403' 4" LOA
50' beam
30' draft when loaded
43,000 sq ft' of sail
11,000 tons coal capacity

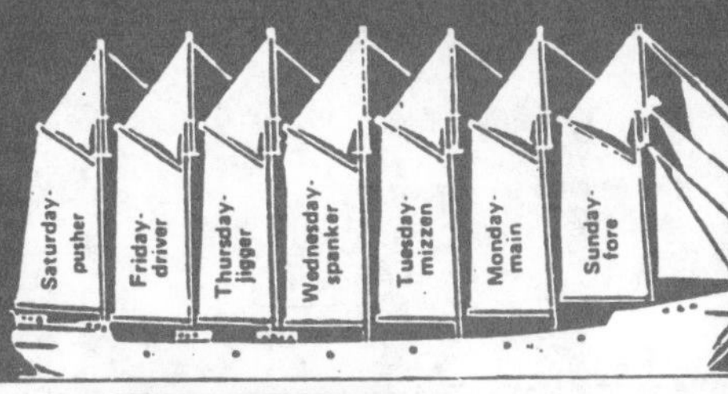
Saturday-pusher
Friday-driver
Thursday-jigger
Wednesday-spanker
Tuesday-mizzen
Monday-main
Sunday-fore

Preussen

The largest **windjammer** *had a maximum 17 knots carrying up to 48 sails. On a hazy November 1910 night sailing down the English Channel, a tiny British steamer crossed her bow against the rules. The collision damaged her bow tearing away her bowsprit rigging. Her steerage was lost in an increasing gale. She was totalled on rocks off the Cliffs of Dover mid afternoon the next day, carrying a load of pianos to Chile.*

The downwind square riggers.

My first advisers, most claiming to sail around the Horn, said the change from square rig to fore-and-aft schooner rig was due to smaller crews to make more profit for owners. Forty years later we find more variables starting with heritage.

Running down the trades. Square rigs were well adapted to sail the southern tradewind route to the New World. The return was the northern route, as they romped downwind headed for Europe.

Northern Atlantic commerce. Europeans with ample winds found the square rig practical to ship cargo and passengers from port to port, and eventually, across the Atlantic delivering colonists to the new world. Small square riggers slowly grew larger to improve profit margins.

A basic rule- *systematically put enough money aside from the profits in ten years to build a new vessel of equal or larger size.*

148 **In 1812** small packets started regular North Atlantic delivery service. By 1850 *wooden hull* square rig clippers were carrying light cargo with delivery time making new records. By 1860 larger *iron windjammers* were delivering larger cargo loads with better profits for owners and shippers.

Sailing
Illustrated
Volume II

Santa Maria

80 (tuns)- wine casks
78'6" stem to stern
55'6" keel length
26' beam
3500 sq.ft. sail

The reaching lateener.

N

Lateeners probably started with early Arab and Phoenician traders in the eastern Mediterranean. They started a new sail rig as winds were too light or too strong for early square sails. It had to be practical as Phoenicians sailed long distances to trade with Vikings for many decades. The lateen rig was inherited by other Mediterranean countries for commerce and fishing.

The Spanish compromise was reached with lateeners to the south, and square rigs to the north. The best known, was the ***Santa Maria*** sailed by Columbus in 1492. The clumsy aft lateen sail was replaced with a square sail in the Canary Islands for running down the trades.

The only lateen rigs in the U.S. were used by Italian fishermen just arriving to the west coast. A photo shows them returning to San Francisco thru the Golden Gate after a day of fishing in strong winds. They rapidly changed to gasoline powered, small double-ended, very seaworthy *Monterey trollers and draggers.* San Francisco had large fleets of Montereys to which Italian fisherman added their own ideas, painting them bright colors.

Thomas W. Lawson

The 7 masted **Thomas W. Lawson,** *was an Atlantic bulk carrier for five years. It was rebuilt with permanent oil tanks, our first oil tanker. On its first trip to Europe it faced a storm of once in a hundred years wiping out all sails. It anchored, with a link breaking in the chain, driven onto rocks, breaking in half. Only 2 of 17 survived.*

The reaching schooners.

Opportunists and inventors are fascinating with questioning open minds looking for unusual opportunites. The chaotic growing port of San Francisco is an outstanding example.

Trade wind sailing. A parallel situation exists using downwind NE trades to Japan, with westerlies for the northern downwind return to the U.S. It requires at least seven times as many days, also we had little interest to trade with Japan. Square rig was excellent for the Pacific, yet more flexibility was needed.

The Mexican government was interested in endless tariffs, and taxes. All vessels were required to enter Monterey, their headquarters. to be cleared, expecting a big tax source. They ignored expanding commerce to improve their finances..

It was taken from Mexico in 1846 by the U.S., becoming our major west coast port, especially provisioning and .repairs, the new homeport for our large whaling fleets.

1949 gold rush. Every sailing vessel able to sail around the Horn found passengers that would pay any price. Even crews jumped ship in San Francisco, sometimes before the anchor was down. An 1853 photo shows hundreds of these sailing vessels becoming derelicts, ready to be scrapped for firewood..

Two New Englanders left their shipbuilding business to join the gold rush, soon running out of money. As they analyzed their situation, they began to realize they found the real gold surrounding them, were the best virgin forests in the world.

They headed for San Francisco to build small schooners called **outside porters** that could move into the tiniest **dog holes** on a hostile rocky coast. They loaded redwood, Oregon pine, and Douglas fir which was sailed to San Francisco. Many of these holes would defy our sailors with similar size vessels in good weather using the best equipment to sail in, and sail out.

Lumber from 500 outside porters was reloaded on larger schooners for trade over the vast Pacific from San Diego, to Australia and China, plus all the islands between.

Pacific schooner timber fleet included larger two-masters, over 125 three-masters, over 180 four-masters, around 100 five-masters, plus brigantines and.barkentines.

Chinese junk masts. 60 year old Oregon Pine to 90' tall, was the favorite choice with several metal band stiffeners. These masts without stays or shrouds, are usually worth more than the hull. Some of the masts have seen active service for 100 years.

Windjammers of the Pacific Rim--Jim Gibbs. It has excellent coverage of schooners, barkentines, etc., built on the Pacific Coast from 1850 to 1921. The appendix lists all these vessels with their specifications. *Schiffer Pub. Ltd., 1469 Morstein Rd., West Chester,PA 19830*

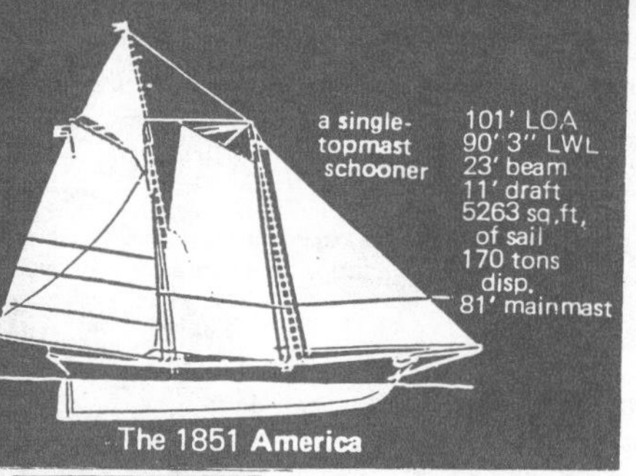
a single-topmast schooner
101' LOA
90' 3" LWL
23' beam
11' draft
5263 sq.ft. of sail
170 tons disp.
81' mainmast
The 1851 America

Baltimore Clippers

British navy officers in 1776 captured all of our vessels. The exception, Baltimore Clippers. One captured, was sailed to England, drydocked, & measured. Was it destroyed in anger?

Pride of Baltimore

first
Pride of Baltimore

LOA 137'
LWL 77'
draft 9'9"
sail area
9523 sq.ft.
121 long tons

America

Square rig vs schooner rig.

Wind is the major factor. Most of our U.S. lives in the land of the westerlies. Prevailing winds continue to flow across the Atlantic to Europe, China, across the North Pacific, and back to the U.S.

Ocean sea breezes on our U.S. west coast increase in the afternoon to ***combine*** with the westerlies similar to the west coast of England and Europe, only stronger with Europe in the latitude of Canada. Stoutly built and somewhat clumsy British warships and cargo vessels still have ample wind for maneuverability.

Ocean sea breezes on the east coast *flow westward* fighting the prevailing winds flowing eastward across the U.S., **cancel** the other out... ***no afternoon wind.*** At night the land breeze going to the cooler ocean, combine with the prevailing westerlies. They are seldom on the surface, raised by the heat of the land cooling off.

Light winds aloft, not on the surface, are the major part of the situation. As wave action is minimum compared to our west coast, hulls had to be lighter with finer lines to sail in the Chesapeake Bay producing different sail and hull designs. Readers now know the frustrations of British officers trying to find the hull secrets by measuring... when geography was their missing answer.

second
Pride of Baltimore

LOA 157' 3"
LWL 91'
draft 12'4"
sail area
10,422 sq. ft.
185.5 long tons

Sailing Illustrated Volume II

The three clippers were designed by **Thomas C. Gilmer**

Californian

LOA 93'6"
LWL 83'
draft 9'6"
sail area
7.000 sq.ft.
130 long tons

PRIDE OF BALTIMORE II

Sailing Illustrated Volume II

Time 11:30 1/23/83. The first ***Pride of Baltimore*** entered Newport Harbor. I met skipper Armin Elsaesser the next day that was wet and overcast, for a 2 1/2 hour lunch. He was polite as we discussed several technical ideas..

While enjoying many spirited idea exchanges with professional west coast skippers, I felt a major problem was unfolding as Armin had no flexibility nor humor. .

He said they did everything to follow traditional thinking, yet below it has the latest in safety equipment. I asked, ***"Do you have a cheap AM radio for storm prediction?"*** We had a very quiet, frosty ride back to his dock.

.I no sooner got home, to be handed a **L.A. Times** negative article on *Pride.* Copies of my answer were hand delivered to Armin, and mailed to his Mayor, and our newspaper. We. summarized the editorials *only contribution, was* for the bottom of bird cages. *Back to the pasta recipes.*

A few days later it was necessary to deliver papers to *Pride* in Marina del Rey, a crew member not letting me aboard. "Let him thru", came from a temporary professional crew member. He had been working with me on supertankers.

I joked, "How many seasick pills do you have?" His grin disappeared. "It seems we may have a wet ride". His next contact was from San Francisco. "I'm not the only seaman jumping ship. What we expected as ***our*** normal weather, the bow went under three waves... going thru the fourth".

My last information from Armin was a postcard dated 11/19/83. "She's home, safe and sound, to a tumultous welcome with the mayor and governor in attendance. A spectacular final!" *Good Sailing, Armin*

I lost touch until finding she had been lost 5/13/1986. Many speculations were coming thru. The first concise record was ***Reader's Digest,*** November 1986, pg. 128.

Call the microburst an excuse. How I argued with Armin to use a cheap AM radio playing constantly in bad weather. Increasing static should have been horrible two or more hours before the microburst hit. With all sails down and hatches sealed, ***Pride's*** crew could have easily survived.

I am privy to much information never to be released. This is the exception with ***Pride's*** hull and rigging designed for protected one-of-a-kind Chesapeake weather... *and a skipper not questioning nor analyzing AM radio potentials..*

For more information- **Pride of Baltimore, *The Story of the Baltimore Clippers*** by Thomas C. Gilmer, published by International Marine in 1992, *ISBN 0-87742-309-1. .*

P.S. A good chunk of Machic or black cabbage bark,used in the keel of the first ***Pride,*** *is next to me writing this page. It arrived just in time to be the centerpiece for our 45th Anniversary. Thanks to Tom Maple, Frederick, MD*

Six U.S. 36-gun, and 44-gun Frigates — *Constitution, Constellation, Congress, Chesapeake, United States,* and *President.*

Eight miles of running rigging were required to handle sail area larger than a football field.

A nine foot ***long gun*** is shown a
a four foot ***carronade*** is shown

HMS Victory

main royal

fore royal

mizzen royal

main topgallant

fore topgallant

mizzen topgallant

main topsail

fore topsail

mizzen topsail

fore topgallant staysail

fore topmast staysail

outter jib

flying jib

spanker

mainsail

foresail

spar deck

gun deck

berthing deck

U.S.S Constitution

British Rater Sys
1st rater-100 gu
2nd rater- 90-98 g
3rd rater- 64-80 g
4th rater- 50 to 60

5th rater- 36-44 g
called frigates

First Rater *HMS Victory*
100 cannon, 850 crew
launched 5/7/1756
commissioned 1778

"Old Ironsides"
launched Oct. 21, 1797
will sail again in 1997
on her 200th birthday,
the first time under
sail in 116 years.

LOA 204'
Beam 43'6"
Draft 22'6"
Disp. 2,200 tons
Hull planking-
25" thick oak
13.5 knots top speed

Warships are floating gun platforms including ***HMS Victory, USS Constitution,*** and ***USS Missouri.***

USS Constitution was one of six frigates authorized in 1794 by Congress.

1783. Almost all our trading and fishing vessels were captured by the British except for some Baltimore Clippers. The Treaty of Versailles ended the war. Our Army and Navy were dispanded, and our last Naval vessel ***Alliance*** was auctioned in 1785. We had to rebuild a new Navy to protect our commerce starting in the Mediterranean where Barbary Corsairs were capturing our merchant fleet, imprisoning our crews, and holding them for ransom.

1797. The oldest commissioned warship afloat in the world was launched three years after laying her keel. Her normal crew was 400, with 450 when she fought ***Guerriere*** August 19, 1812. She captured 22 vessels between the Barbary War and the War of 1812. Over 2 million board feet of wood was used in her construction, another estimate was 3000 trees. Her frames were of **live oak** assembled in pairs with 2" between each pair, while the hull is of **white oak. Enemy shot** bounced off this solid wall of oak. the reason her nickname **"Old Ironsides"**. Below the waterline 10 to 12% of the wood is original when she was first launched.

She carried thirty **long guns** over nine feet long on the ***gun deck.*** They could hurl 24 pound 6" dia. solid balls to pierce 20" of wood at 1000 yards with a 6 pound powder charge. The sixteen four foot **carronades** on the ***spar deck*** hurled 32 pound solid balls 400 yards with a 2 1/2 pound powder charge. They were excellent for close-in fighting to crush, not penetrate. The ***fo'c'sle*** carried eight 32 pound **carronades** and two 24 pound **bow chasers.**

Ordnance metallurgy had advanced enough so all guns had to prove themselves before being mounted on her decks. A USN adviser said that a hundred or more years before without testing, many cannons exploded on their first firing. Few lasted long enough for 50 rounds due to metal fatigue. An unfired cannon of this older period was donated to a LA museum. They cut it up to find the foundry expertise of that period. Huge voids in the barrel would have caused it to explode on the first firing. This would have killed and wounded nearby gunners in cramped quarters of early British raters. *Even our 16" battleship guns required rifling replaced after firing 50 rounds.*

Trading broadsides. Warship cannons had little accuracy, elevation the only adjustment. They aimed warships for punishing broadsides. **USS Constitution** could change tack in 20 minutes for another broadside with **Guerriere.** Larger clumsy British raters required 30 to 45 minutes to change tack to enjoy another broadside.

Term **battleship** is derived from 1st, 2nd, and 3rd rater *ships of the line* in the line of **battle.**

Sailing
Illustrated
Volume II

LOA 880'
Beam 108'
38' draft
57,950 tons disp. fully loaded

top speed 33 knots

U.S.S Missouri

Charles W. Morgan

Morgan is detailed carrying one ·f her eight sail rigs used in her ·0 active years on the ocean.

She can be drifting any place n the world with lookouts in he *crows nest.* 28′ whaleboats weighing 2000 pounds fully equipped, are ready at the first call for launching.

After blubber cooking begins, whaling ships can be smelled 5 to 10 miles downwind. Insults are common from passing clipper ships soon disappearing over the horizon.

Whales were carried to starboard with tail forward. Slight forward movement with light sails, keeps the whale carcass close to hull.

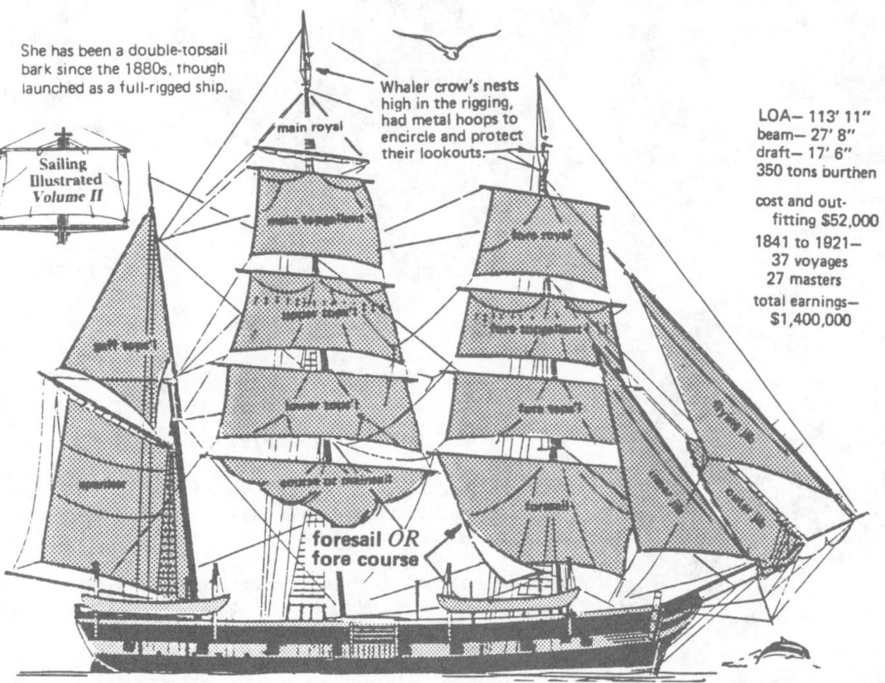
She has been a double-topsail bark since the 1880s, though launched as a full-rigged ship.
Sailing Illustrated Volume II
Whaler crow's nests high in the rigging, had metal hoops to encircle and protect their lookouts.
main royal
foresail OR fore course
LOA— 113′ 11″
beam— 27′ 8″
draft— 17′ 6″
350 tons burthen
cost and out-fitting $52,000
1841 to 1921— 37 voyages 27 masters
total earnings— $1,400,000

When we still had Ocean Life.

I love whales. The most active ocean area in the world up to 1970, was a triangle, Newport Beach, to Catalina, to Long Beach. In 1960 I had to turn off the engines five times and drift for several minutes while taking a twin-screw powerboat to Catalina. We were in huge schools of minnows. They could be pulled into our engine cooling water intake, plugging the engines.

Huge forests of kelp along our shores were denuded by floating cutter vessels breaking the food chain, while the minnows were scooped up by the millions for fertilizer. The last damage comes from sewage plants. A thin film of soap decreases oxygen content over large areas of our local ocean, trapping the irritant chlorine below. This little recognized problem, plus scarcity of minnows, chases the ***big-eye gamefish*** further offshore.

Whale encounters to avoid collisions includes a 40 footer deep inside our jetty, were so numerous in past years I lost count. Near Catalina in an upper force 5, *Pink Cloud* hit a submerged whale that wiped out six feet of our new bottom paint. He panicked. His head went down, and tail up, called *sounding.* Our bow soared skyward as our stern went under. *That was a real martini mixer.*

Pacific Whale Hunting.

Seven Yankee whalers were operating in the Pacific by 1791. By 1830 the American whaling fleet increased to over 400 vessels with most hunting in the Pacific.

San Fransisco Bay was a favorite whaling port from 1822. Continuous hassling by the Mexican government to collect taxes seemed to never end. Sausalito was a favored supply port anchorage, difficult for tax collectors to reach.

The **Charles W. Morgan** *was the first whaler in 1844 to be assessed the new Mexican custom charges, causing many whalers to center their operations in the Hawaiian Islands (Sandwich Islands). When Americans took control of San Fransisco July 1846, it was the peak whaling year as San Francisco became most whalers home port.*

The Last Survivor.

Charles W. Morgan, launched July 1841.The 351 ton whaling ship left New Bedford in September on her first voyage, her only motive, profit. She was heavy, typical of full-rigged, broad-beam, blunt bow and square stern whalers of that period.

She had square sails on all masts, rerigged as a **bark** in 1867. She was extensively refitted in 1874. And in her1881 refitting, her large main topsail became double topsails. During her 17th voyage, double topsails were also added to the foremast. for easier handling. This 5-year voyage ended in 1886.

October 1886- she was refitted for arctic whaling, leaving New Bedford for San Fransisco, her new home port for the rich Pacific whaling grounds. She no longer had to return to New England to deliver her whale oil. Shipping by Union Pacific was less hazardous no longer having to round the *Horn*, plus being more econmical.

June 1906- *Morgan* returned after nearly 20 years to New Bedford. After her 33rd voyage in 1913, she was stripped and laid up. By 1918 Provincetown became her home port with a new owner for her 35th voyage.

May 1921. She returned from her 37th and last voyage. In 1941 at age 101, she was acquired by Mystic Museum as a derelict. She was towed to Mystic less than a month before WW II was declared. Restoration that began 1947, has been a continuous process up to the present.

She awaits anyone interested wanting to walk her decks, the only wooden whaling vessel survivor from the last century.

Whaling vessels had few enthusiasts except wealthy owners. Crews had a difficult, hazardous life away from their home port for one to five years. Their only inducement, whaleships worked on the share system sliding scale. So many for the captain, and one for each crew member, both profited together.

The *Charles W. Morgan,* 1973, by John F. Leavitt; 136 pages ISBN 0-913372-10-2 7 x 10 *Mystic Seaport,* box 6000, Mystic, CN 06355-0990. While we researched endless books on *"Morgan",* we only recommend artist Levitts excellent book.

Your sailing heritage—
how many sail rigs
can you recognize?
1
2
3
4
5
6
7
8

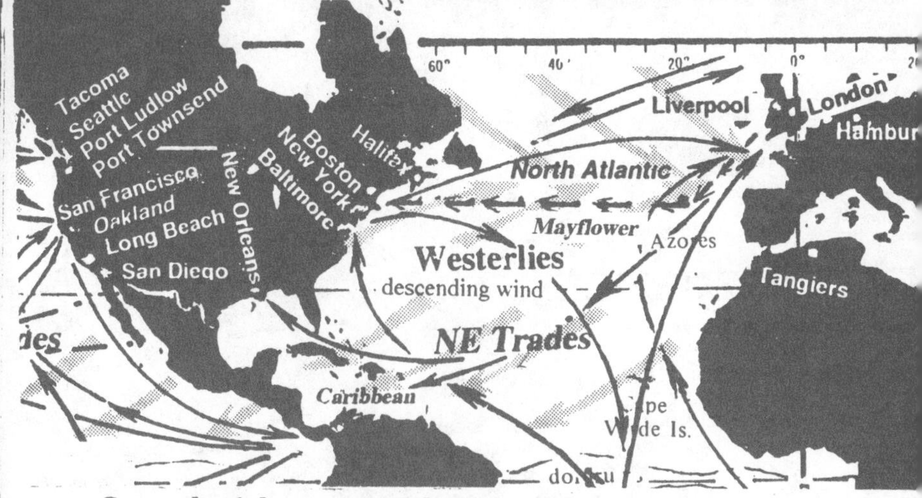

60°
40°
20°
0°
Tacoma
Seattle
Port Ludlow
Port Townsend
San Francisco
Oakland
Long Beach
San Diego
New Orleans
Boston
New York
Baltimore
Halifax
Liverpool
London
Hamburg
North Atlantic
Mayflower
Azores
Westerlies
descending wind
Tangiers
NE Trades
Caribbean

Our colonial commerce began on the water.

Newly arrived colonists seeing endless forests on our eastern seaboard, often began building boats soon after arrival. As most early settlements were isolated, the best transportation was by water, with many new ways to make a profit.

Quality wood was becoming scarce after many centuries of boatbuilding in England and Europe. The ***HMS Victory***, Nelson's Flagship for example, required 60 acres of quality live oak from a century-old forest.

At the time of the Revolutionary War, a third of the tonnage under British Flag, was made in the colonies. Wood cost and quality were excellent, with labor cost less than Europe. During the war British captured the rest of our vessels they hadn't purchased. The exception was a few Baltimore Clippers that outsailed heavier British vessels.

A new era of boatbuilding began in the colonies. We learned from that war that we had to build faster, better maneuverable vessels than the British having made few changes in the last two centuries.

Navigating the North Atlantic.

1620 navigation. The *Mayflower* carried 135 aboard, 102 were passengers. She was 180 tons, 90 foot long, 25 feet beam, with a 100 foot mainmast. Common practice was to sail down to the ***latitude*** of their destination, then sail due west across the Atlantic. *Mayflower* had a stormy trip taking 66 days fighting headwinds. The dotted line shows her course sailed against the prevailing winds to New England..

1957-337 years later. *Mayflower II* with 33 aboard, sailed a much longer course of 5000 miles to reach the prevailing southerly trade winds. It was a downwind romp in a cranky 17th Century ship making her landfall at Cape Cod in 56 days, ten days less.

The Gulf Stream. Benjamin Franklin seems one of the first to realize voyage time is reduced by sailing the northerly route to Europe, and the southerly return route as square riggers handle easier sailing downwind. American captains around 1800 made better time sailing longer routes, puzzled British captains.sailing shorter latitude routes with longer passages, usually fighting prevailing headwinds and the Gulf Stream.

Sailing downwind courses across the Atlantic. *By 1850 most captains chose the northerly course sailing to Europe with prevailing winds on the stern.*

For the return trip, they took the southerly course with the prevailing winds hauling aft of the beam to the stern. On the illustration above it is easy to see how the prevailing winds are ideal for square riggers to reach all ports in the Caribbean from Texas to Florida, and our east coast north to Halifax, Canada.

European wood market. It peaked under sail from 1850 to 1900..Outward bound timber vessels followed the cold northerly downwind course across the Atlantic. They supplied ports from England, to Europe, and Scandinavia. It was a surprise to find in the 1960s most wooden power & sailboats imported from Europe, were made of wood from Oregon.

The return trip to the U.S. was the problem for profit-making captains. Their sailing vessels with an empty hold needed ballast to avoid capsizing, occasionally happening dockside as masts and rigging made empty sailing vessels top heavy. They could carry stone for return ballast with loading and unloading costs.

Sail Rig definitions- pages 282-3, *Sailing Illustrated*- Volume I.

A huge, lonely **Celtic Cross** overlooks an estimated 15,000 Irish buried in unmarked mass graves, the graveyard of our ancestors, sacred to the memory of 1847 Potato Famine victims. Nearby residents call it the *"Irish Island"*.

Grosse Ile is a small island that once served as a quarantine station for immigrants. It is on the St. Lawrence River, a few miles downstream from Quebec, Canada. This island was the first stop of an estimated 110,000 Irish refugees sailing to Canada to escape the 1847 Irish Potato Famine. Grosse Ile was often their first stop in the New World.

Coffin ships. Timber trade vessels carried lumber to Europe. They carried Irish immigrants on the return trip as paying ballast. Mortality rates from sickness, and/or starvation was an estimated one in four. Most were buried at sea. Up to 15,000 died on vessels at anchor, or in island tents and sheds. Over 2000 immigrant children were adopted by nearby residents that summer.

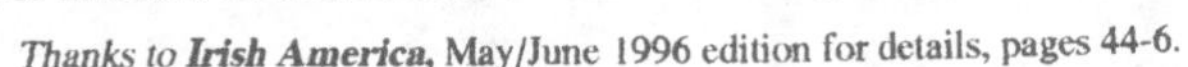

*Thanks to **Irish America,*** May/June 1996 edition for details, pages 44-6.

Sailing
Illustrated
Volume II

The immigrant comes aboard.

Sailing vessels carried cargo and passengers from the early days of Greece and Rome. The goal was to have a full cargo in the hold, then sail in good weather. The practice continued into the 1800s when mail going across the Atlantic became a growing problem. Businessmen often sent identical letters on various ships hoping one might arrive, usually taking six months or longer.

Packets. It applied to a variety of vessels delivering urgent cargo and passengers that sailed on regular schedules. The first was by the Blackball Lines in 1/5/1818 establishing regular schedules between New York and Liverpool. They soon averaged 24 days outbound following the northern route, and 40 days, following the traditional ***latitude return course.***

By 1843 up to 24 packets were following regular schedules from New York to Liverpool, London, and to Europe. River packets served the Hudson and Mississippi Rivers.

Packet passenger ships. The wealthy enjoyed cabins, and up to five meals daily if they bribed the cooks. Minimum cost passengers were assigned to the hold called steerage, often crammed to capacity with up to four persons in a 6 x 6 bunk.

They were required to take their own food.With large groups aboard and too few cooking grates, fights often broke out. Immigrants were lucky to cook one meal a day in good weather; cooking grates were sealed in stormy weather. Drinking water was limited, often poor quality.

Toilets in steerage if any, were buckets with little privacy. In heavy weather with many seasick persons in the hold... the misery was beyond belief. 10% deaths were normal, much higher if contagious diseases broke out. Those surviving left the ships weak and in poor health, bitter with the experience.

1847- my four grandparents leave Ireland.

The 1847 potato faminine. Roads were clogged on the way to seaports with men, women, children and meager possessions to avoid starvation. Liverpool was the largest English port on its west coast, with up to 30 ships leaving on the same tide.

Immigrants had to find an agent knowing when and where bunks were available. Immigrants paid in advance. They were assigned to a waiting house, probably in the worst local slum. They were surrounded by con artists from all over the world trying to steal their gold and possessions.

Lumber ships become passenger ships.

Crude, hastily made bunks were installed close together in tiers to carry as many immigrants as possible. They filled the hold high as possible, especially under the hatches. All passengers were met by an officer as they came aboard to see if they had enough food rations for the trip, plus cooking pot and utensils. Then they were assigned to bunks. Baggage was often stolen on the docks in full sight while boarding.

1847 was probably the worst, with over-loaded and unseaworthy sailing vessels.

Discipline could be harsh as they were under the same life and death rules at sea facing seamen. They were awakened at 7 a.m., to be in their bunks at 10 p.m. Sunday they could sleep to 10 a.m., then have a religious service. Men over 14 were chosen as sweepers in daily rotation. Women had to tidy up their areas and keep them clean.

While conditions were harsh on packet ships designed for regular service, hazards seemed greater on the *temporary* passenger ships. Many were poorly equipped, with crews not trained to carry and control large numbers of passengers. Minor problems often changed to disaster, especially with panic by those on the ocean the first time.

We take 1847 as the benchmark for our discussion when Northern European immigration peaked. In the four following years, almost 60 immigrant ships were reported lost, with few survivors.

Enter Samuel Plimsol. As the windjammer era started around 1870, he proved a major cause of loss of life was overloading. He wanted a **load line** painted on all sail and steam vessels. It was finally passed in 1890 by Parliment, later adopted in 1930 by most nations.

Back to 1847- all quarantine hospitals in New York were full with contagious diseases, as well as newly built ware-houses on Staten Island. During a four month period in 1853, one in eight ships entering New York had contgious diseases aboard,with almost 2000 passengers buried at sea. The U.S.finally decided to refuse entry to vessels with contagious diseases aboard.

The vessels had to return to sea carrying low water, minimum food, with their dead and dying aboard. Many vessels headed for Canadian entry on the St. Lawrence River. The Grosse Island quarantine station had more contagious disease victims of typhus, cholera, and ship-fever, than New York.

Mothers parents the O'Shaughnesseys, landed in Boston where her father made and sold shoes. They eventually moved to Stillwater, Minnesota where they raised seven children. Dads parents the Royces, moved straight to Nebraska where they raised a large family to operate their farm. Mother and dad met in Casper, Wyoming where they were married in 1920. *Only after writing this page at age 74 did I begin to realize why 1st and 2nd generation relatives and immigrant friends had such distrust, and lack of interest in the ocean... and sailing.*

Soverign of the Seas

LOA 258' 2''
keel 245'0''
beam 44'7''
draft 20'0''
disp.2403 long ton
hold depth-23'
canvas-12,000 yds.
crew-105 men,boys

Bering Sea
Bristol Bay
Nushaugar
Nanaker
Gulf of Alaska
Unimak Pass
North Pacific
Westerlies
descending wind
Midway
Hawaii
NE Trades
Yokohama
Japan
Wake
Marianas
Philippines
Carolines
Marshalls
Johnston I.
Christmas
doldrums-rising wind
Marquesas
Galapagos
Solomons
Samoa
Tahiti
Society Is
South Pacific
Fiji Is
Tonga
Cook Is
Tuamotus
SE Trades
descending wind
Juan Fernando
Java
Freemantle
Adelaide
Melbourne
Newcastle
Coral Sea
Tasman Sea
New Zealand
Tasmania
East Longitude
West Longitude
Tacoma
Seattle
Port Ludlow
Port Townsend
San Francisco
Oakland
Long Beach
San Diego
New Orleans
New York
Baltimore
Boston

The clipper ship era was less than a decade old when one of the first true clipper ships,the *Soverign of the Seas,* afloat for less than a year,left Honolulu.

She was deep in the South Pacific heavily laden with oil heading for Cape Horn,then NE to New York City. She was facing continuous rain squalls since midnight charging thru mountainous cresting seas...while still carrying her royals.

The next morning March 18,1853 at 1000 the mate reported,''Nineteen knots again,sir''. The captain replied,''Now you can take the royals off her mister''.

This released some of the pressure,yet at 1100 she was still making 18 knots.The skipper and mate looked at each other.Though they still had an hour to go...this was the first time in history a vessel had sailed more than 400 sea miles in 24 hours,averaging 16.6 knots– *excerpt reprinted by permission of G.P. Putnam's Sons from* **Clipper Ships and Their Makers ©1966** by professor Alexander Laing,deceased.

Another hundred years were required for the first big catamarans to easily hold 20 knots...with *Aikane* in 1959 covering 178 sea miles in 12 hours,while in 1966 *Pattycat II* covered 316 miles in 24 hours.

royals

Sovereign of the Seas

The lieutenant who did his homework.

A passenger on his first ocean trip that was trying to impress his square rigger's captain reported a high moving in.The reply,"Give me a low to blow my ship home in record time",was in a tone that could remove 18 layers of varnish.He remembered a square rigger becalmed for two months in a South Sea high with the same island staying on the distant horizon.The vessel was floating in a carpet of that captain's empty,clanking wine bottles surrounding what would be his last command.

Lt.Matthew Maury *page 66,* produced the first Wind and Current Charts in 1847, available to any skippers desiring such information.Square rigger captains who gained their authority by proven performance didn't take kindly to the ideas of a landbound naval officer with less than a decade of sea duty,who gained his expertise from a study of ships logs which eventually began to indicate basic weather patterns.

The shortest route to Rio was 55 days with vessels facing long doldrum periods. Maury suggested sailing east to mid-Atlantic before turning SSW to Rio which was 3 times the distance.Captain Jackson on the *W. H. D. C. Wright* tested the new idea reaching Rio in 38 days...he then returned in 37 days.

The hard-nose captains took another look at Maury's predictions,turning in their reports to update his charts which eventually covered all the world's oceans.Timing was ideal helping ***clippers*** with their flax sails,wooden hulls,masts,and yards with hemp rigging producing sailing records that still haven't been equalled.

They were followed by much larger ***windjammers*** using flax sails with tremendous bulk-cargo carrying capacity.The hulls,masts,yards,and standing rigging were made of steel.The steel running rigging however had organic rope tails for easier handling.

The Laeisz Line of Hamburg,Germany,operated their Cape Horn windjammers for a century,taking weather reporting to a new plateau that reduced time underway from port to port.Every master received a thorough briefing month by month of the weather he would face.After he returned he would have to submit a detailed accounting of his records and any ideas to improve the performance of their vessels.

After sailing efficiency peaked,it was replaced by steam.A new generation of deep-sea cargo and fishing wind machines may evolve following traditional square rig sailing routes around the world.The first oil tankers and bulk carriers for several decades were sailing vessels starting with the iron-hull *Atlantic,* launched in 1863.The seven-masted schooner *Thomas W.Lawson,* text page 269,converted to carry bulk oil in tank compartments, was lost on her first trip to the English Channel on her new assignment.

Basic weather pattern boundaries above have short-time variations due to seasonal changes...plus local conditions such as world-wide **Feons**, *page 68,*

Monsoons are massive seasonal tropical disturbances,while–

El Niño causes complex normal weather patterns to fall apart with unpredictable time patterns.

The Pacific high *pg.67,* weakens, with ocean temperatures soaring in the eastern Pacific doldrums. As the trade winds diminish *the child* grows to an unpredictable, all-powerful monster.It caused considerable local damage in 1982-3 in our buffer zone *pg.61.*

N

is a new generation of sailing cargo and fishing wind machines practical...

SCG Eagle

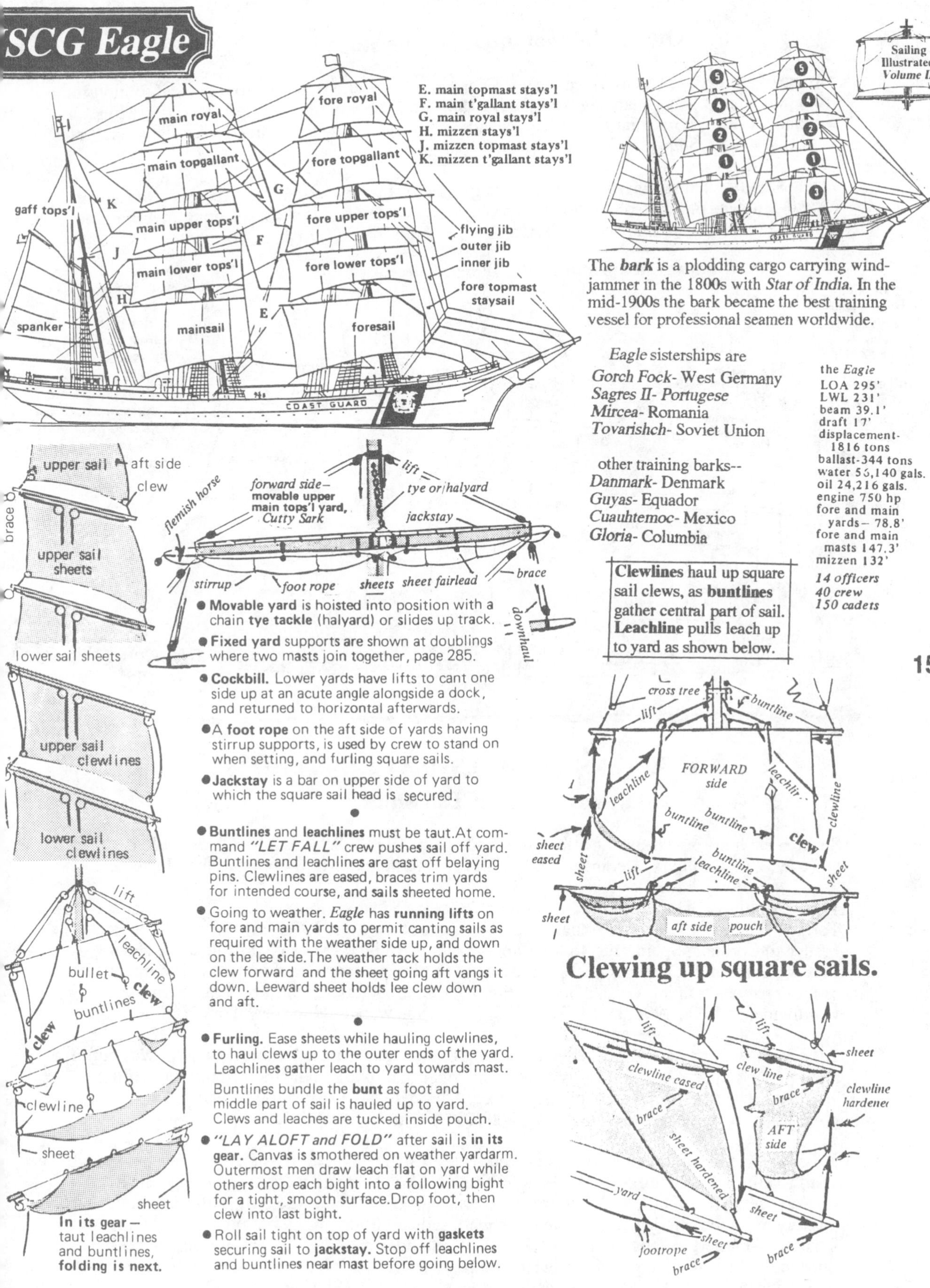

Sailing Illustrated Volume II
main royal
fore royal
main topgallant
fore topgallant
gaff tops'l
K
G
main upper tops'l
fore upper tops'l
J
F
main lower tops'l
fore lower tops'l
H
E
spanker
mainsail
foresail
E. main topmast stays'l
F. main t'gallant stays'l
G. main royal stays'l
H. mizzen stays'l
J. mizzen topmast stays'l
K. mizzen t'gallant stays'l
flying jib
outer jib
inner jib
fore topmast staysail
COAST GUARD
5
4
2
1
3
the Eagle
LOA 295'
LWL 231'
beam 39.1'
draft 17'
displacement-1816 tons
ballast-344 tons
water 56,140 gals.
oil 24,216 gals.
engine 750 hp
fore and main yards– 78.8'
fore and main masts 147.3'
mizzen 132'
14 officers
40 crew
150 cadets
upper sail
aft side
clew
brace
upper sail sheets
lower sail sheets
upper sail clewlines
lower sail clewlines
lift
leachline
bullet
clew
buntlines
clew
clewline
sheet
sheet
flemish horse
forward side– movable upper main tops'l yard, Cutty Sark
lift
tye or halyard
jackstay
stirrup
foot rope
sheets
sheet fairlead
brace
downhaul
cross tree
buntline
lift
FORWARD side
leachline
leachline
clewline
buntline
buntline
clew
sheet eased
sheet
buntline
leachline
lift
sheet
sheet
aft side
pouch
lift
lift
sheet
clewline eased
clew line
clewline hardened
brace
brace
brace
AFT side
sheet hardened
yard
sheet
sheet
footrope
brace
brace

The **bark** is a plodding cargo carrying windjammer in the 1800s with *Star of India.* In the mid-1900s the bark became the best training vessel for professional seamen worldwide.

Eagle sisterships are
Gorch Fock- West Germany
Sagres II- Portugese
Mircea- Romania
Tovarishch- Soviet Union

other training barks--
Danmark- Denmark
Guyas- Equador
Cuauhtemoc- Mexico
Gloria- Columbia

Clewlines haul up square sail clews, as **buntlines** gather central part of sail. **Leachline** pulls leach up to yard as shown below.

- **Movable yard** is hoisted into position with a chain **tye tackle** (halyard) or slides up track.
- **Fixed yard** supports are shown at doublings where two masts join together, page 285.
- **Cockbill.** Lower yards have lifts to cant one side up at an acute angle alongside a dock, and returned to horizontal afterwards.
- A **foot rope** on the aft side of yards having stirrup supports, is used by crew to stand on when setting, and furling square sails.
- **Jackstay** is a bar on upper side of yard to which the square sail head is secured.

•

- **Buntlines** and **leachlines** must be taut. At command *"LET FALL"* crew pushes sail off yard. Buntlines and leachlines are cast off belaying pins. Clewlines are eased, braces trim yards for intended course, and **sails** sheeted home.
- Going to weather. *Eagle* has **running lifts** on fore and main yards to permit canting sails as required with the weather side up, and down on the lee side. The weather tack holds the clew forward and the sheet going aft vangs it down. Leeward sheet holds lee clew down and aft.

•

- **Furling.** Ease sheets while hauling clewlines, to haul clews up to the outer ends of the yard. Leachlines gather leach to yard towards mast.

  Buntlines bundle the **bunt** as foot and middle part of sail is hauled up to yard. Clews and leaches are tucked inside pouch.
- *"LAY ALOFT and FOLD"* after sail is **in its gear.** Canvas is smothered on weather yardarm. Outermost men draw leach flat on yard while others drop each bight into a following bight for a tight, smooth surface. Drop foot, then clew into last bight.
- Roll sail tight on top of yard with **gaskets** securing sail to **jackstay.** Stop off leachlines and buntlines near mast before going below.

In its gear – taut leachlines and buntlines, **folding is next.**

Clewing up square sails.

Sailing
Illustrated
Volume II

Our traditional square rig heritage

Square rig merchantmen. Since before recorded history, the best way to move cargo in volume from port to port was square rig vessels. By **1880 half the worlds tonnage** was still being shipped worldwide by square rig clippers and deep watermen windjammers. We show examples with *Cutty Sark, Star of India,* and *Soverign of the Seas.*

Steam slowly, then steadily took over. Though steam shipping was more expensive, shipment arrival date was more predictable. 1957 proved the last shipment of windjammer merchantmen as *Passat* delivered a bulk cargo of barley from Buenos Aires to Lisbon, Portugal.

Argentina's Ambassador in the World Seas.

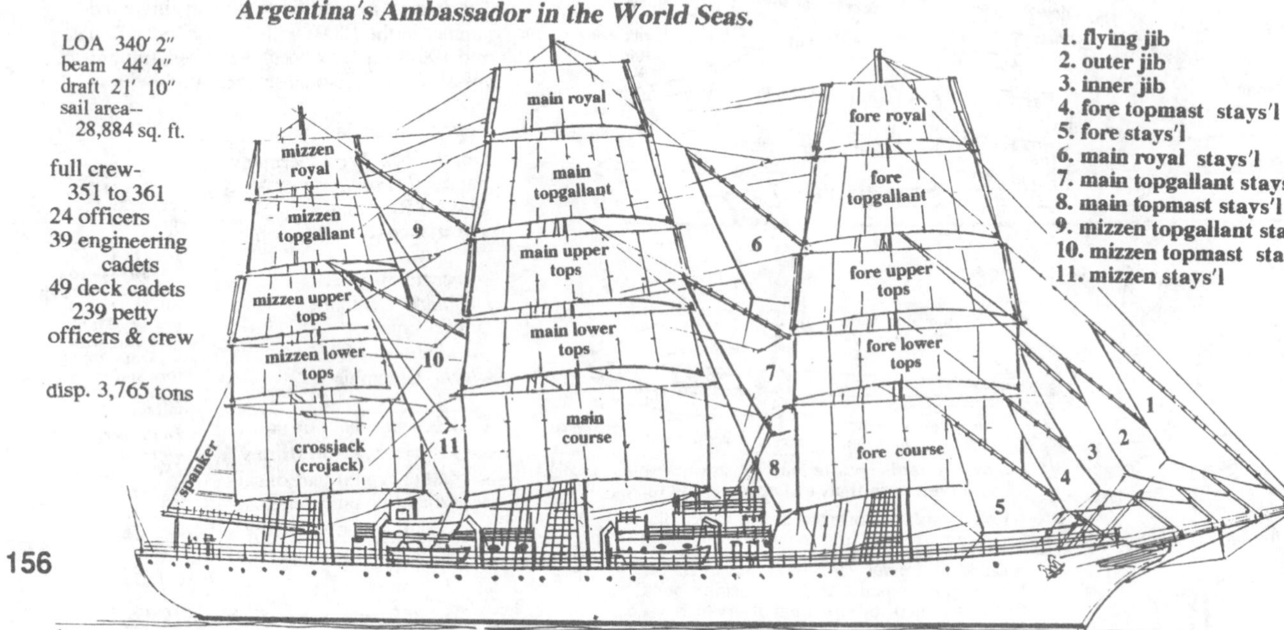
LOA 340′ 2″
beam 44′ 4″
draft 21′ 10″
sail area--
28,884 sq. ft.
full crew-
351 to 361
24 officers
39 engineering
cadets
49 deck cadets
239 petty
officers & crew
disp. 3,765 tons
1. flying jib
2. outer jib
3. inner jib
4. fore topmast stays'l
5. fore stays'l
6. main royal stays'l
7. main topgallant stays
8. main topmast stays'l
9. mizzen topgallant sta
10. mizzen topmast sta
11. mizzen stays'l
main royal
main topgallant
main upper tops
main lower tops
main course
fore royal
fore topgallant
fore upper tops
fore lower tops
fore course
mizzen royal
mizzen topgallant
mizzen upper tops
mizzen lower tops
crossjack (crojack)
spanker
1
2
3
4
5
6
7
8
9
10
11

A.R.A. (ARMADA ARGENTINA) *Libertad*

The new world of Tall Ships.

Square rig training ships. Several were made from 1930 to 1940... 238′ *Christian Radich*- Norway; 253′ *Danmark*- Denmark; 259′ *Mircea*- Roumania; 318′ *Nippon Maru*- Japan, etc.

1956 Tall Ships. The English Sail Training Association sponsored the first Tall Ship race from Torbay, England to Lisbon, Portugal for European competitors. 1958 saw the race from Brest, France to Corunna, Spain, then to the Canary Islands. In 1960 they sailed from Oslo, Norway to Ostend, Belgium.It opened a new square rig era to be repeated every two years. The interest grew as more nations training vessels joined the races and regattas. Locations began to move worldwide. In 1964, 1976, and 1986 Tall Ship regattas were held in New York Harbor.

Libortad *(Liberty)* was launched May 30, 1956, the latest generation training ship, was built for and operated by the Argentina Navy. We remember that date as our first printing of ***Sailing Illustrated*** was delivered a couple days later. After extensive sea trials she was formerly commissioned into the Argentina Navy 5/28/1963 to train naval cadets.

Libertad has a steel hull, easily recognized by her flush deck. Her masts are spaced far enough apart to eliminate chafe-protection baggywrinkles. She has a rare pilot house bridge deck forward of the mainmast, with wings to port and starboard. She is the only **Tall Ship** built entirely in Latin America. While she has square sails on three masts, her preliminary plans were for a four-masted brigantine. Her 13.5 knot speed under power with 2400 horsepower, is outstanding for her 3,765 tons displacement. Note smokestack between main and mizzen masts. She trains up to 120 4th year naval cadets in lenghty cruises. She has made 30 lengthy yearly training cruises to time of writing.

Argentine weather patterns are in the Roaring Forties.

Square rig crossroads. Examine global winds page 147, to find much of Argentina is in the ***Roaring Forties.*** Note various square rig routes with Rio and Buenos Aires excellent stop over harbors to repair ships, load food and water beginning with whalers possibly 350 years ago. Sailing ships from Europe and the U.S. regularly stopped in Argentina harbors before heading east for India, Australia, New Zealand and the Pacific, as well as ships before, or after **rounding** Cape Horn. Argentina has ample wind for square riggers. The high Andes moderate wind along the coast, regaining full strength farther offshore.

sails are cut flat
Four 47mm salute guns are carried forward of bridge.
163′ tall mainmast
A.R.A. LIBERTAD
flush deck
pilothouse with
bridge & wings
engine funnel
between main
& mizzen
13.5 knots
under power
two 1200 hp
engines
RÖYCE

Thirty training and goodwill cruises to 1995-

654,070 nautical miles... 5432 days underway.

1963. Her first cruise was approximately 18,000 nautical miles from June 16 to Dec. 6. Stops included Puerto Rico, Boston, Bermuda, Portugal, France, Germany, London, Spain, Africa, Brazil, Uruguay, to homeport Buenos Aires.

1966. She broke the sailing record from Cape Race, Newfoundland, to the Dublin/Liverpool finish. She was also awarded the Boston Teapot Trophy from Cape Race to Dorsey Island, Ireland. Distance was 1,335 miles in 124 hours totally under sail, established by the Sail Training Organization.

1970. She was in the Sydney **Tall Ship Parade** celebrating the 200th Anniversary discovery of Australia.

1976. She was in the **Tall Ship Race** from Bermuda to Newport, Rhode Island. She again won the Boston Teapot Trophy for 1,247 nautical miles under sail. She sailed to New York for **OP SAIL 76 Regatta,** participating in the celebration of our 200th year of U.S. Independence.

1979. On her 15th cruise, it was between Recife, Brazil to Santao Domingo in the Caribbean, sailing 1,029 nautical miles. **1985.** She participated in **OP Sail 85** in Amsterdam, Holland.

1986. She participated in **OP Sail 86, Tall Ship Review** in New York celebrating the 100th Anniversary of our *Statue of Liberty*. She also participated in the **Tall Ship Parade** in the Wessen River, Bremenhauen, Germany.

1987. She logged 1,790 nautical miles from Recife, Brazil to La Gueyra, Venzuela in the Caribbean.

1990. She celebrated the Bicentenary of the French Revolution in Le Havre. Also the **Tall Ship reviews** in Belgium and Amsterdam. **1990.** It was spent at the Argentian Puerto Pelgrano Naval Base for a major refit.

1992. She was in the **Columbus 92 Quicentenary Grand Regatta** sailing from Europe to the Canaries to New York. July 4th she was in **Op Sail** on the Hudson River, New York; and July 12th, **Sail Boston.** She sailed to Liverpool, to the Canary Islands, returning to Brazil ports, then to Buenos Aires. **1996.** Extensive shipyard work.

Reference book; **Manrique Zago, *La Fragata Libertad, Argentina Ambassador in the World Seas.* Manrique Zago Ediciones, 1995. ISBN 850-9517-57-7**

Your sailing heritage--
how many sail rigs
can you recognize?
1
2
3
4
158
5
6
7
8

Square rig family
pages 282-3
SI- Volume 1

INDEX

R of INDIA

Explore her decks as she is today.

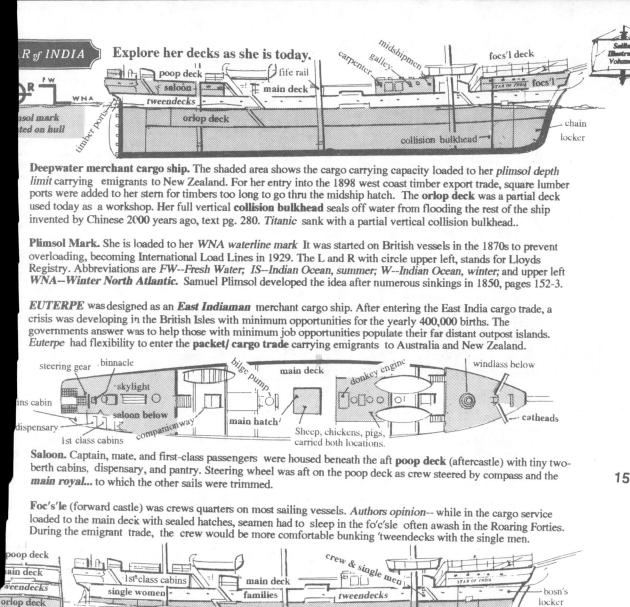

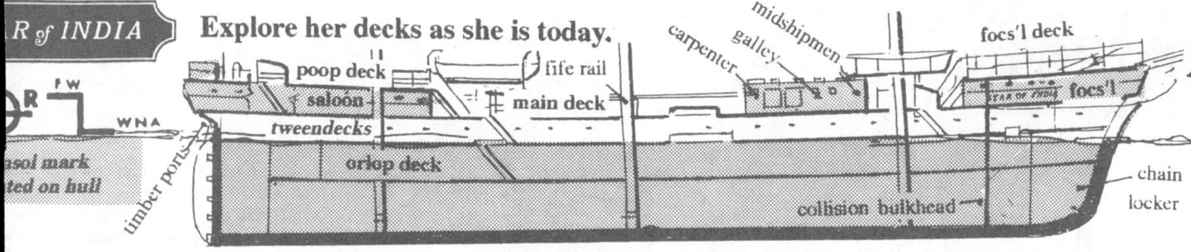

Deepwater merchant cargo ship. The shaded area shows the cargo carrying capacity loaded to her *plimsol depth limit* carrying emigrants to New Zealand. For her entry into the 1898 west coast timber export trade, square lumber ports were added to her stern for timbers too long to go thru the midship hatch. The **orlop deck** was a partial deck used today as a workshop. Her full vertical **collision bulkhead** seals off water from flooding the rest of the ship invented by Chinese 2000 years ago, text pg. 280. *Titanic* sank with a partial vertical collision bulkhead..

Plimsol Mark. She is loaded to her *WNA waterline mark* It was started on British vessels in the 1870s to prevent overloading, becoming International Load Lines in 1929. The L and R with circle upper left, stands for Lloyds Registry. Abbreviations are *FW--Fresh Water; IS--Indian Ocean, summer; W--Indian Ocean, winter;* and upper left ***WNA--Winter North Atlantic.*** Samuel Plimsol developed the idea after numerous sinkings in 1850, pages 152-3.

EUTERPE was designed as an ***East Indiaman*** merchant cargo ship. After entering the East India cargo trade, a crisis was developing in the British Isles with minimum opportunities for the yearly **400,000** births. The governments answer was to help those with minimum job opportunities populate their far distant outpost islands. *Euterpe* had flexibility to enter the **packet/ cargo trade** carrying emigrants to Australia and New Zealand.

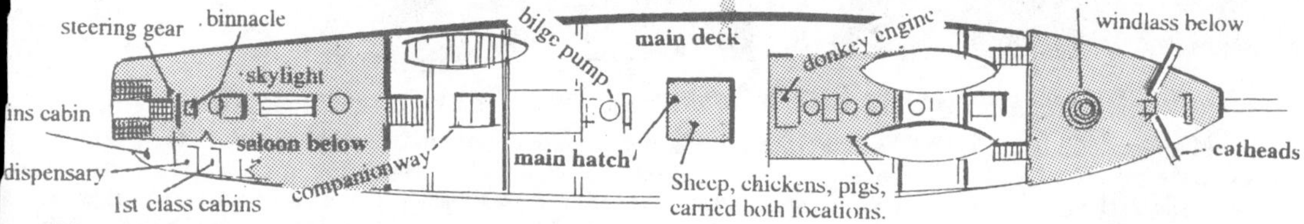

Saloon. Captain, mate, and first-class passengers were housed beneath the aft **poop deck** (aftercastle) with tiny two-berth cabins, dispensary, and pantry. Steering wheel was aft on the poop deck as crew steered by compass and the ***main royal...*** to which the other sails were trimmed.

Foc's'le (forward castle) was crews quarters on most sailing vessels. *Authors opinion--* while in the cargo service loaded to the main deck with sealed hatches, seamen had to sleep in the fo'c'sle often awash in the Roaring Forties. During the emigrant trade, the crew would be more comfortable bunking 'tweendecks with the single men.

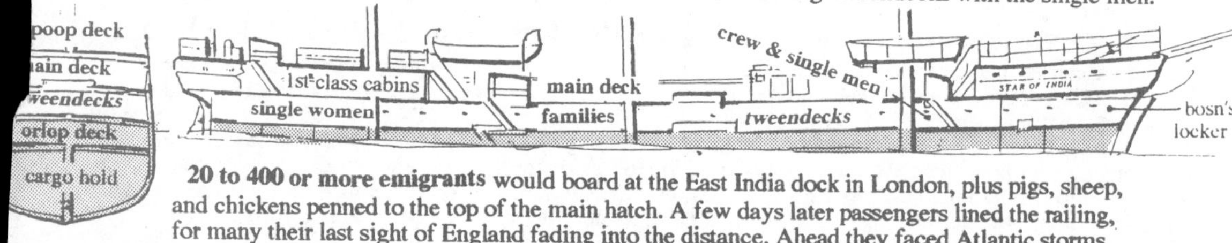

20 to 400 or more emigrants would board at the East India dock in London, plus pigs, sheep, and chickens penned to the top of the main hatch. A few days later passengers lined the railing, for many their last sight of England fading into the distance. Ahead they faced Atlantic storms, hot doldrums, plus the cold wet **Roaring Forties** for an avereage 123 days to New Zealand.

'Tweendecks required flexibility. Single women were usually quartered in the aft end behind a temporary bulkhead. Married couples with children were in the middle with their own children separated by flimsy curtains. Single men were bunked forward with a temporary bulkhead. While we concentrate on sailing operation, we recommend you read----

EUTERPE" by Craig Arnold covering her story from another view. Readers find they suddenly are emigrants coming aboard into a strange new world. Many stories are quoted by passengers of life aboard. Food varied considerably for 1st, 2nd class, emigrants, and crew. This excellent coverage of life 120 years ago, happened on a deepwater sailing ship you can board in San Diego.
Maritime Museum Association, 1306 North Harbor Drive, San Diego, CA 92101: (619) 234-9153

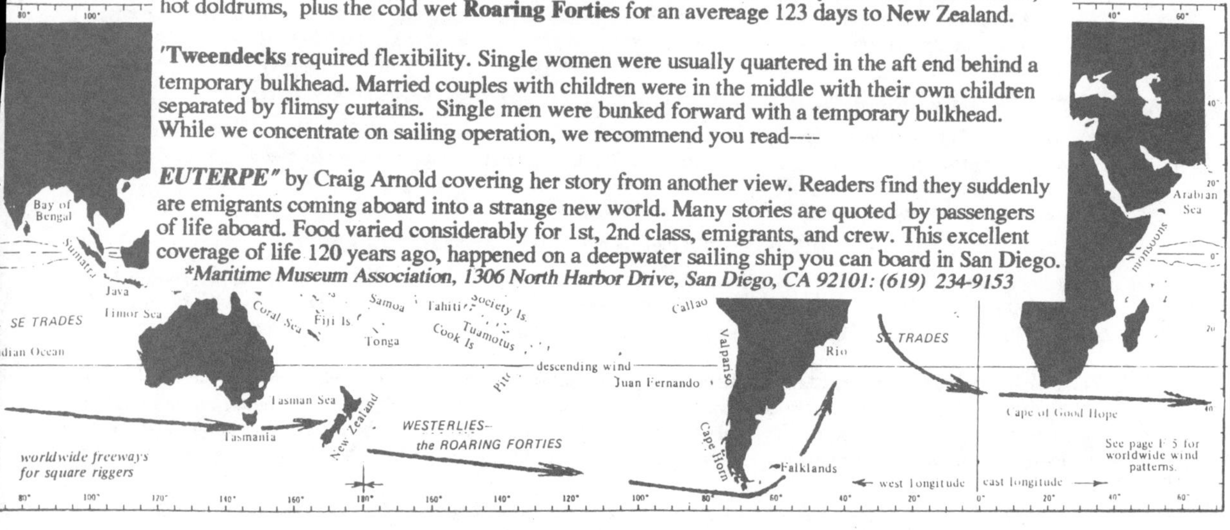

worldwide freeways for square riggers

See page 15 for worldwide wind patterns.

The San Diego Iron Lady as you see her under way today.

STAR of INDIA

Edward King, long deceased, was the most stimu
sailor I've known, page 101. We were enjoying a
heated discussion over a cup of coffee below
Igdrasil. His ever present smile disp
the first time he became s

"A year ago I was a fleet admiral, one of th
powerful men in the world. After a l
at sea, my peaceful civilian life is mis
All I have is my sailboat, and a
author who enjoys chal
an old sailor (a

.Ed ran away from his V
home at an early age to g
At age nine he became
boy on the *Star o*

main royal
fore royal
main topgallant
fore topgallant
main t'g't stays'l
gaff tops'l
mizzen topmast stays'l
main upper tops'l
fore upper tops'l
main lower tops'l
fore lower tops'l
main topmast stays'l
flying jib
outer jib
inner jib
spanker
mizzen stays'l
main course
fore course
port tack- *full & by*
Royce

Sailing Illustrated Volume II

This deepwater iron ship made 21 round-the-world voyages before 1900.

November 14, 1863. The ***EUTERPE*** (Eu-ter-pe, Greek *muse of music)* was launched at Ramsey on the Isle of Man, in the Irish sea. East India merchants were her first owners, Wakefield & Nash. She was a deepwater ship with square sails on three masts listed with eight staterooms, plus bath and waterclosets in the (aftercastle) **saloon** under the poop deck. Forward of the midship galley were 14 berths for midshipmen and petty officers. The **foc'sl'e** (forward castle) had 25 crew berths. plus a windlass, and capstan on the deck above. It required ***Svedish steam*** (manpower) to take in her anchors secured to catheads port and starboard.

She made six round trips to India for the jute trade. On her maiden voyage four days out of Liverpool for Calcutta, she was in a foggy weather collision with a steamer at 0500. She returned to port as her jib boom and several headsails were carried away. A mutiny followed with 17 crew members sentenced to 14 days of hard labor. On her return trip eight months later, a fire broke out dockside, soon extinguished. It wasn't a dull maiden voyage.

An intentional dismasting during a 3 day hurricane in the Indian Ocean.

She was anchored in an open roadstead at Madras, SE India on her last India voyage. As a major hurricane was moving in she slipped her anchor cables, heading for the open ocean. She was pounded for three days with this brutal storm until the wind shifted catching her broadside. With lee rail under, Captain Storry ordered the weather hemp standing rigging cut away at the deck, with masts and rigging going overboard. She was dead in the water, slowly coming upright. Her crew made a jury rig sailing to Ceylon for three months emergency repair to patch up ship and crew. Under improved jury rig she headed for a Calcutta shipyard for major repairs. When she was again underway for the British Isles, Captain Storry died 13 days later, followed by a burial at sea.

N

For the 1867-71 period her new owner was David Brown, also an East India merchant. A series of major storms hit her. She had to dump part of her cargo overboard to save the ship before reaching the tip of Africa *Cape of Good Hope*. Her 1868-70 voyages were easier. Returning from Bombay in 1871, her new owners became Shaw Savill.

New Zealand emigrant trade required 16 month voyages round-the-world.

London around the world to New Zealand... back to London. Her next ten voyages under Captain Phillips carried emigrants to New Zealand, some to Australia. She then had to pick up paying cargo such as wool, or coal from Newcastle for her return trip. **Returning in ballast without cargo.** Large boulders were normally used requiring expensive loading and unloading charges. Would you buy the boulders after their expensive sea voyage?

Square- rigged cargo vessels can capsize dockside.

Dockside capsize. This became a hazardous risk. As cargo is being discharged, the masts, spars, and rigging at a certain point could make her topheavy. When ***Euterpe*** was hauled in October 1898, ***300 tons of ballast were left aboard.*** Pilings still existed in 1950 on the New York East River to support sailing vessels from capsizing.

Total Volume-- **1246 tons register; Packers 1318 gross tonnage.** The Columbus 1492 *Santa Maria* was listed as "80 tuns or tonelades", able to carry ***80 tuns of wine.*** The ***tun*** evolved into 2,240 pounds today, basically 100 square feet. **Registered tonnage** is a vessels cubic content divided by 100, an estimate for port charges and taxes for commercial craft. **Gross tonnage** is measurement of all spaces below upper deck. **Net tonnage** uses gross tonnage with areas deducted not carrying cargo..

MAINS'L HAUL --A *Journal of Maritime History,* is excellent, published quarterly by the San Diego Maritime Museum, 1306 N. Harbor Drive, San Diego, CA 92101 (619) 234-9153